chapter 6

π The proportion of elements in a population which possess the attribute under consideration (π = Greek letter pi)

p The proportion of elements in a sample which possess the attribute under consideration. If X is the number of elements in the sample which possess the attribute, then $p = X/n$

e The mathematical constant, 2.71828. . . .

chapter 7

$f(X)$ The density function for a continuous random variable X

Z The standard normal random variable

$>$ Greater than

$\geq$ Equal to or greater than

$<$ Less than

$\leq$ Equal to or less than

$s_{\bar{X}}$ The estimate of the standard error of $\bar{X}$

Π The mathematical constant, 3.1416. . . .

chapter 8

t The random variable t

ν The degrees of freedom for a probability distribution (ν = Greek letter nu)

chapter 9

p-value The probability of obtaining the observed sample result when the null hypothesis is true

α The level of significance specified before an hypothesis is tested (α = Greek letter alpha)

chapter 10

χ^2 The random variable chi-square (χ = Greek letter chi)

f_o The observed frequency of observations in a category

f_e The expected frequency of observations in a category

Statistics for Management Decisions

Statistics for
Management Decisions

DONALD R. PLANE

Professor and Head,
Division of Management Science
University of Colorado

EDWARD B. OPPERMANN

Associate Professor of Management Science
University of Colorado

 1977

BUSINESS PUBLICATIONS, INC.   Dallas, Texas   75243

Irwin-Dorsey Limited   Georgetown, Ontario   L7G 4B3

To Margey, Dennis, Brian, and Rosemary
and to Kurt, Kim and Jody

3 4 5 6 7 8 9 0 K 5 4 3 2 1 0 9 8

ISBN 0-256-01814-6
Library of Congress Catalog Card No. 76–47723
Printed in the United States of America

Preface to the Instructor

This book is designed to serve as a basic statistics text for students of business or economics. The presentation is oriented to the student who is expected to grasp the concepts and apply the techniques of data presentation, data analysis, statistical inference, and statistical decision analysis.

The mathematical background that a student is expected to have is no more than a good course in high school algebra. But as in any quantitative course in the social sciences, the student who has studied more mathematics is able to grasp statistical concepts and techniques more quickly. Without sacrificing precision and correctness, this book is written for students whose basic "bent" is something other than mathematics.

The book can be used in many sequences, to accommodate courses of a quarter, a semester, or longer, as indicated on the diagram on the following page. Those courses that utilize this text for two quarters or longer should be able to cover all 17 chapters. Depending upon the objectives of the course and the student background, a full year course may include substantial projects in multiple regression, time series analysis, decision analysis and optimal sample size, and other topics. Courses designed to emphasize decision theory may choose to discuss Chapters 16 and 17 much earlier in the course, so that an "end of the course crunch" does not short-change these topics. Other courses may prefer to discuss Chapters 14 and 15 much earlier in the course, in order to show relationships between economic analysis and statistical analysis. (Time Series Analysis may be discussed without a complete treatment of regression analysis, if desired.) There are many other sequences which make sense in other courses.

One of the unique features of this text is a set of notes for students. The notes are primarily a compilation of the mathematical development of numerous concepts of statistical analysis. Furthermore, the notes are supplementary material, intended for those students who are interested in this more abstract aspect of statistics. Since the textual material is complete without the notes, the notes are placed at the end of the text and are referenced in the chapters. In addition, the chapter and section for which each note is appropriate is indicated with each note. Thus the notes are available for the mathematically inclined student to be able to investigate some of the richness behind statistics, while the student who is made uncomfortable by too much exposure to algebra is not forced into directions that may be counter-productive.

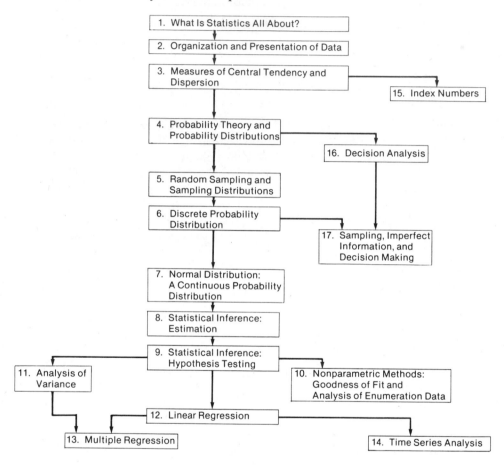

There are several other features that set this book apart from other texts. One is the clear distinction between statistical inference and statistical decision theory. Both estimation and testing are presented as *information models* which describe the results of a statistical experiment; testing is not presented in its "classical" framework of "decision-making." However, the chapters on statistical decision theory present *decision models,* heavily oriented toward procedures that have direct applicability in a decision process. This division is intended to end the confusion of "when do I test a hypothesis, and when do I draw a decision tree?"

Another unique feature of the book is the construction of the statistical tables. Every tabulated probability distribution is presented as a right-tail probability. Furthermore, more extensive tables are provided for the binomial, chi-square, F, and t distributions. Although technically redundant, the binomial tables extend to parameter values above .5; this reduces confusion and tedious explanations, without any real loss of learning. Extensive tables for the chi-square, F, and t distributions are provided so that probabilities other than the traditional .1, .05, .025, .01, and .001 may be appropriately used.

The problems provided for the student are extensive, allowing the instructor to choose those problems that emphasize the most important concepts for a particular group of students. There is a solutions manual for the instructor, and the appendix with answers to a number of the problems (marked *) provides incentive to the student to keep working problems!

We are indebted to many people who have assisted in preparing this manuscript. We especially want to thank Norman L. Chervaney, David M. Beveridge, W. W. Thompson, P. S. Wang, Lotus Blackwell, and Joe Van Matre, who made many helpful comments about the manuscript. A special gratitude is expressed to William Whitaker, who prepared early drafts of several of the chapters. Perhaps the true contributors are the many students who have suffered through various versions of this text over the years. At this point we wish we could break with tradition and blame someone for the errors that may remain; tradition wins.

DONALD R. PLANE

EDWARD B. OPPERMANN

January 1977

Preface to the Student

There are several things a student can do to make a study of statistics more productive. Although these comments are certainly not complete—and they may not help every student—we want to pass along to the users of this text some ways which we have found to make statistics a bit easier.

1. Read the text carefully, with a scratch pad and a calculator handy. Don't read this book like a novel. Every time a number is encountered, ask yourself where the number came from. If it came from a table in the back of the book, go to that table and verify the number. If it came from a calculation, do that calculation to reinforce previous topics. If it appears to come out of thin air, back up a few paragraphs or pages, and try to find out where it came from. If that doesn't work, ask your instructor.

2. Some students find it helpful to scan a chapter first, to see where it is heading. After this scanning, reread the chapter carefully as suggestion (1) describes.

3. Work many, many problems. Exercises with answers provided in Appendix L are marked with an asterisk (*). Students sometimes read a section and say, "That looks easy." Then they find out on exams that some key point was missing in their understanding. If that is the case, that key point probably would have been discovered and understood in solving problems.

4. Use a calculator when solving problems. If the time to solve problems can be reduced, more problems can be solved; that means more learning!

5. If you are a student who likes to know a lot more about "why is that true," we refer you to the section at the end of the book called "Notes for the Student." These notes are written for you. But if you are satisfied with a statement or a numerical example, you may prefer to ignore the notes.

6. Statistics is definitely not an easy subject, but it can be interesting and even fun at times. We hope this text helps to make the course both of these things for you.

January 1977   D. R. P.
                                                      E. B. O.

Contents

1

What Is Statistics All About?

There is a good chance you did not buy this book because you really wanted to read it. Probably you are taking this course because it's a requirement, and you would just as soon not be facing a term of statistics. But have you seriously thought about the useful reasons for studying statistics? Did it ever occur to you that perhaps statistics is a useful tool for managerial decisions? Believe it or not, the chances are rather good that you will successfully complete the course, and may even enjoy the subject. Furthermore, statistics *is* useful, and the study of statistics can be interesting and rewarding.

1.1 STATISTICS: MAKING SENSE OUT OF NUMBERS

Almost everyone has used the term statistics in an ordinary conversation. The radio broadcast at a football game is usually concluded by a report on the statistics of the game. The Bureau of Vital Statistics keeps track of births, deaths, marriages, and other data on individuals. But what does a statistician really do? In a football game, the statistician records things as they occur, summarizes them, and prepares a report for the listening audience. The statistician's job is to prepare meaningful numbers, often involving summaries of numbers or other data. The statistician must present such data in a form which is *useful* to the recipient of that data. How useful would you find the statistics in the following report:

On the first play of the game Smith carried for seven yards. On the second play of the game Jones received a pass from the quarterback for 19 yards. He fumbled when he got the ball. On the third play of the game, they had a quick kick that went for 14 yards. On the first play of the next series of downs. . . .

This kind of boring rehash has not been summarized; it has not been presented in a form *useful* to the typical recipient of the data. The listener would probably change to another station, rather than listen to a dry and

1

overly detailed rerun of the game. The typical listener wants a concise statistical summary of the game.

Even reporting the score at the end of the game reflects a useful summarization. The score could have been reported as first quarter 7 to 2, second quarter 9 to 0, third quarter 0 to 7, and fourth quarter 3 to 3. The useful summarization that has been omitted here is adding the quarterly scores and reporting who won the game.

You might comment that this kind of summarization is nothing more than common sense. Agreed! Statistical presentation of data is nothing more than organizing numbers into common sense, so that the numbers are useful, meaningful, and helpful.

Another very important task of a statistician may be to make sense of economic data concerning the economic performance of a firm, an industry, or the economy as a whole. Special statistical techniques are necessary to make these kinds of data useful. Sections of this text relate to the development and understanding of index numbers and the analysis of data which occur as time series. We are all familiar with the Consumer Price Index or the "Cost of Living Index." Part of the truly useful task in learning statistics is to understand how this price index (and other indices) are computed, and how they should be interpreted. We also are familiar with changes in the level of aggregate economic activity, the Gross National Product. We hear and read about the terms *recession, inflation, recovery,* and *depression.* Statistical methods have been developed to aid in understanding measurements of economic activity.

1.2 STATISTICS: DEALING WITH UNCERTAINTY

Over the past several decades, the primary emphasis of statistics has switched from data presentation to the development of procedures that managers can use to deal with uncertainty. After all, most decisions regarding resource allocations in profit and nonprofit organizations are made under uncertainty. The decision maker never knows exactly what is going to happen. There are two primary aspects of statistics that deal with such uncertainty: communicating information under uncertainty, and analyzing decisions under uncertainty.

1.21 Communicating Information under Uncertainty

Statistical inference is used to convey information from one person (the statistician) to another (the user of the information). One type of statistical inference is the estimate of an uncertain quantity and the amount of uncerainty in that estimate. One of the primary statistical procedures is to take a *sample* of items from a *population* (or universe) of interest. For example, a statistical inference is made when a sample of 100 supermarket customers is analyzed to infer or discover something about the spending of all of the store's customers (the population). Since this statistical procedure involves a sample, there is uncertainty about how well the sample estimates the average spending of the entire population. Statistical inference provides measures of this uncertainty in terms of how much the estimate may be in error, and the chances that it may be that much in error.

1.22   Decision Analysis

Statistical inference is not a decision process; it is a communication process. The use of statistical methods in decision making is called *decision analysis*. Decision analysis breaks down a managerial problem under uncertainty into its several components, and then develops ways of combining all these components (which may reflect a great deal of the decision maker's judgment, experience, intuition, and managerial skill) into a rational procedure which will lead to the choice of one best act.

One of the most valuable aspects of decision analysis is that it provides a method for evaluating information. One of the most difficult problems faced in many managerial situations is that of "When should I decide?" But this question is really, "How much information should I have before I decide?" These questions are the same because delaying a decision will provide time in which to gain more information. Decision analysis is a way of deciding whether to decide now or to wait and obtain more information (usually at a cost) before reaching a final decision.

1.3   EXAMPLES OF MANAGERIAL SITUATIONS UTILIZING STATISTICS

In order to appreciate more fully the broad applicability of statistical methods, several applications of statistical methodologies are presented. These are only a few examples in which statistical methods are used in a managerial situation, but they will give the reader some basis for this odyssey into the study of statistics.

1.31   Summarizing Sales Information

The buyer for the women's sportswear department of a large clothing store is interested in "what's happening" to sales of the department. Although daily reports are available on sales volume, there is little detail on just which items are selling. Furthermore, information on what the customers want cannot be obtained from long-term sales data, because everything the store purchases is sold eventually, by lowering the price during special sales. In order to find out the current "pulse" of the department,

during the first two weeks of the spring selling season detailed records are
kept on every sale. This record keeping is possible because electronic
"point of sale" computer terminals have been installed to replace cash
registers, so that the sales force is not burdened by excess clerical work.

When the data are available at the end of the two weeks, a variety of
reports are prepared. All the reports reflect a great deal of summarization,
converting raw data into information. Among the reports are tables and
charts summarizing these items:

Number of clothing items sold, classified by color.

Number of clothing items sold, classified by size.

Number of clothing items sold, classified by both color and size, to see
if different size women prefer different colors.

Number of clothing items sold, classified by price.

Number of clothing outfits sold, classified by "skirt" or "pant."

Number of clothing items sold, classified by manufacturer.

As the buyer receives these reports, several factors come to mind: Should
I be dealing with the *number* of items, or the *percent* of items? Should I
be dealing with the number of items, or the *dollar volume* of items? Should
it be *total* dollars or dollar sales expressed as a *percent* of total sales?
Descriptive statistics can be used to summarize any of these measures,
according to the desire of the user of the data.

After the buyer has become familiar with these reports, further uses of
information are suggested.

What value is advertising?

What value is in-store display?

What is the effect of displaying merchandise by similarity and compati-
bility of color, rather than by size?

To investigate these questions, experiments are designed. A two-week
period is split into two periods. During the first period, a group of items is
not advertised. During the second period, it is advertised. Sales of the
items are compared for the two periods. Similar experiments are used for
type of in-store display. From a descriptive standpoint, the buyer can obtain some insight into the importance of the factors of the experiment.
From a statistical inference standpoint, a statistician can investigate
whether observed differences in sales are caused by chance or by the
experiment.

Although it is quite possible that most of the information gathered in a
study of this type will reinforce the experience and intuition of the buyer,
routine reports of the type described here assist in spotting new trends and
other factors which are very important in managing the department.

1.32 Which Candidate Should Get the Job?

The personnel director of a large firm is often faced with the decision of which of several candidates should receive a job offer. If the decision were made under certainty, the future job success of each candidate would be known *before* the decision had to be made. Under uncertainty, only imperfect predictions are available to make the decision. The candidate's placement scores, past employment record, and other factors would be known, but the crucial knowledge of future job success is unknown. Statistical methods can be used to relate the measurable factors (placement scores, etc.) to the job success of current employees. Although none of these job success predictors is perfect, statistical methods (such as regression analysis) are useful in giving insight to the personnel director who must decide which candidate to hire.

1.33 How Large a Sample Should I Have?

The head of the accounting department for a large wholesale firm has been given the task of estimating (on a weekly basis) the interest costs incurred by the firm for overdue accounts receivable. The number of such accounts runs into thousands; the costs of a complete weekly audit would be large. As the number of overdue accounts is easy to obtain, an estimate of the average amount overdue is needed. Statistical inference permits taking a sample in order to make this estimate. But how large a sample should be taken? This depends on how close to the true average the estimate needs to be, and with what confidence. Statistical methods are available to calculate the correct sample size.

1.34 Which Advertising Plan Should We Adopt?

The vice president for marketing is faced with the choice between two advertising plans, both of which will cost millions of dollars. The vice president has conducted a pilot study of three cities for each of the two advertising plans. Each plan has produced different sales results. There are statistical methods for answering the question of whether these two plans differ in effectiveness, or whether the difference in the pilot studies is due to chance.

1.35 Should I Send the Lot Back?

The quality control manager of an electronics firm has just received a shipment of parts. There has been some damage in the shipment, which leads the quality control manager to believe there may be damage to the parts. However, a delay in receiving replacement parts will cause a substantial cost increase. Several courses of action are available. These include sending the lot back, going ahead and using the lot as it is, or testing some of the parts for damage and then determining whether to keep the shipment or send it back. But how many parts should be tested?

This question fits into the framework of "How much information should I have before I decide?" Information costs money. In this case testing and the delay in using the parts may be expensive. But acting without the additional information may be even more expensive. Future production may be faulty and delayed if damaged parts are used. Statistical methods are useful in determining whether a sample should be taken, how large a sample, and what to do with the sample information after it has been received.

1.36   Statistical Applications in a Nonprofit Organization: Where to Build a Firehouse?

In order to decide where to build a firehouse, it is necessary to know how long it takes to get from "here" to "there," where "here" is any place where we might build the firehouse and "there" is any place a fire might occur. Statistical methods are used to determine how long it takes to get from "here" to "there," when one knows the distance from "here" to "there." Distance can be measured on a map, so it is possible to determine the time necessary to get from "here" to "there" with a fire vehicle. This information is necessary in order to decide the consequences of any distribution of firehouses, because the distribution can be evaluated quite logically by summarized information on how long it takes to travel from various firehouses to various locations where fires might occur.

Another useful application of statistics in managing a fire department is the summarization of other data. If a fire chief does *not* know that 40 percent of all false alarms are reported by fire alarm boxes rather than by telephone, it is impossible to decide rationally whether to have fire alarm boxes. Good statistical data on the incidence of false alarms and fires can be very useful for decisions of this type. This a situation in which many pieces of data are available in voluminous file drawers and storage boxes; however, very little useful information is really available until it has been summarized and presented in a meaningful manner.

1.4   SUMMARY

Hopefully, these examples have served to demonstrate the relevance of statistical analysis in managerial decision problems. We are *not* presenting statistics as a set of derivations which are primarily of interest for their mathematical beauty. We are *not* presenting statistics as a set of formulas for you to memorize for "plug and chug." Although formulas are necessary, we hope in the material that follows to show how statistics can be used in many situations, and how you as a potential analyst in private, business, and public life can perform useful statistical analyses.

EXERCISES

Each of the following scenarios has some internal inconsistencies in it. Since statistical methodologies deal with making sense out of numbers, it is good practice to look at numbers and see if they make sense. For each of the following, point out things which are obviously inconsistent with each other, based on common sense and what you already know about the world.

1.1 I'm marketing a new sailboat seat for boats used on small lakes. Each sailboat needs one or two of these seats, depending on the size of the boat. If I price them low enough, I ought to be able to sell about 40 million seats a year in the United States.

1.2 This year-old car has been driven 600,000 miles. Most of it was on the streets of Manhattan.

1.3 A fire truck with four people on duty at one time, around the clock, costs about $40,000 a year for staffing.

1.4 In the National Football League, the quarterback for the local team threw 637 touchdown passes last year.

1.5 Using a factor of three out-of-class study hours for every in-class hour, the typical student load should be 24 hours of classes each week. That leaves plenty of time for relaxation, sleep, eating, and just "goofing off."

1.6 If each student enrolls in 18 credit hours, the average class size is 50 students, and each faculty member teaches nine credit hours, we would need 75 faculty members for 1,000 students.

1.7 If busses average about five times as many passenger miles per gallon as the automobile (with one passenger), busses are five times as fuel-efficient as cars.

1.8 It takes about twice as long to ski down a particular run as it does to ride the lift up for the run. The lift serves two similar ski runs. Two people board the lift every 15 seconds; the lift ride takes ten minutes. Thus, with 5,000 people using the two runs and the lift, we should expect very short lift lines, if any. (A lift line is a group of people waiting to board the ski lift.)

1.9 From looking at houses under construction, I know that those vertical pieces of wood that go inside the walls (called *studs*) are spaced somewhere between one and three feet apart. In fact, I have no trouble walking between them sideways, but my shoulders are too broad to walk straight through. I'm building a one-story house with an area of 1,200 square feet. I guess I'd better order 40 studs. That should give me about 5 percent for breakage and mistakes.

1.10 The safe-driving rules often suggest a one-car-length interval between cars for each ten mph of speed. This four-lane highway (two lanes each way) should be able to deliver enough people to this town to fill our 40,000-seat football stadium in one hour, even allowing for a substantial "jam up" at the turn-off for the stadium.

1.11   This one-pump gas station can sell 20,000 gallons of gasoline on a good day.

1.12   The HKO Company, which manufactures children's clothing, sells about 4 million pairs of plaid jeans, red color, size four (small children, about three or four years old) each year. But their big seller does even better.

1.13   I drove from New York City to San Diego in 28 hours.

REFERENCES

Campbell, Stephen K.   *Flaws and Fallacies in Statistical Thinking*. Englewood Cliffs, N.J.: Prentice-Hall, Inc., 1974.

Mansfield, E., ed.   *Elementary Statistics for Economics and Business: Selected Readings*. New York: W. W. Norton, 1970.

Naiman, Arnold; Rosenfeld, Robert; and Zirkel, Gene.   *Understanding Statistics*. New York: McGraw-Hill Book Co., 1972.

Sielaff, Theodore J.   *Statistics in Action*. San Jose, California: Lansford Press, 1963.

2

Organization and Presentation of Data

2.1 DATA: THE BASIC INGREDIENT OF STATISTICS

Statistics is the science of assembling, classifying, tabulating, and analyzing numerical facts or data. The basic ingredient is data. Before any statistical investigation has meaning, meaningful data must first be obtained. Such data exist throughout our environment, although frequently we fail to realize their existence and sources.

Business and government enterprises generate data of many forms. Every activity performed by an organization may have numerical aspects which can be studied. The economy, with inflation, unemployment, economic growth, and the balance of payments, is also a creator of voluminous data to be sifted, sorted, and reported. In general, we view the sources of these data as being either *internal* or *external* to the basic organization being studied.

2.11 Internal Data

When an organization seeks data for decision-making purposes, it may be its own best source. Virtually all organizations produce masses of data on their own operations. A business firm generates financial data; balance sheets and income statements are examples of reports based on these data. Data on personnel are maintained for use by management. Production reports reflect data on operations. When an organization acts as its own source of data, such data are *internal* data. Accountants provide much of a firm's internal data.

2.12 External Data

External data are those data not produced within the using organization. External data are usually obtained from published documents, which in turn are classified as *primary* or *secondary* sources. A primary data source is a compilation and publication produced by the data-gathering agency. A secondary data source is a publication of data gathered by another agency. Both primary and secondary data are published by government agencies, trade associations, private research organizations, and other business firms and agencies, as listed in Figure 2.1.

Figure 2.1

Brief Listing of Sources of External Data

1. *Statistical Abstract of the United States.* U.S. Bureau of the Census. This annual volume is perhaps the most versatile single source of data on the United States. Comprehensive data on population, economics, industrial activity, and many other areas are included. This source is particularly useful because it describes the primary source of the data reported in the *Abstract*.

2. *Economic Report of the President.* U.S. President. This annual report contains a statistical supplement which is a compact summary of statistical tables relating to income, employment, and production.

3. *Handbook of Basic Economic Statistics.* Economic Statistics Bureau of Washington, D.C. Both current and historical statistics on many aspects of the U.S. economy are reported in this annual volume.

4. *Business Statistics.* U.S. Department of Commerce. A historical record of statistical series which appear currently in the *Survey of Current Business*. These two sources provide both historical and current data on national income, national product, and the components of each.

5. *Business Conditions Digest* (BCD). U.S. Bureau of the Census. This source contains charts of many economic time series, grouped in accordance with the National Bureau of Economic Research determinations of leading, coincident, and lagging indicators.

6. *Monthly Labor Review.* U.S. Bureau of Labor Statistics. A primary source of data on employment, unemployment, hours and earnings, and prices.

7. *National Economic Projections Series.* National Planning Association, Center for Economic Projections. Long-range forecasts for items such as economic statistics, industrial growth patterns, and population for the states and metropolitan regions.

8. *The Fortune Directory.* This listing of the 500 largest U.S. industrial corporations, the second largest 500 U.S. industrial corporations, and the 200 largest foreign industrial corporations is published each year in *Fortune* magazine.

9. *The Wall Street Journal.* This newspaper, published every business day, contains vast amounts of current data on corporations, stock prices, economic indicators, and many other items of interest to a student of business or economics.

Figure 2.1 (*continued*)

10. *Moody's Investors Service.* This set of six annual volumes covers financial data, company histories, and other useful information for many United States corporations and governments.

11. *Marketing Information Guide.* Marketing Information Guide, Inc. This reference is not a source of data, but is a source for sources of data. It is an annotated listing of publications of universities, government agencies, trade associations, and many other publishers of data. This is a particularly useful source for finding out where to find out.

12. *Directory of Federal Statistics for States; A Guide to Sources,* and *Directory of Non-Federal Statistics for State and Local Areas; A Guide to Sources.* U.S. Bureau of the Census. These two volumes are a comprehensive guide to data useful for state or regional analysis.

13. Sources for Industry Analysis:
    Appliance magazine contains an annual statistical review in April.
    Automobile Facts and Figures. Automobile Manufacturer Association.
    Chemical and Engineering News contains an annual statistical review in September.
    Construction Review. U.S. Bureau of Domestic Commerce.
    Housing and Urban Development Trends. U.S. Department of Housing and Urban Development.
    Gas Facts: A Statistical Record of the Gas Utility Industry. American Gas Association.
    Electronics. "U.S. Markets Forecasts" is published with a January issue.
    Agricultural Statistics. U.S. Department of Agriculture.
    Insurance Facts. Insurance Information Institute.
    Savings and Loan Fact Book. United States Savings and Loan League.
    Statistics of Paper and Paperboard. American Paper Institute.
    Petroleum Facts and Figures. American Petroleum Institute.
    Highway Statistics. U.S. Federal Highway Administration.
    Transport Statistics in the United States. U.S. Interstate Commerce Commission.
    Federal Reserve Bulletin. Federal Reserve System. Primary data on banking.

Source: Abstracted from Lorna M. Daniells, *Business Reference Sources,* Graduate School of Business Administration, Harvard University, 1971.

As a general rule, primary sources of data are preferred to secondary sources. The primary source typically provides more detail. Also, the primary source generally contains much pertinent information about collection methods and limitations associated with the data.

The amount of external data available is staggering. It includes information about prices, production, incomes, employment, population, inventories, profits, and consumption. The amount of detail and accuracy varies from one source to another. Data from external sources are often misused because they are not thoroughly understood. Thus, it is imperative for an analyst to have complete knowledge of the definitions and descriptions of the data.

2.13 Variables

Once data have been collected, whether from internal or external sources, the data must be organized for proper analysis and inference. The first step in analysis is to identify those characteristics or features for which data are required. These characteristics are called *variables*.

A *variable* is a characteristic which may take on different values at different times, places, or situations.

Every item on an accounting statement is a variable. Each characteristic or financial variable may take on different values over time for the given company of interest. A firm's profit (over time) is a variable; 1972 profit is known, and not variable. Personnel records, customer accounts, production performance reports, and many other internal documents provide a series of observations on many characteristics which constitute many variables.

The data from external data sources also are variables. Population, employment, income, prices, interest rates, and wages are all examples of variables which may be obtained for the U.S. economy from published external data sources.

2.14 Time Series and Cross-Sectional Data

In any business enterprise, nearly any characteristic assumes different values from time to time. There are variations in revenues, profits, inventories, production costs, marketing costs, and articles produced in the manufacturing process. Such variations occur both in data observed at a point in time as well as in data occurring over a period of time. Data which are observed at one point in time are referred to as *cross-sectional data,* such as the wages of each of 100 company employees in March of this year. Time has been stopped and the variable (wages) assumes different values from worker to worker. A set of figures observed over a period of time is called *time series data,* such as the number of boxes of cereal produced each day for a month or a company's annual production of electrical switches since 1950.

2.2 FREQUENCY DISTRIBUTIONS: UNGROUPED DATA

Frequency distributions facilitate organization and presentation of data. This technique of presentation deals with data where the order in which the observations are recorded is of no importance, as in the case of wages of all machinists in a certain plant, the total profits of all steel companies in the United States in 1972, or the batting averages of all second basemen in the major leagues.

A _frequency distribution_ for ungrouped data shows the number of times each value of a variable occurs.

This concept is better understood by applying an example. The Pure Chemical Company produces a chemical product in ten similar curing vats. The number of gallons produced in each vat on January 19, 1976, is shown in Figure 2.2.

Figure 2.2

Output of Ten Curing Vats (Pure Chemical Company, January 19, 1976)

Vat	Gallons Produced
A	65
B	67
C	66
D	68
E	66
F	67
G	66
H	65
I	64
J	68

2.21 Ordered Array

The first step in constructing a frequency distribution may be to develop an _ordered array_ of the raw data.

An _ordered array_ is a listing of the recorded observations in order of magnitude, either ascending or descending.

An ordered array of the output of the ten vats of Pure Chemical Company is:

$$64, \ 65, \ 65, \ 66, \ 66, \ 66, \ 67, \ 67, \ 68, \ 68$$

It is easily discernible from this ordered array that the extreme values are 64 gallons and 68 gallons, and that for the ten vats, only five different categories appear in the data (i.e., the number of units produced each day can be expressed by one of five numbers).

2.22   Frequency Distribution Table

The presentation of the above information in the form of a table summarizing the number of occurrences is called the *frequency distribution* table. The number of occurrences is called *frequency* or *absolute frequency*. When frequencies are expressed in terms of proportions in each of the categories, the table is called a *relative frequency distribution*. The distribution of output of Pure Chemical Company's vats is summarized in Figure 2.3. The relative frequencies were determined by dividing the absolute frequency for each category by the total of the absolute frequencies, which is ten (number of vats for which output is recorded) in this case.

Figure 2.3

Frequency Distribution (Pure Chemical Company curing vat output, January 19, 1976)

Output (gallons)	Frequency Absolute	Frequency Relative
64	1	1/10 = 0.1
65	2	2/10 = 0.2
66	3	3/10 = 0.3
67	2	2/10 = 0.2
68	2	2/10 = 0.2
Totals	10	1.0

The frequency distribution is a valuable tool. For example, it shows at a glance that 66 gallons of output was more prevalent than any other level, and it also shows the frequency of any other value of the variable.

2.23   Histogram

Graphs are often used to present a more effective picture of the pattern of variation in statistical data. The graph used for this purpose is called a histogram.

A *histogram* is a bar chart or graph showing the frequency of occurrence of each category of the variable being analyzed.

A segment of the horizontal scale of the histogram represents each category, while the vertical scale represents the frequency of each category in the table. The vertical scale must start from zero, but the horizontal scale is labeled with a scale that represents the exhaustive categories of the variable. There are often two vertical scales, one on the left side of the histogram to measure absolute frequencies and one on the right side

Figure 2.4

Histogram (Pure Chemical Company curing vat output, January 19, 1976)

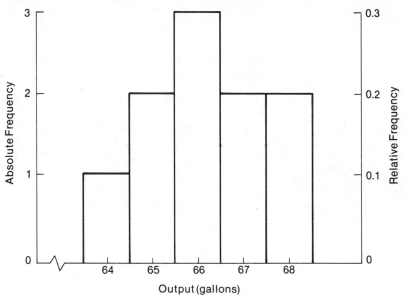

Output (gallons)

to measure relative frequencies. A histogram is constructed by erecting a rectangle equal in height to the frequency of each category. A histogram for the production of the Pure Chemical Company's vats is shown in Figure 2.4.

2.24 Frequency Polygon

Another type of graphical presentation for displaying data from the frequency distribution table is the frequency polygon. A frequency polygon is obtained by joining dots at the appropriate height (or frequency) for each category of data being analyzed. In other words, the frequency polygon is formed by joining the midpoints of the tops of the rectangles in a histogram. When these dots are connected, a many-sided figure (polygon) is formed. It is accepted practice to close the polygon at both ends of the distribution by drawing a line from the dot representing the frequency of the lowest category to a point on the horizontal axis half a bar width to the left. This same procedure is also followed on the right side of the horizontal axis for the highest category. This procedure makes the area under a frequency polygon equal to that under a histogram. A frequency polygon for the production of the Pure Chemical Company's vats is presented in Figure 2.5.

Figure 2.5

Frequency Polygon (Pure Chemical Company curing vat output, January 19, 1976)

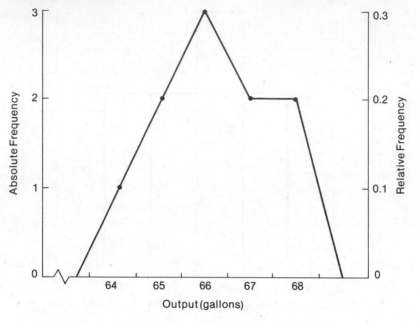

Figure 2.6

Frequency Polygon and Smooth Curve (Pure Chemical Company curing vat output, January 19, 1976)

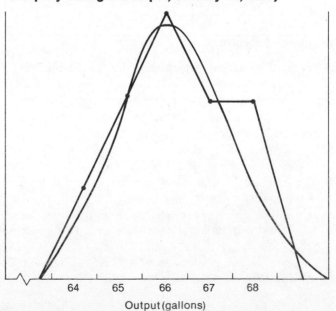

It is important to realize that the line segments are drawn for convenience in reading the graph. The only meaningful points on the graph are the dots representing frequencies of each category.

The very small population plotted above as a frequency polygon results in a series of straight lines. If a much larger population of output values were plotted, the resulting frequency polygon might approach a smoothed curve, as shown superimposed in Figure 2.6.

2.25 Cumulative Frequency Distribution Table

In many analyses, it is of interest to know the number of cases that lie at or below a specified value, rather than within an interval as shown in a frequency distribution. In these situations, a cumulative frequency distribution is used rather than the frequency distribution.

A cumulative frequency distribution shows the number of observations less than or equal to each value of the variable.

The cumulative frequency distribution table for the output of the Pure Chemical Company's vats is shown in Figure 2.7. This table is sometimes

Figure 2.7

Cumulative Frequency Distribution (Pure Chemical Company curing vat output, January 19, 1976)

Output (gallons)	Frequency		Cumulative Frequency (less than or equal to)	
	Absolute	Relative	Absolute	Relative
64	1	0.1	1	0.1
65	2	0.2	3	0.3
66	3	0.3	6	0.6
67	2	0.2	8	0.8
68	2	0.2	10	1.0
Totals	10	1.0		

called a "less than" cumulative distribution table. This name is derived from the information that can be obtained from the table. For example, for six of the ten vats, the output was 66 gallons or less, or the output was "less than or equal to" 66 gallons for six vats.

2.26 Cumulative Frequency Distribution Graph

The graph of a cumulative frequency distribution for the Pure Chemical Company data is displayed in Figure 2.8. The plotted points represent the

Figure 2.8

"Less Than or Equal To" Cumulative Frequency (Pure Chemical Company curing vat output, January 19, 1976)

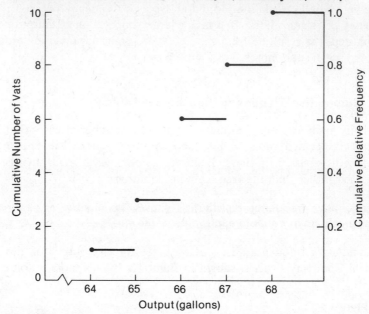

ungrouped

number of occurrences (vats) having "less than or equal to" the number of gallons of output shown on the horizontal axis directly below the plotted point. The configuration shown is typical of the appearance of the "less than or equal to" curve. Cumulative frequency tables and graphs showing "greater than or equal to" can also be prepared.

2.3 FREQUENCY DISTRIBUTIONS: GROUPED DATA

Thus far, this chapter has been devoted to a description of presentations pertaining to observations which can be treated individually without a requirement to be grouped. For the Pure Chemical Company example, each vat was represented by an integer number of gallons; it was not necessary to group several integers into one category. This section treats the case where large numbers of observations are placed in arbitrarily chosen classes or categories to accommodate the analysis. The only definite rules that apply to the construction of frequency distributions for grouped data are that the classes must be *exhaustive* (there is a class for every observation) and *mutually exclusive* (an observation cannot fall into more than one

Figure 2.9

Output, Pure Chemical Company (50 aging vats)

465.64	614.87	502.81	578.12	527.47
560.17	552.46	560.16	512.09	538.86
523.97	592.24	557.17	593.07	506.34
587.56	473.76	571.29	487.52	604.77
554.37	536.39	529.91	533.48	488.08
579.61	508.64	636.02	552.33	524.06
431.91	525.53	496.36	582.59	478.26
545.18	471.15	532.67	591.43	457.69
561.22	546.07	575.79	578.66	567.83
573.35	517.79	567.82	569.84	538.96

class). Other than this rule, each case is dependent on the specific design of the analyst.

A *frequency distribution* for grouped data shows the number of times the value of a variable occurs in each category or class. The classes must be selected so that they are mutually exclusive (do not overlap) and exhaustive (everything is included).

As in the previous sections of this chapter, these concepts are better understood by studying an example. The number of gallons of a different chemical product manufactured in a total of 50 aging vats by the Pure Chemical Company is presented in Figure 2.9, for February 28, 1976. These data will be used throughout this section to demonstrate the concepts of frequency distribution as applied to grouped data.

2.31 Ordered Array

The first step in the development of a frequency table is to organize the raw data in an ordered array as shown in Figure 2.10. It is observed from

Figure 2.10

Ordered Array of Output, Pure Chemical Company (50 vats)

431.91	506.34	533.48	560.16	578.66
457.69	508.64	536.39	560.17	579.61
465.64	512.09	538.86	561.22	582.59
471.15	517.79	538.96	567.82	587.56
473.76	523.97	545.18	567.83	591.43
478.26	524.06	546.07	569.84	592.24
487.52	525.53	552.33	571.29	593.07
488.08	527.47	552.46	573.35	604.77
496.36	529.91	554.37	575.79	614.87
502.81	532.67	557.17	578.12	636.02

this ordered array that the extreme values are 431.91 gallons and 636.02 gallons.

2.32   Classes: Number and Width

After data are ordered into an array, it is necessary to determine classes into which the data fall. *Classes* are specific ranges within which all data can be placed. Questions are frequently asked about how many classes are useful and what size should they be. There is no "correct" answer for every set of data. Each case must be treated separately; each frequency table must be designed individually. More detail can be shown in larger numbers of classes; however, if the number of classes is too large, the classification loses its effectiveness as a means of summarizing data. On the other hand, if the number of classes is too small, the data will be condensed so much that little or no insight can be gained into the nature of the pattern of variation. The number of classes in a frequency table generally ranges from four to twenty, with seven to twelve quite typical.

The choice of class width is directly related to the number of classes. It is best if all classes are the same width. This provides ease in the interpretation of the distribution. However, in certain cases, unequal class intervals must be used. Such would be the case for salary ranges for a large number of people: narrow class widths would be used for values of the variable where many data points fall, and wider class widths would be used where the number of occurrences is relatively small.

In the example in the previous section, seven intervals with a class width of 30 gallons will fit very nicely; however, 11 intervals of 20 gallons each or six intervals of 40 gallons would also have been acceptable. Once the classes have been selected, the number of items in each class is determined by counting. The general form to present this tally is shown in Figure 2.11.

In specifying class limits, the analyst should avoid ambiguity. For

Figure 2.11

Tally Table for Constructing Frequency Distribution of Output (Pure Chemical Company curing vats)

Output (gallons)			
At Least	But Less Than	Tally	No. Vats
430	460 11		2
460	490 .... ̶H̶l̶l̶ 1		6
490	520 .... ̶H̶l̶l̶ 1		6
520	550 .... ̶H̶l̶l̶ ̶H̶l̶l̶ 11		12
550	580 .... ̶H̶l̶l̶ ̶H̶l̶l̶ ̶H̶l̶l̶ 1		16
580	610 .... ̶H̶l̶l̶ 1		6
610	640 11		2
			Total 50

example, limits such as 430–460 and 460–690 are not clear, because 460 could be assigned (erroneously) to both classes. If the class limits are "at least 430 but less than 460," etc., there is no doubt into which class an item falls.

2.33 Class Midpoint

While class limits are important in frequency distribution construction, the class midpoint is extremely important in calculations regarding the distribution. The midpoint of a class is the number which lies halfway between the lower and upper limits of the class, or the average of the two limits of that class. The midpoints for the classes being used in the Pure Chemical Company example are shown in Figure 2.12.

Figure 2.12

Frequency Distribution for Output (Pure Chemical Company curing vats)

Class Interval (gallons)		Midpoint	Frequency Number of Vats	Relative Frequency
At Least	But Less Than			
430	460	445	2	0.04
460	490	475	6	0.12
490	520	505	6	0.12
520	550	535	12	0.24
550	580	565	16	0.32
580	610	595	6	0.12
610	640	625	2	0.04
			Total 50	1·00

The first class interval begins at 430 and ends just below 460 at 459.99 . . . ; this clearly indicates that 460 falls in the second, not the first, class interval. For computational purposes, the midpoint of the class is calculated by averaging 430 and 460, producing a value of 445 for the midpoint of the first class.

If the variable is something which is counted rather than measured, the class intervals would appear with integer limits such as 200–229; 230–259; etc. In this case, the midpoints would be 214.5, 244.5, etc. If the variable is measured and before tallying rounded to, say, an integer, the midpoint will still be the average of the class limits, which are the largest and smallest (rounded) values that can fall in that class.

2.34 Histogram

A histogram for the grouped data in Figure 2.13 is identical in concept to the histogram for the ungrouped data in Figure 2.4. The histogram of

Figure 2.13

Histogram of Output (Pure Chemical Company, 50 curing vats)

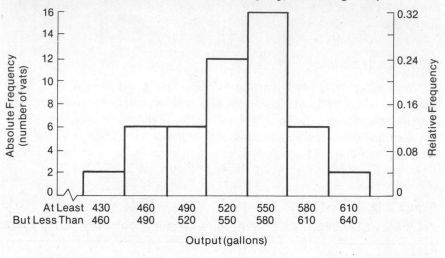

Figure 2.13 is constructed for 50 vats, with the classes and frequencies previously developed.

2.35   Frequency Polygon

The frequency polygon was described in relation to ungrouped data in Section 2.24. Using this description and the output data for the aging vats of the Pure Chemical Company, the polygon in Figure 2.14 is constructed.

Figure 2.14

Frequency Polygon (Pure Chemical Company, 50 curing vats)

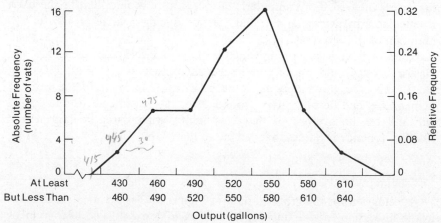

2.36 Frequency Density

If a histogram (or other graphical display) is to be prepared for a frequency distribution of grouped data, special care needs to be taken if the class intervals are of unequal width. To see why this is true, the array of Figure 2.10 has been tabulated into a frequency distribution with unequal class intervals; see the left-most three columns of Figure 2.15. The "histogram" which would result from this set of frequencies would not look like the correct histogram of Figure 2.13. In fact, its (incorrect) shape would be an upright ∪, while the correct histogram shape is similar to ∩. To correct for the unequal class intervals, one would find for each

Figure 2.15

Frequency Distribution with Unequal Class Intervals for Output (Pure Chemical Company curing vats)

Output (gallons)		Frequency (number of vats)	Relative Frequency	Class Width	Frequency Density	Relative Frequency Density
At Least	But Less Than					
430	500	9	0.18	70	0.129	0.00257
500	530	10	0.20	30	0.333	0.00667
530	540	5	0.10	10	0.500	0.01000
540	570	12	0.24	30	0.400	0.00800
570	640	14	0.28	70	0.200	0.00400
	Totals	50	1.00			

class the *frequency density* or the *relative frequency density*. The frequency density is the frequency for that class divided by the width of that class. The relative frequency density is the relative frequency divided by the class width. A histogram or frequency density polygon constructed from these density values would have the same general appearance as the corresponding graphical display developed from equal class intervals. The frequency densities and relative frequency densities are shown in the right-most columns of Figure 2.15. For frequency densities in which the data are integers, the class width is the number of distinct integer values in the class.

2.37 Cumulative Frequency Distribution

Cumulative frequency distributions were described for the ungrouped data situation in Sections 2.25 and 2.26. The variable for the grouped data situation is represented by one of the limits of each class interval. The

Figure 2.16

Cumulative Frequency Distribution for Output (Pure Chemical Company, 50 curing vats)

Output (gallons)	Cumulative Frequency (less than or equal to) Absolute	Relative
460............................... 2		0.04
490............................... 8		0.16
520...............................14		0.28
550...............................26		0.52
580...............................42		0.84
610...............................48		0.96
640...............................50		1.00

Figure 2.17

Cumulative Frequency Distribution for Output (Pure Chemical Company, 50 curing vats)

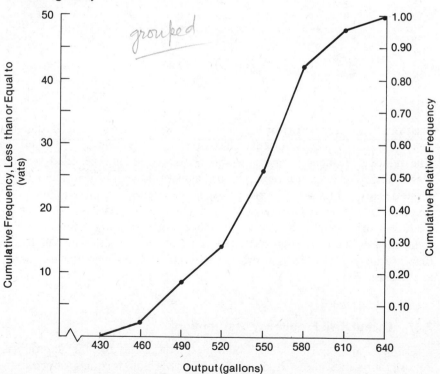

cumulative frequency distribution table for the output of the Pure Chemical Company 50 curing vats is shown in Figure 2.16, and graphically in Figure 2.17.

2.4 SUMMARY

The basic ingredient of statistics is data. The basic sources of data are either internal or external to the organization. In order to analyze the collected data it must be organized into some useful format. Data may be used in an ungrouped form, but usually are grouped into intervals. Data may also be usefully displayed by a histogram or polygon. Relative frequency distributions may be calculated on the basis of individual class intervals or on a cumulative basis.

EXERCISES

* 2.1   Classify each of the following into internal data or external data:
    a. The population, by census tract, of the county in which you are doing business.
    b. The number of your customers, by census tract, in the county in which you are doing business.
    c. Sales volume, by department, for the XYZ Industries.
    d. Industrial production, by industry classification, as reported by the Federal Reserve Board.
    e. Profit margin for each of your 43 product lines.
    f. Average profit margin, by industry classification, for each of 43 major industries.
    g. Bad debts your firm incurred in 1975.

* 2.2   Classify each of the following as time series data or cross section data:
    a. False alarm rate, Denver Fire Department, 1962–75.
    b. False alarm rate, Denver Fire Department, by census tract, 1975.
    c. Population of San Mateo County, 1947–74.
    d. Population of California, by county, 1974.
    e. The number of your customers, by census tract, for 1975.
    f. Sales volume, by department, for the XYZ Industries, 1963.
    g. Unemployment claims, monthly, 1970–75.

2.3   The number of children in ten families is 0, 4, 2, 1, 1, 0, 0, 3, 2, 1. Construct:
    a. An ordered array.
    b. A frequency distribution.
    c. A relative frequency distribution.
    d. A cumulative frequency distribution.

* Answers to exercises marked with an asterisk (*) are in Appendix L.

2.4   For October, the eight sales people of the Edeo Realty Company reported these results:

Salesperson	Number of Sales
JT	0
HT	2
PD	4
EO	2
BO	1
QU	3
FH	3
JR	3

a.   Construct a frequency distribution, a histogram, and a frequency polygon for these sales data.

b.   Construct a cumulative frequency distribution table for these data.

* 2.5   The dean of the business school of a large state university wanted to prepare a justification for more faculty positions. One of the justifications was the large class size within the school. For the previous semester, 40 classes had been offered, with the following initial student enrollments:

37	48	59	23	46	105	103	97
74	21	8	14	46	72	81	36
50	40	15	70	74	77	106	47
24	18	48	58	78	61	82	80
32	20	82	74	63	91	32	19

a.   Construct an ordered array for student enrollment.

b.   Using an appropriate grouping, present the data in a frequency distribution table.

c.   Prepare a histogram for the dean to use in the justification. Make sure all titles, labels, etc., are correcly shown on the histogram.

2.6   In trying to understand the buying habits of its customers better, the Pine Tree Sales Corporation gathered information on the number of times each customer made a purchase. (This was possible because every customer was routinely asked for her/his name and address for sales brochure mailings.) For the year 1975, the data were tabulated as shown below:

Number of Purchases in 1975	Number of Customers
1	95
2	86
3	94
4	63
5	72
6	80
7	65
8	40
9	53

Number of Purchases in 1975	Number of Customers
10	20
11	13
12	11
13	10
14	14
15	9
16	6
17	7
18	5
19	8
20	4
21	3
22	8
23	7
24	5
25	2
26	4
27	0
28	0
29	1
30	1
33	1
36	2
40	1
47	1
52	1

a. Using an appropriate set of equal class intervals, prepare a frequency distribution and a histogram to represent these data.

b. Using a set of class intervals with *unequal* class intervals, prepare a relative frequency density histogram to represent these data.

* 2.7 The cumulative frequency distribution for the number of rooms (as defined by the Bureau of the Census) in a house, for a census tract in a large city, is:

Number of Rooms	Number of Houses with at Least this Number of Rooms
1	950
2	950
3	950
4	950
5	950
6	942
7	630
8	247
9	41
10	8
11	1
12	1
13	0

    a.   Construct the frequency distribution table for the number of rooms in houses in the census tract.

    b.   Construct the cumulative frequency distribution table showing the opposite accumulation, i.e., the number of houses with the stated number of rooms or fewer.

2.8   There are several errors or improper procedures illustrated in the following frequency distribution for the number of TV sets sold by the Boob Tube Shop salespeople. Describe as many errors or poor procedures as you think exist.

Number of Sets Sold	Number of Salespeople (frequency)
fewer than 30	2
30–35	3
35–40	1
40–50	4
50–54	3
more than 54	9

2.9   In making a presentation to the sales committee of the Sunflake Corporation, you need to present the data showing profit margin on each of five product lines produced by the Sunflake Corporation. Which one or two of the following would you use in presenting the information? Explain why you would not use any you choose to omit.

    a.   Frequency table.

    b.   Ordered array.

    c.   Histogram.

    d.   Frequency polygon.

    e.   Cumulative distribution table.

    f.   Frequency density table.

    g.   A listing showing the name of each product line (in alphabetical order) and the profit margin for that line.

    h.   A listing showing the name of each product line and the profit margin for the line, arranged in order of decreasing profit margin.

2.10   In making a presentation to the sales committee of the Sunflake Corporation, you need to present data showing the size of purchase of Sunflake's 83,246 customers. Which one or two of the following would you use in presenting the information? Explain why you would not use any you choose to omit.

    a.   Frequency table, grouped data, equal class intervals.

    b.   Frequency table, grouped data, unequal class intervals.

    c.   Ordered array.

    d.   Histogram.

    e.   Frequency density histogram.

    f.   Frequency density polygon.

    g.   A listing showing the name of each customer (in alphabetical order) and the size of purchase for that customer.

    h.   A listing showing the name of each customer and the size of that customer's purchase, arranged in order of decreasing purchase size.

REFERENCES

Ehrenberg, A. S. C.   *Data Reduction*. New York: John Wiley & Sons, Inc., 1975.

Hoel, Paul G.   *Elementary Statistics*. 2d ed. New York: John Wiley & Sons, Inc., 1966.

Leabo, Dick A.   *Basic Statistics*. 5th ed. Homewood, Ill.: Richard D. Irwin, Inc., 1976.

McCollough, Celeste, and Van Atta, Locke.   *Statistical Concepts*. New York: McGraw-Hill Book Co. 1963

3

Measures of Central Tendency and Dispersion

3.1 DISTRIBUTIONS AND THEIR CHARACTERISTICS

In the previous chapter, data collection and organization were discussed. The discussion did not distinguish between complete sets of data and subsets of data. It is necessary to clarify the distinction between a population and subsets of this population.

A *population* is the set of all possible units (people, places, things) from which meaningful information can be obtained relative to a characteristic of interest.

A population consists of the units from which information is desired, rather than the information itself. If information is desired on employees' wages, the employees themselves are the units which make up the population. Wages are the characteristic of interest and, as a variable, take on different values. Business-related populations might consist of employees, suppliers, consumers, stockholders, units of production, units of inventory, pieces of equipment, accounts receivable, accounts payable, or any other similar grouping of units about which the decision maker might desire information.

One purpose of this chapter is to discuss numerical characteristics of populations.

Numerical characteristics of populations are called *parameters*. Population parameters are generally given a Greek letter as their statistical label.

Later in this chapter the concept of a sample (a subset of a population) is discussed.

3.2 MEASURES OF CENTRAL TENDENCY

Data may be organized and presented in many ways, some using all data in its original form while others use all the data in a reduced or representative form. The methods presented in Chapter 2 involve using all the data in either original or grouped form. The measures of central tendency and measures of dispersion discussed in this chapter constitute data reductions or transformations. A single value will be obtained which represents some characteristic of an entire set of data.

The measures which describe central tendency are similar to the everyday concept of average. These measures are concerned with finding that value which best represents the center of the data array. The primary measures of central tendency include the mean, the median, and the mode.

3.21 Mean

For a set of data, the mean is the average value of the data. Stated differently, the mean of a variable X is the sum of the observations on X divided by N, where N is the total number of observations.

$$\mu_X = \frac{X_1 + X_2 + \cdots + X_N}{N}$$

The symbol μ_X (μ is the Greek letter *mu*) is the accepted notation for the mean of a population. As such, it is a *parameter*.

Consider the following observations of a variable: 7, 9, 10, 10, 11, 13. For this data array, μ_X may be found by adding and dividing by six.

$$\mu_X = \frac{X_1 + X_2 + X_3 + X_4 + X_5 + X_6}{6} = \frac{7 + 9 + 10 + 10 + 11 + 13}{6}$$

$$= \frac{60}{6} = 10$$

In order to simplify the notations used in the definition of the mean and subsequent measures, the summation notaton Σ and the subscript i are introduced. The symbol Σ is the symbol for summation; it is the notation for "the sum of." The subscript i is used with Σ in order to define what is to be added. In the example, six numbers were added. If we consider these six numbers generally as X_1 (the first observation), X_2 (the second observation) X_3, X_4, X_5, and X_6, we have a sequence of subscripts on X ranging from one to six. So the desired operation actually becomes "sum X_i as i goes from one to six." Using notation,

$$\mu_X = \frac{\sum_{i=1}^{6} X_i}{6} = \frac{X_1 + X_2 + X_3 + X_4 + X_5 + X_6}{6}$$

For the more general case,

$$\mu_X = \frac{\sum_{i=1}^{N} X_i}{N} = \frac{X_1 + X_2 + \cdots + X_N}{N}$$

One characteristic of the mean is the potential impact on the mean of a single unusual observation. Consider the previous example with one more observation, 7, 9, 10, 10, 11, 13, 31. The mean of X would be

$$\mu_X = \frac{\sum_{i=1}^{7} X_i}{7} = \frac{7 + 9 + 10 + 10 + 11 + 13 + 31}{7} = \frac{91}{7} = 13$$

By including one extreme value, 31, the mean increased from 10 to 13. Another measure of central tendency, the median, reduces the impact of extreme values.

3.22 Median

The median is obtained by creating an ordered array of the observations on X and then finding the value at the middle position in the array. For the example containing the extreme value,

7
9
10
10◄————Value at middle position of array = Median = 10
11
13
31

For the example chosen, finding the median was simplified by the fact that an odd number of observations of X were presented. When an even number of observations are listed, there may be no single middle position value.

7
9
10
11   ◄————Two middle position values
13
31

A median for an even number of observations may be found by averaging the two middle position values,

$$\text{Median} = \frac{10 + 11}{2} = \frac{21}{2} = 10.5$$

Expressing these definitions of the median in a more general manner, let $X_1, X_2 \ldots , X_N$ be an ordered array of observations of X with X_1 the smallest observation and X_N the largest observation. If N is an odd number, then the median, denoted as MED, is symbolically.

$$\text{MED} = X_{\frac{N+1}{2}}$$

For the case where $N = 7$,

$$\text{MED} = X_{\frac{7+1}{2}} = X_4$$

and the fourth term in the ordered array is chosen as the median.

If N is an even number, then a median is obtained by,

$$\text{MED} = \frac{X_{\frac{N}{2}} + X_{\frac{N}{2}+1}}{2}$$

For the case where $N = 6$,

$$\text{MED} = \frac{X_{\frac{6}{2}} + X_{\frac{6}{2}+1}}{2} = \frac{X_3 + X_4}{2}$$

The third and fourth terms in the ordered array are averaged to obtain a median.

3.23   Mode

Frequently, it is desirable to know what value in a distribution or array of observations occurs with the greatest frequency. Such a value is defined to be the *mode* and is denoted as Mo. This definition implies a single mode for any distribution. However, there are distributions where multiple modes appear; a definition compatible with multiple occurrences would be desirable. Therefore, the mode is more correctly defined as any value at which the frequency density is at a peak, or local maximum. For the first distribution in Figure 3.1, there is only one peak or one most frequent

Figure 3.1

Unimodal and Bimodal Distributions

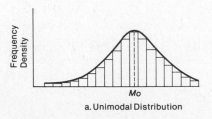

a. Unimodal Distribution

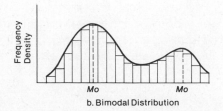

b. Bimodal Distribution

value; there is only one local maximum. For the second distribution, there are two peaks, or two local maximums. Although one peak is definitely higher than the other, there are still two peaks for the distribution. Such a distribution is called a *bimodal distribution*.

A uniform distribution, as shown in Figure 3.2, has no mode. A uniform distribution is one where all values of X occur with the same frequency. Therefore, no single value of X occurs more frequently than any other value.

For the data array 7, 9, 10, 10, 11, 13, the mode is ten, because this value of X occurs twice while all other values occur only once. If one of the tens had been omitted from the set, there would be no modal value.

Figure 3.2

Uniform Distribution, Having No Mode

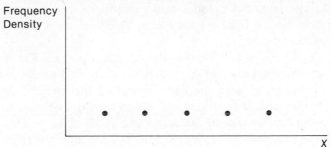

As a measure of central tendency, the mode has obvious limitations. Some distributions have more than one mode, while other distributions have no mode. It is the most typical value or values, but it does not always provide a good measure of the middle or center of a distribution. However, when one is measuring the most popular color or style, the mode is unique in its descriptive ability.

3.24   Comparison of the Mean, Median, and Mode

As measures of central tendency, three alternatives have been examined; mean, median, and mode. There are definite relationships that exist between these measures when the distribution being examined is unimodal.

In Figure 3.3, the distribution presented is unimodal and symmetric. Symmetry means that the distribution's left side is a mirror image of its right side. For a distribution that is both unimodal and symmetric, the mean, median, and mode all occur at the same value of X.

In Figure 3.4, the distributions are unimodal but not symmetric. A distribution which is not symmetric is called a *skewed* distribution. The

Figure 3.3

Unimodal and Symmetric Distribution

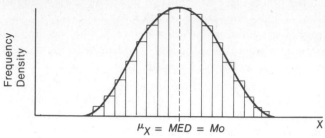

$$\mu_X = MED = Mo$$

distribution in Figure 3.4(a) is skewed to the right, while the distribution in 3.4(b) is skewed to the left. Right skewness means extreme values are typically to the right of the modal value, and therefore cause the mean to be higher than (to the right of) the mode. The converse is true of a distribution skewed to the left.

When a unimodal distribution is skewed, the mean, median, and mode all occur at different values of X. The mode is located at the peak of the distribution; the mean is to the right or left of the mode depending on whether the concentration of extreme values is to the right or to the left; and the median falls between the mean and mode. The median is therefore the preferred measure of central tendency for highly skewed distributions, as for example income distributions. It is often more meaningful to know the median income level, at which half of the population earns less and half earns more. The mean can be greatly affected (raised) by a few extremely high incomes.

The purpose of measures of central tendency is to locate the middle of a set of numerical observations. The mean, median, and mode are alternative methods for measuring this basic concept. The mean is the most generally used measure, and is used predominately throughout the remainder of this text.

Figure 3.4

Unimodal and Skewed Distributions

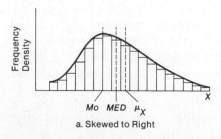

a. Skewed to Right

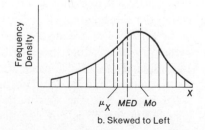

b. Skewed to Left

3.3 MEASURES OF DISPERSION

Once the mean has been determined, the next question is, "How far from the mean do the data fall?" Do they cluster tightly about the mean? Or do they vary widely, with considerable dispersion between the X values and the mean, μ_X?

The question of data dispersion has attracted sufficient attention to result in numerous measures of this basic concept. Some of these will be examined in the next portion of this chapter. The major measures of dispersion to be covered include: range, average deviation, variance, and standard deviation.

3.31 Range

One of the simplest measures of dispersion is the *range,* which is defined as the difference between the largest and smallest value of X.

$$\text{Range} = X_{\max} - X_{\min}$$

where $X_{\max}$ is the largest value and $X_{\min}$ is the smallest.

However, as a measure of dispersion, it is very limited in usefulness. The problem with the range as a dispersion measure is its total reliance on only two extreme data points. If one data point is an extreme point, it leads to a distorted dispersion measure. For example, consider the following data:

$$X = 3,3,5,7,7,49$$

For this group of data, the range is found by subtraction of the minimum value (3) from the maximum value (49). However, examination of the data indicates that 49 is an extreme value; an average expression of dispersion would be much smaller.

3.32 Average Deviation

Given that the range is often unacceptable as a measure of dispersion, alternative expressions of dispersion must be sought to alleviate some of the problems of the range. A new question is posed and answered: What is the average amount by which the data in the data set differ from the mean?

Each data point of observation differs from the mean by a measurable amount. This can be measured in a general sense by the expression,

$$d_i = X_i - \mu_X$$

where d_i is the difference between any specific data point, X_i, and the mean, μ_X. Consider the following data,

$$X = 7, \quad 9, \quad 10, \quad 10, \quad 11, \quad 13$$

Obtain the mean of the data,

$$\mu_X = \frac{\sum_{i=1}^{N} X_i}{N} = \frac{7 + 9 + 10 + 10 + 11 + 13}{6} = \frac{60}{6} = 10$$

Now calculate the deviation of each data point from its mean,

i	X_i	$d_i = X_i - \mu_X$
1.	7	$7 - 10 = -3$
2.	9	$9 - 10 = -1$
3.	10	$10 - 10 = \;\;\;0$
4.	10	$10 - 10 = \;\;\;0$
5.	11	$11 - 10 = \;\;\;1$
6.	13	$13 - 10 = \;\;\;3$

The average of a group of data is found by summing all observations and dividing by the number of observations summed. In this case, the average of the deviations is

$$\frac{\sum_{i=1}^{N} d_i}{N} = \frac{(-3) + (-1) + 0 + 0 + 1 + 3}{6} = \frac{0}{6} = 0$$

There is an obvious problem here. The average amount by which the six observations deviate from the mean has been found to be zero, yet all six observations are not tens. This is not a special case; for any data set, the average of the deviations about the mean is zero.

This situation arises because the negative values offset the positive values; something needs to be done to eliminate the negative signs. Two mathematical procedures immediately come to mind which will accomplish this result: taking the absolute value[1] of all deviations, or squaring all deviations. Either procedure will convert all signs to positive signs. First examine the results when absolute values are taken prior to averaging the deviations.

i	X_i	$X_i - \mu_X$	$|X_i - \mu_X|$
1.	7	-3	3
2.	9	-1	1
3.	10	0	0
4.	10	0	0
5.	11	1	1
6.	13	3	3
Totals	60	0	8

---

[1] The absolute value of a number is obtained by ignoring any negative sign. It is noted by a pair of vertical bars around the number. Thus:

$$|3| = 3$$
$$|-3| = 3$$
$$|-27.2| = 27.2$$

The average of the absolute deviations, called the *average deviation* becomes:

$$\text{Average Deviation} = \frac{\sum_{i=1}^{N} |X_i - \mu_X|}{N} = \frac{3 + 1 + 0 + 0 + 1 + 3}{6} = \frac{8}{6}$$
$$= 1.333$$

A serious problem in using the average deviation is that of mathematical manipulation. By using the absolute value operation in order to eliminate negative signs, severe restrictions are placed upon the subsequent mathematical operations which may be used in developing the theory of sampling and the techniques of statistical inference. Some mathematical operations become quite restricted by absolute values. This problem is so critical that an alternative measure of dispersion is needed with better mathematical properties.

3.33   Variance and Standard Deviation

As mentioned in the discussion of the average deviation, there are two simple methods of dealing with the problem of signs in averaging deviations about the mean: absolute values and squares. The average deviation was found by averaging the absolute values of the deviations. Now the result of squaring the deviations is examined.

Returning to the prior example and squaring the deviations, we have:

i	X_i	$X_i - \mu_X$	$(X_i - \mu_X)^2$
1	7	-3	9
2	9	-1	1
3	10	0	0
4	10	0	0
5	11	1	1
6	13	3	9
Totals	60		20

Thus, the sum of the squared deviations is 20 for this example. The average or mean squared deviation is found by dividing by 6 (the number of observations):

$$\frac{\sum_{i=1}^{N} (X_i - \mu_X)^2}{N} = \frac{9 + 1 + 0 + 0 + 1 + 9}{6} = \frac{20}{6} = 3\tfrac{1}{3}$$

The mean squared deviation is also called the *variance,* and is denoted by the symbol σ_X^2 (σ is the Greek letter *sigma*). Thus

$$\text{Variance} = \sigma_X{}^2 = \frac{\sum_{i=1}^{N} (X_i - \mu_X)^2}{N}$$

is the general expression for the variance, and for the example

$$\text{Variance} = \sigma_X{}^2 = 3\tfrac{1}{3}$$

Variance is quite different from the average deviation discussed in the previous section. Whereas the average deviation carried the same units as the original observations, the variance is expressed in squared units. This may be corrected by taking the square root of the variance. In order to distinguish the variance from its square root, the square root of the variance is called the *standard deviation*.

$$\text{Standard Deviation} = \sigma_X = \sqrt{\sigma_X{}^2}$$

and therefore

$$\text{Standard Deviation} = \sigma_X = \sqrt{\frac{\sum_{i=1}^{N} (X_i - \mu_X)^2}{N}}$$

For the example,

$$\sigma_X = \sqrt{\frac{\sum_{i=1}^{N} (X_i - \mu_X)^2}{N}} = \sqrt{\frac{9 + 1 + 0 + 0 + 1 + 9}{6}} = \sqrt{\frac{20}{6}} = 1.826$$

The standard deviation is expressed in the same units as the original observations.

The variance and standard deviation, as measures of dispersion, are amenable to further mathematical manipulation and therefore serve as the most desirable of the discussed measures of dispersion. Their use will be extensive in the development of the various techniques of statistical inference which are presented in the remainder of this book.

3.34   Alternative Formulas: Variance and Standard Deviations

An alternative formulation of both the variance and standard deviation can be obtained through simple mathematical manipulation (shown in note 3.34, following Chapter 17 of the text). These are:

$$\sigma_X{}^2 = \frac{\sum_{i=1}^{N} (X_i - \mu_X)^2}{N} = \frac{\sum_{i=1}^{N} X_i{}^2 - \frac{\left(\sum_{i=1}^{N} X_i\right)^2}{N}}{N}$$

and

$$\sigma_X = \sqrt{\dfrac{\displaystyle\sum_{i=1}^{N} X_i^2 - \dfrac{\left(\displaystyle\sum_{i=1}^{N} X_i\right)^2}{N}}{N}}$$

This alternative formulation is especially convenient to use when the arithmetic mean is not a whole number or an easy number to subtract from each observation. Further, it simplifies the amount of work required on a worksheet prior to formula substitution and solution. The comparative worksheets of Figure 3.5 demonstrate these points.

Figure 3.5

Comparative Worksheets

Worksheet A for $\sigma_X^2 = \dfrac{\Sigma(X - \mu_X)^2}{N}$

X	$X - \mu_X$	$(X - \mu_X)^2$
2	−3.8	14.44
5	−0.8	0.64
7	1.2	1.44
7	1.2	1.44
8	2.2	4.84
29	0	22.80

$$\mu_X = \frac{29}{5} = 5.8$$
$$\sigma_X^2 = \frac{22.80}{5} = 4.56$$
$$\sigma_X = \sqrt{4.56} = 2.14$$

Worksheet B for $\sigma_X^2 = \dfrac{\Sigma X^2 - \dfrac{(\Sigma X)^2}{N}}{N}$

X	X^2
2	4
5	25
7	49
7	49
8	64
29	191

$$\mu_X = \frac{29}{5} = 5.8$$
$$\sigma_X^2 = \frac{(191) - \frac{(29)^2}{5}}{5} = \frac{191 - 168.2}{5} = 4.56$$
$$\sigma_X = \sqrt{4.56} = 2.14$$

Worksheet A requires three columns; Worksheet B requires only two. Furthermore, the squaring operations on Worksheet A have produced figures with two decimal places in the third column. Fewer columns and simpler squares are shown on Worksheet B. In general, it is best to use Worksheet A when the mean is a whole number, and Worksheet B when the mean is not a whole number. Also note in Figure 3.5 that a simpler notation has been used by omitting subscripts. Thus:

$$\sum_{i=1}^{N} X_i \quad \text{simplifies to } \Sigma X$$

$$\sum_{i=1}^{N} (X_i - \mu_X)^2 \text{ simplifies to } \Sigma(X - \mu_X)^2$$

3.4 SKEWNESS

The concept of skewness has been illustrated in Figure 3.4. Numerical descriptions of skewness are also possible. A commonly used measure of skewness is Pearson's measure, the *coefficient of skewness*. Recall that as skewness increases, the mean and median become further apart. Also, a right-tail skewness has the mean to the right of the median. Thus, the measure of skewness:

$$Sk = \frac{3(\mu_X - \text{MED})}{\sigma_X}$$

increases as the mean and median diverge. It is positive for right-tail skew, and negative for left-tail skew.

3.5 MEAN AND STANDARD DEVIATION FOR FREQUENCY DISTRIBUTIONS

The calculations for a population mean and standard deviation that have just been described assume the statistician is working with raw data rather than with data from a frequency distribution. In the previous chapter, frequency distributions were presented both for ungrouped data and for grouped data.

3.51 Mean for a Frequency Distribution

The method for finding the mean states that the observations of the variable X are to be added (i.e., ΣX). This sum is then divided by the number of observations, N, for example,

$$\mu_X = \frac{\Sigma X}{N}$$

However, when a set of data is presented as a frequency distribution, some values (for example $X = 10$) may occur more than once. The symbol f_i is used to denote the number of times the value X_i occurs in the data. The total number of observations in the set of data is $N = \Sigma f_i$. Furthermore, since the value X_i occurs f_i times, then the expression $f_i X_i$ represents the sum of the observations which have the value X_i. Hence, to find the sum of the observations of the variable X, simply multiply each value X_i, by its frequency f_i and add these products for all values of the variable X. Thus, for a frequency distribution:

$$\mu_X = \frac{\Sigma f X}{N}$$

where the summation is preformed over all distinct values of X. For example, the data

$$X = 3,4,4,5,7,7,7,8,8,9$$

Figure 3.6

Arithmetic Mean for a Frequency Distribution

X	f	fX
3	1	3
4	2	8
5	1	5
7	3	21
8	2	16
9	1	9

$$N = \Sigma f = \overline{10} \qquad \Sigma fX = \overline{62}$$

$$\mu_X = \frac{\Sigma fX}{N} = \frac{62}{10} = 6.2$$

$N = \Sigma f_i$

can be represented as the frequency distribution shown in the first two columns of Figure 3.6. The third column shows the products fX and their sum. At this point, you can add the original observations (3,4,4,5,7,7,7, 8,8,9) and observe that the two sums have the same value. From this sum, the mean is easily calculated as shown in Figure 3.6.

3.52 Standard Deviation for a Frequency Distribution

The same ideas apply to the standard deviation of a set of data presented as a frequency distribution. Figure 3.7 compares the expressions encountered in the previous computations of the standard deviation and their corresponding expressions using a frequency distribution. Although the formulas may appear different, they are different only because a particular value, X_i, appears f_i times; this repeated occurrence needs to be ac-

Figure 3.7

Comparison of Expressions for Standard Deviation Calculation

Raw Data Expressions	*Frequency Distribution Expressions*
ΣX	ΣfX
ΣX^2	ΣfX^2
$(\Sigma X)^2$	$(\Sigma fX)^2$
$\Sigma(X - \mu_X)^2$	$\Sigma f(X - \mu_X)^2$
$\sigma_X = \sqrt{\dfrac{\Sigma(X - \mu_X)^2}{N}}$	$\sigma_X = \sqrt{\dfrac{\Sigma f(X - \mu_X)^2}{N = \Sigma f}}$
$\sigma_X = \sqrt{\dfrac{\Sigma X^2 - \dfrac{(\Sigma X)^2}{N}}{N}}$	$\sigma_X = \sqrt{\dfrac{\Sigma fX^2 - \dfrac{(\Sigma fX)^2}{N}}{N = \Sigma f}}$
Σ denotes summation over all *observations* in the distribution.	Σ denotes summation over all *values* in the frequency distribution.

Figure 3.8

Standard Deviation for a Frequency Distribution

X	f	fX	X^2	fX^2
3	1	3	9	9
4	2	8	16	32
5	1	5	25	25
7	3	21	49	147
8	2	16	64	128
9	1	9	81	81
	$\Sigma f = \overline{10}$	$\Sigma fX = \overline{62}$		$\Sigma fX^2 = \overline{422}$

$$\sigma_X = \sqrt{\frac{\Sigma fX^2 - \frac{(\Sigma fX)^2}{N}}{N}} = \sqrt{\frac{422 - \frac{(62)^2}{10}}{10}} = \sqrt{3.76} = 1.94$$

counted for in the formula. The standard deviation for the data of Figure 3.6 is calculated in Figure 3.8, using the methods that were illustrated in Figure 3.7.

3.6 DESCRIPTIVE MEASURES FOR GROUPED DATA

In a frequency distribution with ungrouped data, each observation in a class has the same value. When the data have been grouped into a frequency distribution, many different values are present in a group; the identity of each observation is lost.

In order to find the mean and variance using grouped data, it is assumed that each observation falls at the midpoint of the class.

To find the mean or variance, the procedures discussed above for a frequency distribution are used with the class midpoints as the values of X.

To find the median of grouped data, it is assumed that the observations are uniformly spread throughout each interval. Then if, for example, one wants to estimate the fifth number in a class with 25 numbers, it would be estimated as the value 5/25, or 1/5 of the way into the class. These concepts are illustrated in the example of Figure 3.9.

3.7 PERCENTILE: ANOTHER DESCRIPTIVE MEASURE

A descriptive measure commonly used in reporting scores is the percentile. A person receiving a score of the 82 percentile scored better than 82 percent of the reference group taking the exam. The median is the 50 percentile. Other percentiles have special names; the 75 percentile is called the *third quartile* (three fourths below), and the 25 percentile is called

Figure 3.9

Calculations of Mean, Variance, Standard Deviation, and Median Using Grouped Data

Hourly Wage						
At Least	But Less Than	Midpoint, X	X^2	f	fX	fX^2
$1.00	$1.80	$1.40	1.96	12	16.8	23.52
1.80	2.60	2.20	4.84	27	59.4	130.68
2.60	3.40	3.00	9.00	23	69.0	207.00
3.40	4.20	3.80	14.44	21	79.8	303.24
4.20	5.00	4.60	21.16	7	32.2	148.12
				90	257.2	812.56

Mean:
$$\mu_X = \frac{\Sigma fX}{N} = \frac{257.2}{90} = 2.858$$

Variance:
$$\sigma_X{}^2 = \frac{\Sigma fX^2 - \frac{(\Sigma fX)^2}{N}}{N} = \frac{812.56 - \frac{(257.2)^2}{90}}{90} = \frac{812.56 - 735.02}{90}$$

$$\sigma_X{}^2 = 0.8616$$

Standard Deviation: $\sigma_X = \sqrt{0.8616} = 0.9282$

Median: Since $N = 90$, there are 45 numbers on each side of the median. The first class contains 12 observations; the first two contain $12 + 27 = 39$ observations; the first three contain $12 + 27 + 23 = 62$ observations. The median is approximately the $45 - 39 = $ 6th observation in the third class, or about 6/23 of the width of the class away from the boundary—a distance of $6/23 \times 0.80 = 0.21$. Thus, the median is about 2.60 (the lower limit of the class) + 0.21, or about $2.81.

the *first quartile* (one fourth below). Similarly, the *first decile* has one tenth below, and so on. The procedures for finding the median have their obvious extension to finding other percentiles.

3.8 TCHEBYCHEFF'S THEOREM

In developing measures of dispersion, the standard deviation was presented as the most frequently used measure. It has mathematical properties which facilitate development of statistical theory. It carries the same units as the variable, whereas the variance is expressed in squared units.

Further insight into the role and meaning of the standard deviation can be gained through examination and use of a theorem developed by the Russian mathematician, Tchebycheff. The theorem states that, given a group of N numbers, at least the proportion $1 - (1/k)^2$ of the N observations will lie within k standard deviations of the mean. The symbol k is simply a number of standard deviations. The theorem may be quantified for any desired value of k.

Graphically, the essence of the theorem is seen in Figure 3.10. Begin-

Figure 3.10

Tchebycheff's Theorem Graphically

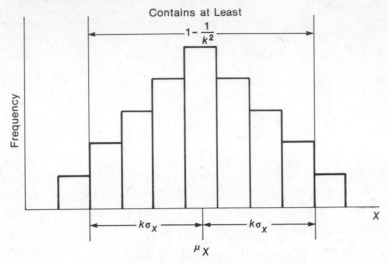

ning at the mean, μ_X, an interval is created along the X axis by the addition and subtraction of k standard deviations. This interval, once obtained, will contain at least $1 - (1/k)^2$ of the total observations of X. Each different value of k produces a new interval with different minimum proportions of observations encompassed.

To illustrate, let $k = 1,2$, and 3. When $k = 1$, the interval created is the mean plus and minus one standard deviation, $\mu_X \pm 1\sigma_X$. For this value of k, the minimum proportion of observations contained in the interval is $1 - (1/k)^2 = 1 - 1/1 = 0$. When $k = 2$, the interval is $\mu_X \pm 2\sigma_X$, and the minimum number of observations in the interval is $1 - (1/2)^2 = 3/4$. When $k = 3$, 8/9 or more of the observations will fall within three standard deviations of the mean.

k Values	Ranges	*Minimum Proportion of Observations*
1	$\mu_X \pm 1\sigma_X$	0
2	$\mu_X \pm 2\sigma_X$	¾ or 75 percent
3	$\mu_X \pm 3\sigma_X$	8/9 or 88.89 percent

The proportion of the observations falling with in the various intervals are all minimums. At *least* that percentage of observations will fall in that interval. These minimums hold regardless of the distribution being investigated.

For the example of Section 3.33, where $X = 7,9,10,10,11,13$, $\mu_X = 10$ and $\sigma_X = 1.826$:

$\mu_X \pm k\sigma_X$	Observations Included	Actual Proportion	Tchebycheff's Minimum Proportion
$10 \pm 1(1.826)$ or 8.174 to 11.826	9,10,10,11	$\frac{4}{6} = \frac{2}{3}$	0
$10 \pm 2(1.826)$ or 6.348 to 13.652	7,9,10,10,11,13	$\frac{6}{6} = 1$	$\frac{3}{4}$
$10 \pm 3(1.826)$ or 4.522 to 15.478	7,9,10,10,11,13	$\frac{6}{6} = 1$	$\frac{8}{9}$

It is obvious that the actual proportion of observations which were encompassed by the respective intervals easily exceed the Tchebycheff minimums.

3.9   SAMPLES AND STATISTICS

Earlier in this chapter a population was defined as the set of all possible units (people, places, things) from which meaningful information can be obtained about a characteristic of interest. The previous sections of this chapter have dealt with developing and computing summary measures, called parameters, which describe the central tendency and dispersion of a variable possessed by the elements of a population.

In many statistical investigations, it is not feasible or economically desirable to find the value of the variable of interest for each element of the population. When this is the case, a sample of the population will be investigated.

A *sample* is a subset of a population. It is a collection of *n* elements taken from the population of *N* elements.

As shall be seen in Chapter 5, there are certain procedures which must be followed for the selection of the sample, if the sample is to be used in statistical investigations. However, our purpose in this chapter is to show how characteristics resulting from a sample are to be calculated. These sample characteristics are called *statistics;* the corresponding population characteristics described in this chapter are called *parameters.*

A sample *statistic* is a number calculated from the values of a variable possessed by elements of a sample.

Corresponding to the parameter called the *population mean,* there is the sample statistic called a *sample mean.* Similarly, corresponding to the *population variance* and the *population standard deviation,* there are the statistics called the *sample variance* and *sample standard deviation.*

The population parameter symbols are μ_X, σ_X^2, and σ_X; the corresponding sample statistic symbols are $\bar{X}$, s_X^2, and s_X.

3.91   Sample Mean, Variance, and Standard Deviation

For the n elements in a sample, the sample mean, $\bar{X}$, is defined as:

$$\bar{X} = \frac{\Sigma X}{n}$$

This is, of course, analogous to the definition of the population mean.

The variance of the observations in a sample is called the sample variance, s_X^2. It is defined as:

$$s_X^2 = \frac{\Sigma(X - \bar{X})^2}{n - 1} = \frac{\Sigma X^2 - \frac{(\Sigma X)^2}{n}}{n - 1}$$

The sample standard deviation, s_X, is therefore:

$$s_X = \sqrt{s_X^2} = \sqrt{\frac{\Sigma(X - \bar{X})^2}{n - 1}}$$

In comparing the sample variance with the population variance, the primary difference is that the denominator for the sample variance is $n-1$ whereas the denominator for the population variance is N. There is a theoretical reason which makes the $n-1$ divisor appropriate. This reason relates to the fact that $\bar{X}$ is used instead of μ_X in the calculation of the sum of the squared deviations in the numerator of the expression.

If sample statistics are computed from a frequency distribution or from grouped data, the procedures are similar to those already described. Figure 3.11 shows all of these formulas in summary form.

In Chapter 8 we will more fully discuss the use of sample statistics as estimates of population parameters.

3.10   SUMMARY

Measures of central tendency such as the mean, mode, and median were discussed in this chapter. Measures of dispersion such as the range, variance, and standard deviation were also discussed at length. Formulas and computational methods for calculation of the mean, variance, and standard deviation were developed and demonstrated for ungrouped data, grouped data, and frequency distributions. Formulas were developed for both a population and a sample.

Special topics concerning skewness, quartiles, deciles, and percentiles were also described.

Figure 3.11
Summary of Formulas

Parameter

statistics

Case	*Population*	*Sample*
Mean, original data	$$\mu_X = \frac{\Sigma X}{N}$$ Where the summation operation is performed over all elements of the population.	$$\overline{X} = \frac{\Sigma X}{n}$$ Where the summation operation is performed over all elements of the sample.
Mean, frequency distribution data	$$\mu_X = \frac{\Sigma fX}{N = \Sigma f}$$ Where the summation operation is performed over all distinct values of X in the population.	$$\overline{X} = \frac{\Sigma fX}{n = \Sigma f}$$ Where the summation operation is performed over all distinct values of X in the sample.
Mean, grouped data	$$\mu_X = \frac{\Sigma fX}{N = \Sigma f}$$ Where each value of X represents the midpoint of its class, and the summation operation is performed over all classes.	$$\overline{X} = \frac{\Sigma fX}{n = \Sigma f}$$ Where each value of X represents the midpoint of its class, and the summation operation is performed over all classes.
Variance, original data	$$\sigma_X^2 = \frac{\Sigma(X - \mu_X)^2}{N}$$ Or $$\sigma_X^2 = \frac{\Sigma X^2 - \frac{(\Sigma X)^2}{N}}{N}$$ Where the summation operation is performed over all elements of the population.	$$s_X^2 = \frac{\Sigma(X - \overline{X})^2}{n - 1}$$ Or $$s_X^2 = \frac{\Sigma X^2 - \frac{(\Sigma X)^2}{n}}{n - 1}$$ Where the summation operation is performed over all elements of the sample.
Variance, frequency distribution data	$$\sigma_X^2 = \frac{\Sigma f(X - \mu_X)^2}{N = \Sigma f}$$ Or $$\sigma_X^2 = \frac{\Sigma fX^2 - \frac{(\Sigma fX)^2}{N}}{N}$$ Where the summation operation is performed over all distinct values of X in the population.	$$s_X^2 = \frac{\Sigma f(X - \overline{X})^2}{n - 1 = \Sigma f - 1}$$ Or $$s_X^2 = \frac{\Sigma fX^2 - \frac{(\Sigma fX)^2}{n}}{n - 1 = \Sigma f - 1}$$ Where the summation operation is performed over all distinct values of X in the sample.
Variance, grouped data	$$\sigma_X^2 = \frac{\Sigma f(X - \mu_X)^2}{N = \Sigma f}$$ Or $$\sigma_X^2 = \frac{\Sigma fX^2 - \frac{(\Sigma fX)^2}{N}}{N}$$ Where each value of X represents the midpoint of its class, and the summation operation is performed over all classes.	$$s_X^2 = \frac{\Sigma f(X - \overline{X})^2}{n - 1 = \Sigma f - 1}$$ Or $$s_X^2 = \frac{\Sigma fX^2 - \frac{(\Sigma fX)^2}{n}}{n - 1 = \Sigma f - 1}$$ Where each value of X represents the midpoint of its class, and the summation operation is performed over all classes.
Standard deviation, any situation	$$\sigma_X = \sqrt{\sigma_X^2}$$	$$s_X = \sqrt{s_X^2}$$

EXERCISES

3.1   Distinguish between *central tendency* and *dispersion*. Give examples of measures of each.

3.2   In determining whether to wade across a stream, would the average depth of the water be a sufficient guide to action for a nonswimmer? If not, what characteristics of the water depth would be important?

3.3   If the average wealth of state governors is $1,437,000, is it necessarily true that the "typical" governor has a wealth of $1,437,000? If not, what measures would you desire in order to describe the wealth of a "typical" governor?

3.4   Why is the *median* income often preferred to the *mean* income?

*   3.5   The ages of the children who live in the 2700 block of Iliff Street are 1, 4, 8, 4, 11, 7, 3, 11, 15, 9, 7, 3, 18, 3, 7 and 8.
           What is the average age of these children?

*   3.6   Find the median age of the children in Exercise 3.5.

*   3.7   Find the modal age of the children in Exercise 3.5.

*   3.8   What is the range of the age of the children in Exercise 3.5?

*   3.9   What is the variance of the age of the children in Exercise 3.5?

*   3.10   What is the standard deviation of the age of the children in Exercise 3.5?

*   3.11   How many children have an age within one, two, and three standard deviations on either side of the mean? How does this compare with Tchebycheff's theorem?

3.12   Compute the variance of the age of the children in Exercise 3.5 by using a different method than in Exercise 3.9. Make sure your answers agree with each other. Which method do you prefer? Why?

3.13   Differentiate between a *sample* and a *population*. Give examples of each.

3.14   Differentiate between a *statistic* and a *parameter*. Give examples of each.

*   3.15   The Denver Fire Department took a sample of 100 runs of fire trucks to fires. The time required for each run was recorded to the nearest minute. On the same worksheet, information was recorded to show the square of the time required for each run, as well as the number (from 1 to 100) of the particular run being timed. The worksheet appeared as shown below, with some of the data (but none of the totals) omitted:

Run Number	Time Required, X, Minutes	X^2
1	3	9
2	4	16
3	1	1
4	5	25
.	.	.
.	.	.
.	.	.
99	2	4
100	3	9
Totals	300	1,197

* Answers to exercises marked with an asterisk (*) are in Appendix L.

Find the average run time, the variance of run time, and the standard deviation of run time.

* 3.16 The Colorado Springs Fire Department took a sample of 100 runs of fire trucks to a fire. However, the work sheet used in Colorado Springs was considerably different from the Denver worksheet shown in Exercise 3.15. For the Colorado Springs data shown below, find the average time and the standard deviation of run time.

Time Required, X, Minutes	Number of Runs
1	6
2	28
3	36
4	17
5	9
6	3
7	1
8 or more	0

* 3.17 A family has lived in five different cities. The number of years in each city was: 5 years, 16 years, 1 year, 3 years, and 8 years. Find the average number of years in a city, and the standard deviation of time in a city.

* 3.18 A random sample of five families was selected. The number of years each family had lived in the city was: 5 years, 16 years, 1 year, 3 years and 8 years. Find the average number of years in the city, and the standard deviation for the time in the city.

3.19 Compare your answers to Exercises 3.17 and 3.18. Which answers are identical? Which answers are different? Why?

* 3.20 Use the raw data from Exercise 2.5 to find the mean and standard deviation of class size. Treat class as a sample.

3.21 Use the grouped data frequency distribution you prepared for Exercise 2.5(b) to find the mean and standard deviation of class size. Will this result be the same as the answer to Exercise 3.20? Why or why not?

3.22 For the data given in Exercise 2.7, find the average number of rooms in a house, and the standard deviation.

* 3.23 The Sunflake Corporation has presented you with data on the profit margin (profit per unit divided by the selling price of the unit) for each of five products:

Product	Profit Margin (percent)	Selling Price	Number sold in 1975
Stuffed dog	8.3	$ 6	100
Stuffed cat	10.4	5	200
Backpack	25.0	6	5
Doll	7.2	9	1,000
Doll House	19.2	18	100

a. Find the average of the five values of profit margin shown above.
b. Find the profit for each product in 1975, by finding the gross sales

for that product (selling price × number sold), and multiplying the sales volume by the profit margin for the product.

c. Find the total profit for all five products for Sunflake.

d. Find the total gross sales for all five products for Sunflake.

e. Find the profit margin for all sales made by Sunflake.

f. Compare your answers to parts *a* and part *e*. Why are they different?

* 3.24 A motorist drove 100 miles, averaging ten miles per gallon. Next, the motorist drove 100 miles over a different course, averaging 20 miles per gallon. What was the average miles per gallon for the 200 miles? (Hint: it is *not* 15 mpg. Note that consumption of gasoline is 15 gallons.)

REFERENCES

Freund, John E. *Modern Elementary Statistics.* 4th ed. Englewood Cliffs, N.J.: Prentice-Hall, Inc., 1973.

Hoel, Paul G. *Elementary Statistics.* 2d ed. New York: John Wiley & Sons. Inc., 1966.

Neter, John; Wasserman, William; and Whitmore, G. A. *Fundamental Statistics for Business and Economics.* 4th ed. Boston: Allyn & Bacon, Inc., 1973.

Yule, G. Udny, and Kendall, M. G. *An Introduction to the Theory of Statistics.* 14th ed. London: Charles Griffin, 1950.

4

Probability Theory and
Probability Distributions

4.1 PROBABILITY

Management decisions are made in an environment of uncertainty. Under uncertainty, the decision maker does not know which of several events or outcomes will occur in the future. Because decisions are made under uncertainty, a precise terminology for dealing with uncertainty is needed. Probability theory is such a precise terminology.

Before probability theory can be studied, some notation, concepts, and terminology are needed. The notation used is set theory because there are very close relationships between sets and probabilities.

4.2 SETS AND SUBSETS

A *set* is any collection of objects. The objects are called *elements* of the set. The objects belong to the set. Sets may be presented in several ways. The way used here is to list all elements of the set. The label for the set, *S,* is equated to a complete itemization of all elements in the set, contained in braces, such as:

$$S = \{1, 2, 6, 12\}$$

The set need not contain numerical elements. For example,

$$S = \{\text{Bob, Carol, Ted, Alice}\}$$

has nonnumerical elements.

A *subset* is a set of elements whose elements are wholly contained in another set. For example, {Bob, Ted} is a subset of {Bob, Carol, Ted, Alice}.

4.21   Set Theory and the Sample Space

The probability equivalent of a set is a sample space. If one knows what will happen in the context of a given decision problem, the only outcome of interest is that outcome which is going to happen. But when many different things can happen, there are many outcomes that are of interest. The collection of all possible outcomes is called a *sample space*. A sample space is a special case of the general concept of a set. A set is defined as a collection of objects. An *experiment* is finding out what happens in an uncertain situation. A sample space is the collection of the outcomes of an experiment.

A *sample space* is the set of all possible outcomes of an experiment.

Within the sample space are individual elements which are called *simple events*. A simple event is a single outcome of the experiment. It is the smallest unit of a sample space, and cannot usefully be further decomposed. A simple event of a sample space corresponds to an element of a set.

A single outcome of an experiment, the smallest unit of a sample space, is called a *simple event*. The set of all simple events is constructed so that exactly one simple event must occur. Thus, the simple events are said to be mutually exclusive and exhaustive.

Figure 4.1

Venn Diagram of the Sample Space for Statistics Course Decision

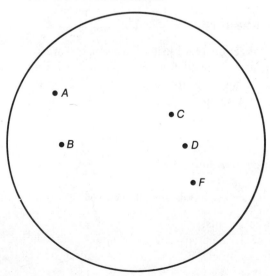

As an example of a sample space, consider a student's decision problem of whether to enroll in a first-semester statistics course in the sophomore year. Assuming that the student is only interested in the grade for the course, there are five possible outcomes or simple events in the sample space. The student could take the course and receive any of the following grades: A, B, C, D, or F. This sample space is shown in Figure 4.1, a figure generally called a *Venn diagram*.

Frequently, it is desirable to speak of a collection of simple events, which is then called an *event*. An event is equivalent to a subset in set theory. At one extreme, an event may be the entire sample space. On the other hand, the event may be a single outcome or simple event.

An *event* is a subset of simple events from the set of simple events constituting a sample space.

Referring back to the example of grades for a statistics course, an event might be defined as passing the course. This event contains four of the five points in the sample space: A, B, C, and D. The point associated with F is not included in the event, because it does not meet the definition of passing the course.

4.22 Sample Space and Probability Functions

For the sample space to be useful in decision making, it is necessary to attach to each simple event a probability of its occurrence. This probability should indicate the likelihood of the occurrence of that event.

A *probability function* is defined as a function or rule which assigns a probability value to every simple event in the sample space. It is required that each assigned probability be greater than or equal to zero, and that the sum of all of the assigned probabilities for the simple events be equal to one.

A *probability function* is a function which assigns a probability, *P(E)*, to each simple event *E* of a sample space *S* subject to two conditions:

1. $P(E) \geq 0$ for each simple event E
2. $\Sigma P(E) = 1$

Any function which deals with the likelihood of events and meets these two conditions may qualify as a probability function. For specific cases, however, greater knowledge of the experiment or process is usually required in order to find the probability function that is relevant to the problem.

4.3   THREE APPROACHES TO DEFINING PROBABILITIES

Depending upon the type of experiment to be performed, there are various ways of assigning probabilities to the simple events in a sample space. The method for assigning probabilities to the roll of a pair of dice does not work for assigning a probability to whether the United States will be wholly dependent on imported crude oil in the year 2000. Hence three different approaches to probabilities are discussed: an *equally likely* approach, a *relative frequency* approach, and a *subjective* (or personalistic) approach.

4.31   Probabilities Based on Equally Likely Simple Events

In many situations there is reason to believe that the various simple events which constitute the sample space are all *equally likely* to occur. Most of these equally likely situations are based on some mechanical device, such as a gambling mechanism. It is usually assumed that a roulette wheel is constructed so that each of the positions is equally likely to be the one in which the ball stops. For a well shuffled deck of cards, each of the cards in the deck is equally likely to be, say, the thirteenth card from the top of the deck. When lottery tickets are placed in a large urn and mixed well, there is good reason to believe that each ticket in the urn is equally likely to be selected. In each of these situations, a conscious effort has been made to produce equally likely outcomes. We shall see in the next chapter that sampling is often done so that each element of the population has an equally likely chance of being selected.

When an equally likely situation arises, it is easy to associate a probability with each simple event in the sample space. If there are $N(S)$ simple events in the sample space S, and each of them is equally likely to occur because of some physical mechanism or arrangement, one can say that the probability of any particular simple event is $1/N(S)$. This definition satisfies the probability function conditions that the probabilities add up to one, and that the probabilities assigned are not negative. When one die from a pair of dice is rolled, the probability of a particular face appearing is one out of six, or $\frac{1}{6}$, because there are six faces on a die. This sample space with associated probabilities is shown in Figure 4.2.

Extending this concept, the formal equally likely definition of the probability of an event states:

If the list of all N(S) equally likely simple events contains N(A) simple events which indicate the occurrence of an event A, then the *probability* that event A will occur is:

$$P(A) = \frac{N(A)}{N(S)}$$

Figure 4.2

Sample Space for One Roll of a Die, with Probabilities

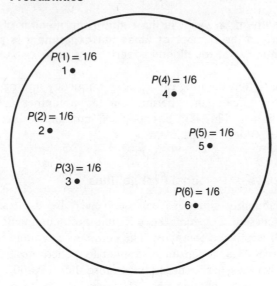

For example, consider the probability of obtaining an odd number of dots on one roll of a true die. There are six sides to the die with dots on each side from one through six inclusive; $N(S) = 6$. Exactly three of the six sides have an odd number of dots; $N(A) = 3$, therefore,

$$P(\text{odd}) = \frac{3}{6} = \frac{1}{2}$$

4.32   Probabilities as Relative Frequencies

After an item has been manufactured, it is either within the specifications (good) or not within the specifications (bad). Even though there are two outcomes, good and bad, it does *not* necessarily follow that $P(\text{good}) = P(\text{bad}) = \frac{1}{2}$. In this situation a different definition is needed to replace the equally likely approach to probability.

What is the probability of obtaining a good item? Suppose you make 100 items and obtain 85 good ones. You should be inclined to make a statement to the effect that the probability of obtaining a good one is approximately 0.85. But suppose you then make another 100 items and obtain a total of 172 good ones in the 200. You should then be inclined to say that the probability of a good one is about 172/200 or 0.86. As you continue to obtain experience, the ratio of the number of good ones obtained to the total number of items made may tend to cluster closely about some number. This suggests a long run *relative frequency* approach to probabilities. This approach to probabilities defines the probability of an event as:

The *probability* of an event is the ratio of the number of times the event occurs to the number of times the experiment is performed, where the number of repetitions is very, very large.

Note carefully that the long run relative frequency approach assumes it is possible to duplicate an experiment a large number of times under identical conditions. This is a strenuous, if not impossible, requirement for many business decision problems.

4.33   Subjective or Personal Probabilities

Not all probability situations can be viewed by the two approaches previously discussed. Consider the decision problem facing the product manager of an appliance company. The company is going to introduce to the marketplace a new consumer appliance called an "electric back-washer." The backwasher is successful if more than 10,000 are sold at the full retail price in the coming year. The product manager is concerned about the probability that the backwasher will be a success. A believer in the equally likely approach to probability might be tempted to conclude that the probability that the backwasher will be successful is 0.5 (on the faulty reasoning that there are two possible events, success and failure, and the probability of each is therefore ½). This reasoning is fallacious because there is no reason to believe that the two events, success and failure, are equally likely.

A person trained in the relative frequency approach to probabilities might be tempted to suggest that the product be introduced a large number of times in the coming year and that one simply counts the number of times it is successful. This obviously does not make sense, because it is impossible to introduce the same product as a "new" product more than once. In other words, this experiment cannot be repeated.

For the backwasher, both the equally likely and relative frequency approaches to probability are inappropriate. However, this does not mean that one cannot talk about the probability that the backwasher will be successful. For example, it is common to talk about the probability of rain tomorrow, even though tomorrow will occur only once. People talk about the probability that the horse named "Hoe" will win the sixth race tomorrow, even though there will be only one sixth race tomorrow. Sports fans talk about the probability that a favorite football team will win the big game on Sunday, even though the game will be played only once. None of these probabilities can be assessed by either the equally likely or relative frequency approaches, yet they are meaningful to those who use them. These probabilities are called *subjective* (or personal) probabilities.

A *subjective probability* represents the individual's degree of belief in the occurrence of an event.

The product manager who says "the probability is 0.7 that the electric backwasher will be successful" is using accumulated judgment, experience, and "gut feeling" of the situation to convey a personal "70 percent sure" that the product will be successful.

It is important to note that various decision makers, assessing the probability of the same event, may reach different conclusions about the "correct" probability. This occurs because different people have different experience and judgment. However, the probability assessed by a particular decision maker is useful to that person for the decision problem being studied.

It is also useful to note that there is typically a great deal of subjectivity in determining any probability, whether it is a probability determined by an equally likely or a relative frequency approach. The equally likely approach has used a *subjective* judgment that the events in the event space are indeed equally likely. A relative frequency probability is based on the assumption that an experiment has been performed repeatedly under identical conditions. Whether the conditions were indeed identical is a *subjective* evaluation on the part of the decision maker. Thus, it can be argued that any business decision under uncertainty involves *subjective* probabilities.

4.34   Which Approach to Probability Should Be Used?

There is no unique answer to the question of which probability approach is most useful. Each is useful in some situations. In many statistical problems one can artificially create an equally likely situation in the process of sampling. In a sampling procedure one can artificially place many elements in an urn and then select the sample from that urn, much as in a lottery drawing. Hence, an equally likely model has been placed into the decision process. Other times there will be enough data about a situation which has been repeated under identical (or nearly identical) situations over a long period of time. When data are available, and when the conditions under which the data were collected are similar to the conditions anticipated for the future, the data can be used as a long run relative frequency probability. When neither of these conditions exists, a subjective approach to probability must be used. In the business world, conditions are very seldom stable long enough to avoid the use of some subjective elements in the assignment of probability numbers to simple events. It is typical to start with relative frequencies, and then make

Figure 4.3

Unions and Intersections

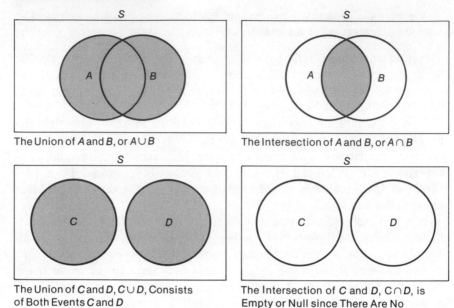

The Union of A and B, or A∪B

The Intersection of A and B, or A∩B

The Union of C and D, C∪D, Consists of Both Events C and D

The Intersection of C and D, C∩D, is Empty or Null since There Are No Simple Events That Belong to Both C and D

modifications to account for changes or differences for the particular situation.

4.4 EVENTS, UNIONS, AND INTERSECTIONS

In the previous sections, three approaches have been discussed which may be useful in assigning probability numbers to simple events. In addition to these probabilities for simple events, one is often interested in the probability of an event. An event has already been defined to be a subset or group of simple events. The probability of an event is given by this definition:

> The *probability of an event* is the sum of the probabilities of the simple events that make up the event.

When dealing with events it is useful to use the definitions of *union* and *intersection* of events. These definitions are adapted from set notation:

> The *union* of two events A and B, denoted A ∪ B, is the event which contains all simple events which belong to either A or B, including those which belong to both A and B.

The *intersection* of two events A and B, denoted A ∩ B, is the event which contains all simple events which belong to both A and B.

Figure 4.3 illustrates the unions and intersections for two events. The top two diagrams show a situation in which the events A and B overlap. The lower diagrams show a situation in which the events C and D do not overlap; i.e., C and D are *mutually exclusive*.
Therefore:

Two events C and D are *mutually exclusive* if there are no simple events that belong to both C and D. In other words, C and D are mutually exclusive if they have no intersection. Two mutually exclusive events cannot both occur at the same time.

$$P(A \cap B) = 0$$

Figure 4.4

Set Theory and Probability

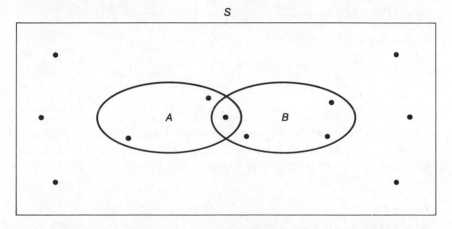

In Figure 4.4, a diagram is used to define the probability of both a union and an intersection of two events. Altogether, there are twelve points in the sample space S. Six of these points do not appear in either A or B, three points appear in A, four appear in B, and one point is in the intersection of A and B. Assuming each point is equally likely, the probability of each point is $1/N(S) = \frac{1}{12}$.

Since the simple events are equally likely, it can be stated that:

$$P(A) = \frac{N(A)}{N(S)} = \frac{3}{12} = \frac{1}{4}$$

$$P(B) = \frac{N(B)}{N(S)} = \frac{4}{12} = \frac{1}{3}$$

The above states that the probability of the event A equals the number of simple events in A, N(A), divided by the total number of simple events in S, $N(S)$. Therefore in Figure 4.4, $P(A) = \frac{3}{12} = \frac{1}{4}$. In like manner, $P(B) = \frac{4}{12} = \frac{1}{3}$.

The probability of the event $A \cap B$ equals the number of points in the intersection of A and B divided by the number of simple events in S, $N(S)$. In Figure 4.4,

$$P(A \cap B) = \frac{N(A \cap B)}{N(S)} = \frac{1}{12}$$

This is also called the *joint probability* of A and B.

For the union of A and B, $P(A \cup B)$ equals the number of elements in A plus the number of elements in B, minus the number of elements in the intersection A and B, all divided by the total count of simple events in the sample space. When calculating the probability of the union of A and B, one must subtract the elements in the intersection in order to prevent their being double-counted. For Figure 4.4,

$$P(A \cup B) = \frac{N(A) + N(B) - N(A \cap B)}{N(S)} = \frac{3 + 4 - 1}{12} = \frac{1}{2}$$

Or restating $P(A \cup B)$:

$$P(A \cup B) = \frac{N(A) + N(B) - N(A \cap B)}{N(S)} = \frac{N(A)}{N(S)} + \frac{N(B)}{N(S)} - \frac{N(A \cap B)}{N(S)}$$

$$= P(A) + P(B) - P(A \cap B)$$

The relationship above is used to find the probability of the union of any two events. Although it has been developed using equally likely simple events, it is applicable to *any* events.

Figure 4.5

Mutually Exclusive Events C and D

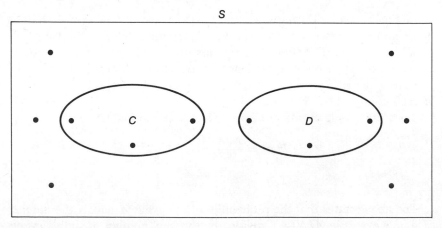

The additive law of probability states that the probability of the union of two events, *A* and *B*, is equal to:

$$P(A \cup B) = P(A) + P(B) - P(A \cap B).$$

When there are no common simple events between two events, then there is no intersection, and such events have been defined as mutually exclusive events. The probability of the union of two mutually exclusive events equals the sum of the probabilities of each event, since the probability of their (empty or null) intersection is zero. Figure 4.5 shows such a situation.

A special case of two mutually exclusive events is *complementary events*.

The *complement* of the event *A* is all simple events that are not in *A*. The complement of *A* is noted *A'*.

If the event *A* is "Jan will pass the course," the complement event, *A'*, is "Jan will not pass the course." From the additive law of probabilities for these mutually exclusive events:

$$P(A') = 1 - P(A)$$

and

$$P(A) = 1 - P(A')$$

because the probability for the entire sample space $(A \cup A')$ is one.

Example. A class has the following student characteristics:

Characteristic	Percent of Class
Male (M)	40
Female (F)	60
Wear glasses (G)	30
Long hair (H)	80
Long hair and male (H ∩ M)	35
Female wearing glasses (F ∩ G)	10

1. What is the meaning of:
    a. $H \cap M$? — and / intersection / together
    b. $H \cup M$? or / either or / union

    a. $H \cap M$ means a student who is both long haired and male; it is the intersection of *H* and *M*.
    b. $H \cup M$ means a student who is either long haired or male (or both); it is the union of *H* and *M*.

2. For a student selected at random from the class, calculate
    a. $P(H \cap M)$
    b. $P(H \cup M)$

    a. $P(H \cap M) = 0.35$ (given)

b. $P(H \cup M) = P(H) + P(M) - P(H \cap M)$ (additive law of probabilities)

$P(H \cup M) = 0.80 + 0.40 - 0.35 = 0.85$

3. Which of the following event pairs is a pair of mutually exclusive events?
    a. M,H
    b. M,F
    c. F,G

    a. M,H cannot be mutually exclusive, because some students are both male and long haired.

    b. M,F are mutually exclusive; a student cannot be both male and female simultaneously.

    c. F,G cannot be mutually exclusive, because some female students wear glasses.

4.5 CONDITIONAL PROBABILITIES

There are many cases where the probability of the occurrence of one event depends upon whether or not another event has occurred. Up to this point, probabilities of events have been presented relative to or contingent upon the entire sample space, S. It may also be desired to obtain the probability of occurrence of an event A given that event B has occurred. What this does is reduce the relevant sample space from S to B; thus, B becomes a new sample space. In other words, when one knows event B has occurred, the information available has changed. As information changes, probabilities may change.

Consider again the diagram of Figure 4.4 in which each point in the sample space S is equally likely. There are twelve points in the sample space S, and the probability of any specific point occurring, given the point will be selected from S, is $\frac{1}{12}$. Constraining your consideration only to B (rather than S), notice that there are four points in B, all equally likely. Therefore, the probability of occurrence for any point in A, *given* that B has occurred, is $\frac{1}{4}$. By imposing the special condition, reference to B rather than S, the probabilities attached to the points are altered.

All probabilities are contingent upon some base. It is useful to develop special relationships for cases when an original sample space S is defined and then a second base, say the event B, is introduced. The conditional probability of an event A, *given* that the event B has occurred, is noted as

$$P(A|B)$$

where the event that is given appears to the right of the vertical line and the event whose probability is desired over the new base of reference is to the left of the vertical line. $P(A|B)$ is read, "Probability of A *given* B."

In Figure 4.4, each point in S has a probability of $\frac{1}{12}$ when S is the base. Each point in B has a probability of $\frac{1}{4}$ when B is the base. Given B as the base, there is only one point in A which also is in B. Therefore,

$$P(A|B) = 1/4$$

If the event A is the base, then there are three points to be considered. Only one of these is in B, so the probability would be $\frac{1}{3}$. Therefore,

$$P(B|A) = 1/3$$

The process of reassigning probabilities to each and every simple event when the reference base changes can become tedious. The use of a simple relationship can expedite the calculations of conditional probability:

The *conditional probability* of an event *A*, given that *B* has occurred, is defined as

$$P(A|B) = \frac{P(A \cap B)}{P(B)}$$

To understand this definition, return to Figure 4.4 to calculate again the probability of A, given B, which is written as $P(A|B)$. There are four points in B and only one of them is also contained in A. Therefore, the conditional probability of event A, given B, is:

$$P(A|B) = \frac{N(A \cap B)}{N(B)} = 1/4$$

Divide the numerator and denominator by $N(S)$, and obtain:

$$P(A|B) = \frac{N(A \cap B)/N(S)}{N(B)/N(S)} = \frac{P(A \cap B)}{P(B)}$$

as defined above.

This relationship is rewritten to obtain the multiplicative law of probability:

The *multiplicative law of probability* states that the probability of the intersection of two events, *A* and *B*, is

$$P(A \cap B) = P(A) \cdot P(B|A)$$

$$P(A \cap B) = P(B) \cdot P(A|B)$$

This law also touches upon a most important relationship between events. Two events are said to be *independent* of each other in a statistical sense if the occurrence of one event does not affect the probability of occurrence of the other event. One should anticipate that the probability that it will rain tomorrow is not affected by the knowledge (given) that tomorrow is Saturday; hence, rain and the day of the week are independent. In the notation of probability, two events E and F which are independent of each other have the property that

$$P(E|F) = P(E)$$

$$P(F|E) = P(F)$$

For two *independent* events the multiplicative law of probabilities is simplified. If E and F are independent of each other, the probability of their intersection is

$$P(E \cap F) = P(E) \cdot P(F)$$

4.6 PROBABILITY LAWS: A RECAPITULATION AND EXAMPLES

In the sections above two probability laws have been developed. The additive law is used to find the probability of the *union* of two events, and the multiplicative law is used to find the joint probability of the *intersection* of two events. Again:

$P(A \cup B) = P(A) + P(B) - P(A \cap B)$ for any two events, A and B

$P(A \cap B) = P(A) \cdot P(B|A) = P(B) \cdot P(A|B)$ for any two events A and B

If C and D are two events which are mutually exclusive (or disjoint), the additive law becomes:

$$P(C \cup D) = P(C) + P(D)$$

as

$$P(C \cap D) = 0$$

The additive law can be expanded to handle more then two mutually exclusive events, e.g.,

$$P(H \cup I \cup J) = P(H) + P(I) + P(J)$$

and so on, for a number of mutually exclusive events.
For any two independent events, E and $F,$ the multiplicative law is:

$$P(E \cap F) = P(E) \cdot P(F)$$

The multiplicative law can also be expanded to handle more than two independent events, e.g.,

$$P(E \cap F \cap G) = P(E) \cdot P(F) \cdot P(G)$$

and so on, for any number of independent events.

The special cases of independent and mutually exclusive events should not be confused with each other. The two situations are different from each other and do not occur simultaneously for two events which have nonzero probabilities.

Example: The personnel officer of a large manufacturing firm is studying the source of new employees and their success in their new jobs. The breakdown of new employees is:

Success	Source of Employee Want-Ads (W)	Agency (A)	Letter (L)	Totals
High (H)	30	14	11	55
Moderate (M)	5	1	14	20
None (N)	10	5	10	25
Totals	45	20	35	100

a. From the table, find each of the following probabilities for one of the 100 employees selected on a basis that each employee has an equally likely chance of selection.

$$P(H), P(M), P(N), P(W), P(A), P(L), P(H \cup M), P(H \cup W),$$
$$P(A \cup N), P(H \cap M), P(H \cap W), P(A \cap N), P(L|H), P(H|W),$$
$$P(N|A), P(H|M)$$

When selecting one of the 100 employees on an equally likely basis, a sample space with 100 simple events has been created. To find $P(H)$, count the 55 employees who make up the event H (or add the probability 0.01 attached to each), and obtain:

$$P(H) = 0.55$$

Similarly,

$$P(M) = 0.20$$
$$P(N) = 0.25$$
$$P(W) = 0.45$$
$$P(A) = 0.20$$
$$P(L) = 0.35$$

To find the probability of $H \cup M$, envision the simple events that comprise $H \cup M$, count the employees that make up the events H and M, (or add the probability 0.01 attached to each), and obtain:

$$P(H \cup M) = \frac{55 + 20}{100} = 0.75$$

To count the simple events that belong to $H \cup W$, use the first row and the first column, and obtain

$$P(H \cup W) = \frac{55 + 45 - 30}{100} = 0.70$$

$$P(A \cup N) = \frac{20 + 25 - 5}{100} = 0.40$$

$$P(H \cap M) = 0 \ (H \text{ and } M \text{ have no intersection})$$
$$P(H \cap W) = 30/100 = 0.30$$
$$P(A \cap N) = 5/100 = 0.05$$

$P(L|H)$ refers only to the first (H) row, which has 55 employees. Of these 55, 11 employees belong to L. Hence,

$$P(L|H) = \frac{11}{55} = 0.20$$

and

$$P(H|W) = \frac{30}{45} = 0.667$$

$$P(N|A) = \frac{5}{20} = 0.25$$

$$P(H|M) = 0$$

(An employee who is moderately successful cannot be highly successful.)

b. Use the appropriate probability laws to find:

$$P(M \cup W), P(M \cup L), P(A \cup L)$$

All of these probabilities are unions; the additive law is appropriate.

$$P(M \cup W) = P(M) + P(W) - P(M \cap W)$$
$$= 0.20 + 0.45 - 0.05 = 0.60$$
$$P(M \cup L) = P(M) + P(L) - P(M \cap L)$$
$$= 0.20 + 0.35 - 0.14 = 0.41$$
$$P(A \cup L) = P(A) + P(L) - P(A \cap L)$$
$$= 0.20 + 0.35 - 0 = 0.55$$

or

$$P(A \cup L) = P(A) + P(L) \text{ (Since } A \text{ and } L \text{ are mutually exclusive)}$$
$$= 0.20 + 0.35 = 0.55$$

c. Use the appropriate laws of probability and answers from part a of this example to find $P(A \cap N)$, $P(H \cap M)$, and $P(H \cap W)$.

$$P(A \cap N) = P(A) P(N|A) = 0.20(0.25) = 0.05$$
$$P(H \cap M) = P(M) P(H|M) = 0.20(0) = 0$$
$$P(H \cap W) = P(W) P(H|W) = 0.45(0.667) = 0.30$$

d. Use the definition of conditional probability to find:

$$P(H|W), P(H|M)$$

From the answers to part a, $P(H \cap W) = 0.30$. Thus,

$$P(H|W) = \frac{P(H \cap W)}{P(W)} = \frac{0.30}{0.45} = 0.667$$

and

$$P(H|M) = \frac{P(H \cap M)}{P(M)} = \frac{0}{0.20} = 0$$

Note that these answers agree with the answers from part a for these same probabilities.

e. Are the events, "High Success" and "Want-Ads" independent? It has been found that:

$$P(H) = 0.55$$
$$P(H|W) = 0.667$$

Since $P(H) \neq P(H|W)$, H and W are not independent.

Example. The probability that a randomly selected Denver Bus rider is a regular commuter (RC), and not an occasional rider (OR), is 0.9. The probability that a randomly selected Denver Bus rider (who is known to be a regular commuter) is employed in the downtown area is 0.8. The probability that a randomly selected Denver Bus rider is employed in the downtown area (ED) is 0.75. What is the probability that a randomly selected Denver Bus rider (who is known to be employed in the downtown area) is an occasional rider of the Denver Bus?

Solution. The first step in solving a problem such as this is to state symbolically what is known, and also state what is to be found. These are:

Known: 1. $P(RC)$ $= 0.9$
            2. $P(ED|RC) = 0.8$
            3. $P(ED)$ $= 0.75$

Find: $P(OR|ED)$ $= ?$

A helpful device in solving this type of problem is a table of joint probabilities for the variables—frequency of ridership and location of employment. The procedure to be followed is to develop the table of joint probabilities to answer the question, using the laws of probability. In Figure 4.6a, the initial framework of the joint probability table is shown, using items one and three in the listing of "knowns" above. The move from Figure 4.6a to Figure 4.6b is straightforward: Item 2 from the list of "knowns" says that 0.8 of the RC column must be in the ED row; therefore, $0.9 \times 0.8 = 0.72$ is entered in the upper left corner of the table. Further, since the row totals must add to one, and the column totals must add to one, the remaining row and column totals (0.1 and 0.25) are obvious. To obtain Figure 4.6c, the three remaining items are entered so that each row and each column adds to its already determined total probability. Now that this table of joint probabilities is completed, it is straightforward to find $P(OR|ED)$, using the definition of conditional probabilities:

$$P(OR|ED) = \frac{P(OR \cap ED)}{P(ED)} = \frac{0.03}{0.75} = 0.04$$

where $P(ED) = 0.75$ and $P(OR \cap ED) = 0.03$ were read directly from the table. The laws of probability were used throughout the construction of the table of joint probabilities. The upper left entry, 0.72, was made using the multiplicative law of probabilities, as:

$$P(RC \cap ED) = P(RC) \cdot P(ED|RC) = 0.9 \times 0.8 = 0.72$$

The row totals were determined so that they add to one, using the property that the sum of the probabilities over a set of mutually exclusive and exhaustive events must be one. When the remaining items in the body of the table (0.03, 0.18, and 0.07) were entered (so that each row and each column

Figure 4.6

Joint Probability Table

a.

Ridership / Employment	RC	OR	Totals
ED			0.75
ED'			
Totals	0.90		

b.

Ridership / Employment	RC	OR	Totals
ED	0.72		0.75
ED'			0.25
Totals	0.90	0.10	1.00

c.

Ridership / Employment	RC	OR	Totals
ED	0.72	0.03	0.75
ED'	0.18	0.07	0.25
Totals	0.90	0.10	1.00

(handwritten notes in margin:) Joint Prob. $P(RC \cap ED) = P(RC/ED) \cdot P(ED)$ $0.8 \times 0.9 = 0.72$

had the already determined total probability), the additive law of probabilities was used. For example, the event *ED* is logically the union of the two events *(ED ∩ OR)* and *(ED ∩ RC)*, because anyone who is employed downtown *(ED)* is either employed downtown and occasional rider *(ED ∩ OR)*, or is employed downtown and a regular commuter *(ED ∩ RC)*. These two events are mutually exclusive and, therefore,

$$P(ED) = P(ED \cap OR) + P(ED \cap RC)$$
$$P(ED \cap OR) = P(ED) - P(ED \cap RC) = 0.75 - 0.72 = 0.03$$

Similar relationships are used to find:

$$P(ED' \cap RC) = 0.18$$
$$P(ED' \cap OR) = 0.07$$

which completes the table.

Figure 4.7a

**Sample Space and Sample Events: The Six
Sides of a Die**

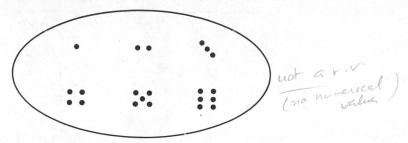

not a r.v.
(no numerical value)

4.7   RANDOM VARIABLES

In the previous sections of this chapter, the concepts of probability have been defined from several different viewpoints. These concepts will now be advanced to the consideration of two new concepts, *random variable* and *probability distribution*.

A *random variable* is a function or rule which assigns numerical values to each simple event of a sample space.

In Figure 4.7*a*, a sample space is depicted with six simple events; the six sides of a die. As such, the simple events do not constitute a random variable because they do not carry numerical values. If we count the number of dots on each side of the die, we now have a random variable as in Figure 4.7*b*.

As another example, consider the sample space created by tossing two coins. This sample space contains four simple events: (*H,H*), (*H,T*), (*T,H*), (*T,T*). Until these simple events have been assigned numerical values, they are not a random variable. Counting the number of heads in

Figure 4.7*b*

**A Random Variable: The Number of Dots on
Each Side of a Die**

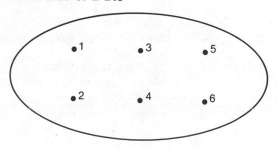

Figure 4.8

Random Variable for the Tossing of Two Coins: Counting Heads

Simple Events	Assigned Numerical Values (number of heads)
(H,H)...........................	2
(H,T)...........................	1
(T,H)...........................	1
(T,T)...........................	0

each outcome and assigning that number to each simple event, defines a random variable, as in Figure 4.8.

Thus, a random variable is a function or rule for assigning a numerical value to each simple event in a sample space. In the coin tossing example, the random variable is the rule of counting heads. In rolling a die, it is counting the number of dots on the top face.

A random variable exists when an experiment has a numerical outcome. Examples include the length of a piece of cloth, the number of defective radios, the dollar amount of an invoice, and the salary of an employee.

4.71 Types of Random Variables

Random variables are classified as being either *discrete* or *continuous*.

A *discrete* random variable is a rule or function which assigns only specified numerical values (often integers) to the simple events of a sample space.

In producing two radios, either of which may be good or bad, four simple events constitute the sample space. These four are (good, good), (good, bad), (bad, good), and (bad, bad). By assigning a numerical value equal to the count of good radios in each outcome, a random variable is defined. This random variable is restricted to the specified numerical values of 0, 1, or 2. Therefore, it is classified as a discrete random variable.

A *continuous* random variable is a rule or function which may assign any numerical value (within some limits) to simple events.

This means the number of potential values of the random variable is infinite. Since the random variable can assign only one number to any given simple event, and since an infinite quantity of numerical values may be assigned, it follows that an infinite sample space is required. A continuous random variable typically results from a measurement of some sort, when the simple event from the sample space is the selection of one item from an infinity of such items arising from apparently similar situations. The random variable is the measurement of some attribute of this item. As an example, a metal-working machine cuts a piece of steel. There are (conceptually) an infinite number of places the cut could be made under apparently identical situations. The continuous random variable could be the length of the piece of steel cut off.

As another example of the difference between a discrete random variable and a continuous random variable, consider the case of a person walking down a flight of stairs and another person walking down an inclined ramp. Both start at the same time and stop when the command "stop" is shouted. Each then reports his position from the beginning of the descent. The person on the stairs would report "I am five steps from the top" while the person on the ramp would report "I am 4.7 feet from the top." The *count* of the number of steps is a discrete random variable. The *measurement* of the position from the top of the ramp is a continuous random variable. When steps are counted, an integer must be the result. When the position on the ramp is measured, the result can be any value between zero and the length of the ramp. If a very precise measuring device is used to find the position, there will be many digits past the decimal point in the reported position. Continuous random variables are discussed further in Chapter 7.

4.72 Probability Distributions for Discrete Random Variables

A random variable is a procedure for assigning numerical values to the elements of a sample space; a random variable has a probability distribution associated with it.

A *probability distribution for a discrete random variable* is an assignment of probabilities to each of the distinct numerical values of the random variable.[1]

Returning to the simple events of Figure 4.7b and assuming each outcome to be equally likely (a fair die), the probability associated with each numerical value is ⅙.

$$P(X) = \frac{1}{6} \text{ where } X = 1, 2, 3, 4, 5, 6$$

The probability distribution for the coin tossing experiment of Figure 4.8 is more involved because two elements in the event space were assigned the same numerical value, $(H,T) = 1$ and $(T,H) = 1$. In order to

---

[1] A probability distribution for a discrete random variable is also called a probability mass function.

Figure 4.9

Probability Distribution for the Experiment of Tossing Two Coins and Counting Heads

Values of the Random Variable X	Probabilities Assigned the Values of the Random Variable P(X)
0	¼
1	½
2	¼
	1

find the probability for a particular value of the random variable X, it is necessary to add the probabilities of the simple events which have been assigned that particular numerical value. This yields

$$P(X = 0) = P(T,T) = \frac{1}{4}$$

$$P(X = 1) = P(H,T) + P(T,H) = \frac{1}{4} + \frac{1}{4} = \frac{1}{2}$$

$$P(X = 2) = P(H,H) = \frac{1}{4}$$

which is summarized in Figure 4.9.

Consider the experiment of simultaneously choosing a student out of five to serve as leader of a project. The complete listing of simple events, or leaders for five students is their names: Beth, Bill, Charles, Susan, and Sam.

Next, replace each student's name by age:

Student	Age
Beth	18
Bill	18
Charles	20
Susan	20
Sam	22

Now imagine the experiment of randomly selecting one student from the five and noting the age. This defines a *random variable* with the probability distribution:

Age of Selected Student, X	Probability P(X)
18	⅖ = 0.4
20	⅖ = 0.4
22	⅕ = 0.2
	1.0

Note that the average of the population of student ages is

$$\mu_X = \frac{18 + 18 + 20 + 20 + 22}{5} = 19.6 \text{ years.}$$

This will be used in the section.

4.8 DESCRIPTIVE MEASURES OF A DISCRETE PROBABILITY DISTRIBUTION

The mean of this or any discrete probability distribution is defined as follows.

The *mean of a discrete probability distribution* is

$$\mu_X = \Sigma XP(X)$$

where the summation is performed over all values of the random variable, X. This mean is also called the *expected value* of the random variable, noted E(X). Hence,

$$E(X) = \Sigma XP(X)$$

For the probability distribution of student age, the mean is:

$$E(X) = \mu_X = 18(0.4) + 20(0.4) + 22(0.2) = 19.6 \text{ years}$$

which is the same as the mean age calculated when the students were viewed as a population with five members. Thus, a probability distribution and a population are alternative ways of viewing the same situation.

A probability distribution also has a variance and standard deviation, just as a population has these two measures of dispersion.

The *variance of a discrete probability distribution* is:

$$\sigma_X{}^2 = \Sigma(X - \mu_X)^2 P(X) \quad = \quad (\mu_{X^2}) - (\mu_X)^2$$

$$\left(\Sigma X^2 P(X) \text{ mean of } X^2 \right)$$

where the summation is performed over all values of the random variable X.

The *standard deviation of a probability distribution* is:

$$\sigma_X = \sqrt{\sigma_X{}^2}$$

This definition of the variance is completely consistent with the definition of the variance of a population as discussed in Chapter 3. For the probability distribution of student age:

$$\sigma_X{}^2 = (18 - 19.6)^2 (.4) + (20 - 19.6)^2 (.4) + (22 - 19.6)^2 (.2) = 2.240$$

and

$$\sigma_X = \sqrt{2.240} = 1.497$$

4.9 SUMMARY

Probability theory is the terminology of uncertainty; it is useful for studying managerial decisions made under conditions of uncertainty. There are three approaches to defining probability: The *equally likely* approach, the *relative frequency* approach, and the *subjective* (or personal) approach. Each is useful in certain situations.

The outcomes of a given probabilistic situation are collected into a sample space. The simple events that make up a sample space are mutually exclusive (disjoint or nonoverlapping) and exhaustive (nothing else can happen). An event is a collection of simple events. The additive and multiplicative probability laws are useful to find the probabilities of events. The additive law is used to find the probability of the union of two events; the multiplicative law is used to find a joint probability, or the probability of the intersection of two events. The additive law has a special case for mutually exclusive events; the multiplicative law has a special case for independent events.

A random variable and a probability distribution are directly associated with a sample space. A random variable gives a numerical value to each simple event. A probability distribution is a method of stating or finding the probability for the occurrence of any numerical value of the random variable. A probability distribution also has a mean and variance, which are properties of that distribution.

EXERCISES

4.1   What is a sample space? a simple event? an event?

4.2   Describe the meaning of the symbol $\cup$.

4.3   Describe the meaning of the symbol $\cap$.

4.4   Discuss: "I am so certain the Miami Dolphins will win the next Super Bowl that I assign the probability of 1.1 to that event."

4.5   For a set of numbers to constitute a set of legitimate probabilities for the simple events in a sample space, what conditions must be met?

4.6   Discuss: "In this standard deck of cards, well shuffled, I know that the probability of randomly selecting a red card is 0.5. I also know that the probability of randomly selecting either a spade or a diamond is 0.5. Since these two numbers add to one, I know that I will draw either a red card, or a diamond or spade."

4.7   Give an example of a probability which has been determined by using the equally likely approach to probabilities.

4.8   Give an example of a probability which has been determined by using the relative frequency approach to probabilities.

4.9   Give an example of a probability which has been subjectively determined.

4.10 Classify each of the following into one of the three approaches to probabilities:
- a. The draw of July 20 in the draft lottery.
- b. The odds of the Oakland Raiders winning the next Super Bowl are 3:2 (meaning that the chances are 3 out of 3 + 2, or a probability of 0.6).
- c. Based on meterological records, January precipitation has been below average 60 percent of the years; hence, the probability that the precipitation in January, 1978, will be below average is 0.60.
- d. Three out of four job applications received in response to a newspaper ad have been unqualified for this job; hence, John Doe (whom I interviewed yesterday) has a 0.75 probability of being unqualified for this job.
- e. This machine produces defective springholders randomly, averaging 5 percent defective. I just picked up this springholder from the bin of finished springholders just produced by this machine. Hence, its probability of being satisfactory is 0.95.
- f. The national average of "successes" for new products in this industry is 0.2. But my product is far superior; hence, I believe its probability of "success" is 0.6.
- g. For this well shuffled deck of cards, the probability of drawing the ace of hearts is 1/52.

4.11 Discuss: "All probabilities have some degree of subjectivity in them."

* 4.12 A set of events is described by the faces of a single die from a pair of dice.

    Let event A be 1, 2, 3, 4
    Let event B be 4, 5, 6
- a. What is $P(A)$? $P(B)$?
- b. What is $P(A \cap B)$?
- c. What is $P(A \cup B)$?
- d. What is $P(A|B)$? $P(B|A)$?
- e. Are A and B independent?
- f. Are A and B mutually exclusive?

4.13 If $P(A) = \frac{2}{3}$, $P(B) = \frac{1}{3}$, and $P(A|B) = \frac{1}{2}$, what is:
- a. $P(A \cap B)$?
- b. $P(A \cup B)$?
- c. $P(B|A)$?
- d. Are A and B independent?
- e. Are A and B mutually exclusive?
- f. Are A and B exhaustive? $\longrightarrow$ $P(A) + P(B) = 1$ -yes

* 4.14 If two events are mutually exclusive, what is the maximum number of simple events that they may have in common?

* 4.15 Find as many pairs of mutually exclusive events as you can from this list:

---

* Answers to exercises marked with an asterisk (*) are in Appendix L.

    a. The order was sent in by Grace Jones.
    b. The order requested five pounds of turkey.
    c. The order requested six boiling chickens.
    d. The order was sent in by Tom Monarch.
    e. The order was mailed on January 15, 1975.
    f. The order was mailed in March, 1974.

* **4.16** The probability that a randomly selected order sent to the Shorthill Turkey Processor requests turkey sausage is 0.4. What is the probability that a randomly selected order does not request turkey sausage?

$1 - 0.4 = 0.6$

* **4.17** The Dennis Company has been in business for three years. 30 percent of its current customers started doing business with Dennis in its first year and 35 percent in the second year. What is the probability that a randomly selected customer started doing business with Dennis in the third year?

$1 - .35 - .3 = .35$

* **4.18** Two "dunning letters" are sent to customers with overdue accounts. It is known that the probability the letter will elicit a payment is 0.3. If the two customers are independent of each other, what is the probability that both letters will elicit a payment?

$0.3 \times 0.3 = 0.09$

* **4.19** A firm polled its executives to find out what business publications they regularly read. The questions asked, and the responses were:

Question	Percent Saying "Yes"
Do you read The Wall Street Journal?...............	45
Do you read Business Week?........................	36
Do you read Fortune?.............................	25

Further analysis of the questionnaire showed these results:

"Yes" to both Wall Street Journal and Business Week.........	9%
"Yes" to both Wall Street Journal and Fortune...............	5%
"Yes" to both Business Week and Fortune...................	6%

    a. What proportion of the executives read either The Wall Street Journal or Business Week?
    b. What proportion of the executives read either Fortune or Business Week?
    c. If the responses to the three basic questions, "Do you read the . . ." are summed, the total is 106 percent. Why is the total greater than 100 percent?
    d. What proportion of the executives read either Fortune or The Wall Street Journal?

* **4.20** An investor had been purchasing the list of recommendations of an advisory firm for the past year. The firm had made 100 "buy" recommendations at the beginning of the year; now that the year was finished, the results could be tabulated. The investor was particularly interested in the risk perceived in each recommendation (which had been recorded at the beginning of the year), and the subsequent performance of the recommended security. The results were:

Performance Risk	Poor	OK	Good	Totals
High	3	0	2	5
Medium	19	22	19	60
Low	3	19	8	30
None	0	4	1	5
Totals	25	45	30	100

a. What proportion of the recommendations were either *OK* or *Good* performers?

b. What proportion of the recommendations were rated as *Medium* or below in risk?

c. What proportion of the *High* risk recommendations were *Good* performers?

d. What proportion of the *Poor* performers were *Medium* risk?

e. What proportion of the recommendations were either *Poor* performers or *High* risk?

f. What proportion of the recommendations were both *Good* performers and *Low* risk?

g. What proportion of the *OK* performers were *High* risk?

h. What proportion of the *Medium* risk *Good* performers were *High* risk?

i. What proportion of the *OK* performers were also *Good* performers?

j. What proportion of the recommendations were either *OK* performers or *Medium* risk?

k. What proportion of the recommendations were *Good* performers or *Low* risk?

l. What proportion of the recommendations were *Poor* or *OK* performers?

m. What proportion of the *Good* performers were *High* risk?

4.21   In Exercise 4.20, is performance independent of risk? Why or why not?

4.22   A mail order firm was experimenting with three different brochures. The list of customers was randomly split into three equal groups; each group was sent a different brochure. The dollar value of orders (as measured by selling price) was compiled for each brochure.

a. What is the probability that a randomly selected customer received Brochure *A*?

b. What is the probability that a randomly selected customer placed an order?

c. What is the probability that a randomly selected customer placed an order that was larger than $10.00?

d. What proportion of the customers who placed orders over $50.00 received Brochure *B*?

Value of Orders Received \ Brochure	A	B	C	
No Order	62	70	68	200
$0.01–$10.00	20	10	20	50
$10.01–$50.00	15	15	10	40
Over $50.00	3	5	2	10
	100	100	100	300

e. What proportion of all customers placed orders from $0.01 to
    $10.00 and received Brochure *A?*

f. What is the probability that a randomly selected customer either
    received Brochure *C* or placed no order?

g. What is the probability that a customer known to have received
    Brochure *B* placed an order over $50.00?

h. What is $P($Brochure $A \mid$ *No Order*$)$?

i. What is the probability that a customer received either Brochure
    A, B, or *C* and also placed an order of $10.00 or less?

j. Use the additive law of probability to find the probability that a
    randomly selected customer received Brochure *C* or placed an order
    over $50.00.

k. Are the categories, "No Order" and "Over $50.00" mutually ex-
    clusive?

l. Are the categories, "No Order" and "Over $50.00" independent?

* 4.23 Two copies of a contract were mailed to Los Angeles from Boston. One
    was sent air mail; the other first class. From past studies:

$$P(\text{First class arrives in two days}) = 0.4$$
$$P(\text{Air Mail arrives in two days}) = 0.5$$

Assuming independence, what is the probability that at least one contract will arrive in Los Angeles in two days?

* 4.24 For air mail from Boston to Los Angeles, the probability distribution of
    time to delivery (number of days) is:

X	P(X)
0	0.0
1	0.1
2	0.4
3	0.2
4	0.1
5	0.1
6	0.05
7	0.05

a. What is the mean time to delivery?

b. What is the standard deviation of time to delivery?

c. What is the probability the time to delivery is five or more days?

* 4.25   For first class from Boston to L.A., the probability distribution of time to delivery is:

Y	$P(Y)$
0	0
1	.05
2	.35
3	.30
4	.10
5	.10
6	.05
7	.05

If two letters are mailed, one air mail and one first class, what is the probability of:
a. One (either) arriving in exactly one day, the other in exactly two days?
b. One (either) arriving exactly four days after the other?
Assume independence, and use data from Exercise 4.24.

* 4.26   In a particular job category, it is known that 40 percent of the employees are female. It is also known that 50 percent of the employees are above the median salary (Why?). If two-thirds of the male employees are above the median salary, what is the probability that an employee who is below the median salary is female? Use a table of joint probabilities.

* 4.27   In producing high quality stainless steel weldings, it is often desirable to use an X-ray technique to evaluate the strength of the weld. However, there will be occasional technical errors in a particular application that renders the X-ray process "acceptable" in only 80 percent of the uses. Each use of the X-ray procedure is independent of other uses.
a. What is the probability of an "acceptable" X-ray if the procedure is used twice?
b. It is known that the first use of the X-ray is not acceptable. What is the probability that the second use will produce an acceptable X-ray?
c. If the X-ray is used twice, what is the probability that both X-rays will be unacceptable?
d. If the X-ray is used three times, what is the probability that all will be unacceptable?
e. If it is required that the probability of a successful X-ray must be at least 0.999, how many X-rays must be taken?
f. The X-ray device costs $400 per application. Another device, costing $1,000 per application, is being considered; this new device will have a probability of producing an acceptable X-ray of 0.90. If enough X-rays (of the type being used) must be taken to yield a 0.999 probability of a successful X-ray, which device should be used?

* 4.28   A "funky" sweatshirt comes in two colors, red and green, and in two sizes, large and small. If the probability that an order is for a large sweatshirt is 0.3, and the probability that an order is for a green sweatshirt is 0.4, and half of all green sweatshirts are ordered in the large size, what is the probability that an order for a red sweatshirt will be for the small size?

4.29   Consider this statement: "A condition placed on a probability statement is intended to change the information contained in the statement. For example, I might say that the probability the sun is shining is 0.80. But if you tell me that it is snowing, you have given me additional information. My conditional probability that the sun is shining, given that it is snowing is 0.05." Do you agree with this interpretation of conditional probabilities?

4.30   A typist makes errors on 5 percent of the pages, on the average. Do you think it is realistic to assume that the probability that a particular page will be error-free is independent of the state (with errors, or error-free) of the previous page? (Hint: you might want to consider factors such as time of day, time until break, day of the week, etc.)

* 4.31   A workbench contains ten similar components; six of them are made by Manufacturer A and four by B. Assume the components are identical in appearance, and that they have been thoroughly mixed up on the workbench. One of the components has been removed from the bench.
   a.   What is the probability that the one removed is made by A?
   b.   Given that the first one removed is made by A, what is the probability that the next one removed from the workbench is made by A?
   c.   Are the two "draws" of components from the workbench independent of each other?

* 4.32   A batch of 15 orders has been filled by the order-picker. Based on many other 15-order batches, the following probability distribution of the number of orders with errors has been compiled:

No. of Orders with Errors, X	P(X)
0	0.80
1	0.10
2	0.05
3	0.04
4	0.01

   a.   What is the random variable in this situation?
   b.   What is the mean of this probability distribution?
   c.   What is the expected value of the random variable?
   d.   What is the variance of the random variable?
   e.   What is the standard deviation of the random variable?

4.33   For the order-filling operation described in Exercise 4.32, the costs of errors in a batch of 15 orders is $10.00 multiplied by the square of the number of orders with errors.
   a.   Construct the probability distribution for the random variable, Cost of Errors.
   b.   What is the expected cost of errors?

  c. What is the probability that the cost of errors will be greater than $50.00?

4.34 What is a random variable?

* 4.35 Does the following probability table depict a random variable? Why or why not?

Color Requested in the Order	Probability
Red	0.4
Orange	0.3
Green	0.2
Purple	0.1

4.36 Distinguish between a discrete and a continuous random variable.

4.37 Discuss: "My random variable of interest is the number of times I must flip a coin to receive the first head. Conceivably, this could require any number of flips. Since this random variable can be any positive integer (of which there is an infinite number), I am dealing with a continuous random variable."

REFERENCES

Cramer, Harold. *The Elements of Probability Theory.* New York: John Wiley & Sons, Inc., 1955.

Feller, William. *An Introduction to Probability Theory and Its Applications,* vol. 1. 3d ed. New York: John Wiley & Sons, Inc., 1968.

Hadley, G. *Introduction to Probability and Statistical Decision Theory.* San Francisco: Holden-Day, Inc., 1967.

Mosteller, Frederick; Rourke, Robert E. K.; and Thomas, George B., Jr. *Probability with Statistical Applications.* 2d ed. Reading Mass.: Addison-Wesley Publishing Co., Inc., 1970.

5

Random Sampling and Sampling Distributions

Parameters (μ_x, σ_x)
constants

Statistics $(\bar{x}, s_x)$
variables

5.1 POPULATIONS AND SAMPLES

The objective of statistical inference is to use information obtained from a sample in order to draw conclusions about a population. In Chapter 3, the concepts of a population and a sample were introduced and discussed. A population is a collection of N elements (people, places, or things). Parameters are characteristics of a population and are constants. The population mean, μ_x, and population variance, σ_x^2, are examples of parameters for which formulas were presented in Chapter 3.

A sample is a subset of a population. It is a collection of n elements taken from the given population of interest. Characteristics of samples are called statistics and they are *variables* (i.e., they vary in value from sample to sample). The sample mean, $\bar{X}$, and sample variance, s_x^2, are sample statistics.

5.2 SIMPLE RANDOM SAMPLING

As a prelude to defining simple random sampling, it is helpful to give an example of a procedure for drawing a simple random sample. Suppose there is a population of $N = 100$ employees. Let us number these 100 employees 00 through 99. A random sample of size $n = 10$ is desired from this population to investigate employee attitude toward unionization. One procedure is to place the numbers 00 through 99 on ping pong balls, put the balls in a big urn, stir them very well, and then (blindfolded) draw a ball from the urn. Having noted the number on the selected ball, the correspondingly numbered element from the population would then be in the sample. Another ball is drawn, and its number noted. This process is repeated ten times. The ten employees, corresponding to the ten numbers, constitute a simple random sample of the population.

Such a mechanical selection procedure is tedious. Instead, one may use a table of random numbers to accomplish the same thing. A table of random numbers is furnished as Appendix C. In this table notice that the numbers are in groups of five digits. Only two are needed for our example. One could decide to use the first two digits (or two in the middle, or on the end, or whatever) as corresponding to ping pong ball numbers. The next step is the arbitrary selection of a starting point and a direction of movement. Suppose the start is made in row 21, column 6; the five digit number is 85611. Taking only the first two digits, the corresponding ping pong ball number (and the correspondingly numbered population element) is 85. If the direction is to move down, the next nine two-digit numbers are 11, 12, 04, 70, 56, 73, 27, 70, and 91. Note that 70 appears twice. In sampling, the second 70 could not be in the sample. It would be ignored, and the next random number in succession, 62, would be selected. Note that these ten numbers are identification numbers of population elements and not the values of any variables associated with these elements.

What does the previous paragraph mean by *arbitrary* selection of starting point and direction of travel? The selection is arbitrary as long as the selections are made without the influence of the numbers themselves; then the procedure is considered to be random. It is a good idea to use a different scheme each time the table is used.

What would be necessary if the population had 500 elements in it? It would be necessary to use three-digit random numbers, arbitrarily selected from the five digits as before. But what does one do when digits such as 837 appear? There is no corresponding element of the population, hence, one simply ignores random digits which have no corresponding population elements. For $N = 500$, one could use the digits 000 to 499, or the digits 001 to 500, or other sets of digits. The remaining digits would simply be ignored.

More formally, in order for a method of selecting a sample to produce a *simple random sample,* it is necessary that the method meet the following criterion:

The method used for random sampling must be so designed that every possible sample of size *n* has the *same probability* of being drawn.

If this criterion is met, then a necessary corollary is that the method used is so designed that each *element* of the population has the same probability of being included in the sample.

In order to obtain an estimate of the opinion of the University student body (20,000 students) on the issue of the dormitory visitation policy, it was decided to select 400 students at random and obtain their opinions. The proportion of the sample favoring the proposed policy (a statistic) would be used as an estimate of the *unknown* proportion of the population favoring the proposed policy (a parameter). Three alternative methods of selecting the sample of 400 were proposed. Your assignment is to determine which method or methods produce simple random samples.

Selection Method A: There are 20,000 students. A sample of 400 is desired, i.e., one out of every 50 students. From a listing of students arranged by grade point average, select the 20th name on the list and every 50th name thereafter.

Selection Method B: Select a number from a random number table between one and 50 inclusive. Use this number to find the first student included from the grade point ranking. Then take every 50th student thereafter.

Selection Method C: From a random number table, select 400 different numbers between 1 and 20,000. Using the 400 random numbers, select the sample from the grade point ranking of students. (If one of the random numbers is 489, then select the 489th student down the list, and so forth.)

Of the three methods proposed for sample selection, only Method C conforms to the definition of a simple random sample. Both Methods A and B can easily be eliminated through the definition of simple random sampling, which requires that *all possible samples* of size 400 have an equal probability of being drawn.

For Method A, only one of the possible samples based on 20,000 students taken 400 at a time can occur. This sample begins with the 20th student and has a probability of occurrence equal to one. All other sample possibilities have a zero probability of occurrence.

For Method B, there are 50 different samples which may be selected, each with a probability of occurrence equal to 1/50. However, there are many other possible samples which are not allowed to occur in this particular method and are assigned a zero probability, therefore violating the definition of random sampling. For example, any sample containing the first *and* second students cannot be selected.

In Method C, all possible combinations of 400 of the 20,000 students can actually occur. No combinations are restricted from occurring by this method of selection. Furthermore, using a random number table for element selection guarantees that each and every possible sample has an equal probability of occurring.

The manner in which the population is itemized, whether by grade point, alphabetically by last name, or numerically by social security number, or any other scheme, does not affect the random nature of the sample. Randomness is based on the manner of selection from the list, *not* the manner of producing the particular ordering occurring in the list. As long as an equal probability for all possible samples is maintained, the ordering of the complete population does not affect randomness in sampling.

Frequently, it is not economically desirable to use simple random sampling. When such is the case, there are several alternative random sampling designs or schemes which might be used. Two such schemes, stratified sampling and cluster sampling, are discussed later in this chapter.

5.3 SAMPLING DISTRIBUTION (*without replacement*)

It is useful to view the manner in which statistics (sample characteristics) vary from one random sample to another random sample. In order to structure the examination of sample-to-sample statistic behavior, the discussion will be restricted to a given population, a given sample size, and repeated random samples of the selected size. In other words, a sampling distribution will be developed.

In practice, one does not typically take more than one sample (of n observations) from a population. The concept of taking repeated samples is useful to understand a sampling distribution.

A sampling distribution is defined as follows:

A *sampling distribution* is a probability distribution showing the values of a sample statistic and the corresponding probability distribution for these values.

A sampling distribution is first of all a probability distribution; it is a procedure for assigning probabilities to values of a random variable. The distinguishing feature of sampling distributions is that the value of the random variable is the value of the sample statistic.

The procedure for constructing a sampling distribution for purposes of studying the behavior of statistics from sample to sample is relatively simple and can be summarized in six procedural steps.

In order to see how this procedure works, follow through this example step-by-step.

1. Define the population to be sampled. Let the population be five ping pong balls which have been placed in a bowl. Each ball has a number written on it. The numbers are 1, 3, 5, 7, and 9. The ping pong balls themselves are the population. The variable is the number on the balls.

2. Choose a sample size, n. We will choose samples of size two.

3. Identify all possible simple random samples of size $n = 2$ which may be obtained from the population. Altogether, there are 20 possible simple random samples of size two which may be drawn from this population of ping pong balls. These samples are presented in column one of Figure 5.1 with the numbers as the identifying feature of each ball. Note that (3,1) is distinct from (1,3). The order in the parentheses is the order of draw.

4. Create a random variable over the sample space. For this example, it was decided to examine the sample mean. The sum of each sample is divided by the sample size. The 20 calculated values of $\bar{X}$ are presented in column two of Figure 5.1.

Figure 5.1

Sampling Distribution Worksheet

All Possible Distinct Simple Random Samples (X_1, X_2)	Sample Means $\left(\bar{X} = \dfrac{X_1 + X_2}{2}\right)$	Probabilities $P(\bar{X})$
(1,3)	2	1/20
(1,5)	3	1/20
(1,7)	4	1/20
(1,9)	5	1/20
(3,1)	2	1/20
(3,5)	4	1/20
(3,7)	5	1/20
(3,9)	6	1/20
(5,1)	3	1/20
(5,3)	4	1/20
(5,7)	6	1/20
(5,9)	7	1/20
(7,1)	4	1/20
(7,3)	5	1/20
(7,5)	6	1/20
(7,9)	8	1/20
(9,1)	5	1/20
(9,3)	6	1/20
(9,5)	7	1/20
(9,7)	8	1/20
		20/20 = 1

5. Assign probabilities to each simple event in the sample space. Since simple random sampling has been used to obtain the list of samples, each sample is equally likely. With 20 samples, each has 1/20 probability of occurrence.

6. Combine the random variable values and probability values into a probability distribution. By scanning the various values of $\bar{X}$, seven distinct values can be seen, the integers from two to eight. These are listed in column one of Figure 5.2. To finish development of the sampling distribution, the probabilities for each distinct value of $\bar{X}$ are obtained by summing the probabilities for the number of times each distinct value

Figure 5.2

Sampling Distribution of $\bar{X}$

Sample Mean $\bar{X}$	Probability $P(\bar{X})$
2	2/20
3	2/20
4	4/20
5	4/20
6	4/20
7	2/20
8	2/20
	20/20 = 1

occurred. These probabilities are presented in column two of Figure 5.2, concluding the development of the sampling distribution of $\bar{X}$ for this example. In addition to presenting the sampling distribution in table form, it is possible to present the results graphically, as in Figure 5.3. The graphical approach helps visualize the shape of the distribution, a feature more difficult to see from a table.

Figure 5.3

Sampling Distribution of $\bar{X}$

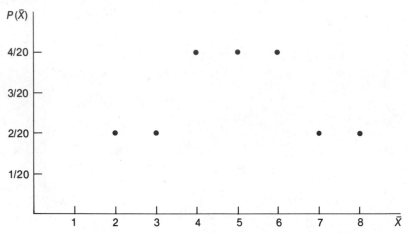

In this example, the sample mean was the statistic calculated for each sample. Therefore, the result is called the *sampling distribution of the mean*. If a different statistic were used, the title of the result would change accordingly; the *sampling distribution of the proportion* and the *sampling distribution of the variance* are examples.

5.31   Comparison of Population and Sampling Distribution Characteristics

The development of sampling distributions facilities the subsequent development of methods for statistical inferences about a population. The sampling distribution serves as a link between the sample and population. The starting point in studying this link is the manner by which the sampling distribution and the population distribution are related.

The sampling distribution of $\bar{X}$ was developed for the ping pong ball example through application of the six steps by which a sampling distribution is created. Selected characteristics of the population distribution and the sampling distribution are calculated and presented in Figures 5.4 and

Figure 5.4

Population Distribution with Mean and Variance, $n = 1$

X	$P(X)$	$XP(X)$	$(X - \mu_X)$	$(X - \mu_X)^2$	$(X - \mu_X)^2 P(X)$
1.........	1/5	1/5	-4	16	16/5
3.........	1/5	3/5	-2	4	4/5
5.........	1/5	5/5	0	0	0
7.........	1/5	7/5	2	4	4/5
9.........	1/5	9/5	4	16	16/5
	$5/5 = 1$	$25/5 = 5 = \mu_X$			$40/5 = 8 = \sigma_X^2$

Figure 5.5

Sampling Distribution of $\bar{X}$ with Mean and Variance, $n = 2$

$\bar{X}$	$P(\bar{X})$	$\bar{X}P(\bar{X})$	$(\bar{X} - \mu_{\bar{X}})$	$(\bar{X} - \mu_{\bar{X}})^2$	$(\bar{X} - \mu_{\bar{X}})^2 P(\bar{X})$
2.....	2/20	4/20	-3	9	18/20
3.....	2/20	6/20	-2	4	8/20
4.....	4/20	16/20	-1	1	4/20
5.....	4/20	20/20	0	0	0
6.....	4/20	24/20	1	1	4/20
7.....	2/20	14/20	2	4	8/20
8.....	2/20	16/20	3	9	18/20
	$20/20 = 1$	$100/20 = 5 = \mu_{\bar{X}}$			$60/20 = 3 = \sigma_{\bar{X}}^2$

5.5. The population distribution and the sampling distribution have means, μ_X and $\mu_{\bar{X}}$, respectively. The mean of the population distribution for the example is $\mu_X = 5$. The mean of the sampling distribution for the example is $\mu_{\bar{X}} = 5$. This suggests that μ_X *and* $\mu_{\bar{X}}$ are equal. This is true, both for the example and for the general case.

> The *mean of the population* distribution and the *mean of the sampling distribution of $\bar{X}$* derived from the population are equal:
> $$\mu_X = \mu_{\bar{X}}$$

Since a relationship was found between the means of the population and the sampling distribution of $\bar{X}$, it is logical to expect some form of relationship between the variances of the two distributions. In the example, $\sigma_X^2 = 8$, while $\sigma_{\bar{X}}^2 = 3$. The relationship is:

$$\sigma_{\bar{X}}^2 = \frac{\sigma_X^2}{n}\left(\frac{N - n}{N - 1}\right)$$

For this example,

$$\frac{\sigma_X^2}{n}\left(\frac{N - n}{N - 1}\right) = \frac{8}{2}\left(\frac{5 - 2}{5 - 1}\right) = \frac{8}{2}\left(\frac{3}{4}\right) = 3$$

as found in Figure 5.5.

The equation

$$\sigma_{\bar{X}} = \frac{\sigma_X}{\sqrt{n}} \sqrt{\frac{N-n}{N-1}}$$

expresses the relationship between the standard deviations. The standard deviation of the sampling distribution of $\bar{X}$ is often called the *standard error* of the sample mean.

An additional feature or characteristic of the population distribution and the sampling distribution of $\bar{X}$ which might be compared is the shape of the distributions. For our example, the population distribution was uniform; each value of the random variable X was equally likely. The population distribution is shown in Figure 5.6.

Figure 5.6

Graph of Population Distribution

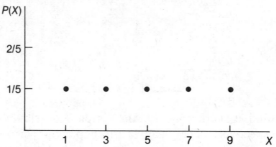

The sampling distribution of $\bar{X}$ which resulted from this uniform population distribution has a somewhat peaked appearance, as shown in Figure 5.3. Based on a comparison of these two distribution shapes, it is impossible at this point to arrive at a final conclusion regarding shape relationships. However, the factor which governs shape is a special theorem of statistics. Since this special theorem requires additional conceptual development, its discussion is postponed to Chapter 7 when the central limit theorem is formally introduced.

5.32 Sampling from a Very Large (or Infinite) Population *(with replacement)*

By way of summary, the following relationships have been established between the characteristics of the population distribution and the sampling distribution of $\bar{X}$:

Means: $\mu_{\bar{X}} = \mu_X$

Variances: $\sigma_{\bar{X}}^2 = \frac{\sigma_X^2}{n}\left(\frac{N-n}{N-1}\right)$

without replace. finite → hypergeometric
with replacement or infinite → Multinomial

$$\text{Standard Deviations:} \quad \sigma_{\bar{X}} = \frac{\sigma_X}{\sqrt{n}} \sqrt{\frac{N-n}{N-1}}$$

$\left(\frac{N-n}{N-1} \right)$

The term $(N-n)/(N-1)$ is sometimes called the *finite population multiplier*, because it is used when the population is finite, and is not necessary when the population is infinite or very large. Throughout this text, the term *large population* means a population that is large *relative to the sample size.* In practice, a population 20 times as large as the sample is considered large.

Note that when the population is much larger than the sample, the multiplier has a value very near one. In this case, these relationships hold:

Means: $\qquad\qquad\qquad \mu_{\bar{X}} = \mu_X$

Variances: $\qquad\qquad\quad \sigma_{\bar{X}}^2 = \frac{\sigma_X^2}{n}$ $\qquad N \to \infty$

Standard Deviations: $\quad \sigma_{\bar{X}} = \frac{\sigma_X}{\sqrt{n}}$

(These relationships are proved in note 5.32 c and note 5.32 f, following Chapter 17.

In many applications, N is so much larger than n that the finite population multiplier is ignored. Throughout the remainder of this text, if a value of N is not given, it is assumed that N is sufficiently large to ignore the finite population multiplier.

It is worth noting that in the extreme case of $n = N$ (a census), the multiplier has a value of zero, so $\sigma_{\bar{X}} = 0$. This correctly states that the standard error for the mean of a census is zero, because a census mean is a population mean which is a constant; a constant has no variance.

5.33 Example

In some cases it is necessary to find a sampling distribution when the population is given as a probability distribution. This implies a large population, because the probabilities remain the same from one observation to the next. For example, find the sampling distribution of $\bar{X}$, given $n = 2$, from this population:

X	P(X)
0	0.5
1	0.3
3	0.2
	1.0

Using two numbers in sequence to denote the two observations, the possible samples plus their probabilities and the resulting sampling distribution of $\bar{X}$ are shown in Figure 5.7.

Figure 5.7

Sampling Distribution Worksheet

Samples (X_1, X_2)	Sample Means $\bar{X} = \dfrac{X_1 + X_2}{2}$	Probabilities $P(X_1) \cdot P(X_2) = P(X_1 \cap X_2) = P(\bar{X})$
(0,0)	0.0	$0.5 \times 0.5 = 0.25$
(0,1)	0.5	$0.5 \times 0.3 = 0.15$
(0,3)	1.5	$0.5 \times 0.2 = 0.10$
(1,0)	0.5	$0.3 \times 0.5 = 0.15$
(1,1)	1.0	$0.3 \times 0.3 = 0.09$
(1,3)	2.0	$0.3 \times 0.2 = 0.06$
(3,0)	1.5	$0.2 \times 0.5 = 0.10$
(3,1)	2.0	$0.2 \times 0.3 = 0.06$
(3,3)	3.0	$0.2 \times 0.2 = \underline{0.04}$
		1.00

Collecting probabilities for identical values of $\bar{X}$ results in:

$\bar{X}$	$P(\bar{X})$
0.0	$0.25 = 0.25$
0.5	$0.15 + 0.15 = 0.30$
1.0	$0.09 = 0.09$
1.5	$0.10 + 0.10 = 0.20$
2.0	$0.06 + 0.06 = 0.12$
3.0	$0.04 = \underline{0.04}$
	1.00

Demonstrating that $E(\bar{X}) = E(X)$ or $\mu_{\bar{X}} = \mu_X$:

$$E(X) = \Sigma XP(X) = 0(0.5) + 1(0.3) + 3(0.2) = 0.9$$
$$E(\bar{X}) = \Sigma \bar{X}P(\bar{X}) = 0(0.25) + 0.5(0.30) + 1.0(0.09) + 1.5(0.20) + 2.0(0.12)$$
$$+ 3.0(0.04) = 0.9$$

Demonstrating that $\sigma_{\bar{X}}^2 = \sigma_X^2/n$:

$$\sigma_X^2 = \Sigma[X - E(X)]^2 P(X) = (0 - 0.9)^2\, 0.5 + (1 - 0.9)^2\, 0.3 + (3 - 0.9)^2 0.2$$
$$= 1.29$$

$$\sigma_{\bar{X}}^2 = \Sigma[\bar{X} - E(\bar{X})]^2 P(\bar{X}) = (0 - 0.9)^2\, (0.25) + (0.5 - 0.9)^2\, (0.30)$$
$$+ (1 - 0.9)^2\, (0.09) + (1.5 - 0.9)^2\, (0.20)$$
$$+ (2 - 0.9)^2\, (0.12) + (3 - 0.9)^2\, (0.04) = 0.645$$

$$\sigma_{\bar{X}}^2 = 0.645 = \frac{1.29}{2} = \frac{\sigma_X^2}{n}$$

This same procedure could be used for any number of values of X, and for any sample size. However, the number of arrangements of X values grows rapidly, making this enumeration approach to finding the sampling distribution of $\bar{X}$ a very cumbersome approach. This chapter emphasizes finding sampling distributions primarily to illustrate clearly the concept of the sampling distribution of $\bar{X}$, and also to demonstrate the relationships between the parameters of the population and the parameters of the sampling distribution.

5.4 OTHER SAMPLING PLANS

In Section 5.2, simple random sampling was discussed because of the dominant role played by simple random sampling in statistics. However, in many cases, it is neither feasible nor desirable to use the technique of simple random sampling. When such is the case, a number of alternative approaches to choosing the elements to be included in the sample exist. Two such techniques are Stratified sampling and Cluster sampling. The discussion that follows indicates when one would want to consider stratified or cluster sampling.

5.41 Stratified Sampling

The methods of stratified sampling tend to be economically desirable if the population to be sampled can be divided into relatively homogeneous subdivisions or strata. Stratified random sampling is the procedure of dividing the population into *strata* (relatively homogeneous groups) and then taking a simple random sample from each stratum. If stratification could be done so that there is complete homogeneity within a stratum, a sample of $n = 1$ from each stratum would be equivalent to a census.

In order for stratified random sampling to be effective it is necessary to be sufficiently familiar with the population to know a logical scheme for stratification. The procedure adopted for population stratification depends on the structure of the population relative to the characteristic of interest. When interested in mean family income for a particular geographically area, it may be appropriate to stratify families by the occupation of the head of the household, or by assessed value of home, or by years of college. Familiarity with the composition of the population is required for effective stratification.

Once the strata have been defined and the population elements of each stratum identified, then a random sample is selected from each stratum and special statistical methods are used to estimate the population parameters on the basis of the sample statistics from all strata.

If the population cannot be meaningfully divided into strata or if the strata elements cannot be identified, then stratified sampling is not effective and simple random sampling or some alternative sampling method must be used.

5.42   Cluster Sampling

With stratified sampling, the desire was to divide the population into homogeneous strata which differ from one another. With cluster sampling, the desire is to divide the population into different clusters, which are heterogeneous within each cluster, but relatively similar from cluster to cluster. If clustering could be done perfectly, each cluster would be a miniature of the population. In this case, a census of one cluster would be equivalent to a census of the population.

Market analyses frequently are conducted using cluster sampling. The geographical area of interest is divided into a number of subdivisions (city blocks, etc.) which are called clusters. A random sample of clusters is then drawn, and either a census or a sample of each included cluster is taken. When a census is taken for each selected cluster, the procedure is called *single stage sampling*. However, when each included cluster has only a sample of its elements included, then the procedure is called *multi-stage sampling*. After the appropriate information is collected from selected clusters, special statistical methods are used to combine cluster statistics into population estimates.

Consider the problem of estimating the average number of children per household in a large city. To use cluster sampling, the city can first be divided geographically into clusters.[1] After the clusters (assume blocks in this case) have been identified, each family in the included blocks can be examined for the number of children. If a multistage approach were desired, only a sample of families in the block would be used in the overall sample.

The situation just described constitutes the most widely adopted application of cluster sampling, and has come to be labeled *area sampling*. Area sampling produces great economies in data collection when studying geographical areas, because data collection is concentrated in a limited number of clusters rather than randomly over the entire area. Although the cost per observation is relatively low for cluster sampling, cluster sampling typically requires larger samples than is required with simple random sampling in order to achieve any given level of precision.

5.5   SUMMARY

Two important concepts have been developed in this chapter: (1) the concept of simple random sampling, and (2) the concept of a sampling

---

[1] The Bureau of the Census has divided all major cities (Standard Metropolitan Statistical Areas) into census tracts of approximately 4,000 persons, block groups of approximately 1,000 persons, and blocks of approximately 100 persons each.

distribution. Particular emphasis has been placed upon the sampling distribution of the mean.

A simple random sample is usually selected with the aid of a table of random numbers. It has the characteristic that every element of the population is equally likely to be included in the sample. A definition of a simple random sample is that every possible sample of size n is equally likely to be the selected sample. All of the samples used in later chapters of this book are simple random samples, although they may be taken from either finite or infinite populations.

A sampling distribution is nothing more than a probability distribution; it shows the probability of obtaining possible values of the sample statistic of interest. When dealing with the sampling distribution of $\bar{X}$, it was observed that the following relationships are true:

mean of $\bar{X} \longrightarrow \mu_{\bar{X}} = \mu_X$ ———— mean of x

var. of $\bar{X} \longrightarrow \sigma_{\bar{X}}^2 = \dfrac{\sigma_X^2}{n} \cdot \dfrac{N-n}{N-1}$ —— variance of x

" $\bar{X} \longrightarrow \sigma_{\bar{X}}^2 = \dfrac{\sigma_X^2}{n}$ (large population) "

It was also observed that the shape of the sampling distribution of $\bar{X}$ was different (more peaked) from the distribution of the population from which the sample was taken.

Under special circumstances, it may be appropriate to use sampling techniques such as stratified sampling and cluster sampling, but these special techniques are not pursued further in this text.

EXERCISES

5.1   Describe a procedure using a table of random numbers for drawing a simple random sample.

5.2   What should be done when a random number appears more than once?

* 5.3   In a simple random sample, every element of the population has an equal chance of belonging to the sample. Is the converse true (i.e., if every element of the population has an equal chance of belonging to the sample, is it necessarily a simple random sample)?

5.4   A sample is to be drawn from a population of 1,000 men and 1,000 women. Since the overall sample size is to be 100, 50 men are randomly selected from the 1,000 men and 50 women are randomly selected from the 1,000 women.

   a. Does every element in the population have the same chance of being selected?

   b. Is it true that in a simple random sample every element in the population has the same chance of being selected?

———————

* Answers to exercises marked with an asterisk (*) are in Appendix L.

     c. Does the procedure described yield a simple random sample from the entire population? If not, what procedure could be used to generate a simple random sample from the entire population?

     d. In the procedure described, what is the probability that the sample of 100 could contain 45 men and 55 women?

5.5 Technically, neither of the following procedures is a correct procedure to draw a simple random sample. However, one of the procedures may yield a sample which has properties similar to those of a simple random sample. The procedures are:

1. Use a listing of households, alphabetical by street and then numerically by street number. The listing contains 20,000 names. A sample of size 800 is desired. Randomly select a number from 1 to 25, start with that position on the list, and take every 25th name from there forward.

2. Use a listing of households, alphabetical by family name. The listing contains 20,000 names. A sample of size 800 is desired. Randomly select a number from one to 25. Start with that position on the list, and take every 25th name from there forward.

     a. Do you think people living on the same street would tend to have similar characteristics? Why or why not?

     b. Do you think people adjacent on the alphabetical list would tend to have similar characteristics? Why or why not?

     c. Which procedure would tend to yield a sample with characteristics similar to a simple random sample?

     d. Which procedure would tend to yield a sample with characteristics similar to a stratified random sample?

     e. Suppose it is true that our school systems have tended to show preference to people whose name appears early in an alphabetical listing by providing advantageous seating to those people. How would this affect your answers?

5.6 In a pinch, some statisticians have been known to use all or part of the serial number on a dollar bill as a random number. Which do you think would tend to be more nearly similar to a table of random numbers, the first two digits or the last two digits of the bill closest to the front of your wallet? What about the first and second bills if you had just secured crisp bills for birthday presents?

5.7 What is a sampling distribution? How is it similar to a probability distribution?

* **5.8** A random sample of size, $n = 10$, is taken from a population of size, $N = 100$. The population variance is 100. What is the standard error of $\bar{X}$?

5.9 Ten employees are selected at random and asked how many years of service they have completed with the company. Since the company is only two years old, their replies will be either zero, one, or two. These replies are then to be averaged. What are the 21 possible results of this procedure? What other information would be needed to develop a sampling distribution for the average numbers of years of service for the sample of employees?

5.10 What is the meaning of the symbol, $\mu_{\bar{X}}$? $\sigma_{\bar{X}}$?

5.11 A population is composed of the observations 4, 4, 6, 8, 8. Samples of size $n = 2$ are to be selected from the population. Construct the sampling distribution of $\bar{X}$.

5.12 Find the mean and variance of the sampling distribution from Exercise 5.11.

* 5.13 An airline is planning to take a simple random sample of two routes from the four routes being investigated. The mileages of the four routes are:

Route	Mileage
A	100
B	100
C	200
D	200

a. Construct a probability distribution for the mileage in the population of four routes.

b. Find the mean and variance of the probability distribution of mileage.

c. List all possible combinations of two routes. Then, for each of the combinations, find the sample average of mileage for the two routes. Notice that each of these combinations has an equal chance of being selected.

d. Construct a sampling distribution for the mean, i.e., the average mileage in the sample of two routes.

e. Find the mean and variance of the sampling distribution of the mean, using the results of part d.

f. Find the mean and variance of the sampling distribution of the mean, using the results of sampling theory and the results of part b.

g. Compare your answers to e and f. If they do not agree, find your error.

* 5.14 Find the sampling distribution of $\bar{X}$ for a sample of two taken from this very large population:

X, Number of Children in the Family	Probability, P(X)
0	0.3
1	0.4
2	0.2
3	0.1

* 5.15 From the sampling distribution of Exercise 5.14, find the mean and variance of the sampling distribution of $\bar{X}$. Find the parameters of the sampling distribution in a different way.

* 5.16 For the sampling distribution of Exercise 5.14, what is the probability that the sample mean will fall within one child of the population mean?

* 5.17   A sample of size 64 is taken from a population with mean, $\mu_x = 500$ and the standard deviation, $\sigma_x = 100$.

    a.   If the population has a very large number of elements, what are the mean and variance of the sampling distribution of $\bar{X}$.

    b.   If the population has 100 elements, what are the mean and variance of the sampling distribution of $\bar{X}$?

* 5.18   Use Tchebycheff's theorem and sampling theory to show that the following statement is incorrect: "I know that the average family income in Rocktown is $12,000 and that the standard deviation of family income in Rocktown is $3,000. If I take a simple random sample of nine families, the chances are greater than one in five that the average income for the sample will be greater than $15,000 or less than $9,000."

5.19   What is stratified sampling?

5.20   What is cluster sampling?

5.21   What advantages, if any, would cluster sampling have for a sample to be conducted through the mail?

5.22   Would a doubling in the hourly wage rate for interviewers tend to make cluster sampling more or less attractive for a sample to be taken in a suburban area?

5.23   In determining strata for a sampling plan, which would be the more attractive plan for a sample to investigate family income?

    a.   Strata developed by dividing an alphabetical list into groups of adjacent names.

    b.   Strata developed by dividing a list of addresses (alphabetical by street name, then numerical by street number) into groups of adjacent names.

    c.   Strata developed by dividing a list of families (arranged by decreasing assessed valuation of the dwelling unit) into groups of adjacent names.

REFERENCES

Cochran, William G.   *Sampling Techniques,* 2d ed. New York: John Wiley & Sons, Inc., 1963.

Deming, W. Edwards.   *Sample Design in Business Research.* New York: John Wiley & Sons, Inc., 1960.

Solnim, Morris James.   "Sampling in a Nutshell," *Journal of the American Statistical Association,* vol. 52, No. 278 (June 1957).

Yamane, Taro.   *Elementary Sampling Theory.* Englewood Cliffs, N.J.: Prentice-Hall, Inc., 1967.

6

Discrete Probability Distributions

6.1 DISCRETE PROBABILITY DISTRIBUTIONS

There are two types of random variables, discrete and continuous. Associated with any random variable is a probability distribution of either a discrete or a continuous nature. This chapter contains an examination of several discrete random variables and their associated discrete probability distributions.

A discrete random variable begins with a sample space for an experiment. The random variable is created when a numerical value is assigned to each outcome. The discrete probability distribution occurs when a probability is assigned to each of the distinct numerical values of the random variable.

There are numerous different discrete probability distributions. In this chapter the Bernoulli probability distribution is developed first, followed by the binomial, and the Poisson probability distributions.

6.2 BERNOULLI DISTRIBUTION

A Bernoulli process is an experiment or process which has _only two_ possible outcomes. Consider a manufacturing process where each unit produced is either of acceptable or unacceptable quality; these are the two outcomes. Another example of a Bernoulli process is the favorable or unfavorable individual reaction to an advertising campaign (only two possible outcomes). If neutral, slightly favorable, or slightly unfavorable responses to the advertising campaign are added as possible replies, the requirement for only two possible outcomes is violated and the process is no longer called a Bernoulli process.

In order to standardize the statistical vocabulary, it is conventional to label one of the possible Bernoulli outcomes as a _success_ and the other as a _failure_. Unfortunately, this convention carries the unnecessary connotations of good and bad. The purpose of the labels is solely to distinguish between the two outcomes, without any good or bad distinctions.

The sample space for a Bernoulli process also has only two simple events: one is called *success* and the other is called *failure;* thus, $S =$ {success, failure}. In order to convert these points to a random variable, it is necessary to assign a numerical value to each. The Bernoulli random variable is obtained by assigning the value one to a success and the value zero to a failure; $S = \{1,0\}$. The values one and zero are numbers which are mathematically convenient.

A Bernoulli probability distribution is obtained when probabilities are assigned to the distinct values of the Bernoulli random variable. The symbol π (the Greek letter *pi*) is used to label the probability assigned to the sample space event of *success* (value of one). This requires that the probability assigned to the sample space event of failure (value of zero) to equal $1 - \pi$. As there are only two sample space events, the sum of the assigned probabilities must equal unity. Thus, if $P(1) = \pi$, then $P(0) = 1 - P(1) = 1 - \pi$, and $P(1) + P(0) = 1$.

6.21   Bernoulli Distribution: Mean and Variance

As with all probability distributions, the Bernoulli distribution has a mean and variance. Figure 6.1 shows the calculation of the mean and

Figure 6.1

Calculation of Bernoulli Mean and Variance

X	$P(X)$	$X \cdot P(X)$	$X - \mu_X$	$(X - \mu_X)^2$	$(X - \mu_X)^2 \cdot P(X)$
0	$1 - \pi$	0	$0 - \pi$	π^2	$\pi^2 - \pi^3$
1	π	π	$1 - \pi$	$1 - 2\pi + \pi^2$	$\pi - 2\pi^2 + \pi^3$
	1	$\mu_X = \pi$			$\sigma_X^2 = \pi - \pi^2$

$$\mu_X = E(X) = \Sigma X \cdot P(X) = \pi$$
$$\sigma_X^2 = \Sigma(X - \mu_X)^2 \cdot P(X) = \pi - \pi^2 = \pi(1 - \pi)$$

variance of the Bernoulli distribution, using the definitions given in Chapter 4. The mean, π, and the variance, $\pi(1 - \pi)$, are parameters of the Bernoulli distribution.

6.3   BINOMIAL DISTRIBUTION (*good for only large population*)

If it is only desired to assign probabilities to the outcomes of a *single* outcome or trial of a Bernoulli process, then the Bernoulli probability distribution is adequate. However, if it is desired to assign probabilities to the event "X successes in n trials of a Bernoulli process," a new probability distribution is required: the binomial distribution.

The *binomial distribution* is a sampling distribution which arises when one counts the number of successes in *n* trials of a constant Bernoulli process. Thus, a binomial distribution describes the number of successes in a simple random sample of size *n* selected from a large population whose events either possess some characteristic (success), or do not possess the characteristic (failure).

The binomial random variable is similar to the Bernoulli random variable since both are "counters" of "successes." Since only a single experiment was involved with the Bernoulli process, only zero (failure) or one (success) was possible. On the other hand, a binomial random variable can take on any *integer* value from 0 to *n,* because the number of successes which may occur during *n* repetitions of a Bernoulli process may range from zero successes to *n* successes. The binomial random variable is simply the sum of numbers which are zeros or ones. For example, if seven repetitions of a Bernoulli process produces the results (1,1,0,1,0,0,1), then the value of the binomial random variable is the sample sum and, therefore, equals four:

$$X = 1 + 1 + 0 + 1 + 0 + 0 + 1 = 4$$

Observing the sex of a customer may be viewed as a Bernoulli process. Outcomes are therefore restricted to only two possible events, male or female. Assume a simple random sample of three customers is to be selected where the events male and female are equally likely, and assume the sex of each customer is independent of the other customers. Figure 6.2 shows the possible samples, the values of the binomial random variable, and the probabilities of each binomial random variable. These columns are similar to those in Chapter 5 which were used in constructing sampling distributions. First, all possible samples are identified, then as-

Figure 6.2

Binomial Distribution for Number of Females in Three Customers

Possible Samples	Random Variable X, Number of Females	Probability P(X)
MMM*	0	$\frac{1}{2} \times \frac{1}{2} \times \frac{1}{2} = \frac{1}{8}$
FMM	1	$\frac{1}{2} \times \frac{1}{2} \times \frac{1}{2} = \frac{1}{8}$
MFM	1	$\frac{1}{2} \times \frac{1}{2} \times \frac{1}{2} = \frac{1}{8}$
MMF	1	$\frac{1}{2} \times \frac{1}{2} \times \frac{1}{2} = \frac{1}{8}$
FFM	2	$\frac{1}{2} \times \frac{1}{2} \times \frac{1}{2} = \frac{1}{8}$
FMF	2	$\frac{1}{2} \times \frac{1}{2} \times \frac{1}{2} = \frac{1}{8}$
MFF	2	$\frac{1}{2} \times \frac{1}{2} \times \frac{1}{2} = \frac{1}{8}$
FFF	3	$\frac{1}{2} \times \frac{1}{2} \times \frac{1}{2} = \frac{1}{8}$
		$\frac{8}{8} = 1$

* M = Male, F = Female.

Figure 6.3

Binomial Distribution for Number of Females in Three Customers

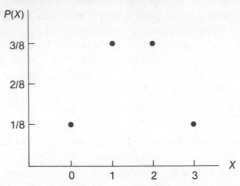

signed numerical values, and then summarized into a probability distribution. The binomial probabilities are shown graphically in Figure 6.3.

The procedure for obtaining the binomial probabilities in Figure 6.2 was easy, because a small sample was used. In the general case, for all sizes of n, the binomial probabilities are obtained by use of the binomial distribution formula[1]:

$$P(X|n,\pi) = \frac{n!}{X!\,(n-X)!}\,\pi^X(1-\pi)^{n-X} \text{ for } X = 0, 1, 2, \ldots, n$$

The probability for a given X value is obtained by using that X value, the value of n, and the value of π in the binomial formula.

To understand this formula more fully, it is helpful to view it as two parts:

$$P(X|n,\pi) = \left[\frac{n!}{X!\,(n-X)!}\right] \cdot \left[\pi^X(1-\pi)^{n-X}\right]$$
$$\text{Part A} \qquad \cdot \qquad \text{Part B}$$

Part B is the probability of a *specific* sequence of X successes and $(n-X)$ failures. This part follows directly from repeated application of the multiplicative law for independent events. There are many sequences of X successes and $n-X$ failures, and each sequence has the probability given in Part B. The *number* of such sequences is given by Part A. Applying the additive law for mutually exclusive events completes the expression for $P(X|n,\pi)$, and the resulting probability of X successes.

---

[1] Part of the binomial formula involves *factorial* notation, which is:

$$n! = n \cdot (n-1) \cdot (n-2) \cdot \ldots \cdot 3 \cdot 2 \cdot 1$$
$$0! = 1, \text{ by definition.}$$

As an example, observe that

$$\frac{n!}{X! \ (n - X)!}$$

is indeed the number of sequences of X successes in n trials for the situation in which $n = 5$ and $X = 2$. The *number* of sequences, according to the formula, is:

$$\frac{n!}{X! \ (n - X)!} = \frac{5!}{2! \ (5 - 2)!} = \frac{5 \times 4 \times 3 \times 2 \times 1}{(2 \times 1) \times (3 \times 2 \times 1)} = 10$$

The listing of the sequences (S = Success, F = Failure) is:

S	S	F	F	F		F	S	F	S	F
S	F	S	F	F		F	S	F	F	S
S	F	F	S	F		F	F	S	S	F
S	F	F	F	S		F	F	S	F	S
F	S	S	F	F		F	F	F	S	S

There are ten sequences, in agreement with the formula.

Suppose it is known that a production line produces 30 percent defectives, and that each unit's condition (good or defective) is independent of the condition of other units. On Tuesday, four units were produced. What probabilities would be assigned to the values of X, the number of defectives?

$$P(X|n,\pi) = \frac{n!}{X! \ (n - X)!} \cdot \pi^X (1 - \pi)^{n-X}$$

$$P(X = 0|4,0.3) = P(0) = \frac{4!}{0!4!} (0.3)^0 (0.7)^4 = 0.2401$$

$$P(X = 1|4,0.3) = P(1) = \frac{4!}{1!3!} (0.3)^1 (0.7)^3 = 0.4116$$

$$P(X = 2|4,0.3) = P(2) = \frac{4!}{2!2!} (0.3)^2 (0.7)^2 = 0.2646$$

$$P(X = 3|4,0.3) = P(3) = \frac{4!}{3!1!} (0.3)^3 (0.7)^1 = 0.0756$$

$$P(X = 4|4,0.3) = P(4) = \frac{4!}{4!0!} (0.3)^4 (0.7)^0 = 0.0081$$

Those probabilities are shown graphically in Figure 6.4. It is important for the reader to recall that the binomial distribution is based on random sampling from a very large population. Thus, the probability of success is not (noticeably) changed from one observation to the next. If the population is small, use of the binomial distribution is invalid; the hypergeometric distribution (discussed in Note 6.3 following Chapter 17 in this text) should be used instead.

Figure 6.4

**Binomial Distribution for Number of Defectives
in Four Units of Production.**

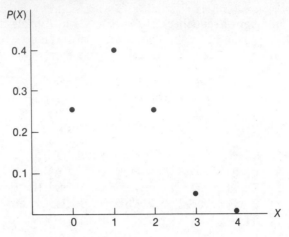

6.31   Tables of the Binomial Distribution

The binomial distribution formula is relatively easy to use when the sample size is small. However, the arithmetic becomes cumbersome as n increases. The calculations required by the formula are extensive, so tables have been developed containing the binomial probabilities. Tables of binomial probabilities are presented in Appendix D.

The binomial distributions of Appendix D have four key features of their organization: (1) the sample size (or number or trials) of the Bernoulli process, labeled n; (2) the probability of success, labeled π; (3) the binomial random variable, labeled X, and (4) the body of the table which shows the probabilities generated from application of the binomial distribution formula.

The five probabilities calculated for the production line example, where $\pi = 0.30$ and $n = 4$, can be verified from the table. First, locate the portion of the table devoted to samples of size $n = 4$; then locate the column which corresponds to the value of $\pi = 0.30$ and find the following numbers for $P(X|n = 4, \pi = 0.30)$:

X	$P(X)$
0	0.2401
1	0.4116
2	0.2646
3	0.0756
4	0.0081
	1.0000

These values are identical to those obtained by use of the binomial distribution formula.

There are also situations which require the probability of, say, three or more successes in a binomial situation. By the additive law for mutually exclusive events, for $n = 4$:

$$P(X \geq 3) = P(X = 3) + P(X = 4)$$

Letting $\pi = 0.30$:

$$P(X \geq 3) = 0.0756 + 0.0081 = 0.0837$$

For small values of n, this summation process is simple. However, for larger values of n, it would be tedious to add together a large number of these probabilities; therefore, tables of cumulative right-tail binomial probabilities are provided in Appendix E. The values in the body of the table give the probability of X or more successes for the specified values of n and π. Reading from the table, for $n = 4$ and $\pi = 0.3$:

$$P(X \geq 3) = 0.0837$$

Appendix E does not contain rows for $X = 0$, because $P(X \geq 0) = 1$ for any binomial distribution.

In order to find the probability of X or fewer successes, which cannot be obtained directly from the cumulative table, recall that the total probability of all possible events is one. If one finds the probability of, say, three or more successes and subtracts this from one, then one has obtained the probability of two or fewer successes. Thus:

$$P(X \geq 3) + P(X \leq 2) = 1$$
$$P(X \leq 2) = 1 - P(X \geq 3)$$
$$P(X \leq 2) = 1 - 0.0837$$
$$P(X \leq 2) = 0.9163$$

This is illustrated in Figure 6.5.

In a similar manner, the cumulative binomial table can be used to find

Figure 6.5

Left-Tail Binomial Probability

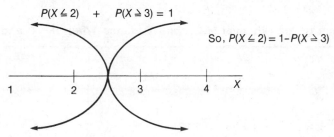

Figure 6.6

Binomial Probability for an Interval

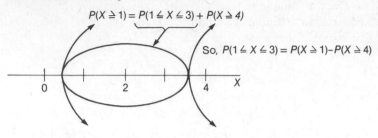

the probability that X falls in a *specific interval*. When $n = 4$ and $\pi = 0.3$, the probability that $1 \leq X \leq 3$ is:

$$
\begin{aligned}
P(1 \leq X \leq 3) &= P(X \geq 1) - P(X > 3) \\
&= P(X \geq 1) - P(X \geq 4) \\
&= 0.7599 - 0.0081 \\
&= 0.7518
\end{aligned}
$$

This is illustrated in Figure 6.6.

6.32   Binomial Distribution: Mean and Variance

As with the Bernoulli distribution, the binomial distribution has a mean and variance. The mean of a binomial distribution can be obtained by calculation of the expected value of the binomial random variable.

$$
\mu_X = E(X) = \sum_{X=0}^{n} XP(X)
$$

The binomial probability distribution for $n = 3$, $\pi = 0.5$ is presented in Figure 6.7, along with the computations of the mean and variance of the distribution. For this case,

$$
\mu_X = E(X) = 1.5
$$

Figure 6.7

Calculation of the Binomial Mean and Variance When $n = 3$ and $\pi = 0.5$

X	$P(X)$	$XP(X)$	$X - \mu_X$	$(X - \mu_X)^2$	$(X - \mu_X)^2 P(X)$
0.......	1/8	0	$-3/2$	9/4	9/32
1.......	3/8	3/8	$-1/2$	1/4	3/32
2.......	3/8	6/8	1/2	1/4	3/32
3.......	1/8	3/8	3/2	9/4	9/32
	8/8 = 1	$\mu_X = 12/8 = 1.5$			$\sigma_X^2 = 24/32 = 0.75$

A simpler formula to use for the mean of a binomial distribution is:

$$\mu_X = n\pi$$

mean

where again n is the sample size and π is the probability of success. (This relationship is proved in Note 6.32a following Chapter 17 in this text.) For $n = 3$, $\pi = 0.5$:

$$\mu_X = n\pi = 3(0.5) = 1.5$$

This result agrees with the result in Figure 6.7.

The formula for the variance of the binomial distribution can be developed in a similar manner. From previous discussions of the mean and the variance in Chapter 4, it is known that:

$$\sigma_X^2 = \sum_{X=0}^{n} (X - \mu_X)^2 \cdot P(X)$$

Referring to Figure 6.7, the variance of a binomial distribution, where $n = 3$ and $\pi = 0.5$, can be found as follows:

$$\sigma_X^2 = \Sigma(X - \mu_X)^2 \cdot P(X) = 24/32 = 0.75$$

Just as there is a simpler formula for the mean, the same is true for the variance of the binomial distribution. Rather than using the summation approach, the binomial distribution variance may be calculated by the following:

$$\sigma_X^2 = n\pi (1 - \pi)$$

Variance

(This relationship is proved in Note 6.32b following Chapter 17.) When $n = 3$ and $\pi = 0.5$:

$$\sigma_X^2 = n\pi (1 - \pi) = 3(0.5)(0.5) = 0.75$$

The standard deviation is the square root of the variance; the standard deviation of the binomial distribution is:

$$\sigma_X = \sqrt{\sigma_X^2}$$
$$\sigma_X = \sqrt{n\pi (1 - \pi)}$$

standard deviation

For the example where $n = 3$ and $\pi = 0.5$,

$$\sigma_X = \sqrt{\sigma_X^2} = \sqrt{0.75} = 0.866$$

6.33 Binomial Distribution Shape

A distribution characteristic which is frequently as important as the values of the mean and variance is the shape of the distribution, and the changes in the shape which occur for different sample sizes. In Figure 6.8, various shapes of the binomial are presented. When $\pi = 0.5$, the

Figure 6.8. Binomial Distributions

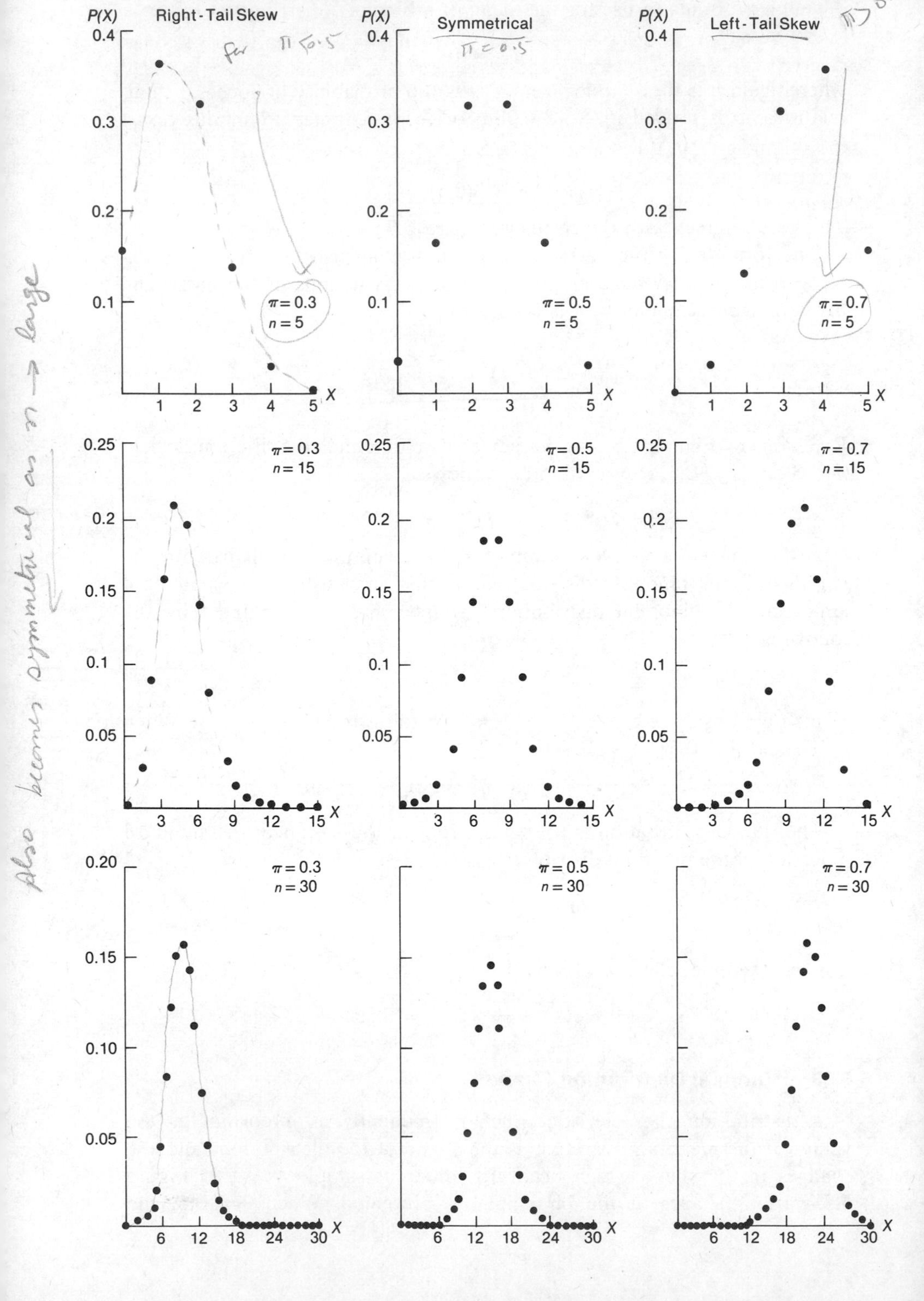

Handwritten annotations:
- *for $\pi < 0.5$* (top left panel)
- *$\pi = 0.3$, $n = 5$* (circled, top left panel)
- *$\pi = 0.5$* (top center panel)
- *for $\pi > 0.5$* (top right, above panel)
- *$\pi = 0.7$, $n = 5$* (circled, top right panel)
- *Also becomes symmetrical as $n \to$ large* (left margin, vertical)

Top row, left panel — **Right-Tail Skew**, $P(X)$ vs X, $\pi = 0.3$, $n = 5$

Top row, center panel — **Symmetrical**, $P(X)$, $\pi = 0.5$, $n = 5$

Top row, right panel — **Left-Tail Skew**, $P(X)$, $\pi = 0.7$, $n = 5$

Middle row, left panel — $\pi = 0.3$, $n = 15$

Middle row, center panel — $\pi = 0.5$, $n = 15$

Middle row, right panel — $\pi = 0.7$, $n = 15$

Bottom row, left panel — $\pi = 0.3$, $n = 30$

Bottom row, center panel — $\pi = 0.5$, $n = 30$

Bottom row, right panel — $\pi = 0.7$, $n = 30$

distribution is symmetric (the left side of the distribution is a mirror image of the right side). On the other hand, when $\pi = 0.3$, the distribution is skewed with a long right tail, and when $\pi = 0.7$, it is skewed with a long left tail.

Just as π has an influence on the binomial distribution shape, so does the sample size. As the sample size (number of trials of the Bernoulli experiment) increases, the shape of the binomial distribution approaches symmetry. In Figure 6.8, where $\pi = 0.5$ there is symmetry at all sample sizes. But regardless of π, the shape approaches symmetry as n is increased. Where $\pi = 0.3$ and $\pi = 0.7$, the lack of symmetry is obvious for small samples. However, as the sample size increases, the shape of the distribution approaches symmetry.

6.4   SAMPLING DISTRIBUTION OF THE PROPORTION

The sample proportion, denoted p, measures the proportion of successes in n trials of a Bernoulli process while the binomial random variable X measures the number of successes in n trials. Definitionally, the sample proportion is

$$p = \frac{X}{n}$$

success X in n trial

p is random variable

where X is the binomial random variable, and n is the number of trials of the Bernoulli process. If $n = 50$, $X = 13$, then $p = 0.26$.

The random variable p takes on numerical values from zero to one. This can be seen from the definition of p; values of X are restricted to the interval from zero to n. When $X = 0$, $p = 0$. When X reaches its maximum value of $X = n$, $p = 1$.

In the discussion of the binomial distribution, the example of counting the number of females in three customers was presented. Figure 6.9 shows the values of the binomial random variable X for this example, along with the binomial probabilities. The table contains values of the random variable X from zero to three and values of the random variable p from zero to one.

$0 \le p \le 1$ always

Figure 6.9

Binomial Distribution for p and X

three customers $n = 3$

X	$P(X)$	$p = \dfrac{X}{n}$	$P(p) = P(x)$
0.............	1/8	0	1/8
1.............	3/8	1/3	3/8
2.............	3/8	2/3	3/8
3.............	1/8	1	1/8
	8/8 = 1		8/8 = 1

Figure 6.10

Probability Distribution of Sample Pro-portion

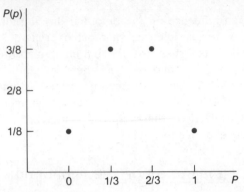

The probabilities assigned each value of the <u>random variable p</u> in Figure 6.9 are <u>the same as those</u> assigned the random variable X in Figure 6.7. This is not a coincidence. The probability distribution function for p is exactly the same as the binomial probability distribution function

$$P(p) = P(X) = \frac{n!}{X!\,(n - X)!}\,\pi^X(1 - \pi)^{n-X}$$

This is intuitively acceptable because the probability of one third of the three trials being successes is the same as the probability of one success in three trials, and so on.

Since the probabilities assigned the random variable p are binomial probabilities, the shape of the distribution of the sample proportion is the same as the shape of the binomial distribution. For the example of count-ing the number of females in three customers, the graph of the distribution of the sample proportion is shown in Figure 6.10, which has the same shape as the corresponding distribution of X, shown in Figure 6.3.

6.41   Mean and Variance of the Sampling Distribution of the Proportion

The mean of the sampling distribution of the proportion is given by the expression:

$$\mu_p = E(p) = \pi$$

Thus, the mean of the sampling distribution of the proportion p equals the probability of success π for a Bernoulli trial.

The variance of the sampling distribution of the proportion, σ_p^2, is given by:

$$\sigma_p{}^2 = \frac{\pi(1-\pi)}{n}$$

variance

(These relationships are proved in Notes 6.41*a* and 6.41*b* following Chapter 17.)

The standard deviation of the sampling distribution of the proportion is obtained by:

$$\sigma_p = \sqrt{\sigma_p{}^2}$$

$$\sigma_p = \sqrt{\frac{\pi(1-\pi)}{n}}$$

Standard Dev.
or
Standard error

The standard deviation of the sampling distribution of p is often called the *standard error* of the sample proportion.

It is worthwhile to note that p and π are both *means*. The sample proportion, p, is the average number of successes per observation in the sample of size n, and π is the average number of successes per element in the population. Thus, from sampling theory:

$$\mu_{\bar{x}} = \mu_x$$
$$\mu_p = \pi$$

because p is a sample mean, and π is a population mean. Similarly, from sampling theory:

$$\sigma_{\bar{x}}{}^2 = \frac{\sigma_x{}^2}{n}$$

thus

$$\sigma_p{}^2 = \frac{\sigma_x{}^2}{n} = \frac{\pi(1-\pi)}{n}$$

because it was shown before that the variance of a Bernoulli population is $\pi(1-\pi)$.

6.5 POISSON DISTRIBUTION

Another important discrete probability distribution is the Poisson distribution. This distribution is frequently applied to the random variable created by counting the number of items or events in either a unit of *time* or *space*.

One situation for which the Poisson distribution might be appropriate is the assigning of probabilities to the different numbers of cars which might arrive at a gasoline station in a one minute period of time. Another situation is the assigning of probabilities to the number of defects in a painted surface, a situation which involves a unit of space.

/ Time

/ space

The Poisson distribution may be used for counting the number of events that occur over time or space when:

1. The average number of events per unit of time or space remains stable for some rather long period of time or amount of space.
2. This is the most that can be said about how events occur. Knowing what happens in one part of time or space does not affect what happens in another part of time or space.

As an example of a Poisson process generating a Poisson random variable, consider throwing darts at a dart board. Assume that you are "randomly" throwing these darts so that each dart is as likely to fall at one place as another on the board. If you threw, say, 100 darts at a board with an area of 100 square inches, you would average one dart per square inch. Then the number of darts in a square inch of the board would be (approximately) described by the Poisson probability distribution, since the most that can be said (given random throws) is that the expected or average number of darts for a square inch is one.

Consider the gasoline station situation, where the basic unit is one minute of time. Within a given minute, zero cars may arrive, one car may arrive, two cars may arrive, and so forth. Here, in effect, you are "throwing" cars at a time line, so that each car is as likely to "hit" on one spot as any other on the time line. The most that can be said about the arrival of cars is the expected, or average, number of arrivals in one minute.

The Poisson probability distribution formula assigns probabilities to the values of the Poisson random variable. The Poisson distribution depends on the specified value of the parameter μ_X, the mean number of events in the specified unit of time or space. The Poisson probability distribution formula is:

$$P(X|\mu_X) = e^{-\mu_X} \frac{(\mu_X)^X}{X!}$$

where e is the mathematical constant, 2.71828 . . . , μ_X equals the mean number of events, and X is the Poisson random variable. (The Poisson distribution formula is derived from the binomial distribution in Note 6.5b following Chapter 17.)

The formula is difficult to use without the assistance of tables. Thus, in Appendix F, values for the Poisson probability formula are given. For example, if the mean number of cars which may arrive at a gas station in one minute is two, then one uses the column of Poisson probabilities for $\mu_X = 2$, and reads the following for $P(X|\mu_X = 2)$:

$P(0) = 0.135$ $P(5) = 0.036$
$P(1) = 0.271$ $P(6) = 0.012$
$P(2) = 0.271$ $P(7) = 0.003$
$P(3) = 0.180$ $P(8) = 0.001$
$P(4) = 0.090$ 0.999 (rounding)

Just as in the case of the binomial, it can be tedious calculating $P(X \geq 5|\mu_X = 2)$, by adding $P(5) + P(6) + P(7) + P(8) = 0.036 + 0.012 + 0.003 + 0.001 = 0.052$. Therefore, in Appendix G, a table of cumulative right-tail Poisson probabilities are presented. The calculated values for $P(X \geq 5|\mu_X = 2)$ can be checked by referring to the portion of the table associated with $\mu_X = 2$, and reading the value 0.053. (This value is more accurate than 0.052, calculated above, because of accumulated rounding errors.)

[margin note: cumulative / Appendix G]

6.51   Poisson Distribution: Mean and Variance

The Poisson distribution mean and variance are presented:

$$\mu_X = E(X)$$
$$\sigma_X^2 = \mu_X$$

[margin note: Imp]

The Poisson distribution has a mean and variance which are both equal to μ_X, the mean number of events per unit of time or space. (These relationships are proved in Notes 6.51a and 6.51c.)

6.52   Units for the Poisson Distribution

Suppose you are dealing with arrivals at a gas station where cars arrive at an average of two per minute; thus $\mu_X = 2$ for one minute. But suppose you are concerned with the probability of, say, five arrivals in four minutes. For a four minute interval, the Poisson process no longer has a mean of two. The Poisson mean instead is the average number of arrivals in four minutes. It is obvious that if the average for one minute is two arrivals, then the average for four minutes is eight arrivals. From this,

[margin note: = 8]

$$P(5 \text{ arrivals in 4 minutes}) = P(X = 5|\mu_X = 8) = 0.092$$

[margin note: Prob. of 5 arrivals in 4 minutes]

from the Poisson table in Appendix F.

This conversion of units can also be made for a smaller unit of time or space as well. Suppose you are interested in the probability of at least one arrival in 15 seconds. Since 15 seconds equals ¼ minute, the mean here is ¼ × 2 = 0.5. From Appendix G, $P(X \geq 1|\mu_X = 0.5) = 0.393$.

[margin note: x ≥ 1 / Prob. of 1 arrival in 15 sec.]

[margin note: cumulative]

6.53   Poisson Approximation to the Binomial

As n becomes very large, and π becomes very small, a binomial distribution approaches the Poisson distribution. The Poisson distribution which approximates a binomial distribution will have:

Use Poisson $\xrightarrow{\text{?}}$ Binomial $\begin{cases} n\pi < 5 \\ n \geqslant 50 \end{cases}$ $\begin{cases} n \text{ large} \\ \pi \text{ small} \end{cases}$

$$E(X) = n\pi = \mu_X$$

The use of the Poisson approximation is usually limited to those binomial values of n and π where $n\pi < 5$ and $n \geq 50.$

6.54   Example of Poisson Approximation to the Binomial

Use the Poisson approximation to the binomial to find the distribution of X for $n = 50$ and $\pi = 0.01$. Then, for the Poisson:

$$\mu_X = E(X) = n\pi = 0.5$$

And, the Poisson probabilities (Appendix F) are:

X	$P(X)$
0	0.607
1	0.303
2	0.076
3	0.013
4	0.002
5	0.000
	1.001 (rounding)

And, from Appendix D, the binomial probabilities are:

X	$P(X)$
0	0.6050
1	0.3056
2	0.0756
3	0.0122
4	0.0015
5	0.0001
	1.0000

which illustrates the closeness of the approximation.

6.6   SUMMARY

In this chapter we have developed special probability models for the binomial and Poisson probability distributions. These special probability models are useful because many probability situations are well described by these models. By examining these models in detail, we have really "prethought" many probability situations.

The binomial probability distribution arises in observing n trials of a constant Bernoulli process, and counting the number of successes. This is equivalent to saying that one is looking at n trials of a process which generates two outcomes called *success* and *failure* and counting the number of successes, where on each of these trials, the probability of success is constant, and the outcome of the trial is independent of all other outcomes.

A Poisson random variable typically arises in situations in which phenomena occur "randomly" over time or space, and one wants to count the number of times the event occurs. Typical examples are arrivals of telephone calls at a switchboard during the lunch hour, vacancies on the Supreme Court, injuries due to accidents, defects in a continuous manufacturing process, arrival of customers at a store, and so on.

These special probability models have their own probability distribution formulas. For the binomial distribution:

Binomial

$$P(X|n,\pi) = \frac{n!}{X!\,(n-X)!}\,\pi^X(1-\pi)^{n-X}$$
$$\mu_X = E(X) = n\pi$$
$$\sigma_X^2 = n\pi(1-\pi)$$

For the distribution of sample proportions:

$$P(p) = P\left(\frac{X}{n}\Big|n,\pi\right) = \frac{n!}{X!\,(n-X)!}\,\pi^X(1-\pi)^{n-X}$$
$$\mu_p = E(p) = \pi$$
$$\sigma_p^2 = \frac{\pi(1-\pi)}{n}$$

For the Poisson distribution:

Poisson

$$P(X|\mu_X) = e^{-\mu_X}\frac{(\mu_X)^X}{X!}$$
$$\mu_X = E(X)$$
$$\sigma_X^2 = \mu_X$$

$$\mu_X = E(x)$$
$$\sigma_X^2 = \mu(x)$$
(note square)

EXERCISES

6.1   What is a Bernoulli process?

* 6.2   A person, selected at random from the listing of all students at the University of Colorado, is to be interrogated to determine whether he or she has a bachelor's degree.

   a.   Draw the sample space for this experiment.
   b.   If 30 percent of the students have bachelor's degrees, attach probabilities to the simple events in the sample space.
   c.   Define a random variable which associates zero with "no bachelor's degree" and one with "has a bachelor's degree." Construct a probability distribution for this random variable.
   d.   Find the mean and variance of the probability distribution, using

---

* Answers to exercises marked with an asterisk (*) are in Appendix L.

the definitions of mean and variance for a probability distribution, from Chapter 4.

e. Does this situation describe a Bernoulli process?

6.3   A particular Bernoulli process has a 30 percent chance of yielding a "success." Find the mean and variance of this Bernoulli probability distribution, using the formulas given in the chapter. Compare your results with 6.2 *d.*

6.4   Describe, in general terms, the conditions that lead to a binomial probability distribution.

* 6.5   Using the formula for the binomial probability distribution, find the complete probability distribution for the number of heads on three flips of a fair coin.

* 6.6   Using the formula for the binomial probability distribution, find the complete probability distribution for the number of nonresident students in a simple random sample of four students, when it is known that 40 percent of all students are nonresidents.

* 6.7   Find the mean and variance of the probability distribution in Exercise 6.6, using the formulas from Chapter 4. Compare your results with the appropriate formulas from Chapter 6.

6.8   Verify your answers to Exercises 6.5 and 6.6 by using the tables of the binomial distribution.

* 6.9   Using the binomial tables, find:
a. $P(X = 3 \mid n = 7, \pi = 0.3)$
b. $P(X = 3 \mid n = 7, \pi = 0.6)$
c. $P(X = 5 \mid n = 10, \pi = 0.5)$
d. $P(X \geq 3 \mid n = 10, \pi = 0.4)$
e. $P(X \leq 2 \mid n = 10, \pi = 0.4)$
f. $P(X > 6 \mid n = 10, \pi = 0.6)$
g. $P(X \leq 7 \mid n = 10, \pi = 0.6)$

* 6.10   Using the binomial tables, find:
a. $P(X \leq 5 \mid n = 8, \pi = 0.7)$
b. $P(X \geq 6 \mid n = 8, \pi = 0.7)$
c. $P(X = 0 \mid n = 1, \pi = 0.3)$
d. $P(X = 7 \mid n = 6, \pi = 0.4)$
e. $P(X \geq 4 \mid n = 4, \pi = 0.4)$
f. $P(X = 3 \mid n = 9, \pi = 0.5)$
g. $P(X \leq 6 \mid n = 9, \pi = 0.8)$

* 6.11   Using the binomial tables, find:
a. $P(3 \leq X \leq 7 \mid n = 10, \pi = 0.5)$
b. $P(12 \leq X \leq 15 \mid n = 20, \pi = 0.8)$
c. $P(1 \leq X \leq 3 \mid n = 20, \pi = 0.8)$
d. $P(-3 < X < -2) \mid n = 5, \pi = 0.4)$ $\times$ can't be negative

* 6.12   Use the table of the Poisson distribution to find:
a. $P(X = 3 \mid \mu_x = 1.4)$
b. $P(X > 3 \mid \mu_x = 2.0)$
c. $P(X = 4 \mid \mu_x = 4)$

     d.   Using the Poisson approximation to the binomial, find $P(X = 4 \mid n = 100, \pi = 0.02)$

* 6.13   In a quality control application, a random sample of ten items is selected from the hourly output of the machine. If the machine has been working correctly that hour, the defect rate is 30 percent of the items. When it is not working correctly, the defect rate is 60 percent. The probability that the machine is working correctly for a randomly selected hour is 0.20. What is the probability that exactly two of the ten, selected at random from a randomly selected hour's production, will be defective? What is the probability that more than two will be defective? A table of joint probabilities showing entries such as P (correct $\cap$ $X = 2$) is very helpful.

* 6.14   An urn contains 100,000 balls, of which 40,000 are green. A random sample of five balls is taken. What is the probability that two of the five balls will be green?

* 6.15   An urn contains ten balls, of which four are green. A random sample of five balls is taken. Is the probability that two of the five balls will be green the same as in Exercise 6.14? Why or why not?

* 6.16   To determine which three soldiers to assign to an unpleasant detail, the Sergeant puts the names of the eight candidates for the detail in a hat, stirs well, and draws out three. Of the eight candidates, two are women. Is it correct to say that the probability that two women and one man will will be assigned to the detail is 0.1406, as determined from the binomial table? Think about population size.

* 6.17   A coin is flipped four times, and the number of tails is counted. You have a wager with a friend, which requires you to pay $50 if no tails appear, pay $10 if one tail appears, receive $10 if two tails appear, receive $30 if three tails appear, and receive $10 if four tails appear. What is the expected value of the random variable defined as the amount of money you receive (where a negative value indicates money you pay out)?

* 6.18   A purchasing agent to whom the Rile Corporation sells roofing materials calls the Rile Corporation with this comment: "You folks at Rile say that only 2 percent of the roofing bundles have bad shingles in them. I just bought ten bundles, and two of them had bad shingles in them. Are you guys picking on me?"
     a.   If Rile actually produces only 2 percent bad bundles, what is the probability that the purchasing agent would receive two bad bundles out of ten?
     b.   Do you think Rile is picking on the agent? Why or why not?

6.19   Discuss: "If I know the probability distribution for X, the number of successes in a binomial situation, I also know the probability distribution for p, the sample proportion of successes in the same situation."

6.20   In what way is a sample proportion (for a binomial sampling situation) similar to a sample mean?

* 6.21   Using the binomial probability distribution for the sample proportion, find the probability that half of a sample of size four will be "good" when 40 percent of the population is "good."

* 6.22   Using the tables of the binomial probability distribution, find:
  a. $P(p = 0.25 \mid n = 8, \pi = 0.3)$
  b. $P(p \geq 0.25 \mid n = 8, \pi = 0.3)$
  c. $P(p \leq 0.25 \mid n = 8, \pi = 0.3)$
  d. $P(p \geq 0.20 \mid n = 8, \pi = 0.3)$
  e. $P(p = 0.20 \mid n = 8, \pi = 0.3)$
  f. $P(p < 0.20 \mid n = 8, \pi = 0.3)$

* 6.23   What are the mean and variance for the sample proportion for a sample of 100 taken from a binomial population with $\pi = 0.8$?

* 6.24   What are the mean and variance for the number of successes for a sample of 100 taken from a binomial population with $\pi = 0.8$?

* 6.25   Between 9:30 and 10:30 AM, customers arrive at the QueenMart according to the Poisson distribution. The number of customers arriving during that hour averages five. What is the probability that exactly five will arrive during that hour tomorrow? What is the probability that three or more will arrive during that hour tomorrow?

  6.26   If you knew that the QueenMart is a major grocery store, would you think your answers to Exercise 6.25 would apply to the day before Thanksgiving?

* 6.27   For the QueenMart, with its Poisson arrivals between 9:30 and 10:30 averaging five per hour, what is the probability that exactly three customers will arrive between 9:30 and 10:00?

* 6.28   Consider the arrivals of fire alarms at the Golden Fire Alarm Headquarters. It is known that the average rate of fire alarms for Golden, between 5:00 PM and 10:00 PM on a weekday evening in August is 1.00 per hour. Thus, for a two hour period (as from 6:00 PM to 8:00 PM), the average number of fire alarms to arrive is 2.00.
  a.   What is the probability of no fire alarms between 5:00 PM and 6:00 PM?
  b.   What is the probability of no fire alarms between 6:00 PM and 7:00 PM?
  c.   Using your answers to a and b, and the fact that the two hours are independent of each other (which must be true for the Poisson process to apply), what is the probability of no fire alarms between 5:00 PM and 7:00 PM?
  d.   Use the table of the Poisson distribution, with a mean of 2.00 to verify your answer to c.
  e.   To receive exactly one alarm between 5:00 PM and 7:00 PM, it must arrive either between 5:00 PM and 6:00 PM or between 6:00 PM and 7:00 PM. Use the Poisson distribution with a mean of 1.00 to find the probability of zero alarms in an hour, and the probability of one alarm in an hour. Then use the appropriate laws of probability, (multiplicative laws for independent events, additive law for mutually exclusive events) to find the probability of exactly one alarm between 5:00 PM and 7:00 PM, using only information

you have developed in this question. Then verify your answer using the Poisson distribution with a mean of 2.00.

* 6.29 A piece of equipment breaks down once every five days, on the average. The Poisson distribution describes the number of breakdowns in a unit of time.

    a. What is the probability of one breakdown in the next day of operation?

    b. What is the probability of one breakdown in the next two days of operation?

    c. What is the probability of more than two breakdowns in the next ten days of operation?

Assume that repair time is very quick, so that no substantial amounts of productive time are lost during repair.

REFERENCES

Feller, W. *An Introduction to Probability Theory and Its Applications,* vol. 1, 3d ed. New York: John Wiley & Sons, Inc., 1968.

Gangolli, R. A. and Ylvisaker, Donald. *Discrete Probability.* New York: Harcourt, Brace & World, Inc., 1967.

Goldberg, Samuel. *Probability, An Introduction.* Englewood Cliffs, N.J.: Prentice-Hall, 1960.

7

Normal Distribution: A Continuous Probability Distribution

7.1 CONTINUOUS PROBABILITY DISTRIBUTIONS

In the previous chapter, the discussion centered on probability distributions associated with *discrete* random variables. In this chapter, probability distributions associated with *continuous* random variables are discussed. A continuous random variable is one which may take on any value within some interval.

Many types of data used by business managers, economists, and public officials are of a continuous nature. For practical purposes, data expressed in dollars and cents can be viewed as continuous random variables. Indices of prices, incomes, wages, outputs, and most other economic phenomena also qualify as continuous. Further examples of continuous variables can be presented at length. In the general case, any random variable associated with measurement, as opposed to counting, may qualify as a continuous random variable.

For a continuous random variable, the probability distribution is referred to as a *probability density function*. To see more clearly the relationship between a discrete probability distribution and a probability density function for a continuous random variable, consider the property tax paid on single-family dwellings in a large city. If a histogram is constructed with class intervals having widths of $400, then $200, and then $100, a series of histograms might occur such as shown in Figure 7.1. These histograms are constructed to show the relative frequency density, as discussed in Chapter 2. Recall that the area of such a histogram bar shows the proportion of the population that falls in that class. If the random variable under consideration is the property tax paid on a

Figure 7.1

Three Histograms for Property Tax

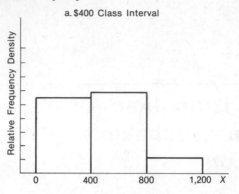

a. $400 Class Interval

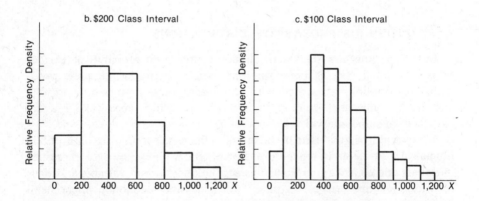

b. $200 Class Interval

c. $100 Class Interval

randomly selected single-family dwelling, the area of the histogram bar shows the probability that the property tax paid will fall in that class.

Notice that narrowing the class interval gives more detail in the histogram, and also to the corresponding probability distribution. If the class intervals grow continually smaller, the tops of the histogram bars approach a smooth curve, as shown in Figure 7.2. If one were to draw (on Figure 7.2) the class limits from any histogram bar from Figure 7.1*a, b,* or *c,* the area under the smooth curve would be the same as the area of the corresponding histogram bar. Since the area contained in the histogram bars can be viewed as the probability distribution for a random variable, the area under the smooth curve of Figure 7.2 can also be seen to represent

Figure 7.2

Smooth Curve as the Limit of a Histogram as the Class Interval Gets Smaller

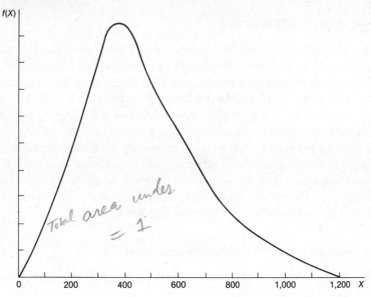

the probability distribution for a random variable. This smooth curve is the *probability density function.*

There is an important distinction between the histograms and the probability density function. For a histogram, the value of the tax paid was identified only as one of twelve (or fewer) classes. This is an example of a discrete probability distribution. For the probability density function of the continuous variable, one could discern values of tax paid for any interval, not just twelve (or fewer) classes. This is an example of a continuous probability distribution.

Note carefully that the probability density function cannot furnish the probability of the occurrence of an *individual* value of the random variable. Since a probability is an area of a region under a probability density function (rather than a height), only probabilities of occurrence for *ranges* of values may be produced by a density function. The probability of occurrence is the area of a region under the probability density function between the two endpoints of the interval of interest for the random variable. The total area under the probability density function must equal one. (Some properties of density functions are developed in Notes 7.1*a* and 7.1*b*.)

For a continuous random variable, the probability that its value will be in a specified interval is represented by the area under the density function between the endpoints of the interval.

7.2   NORMAL DISTRIBUTION

Of all continuous distributions, the one of greatest importance is the normal distribution. There are several reasons for this importance. First, many variables encountered in life have probability distributions which are close to the normal. Examples include the diameter of machined parts, weight of cereal in boxes, height of women, and the accuracy of artillery fire. Second, the sampling distributions of many sample statistics (especially the sample mean) follow approximately a normal distribution regardless of the shape of the population distribution. The central limit theorem, discussed later in this chapter, refers to shape of the sampling distribution of the mean. Third, the normal distribution is useful in approximating many discrete probability distributions.

7.21   Properties of the Normal Distribution

The normal probability distribution is described by this probability density function:

$$f(X) = \frac{1}{\sigma_X \sqrt{2\Pi}} e^{-(X-\mu_X)^2/2\sigma_X^2}$$

where X is the continuous random variable, μ_X is the mean of the distribution, σ_X is the standard deviation of the distribution, and Π and e are mathematical constants.

The probability density function is a mathematical expression that yields a value for $f(X)$ when a value of the random variable, X is introduced on the right-hand side of the equation. By plotting the values of $f(X)$ against their associated X values, the appearance of a normal probability distribution can be obtained, as in Figure 7.3. Note that $f(X)$ means the value of the density function (height of the curve); it does *not* mean multiplication. It is read "f of X" (*not* frequency).

There are two features of the normal distribution which are visually obvious:

1.   The normal distribution is bell-shaped and has one mode.
2.   The normal distribution is symmetric about its mean.

Additional features of the normal distribution can be obtained from examination of the probability density function. One such feature is:

3.   A specific normal distribution is uniquely determined by its mean *and* standard deviation.

Figure 7.3

Graph of a Normal Distribution

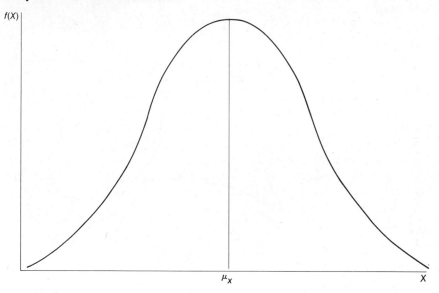

Without specification of both the mean and standard deviation, no single normal distribution can be drawn. If only the mean is specified, a family of normal distributions is identified with equal means but differing measures of dispersions, as depicted in Figure 7.4. On the other hand, specifying only the standard deviation yields a family of normal distributions with an equal measure of dispersion but dissimilar means, as shown in Figure 7.5. Only the specification of values for *both* the mean *and* the standard deviation yields a unique normal distribution.

As with all probability density functions, two additional features of the probability density function for the normal distribution are:

4. The total area under the normal distribution curve equals one.
5. The area of a region under the normal distribution curve between any two values of the random variable equals the probability of observing a value in that range, when randomly selecting an observation from the distribution.

A final property of the normal distribution is:

6. The normal distribution has the property that the area between the mean and k (a number) standard deviations from the mean is the same for all normal distributions, regardless of what the mean and

Figure 7.4

Normal Distributions with the Same Mean but Different Standard Deviations

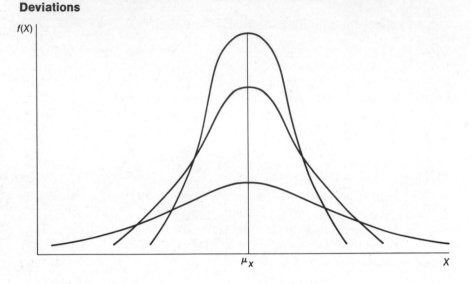

Figure 7.5

Normal Distributions with Different Means but the Same Standard Deviation

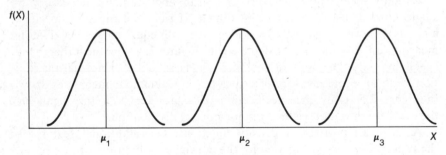

standard deviation are. This may be called the *proportional* property of the normal distribution.

7.22 Standard Normal Distribution $\mu_x = 0$

The discussion now turns to a special distribution called the *standard normal distribution*. The standard normal distribution has the same features as any normal distribution. However, the mean of the standard normal distribution is zero, and the standard deviation is one, which is helpful in providing probability tables for the standard normal distribution. (These characteristics are developed in Notes 7.22*a* and 7.22*b*.)

7.23 Table of the Standard Normal Distribution

Appendix
H

The most practical reason for discussing the standard normal distribution is that one normal distribution probability table is preferred to many. The standard normal distribution is convenient to use. With the standard normal distribution, there is need for only *one* table for *all* normal distributions. Therefore, Appendix H is based on the standard normal distribution. With this table, probability values can be found for any normal distribution.

Appendix H is characterized by a left border and an upper border which contain possible values of the standard normal random variable, labeled Z. The values in the left border show one decimal place, while the values across the top furnish a second decimal place for Z. For example, a Z value of 1.9 is associated with a row of entries across the table. The particular column chosen depends upon the value desired in the second decimal place. A Z value of 1.96 is the 1.9 row and the 0.06 column, which is associated with the probability value of 0.0250.

The meaning of the probability values in the body of the table is the area (probability) under the standard normal distribution (curve) to the right of any positive Z value selected. Obviously, the same table can be used to find the area (probability) under the standard normal distribution (curve) to the left of any negative Z value selected. In the case of continuous probability distributions, the area under the curve and the probability of occurrence in that range are identical. Therefore, the table entry of 0.0250 means that 2.5 percent of the area under the curve lies to the right of a Z value of 1.96. In turn, a Z value of −1.96 means that 2.5 percent of the area under the curve lies to the left of that Z value. This is shown in Figure 7.6.

area to the
right only

In order to strengthen your understanding of the table, determine the probability of Z being less than −1.25 (answer: 0.1056), the probability of Z being greater than 1.51 (answer: 0.0655), and the probability of Z falling between −1.25 and 1.51 [answer: (0.5000 − 0.1056) + (0.5000 − 0.0655) = 0.8289]. These are illustrated in Figure 7.7.

The truly useful feature of the standard normal distribution is that there is a simple transformation formula which will take any value, X, from any normal distribution and transform it into an equivalent value, Z, for the standard normal distribution. Equivalent, as used here, means the same area under the curve; hence, the same probability. For example, if 37 percent of the area lies to the left of a given X value, then 37 precent of the area lies to the left of its transformed Z value. This transformation follows from the proportional property of the normal distribution.

Figure 7.6

Standard Normal Distribution

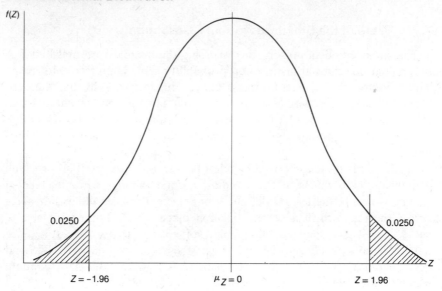

Figure 7.7

Probabilities for the Standard Normal Distribution

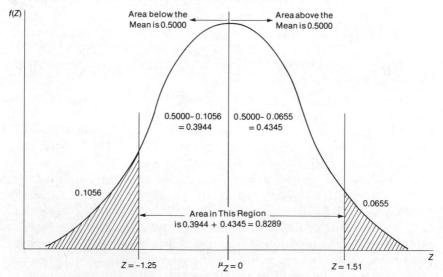

The form of the transformation is as follows: *Transformation for non zero μ_X*

$$Z = \frac{X - \mu_X}{\sigma_X}$$

where X is a normally distributed random variable which has a mean μ_X and a standard deviation σ_X, and Z is the number of standard deviations X is from μ_X. This transformation is always conceptually the same for any random variable which is normally distributed, although the symbols may vary in special cases. For example,

$$Z = \frac{\bar{X} - \mu_{\bar{X}}}{\sigma_{\bar{X}}}$$

where

$$\sigma_{\bar{X}} = \frac{\sigma_X}{\sqrt{n}}$$

In this example, Z is formed by taking a normally distributed random variable (the sample mean), subtracting the mean of that normal variable ($\mu_{\bar{X}}$) and dividing by the standard deviation of the same normal variable ($\sigma_{\bar{X}}$). In general,

$$Z = \frac{\text{Normal random variable} - \text{Mean of the variable}}{\text{Standard deviation of the variable}}$$

general

Once the Z transformation is calculated, finding areas (and therefore probabilities) under any normal distribution can be accomplished with the table of the standard normal distribution. For example, find $P(5 \leq X \leq 20)$ for a normal distribution with $\mu_X = 10$ and $\sigma_X = 5$. The relevant transformation in this case are:

$$Z_1 = \frac{X_1 - \mu_X}{\sigma_X} = \frac{5 - 10}{5} = -1; X_1 = 5 \text{ is one standard deviation below the mean (negative sign indicates below).}$$

$$Z_2 = \frac{X_2 - \mu_X}{\sigma_X} = \frac{20 - 10}{5} = 2; X_2 = 20 \text{ is two standard deviations above the mean.}$$

The question can now be stated as: find the area under the standard normal distribution between $Z_1 = -1$ and $Z_2 = 2$ (see Figure 7.8).

$$\text{Area} = [0.5000 - P(Z > 2)] + [0.5000 - P(Z < -1)]$$

or

$$P(-1 \leq Z \leq 2) = (0.5000 - 0.0228) + (0.5000 - 0.1587)$$
$$= 0.4772 + 0.3413 = 0.8185$$

This could also be calculated as $1 - P(Z < -1) - P(Z > 2) = 1 -$

Figure 7.8

Example of the Z-Transformation

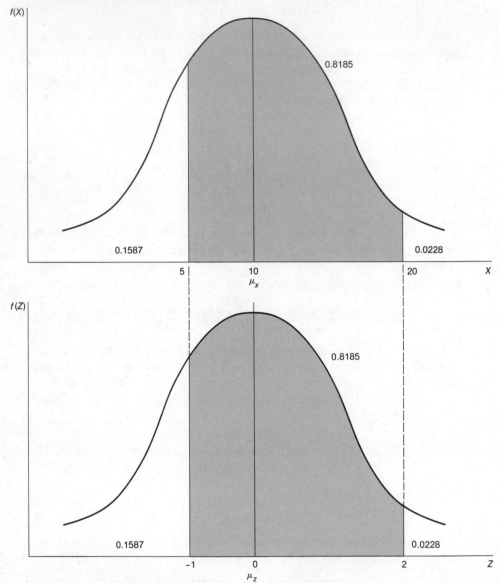

$0.1587 - 0.0228 = 0.8185$. Note that $P(Z > 2)$ could have been stated as $P(Z \geq 2)$, since Z is a *continuous* random variable, and the area of a line is zero, i.e., and $P(Z = 2) = 0$. Similarly, $P(Z < -1) = P(Z \leq -1)$.

7.24 Example of the Normal Distribution

A personnel manager is considering the use of an aptitude test as a screening device for prospective employees. The publisher of the test claims the test scores are normally distributed with a mean of 500 and a standard deviation of 100. If the test is given to prospective employees, calculate the probability that a randomly selected prospective employee will have a test score:

a. Below 300: (see Figure 7.9)

$$P(X < 300) = P\left(Z < \frac{300 - 500}{100}\right) = P(Z < -2) = 0.0228$$

Figure 7.9

Probability that the Value of the Random Variable Will Be Less than 300

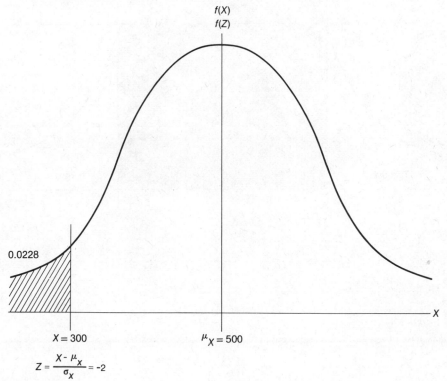

b. Between 400 and 600: (see Figure 7.10)

$$P(400 \leq X \leq 600) = P\left(\frac{400 - 500}{100} \leq Z \leq \frac{600 - 500}{100}\right)$$
$$= P(-1 \leq Z \leq 1)$$
$$= 0.5000 - P(Z < -1) + 0.5000 - P(Z > 1)$$
$$= (0.5000 - 0.1587) + (0.5000 - 0.1587)$$
$$= 0.6826$$

Figure 7.10

Probability that the Value of the Random Variable Will Be between 400 and 600

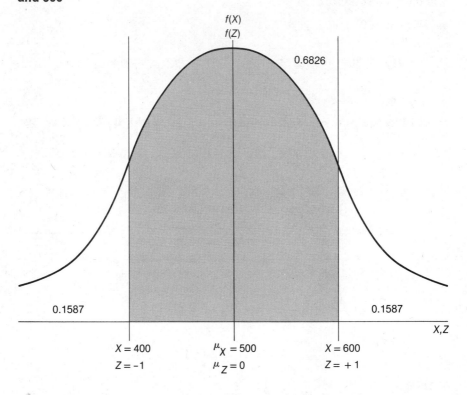

$f(X)$
$f(Z)$

0.6826

0.1587

0.1587

X,Z

$X = 400$ $\mu_X = 500$ $X = 600$
$Z = -1$ $\mu_Z = 0$ $Z = +1$

c. Above 675: (see Figure 7.11)

$$P(X > 675) = P\left(Z > \frac{675 - 500}{100}\right) = P(Z > 1.75) = 0.0401$$

Figure 7.11

Probability that the Value of the Random Variable Will Be Greater than 675

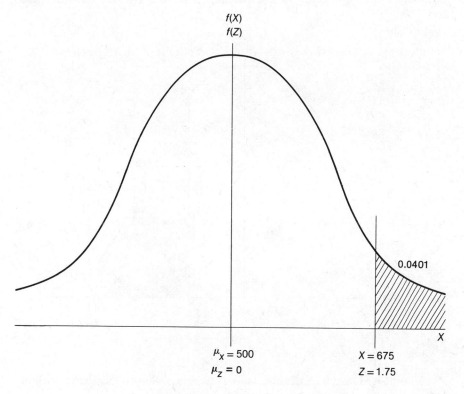

d.   Between 550 and 625: (see Figure 7.12)

$$P(550 \leq X \leq 625) = P\left(\frac{550 - 500}{100} \leq Z \leq \frac{625 - 500}{100}\right)$$
$$= P(0.5 \leq Z \leq 1.25) = P(Z > .5) - P(Z > 1.25)$$
$$= 0.3085 - 0.1056 = 0.2029$$

Figure 7.12

Probability that the Value of the Random Variable Will Be between 550 and 625

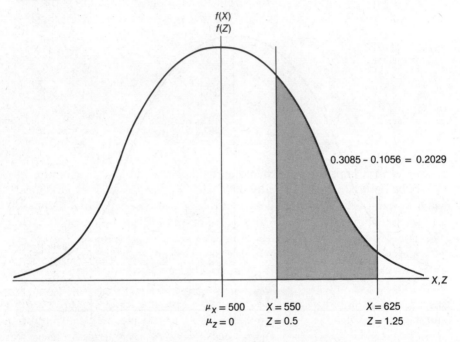

Recall that $\leq$ is equivalent to $<$ and $\geq$ is equivalent to $>$ for a continuous distribution. Not so for a discrete distribution.

7.3   CENTRAL LIMIT THEOREM

Perhaps the most important theorem in the development of statistical theory and application is the central limit theorem. This theorem can be defined as follows:

   Central Limit Theorem: **For any population,[1] the sampling distribution of $\overline{X}$ approaches a normal distribution as the sample size increases.**

---

   [1] Technically, the population must have a finite variance. Although there are populations with an infinite variance, for business decision situations this condition of finite variance is almost invariably met.

The central limit theorem is important because it predicts the normal distribution as the shape which the sampling distribution of $\bar{X}$ approaches as larger samples are used to construct the sampling distribution. Frequently, it is necessary to make inferences regarding a population when the shape of the population distribution is unknown. The central limit theorem permits one to draw conclusions based on sample information from any population. Since the sample mean is often the relevant statistic (in Chapter 8 $\bar{X}$ is used to make inferences about the population mean), the central limit theorem often applies.

In Chapter 5 it was established that the sampling distribution of $\bar{X}$ is centered on the mean of the population and possesses these properties:

$$\mu_{\bar{X}} = \mu_X$$
$$\sigma_{\bar{X}}^2 = \frac{\sigma_X^2}{n} \cdot \frac{N - n}{N - 1}$$

or

$$\sigma_{\bar{X}}^2 = \frac{\sigma_X^2}{n} \text{ for large population}$$

The central limit theorem then states that the sampling distribution of $\bar{X}$ will be approximately normally distributed for large values of n. Hence, we now know all (central tendency, variance, and shape) that is required to specify completely the sampling distribution of $\bar{X}$ for large values of n. For populations which are fairly close to symmetric, a sample size of 30 is typically assumed to be sufficient to apply the central limit theorem.[2]

As an example of a situation in which the central limit theorem is useful, consider the random variable of the number of people in cars passing an inspection station on a freeway. The population distribution of the number of people in a car is not described by the normal distribution. This population distribution might be shaped like a "reverse J" because the mode might be one person per car. However, if one were to imagine taking a random sample of 400 cars, the sampling distribution of $\bar{X}$ for this experiment would be described by the normal distribution, according to the central limit theorem. Thus, the population distribution of X is not normal; the sampling distribution of $\bar{X}$ is approximately normal, according to the central limit theorem. If μ_X and σ_X are known, one can make probability statements about $\bar{X}$ using the normal distribution, even though X is not normal.

For example, $\mu_X = 1.40$ people and $\sigma_X = 0.97$ people for the freeway. What is the probability that the average number of people in a random sample of 400 cars will exceed 1.50?

---

[2] When sampling from a finite population both n and $N - n$ should be large for the central limit theorem to apply. Typically, 30 or more is considered large, unless the population is highly skewed.

To find out how many standard deviations 1.50 is from 1.40,

$$Z = \frac{\overline{X} - \mu_{\overline{x}}}{\sigma_{\overline{x}} = \frac{\sigma_X}{\sqrt{n}}} = \frac{1.50 - 1.40}{\frac{0.97}{\sqrt{400}}} = \frac{0.10}{\frac{0.97}{20}} = 2.06$$

Then, from Appendix H,

$$P(Z > 2.06) = P(\overline{X} > 1.50) = 0.0197$$

7.4 NORMAL DISTRIBUTION AS AN APPROXIMATION TO OTHER DISTRIBUTIONS

It has been mentioned before that one of the reasons for the importance of the normal distribution is the central limit theorem, which states that the sampling distribution of $\overline{X}$ will be approximately normal for large samples. Another reason for the importance of the normal distribution is that the normal is very useful as an approximation to other distributions. Two such approximations will be discussed: the normal approximation to the binomial distribution and the normal approximation to the Poisson distribution.

7.41 Normal Approximation to the Binomial Distribution

In the previous chapter it was shown that the binomial distribution becomes more nearly symmetrical as the value of π approaches 0.5 and as the value of n is increased. It was shown that the binomial distribution has these parameters: $\mu_X = n\pi$ and $\sigma_X^2 = n\pi(1 - \pi)$. The normal distribution is a good approximation to the binomial when n is sufficiently large and π is close to 0.5, so that the binomial distribution is sufficiently symmetrical. Specifically, the normal distribution is a reasonably good approximation to the binomial whenever $n\pi$ and $n(1 - \pi)$ are both ≥ 5. The approximation is made by finding the probability under the normal curve with the same mean and variance as the binomial distribution which is being approximated. For example, if one is interested in approximating a binomial distribution with $n = 30$ and $\pi = 0.20$, the calculations are:

1. To see if the normal approximations can be used:

$$n\pi = 30(0.20) = 6 > 5$$
$$n(1 - \pi) = 30(1 - 0.20) = 30(0.80) = 24 > 5$$

2. Since both conditions are met,

$$\mu_X = n\pi = 30(0.2) = 6$$
$$\sigma_X^2 = n\pi(1 - \pi) = 30(0.2)(0.8) = 4.8$$
$$\sigma_X = \sqrt{4.8} = 2.191$$

These parameters are used for the approximating normal distribution.

When approximating the binomial with the normal, one additional problem arises. Recall that the binomial distribution is a discrete distribution and takes on only integer values. However, the probability that a normally distributed random variable will take on an exact integer value is trivial. To cope with this problem, it is assumed that the area under the approximating normal curve from, say, 7.5 to 8.5 is approximately equal to the binomial probability corresponding to $X = 8$. In effect, a half-unit correction has been made on either side of the binomial value of interest. To calculate the probability $P(X = 8 \mid n = 30, \pi = 0.2)$ by the normal approximation: ± 0.5 correction

$$P(X = 8) = P\left(\frac{7.5 - \mu_X}{\sigma_X} \leq Z \leq \frac{8.5 - \mu_X}{\sigma_X}\right)$$

or

$$P\left(\frac{7.5 - 6}{2.191} \leq Z \leq \frac{8.5 - 6}{2.191}\right) = P(0.68 \leq Z \leq 1.14) = P(Z \geq 0.68)$$
$$- P(Z \geq 1.14)$$
$$= 0.2483 - 0.1271 = 0.1212$$

From the binomial table:

$$P(X = 8 \mid n = 30, \pi = 0.2) = 0.1106$$

which shows the closeness of the approximation. The normal approximation is shown in Figure 7.13.

Consider a firm marketing a new industrial product. If 40 percent of the customers will buy the product under the specified terms of sale, what is the probability that a random sample of 50 customers will reveal that 21 to 25 customers of the sample will buy?

The desired probability for this problem is:

$$P(21 \leq X \leq 25)$$

where X is a binomial random variable and $n = 50$, $\pi = 0.4$. If tables with sufficiently large values of n were not available, a normal approximation would be necessary. The first step is to see if the normal approximation is adequate by computing:

$$n\pi = 50(0.4) = 20 > 5; n(1 - \pi) = 50(0.6) = 30 > 5$$

Since both are greater than five, it is reasonable to use the normal approximation. The aproximating normal will have these parameters:

$$\mu_X = n\pi = 20$$
$$\sigma_X = \sqrt{n(\pi)(1 - \pi)} = \sqrt{50(0.4)(0.6)} = \sqrt{12} = 3.464$$

Figure 7.13

Normal Approximation to the Binomial

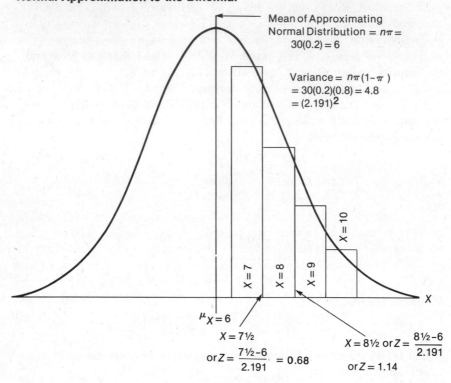

Using the approximate half-unit corrections, it is necessary to find the area under the standard normal curve between 20.5 and 25.5. Standardizing these values:

$$P(20.5 < X < 25.5) = P\left(\frac{20.5 - 20}{3.464} \le Z \le \frac{25.5 - 20}{3.464}\right)$$
$$= P(0.14 \le Z \le 1.59) = P(Z > 0.14) - P(Z > 1.59)$$
$$= 0.4443 - 0.0559 = 0.3884$$

Based on the binomial distribution for $\pi = 0.4$ and $n = 50$, it is 0.3817.

7.42   Example of the Normal Approximation to the Binomial Proportion

The normal distribution can also be used to approximate the sampling distribution of p. Consider a political candidate who is favored by 50 percent of the voters. What would be the probability that a random sample of $n = 200$ would have a value of $p \geq 0.6$? Again the first step is to be sure that the normal approximation is adequate by computing:

$$n\pi = 200(0.5) = 100 > 5; \; n(1 - \pi) = 200(0.5) = 100 > 5$$

It is adequate.

The approximating normal distribution will have these parameters:

$$\mu_p = \pi = 0.5$$

$$\sigma_p = \sqrt{\frac{\pi(1 - \pi)}{n}} = \sqrt{\frac{0.5(0.5)}{200}} = 0.0354$$

Standardizing this value:

$$P(p \geq 0.60) = P\left(Z \geq \frac{p - \mu_P}{\sigma_P}\right) = P\left(Z \geq \frac{0.60 - 0.50}{0.0354}\right)$$

$$= P(Z \geq 2.82) = 0.0024$$

This calculation has neglected the half-unit corrections which could have been made. A sample proportion $p \geq 0.60$ implies 120 or more voters, which is "corrected" to 119.5. The value of p that corresponds to $X = 119.5$ is $119.5/200 = 0.5975$, which would lead to a somewhat different (and more nearly correct) probability. In most cases in the remainder of this text, the half unit correction for values of p, the sample proportion, will be ignored for computational convenience.

7.43   Normal Approximation to the Poisson Distribution

$\mu_x \geq 10$

As the value of the parameter, μ_X, for the Poisson distribution increases, the distribution becomes less and less skewed, and approaches the normal distribution in shape. Thus, for values of $\mu_X \geq 10$ (not obtainable in the Poisson table) one can use the normal approximation for the Poisson distribution.

The normal approximation for the Poisson distribution will use the values of parameters based on the Poisson parameters. Thus, for the normal approximation, the Poisson mean (μ_X) is used for the normal mean (μ_X) and the Poisson standard deviation ($\sqrt{\mu_X}$) is used for the normal standard deviation (σ_X).

Now assume that one wants Poisson probability values for a Poisson distribution with $\mu_X = 10$. The question is asked, what is $P(X = 11 \mid \mu_X = 10)$? As with the approximation for the binomial, it is necessary to recognize that the Poisson is a discrete distribution, and the half-unit correction is again necessary. Therefore, the question restated as a normal approximation is:

$$P(X = 11 | \mu_X = 10) = P(10.5 \leq X \leq 11.5)$$

where $\mu_X = 10$ and $\sigma_X = \sqrt{10} = 3.162$. Thus

$$P(10.5 \leq X \leq 11.5) = P\left(\frac{10.5 - \mu_X}{\sigma_X} \leq Z \leq \frac{11.5 - \mu_X}{\sigma_X}\right)$$

$$= P\left(\frac{10.5 - 10}{3.162} \leq Z \leq \frac{11.5 - 10}{3.162}\right)$$

$$= P(0.16 < Z < 0.47)$$

$$= P(Z \geq 0.16) - P(Z \geq 0.47) = 0.4364 - 0.3192$$

$$= 0.1172$$

The probability from the Poisson table in Appendix F for $\mu_X = 10$ is 0.114.

A general rule that is reasonably good to follow is use the normal approximation for the Poisson distribution when $\mu_X > 10$.

7.44   Other Continuous Probability Distributions

The normal distribution is by no means the only continuous probability distribution. In subsequent chapters of this book, additional continuous distributions will be introduced as the appropriate situations arise and are discussed. In particular, discussions are forthcoming on the t-distribution, the chi-square distribution, and the F-distribution. The exponential distribution, which is related to the Poisson distribution, is discussed in Note 7.44.

7.5   SUMMARY

This chapter has illustrated the use of a probability density function to describe a probability distribution for a continuous random variable. The area between the density function, the X-axis, and the vertical lines at X_1 and X_2 is the probability that the value of X will fall between X_1 and X_2.

The normal distribution is one of the most important concepts in statistics, primarily because of the central limit theorem. This theorem states that the shape of the sampling distribution of $\bar{X}$ approaches the normal distribution as n gets large. This theorem, along with concepts of sampling theory (Chapter 5), enable one to make probability statements about $\bar{X}$ (the mean of a sample yet to be selected) even when the shape of the population is not known. Putting these concepts of sampling theory and the central limit theorem together in capsule form:

$$\mu_{\bar{X}} = \mu_X$$

$$\sigma_{\bar{X}} = \frac{\sigma_X}{\sqrt{n}}\sqrt{\frac{N - n}{N - 1}}$$

or

$$\sigma_{\bar{X}} = \frac{\sigma_X}{\sqrt{n}} \text{ for large populations.}$$

ignore $\sqrt{\frac{N-n}{N-1}}$ for $N \geqslant 20n$

The shape of the sampling distribution of $\bar{X}$ is normal if n is sufficiently large (typically, about 30).

The normal distribution has two parameters, its mean and variance (or standard deviation). When these are known, the table of the standard normal distribution may be used to find any probability for any normal distribution.

The normal distribution is also used to approximate other distributions. The normal distribution may be used to approximate the binomial distribution if both $n\pi$ and $n(1-\pi)$ are at least five. The approximation is accomplished by using the mean $(n\pi)$ and the standard deviation $(\sqrt{n\pi[1-\pi]})$ of the binomial distribution as the parameters of the approximating normal distribution.

$n\pi > 5$

$n(1-\pi) > 5$

The normal distribution may be used to approximate the Poisson distribution if the Poisson mean is larger than ten. The approximation is accomplished by using the mean (μ_X) and the standard deviation $(\sqrt{\mu_X})$ of the Poisson distribution as the parameters of the approximating normal distribution.

$\mu_X > 10$

EXERCISES

7.1   Give a clear example of a random variable which is usefully described as being continuous, rather than discrete.

7.2   Distinguish between a discrete random variable and a continuous random variable.

7.3   Discuss: "Unless infinitely precise measuring instruments are available, we can never have a truly continuous random variable. Hence, all uses of continuous random variables are actually approximations which, although quite useful, are not theoretically correct."

7.4   In what major way is a relative frequency density histogram similar to a density function?

7.5   Why must the area under a density function always be equal to one?

7.6   Discuss: "Since the area of a line is zero, we must always speak of probabilities for continuous random variables as probabilities for intervals, rather than probabilities for specific values."

*   7.7   Draw on a sheet of graph paper a line from the point $(X = 0, Y = \frac{1}{2})$ to the point $(X = 2, Y = \frac{1}{2})$. Now label the X-axis "X, a continuous random variable" and the Y-axis "$f(X)$, density function for X". You have just constructed a density function for what is called a uniform probability distribution. (The name arises because the height of the density function is uniform.)

   a.   Show that the area under the density function is one.

   b.   Find the probability that the value of the random variable, X, will fall between zero and one.

_____

* Answers to exercises marked with an asterisk (*) are in Appendix L.

      c. Find the probability that the value of the random variable, *X,* will fall between 0.4 and 1.6.

      d. What is the height of the density function where $X = 3$?

7.8 What does the area under a density function represent?

* **7.9** The normal distribution is one of the most important distributions in statistics. Which of the following are true statements about the normal probability distribution?

      a. It represents the probability distribution for a continuous random variable.

      b. It is a distribution for which the mean and mode are equal.

      c. It is symmetrical distribution.

      d. Any normally-distributed random variable can never have a negative value.

      e. A normal distribution is completely specified when the mean and variance are known.

      f. A normal distribution is completely specified when the mean and standard deviation are known.

      g. Although the mean of a normal distribution may be negative, its standard deviation cannot be negative.

      h. The median of a normal distribution is slightly to the right of the mean, since the distribution is slightly skewed.

      i. In order to be able to use the normal distribution, you must be thoroughly familiar with the use of the equation giving its density function.

      j. The normal distribution has only one mode, which is always equal to the mean.

7.10 What powerful uses does the central limit theorem give to the normal distribution?

7.11 The central limit theorem states that "the sampling distribution of the sample mean approaches a normal distribution as the sample size increases." What does this mean?

7.12 Discuss this statement made by a statistical novice: "It is ridiculous to speak of $\bar{X}$ being normally distributed. I just took a sample, and have a value of $\bar{X}$. Now tell me, how can one value have a normal distribution?"

7.13 When we say that the sample mean is normally distributed, is this the same thing as saying that the *X*-values which are used in computing $\bar{X}$ are themselves normally distributed? Why or why not?

* **7.14** Which of the following would you think are approximately described by the normal distribution?

      a. Family income in Los Angeles

      b. Weight of adult males

      c. Scores of NFL football games

      d. Height of children, ages 0–8

      e. Weight of three-year old males

      f. Number of telephone calls arriving at a telephone central office (which is extremely busy) in a randomly selected minute between 3:00 P.M. and 4:00 P.M. weekdays in August.

    g. Length of steel rods cut by an automatic shear operating normally

    h. Grades on a standardized placement test used for college entrance

    i. Grades on an exam in which about half of the students receive 100 percent

    j. Weight of coffee in coffee jars filled by a machine operating normally

7.15 What does it mean to "standardize" a normally distributed random variable?

* **7.16** If we say that a value 1.5 standard deviations above the mean has been observed (and we know that $\mu_x = 10$, $\sigma_x = 5$), what value has been observed?

* **7.17** For a normal distribution with mean 50 and variance 100, 32 is how many standard deviations away from the mean?

* **7.18** For a normal distribution with $\mu_x = 30$ and $\sigma_x^2 = 100$, what value of Z corresponds to $X = 32$?

* **7.19** If X is a normally-distributed random variable, $\mu_x = 100$ and $\sigma_x = 40$, find:

    a. $P(X \geq 100)$ *f.* $P(100 \leq X \leq 140)$ *j.* $P(X = 50)$

    b. $P(X > 100)$ *g.* $P(60 < X \leq 120)$ *k.* $P(X \leq 50)$

    c. $P(X < 60)$ *h.* $P(110 \leq X \leq 130)$ *l.* $P(90 \leq X \leq 260)$

    d. $P(X \leq 0)$ *i.* $P(-10 \leq X \leq 50)$ *m.* $P(X \geq 300)$

    e. $P(X \geq 150)$

It is helpful to draw a density function picture for each question.

* **7.20** If the weight of American males is described by the normal distribution with a mean of 160 pounds and a standard deviation of 15 pounds, how should a store allocate its order of 200 bathrobes into sizes, assuming that it desired to have the same proportion in its inventory as in the population? The weight/size table for this item is:

Weight	Size
Under 120	XS
120–140	S
140–160	M
160–190	L
190–220	XL
Over 220	KS

* **7.21** The time to commute from Chestnut Creek to Mapleland is normally distributed, with a mean time of 0.75 hours. The standard deviation of the commute time is eight minutes. If a commuter leaves Chestnut Creek at 8:30, what is the probability of arriving in Mapleland no later than 9:20? No later than 9:30? Before 9:10? Within five minutes of 9:15?

* **7.22** A grinding machine is set so that its production of shafts has an average diameter of 1.010 inches and a standard deviation of 0.020 inches. The product specifications call for shaft diameters between 1.005 inches and 1.020 inches. What proportion of the output meets the specifications?

* **7.23** The grinding machine (in Exercise 7.22) can be adjusted to any desired mean value, although the standard deviation is determined by how the machine is built, rather than how it is adjusted. The machine is to be used to produce 100 shafts which meet specifications.

  a. For the machine as it is set in Exercise 7.22, about how many shafts must be produced (started) to have 100 good shafts?

  b. What setting of the average diameter will yield the greatest proportion of "good" shafts?

  c. If each shaft started costs $100, and the adjustment process costs $1,000, should the change found in b be accomplished? Why or why not?

* 7.24 A simple random sample of 100 families is taken from the Colorado population. If the average family income for the population is $15,000 and the standard deviation is $2,000, what is the probability that the sample mean will fall between $15,000 and $15,200? Within $150 of the population mean?

* 7.25 An auditor picked 400 purchase orders out of a file, using a table of random numbers to assure a simple random sample. If the properties of last year's population of purchase orders (average amount of order $357, standard deviation $138) still hold true, what is the probability that the average order size for the sample of 400 will exceed $368?

* 7.26 If you take a random sample of size 225 from a population with a standard deviation of $900, what is the probability that $\bar{X}$ will fall within $50 of the population mean?

* 7.27 For the situation of Exercise 7.26, how large must the sample be if you want to have a 90 percent chance that $\bar{X}$ will fall within $50 of the mean?

* 7.28 Under what conditions can the normal distribution be used to approximate the binomial distribution?

7.29 What is the purpose of the half-unit correction in using the normal distribution as an approximation to the binomial distribution?

* 7.30 Find each of the following, using the normal approximation to the binomial:

  a. $P(X = 50 \mid n = 100, \pi = 0.50)$
  b. $P(X \geq 60 \mid n = 100, \pi = 0.55)$
  c. $P(30 \leq X \leq 60 \mid n = 90, \pi = 0.4)$
  d. $P(X \leq 45 \mid n = 50, \pi = 0.1)$

* 7.31 Find each of the following, using the normal approximation to the Poisson:

  a. $P(X = 5 \mid \mu_x = 20)$
  b. $P(X \geq 5 \mid \mu_x = 20)$
  c. $P(X < 15 \mid \mu_x = 20)$

REFERENCES

Alder, H. L., and Roessler, E. B. *Introduction to Probability and Statistics,* 5th ed. San Francisco: W. H. Freeman and Company, 1972.

Chew, Victor. "Some Useful Alternatives to the Normal Distribution," *The American Statistician,* vol. 22 (June, 1968), pp. 22–24.

Hansen, M. H.; Hurwitz, W. N.; and Madow, W. G. *Sample Survey Methods and Theory,* vol. 1. New York: John Wiley & Sons, Inc., 1953.

Neter, John, and Wasserman, William. *Applied Linear Statistical Models.* Homewood, Ill.: Richard D. Irwin, Inc., 1974.

Ross, Sheldon M. *Applied Probability Models with Optimization Applications.* San Francisco: Holden-Day, Inc., 1970.

8

Statistical Inference: Estimation

Up to this point in the text, the major topics which have been considered are data description, probability theory, and sampling theory. Data description deals primarily with ways of presenting data so that the user may easily grasp the essence of a body of data prepared by a statistician. In probability and sampling theory, our discussion dealt with probability models which enable one to make statements about the results of an experiment or sample. These statements are probabilistic in nature; they state the probability that a given outcome will be obtained when the world or population behaves in a specified manner. Sampling theory has been presented as a logical extension of probability theory; it describes the probabilistic outcome of a sample taken from a known population.

In this section of the text, probability and sampling theory are used in a different fashion. Previously, it was assumed that the population was known in order to make probabilistic statements about the outcome of a sample or experiment. In statistical inference, the sample result is known, from which inferences are made about the population being considered. Thus, the probability problem and the statistical inference problem are opposites. In probability theory, the population is known in order to make statements about the sample. In statistical inference, the sample is known and used to make inferences about the unknown population.

8.1 WHAT IS STATISTICAL INFERENCE?

Statistical inference is the process of making statements about a population on the basis of information contained in a sample. Statistical inference has three major branches: point estimation, interval estimation, and hypothesis testing. This chapter describes some concepts of point and interval estimation. Chapter 9 discusses hypothesis testing. The purpose of all of these statistical inferences is the same: to make statements about a population on the basis of a sample. Unfortunately, one never knows

149

whether an inference is right or wrong. The statistician is able to make probability statements about these inferences.

8.11 Judgment Sampling and Random Sampling in Inference

All the methods of statistical inference described in this text assume that the sample which has been selected is a simple random sample. If the sample which has been selected is a "judgment" sample, the statistician has no tools for making inferences. For example, suppose an interviewer has been given the instructions to go to a shopping center to ask a "representative cross section" of shoppers their opinion of a proposed city ordinance. Any inferences which would be made on the basis of a sample of this sort could be no more valid than the interviewer's judgment about the "representativeness" of the sample. If the judgment in choosing the sample was "very good," inferences made from that sample could be "very good." If the judgment was "poor," inferences made from that sample would be "poor." However, if the same type of study had been conducted using a simple random sampling technique, then each shopper would have had an equal chance of being selected, and statistical inferences about the population of all shoppers could be made by a statistician. Changing the method of sample selection from a judgment sample to a simple random sample gives the statistician the basis on which to make inferences for which statistical validity can be ascertained.

The statistician is not required to work only with simple random sampling. The chapter on sampling briefly discussed other sampling procedures, including stratified sampling and cluster sampling. If these techniques are correctly applied, the statistician can proceed to make valid statistical inferences. However, the specific procedures for using sampling procedures other than simple random sampling are beyond the scope of this text. The important concept is that a sample must be drawn by some probability mechanism in order for statistical inferences to be valid. Judgment samples may yield very useful inferences, but they do not constitute valid statistical inferences. They are no more valid than the judgment which went into constructing the samples.

8.12 Nonsampling Errors

Another very important assumption is made whenever sampling is discussed in this text. It assumes that the information revealed by a sample is always completely correct. But this is not always the case; *nonsampling errors* are often a major source of error in statistical research. A nonsampling error arises when a research procedure, such as a question on a questionnaire, does not reveal the information being sought by the researcher. For example, a very straight-forward question on a survey might be concerned with the federal income tax paid by the respondent in 1975. There may be several sources of nonsampling error in such a question. One of these sources is the ambiguity of the question. Is the question referring to the respondent's 1975 federal income tax liability, or is it referring to the cash payments made by the respondent in 1975 for federal income tax? Even if the question is worded unambiguously, other nonsampling errors may arise. The respondent may not know the answer to the question; most of us do not remember such detailed information. Even a respondent who knows the 1975 federal income tax liability may choose not to reveal the information to the researcher. Thus, an apparently innocent question, "What was your 1975 income tax liability?" may yield a nonsampling error because of ambiguity, ignorance, or unwillingness to respond correctly. Any of these nonsampling errors may be more important than the error caused by taking a sample rather than a census of the population.

Another frequent source of nonsampling errors in a statistical research project arises from people who are selected to be in the random sample, but who do not respond to the questionnaire or interview. These *nonrespondents* yield no information, yet the sampling plan has dictated that their information should be included in the sample. For example, suppose that a research project is being undertaken to learn the proportion of homeowners in a city who favor a proposed city ordinance. A list of all homeowners is prepared from the tax assessor's records. From these 10,000 homeowners, a simple random sample of 100 homeowners is selected using a table of random numbers. A questionnaire is sent to these 100 homeowners, and 30 respond to the questionnaire. Although the population of interest is all homeowners, the data base can be used only to make statistical inferences about homeowners on the assessor's list who *would* respond to the questionnaire. If the population of homeowners who *would* respond is similar to the population of homeowners who *would not* respond, the inferences made from the sample will be useful. But if those who favor the ordinance are more or less likely to return questionnaires than those who do not favor the ordinance, the usefulness of the survey will be substantially diminished.

This problem of nonrespondents is one of the most serious problems in statistical methods. This nonresponse error may be reduced by extensive followup procedures. A mail survey may be followed by a reminder if no response is initially received. A third step might be a telephone call, followed by a personal interview if necessary. These steps are often very expensive, but they are necessary if nonresponse error is to be reduced.

The example of a research procedure investigating the attitude of homeowners illustrates still another type of nonsampling error. The list of homeowners was taken from the assessor's records. If these are incorrect, either because of "old" data or other errors, the statistical method will be subject to this same nonsampling error. Statistical inferences assume that a complete list of the population is somehow available. If the list actually used is different from the list sought by the researcher, nonsampling errors will arise. As a further example, a telephone directory is not a complete list of all telephone subscribers. There are differences between the directory and the list of all subscribers because of time lags, unlisted telephone numbers, people moving into the city, and people moving out of the city. Although it may be necessary to use the telephone directory as a listing of telephone subscribers, only the judgment of the researcher, considering the particular problem, can be used to assess the validity of the research plan.

8.13   Sampling Errors

Nonsampling errors, which may be numerous, are not the only errors resulting from a statistical research project. In most cases, the research plan requires that only a subset of the members of the population will be interrogated. Thus, one is dealing with a sample rather than a census. If all elements of the population were interrogated and responded, the only errors remaining would be the nonsampling errors, as a census would have been taken. When a research plan requires a sample instead of a census, a whole new set of errors, called *sampling errors,* arise. The statistician is able to assess the magnitude of these sampling errors. From a statistical standpoint, most of statistical inference deals with assessing the magnitude of sampling errors. Although this is a very useful procedure, its usefulness is limited by the presence of nonsampling errors.

The preceding comments can be summarized by carefully defining nonsampling and sampling errors.

> A *nonsampling error* is an error which arises even if a census of the population is undertaken, using the same procedures which were used in taking a sample. A *sampling error* arises from the difference between a census result and a sample result. Statistical methodology can be used to assess the magnitude of a sampling error. Judgment is usually required to assess the magnitude of a non-sampling error.

8.2   POINT ESTIMATION

A *point estimate* is a single value, calculated from a sample, which is used to estimate the value of a population parameter. Point estimates may be constructed for a population mean, a population variance, a population proportion, or other characteristics of the population. We shall first describe how point estimates are made, and then discuss the statistical properties of point estimates.

8.21   Point Estimate of the Population Mean

The *sample mean,* calculated from a simple random sample selected from the population of interest, is a useful *point estimate* of the *population mean.*

As an example, consider a study undertaken to investigate the average elapsed time from a taxicab company's request for a taxi until the taxi arrived to pick up the passenger. The dispatcher's logs are available, which give the time of the receipt of the call and the time the driver called in to announce arrival at the address. Since all taxicab runs are given a serial number, it is very easy to construct a listing of the population of taxicab runs. A table of random numbers is used to select a random sample of 100 runs. For each run, the elapsed time (from receipt of call to arrival at the address) is calculated from the dispatcher's log. These times are then averaged, giving a value for the sample mean, $\bar{X}$, of 13.3 minutes. The sample mean, $\bar{X}$, is a point estimate of the population mean, μ_X. The population mean is the average elapsed time for *all* taxicab runs; the sample mean is the average for the random sample of 100 taxicab runs. The sample mean is considered to be a good point estimate of the (unknown) population mean.

8.22   Point Estimate of the Population Variance

In the taxicab time study, the random sample of 100 observations was also used to estimate the dispersion of response times. From the sample data, the sample standard deviation, s_X, was calculated. This yielded a value of $s_X = 4.2$ minutes, or a variance of $(4.2 \text{ minutes})^2$. The sample variance, 17.64, is a good point estimate of the population variance.

The sample variance, s_x^2, is a point estimator of the population variance, σ_X^2.

8.23   Point Estimate of the Population Proportion

This same taxicab sample could also address the question of the number of taxi runs which require more than 15 minutes from receipt of a call to arrival of the taxi. From the sample data, it was observed that 40 of the 100, or 40 percent, of the runs required more than 15 minutes. This sample value, $p = 0.40$, is the sample proportion.

The sample proportion, *p,* is a point estimate of the population proportion, π.

From this sample proportion, $p = 0.40$, one can make a point estimate that 40 percent of the population of all taxicab runs requires more than 15 minutes from the receipt of the call to the arrival of the taxi.

8.24   How Good Are These Point Estimates?

All three of these point estimates possess a good property of estimation; they are all *unbiased* estimates.[1] Loosely speaking, an estimation procedure is said to be unbiased if, for many samples, the average value obtained by the estimation procedure equals the value of the population parameter being estimated. For example, suppose that one is using, for some strange reason, a sampling procedure to estimate the mean of a population, when the true value of the population mean μ_X is known to be 90. (Obviously, if one knows that μ_X is 90, one would not be taking a sample.) A sample taken from this population gives a value of $\bar{X}$. This value of $\bar{X}$ may or may not be 90; typically, it would not be 90. However, the value of $\bar{X}$ would still be the point estimate of μ_X. Another sample would yield a different value of $\bar{X}$, and a different point estimate of the population mean, μ_X. In the long run, if many samples were taken from this population, the average of the $\bar{X}$ values would be 90. Because the average of all sample means is the true population mean, this is an unbiased estimate. The same long-run results are true for p and s_X^2. (Note 8.24 proves that s_X^2 is unbiased.)

An unbiased estimate is one whose expected value is the population parameter being estimated.

8.3   INTERVAL ESTIMATION

Although point estimates are often useful, they do have one very serious drawback: in most cases, they are somewhat wrong. They are often "close" to the true parameter value, but if the parameter can in reality have any value within some range, the point estimator has a trivial probability of being exactly correct. Thus, although point estimates may be "close," they are typically wrong. To appraise the error that is associated with point estimates, a point estimate is converted into an *interval* estimate.

Whereas a point estimate consists of a single estimate of a population parameter, an interval estimate has two parts: an *interval* within which the value of the parameter is estimated to lie, and a *confidence* level, expressed as a percentage, associated with that interval. For example, a confidence interval estimate might be stated as follows: On the basis of a simple random sample of students enrolled at the university, I am 90 percent confident that the average student income is between $438 and $962. (Note that this does not say anything about the *range* of incomes for various students.) It is quite conceivable that some students have

---

[1] The sample variance is an unbiased estimate of the population variance only if the population is large.

incomes well in excess of $10,000. What the interval does say is that the average income, where all students are included in the average, is within the $438 to $962 interval with a confidence level of 90 percent.

The confidence interval estimate described here has as its midpoint the point estimate for the population parameter being estimated. Thus, in making an interval estimate for a population mean, the sample mean would be midway between the end points of the interval estimate. (Not all interval estimates are centered on their point estimates, but those described in this text have this property.) It is useful to conceive of the procedure for constructing an interval estimate as starting with the point estimate, and then determining a value to be added to and subtracted from the point estimate to compute the interval estimate.

8.31 Confidence Interval Estimate for a Population Mean with a Large Sample

The first example of a confidence interval will be for the average elapsed time for the taxicab experiment described earlier in this chapter. In that example, a study was conducted to determine the average time from the receipt of a call for a taxi to the arrival of the taxi at the address to pick up the passenger. A sample of 100 taxicab runs from a large population contained these statistics:

$$\bar{X} = 13.3 \text{ minutes}$$
$$s_X = 4.2 \text{ minutes}$$

The point estimate for the population average time, μ_X, is the sample mean, $\bar{X} = 13.3$ minutes. Suppose one desires to establish a confidence interval estimate instead of this point estimate. The first question is to ask what confidence level is desired for the interval. Assume it has been decided that a confidence level of 95 percent is "appropriate" for this desired estimate. The next step is to use the table of the standard normal distribution to find that 95 percent of the area of the standard normal curve is contained within 1.96 standard deviations of the mean of the standard normal curve. This is a Z-value of 1.96; the area to the right of 1.96 is 0.025; the area to the left of −1.96 is also 0.025, for a total of 0.05 or 5 percent. The method for finding the confidence interval is:

$$\text{Confidence interval for } \mu_X, \text{ large sample: } \bar{X} \pm Zs_{\bar{x}} = \bar{X} \pm Z\frac{s_X}{\sqrt{n}}$$

or ± 1.025

For this example, the 95 percent confidence interval for μ_X is:

$$13.3 \pm 1.96 \frac{4.2}{\sqrt{100}} = 13.3 \pm 0.82$$

which is 12.48 to 14.12.   *conf. Interval*

8.32   Why the Interval Estimate Procedure Works

To understand this procedure more fully, it is necessary to bring together the concepts of sampling and probability theory which were developed in earlier chapters. Specifically, sampling theory and the central limit theorem (Chapters 5 and 7) state for sampling from a population where N is much larger than n:

1. The sampling distribution of $\bar{X}$ approaches the normal distribution for a sufficiently large sample size. A sample of 30 or more is typically sufficiently large unless the population is highly skewed.
2. The mean of the sampling distribution of $\bar{X}$ is equal to the mean of the distribution of the original population, $\mu_{\bar{x}} = \mu_X$.
3. The variance of the sampling distribution of $\bar{X}$ is equal to the variance of the population, divided by the sample size (large population):

$$\sigma_{\bar{X}}^2 = \frac{\sigma_X^2}{n}$$

For standard deviations:

$$\sigma_{\bar{x}} = \frac{\sigma_X}{\sqrt{n}}$$

As the next step in understanding the computation of the confidence interval for μ_X, suppose that it is *known* that the population has these parameters: $\mu_X = 14$ minutes and $\sigma_X = 4.0$ minutes. Now there is enough information to make probability statements about the closeness of a sample mean, $\bar{X}$, to the population mean, μ_X. To find the interval within which there is a 95 percent probability that $\bar{X}$ (for a sample of $n = 100$) would lie, one enters the standard normal table. One should find that 95 percent of the area under the standard normal curve lies between $Z = -1.96$ and $Z = 1.96$. From sampling theory:

$$\sigma_{\bar{x}} = \frac{\sigma_X}{\sqrt{n}} = \frac{4.0}{\sqrt{100}} = 0.4$$

It is also known from sampling theory that the distribution of $\bar{X}$ is centered on $\mu_{\bar{x}} = \mu_X = 14$ minutes. From the central limit theorem, it is known that the normal distribution satisfactorily describes the distribution of $\bar{X}$. All of these concepts are placed together in Figure 8.1. It has already been observed that the interval $\mu_{\bar{x}} \pm 1.96\ \sigma_{\bar{x}}$ contained the desired probability of 0.95. The desired 0.95 probability interval is:

Prob. Interval

$$\mu_X \pm 1.96\ \sigma_{\bar{x}} = 14 \pm 1.96\ (0.4)$$

which is 13.22 to 14.78.

To summarize, it was assumed that the population mean and standard

Figure 8.1

Probability Interval for Sample Mean

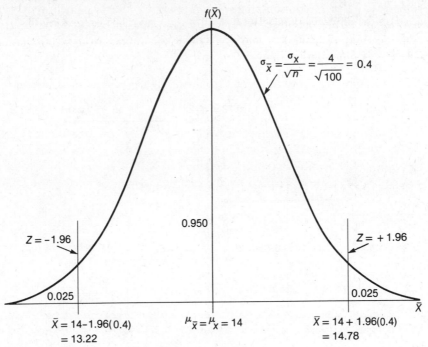

$$\sigma_{\bar{X}} = \frac{\sigma_X}{\sqrt{n}} = \frac{4}{\sqrt{100}} = 0.4$$

$Z = -1.96$ $Z = +1.96$

0.950

0.025   0.025

$\bar{X} = 14 - 1.96(0.4)$ $\mu_{\bar{X}} = \mu_X = 14$ $\bar{X} = 14 + 1.96(0.4)$
$= 13.22$ $= 14.78$

deviation were known. Then it was possible to construct a probability interval for $\bar{X}$. This interval was constructed as:

Probability interval for $\bar{X}$: $\mu_X \pm Z\sigma_{\bar{X}}$ or $\mu_X \pm Z\frac{\sigma_X}{\sqrt{n}}$ *measure of sample error*

Compare this to the confidence interval for μ_X:

Confidence interval for μ_X: $\bar{X} \pm Z\,s_{\bar{X}}$ or $\bar{X} \pm Z\frac{s_X}{\sqrt{n}}$ *sample error measure*

Note that $\bar{X}$, the estimate of μ_X, replaces μ_X, and s_X replaces σ_X. In the probability interval for $\bar{X}$, the standard error of $\bar{X}$, $\sigma_{\bar{X}}$, is a measure of the sampling error, or the difference between $\bar{X}$ and μ_X. In the confidence interval for μ_X, the estimate of the standard error, $s_{\bar{X}} = s_X/\sqrt{n}$, is a measure of the sampling error.

If one is constructing a confidence interval where the population standard deviation is known, the value of σ_X should be used in place of s_X. Suppose one is sampling from a population with $\mu_X = 14$ (unknown) and $\sigma_X = 4$ (known). If a sample of $n = 100$ has a mean of (say) $\bar{X} = 15.0$, does a 95 percent confidence interval of $\bar{X} \pm 1.96\ (4/\sqrt{100})$, or 14.22

Figure 8.2

Confidence Interval

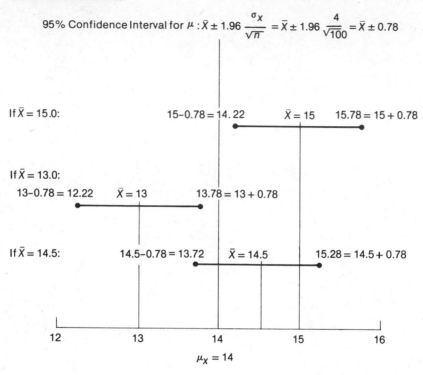

95% Confidence Interval for $\mu : \bar{X} \pm 1.96 \dfrac{\sigma_X}{\sqrt{n}} = \bar{X} \pm 1.96 \dfrac{4}{\sqrt{100}} = \bar{X} \pm 0.78$

If $\bar{X} = 15.0$: $15 - 0.78 = 14.22$ $\bar{X} = 15$ $15.78 = 15 + 0.78$

If $\bar{X} = 13.0$:
$13 - 0.78 = 12.22$ $\bar{X} = 13$ $13.78 = 13 + 0.78$

If $\bar{X} = 14.5$: $14.5 - 0.78 = 13.72$ $\bar{X} = 14.5$ $15.28 = 14.5 + 0.78$

12   13   14   15   16

$\mu_X = 14$

to 15.78, include the true mean, $\mu_X = 14$? Observing Figure 8.2, it does not. Answer the same question for $\bar{X} = 13.0$ (the interval is from 12.22 to 13.78). Again, it does not. However, the opposite answer occurs for $\bar{X} = 14.5$ (the interval is from 13.72 to 15.28); i.e., the 95 percent confidence interval for μ_X includes $\mu_X = 14$. Thus, any time $\bar{X}$ is between 13.22 and 14.78, the 95 percent confidence interval includes $\mu_X = 14$; if $\bar{X} < 13.22$ or $\bar{X} > 14.78$, the 95 percent confidence intervals does not include $\mu_X = 14$. Hence, you *do* include the true mean, $\mu_X = 14$, in the confidence interval 95 percent of the time, because $P(13.22 \le \bar{X} \le 14.78) = 0.95$, and you *do not* include the true mean, $\mu_X = 14$, in the confidence interval 5 percent of the time, as $P(\bar{X} < 13.22 \cup \bar{X} > 14.78) = 0.05$, as shown in Figure 8.1.

$n \le 30$

8.33   Effect of a Small Sample: The *t*-Distribution

The preceding sections described a procedure for finding the confidence interval for the population mean, based on a large sample. This procedure is perfectly general; it does not require any assumption about the shape of the population from which the sample is drawn. Even if the normal distribution does not closely describe the shape of the population, the normal distribution may still be used for constructing the confidence interval of μ_X. The central limit theorem permits use of the normal distribution for describing the distribution of $\bar{X}$, even though the population itself may not be normally distributed, or even nearly so. The only requirement is that the sample be sufficiently large. The more the shape of the population departs from normality, the larger the sample needs to be. A confidence interval for the population mean of a very highly skewed population requires a larger sample than is required for a confidence interval for a population mean of a more nearly symmetrical population.

When a confidence interval is to be constructed for the population mean using a small sample, the central limit theorem is of no use. Hence, it is possible to construct *small* sample confidence intervals only for means of populations which are normally distributed (or nearly normally distributed). In order to construct a confidence interval for the mean of a normal population (or nearly normal population), the procedure is similar to that described above if σ_X is known, which is seldom the case. When σ_X is unknown, the *t*-distribution must be used.

The previous chapter discussed the Z-transformation where a normal random variable X was transformed to a corresponding standard normal random variable Z. For this transformation, the standard deviation of the variable had to be known. Recalling the transformation for a normally distributed sample mean, $\bar{X}$:

$$Z = \frac{\bar{X} - \mu_{\bar{x}}}{\sigma_{\bar{x}}} = \frac{\bar{X} - \mu_{\bar{x}}}{\frac{\sigma_X}{\sqrt{n}}}$$

where $\sigma_{\bar{x}}$ is the standard deviation of the variable $\bar{X}$ and is equal to $\sigma_X/\sqrt{n}$, and where σ_X is the known standard deviation of X.

If the standard deviation of X is unknown and is replaced by its estimated value s_X, the standard deviation of a sample, then the standard error of the sample mean, $\sigma_{\bar{x}}$, is estimated by $s_{\bar{x}} = s_X/\sqrt{n}$. A new transformation is generated:

$$t = \frac{\bar{X} - \mu_{\bar{x}}}{s_{\bar{x}}} = \frac{\bar{X} - \mu_{\bar{x}}}{\frac{s_X}{\sqrt{n}}}$$

The new transformation, in which s_X is used as an estimate of σ_X, no longer transforms $\bar{X}$ to the standard normal distribution. Although the distribution of $\bar{X}$ is normal, the transformation does not produce values of Z because σ_X was estimated and not known. Rather, the transformation of $\bar{X}$ is to a *t*-distribution, but only for situations in which X is normally distributed, or nearly so.

Figure 8.3

t-Distributions for Different Degrees of Freedom

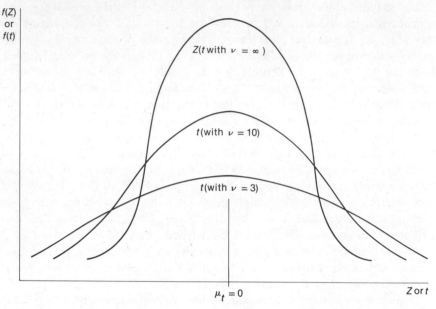

The *t*-distribution is a family of continuous probability distributions which are similar in appearance to the standard normal distribution. These distributions are bell-shaped unimodal, and symmetric. There is a distinct *t*-distribution for each sample size.

Each member of the *t*-distribution family has the same mean as the standard normal distribution, $\mu_t = 0$. The parameter of each *t*-distribution is called the *degrees of freedom*.[2] The symbol ν (the Greek letter *nu*) is used to represent degrees of freedom.

As stated above, there is a distinct *t*-distribution for each sample size. In other words, a particular *t*-distribution is uniquely determined by its degrees of freedom. For this application $\nu = n - 1$.

As the degrees of freedom increases, the *t*-distribution more closely approaches the standard normal distribution. This can be seen graphically in Figure 8.3. Finally, as $\nu = \infty$ (infinity), the areas become identical.

The table for *t*-distributions is presented in Appendix I, for selected values of ν. The *t*-distribution table is organized somewhat differently from the standard normal distribution table presented earlier. The top row of

---

[2] The concept of degrees of freedom refers to the number of independent deviations used in the determination of the estimated value of the standard deviation used in the transformation. In the case of the sample standard deviation being used to replace σ_x, there are $n - 1$ independent deviations because $\overline{X}$ has been calculated from the sample, and therefore $n - 1$ degrees of freedom are associated with its use.

Figure 8.4

Symmetry of *t*-Distribution

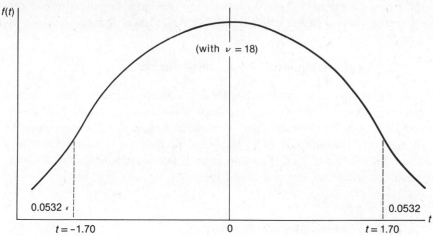

the *t*-table, which is labeled ν, gives the degrees of freedom for each column of the table. Any column of *t*-table could be expanded into a table the size of the standard normal if space permitted.

The left-hand column of the *t*-table lists the various *t* values which, when combined with a given degrees of freedom column, provide the area under the *t*-distribution which is to the right of that *t* value. For example, for the *t*-distribution with 18 degrees of freedom, what area is to the right of the *t* value of 1.70? The answer is 0.0532. For negative values of *t*, the symmetry property of the table is used. For ten degrees of freedom and a *t* value of -1.50, the area is 0.0823, to the left of that *t* value. The symmetry of the *t*-distribution is illustrated in Figure 8.4.

Another use of the *t*-distribution table is demonstrated where one wants to know what value of *t* leaves only 1 percent of the area to its right for a *t*-distribution of, say, 15 degrees of freedom. For this answer, enter the table at the column for 15 degrees of freedom, move down the column until the value of .0100 is found, and then note that this value is in the row for the *t* value of 2.60. When $\nu > 30$, the normal distribution is used to approximate the *t*-distribution, with Z replacing t.

8.34   Confidence Interval for the Population Mean   *using t - distrib.*
from a Small Sample

To calculate a confidence interval for the population mean using a small sample taken from a population which is (nearly) normal, the procedure is similar to the large sample procedure. The difference is that *t* replaces Z.

First, calculate the point estimate for the population mean, using the sample mean as the estimate. Then recognize sampling error by adding and subtracting a term to that point estimate. In this case, however, it is necessary to use the t-distribution. The confidence interval for μ_X is then constructed as:

$$\text{Confidence interval for } \mu_X, \text{ small sample: } \bar{X} \pm t \frac{s_X}{\sqrt{n}}$$

As an example, suppose a production control manager has taken a simple random sample of five bars from a shipment of steel. The tensile strength of each of these five bars is measured, and the five bars have an average tensile strength of 44.16 thousand pounds per square inch with a standard deviation of 3.60 thousand pounds per square inch. The observations and calculations are shown in Figure 8.5.

Figure 8.5

Data for Tensile Strength Problem

BAR	X, Tensile Strength in Thousand Pounds per Square Inch	X^2
1..	48.5	2,352.25
2..	39.7	1,576.09
3..	41.3	1,705.69
4..	46.2	2,134.44
5..	45.1	2,034.01
	220.8	9,802.48

$$\bar{X} = \frac{\Sigma X}{n} = \frac{220.8}{5} = 44.16 \text{ thousand pounds per square inch}$$

$$s_X^2 = \frac{\Sigma(X - \bar{X})^2}{n-1} = \frac{\Sigma X^2 - \frac{(\Sigma X)^2}{n}}{n-1} = \frac{9,802.48 - \frac{(220.8)^2}{5}}{4} = 12.988$$

$$s_X = 3.60 \text{ thousand pounds per square inch}$$

From these data, the confidence interval for the population mean, μ_X, can be constructed as follows:

$$\bar{X} \pm t \frac{s_X}{\sqrt{n}} = 44.16 \pm t \frac{3.60}{\sqrt{5}}$$

The value of t used in this expression depends upon the level of confidence desired for the confidence interval. In order to use the t table, shown in Appendix I, recall that the number of degrees of freedom is $\nu = n - 1$. For a sample of five observations there are four degrees of freedom. To construct a 90 percent confidence interval, one must find the values of t which leave 5 percent of the area in each tail. This accounts for 100 percent of the area: 90 percent in the confidence interval and 5 percent in each of two tails, for a total of 100 percent. For four degrees of freedom, the desired t value is 2.1318. This gives the following confidence interval:

$$\bar{X} \pm t\frac{s_X}{\sqrt{n}} = 44.16 \pm 2.1318\frac{3.60}{\sqrt{5}} = 44.16 \pm 3.43$$

$t_{4,.05}$

or 40.73 to 47.59

8.35 What Confidence Level Is Appropriate?

The question of the appropriate level of confidence for a confidence interval has not been considered. The statistician has nothing very definitive to say about this; however, the statistician can make important contributions in the following way. By increasing the sample size, the width of the interval can be reduced (by decreasing $s_{\bar{x}}$) while holding the confidence level constant, or the confidence level can be increased while holding the width of the interval constant, or some combination of both. By using these trade-offs, the statistician can determine the sample size that will be necessary to produce a confidence interval of the desired width and the desired level of confidence.

For *large* samples, the width of the interval can be cut in half by increasing the sample size by a factor of four. More generally, the width of the interval is inversely proportional to the square root of the sample size. Increasing the sample size by a factor of four produces a confidence interval with a width of $1/\sqrt{4}$ or half of its previous width. Choosing a new sample size which is k times the previous sample will yield an interval which has width of $1/\sqrt{k}$ the previous width.

For small samples, increasing the sample size is slightly more powerful than for large samples, because increasing the sample size reduces $s_{\bar{x}}$ and increases the degrees of freedom which also reduces the corresponding t value.

Changing the level of confidence for a confidence interval also changes the width of the interval. It is easy to see how the confidence level of the interval changes the width of the interval by viewing the Z (or t) values for various levels of confidence. For example, going from an 80 percent confidence interval to a 99 percent confidence interval changes the Z value from 1.28 to 2.58. This approximately doubles the width of the interval. Of course, one could make the interval as small as one desires by letting the confidence level become sufficiently low. If, for some strange reason, one wanted to construct a 1 percent confidence interval, the interval would be very narrow. In effect, one would make a very strong statement (the interval would be very narrow), but one would have practically no confidence in the statement. On the other hand, one could make a very weak statement (a very wide confidence interval), and be very confident in that statement.

[handwritten annotations in top margin: "only for Z distr. since n is to be found."]

8.36   Sample Size

Suppose one desires a 95 percent confidence interval for the tensile strength example of Figure 8.5. Furthermore, suppose one desires to have a total interval width of 2.00 thousand pounds per square inch. The data from Figure 8.5 show a sample estimate of the population standard deviation of 3.60. Also, as the total width of the confidence interval is desired to be 2.00, the term to be added to and subtracted from the sample mean is only half the total width, or 1.00 thousand pounds per square inch. Thus:

$$Z \cdot \frac{s_x}{\sqrt{n}} = 1.00$$

$$(1.96) \frac{3.60}{\sqrt{n}} = 1.00$$

$$\sqrt{n} = \frac{1.96(3.60)}{1.00} = 7.06$$

$$n = (7.06)^2, \text{ or nearly } 50$$

Notice that in this illustration a value of Z was used without knowing the final sample size. It was assumed that the sample size would be large, and a Z value from the standard normal distribution was used in order to start solving the problem. As the required sample size was found to be approximately 50, it is apparent that the assumption was satisfactory.

The procedure illustrated above is typical. A small sample (or pilot sample) is used to get an estimate of the standard deviation of the population. From this estimate, a decision can be made as to the correct sample size that one needs to yield a confidence interval of desired width and level. In the example above, it was calculated that a sample of 50 would be sufficient. This means that 45 additional observations are needed from the population (a pilot sample of five observations had already been taken, as shown in Figure 8.5). It is not necessary to take a pilot sample if there is enough other information to estimate adequately the population standard deviation. Some situations deal with processes whose variability remains nearly unchanged while the central tendency of the population changes. This makes a pilot sample unnecessary.

In both the above large and small sample interval estimates for μ_X, simple random sampling from a large population was assumed. As a general rule, if N is less than $20n$, the finite population multiplier should be used. In such cases, estimate the standard deviation of the sampling distribution of $\bar{X}$ as:[3]

[handwritten annotations in left margin: "fpm" and "N < 20n"]

---

[3] The finite correction factor in this expression is slightly different from the finite correction factor in Chapter 5. Technically, this difference is from a bias in using s_x^2 to estimate σ_x^2, when sampling from a finite population. This bias is removed when the square root has a divisor N instead of $N - 1$.

$$\sigma_{\bar{x}} = \frac{s_X}{\sqrt{n}} \sqrt{\frac{N - n}{N}}$$

$N < 20n$

8.37   Confidence Interval for the Population Proportion

Earlier in this chapter the use of a sample proportion as a point estimate of the binomial population proportion was discussed, using an
example in which 40 percent of the runs in a sample of 100 taxicab runs
required more than 15 minutes from the receipt of the request for a taxi
to the arrival of the taxi at the requested address. This sample value,
$p = 0.40$, is a good point estimate of the binomial population proportion.
It is correct to estimate that 40 percent of all taxicab runs require more
than 15 minutes. In order to expand this point estimate to a confidence
interval estimate, one can use the normal approximation to the binomial
distribution. In Chapter 7, it was shown that the normal distribution is a
useful approximation to the binomial distribution whenever both $n\pi$ and
$n(1 - \pi) \geq 5$. It was also shown in Chapter 6 that the sample proportion, p, is described by the binomial distribution. This is approximated
by a normal distribution with the parameters:

$$\mu_p = \pi$$
$$\sigma_p = \sqrt{\frac{\pi(1 - \pi)}{n}}$$

Since in this case the value of π is not known, one must use the sample
value p to estimate π. The confidence interval is similarly constructed as
for $\bar{X}$ (as p is really a sample mean):

$$\text{Confidence interval for } \pi: \quad p \pm Z \sqrt{\frac{p(1 - p)}{n}}$$

For example, with $p = 0.4$ and $n = 100$, one constructs an 80 percent
confidence interval as:

$$\text{Confidence interval for } \pi: \quad 0.40 \pm 1.28 \sqrt{\frac{0.4(0.6)}{100}} = 0.40 \pm 1.28 \,(0.049)$$
$$= 0.40 \pm 0.063$$

or 0.337 to 0.463.

This procedure may occasionally lead to confidence intervals which go
below zero or above one. This is a natural result of using the approximating
normal distribution. When this occurs, simply end the interval at either
zero or one as appropriate.

In order to determine the sample size necessary to obtain an interval of
the desired width of π with a specified level of confidence, it is necessary to
make some estimate of the value of π in order to determine the standard
deviation, σ_p. A useful (and conservative) procedure is to estimate the

{ Conservative
{ estimate $\pi = 0.5$

value of π to be 0.5 in determining the sample size. This procedure is conservative because it will tend to overstate the necessary sample size if π is near zero or one.

To illustrate this procedure for determining the necessary sample size, consider an example to determine the sample size necessary to construct a 95 percent confidence interval for the proportion of credit card holders who made a purchase during the month of December. The desired confidence interval is to have a total width of no more than four percentage points. This means that the term added to and subtracted from p, the point estimate of π, is to be no larger than two percentage points, or 0.02. Since the value of π is not known, one should make the conservative estimate of $\pi = 0.5$ in order to determine the standard deviation of p. This yields the term:

$4 \Rightarrow \pm 2$
$\Rightarrow .02$

$$1.96\sqrt{\frac{0.5(0.5)}{n}} = 0.02$$

$$\sqrt{n} = \frac{1.96(0.5)}{0.02} = 49$$

$$n = 2,401$$

If one had assumed that the population proportion, π, was 0.2, the sample size calculation would have yielded:

$$1.96\sqrt{\frac{0.2(0.8)}{n}} = 0.02$$

$$\sqrt{n} = \frac{1.96\sqrt{0.16}}{0.02} = 39.2$$

$$n = 1,537$$

It is apparent that the assumption of 0.5 for the population proportion will never underestimate the sample size. It did require a much larger sample size (2,401 versus 1,537) than would have been required if the population proportion had been 0.2. However, since the decision on the width of the confidence interval and the level of confidence are usually judgmental decisions anyway, the validity of the assumption may not be crucial. A pilot sample can be taken before calculating n; the sample proportion would be used in the calculations.

8.38   Confidence Interval for the Difference between Two Population Means

In many situations one is investigating the difference between two population means. For example, these questions are often addressed by looking at the difference between two sample means: What is the difference between January and June? What is the difference between Brand X and Brand Z? What is the difference between Worker A and Worker B? What is the difference between advertising in *The Wall Street Journal* and in *Business Week?*

In order to use the procedures which will be described for constructing estimates about the difference between two population means, the following conditions are necessary:

1. From each population, labeled 1 and 2, a sample must be selected.
2. The two samples must be independent of each other.
3. Each sample must be large enough that the central limit theorem adequately describes the sampling distribution of $\bar{X}$ for each sample.

The two sample means, $\bar{X}_1$ and $\bar{X}_2$, are combined into a single statistic, $(\bar{X}_1 - \bar{X}_2)$. This difference, $\bar{X}_1 - \bar{X}_2$, has its own sampling distributions with these properties:

1. $E(\bar{X}_1 - \bar{X}_2) = \mu_{\bar{X}_1} - \bar{X}_2 = \mu_{X_1} - \mu_{X_2}$ which says that $\bar{X}_1 - \bar{X}_2$ is an unbiased estimator of the difference in population means. This is proved in Note 8.38a.

2. $\sigma_{\bar{X}_1 - \bar{X}_2}^2 = \sigma_{\bar{X}_1}^2 + \sigma_{\bar{X}_2}^2 = \dfrac{\sigma_{X_1}^2}{n_1} + \dfrac{\sigma_{X_2}^2}{n_2}$

   This is proved in note 8.38b.

3. The sampling distribution of $(\bar{X}_1 - \bar{X}_2)$ is normal.

When $\sigma_{X_1}^2$ and $\sigma_{X_2}^2$ are unknown, they are replaced by their estimates, $s_{X_1}^2$ and $s_{X_2}^2$.

To convert the point estimate, $\bar{X}_1 - \bar{X}_2$, to a confidence interval estimate, one uses the following procedure:

$$\text{Confidence interval for } \mu_{X_1} - \mu_{X_2}: \quad (\bar{X}_1 - \bar{X}_2) \pm Z\sqrt{\frac{s_{X_1}^2}{n_1} + \frac{s_{X_2}^2}{n_2}}$$

As an illustration, suppose the taxicab example dealt with a population of taxicab runs in January. A random sample from the population of February runs was also selected. The results of both of these samples are summarized in Figure 8.6. To construct a 98 percent confidence interval, one proceeds as follows:

$$\text{Confidence interval for } \mu_{X_1} - \mu_{X_2}: (\bar{X}_1 - \bar{X}_2) \pm Z\sqrt{\frac{s_{X_1}^2}{n_1} + \frac{s_{X_2}^2}{n_2}}$$

$$= (13.3 - 14.1) \pm 2.33\sqrt{\frac{(4.2)^2}{100} + \frac{(4.7)^2}{120}}$$

$$= -0.8 \pm 2.33\,(0.60)$$

$$= -0.8 \pm 1.40$$

$$= -2.2 \text{ minutes to } 0.6 \text{ minutes}$$

This confidence interval has the obvious interpretation: one is 98 percent confident that the average difference between January and Feb-

Figure 8.6

Data for January–February Taxi Problem

Month	$\bar{X}$	s_X	n
January (1)........................	13.3	4.2	100
February (2).......................	14.1	4.7	120

ruary is between -2.2 minutes and $+0.6$ minutes. The -2.2 minutes means that the average time in February is longer than the average time in January, since one is subtracting February from January. On the other hand, the other end of the confidence interval means that the average time in January is longer than the average time in February.

8.39   Confidence Interval for the Difference between Two Population Proportions

The previous section discussed the difference between two population means. This section discusses the difference between two population proportions, for the case in which all these quantities are at least $5: n_1\pi_1$, $n_1(1 - \pi_1)$, $n_2\pi_2$, and $n_2(1 - \pi_2)$.

A previous example considered the situation in which 40 percent of the taxicab runs required more than 15 minutes from the receipt of the call to the arrival of the taxicab. Suppose this sample came from the population of runs made in January. Suppose that a similar sample was selected from the population of February runs. It is possible to construct estimates for the difference between the proportion of long runs in January and February. The data from these two samples are shown in Figure 8.7. As an

Figure 8.7

Data for Taxicab Problem

Month	Number of Runs with More Than 15 Minutes Elapsed Time	Sample Size n	Sample Proportion p
January (1).....................	40	100	0.40
February (2)...................	60	120	0.50

example, the point estimate for the difference between the proportion of these long runs in January and February using the difference between the sample proportions, is $p_1 - p_2$, or -0.10. Converting a point estimate into a confidence interval for proportions is:

Confidence interval for $\pi_1 - \pi_2$: $(p_1 - p_2) \pm Z\sqrt{\dfrac{p_1(1 - p_1)}{n_1} + \dfrac{p_2(1 - p_2)}{n_2}}$

For the specific data for this example from Figure 8.7, the 80 percent confidence interval is:

$$\text{Confidence interval for } \pi_1 - \pi_2: \quad (0.40 - 0.50) \pm 1.28\sqrt{\frac{0.4(0.6)}{100} + \frac{0.5(0.5)}{120}}$$

$$= -0.10 \pm 1.28\,(0.067)$$

$$= -0.186 \text{ to } -0.014$$

This means that one is 80 percent confident that the difference in the proportion between long runs in January and February is between -18.6 percent and -1.4 percent. As both ends of the confidence interval are negative, it suggests that there is a larger proportion of long runs in February than in January.

8.4 SUMMARY

This chapter has dealt primarily with two types of estimation: point estimates and confidence interval estimates. The general procedure has been to calculate from the sample a point estimate for the population parameter, and then to convert that point estimate into a confidence interval estimate. In converting a point estimate into a confidence interval estimate, there is a common procedure throughout. This common procedure is to build the interval estimate around the point estimate by adding to and subtracting from the point estimate a term to account for the sampling

Figure 8.8

Summary for Interval Estimation When *N* Is Much Larger Than *n*

Situation	Point Estimate	Distribution	Estimated Standard Error
Population mean; large sample	$\bar{X}$	Z	$\dfrac{s_X}{\sqrt{n}}$
Population mean; normal population; small sample	$\bar{X}$	t	$\dfrac{s_X}{\sqrt{n}}$
Population proportion; $n\pi$ and $n(1-\pi) \geq 5$; large sample	p	Z	$\sqrt{\dfrac{p(1-p)}{n}}$
Difference between population means; large, independent samples	$\bar{X}_1 - \bar{X}_2$	Z	$\sqrt{\dfrac{s_{X_1}^2}{n_1} + \dfrac{s_{X_2}^2}{n_2}}$
Difference between population proportion; $n\pi$ and $n(1-\pi) \geq 5$ for both samples; large, independent samples	$p_1 - p_2$	Z	$\sqrt{\dfrac{p_1(1-p_1)}{n_1} + \dfrac{p_2(1-p_2)}{n_2}}$

error in the point estimate. The term which accounts for the sampling error is made up of two factors. The first factor is a value from a probability table; this number, Z or t, depends upon the level of confidence desired, upon the particular population parameter, and upon sample size being investigated. The second factor is a term which is an estimate of the standard error of the point estimate. Figure 8.8 summarizes these various terms for the five cases considered in this chapter.

8.5   COMMENT

Estimation is a very useful tool for conveying from one person (the statistician) to another (the user) the information contained in a sample. If a single number estimate is required, a point estimate is used. If a measure of the precision of the point estimate is required, the point estimate is converted into a confidence interval estimate. However, it is our opinion that confidence intervals are only one informational input into a decision process. The reasons for this are twofold. First, an estimation procedure includes only the information from a sample. In many cases, the decision maker will have information from sources other than the sample. Secondly, an estimation procedure ignores any relevant economic factors in a decision process. For example, a statistician may estimate that the productivity of Worker A is greater than the productivity of Worker B. This does not necessarily mean that Worker A should be retained and Worker B should be fired. The decision maker may have observed the two workers in situations different from those of the samples. Furthermore, there may be different economic costs associated with workers A and B because of seniority, experience, or other factors. Although the sampling and estimation procedures do provide a useful way of conveying the information from the statistician to the decision maker, this does not necessarily mean that the estimation procedure is a decision technique in itself. Hence, we feel that estimation is better viewed as a procedure for supplying information than as a procedure for making decisions. Decision procedures are discussed in chapters 16 and 17.

EXERCISES

8.1   Describe the difference between a sampling error and a nonsampling error.

8.2   Find the flaw(s) in this statement: A general procedure for estimation is to use a population parameter to estimate the value of a sample statistic.

8.3   If one knows the value of the population parameters and is interested in making statements about the results of a sample, is this a problem in probability theory or statistical inference?

8.4 Describe a major difference between point estimation and interval estimation.

8.5 What is an unbiased estimator?

* **8.6** A sample of 400 students yielded these results for X, the number of hours of "A":

$$n = 400$$
$$\bar{X} = 17.2$$
$$s_X = 10.7$$

Construct a 99 percent confidence interval estimate for μ_X, the population average number of hours of "A."

* **8.7** Given these data for a sample of size $n = 100$:

i	X_i	X_i^2
1	37.1	1,376.41
2	14.2	201.64
3	58.0	3,364.00
4	37.6	1,413.76
.	.	.
.	.	.
.	.	.
100	44.4	1,971.36
	2,945.0	91,327.60

a. Construct a point estimate for μ_X.
b. Construct a point estimate for σ_X^2.
c. Construct a 90 percent confidence interval for μ_X.
d. Construct a 99 percent confidence interval for μ_X.

* **8.8** The personnel department of a manufacturing firm conducted a study of the average hours per week worked for a randomly selected sample of 50 employees for the second week in July. These 50 employees worked a total of 2,050 hours. The sum of the squares of the number of hours per week for each of the 50 employees was 84,250. Construct a 99 percent confidence interval for the average number of hours worked for the employees of this firm.

8.9 The t-distribution is used to describe the probability distribution of a random variable defined as

$$t = \frac{\bar{X} - \mu_{\bar{X}}}{\dfrac{s_X}{\sqrt{n}}}$$

a. Explain the meaning of each of the symbols in the expression.
b. What is the degrees of freedom for this t-distribution?

* **8.10** What is the probability that a random variable described by the t-distribution with eight degrees of freedom will exceed 1.00?

---

* Answers to exercises marked with an asterisk (*) are in Appendix L.

* 8.11 What is the probability that a random variable described by the
        t-distribution will exceed 1.5 if the degrees of freedom is:
        a. 1
        b. 5
        c. 10
        d. 20
        e. 1,800

* 8.12 What value will be exceeded with a probability 0.10 by a t-distributed
        random variable with the following degrees of freedom?
        a. 1
        b. 5
        c. 10
        d. 20
        e. 1,800

* 8.13 What value will be exceeded with a probability of 0.90 by a t-distributed
        random variable with the following degrees of freedom?
        a. 1
        b. 5 $P_r(t_1) = -.$
        c. 10
        d. 20
        e. 1,800

  8.14 What would you do if you needed a table of the t-distribution with 482
        degrees of freedom?

* 8.15 The director of sales for an auto manufacturer wants to estimate the
        average dollar damage to new autos when driven into a brick wall at
        20 miles per hour. The director is authorized to use three autos. As-
        suming that the dollar value of damage is normally distributed, and
        the sample results for crashing the three autos are $1,350, $1,450, and
        $1,500:
        a. What is the mean damage for the sample of three autos?
        b. What is the standard deviation of damage for the sample?
        c. What is a point estimate of the average dollar damage for the
              population of all cars of this type manufactured by the company?
        d. Construct a 99 percent confidence interval estimate for the popula-
              tion average dollar damage.

* 8.16 From past experience, a professor knew that the scores on an exam
        would be approximately normally distributed. It was her grading
        procedure to "shuffle" the exams before grading them. She had a very
        large number of exams to grade, but she wanted to make some estimates
        about the average on this exam on the basis of the first five exams she
        graded, because course grades for graduating seniors needed to be
        completed first. These first five exams had scores of 81, 79, 59, 63, and
        91.
        a. What is the mean of the sample of five exams?
        b. What is the standard deviation of the sample of five exams?
        c. Make a point estimate of the average score for this exam.

d. Make a point estimate for the variance of the scores on this exam.

e. Make a 90 percent confidence interval estimate for the average score on this exam.

f. Why would it be inappropriate to use the normal approximation to the binomial distribution to produce a confidence interval estimate for the proportion of exams with scores above 85?

8.17 A small sample is taken from a normal population. The sample observations are 150, 140, 160, and 142.

a. Compute the sample mean and sample standard deviation.

b. Construct a 90 percent confidence interval for the population mean.

* 8.18 A sample poll was taken of public opinion concerning the desirability of the area expansion of a nearby Army post. The sample size was 400. Of these 180 were in favor of the expansion, and 220 were not in favor.

a. What is the point estimate of the population proportion in favor of the expansion?

b. Construct a 99 percent confidence interval of the population proportion in favor of the expansion.

* 8.19 If 897 out of a sample of 1,000 students live off campus, construct a 90 percent confidence interval for the proportion of all students who live off campus. The number of students in the population is very large.

* 8.20 The vice president of marketing for an appliance manufacturer randomly selects 500 purchases of the firm's 1975 model washing machines. Questionnaires are sent to these 500 purchasers. Of the 500, only 200 respond to the questionnaire. Of the 200, 120 replied that they had had no requests for maintenance in the first year of the washing machine's life. The 500 purchasers were selected from the population of purchasers who had returned warranty cards to the manufacturer.

a. Construct a 90 percent confidence interval for the proportion of purchasers who had no maintenance calls during the first year of use. Base this estimate on those responding to the questionnaire.

b. Comment on any difficulties which might arise because not all questionnaires were answered in this study.

c. Comment on the difficulties which might arise because not all purchasers sent in warranty cards for their washing machines.

d. If those who responded to the questionnaire were those who were irritated because of maintenance problems with the washing machine, what would be the direction of bias in the result you reported in *a?*

e. If those who did not send in warranty cards typically had few problems with their washing machines, what would be the direction of bias of the study?

* 8.21 The manager of a grocery store randomly selects 100 periods of one hour each in which to measure the dollar volume of sales. From these one hundred observations, the following statistics are computed: $\bar{X} = \$109.82$; $s_x = \$13.40$.

a. Make a point estimate of the average hourly sales for the store.

    b. Make a point estimate of the variance of hourly sales for the store.

    c. Construct an 80 percent confidence interval for the average hourly sales for the store.

    d. Construct a 95 percent confidence interval for the average hourly sales for the store.

    e. In the same study, 20 of the hours sampled had sales greater than $140.00. Construct a point estimate for the proportion of all hours which have sales greater than $140.00.

    f. Using the data given in *e* above, construct a 90 percent confidence interval for the proportion of hours which have sales in excess of $140.00.

* **8.22** A securities broker is interested in investigating the proportion of his customers who made purchases during January, 1975. He wants to estimate this proportion within three percentage points either way (for a total width of six percentage points). How large a sample is required, so that his interval estimate has an 80 percent confidence?

* **8.23** A small mail order firm is interested in investigating the effectiveness of two different catalog designs. They are particularly interested in the average order size resulting from each brochure. For each type of brochure, 1,000 brochures are sent to randomly selected customers from the very large mailing list of the firm. The first brochure resulted in an average order of $5.00, with a standard deviation of $3.00. The second brochure resulted in an average order size of $4.00 with a standard deviation of $2.00. Construct a 90 percent confidence interval for the difference in average order size for the two brochures.

* **8.24** For the situation described in Exercise 8.23, brochure A resulted in 200 orders, while brochure B resulted in 250 orders. Construct an 85 percent confidence interval for the difference in proportion of catalogs mailed which produce orders.

* **8.25** A university conducts both day and night classes intended to be identical. A sample of 100 day students yields these exam results:

$$\bar{X} = 72.4$$
$$s_X = 14.8$$

A sample of 200 night students yields these exam results:

$$\bar{X} = 73.9$$
$$s_X = 17.9$$

Construct a 90 percent confidence interval for the difference in population average scores between night and day students.

* **8.26** From prior studies it is known that the standard deviation of dollar size of an order received by a large mail order catalog house is $25.00. How large a sample needs to be taken so that a 95 percent confidence interval for the average order size will have a width of $3.00?

* **8.27** The director of industrial relations for the QRS Company is particularly disturbed by an apparently high absentee rate on the day before a holiday. A random sample of 100 employees scheduled to work on the

Wednesday before a Monday holiday revealed 14 absentees. A random sample of 200 employees scheduled to work on the Friday before the Monday holiday revealed 39 absentees. Construct an 80 percent confidence interval for the increase in absentee rate from Wednesday to Friday.

* 8.28   In order to compare the difficulty of two exams, a statistics professor randomly selects 40 students who have completed the course, and administers both exams to each of the 40 students. The score of each student on each exam is reported in this form:

Student	Score, Exam A	Score, Exam B	Difference
1	95	85	10
2	82	80	2
3	73	75	-2
.	.	.	.
.	.	.	.
.	.	.	.
39	80	65	15
40	75	60	15

The professor is interested in a confidence interval for the average difference between the two exams. However, the two exams cannot be regarded as independent samples, because the same students were involved in both exams. Hence, the following procedure is adopted. The difference in score between exam A and exam B is calculated for each student. This difference becomes the measurement for each student. Thus, what appeared to be a two population problem has been converted into a one population problem; that population is the difference in scores for the two exams. The sum of this difference is 400; the sum of the squares of the differences is 6,000. Construct an 80 percent confidence interval for the difference between exam A and exam B.

REFERENCES

Guenther, William C.   *Concepts of Statistical Inference.* New York: McGraw-Hill, 1965.

Li, J. C. R.   *Introduction to Statistical Inference.*   Ann Arbor, Mich.: J. W. Edwards, Publisher, Inc., 1961.

Richmond, Samuel B.   *Statistical Analysis,* 2d ed. New York: Ronald Press, 1964.

Springer, C. H.; Herlihy, R. E.; and Biggs, R. I.   *Statistical Inference.* Mathematics for Management Series, vol. 3. Homewood, Ill.: Richard D. Irwin, Inc., 1966.

9

Statistical Inference: Hypothesis Testing

The discussion of statistical inference began in Chapter 8. Statistical inference is that set of statistical techniques used to make statements about a population, based on information contained in a sample randomly selected from that population. In the previous chapter, estimation procedures were discussed. In this chapter the testing of hypotheses is discussed. Hypothesis testing is used much like statistical estimation procedures. That use is primarily to convey from one person (the statistician) to another person (the user) the information contained in a sample. Statistical inference is not a decision procedure; it is merely a way of stating useful information developed by statistical analysis.

9.1 GENERAL FRAMEWORK FOR HYPOTHESIS TESTING

A statistical hypothesis is merely a statement. As a statement, it may or may not be true. Perhaps supposition is a better word than either hypothesis or statement. The first example illustrating a framework for the testing of a hypothesis is completely nonstatistical in nature, yet it serves as a guideline for the procedures used in testing statistical hypotheses.

9.11 Test of a Nonstatistical Hypothesis

Mr. and Mrs. Proud Parent and their son, Bright, were discussing Bright's performance in school one evening. Bright commented that he was the best speller in his third grade class in school. Of course, Mr. and Mrs. Proud Parent were delighted to hear this good news. On the basis of Bright's statement about his spelling prowess, they believed (accepted) that he was indeed the best speller in his class. This belief is their hy-

Figure 9.1

Flow Diagram for Evaluating a Belief

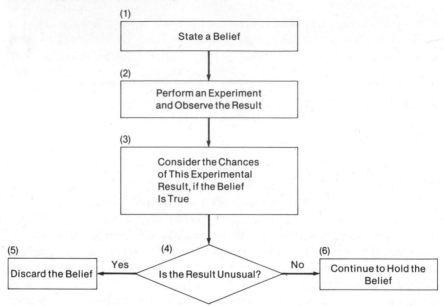

pothesis. They hypothesized or believed that Bright was indeed the best speller in his third grade class.

Mr. and Mrs. Proud Parent later decided to use a bit of caution in assessing their son's spelling capability. They decided to investigate their hypothesis or belief in some detail. However, they would continue to believe that he was the best speller in his class until they had sufficient reason to believe otherwise. After some discussion, they decided that his next report card to come home would be an experimental procedure to investigate the validity of their hypothesis. The results of this experiment were available in three weeks. When Bright brought home his report card, his spelling grade was C. Mr. and Mrs. Proud Parent considered the chances of Bright receiving a C in spelling if he were indeed the best speller in the class. They decided that it would indeed be unusual for the best speller in the class to receive a grade of C; hence, they discarded (rejected) their belief that Bright was the best speller in his class. If Bright had received an A, they would not have considered the result to be unusual or inconsistent with their hypothesis. In that case, they would have accepted or continued to hold their belief that Bright was the best spelling student in his class.

A flow diagram for the general procedure used by Mr. and Mrs. Parent is shown in Figure 9.1. In box 1, they stated a belief: Bright is the best speller in his class. In box 2, they performed an experiment by waiting for his report card. In box 3, they contemplated the chances of receiving a C if he were the best speller in his class. In box 4, they decided the result is unusual, so they proceeded to box 5 and discarded (rejected) the belief. Notice that this procedure did not *prove or disprove* their belief. It only was useful as a way for the Parents to evaluate their belief. Although it is a formal logical procedure, it is not a formal proof or disproof of the belief.

9.12 Test of a Statistical Hypothesis

A new process for producing calculator chips is claimed to have a defect rate of 30 percent, a substantial improvement over the previous process. The quality control department decides to set up a formal test procedure for the process. First, they hypothesize that the probability of a defective chip is 0.3. After all, the process designer is reputable, so the department continues to believe the statement until there is sufficient reason to believe otherwise. They decide on an experimental procedure to test this belief, consisting of taking a random sample of 20 calculator chips from the process. They find eight defective chips in the set of twenty. From the binomial table ($n = 20$, $\pi = 0.3$) they find the conditional probability of obtaining this sample result, *given* that the hypothesis ($\pi = 0.3$) is correct. At this point, the department realizes that, if they throw out the hypothesis after receiving eight defectives in twenty chips, they certainly would want to throw out the hypothesis after observing nine defectives, ten defectives, or any other number in excess of eight. Since the process designer would not understate the performance characteristics, they decided that only a large number of defectives, and not a small number of defectives, will cause them to discard the hypothesis that $\pi = 0.3$. Using the binomial tables, they find that the probability of eight or more defectives is

$$P(X \geq 8|n = 20, \pi = 0.3) = 0.2277$$

They next ask whether this probability is too low to continue believing in the hypothesis. They decide it is not too low and, therefore, do not reject the hypothesis.

A flow diagram for testing this statistical hypothesis is shown in Figure 9.2. In box 1, the department states the hypothesis that the probability of a defective chip is 0.3. A statistician calls this a *null hypothesis,* because it is what is believed in the absence of any data relative to the situation. In box 2, the department randomly selects 20 chips and counts eight defectives. In box 3, they use the binomial table to find the conditional proba-

Figure 9.2

Flow Diagram for Hypothesis Testing

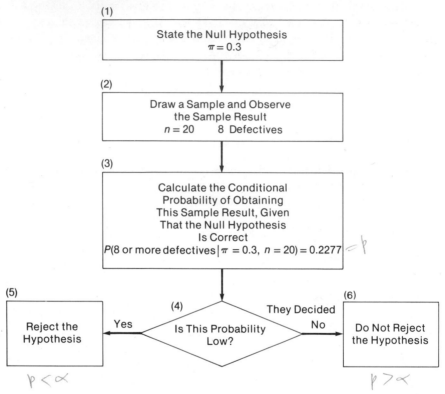

bility of getting eight or more defectives, given that the null hypothesis ($\pi = 0.3$) is correct. In box 4, they decided the probability is not too low, go to box 6, and do not reject the hypothesis.

The statistical analyst has more to say about many of these steps in the flow diagram of Figure 9.2. In box 1, the establishment of the null hypothesis is largely a nonstatistical procedure. The method used to establish the hypothesis is largely a function of the research strategy being used in the particular situation. In one research strategy, the null hypothesis is established as the "status quo," or as the belief that is appropriate in the absence of any further information. It is what one will believe if no sample is taken. In another research strategy, the null hypothesis is a "straw man," meaning that the null hypothesis is established in the hope of being able to discredit (reject) it. As a logical example of this case, the prosecuting attorney in a court of law may hypothesize the accused is innocent. However, the prosecutor hopes this assumption will be destroyed in the process of hearing evidence during the trial. In any case, the hypothesized value comes from some external reference system, such as a previous value, an industry average, a breakeven value, or a legal requirement.

Boxes 2 and 3 in Figure 9.2 draw heavily upon the theory of sampling and probability which have already been described in this text. A simple random sample is selected, and the results are noted. It is then a problem of sampling and probability theory to find the probability of this particular sample result, given that the null hypothesis is correct.

Box 4 of the flow diagram is enhanced by a more formal statement of the statistical criteria for hypothesis testing. This is described in section 9.13.

Boxes 5 and 6, relating to the disposition of the hypothesis, are also enhanced with statistical terminology. In some cases, proceeding to box 5 leads to an error which is called an error of Type I. In some cases, proceeding to box 6 leads to an error called an error of Type II. These error situations are discussed in section 9.14.

9.13   Level of Significance

$.001 < \alpha < 0.1$ Typical

A determination of the *level of significance* for a testing procedure is the same as answering the question, "What is a low probability?" In effect, the level of significance is the dividing line between an "unusual" sample result and an "anticipated" or "not unusual" sample result. The symbol α (Greek letter *alpha*) is used for the level of significance. If the quality control department had specified the level of significance to be $\alpha = 0.25$, box 5 (Figure 9.2) would have been reached, because 0.2277 is smaller than 0.25 and hence "unusual." The specification of the level of significance for a test is a nonstatistical decision. It is typically judgmental, or even arbitrary, in nature. In choosing the level of significance, those involved in the testing procedure should consider the consequences (e.g., the cost) of erroneously reaching box 5 or box 6 in the situation being investigated. Habitually, statisticians tend to use α between 0.1 and 0.001.

The probability value calculated in box 3 of Figure 9.2 may be called the "*p*-value."[1] A "significant" result is said to be obtained whenever the *p*-value is less than α, causing box 5 of the procedure to be reached. This result is said to be "significant," or "unusual," because the null hypothesis has been rejected, which is unexpected if the null hypothesis is the belief held by the researcher at the beginning of the procedure. If, for some fortuitous reason, the prespecified value of α is exactly the same as the *p*-value calculated from the sample, the result is said to be "just significant." Any time this *p*-value is greater than α, box 6 is reached and the

$p < \alpha$
reject

$p > \alpha$
accept

---

[1] The *p*-value is sometimes called the level at which the result would be "just significant."

result is said not to be significant. In order to avoid the arbitrary nature of specifying a level of significance, the statistician often elects to report the p-value. The user, rather than the statistician, then decides whether to reject the null hypothesis.

9.14   Errors in Hypothesis Testing

If the hypothesis testing procedure were always to reject the null hypothesis when it is false and accept the null hypothesis when it is true, there would be no errors in hypothesis testing. However, this is not the case.

When the null hypothesis is rejected, and it is indeed true, a *Type I* error has been made. This is not an error in arithmetic, computation, or logic; it is simply a recognition of the fact that the hypothesis testing procedure may reject true hypotheses as well as false hypotheses.

Whenever one tests a false null hypothesis and reaches box 6, failing to reject the false null hypothesis, a *Type II* error has been made. For Mr. and Mrs. Proud Parent, a Type I error would occur if they were to discard the "best speller" belief when Bright is truly the best speller. A Type II error would occur if they were to continue their belief when he is not the best speller.

For the quality control department in the calculator chip example, a Type I error would occur if the null hypothesis were rejected when π is really less than or equal to 0.30. A Type II error would occur if π were really greater than 0.30, yet the null hypothesis is not rejected. A Type I error might result in not using the new process when the defect rate is satisfactory, while a Type II error might result in using the process when the defect rate is too high. Depending on the startup cost for the new process and the differential operating cost and defect cost for the old versus the new process, either error could be very expensive or trivial.

Much of the power of the testing of statistical hypotheses results from the ability to measure and control the magnitude of Type I and Type II errors. When a level of significance, α, is specified prior to conducting a test, the statistician has automatically set the maximum probability of rejecting a true null hypothesis, because the level of significance is the same as this maximum probability of a Type I error.[2] In many test situations, a Type I error is considered to be the more serious of the two types of errors. Because the level of significance is often specified at a relatively

---

[2] This is strictly true only for situations in which the sample result is a continuous random variable. If the sample result is a discrete random variable, the probability of rejecting a true null hypothesis is never greater than α; it may be less than α, because of the discrete nature of the sample result.

small value (0.10 or less) the procedure is designed so that there is a small (0.10 or less) probability of rejecting the null hypothesis when it is true. Indeed, the null hypothesis is often deliberately established so that its erroneous rejection is a costly error; a low value of α keeps the probability of this costly error small.

The size of a Type II error is somewhat more difficult to discuss. In general, most testing procedures are devised so that the probability of making a Type II error is very *small* when the null hypothesis is false by a *large* amount. However, when the null hypothesis is *nearly correct,* but still false, there is usually a very *large* probability of making a Type II error. The size of the Type II error can be controlled by specifying the sample size. Larger sample sizes have a smaller probability of making a Type II error, all else being equal.

As an example of the statement that a null hypothesis which is false by a large amount has a small probability of being accepted, while a null hypothesis which is very nearly correct has a high probability of being accepted, consider the situation discussed earlier about Mr. and Mrs. Proud Parent and their son Bright. If Bright were really the *worst* speller in the class, his chances of getting a high enough grade on his report card to convince Mr. and Mrs. Parent to retain their belief in his spelling prowess would be quite *small.* However, if he were the *second best* speller in the class, his chances of getting a high enough grade to cause them to retain their belief in his spelling ability would be quite *high.*

9.15   Procedure for Hypothesis Testing: A Recapitulation

One procedure for testing statistical hypothesis is to prespecify a level of significance, α, and then compare it to the conditional probability of the observed sample result (given that the null hypothesis is correct). If this probability, called the *p*-value, is lower than α, the hypothesis is rejected and a "significant" result has been obtained. If a "significant" result occurs even though the null hypothesis is correct, a Type I error has been made.

If the *p*-value is greater than α, the hypothesis is not rejected, and the result is said to be "insignificant" or "not significant." If a sample result is not significant even though the null hypothesis is false, a Type II error has been made. This procedure is shown in the flow diagram of Figure 9.3.

An alternative procedure is to use the sample result to report the *p*-value. In this procedure, there is no reporting of the result as being "significant" or "insignificant." This is left to the user of the test. However, enough information is provided in the *p*-value so that the user may decide whether to call the result significant or not. This procedure is described in Figure 9.4.

Figure 9.3

Flow Diagram for Testing Hypotheses with a Prespecified Level of Significance → *given α*

assume H₀ is True

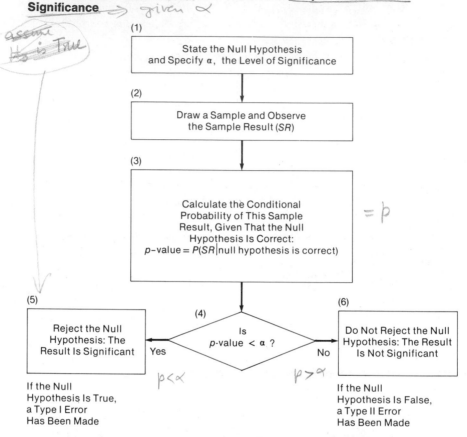

(1)

State the Null Hypothesis
and Specify α, the Level of Significance

(2)

Draw a Sample and Observe
the Sample Result (*SR*)

(3)

Calculate the Conditional
Probability of This Sample
Result, Given That the Null
Hypothesis Is Correct:
p-value = $P(SR|$null hypothesis is correct)

$= p$

(5)

Reject the Null
Hypothesis: The
Result Is Significant

(4)

Is
p-value $< \alpha$?

Yes

(6)

Do Not Reject the Null
Hypothesis: The Result
Is Not Significant

No

$p < \alpha$

$p > \alpha$

If the Null
Hypothesis Is True,
a Type I Error
Has Been Made

If the Null
Hypothesis Is False,
a Type II Error
Has Been Made

9.2 TESTS OF HYPOTHESES ABOUT A POPULATION MEAN

In many cases a statistician is interested in testing a hypothesis about the value of a population mean. The framework already described above is applicable to this situation. It is necessary to be specific only about the probability theory used to calculate the probability in box 3 of the procedures. This probability model depends on the size of the sample which is used in the test procedure. The first case discusses hypothesis testing about a population mean when the sample is large. The second case discusses testing a hypothesis about a mean, when the sample is small, and it is known that the population is approximately normally distributed.

Figure 9.4

Flow Diagram for Reporting the *p*-Value for a Test Result

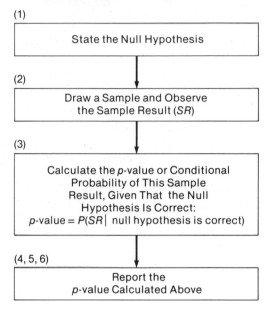

(1)

> State the Null Hypothesis

(2)

> Draw a Sample and Observe
> the Sample Result (*SR*)

(3)

> Calculate the *p*-value or Conditional
> Probability of This Sample
> Result, Given That the Null
> Hypothesis Is Correct:
> *p*-value $= P(SR\mid$ null hypothesis is correct)

(4, 5, 6)

> Report the
> *p*-value Calculated Above

9.21   Tests of Hypotheses about a Population Mean: μ_x Large Sample

To illustrate the test of a hypothesis about a population mean, consider a study conducted by a telephone company which is interested in investigating the number of calls per month made by subscribers in the telephone exchange called Bellwood. The purpose of the study is to justify a higher basic rate for these subscribers, because it is felt that their usage of the telephone system is higher than the usage for all subscribers in the city.

The telephone company knows that the average number of calls per residential subscriber for the entire city is 46 calls per month. The statistical analyst for the telephone company realizes that a public utility commission might be skeptical of the claim that an average Bellwood user makes more calls than the average user from the city. Hence, the statistician states the null hypothesis to be that the average Bellwood subscriber makes 46 or H_0 fewer calls per month, hoping to be able to reject this hypothesis. In this case, the null hypothesis is serving as a "straw man" whose rejection will be convincing to the commission and beneficial to the telephone company.

The statistician also uses a prespecified level of significance, $\alpha = 0.01$. Thus,

$$H_N : \mu_X \leq 46$$
$$\alpha = 0.01$$

A sample of 225 Bellwood subscribers is selected randomly from all residential subscribers in the exchange. Special monitoring equipment is placed on their telephone lines so that a count of the number of outgoing calls can be made for each subscriber. For the month of June, the results are:

$$n = 225$$
$$\bar{X} = 50.50$$
$$s_X = 22.50$$

In order to calculate the probability of obtaining this sample result, given that the null hypothesis is true, the statistician sketched the diagram shown in Figure 9.5. This sketch shows the sampling distribution of $\bar{X}$, given that the null hypothesis is true. The central limit theorem was used in drawing this diagram. Because of the large sample size, the shape of the sampling distribution of $\bar{X}$ is assumed to be normal. The mean of the dis-

Figure 9.5

Sampling Distribution of $\bar{X}$ if the Null Hypothesis Is True

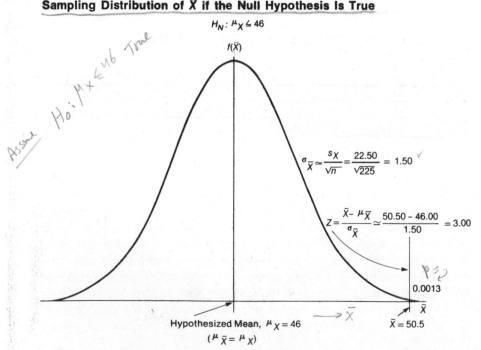

$$H_N : \mu_X \leq 46$$

$$f(\bar{X})$$

$$\sigma_{\bar{X}} \approx \frac{s_X}{\sqrt{n}} = \frac{22.50}{\sqrt{225}} = 1.50$$

$$Z = \frac{\bar{X} - \mu_{\bar{X}}}{\sigma_{\bar{X}}} \approx \frac{50.50 - 46.00}{1.50} = 3.00$$

0.0013

Hypothesized Mean, $\mu_X = 46$
$(\mu_{\bar{X}} = \mu_X)$

$\bar{X} = 50.5$

tribution of $\bar{X}$ is the same as the hypothesized mean of the population, because the diagram represents the sampling distribution of $\bar{X}$ when the null hypothesis is true at the equality. Furthermore, the standard deviation of this sampling distribution of $\bar{X}$ is estimated to be $s_{\bar{x}} = s_X/\sqrt{n}$.

Using Figure 9.5, the statistician reasons that if a sample result, $\bar{X} = 50.50$ calls, causes rejection of the null hypothesis, any number of calls in excess of 50.5 also logically requires rejecting the null hypothesis. (After all, it would not make sense to say, "50.5 calls convinces me that the average is greater than 46, but 53 calls doesn't convince me.") The statistician calculated this probability:

$$p\text{-Value} = P(SR|\text{null hypothesis is true}) = P(\bar{X} \geq 50.5 | \mu_X = 46)$$

$$= P\left(Z \geq \frac{\bar{X} - \mu_{\bar{x}}}{\sigma_{\bar{x}}}\right)$$

$$= P\left(Z \geq \frac{50.50 - 46.00}{22.50/\sqrt{225}}\right)$$

$$= P\left(Z \geq \frac{50.50 - 46}{1.50}\right)$$

$$= P(Z \geq 3.00) = 0.0013 \quad = p$$

Comparing this probability, 0.0013, with the prespecified significance level $(\alpha = .01)$, the result is significant. The statistician concludes that the hypothesis should be rejected. $p < \alpha$ reject

If a prespecified level of significance had not been used, the researcher would have reported that the p-value is 0.0013.

9.22   One- and Two-Tailed Tests

The Bellwood example above is called a "one-tailed test." It is one-tailed because the researcher reports the result to be significant (and rejects the null hypothesis) only if $\bar{X}$ is significantly *greater* than the hypothesized value of μ_X. If $\bar{X}$ had been less than this value μ_X, the result would have given no reason to suspect that the true mean is greater than 46. In other words, only one tail of the sampling distribution of $\bar{X}$, in this case the right or upper tail, causes the result to be reported as significant. Thus, it is called a one-tailed test. Of course, one-tailed tests can apply to either tail of the sampling distribution of $\bar{X}$.

In other situations, two-tailed tests are appropriate. If the commission hearing the petition for the rate increase had conducted the study, a two-tailed procedure might have been used. The commission might have been interested in either raising or lowering the rates for Bellwood, so that either a significantly high value of $\bar{X}$ or a significantly low value of $\bar{X}$ would cause the commission to reject the hypothesis that the average monthly number of calls per Bellwood subscriber is 46. In this situation, the extremes of the right and left tails of the sampling distribution of $\bar{X}$

would be the rejection region; this would be a two-tailed test procedure.

The *alternate hypothesis* is what will be accepted if the null hypothesis is rejected. For the telephone company, the alternate hypothesis would be that the average number of calls for the Bellwood exchange is greater than 46 (H_A: $\mu_X > 46$), which is precisely what the telephone company believes and wants to be correct. From the standpoint of the commission, the alternate hypothesis would be that the average number of calls per month per subscriber for Bellwood is not equal to 46 (H_A: $\mu_X \neq 46$).

H_0: $\mu_X = 46$

9.23 Example of a Two-Tailed Test

The manager of the automobile fleet for the XYZ Corporation is concerned about the gas mileage of the 1978 model automobiles. She knows that the 1977 cars averaged 13.8 miles per gallon over a specified set of driving conditions which the cars often encounter. Thus, she hypothesizes:

$$H_N: \quad \mu_X = 13.8 \text{ miles per gallon}$$

Since she is interested in detecting either an increase or a decrease in gas mileage, she uses a two-tailed test procedure. Her alternate hypothesis is:

$$H_A: \quad \mu_X \neq 13.8 \text{ miles per gallon}$$

She specifies a level of significance of $\alpha = 0.10$ for the test. She randomly selects 50 of the firm's 200 cars for inclusion in the test.

Figure 9.6

Sampling Distribution of $\bar{X}$ if the Null Hypothesis Is True

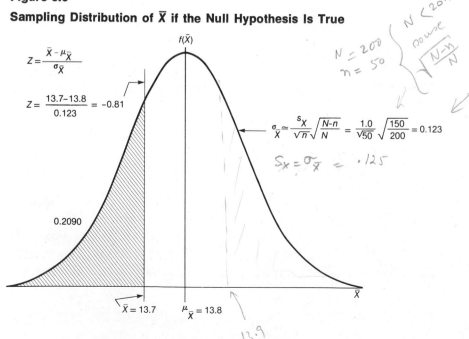

$$Z = \frac{\bar{X} - \mu_{\bar{X}}}{\sigma_{\bar{X}}}$$

$$Z = \frac{13.7 - 13.8}{0.123} = -0.81$$

$$\sigma_{\bar{X}} \approx \frac{s_X}{\sqrt{n}}\sqrt{\frac{N-n}{N}} = \frac{1.0}{\sqrt{50}}\sqrt{\frac{150}{200}} = 0.123$$

$$s_X = \sigma_{\bar{X}} = .125$$

0.2090

$\bar{X} = 13.7$ $\mu_{\bar{X}} = 13.8$

$N = 200$
$n = 50$

$\frac{N-n}{N}$

For the 50 cars, the results of the test are:

$$\bar{X} = 13.7 \text{ miles per gallon}$$
$$s_X = 1.0 \text{ miles per gallon}$$

The sampling distribution of $\bar{X}$, under the assumption that the null hypothesis is correct, is shown in Figure 9.6. Note that the standard deviation of the sampling distribution $\bar{X}$ is calculated using the finite population multiplier (Chapter 8), because a substantial part of the population is included in the sample. The manager reasons that if she were to reject the hypothesis when $\bar{X} = 13.7$ (or 13.9, as this is two-tailed), she would logically need to reject the hypothesis any time $\bar{X}$ is farther from the hypothesized mean than 13.7 or 13.9, given this is a two-tailed test procedure. (Once again, if 13.7 convinces you that the mean is not 13.8, then it does not make sense to claim that 13.5 does *not* convince you.) The manager calculates:

$$P(\bar{X} < 13.7 \cup \bar{X} > 13.9|\mu_X = 13.8) = 2 \cdot P(\bar{X} < 13.7|\mu_X = 13.8)$$

$$= 2 \cdot P\left(Z < \frac{\bar{X} - \mu_{\bar{x}}}{\sigma_{\bar{x}}}\right)$$

$$= 2 \cdot P\left(Z < \frac{13.7 - 13.8}{0.123}\right)$$

$$= 2 \cdot P(Z < -0.81)$$

$$= 2 \cdot 0.2090 = 0.4180$$

Notice in this calculation that the probability of both tails is included; this is accomplished by multiplying the one-tail probability by two. The manager compares this *p*-value, 0.4180, with the specified level of significance, $\alpha = .10$. She concludes that the result is not significant and does not reject the null hypothesis. She can also report that the *p*-value is 0.4180.

9.24 Tests of Hypotheses about a Population Mean: Small Sample

In the previous section, a hypothesis about a population mean was tested using a *large* sample. In this section, a hypothesis about a population mean using a *small* sample is discussed. In the previous section, the central limit theorem permitted use of the normal distribution in the testing process, regardless of the shape of the distribution of the population. In this section, the small sample procedures do not permit using the central limit theorem. This means the population being investigated must be approximately normally distributed.

The primary difference between a large sample and a small sample test of a population mean is that the small sample procedure requires use

Figure 9.7

Data for Catsup Bottle Test

Observation Number	Net Wt., X, oz.	X²
1	9.4	88.36
2	9.0	81.00
3	10.4	108.16
4	10.0	100.00
5	10.4	108.16
6	9.9	98.01
7	10.2	104.04
8	7.5	56.25
9	8.3	68.89
10	10.4	108.16
	95.5	921.03

$$\bar{X} = \frac{\Sigma X}{n} = \frac{95.5}{10} = 9.55 \text{ ounces}$$

$$s_X = \sqrt{\frac{\Sigma(X^2) - \frac{(\Sigma X)^2}{n}}{n-1}} = \sqrt{\frac{921.03 - \frac{(95.5 \times 95.5)}{10}}{9}} = \sqrt{1.0006} = 1.0003$$

of the t-distribution. It has already been discussed in Chapter 8 that the statistic

$$t = \frac{\bar{X} - \mu_X}{\frac{s_X}{\sqrt{n}}}$$

is described by the t-distribution with $v = n - 1$ degrees of freedom.

A small sample test of a population mean can best be illustrated with an example. The HIJ Company uses an automatic filling machine to fill catsup bottles. Before the machine needed an overhaul, it filled bottles with an average of 9.1 ounces of catsup when set for nine ounces. After overhaul, it is hypothesized that the machine will operate as before; that is, the average amount of catsup dispensed will be 9.1 ounces per bottle, when set for nine ounces. The company is interested in detecting either an increase or a decrease from this value, so a two-tailed test is appropriate. The null and alternate hypotheses are:

$$H_N: \quad \mu_X = 9.1 \text{ ounces}$$
$$H_A: \quad \mu_X \neq 9.1 \text{ ounces}$$

$\alpha = .05$

The test is conducted by specifying a 5 percent level of significance, and using a sample of ten observations. The observations and the calculations of the sample mean and standard deviation from these observations are shown in Figure 9.7. Using the sample results that $\bar{X} = 9.55$ and $s_X = 1.0003$, the calculation of the t-statistic is:

$$t = \frac{\bar{X} - \mu_X}{s_X/\sqrt{n}} = \frac{9.55 - 9.1}{1.0003/\sqrt{10}} = 1.42$$

Using the table of the t-distribution with $n-1 = 9$ degrees of freedom, the p-value is found to be $2(0.0948) = 0.1896$. The value of 0.0948 is found by interpolating between 0.0975 for $t = 1.40$ and 0.0839 for $t = 1.50$. The factor of two is used to convert the one-tail probability to a two-tail probability. Since the p-value is greater than α, the sample result is not significant, and the null hypothesis is not rejected. (If the t table had been used without interpolation, the p-value would be calculated as $2[0.0975] = 0.1950$.)

9.3 TESTS OF HYPOTHESES ABOUT A POPULATION PROPORTION

Depending on the situation, there are two procedures which may be appropriate for testing a hypothesis about a population proportion. If the sample size is such that a table of the appropriate binomial distribution is available, the most direct method for testing the hypothesis is to find the required conditional probability value directly from the table. If this is not the case, and if, for the hypothesized value of π, both $n(\pi)$ and $n(1 - \pi)$ are at least five the normal approximation to the binomial may be used. The procedures are identical to those already used, except for the method of calculating the probabilities. Hence, these procedures are illustrated with examples.

An employment agency has received a large number of responses to an employment ad. A random sample of 25 applications reveals that ten of the 25 applicants have completed high school. The owner of the agency is interested in investigating the hypothesis that exactly 30 percent of the applicants from this ad have completed high school. (Another source of applicants, used for a long time, yields 30 percent who have completed high school.) The level of significance is set at $\alpha = 0.05$. Since this test procedure is two-tailed, the p-value is calculated as:

$$p\text{-value} = 2[P\ (X \geq 10 \mid n = 25, \pi = 0.3)] = 2(0.1894) = 0.3788$$

This value is compared to the level of significance, 5 percent. The owner concludes that the result is not significant, and does not reject the hypothesis.

If a level of significance had not been specified for this test, the owner of the employment agency could have reported that the p-value is 0.3788.

The second example of testing a population proportion uses a large sample procedure and the normal approximation to the binomial distribution. After processing many more applications, selected at random from all applications received from the ad, the employment agency owner

Figure 9.8

Sampling Distribution of p if the Null Hypothesis Is True

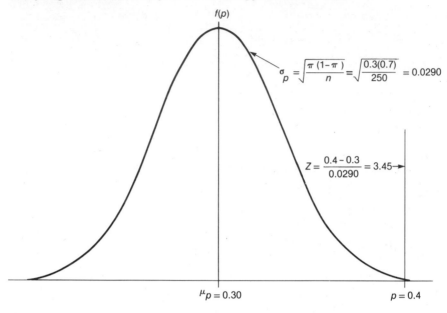

$$\sigma_p = \sqrt{\frac{\pi(1-\pi)}{n}} = \sqrt{\frac{0.3(0.7)}{250}} = 0.0290$$

$$Z = \frac{0.4-0.3}{0.0290} = 3.45 \rightarrow$$

$\mu_p = 0.30$ $p = 0.4$

reports these results: $n = 250$, $X = 100$. The owner then proceeds to use the normal distribution to test the same hypothesis with a large sample size. From the normal approximation to the binomial distribution,

$$\mu_p = \pi$$

$$\sigma_p = \sqrt{\frac{\pi(1-\pi)}{n}}$$

Using the hypothesized value of π, the owner calculates the parameters of the sampling distribution for p as:

$$\mu_p = \pi = 0.30$$

$$\sigma_p = \sqrt{\frac{\pi(1-\pi)}{n}} = \sqrt{\frac{0.3(0.7)}{250}} = 0.0290$$

From these data, the sampling distribution of p is shown in Figure 9.8, given that the hypothesized value of π is true. Since the value of p for the sample is $100/250 = 0.4$, the p-value is calculated as:

$$P(p \geq 0.4 | n = 250, \pi = 0.3) = P\left(Z \geq \frac{p - \mu_p}{\sigma_p}\right) = P\left(Z \geq \frac{0.40 - 0.30}{0.0290}\right)$$

$$= P(Z \geq 3.45) = 0.0003$$

For this two-tail procedure, the p-value $= 2 \times 0.0003 = 0.0006$.

It should be pointed out that in testing this hypothesis about the population proportion, the hypothesized value of π has been used to calculate the standard error of the sampling distribution of p. This hypothesized value of π is used because if it is true that $\mu_p = \pi = .30$, then it must be true that $\sigma_p = \sqrt{\pi(1 - \pi)/n} = .0290$. It would be inconsistent with the hypothesis to estimate σ_p using the sample value, p.

9.4 TESTS OF HYPOTHESES ABOUT THE DIFFERENCE BETWEEN TWO POPULATION MEANS

For t when $n_1 + n_2 - 2 = v$ is degree of freedom $v < 30$. Otherwise use Z-distribution

When one can obtain large independent samples from each of two populations, it is possible to test a hypothesis about the difference between the means of these two populations. The usual hypothesis is that the two population means are equal, or that their difference is zero. The same procedure that is used for testing the hypothesis of the equality of two means may also be used for testing the hypothesis that the difference between two population means is a particular value.

To illustrate this test, recall the example from Chapter 8 of the difference between the average time of taxicab runs in January and February. Using a 2 percent level of significance for a two-tailed test, it is stated:

*H_o *
Type 2

$\alpha = .02$ *Two tail*

$$H_N: \quad \mu_{X_1} = \mu_{X_2} \text{ or } \mu_{X_1} - \mu_{X_2} = 0$$
$$H_A: \quad \mu_{X_1} \neq \mu_X \text{ or } \mu_{X_1} - \mu_{X_2} \neq 0$$

$n_1 = 100$	$n_2 = 120$
$\bar{X}_1 = 13.3$	$\bar{X}_2 = 14.1$
$s_{X_1} = 4.2$	$s_{X_2} = 4.7$

The two samples are independent of each other.

As discussed in Chapter 8, the difference, $\bar{X}_1 - \bar{X}_2$, is normally distributed when the number of observations in each sample is large. It is also true that the estimate of the standard error of the sampling distribution of their difference, $\bar{X}_1 - \bar{X}_2$, is

$$s_{\bar{X}_1 - \bar{X}_2} = \sqrt{\frac{s_{X_1}^2}{n_1} + \frac{s_{X_2}^2}{n_2}}$$

For this example,

$$s_{\bar{X}_1 - \bar{X}_2} = \sqrt{\frac{4.2^2}{100} + \frac{4.7^2}{120}} = 0.60$$

Figure 9.9 shows the sampling distribution for the difference in means, $\bar{X}_1 - \bar{X}_2$, given the hypothesis that there is no difference in the population means. Using this figure, it is seen that the observed difference in sample means is 1.33 standard errors below the mean of $\mu_{X_1} - \mu_{X_2} = 0$. From the table of the standard normal distribution, the probability of being   *→ 0.8*

Figure 9.9

Sampling Distribution for the Taxicab Problem

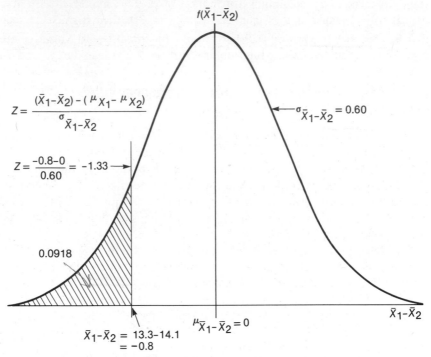

$$Z = \frac{(\bar{X}_1 - \bar{X}_2) - (\mu_{X_1} - \mu_{X_2})}{\sigma_{\bar{X}_1 - \bar{X}_2}}$$

$\sigma_{\bar{X}_1 - \bar{X}_2} = 0.60$

$$Z = \frac{-0.8 - 0}{0.60} = -1.33$$

0.0918

$\bar{X}_1 - \bar{X}_2 = 13.3 - 14.1 = -0.8$

$\mu_{\bar{X}_1 - \bar{X}_2} = 0$

$\bar{X}_1 - \bar{X}_2$

$f(\bar{X}_1 - \bar{X}_2)$

more than 1.33 standard errors below the mean is 0.0918. Since this is a two-tailed test, the probability of obtaining this sample result, or a result even further from zero, is $2(0.0918) = 0.1836$. Comparing this probability with $\alpha = 0.02$, the result is not significant, and the null hypothesis should not be rejected. If a level of significance had not been pre-specified, it could have been reported that the p-value is 0.1836.

9.5 HYPOTHESIS TESTING AND CONFIDENCE INTERVALS

It is instructive to refer to Chapter 8, Section 8.38, in which the confidence interval for the taxicab problem above was discussed and calculated. Since a 2 percent level of significance was used in the hypothesis test above, a 98 percent confidence level was used for the confidence interval, and both examples were two-tailed procedures. It is possible to compare their results and use these results as a discussion of the relationship between confidence intervals and hypothesis tests.

Recall that the null hypothesis was that $\mu_{X_1} - \mu_{X_2} = 0$. Also, this hypothesis was accepted for $\alpha = 0.02$ given the sample results, $\bar{X}_1 - \bar{X}_2 = -0.8$. Then recall that using the same sample results, $\bar{X}_1 - \bar{X}_2 = -0.8$, the confidence interval for $\mu_{X_1} - \mu_{X_2}$ was calculated to be from -2.2 to 0.6. As the null hypothesis value of zero is within the confidence interval, it is correct that the null hypothesis of $\mu_{X_1} - \mu_{X_2} = 0$ would be accepted.

Similarly, the gas mileage example (Section 9.23) can be viewed in both ways. The null hypothesis, $\mu_X = 13.8$, was tested at a level of significance of $\alpha = 0.10$. For the sample result of $\bar{X} = 13.7$ miles per gallon the null hypothesis was accepted.

If a confidence interval is calculated using the same data, the results are determined using a confidence level of 90%. The 90 percent confidence interval for μ_X is:

$$\bar{X} \pm 1.64 \frac{s_X}{\sqrt{n}} \sqrt{\frac{N-n}{N}}$$
$$13.7 \pm 1.64 \left(\frac{1.0}{\sqrt{50}}\right) \sqrt{\frac{150}{200}}$$
$$13.7 \pm 1.64 \,(0.123)$$
$$13.7 \pm 0.202$$
$$13.498 \text{ to } 13.902$$

Again, the null hypothesis value of 13.8 lies within the confidence interval, so the null hypothesis would not be rejected in the test. It is also true that any null hypothesis with μ_X between 13.498 and 13.902 would not be rejected, as long as the same sample is used.

9.6 ERROR CURVES IN HYPOTHESIS TESTING

It has already been pointed out that two types of errors may result from a hypothesis test. A Type I error occurs whenever a true null hypothesis is rejected; a Type II error occurs whenever a false null hypothesis is not rejected. The user of the tests of statistical hypotheses is interested in assessing the risks or probabilities associated with these two types of errors. These probabilities can be demonstrated by the use of error curves for the hypothesis being tested. The calculation of error curves for the one-tailed Bellwood example, and for the two-tailed gas mileage example will be demonstrated.

Before discussing the construction of error curves, one important comment must be made concerning Type II errors. When the null hypothesis about the mean is false, the probability of a Type II error will be large if the true mean is near the hypothesized value of the mean. But the consequences of such an error may be slight, because the true and hypothesized means are near each other. Contrary, if the true mean is far from the hypothesized value of the mean, the probability of a Type II error

Find X_{CV_0} first

will be small but the consequences may be large. This is most fortunate, as the probability of a large error is small and the probability of a small error is large. This point will be demonstrated with the error curve.

The steps necessary to construct an error curve for the test of a hypothesis can be conducted in advance of actually drawing a random sample. However, an estimate of the population standard deviation is always needed. This estimate may be established prior to taking the sample, based on prior knowledge or a pilot study. Or it may be based on the sample standard deviation after the sample has been taken. The steps involved in constructing an error curve are:

1. State the procedure that will be used for testing the hypothesis. The procedure must be consistent with α, the prespecified level of significance.
2. Choose a value of the population mean. Decide whether this value makes the null hypothesis true or false; this determines whether an error resulting from the testing procedure is a Type I or a Type II error.
3. If the chosen value of the population mean makes the null hypothesis true, find the probability (Type I error) of rejecting the hypothesis given the value of the population mean from Step 2 and the procedure from Step 1.
4. If the chosen value of the population mean makes the hypothesis false, find the probability (Type II error) of accepting the hypothesis, given the value of the population mean from Step 2 and the procedure from Step 1.
5. Go back to Step 2 for as many values of the population mean as desired, to provide enough points to sketch the error curve.

For the Bellwood example (Section 9.21) the null hypothesis, the alternate hypothesis, the sample size, the estimate of the population standard deviation, the estimate of the standard error of the sample mean, and the prespecified level of significance are:

$$H_N: \quad \mu_X \leq 46$$
$$H_A: \quad \mu_X > 46$$
$$n = 225$$
$$s_X = 22.50$$
$$\sigma_{\bar{X}} \simeq \frac{22.50}{\sqrt{225}} = 1.50$$
$$\alpha = 0.01$$

$\bar{X} = 50.5$

The prespecified level of significance, $\alpha = 0.01$, indicates that the decision maker is willing to accept a 1 percent chance of rejecting the null hypothesis when it is true. In Figure 9.10a, the sampling distribution of $\bar{X}$ is drawn under the assumption that the null hypothesis is true (that is, the

Figure 9.10

Rejection Region and Error Probabilities for Bellwood Test

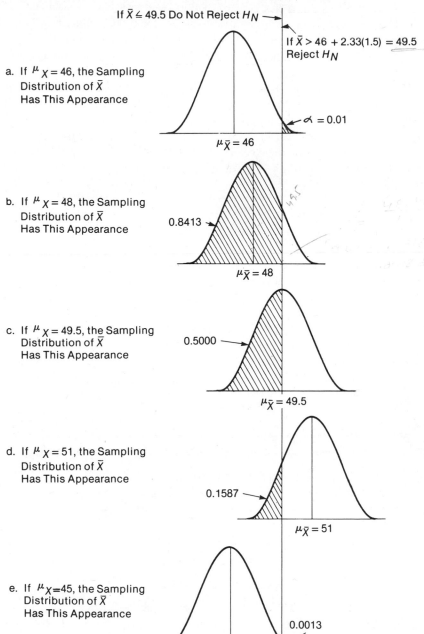

If $\bar{X} \leq 49.5$ Do Not Reject H_N

If $\bar{X} > 46 + 2.33(1.5) = 49.5$
Reject H_N

a. If $\mu_X = 46$, the Sampling
   Distribution of $\bar{X}$
   Has This Appearance

$\alpha = 0.01$

$\mu_{\bar{X}} = 46$

b. If $\mu_X = 48$, the Sampling
   Distribution of $\bar{X}$
   Has This Appearance

0.8413

$\mu_{\bar{X}} = 48$

c. If $\mu_X = 49.5$, the Sampling
   Distribution of $\bar{X}$
   Has This Appearance

0.5000

$\mu_{\bar{X}} = 49.5$

d. If $\mu_X = 51$, the Sampling
   Distribution of $\bar{X}$
   Has This Appearance

0.1587

$\mu_{\bar{X}} = 51$

e. If $\mu_X = 45$, the Sampling
   Distribution of $\bar{X}$
   Has This Appearance

0.0013

$\mu_{\bar{X}} = 45$

average number of calls for Bellwood is 46). It has already been observed that high values of $\bar{X}$, and not low values of $\bar{X}$, cause one to reject the null hypothesis. Therefore, a right-tail rejection region is established with a 0.01 probability; this sets the values of $\bar{X}$ which will cause rejection of the null hypothesis. From Figure 9.10a it is seen that $\bar{X} > 49.50$ will cause a rejection of the null hypothesis. This is the test procedure, listed as *Step 1* above.

The next step in investigating the error characteristics of this testing procedure is to choose some value which the true population mean might assume. Suppose the true population mean, μ_X, is really 48 calls per month. If this is the case, the null hypothesis is obviously false. An error will be made if it is not rejected; it will not be rejected whenever $\bar{X}$ is less than 49.5. The probability of error is illustrated in Figure 9.10b; it is calculated as:

$$P(\text{error}|\mu_X = 48) = P(\text{nonrejection}|\mu_X = 48) = P(\bar{X} < 49.5|\mu_X = 48)$$
$$= P\left(Z < \frac{49.5 - 48}{1.5}\right)$$
$$= P(Z < 1.0) = 1 - 0.1587 = 0.8413$$

This indicates that the probability of making an error when the population mean is really 48 is 0.8413. This is the probability of a Type II error if the true population mean is 48. This completes *Step 2* and *Step 4*.

As another example of the calculation of a Type II error probability, suppose the population mean is really 49.5. Since it has already been established that $\bar{X} = 49.5$ is also the beginning of the rejection region, the symmetry of the normal distribution leads immediately to:

$$P(\text{error}|\mu_X = 49.5) = P(\text{nonrejection}|\mu_X = 49.5)$$
$$= P(\bar{X} < 49.5|\mu_X = 49.5) = P\left(Z < \frac{49.5 - 49.5}{1.5}\right)$$
$$= P(Z < 0) = 0.5000$$

as shown in Figure 9.10c. (Repeat of *Steps 2* and *4*.)

As a final example of the calculation of the probability of a Type II error probability, suppose $\mu_X = 51$; the error probability is:

$$P(\text{error}|\mu_X = 51) = P(\text{nonrejection}|\mu_X = 51)$$
$$= P(\bar{X} < 49.5|\mu_X = 51) = P\left(Z < \frac{49.5 - 51}{1.5}\right)$$
$$= P(Z < -1.0) = 0.1587$$

as shown in Figure 9.10d. (Repeat of *Steps 2* and *4*.)

To find the probability of error when $\mu_X = 46$, recognize that the rejection region was established under the assumption that $\mu_X = 46$, and the calculations can be summarized as:

$$P(\text{error}|\mu_X = 46) = P(\text{rejection}|\mu_X = 46)$$
$$= P(\bar{X} > 49.5|\mu_X = 46) = P\left(Z > \frac{49.5 - 46}{1.5}\right)$$
$$= P(Z > 2.33) = 0.010$$

Notice that in this case the error is a Type I error, because $\mu_X = 46$ means that the null hypothesis is true. This is illustrated in Figure 9.10a. This completes *Step 2* and *Step 3*.

As a final example of the calculation of the probability of a Type I error, assume $\mu_X = 45$. These calculations follow:

$$P(\text{error}|\mu_X = 45) = P(\text{rejection}|\mu_X = 45)$$
$$= P(\bar{X} > 49.5|\mu_X = 45) = P\left(Z > \frac{49.5 - 45}{1.5}\right)$$
$$= P(Z > 3) = 0.0013$$

as shown in Figure 9.10e. (Repeat of *Steps 2* and *3*.)

Figure 9.11

Summary of Type I and Type II Errors

True Population Mean, μ_X	Null Hypothesis	Error	Type Error	Happens if	Probability of Error
48	False	Not Reject	II	$\bar{X} \leq 49.50$	0.8413
49.5	False	Not Reject	II	$\bar{X} \leq 49.50$	0.5000
51	False	Not Reject	II	$\bar{X} \leq 49.50$	0.1587
46	True	Reject	I	$\bar{X} > 49.50$	0.0100
45	True	Reject	I	$\bar{X} > 49.50$	0.0013

The results of these error probabilities are summarized in Figure 9.11. Notice that when the null hypothesis is "close" to being correct ($\mu_X = 48$) there is a high probability of error (0.8413). When the true value of the population mean is "far" from the hypothesized value ($\mu_X = 51$) the probability of error decreases (0.1587).

The error probabilities from Figure 9.11 are shown graphically in Figure 9.12. This curve is called an *error curve*.[3]

For the gas mileage example, the error curve is constructed in a similar fashion. However, since it is a two-tailed testing procedure, the error

---

[3] There are two other curves which are related to the error curve. The first is the *operating characteristic curve*, which shows the probability of not rejecting the hypothesis. For the Bellwood example, the right hand portion of Figure 9.12 is part of the operating characteristic curve. The second curve related to the error curve is called the *power function*. It is the probability of rejecting the null hypothesis. The left half of Figure 9.12 is part of the power function. All three curves—the error curve, the operating characteristic curve, and power function—show the same information in a somewhat different manner.

Find X_{CV_L} & X_{CV_U} (fig)

Figure 9.12

Error Curve for Bellwood Hypothesis

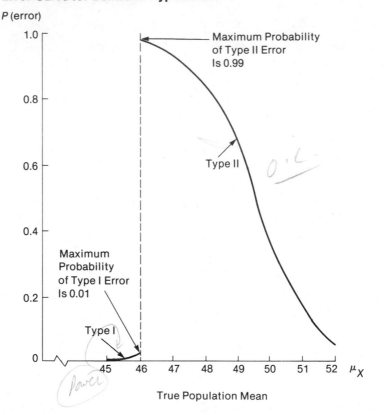

True Population Mean

curve is symmetric about the hypothesized mean. Each Type II error probability calculation gives two points on the error curve. The information needed from the gas mileage example is:

$$H_N: \quad \mu_X = 13.8$$
$$H_A: \quad \mu_X \neq 13.8 \quad \textit{Two tailed Test}$$
$$n = 50$$
$$N = 200$$
$$\sigma_{\bar{x}} \simeq \frac{s_X}{\sqrt{n}} \sqrt{\frac{N-n}{N}} = \frac{1.0}{\sqrt{50}} \sqrt{\frac{150}{200}} = 0.123$$
$$\alpha = 0.10$$

The rejection region is shown in Figure 9.13, which shows the sampling distribution of $\bar{X}$ under the assumption that the null hypothesis is true. When the null hypothesis is true, the level of significance indicates that one is willing to accept a 0.10 chance of rejecting the null hypothesis. This rejection region, which has an area of 0.10, is split into two equal

Figure 9.13

Rejection Region for Gas Mileage Test

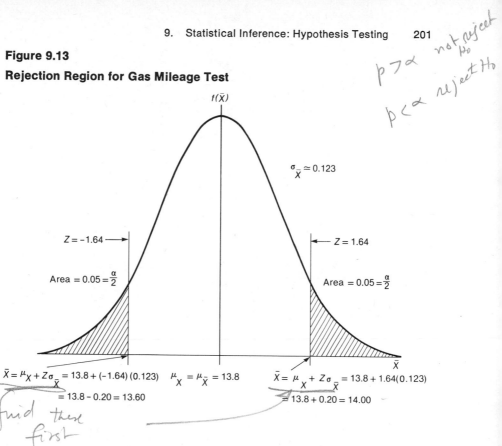

$$f(\bar{X})$$

$$\sigma_{\bar{X}} \approx 0.123$$

$Z = -1.64$

$Z = 1.64$

Area $= 0.05 = \dfrac{\alpha}{2}$

Area $= 0.05 = \dfrac{\alpha}{2}$

$\bar{X} = \mu_X + Z\sigma_{\bar{X}} = 13.8 + (-1.64)(0.123)$ $\mu_X = \mu_{\bar{X}} = 13.8$ $\bar{X} = \mu_X + Z\sigma_{\bar{X}} = 13.8 + 1.64(0.123)$

$= 13.8 - 0.20 = 13.60$ $= 13.8 + 0.20 = 14.00$

find these first

tails, because this is a two-tailed test. From this diagram, it can be seen that the null hypothesis will be rejected whenever $\bar{X}$ exceeds 14.00, or whenever $\bar{X}$ is less than 13.60.

To investigate the error characteristics of this test, the same procedures are followed as in the previous example. In summary, various values are considered which the population mean might take on. Given these values, one determines whether the hypothesis would then be true or false, determines whether rejection or nonrejection would lead to an error, and calculates the probability of this error for the assumed value of the population mean. These steps are shown in Figure 9.14. In calculating the probability in the final column, two separate probability areas must be found because the rejection region is in two parts. Both these parts are shown in the final column of Figure 9.14. The reader is urged to verify these probability values and to be certain that the method for finding the probability of error for a two-tailed test of an hypothesis is understood. Figure 9.15 graphically shows the information from Figure 9.14. In this error curve, note that there is only one point at which a Type I error is represented. This occurs when the null hypothesis is true at its only true value, 13.8 miles per gallon.

Figure 9.14

Error Characteristics for Testing the Gas Mileage Hypothesis

True Population Mean	Null Hypothesis	Error	Type Error	Happens if	Probability
13.5 (or 14.1)	False	Not Reject	II	$13.60 \leq \bar{X} \leq 14.00$ $0.81 \leq Z \leq 4.07$	$0.2090 - 0.0000 = 0.2090$
13.6 (or 14.0)	False	Not Reject	II	$13.60 \leq \bar{X} \leq 14.00$ $0 \leq Z \leq 3.26$	$0.5000 - 0.0006 = 0.4994$
13.7 (or 13.9)	False	Not Reject	II	$13.60 \leq \bar{X} \leq 14.00$ $-0.81 \leq Z \leq 2.44$	$1.0000 - 0.2090$ $-0.0073 = 0.7837$
13.8	True	Reject	I	$\bar{X} < 13.60$ or $\bar{X} > 14.00$ or $Z \leq -1.64$ or $Z \geq 1.64$	$0.0500 + 0.0500 = 0.1000$

H_N: $\mu_X = 13.8$

$n = 50$

$\sigma_{\bar{X}} = 0.123$

With this procedure: If $\bar{X} > 14.00$ or if $\bar{X} < 13.60$, Reject H_N.

Figure 9.15

Error Curve for Gas Mileage Hypothesis

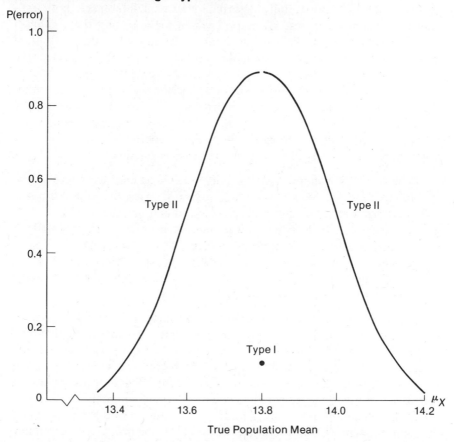

9.61   Error Curve for Population Proportions

Calculations of Type II errors involved in testing a hypothesis about a population proportion are quite similar to those involved in the computations for Figure 9.11, with one notable difference. In Figure 9.14 the standard deviation of the sampling distribution of the sample mean (the standard error of $\bar{X}$) remained constant for various values of the population mean; this is not the case for the standard deviation of the sampling distribution of the sample proportion. Since $\sigma_p = \sqrt{\pi(1 - \pi)/n}$, it is evident that σ_p depends on π, and takes on different values for different values of π. Other than this difference, the procedures for an error curve are identical to those already shown.

9.7 IS HYPOTHESIS TESTING A DECISION PROCEDURE? *NO*

This text has very carefully described statistical inferences, both estimation and hypothesis testing, as procedures for reporting the results of a statistical experiment. It is not uncommon to find other descriptions of hypothesis testing which suggest that hypothesis testing is a decision procedure. This text differs from this view. Statistical inference is a powerful *information model;* i.e., it provides information which may have usefulness in a decision process, if that information is carefully understood by the user. For that reason, the meaning of hypothesis testing has been carefully explained. But we do not believe that hypothesis testing is a decision procedure. There are two primary reasons for this:

1. The only information used in a hypothesis testing procedure is the information provided in the sample. In most cases, the decision maker has other sources of information which should not be ignored.
2. The economic factors involved in a decision process are very difficult to incorporate in a framework of hypothesis testing. Although such economic factors may be considered in specifying the level of significance and the sample size, it is not clear how these economic factors are objectively included.

For these two reasons, other procedures are more powerful for decision making. Decision analysis is discussed in Chapters 16 and 17 of this text.

Another way of looking at the usefulness of inference is to suggest that inferential procedures are useful in research problems. A research problem is one in which the analyst tries to understand the behavior of a system. In scientific investigations, research problems are quite common. In decisions about the allocation of resources in an organization, there are many more decision problems than there are research problems. However, many economic investigations begin as a research problem with the objective of understanding the behavior of a system. Hence, a common analytic framework is to begin a study using inferential procedures to understand a system. As the study nears an end, economic factors become much more important; at this point, decision procedures (such as those described in Chapters 16 and 17) become much more useful than the inferential procedures.

9.8 SUMMARY

Hypothesis testing is a major area of statistical inference which is highly useful in conveying information about a population based on a sample. The sample mean, sample standard deviation, and sample size are used to produce the *p*-value of the sample result. The hypothesis test may be either one-tail or two-tail. The *p*-value may be reported by itself, or it can be compared to a prespecified α level. If the p-value is smaller than α, the test results are considered to be significant and the null hypothesis is rejected; if larger, the null hypothesis is accepted.

[margin handwritten note: $p < \alpha$ reject; $p > \alpha$ accept]

The rejection of a true null hypothesis results in a Type I error. The acceptance of a false null hypothesis results in a Type II error. The plot of Type I error probabilities and Type II error probabilities for various population means given a stated null hypothesis produces an error curve.

Tests of a population mean, differences in population means, and a population proportion were discussed. In any of these tests, one never proves or disproves anything, but information is conveyed to the user.

EXERCISES

9.1   Does testing and rejecting a null hypothesis disprove the hypothesis? Discuss.

9.2   Describe the statistical meaning of a "significant" result and a "not significant" result.

9.3   Discuss the fallacy or fallacies in this statement: "We used a two-tailed test to investigate the difference between two population means. A significant result was obtained. This means that there is a significant difference between the two population means."

9.4   Describe the meaning of a Type I error and a Type II error.

9.5   Does a sample result which is inconsistent with an hypothesis lead to the rejection or nonrejection of that hypothesis?

* 9.6   A bank cashier believes the average service charge for checking accounts is currently \$1.80. Using a 1 percent level of significance, test the null hypothesis that the average service charge is \$1.80. You should be interested in detecting a situation in which the average service charge is either greater than or less than \$1.80. A random sample of 100 accounts had a sample mean of \$1.85, and a standard deviation of 25¢.

9.7   A telephone company salesman has stated that 35 percent of the long distance telephone calls to customers result in an order. You ask him to design an experiment of 64 calls to demonstrate his hypothesis. You have agreed on a 10 percent level of significance for the one-tail test.

    a.   How would the salesman set up the hypotheses so that his claim has the best chance of surviving the test?

    b.   How would you want the test set up if you wanted to be especially careful to avoid the error of using long distance when the productivity of calls is less than 35 percent?

* 9.8   A newspaper is concerned that its want-ad customers are using unusually short ads. Trade publications suggest that the national average is 11.6 words per ad. A sample of 225 ads from the newspaper resulted in this tally sheet:

---

* Answers to exercises marked with an asterisk (*) are in Appendix L.

Ad Number	Number of Words, X	X^2
1...................	10	100
2...................	52	2,704
3...................	9	81
4...................	5	25
....	.	.
....	.	.
....	.	.
225................	8	64
Totals: 25,425	2,573	32,400

Test the hypothesis that this newspaper's ads are at least as long as the national average, and report the p-value.

* 9.9   Another newspaper shares the concern of the newspaper in Exercise 9.8. A similar study yields a sample mean of 14.2 words and a sample standard deviation (for the sample of 225 ads) of 4.1 words. Test the hypothesis that this newspaper is doing at least as well as the national average of 11.6 words per ad.

9.10   In order to test the assertion that the average daily wage of employed workers has increased 3.5 percent or more from last year's census, a sample of 100 workers is taken. Last year the wage rate was $20 per day. The sample for this year has the following results:

$$\bar{X} = \$20.50$$
$$s_X = \$ \ 4.00$$

At the 5 percent level of significance, test the hypothesis that this year's average daily wage rate is 3.5 percent or more above last year's average daily wage rate.

* 9.11   A sample of test scores for five randomly selected XY Co. employees yielded these results:

Employee Number	Score	score^2
1...................	35	1225
2...................	42	1764
3...................	23	529
4...................	40	1600
5...................	26	676
	166	5794

A census of another group of employees yielded an average test score of 40. Test the hypothesis that the XY Co. average score is 40. What is the p-value?

* 9.12   For the data of Exercise 8.16, test the hypothesis that the average score is 90 or more. Report the p-value. $= .03$

* 9.13   A manufacturer of specialty steel products had received a shipment of five expensive rods of high-alloy steel. The end of each rod was carefully cut off and machined for tensile testing. The specifications for this alloy required a tensile strength of at least 250,000 psi. The five test bars had these tested strengths:

(handwritten: $n=5$, $v=4$ degrees)

247,000 psi   *61009*
251,000 psi   *63001*
237,000 psi   *56169*
242,000 psi   *58564*
245,000 psi   *60025*

Test the hypothesis that the lot has an average tensile strength of at least 250,000 psi, using a 10 percent level of significance.

9.14 Would rejection of the hypothesis in the previous exercise be sufficient reason to send back the rods? Would nonrejection of the hypothesis be sufficient reason to use the rods in their intended products? Discuss fully.

* 9.15 A fair coin has a probability of showing heads of 0.5, by definition of "fair." A suspicious coin was flipped eight times, resulting in two heads. Test the hypothesis that this coin is fair, and report the p-value for the test. Describe carefully the meaning of the reported p-value.

* 9.16 A coin was flipped 80 times, resulting in 20 heads. Test the hypothesis that this coin is fair, and report the p-value for the test.

* 9.17 A random sample of 81 employees of a company is selected to investigate the average seniority. The employee's union claims that the average seniority is at least 13 years. The investigation results in a sample mean of 12.5 years, and a sample standard deviation of 2.4 years. Report the p-value for this test, and describe its meaning.

* 9.18 The equality of the means of two populations is being tested. A sample of 64 from the first population has a mean of 10.0 and a standard deviation of 5.0. The sample of 81 from the second population has a mean of 9.5 and a standard deviation of 15. Conduct a two-tailed test of the equality of means at the 15 percent level of significance.

* 9.19 For the data contained in Part e of Exercise 8.21, report the p-value for the test of the hypothesis that the population proportion of hours with sales greater than $140 is at least 0.25.

9.20 A certain television commercial claims that the performance of Product A is "unsurpassed" by Product B. Consider the following imaginary testimony before the Federal Trade Commission regarding this claim. "Yes, it is true that the average performance of Product A was 100 in the sample tests, and that Product B had a performance of 105. Yes, 105 is better performance than 100. No, it is not true that our commercial lies. You see, there is no statistically significant difference between 100 and 105 in our tests. Our statistician used a significance level so very small, $a = 0.001$, that we are above reproach in our claim. After all, if the statistics did not show a significant difference, Product A is apparently unsurpassed."

Except for one statement, this argument makes reasonably good statistical sense. Which statement is a flagrantly incorrect interpretation of hypothesis testing?

* 9.21 For the data contained in Exercise 8.23, test the hypothesis that the two brochures have the same population average order size. Report the p-value.

(handwritten: $\alpha > p$ reject; $p > \alpha$ do not reject or accept)

* 9.22   It is known that the standard deviation of a bank's customer's account balances is $135.00. Last year, a complete census yielded the information that the average balance was $400. For a sample of 100 accounts, what is the range of $\bar{X}$ values for which the hypothesis that $\mu_x = \$400.00$ would not be rejected at a 2 percent level of significance?

* 9.23   Answer Exercise 9.22 for a sample size of $n = 400$.

* 9.24   If, for Exercises 9.22 and 9.23 the average balance is really $420, what is the probability of correctly rejecting the hypothesis for each proposed sample size, 100 and 400?

* 9.25   For the situation of Problem 9.6, what values of $\bar{X}$ would lead to rejection? What is the probability of committing a Type II error when the average service charge is actually $1.78? When it is $1.76? When it is $1.14?

REFERENCES

Dixon, W. J. and Massey, F. J. *Introduction to Statistical Analysis,* 3d ed. New York: McGraw-Hill Book Co., 1969.

Guenther, William C. *Concepts of Statistical Inference.* New York: McGraw-Hill Book Co., Inc., 1965.

Lehman, E. L. *Testing Statistical Hypotheses.* New York: John Wiley & Sons, Inc., 1959.

Mood, Alexander M., and Graybill, Franklin A. *Introduction to the Theory of Statistics,* 3d ed. New York: McGraw-Hill Book Co., 1974.

10

Nonparametric Methods: Goodness of Fit and Analysis of Enumeration Data

Shape of a population

The previous two chapters have dealt with statistical inferences about population parameters. These chapters have described ways of making informational statements about a population parameter, when a random sample drawn from that population is available to the statistician. In some situations (inferences about a population mean using a small sample), it was necessary to assume that the population being studied was approximately normally distributed. One of the purposes of this chapter is to describe a method for making statistical inferences about the shape of a population. This will allow testing of the hypothesis that a sample has been drawn from a normal, a Poisson, or some other distribution.

Another question to be investigated by statistical inference is the question of the independence of several variables. The question of probabilistic independence was discussed at some length in Chapter 4. In this chapter, statistical inference will be used to investigate whether or not there is independence between two factors by using the information in a random sample.

10.1 PREREQUISITE: THE CHI-SQUARE DISTRIBUTION

The statistical inferences described in this chapter will require the use of the chi-square (χ^2) distribution, where the symbol χ is the Greek letter *chi*. The chi-square distribution is a continuous probability distribution. A random variable which is described by the chi-square distribution can take on any positive value. In order to specify exactly which chi-square distribution should be used, it is necessary to specify the parameter called the *degrees of freedom* which is given the symbol v (as with the t distribution). A chi-square distribution is shown in Figure 10.1. The shape of the

Figure 10.1

**Shape of the Chi-Square Distribution
with Eight Degrees of Freedom**

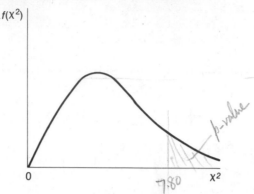

chi-square distribution approaches the normal distribution as ν becomes large. Note that the distribution lies entirely in the positive quadrant; a negative value of a random variable which has a chi-square distribution is impossible.

Appendix J gives chi-square probability distributions in tabular form. Note that in order to use Appendix J, it is necessary to know the degrees of freedom for the particular application. As an example of the use of this table, consider a chi-square random variable with four degrees of freedom. Given the value of a χ^2 statistic, one can use Appendix J to find the right-tail cumulative probability for that χ^2 value. For example, with four degrees of freedom:

$$\nu = 4$$

$$P(\chi^2 \geq 7.80) = 0.0992$$

In the statistical inferences which follow, random samples will be used to calculate statistics which have approximate chi-square distributions.

10.2 GOODNESS OF FIT

Often the question is: "Does this sample come from a population with a specified distribution?" The distribution specified can be a normal distribution, a binomial distribution, a Poisson distribution, or some other specified distribution.

10.21 Goodness of Fit Test for an Arbitrary Distribution

A department store is interested in color preferences for a high fashion woman's accessory. The buyer for the department feels there is an equal probability of red, yellow, and blue preferences. Unless the first 99 items sold show substantial deviation from this pattern, the buyer intends to order in equal quantities for the next shipment of the item. The first 99 purchasers requested 27 red, 31 yellow, and 41 blue items. If the specified distribution (equal probabilities for red, yellow, and blue) is correct, one expects 33 of each color to be requested. The question to be investigated is whether the observed departures from these expected frequencies are sufficient to cause abandonment of the belief of equal probabilities for the colors.

From a statistical standpoint, the null and alternate hypotheses are:

H_N: $P(\text{Red}) = P(\text{Yellow}) = P(\text{Blue}) = \frac{1}{3}$
H_A: The three probabilities are not equal

The statistical procedure for testing this null hypothesis is to calculate a statistic which has a chi-square distribution when H_N is true. This statistic is calculated using the differences between the observed frequencies (27, 31, and 41) and the expected frequencies (33 for each color). This statistic is:

$$\chi^2 = \frac{(27 - 33)^2}{33} + \frac{(31 - 33)^2}{33} + \frac{(41 - 33)^2}{33} = 3.15$$

Note that each term in this statistic is the square of the difference between the observed and expected frequencies, divided by the expected frequency for that category. In symbolic notation, use the symbol f_o to indicate the observed frequency for a category, and the symbol f_e to denote the expected frequency for a category, yielding:

$$\chi^2 = \Sigma \frac{(f_o - f_e)^2}{f_e}, \text{ summing over all categories}$$ ✳

When H_N is true, this statistic is approximately described by a chi-square distribution with degrees of freedom equal to the number of categories less one. In this example, with three categories, $v = 3 - 1 = 2$ degrees of freedom. To explain that degrees of freedom is one less than the number of categories, note that once the total of 99 is given along with 27 and 31, then 41 must occur.

From the construction of the statistic, it is obvious that a large value of the statistic typically will occur when the null hypothesis is not true, because large deviations will occur between observed and expected frequencies. Thus, the null hypothesis is rejected for large values of χ^2. For this example, the tabulated value of the chi-square distribution for the probability $\chi^2 \geq 3.15$ is between 0.2231 and 0.2019, interpolated as 0.2072. This value is the probability of the observed frequencies differing

✳ Karl - Pearson's equation

p = .2072

as much as they have from the expected frequencies, or more, when the null hypothesis is true. This is the p-value for this test. If a prespecified

If α = 0.1

level of significance of 0.10 had been chosen, the test result would not be significant and the null hypothesis of equal preference for the three colors would not be rejected. As with all hypothesis tests, this does not mean that the null hypothesis is true. It is, however, a useful way of providing information about the population, on the basis of the random sample.

As a second example of a chi-square test for goodness of fit, consider a

Ho:

claim made by a manufacturer of a medicine. This claim is that 45 percent of the patients receiving the medication will find their condition is improved, 35 percent will find no change, 15 percent will find a slightly detrimental effect, and 5 percent will find a substantially detrimental effect. A random sample of 200 patients who used the medicine is selected with the following results:

given 200
+82, 75, 39 then 4 has
to recalc. So
ν = 3

82 patients:	condition improved
75 patients:	no change
39 patients:	slightly detrimental effect
4 patients:	substantial detrimental effect

The procedure for testing the manufacturer's claim about the usefulness of this drug has already been illustrated in the previous example. First, compute the expected frequencies for each of the four categories; next, calculate the difference between observed and expected frequencies; square this difference and divide by the expected frequency; and then add the resulting values for the four classes. These calculations are performed in Figure 10.2. From these calculations, Appendix J states that the calculated

p = .061

chi-square value, $x^2 = 7.37$ with three degrees of freedom, has a p-value between 0.0658 and 0.0602, or about 0.0610. The null hypothesis of the manufacturer's claim would not be rejected if α had been prespecified at 0.05, but would be rejected if α had been prespecified at 0.10.

Figure 10.2

Chi-Square Goodness of Test for Medicine Example ($n = 200$)

	Improvement	No Change	Slight Detriment	Substantial Detriment
Hypothesized Proportion...	0.45	0.35	0.15	0.05
Expected Frequencies, f_e....	$200 \times 0.45 = 90$	$200 \times 0.35 = 70$	$200 \times 0.15 = 30$	$200 \times 0.05 = 10$
Observed Frequencies, f_o...	82	75	39	4
$f_o - f_e$..................	-8	5	9	-6
$(f_o - f_e)^2$...............	64	25	81	36
$(f_o - f_e)^2/f_e$.............	0.71	0.36	2.70	3.60

$$x^2 = 0.71 + 0.36 + 2.70 + 3.60 = 7.37$$
$$\text{Degrees of freedom, } \nu = 4 - 1 = 3$$

p > α accept Ho
p < α reject Ho

needs μ_x

10.22   Goodness of Fit for the Poisson Distribution

The previous examples have used a distribution which has been specified by the probabilities for an observation falling into each of several categories. In this section, the same reasoning is applied to testing a hypothesis that a set of observations is from a specific probability model, a Poisson distribution. For this example, consider the alarms received by a fire department of a large city during the first week in August. As discussed in Chapter 5 where the Poisson distribution was introduced, this distribution is often useful for describing the number of occurrences of something which happens "at random." The question to be investigated is whether fire alarms are generated by a Poisson process; that is, does a Poisson distribution adequately describe the number of alarms received during an interval of time?

This particular question is of substantial analytic interest because of a set of tools in management science called *queueing* or *waiting line theory*. Although this text does not describe waiting line theory, many applications of waiting line theory make the assumption that arrivals to a system are adequately described by a Poisson distribution. The chi-square goodness of fit test is one way of investigating this common assumption.

The first week in August is the period of data gathering to investigate the Poisson assumption for the arrival of fire alarms. Since the period from 5 P.M. to 10 P.M. is typically the busiest period for a fire department, and since each hour in this time period has approximately the same work load, this is a reasonable time period for the experiment. This five-hour period is divided into 12-minute intervals. With five intervals in each hour, five hours per day, and five days of data gathering, there are 125 time intervals involved in the experiment. A tally of the number of alarms received in each of these time intervals is shown in Figure 10.3. In this figure, 38 periods had no alarms, 43 periods had one alarm, 29 periods had two alarms, and so on. This figure also shows the total number of alarms received in the entire 25-hour period. There were 150 alarms, an average of six per hour, or an average of 1.20 alarms per 12-minute interval.

To use the chi-square goodness of fit test for this experiment, it is necessary to use the observed frequencies from Figure 10.3, and the expected frequencies calculated from the appropriate Poisson distribution in Appendix F. The appropriate Poisson distribution to use is the Poisson distribution with a mean of 1.20, which is the estimate of the Poisson distribution mean from the sample data.

Figure 10.4 gives the expected frequencies for the chi-square goodness of fit test for the fire alarm data. The first step is to use Appendix F to find the Poisson probabilities for each number of occurrences. Since there are 125 observations, multiplying the sample size, $n = 125$, by the probability for each category gives the expected frequency for each cate-

Figure 10.3

Fire Alarm Data, 12-Minute Periods, 5–10 P.M. Monday–Friday, August 9–13

Number of Alarms in a Time Period, X	Observed Frequency, f_o	(Number of Alarms) × (Frequency)
0...................	38	0
1...................	43	43
2...................	29	58
3...................	13	39
4...................	1	4
5...................	0	0
6...................	1	6
7 or more..........	0	0
	125	150

$$\bar{X} = \frac{150}{125} = 1.20 \text{ per time period} \quad = \frac{\Sigma X f_o}{\Sigma f_o}$$

Figure 10.4

Goodness of Fit Data for Fire Alarm Data

Number of Alarms in a Period, X	Poisson Probabilities $P(X\mid\mu_X = 1.20)$	Expected Frequency, f_e, $125 \cdot P(X\mid\mu_X = 1.20)$
0....................	0.301	37.62
1....................	0.361	45.13
2....................	0.217	27.13
3....................	0.087	10.88
4....................	0.026	3.25 ⎫
5....................	0.006	0.75 ⎬ 4.13
6....................	0.001	0.13 ⎭
7 or more...........	0.000	0.00
	0.9999 (due to rounding)	

gory. Before we can further use these frequencies, it is necessary to describe one important requirement for using the chi-square distribution. The requirement is that the *expected* frequency for *each* category should be at least five. If not, adjacent categories are combined. Slight deviations from this rule are sometimes made with the result that the test is less accurate. Combining the last four categories, 4, 5, 6, and 7 or more alarms into one category results in an expected frequency of 4.13 alarms, which is sufficiently near five for the chi-square distribution to be a useful approximation.

Figure 10.5 gives the calculation of the chi-square statistic for these data. The degrees of freedom for this test is the number of categories, less one, less the number of parameters which have been estimated from the

Figure 10.5

Goodness of Fit Test for Fire Alarm Data

Number of Alarms in a Period, X	Observed Frequency, f_o	Expected Frequency, f_e	$(f_o - f_e)$	$(f_o - f_e)^2$	$\dfrac{(f_o - f_e)^2}{f_e}$
0....................	38	37.62	0.38	0.14	0.004
1....................	43	45.13	−2.13	4.54	0.101
2....................	29	27.13	1.87	3.50	0.129
3....................	13	10.88	2.12	4.49	0.413
4 or more...........	2	4.13	−2.13	4.54	1.099
	$n = 125$	124.89 (rounding)			$\chi^2_{\nu=3} = 1.746$

sample data. Since the sample data were used to estimate the Poisson distribution mean of 1.20, degrees of freedom are:

$$\text{Degrees of freedom} = \nu = 5 - 1 - 1 = 3$$

The chi-square statistic has a value of 1.746. Should the null hypothesis that the population is Poisson distributed be rejected? From Appendix J, observe that about 63 percent of the chi-square distribution is to the right of $\chi^2 = 1.746$. Thus, the p-value is 0.63, which would typically not be small enough to reject the null hypothesis.

10.23   Some Comments on Samples and Populations

In the fire alarm experiment described above, there was no attempt to select randomly a period of time for the observations. It is, therefore, necessary to discuss the interpretation which legitimatizes the use of these data as a random sample. The population about which we are concerned is all possible scenarios of fire alarms that could have occurred during this 25-hour period of interest. There are many fires which could have happened that did not. Random factors prevented some fires and eliminated some alarms during this period of investigation, while other random factors caused some fires and alarms. Hence, the 125 periods may be viewed as a random sample of the large population of potential happenings during that period. It is in this sense that it is considered to be a sample randomly selected from a population.

10.24   Goodness of Fit Test for the Normal Distribution

To use the chi-square test for testing the hypothesis that a sample came from a normal population, no new techniques are needed. To illustrate the test, a random sample of 50 grocery stores is selected by a food processor. For each store, the market share of a new type of potato chip was calculated. The market share is defined as the ounces of the new

Figure 10.6

Market Share Data

[handwritten: cont. variable, so use midpoint]

Market Share X (percent)	Midpoint	Frequency, f_0	$f_0 \cdot$ (Midpoint)	$f_0 \cdot$ (Midpoint)^2
0 < 5.......	2.5	0	0	0
5 < 10.......	7.5	3	22.5	168.75
10 < 15.......	12.5	6	75.0	937.50
15 < 20......	17.5	12	210.0	3,675.00
20 < 25.......	22.5	16	360.0	8,100.00
25 < 30.......	27.5	11	302.5	8,318.75
20 < 35.......	32.5	2	65.0	2,112.50
35 or more.....	67.5	0	0	0
		50	1,035.0	23,312.50

$$\bar{X} = \frac{1,035.0}{50} = 20.70$$

$$s_X = \sqrt{\frac{2,312.5 - \frac{(1035.0)^2}{50}}{49}} = \sqrt{38.53}$$

$$s_X = 6.21$$

brand sold in each store in the previous week, divided by the total number of ounces of potato chips sold by each store, expressed as a percentage. The data which are collected, and the calculation of the sample mean and sample standard deviation, are shown in Figure 10.6.

The test of the hypothesis that the market share (across grocery stores) is normally distributed is shown in Figure 10.7. The procedure is to use the sample statistics $\bar{X}$ and s_X to estimate the parameters μ_X and σ_X of the hypothesized normal distribution. Then the class intervals used in data collection are converted to standardized (Z) values, by subtracting the mean from the upper and lower limits of the interval and dividing by the standard deviation. The probability of that interval is found using the standard normal distribution. Multiplying that probability by the sample size, $n = 50$, gives the expected frequency if the hypothesis of the normal distribution is true. Since some classes have fewer than five expected observations, adjacent classes are combined so that all of the categories (except one) have an expected frequency of 5 or greater. The chi-square statistic is computed, and its value is 1.351. The degrees of freedom are found as in the previous example:

Number of categories − number of parameters estimated − 1
$$= 5 - 2 - 1 = 2$$

From Appendix J for the chi-square distribution, the probability of this value being exceeded when the null hypothesis is true is found to be approximately 0.51; hence, the p-value is 0.51. If a prespecified level of

Figure 10.7
Market Share Data: Goodness of Fit

Prob. of interval (z) = (Expected Rel. freq.)

Expected Rel. freq × Sample size = f_e

Market Share X, percent	Z, Standardized Market Share $\dfrac{X - \bar{X}}{s_X} = \dfrac{X - 20.70}{6.21}$	Expected Relative Frequency	Expected Frequency, f_e	Observed Frequency, f_o	$\dfrac{(f_o - f_e)^2}{f_e}$
0 < 5	< −2.53	0.0057	0.28 ⎫		
5 < 10	−2.53 < −1.72	0.0427 − 0.0057 = 0.0370	1.85 ⎬ 8.93	9	0.001
10 < 15	−1.72 < −0.92	0.1788 − 0.0427 = 0.1361	6.80 ⎭		
15 < 20	−0.92 < −0.11	0.4562 − 0.1788 = 0.2774	13.87	12	0.252
20 < 25	−0.11 < 0.69	1 − 0.4562 − 0.2451 = 0.2987	14.94	16	0.075
25 < 30	0.69 < 1.50	0.2451 − 0.0668 = 0.1783	8.92	11	0.485
30 < 35	1.50 < 2.30	0.0668 − 0.0107 = 0.0561	2.80 ⎫ 3.34	2	0.538
35 or more	> 2.30	0.0107	0.54 ⎭		
		1.0000	50.00	$n = 50$	$\chi^2_{\nu=2} = 1.351$

significance had been, say, $\alpha = 0.10$, the null hypothesis would not be rejected, as the p-value is not sufficiently small.

10.3 ANALYSIS OF ENUMERATION DATA

The independence of two factors was discussed in Chapter 4 on probability theory. Two events (or variables) are independent if the occurrence of one event (variable) does not affect the probability of the occurrence of the other event (variable). If the entire population is known, it is very easy to ascertain whether two variables are independent of each other. When only a sample is available from that population, inferences about independence are in order.

10.31 Test of Independence: Contingency Tables

For the first example of a test of independence, consider a situation faced by a personnel department which is being criticized for advertising job openings only in female-oriented publications. To justify this procedure, the personnel manager is interested in investigating whether passing or failing the preemployment screening tests depends on the sex of the applicant. Company records are randomly sampled for 100 applicants for a particular job opening. Forty men had applied, of which four passed and 36 failed the preemployment screening procedures. Of the 60 women applicants, 26 passed and 34 failed. The hypothesis to be tested is that the variable "pass/fail" is independent of the sex of the applicant. The data are summarized in Figure 10.8, which is called a *contingency table*. It shows an enumeration of pass and fail, contingent upon the sex of the

Figure 10.8
Contingency Table for Employment Data

Sex	Preemployment Test		Total
	Pass	*Fail*	*Total*
Male................	4	36	40
Female..............	26	34	60
	30	70	100

$$\text{Estimates: } P(\text{Pass}) = \frac{30}{100} = 0.3$$

$$P(\text{Fail}) = \frac{70}{100} = \frac{0.7}{1.0}$$

$$P(\text{Male}) = \frac{40}{100} = 0.4$$

$$P(\text{Female}) = \frac{60}{100} = \frac{0.6}{1.0}$$

Exp. freq. = Joint Prob. × sample size (in this example 100)

Figure 10.9

Contingency Table for Employment Data with Observed and Expected Frequencies

| | Preemployment Test | | | | |
| | Pass | | Fail | | |
Sex	Observed Frequency	Expected Frequency	Observed Frequency	Expected Frequency	Total
Male.............	4	12	36	28	40
Female............	26	18	34	42	60
	30	30	70	70	$n = 100$

$$\chi^2 = \frac{(4 - 12)^2}{12} + \frac{(36 - 28)^2}{28} + \frac{(26 - 18)^2}{18} + \frac{(34 - 42)^2}{42} = 12.70$$

applicant. This table also shows an estimate that a randomly selected applicant will pass, the probability that a randomly selected applicant will fail, the probability that a randomly selected applicant is male, and the probability that a randomly selected applicant is female.

If it is true that the preemployment test outcome and sex are independent, then it is easy to estimate the probability that a randomly selected applicant is both male and will pass:

assume indep. + find Joint

$$P(\text{Male} \cap \text{Pass}) = P(\text{Male}) \cdot P(\text{Pass}) = (0.4)(0.3) = 0.12$$

Similarly,

$$P(\text{Male} \cap \text{Fail}) = P(\text{Male}) \cdot P(\text{Fail}) = (0.4)(0.7) = 0.28$$
$$P(\text{Female} \cap \text{Pass}) = P(\text{Female}) \cdot P(\text{Pass}) = (0.6)(0.3) = 0.18$$
$$P(\text{Female} \cap \text{Fail}) = P(\text{Female}) \cdot P(\text{Fail}) = (0.6)(0.7) = 0.42$$

It should be noted that each of these probabilities is based on the hypothesis of independence. If independence does not hold true, these probabilities are, of course, poor estimates of the joint probabilities for each individual category.

The next step is to convert these joint probabilities, based on the hypothesis of independence, into expected frequencies. This is accomplished by multiplying these joint probabilities by the sample size. For example, one would expect to find $0.12 \times 100 = 12$ men passing the test, if the two factors are independent. These expected frequencies are shown in Figure 10.9, along with the observed frequencies. Now that the observed and expected frequencies for each category are available, it is simple to calculate the chi square statistic. As before, it is the square of the difference between observed and expected frequencies, divided by the expected frequency, and summed for the four categories. These calculations are also shown in

Figure 10.9. The degrees of freedom for this statistic is one for this problem. In general, it is:

In each Pass/fail

$$\nu = (\text{Number of rows} - 1) \cdot (\text{Number of columns} - 1)$$

Note that this is the same as the number of categories, less the number of parameters estimated, less one. Two parameters were estimated: the probability of male and the probability of pass. (It was not necessary to estimate the probability of female or fail, because these are determined once the probability of male and the probability of pass are estimated.) Since there are four categories and two estimated parameters, there is $4 - 2 -$

Figure 10.10

Data for Grocery Profitability Example

Profitability	Majority	Mixed	Minority	Total
	Ethnic Composition			
High..........	43	4	3	50
Medium........	55	17	8	80
Low...........	20	10	10	40
Loss..........	12	9	9	30
	130	40	30	$n = 200$

Estimates: $P(\text{High}) = \dfrac{50}{200} = 0.25$ $\qquad P(\text{Majority}) = \dfrac{130}{200} = 0.65$

$P(\text{Medium}) = \dfrac{80}{200} = 0.40$ $\qquad P(\text{Mixed}) = \dfrac{40}{200} = 0.20$

$P(\text{Low}) = \dfrac{40}{200} = 0.20$ $\qquad P(\text{Minority}) = \dfrac{30}{200} = \dfrac{0.15}{1.00}$

$P(\text{Loss}) = \dfrac{30}{200} = \dfrac{0.15}{1.00}$

$1 = 1$ degrees of freedom. From Appendix J for the chi-square distribution, the p-value for this test is between 0.0003 and 0.0004; the null hypothesis would be rejected for any α larger than this. Perhaps the personnel manager should use this as defense for advertising only in female oriented publications.

This chi-square test of independence for enumeration data can of course be applied to larger contingency tables. As an example, consider the data of Figure 10.10, in which the profitability, measured as a percentage of sales volume, is cross classified against the ethnic composition of the neighborhood in which the store is located for 200 stores in a large grocery chain. The management is investigating the hypothesis that profitability is independent of the ethnic composition of the neighborhood.

The first step in testing this hypothesis of independence is to estimate the expected frequency for each combination. To estimate the expected

Figure 10.11

Observed and Expected Frequencies for Grocery Profitability Example

Profitability	Majority		Ethnic Composition Mixed		Minority	
	Observed Frequency	Expected Frequency	Observed Frequency	Expected Frequency	Observed Frequency	Expected Frequency
High.	43	32.5	4	10	3	7.5
Medium.	55	52	17	16	8	12
Low.	20	26	10	8	10	6
Loss.	12	19.5	9	6	9	4.5
	130	130	40	40	30	30

(12 combinations)

$$\chi^2 = \frac{(43 - 32.5)^2}{32.5} + \frac{(4 - 10)^2}{10} + \cdots + \frac{(9 - 4.5)^2}{4.5} = 24.7$$

P(High ∩ Majority) = (0.25)(0.65) = 0.1625
P(High ∩ Mixed) = (0.25)(0.20) = 0.0500
P(High ∩ Minority) = (0.25)(0.15) = 0.0375

P(Medium ∩ Majority) = (0.40)(0.65) = 0.2600
P(Medium ∩ Mixed) = (0.40)(0.20) = 0.0800
P(Medium ∩ Minority) = (0.40)(0.15) = 0.0600

P(Low ∩ Majority) = (0.20)(0.65) = 0.1300
P(Low ∩ Mixed) = (0.20)(0.20) = 0.0400
P(Low ∩ Minority) = (0.20)(0.15) = 0.0300

P(Loss ∩ Majority) = (0.15)(0.65) = 0.0975
P(Loss ∩ Mixed) = (0.15)(0.20) = 0.0300
P(Loss ∩ Minority) = (0.15)(0.15) = 0.0225

P(High)	= 0.25
P(Medium)	= 0.40
P(Low)	= 0.20
P(Loss)	= 0.15
	1.00

P(Majority)	= 0.65
P(Mixed)	= 0.20
P(Minority)	= 0.15
	1.00

frequency for the combination of high profitability and majority neighborhood:

$$P(\text{High} \cap \text{Majority}) = P(\text{High}) \cdot P(\text{Majority}) = (0.25)(0.65) = 0.1625,$$

the expected frequency of (High $\cap$ Majority) $= 200 \times 0.1625 = 32.5$.

Continuing the test concerning the hypothesis of independence, the expected frequencies are shown in Figure 10.11. Note that the smallest expected frequency is 4.5; this is sufficiently close to the rule of thumb that all expected frequencies should be at least five for the chi-square test to be useful. The calculated value of the chi-square statistic is 24.7, which is obtained by using the data from each of the 12 combinations. The degrees of freedom for this statistic is $(4-1) \times (3-1) = 6$. From Appendix J for the chi-square distribution, the p-value is less than 0.0028.

Again, a conceptual discussion of whether these data for the grocery store example constitute a sample or a population is appropriate. If management is interested only in the existing stores for a year for which the data are obtained, this is a population of all results for this particular chain. In that case, a test of significance is of no value, because one would be dealing with a population rather than a sample. But if management is interested in all years in which the general economic condition is similar to the year in which the observations are made, they can assume that other factors which are essentially random in nature generate the observations on profitability for each store. One is then justified in saying that this set of 200 observations constitutes a random sample for all years similar to the year of data gathering, and one can proceed to make inferences about the independence of profitability and ethnic composition.

10.32 Did Several Samples Come from the Same Population: A Test of Homogeneity

In the example of grocery store profitability, cross classified against ethnic composition of the neighborhood, the hypothesis was tested that profitability and ethnic composition are independent. The data were viewed as 200 observations from one population with two factors. The data could have been viewed in a somewhat different fashion; one could have had a sample of 130 observations of stores in a majority neighborhood, a second sample of 40 observations of stores in mixed neighborhoods, and a third sample of 30 observations of stores in minority neighborhoods. There would then have been three groups of stores and each group could be considered a separate population. One would then be interested in testing the hypothesis that the three populations are identical, or are in reality one (homogeneous) population. This is called a *test of homogeneity*. The statistical term for identical populations is *homoge-*

neous; if several populations are said to be homogeneous, that is statistical terminology for saying that they are the same. Computationally, a test of this hypothesis of homogeneity is the same as the test of independence already accomplished.

To illustrate this type of test, consider the question concerning the grades received by students at two universities. The question is whether grades are really different at the two schools; i.e., are they from two different populations, or are they homogeneous and from one population?

Test

Ho:

To test this hypothesis a random sample of grades is taken from each university. The sample results are given in Figure 10.12.

Figure 10.12

Sample Results of Student Grades from Two Universities

Grades	University 1	University 2	Total
A................	15	10	25
B................	25	15	40
C................	50	60	110
D................	5	10	15
F................	5	5	10
	$n_1 = 100$	$n_2 = 100$	200

P(GRADE)
25/200
40/200
110/200
15/200
10/200

$$P(1) = \frac{100}{200} \qquad P(2) = \frac{100}{200}$$

Just as in the testing of independence, the first step is to estimate the expected frequencies for each combination. These expected frequencies are shown, along with calculations, in Figure 10.13.

The χ^2 statistic is calculated using the same procedure as used for the test of independence. Its value is 6.06, and the degrees of freedom are $(5-1) \times (2-1) = 4$. From Appendix J for the chi-square distribution, the *p*-value is between 0.1991 and 0.1847, or about 0.195. If a prespecified α level had been set at 0.05, one would accept the hypothesis that the samples came from the same population. If α had been set at 0.20, one would reject.

p = .195
α = .05
Ho: accept
if α = 0.2
reject

There is a slight difference in the test of independence and the test of homogeneity; that difference is the manner in which the sample is selected. If the test is thought of as a test for homogeneity, there are several "urns" or populations, from which the observations are drawn. The number of observations coming from each urn is controlled by the experimenter. In the test of independence, all observations are drawn from one urn. The experimenter does not control either the row totals or the column totals; these are random variables in a test for independence. This difference is not of particular importance, because the calculations are identical for either situation.

difference

Figure 10.13

Observed and Expected Frequencies for University Grades Example

	University 1		University 2	
Grades	Observed Frequency	Expected Frequency	Observed Frequency	Expected Frequency
A...............	15	12.5	10	12.5
B...............	25	20.0	15	20.0
C...............	50	55.0	60	55.0
D...............	5	7.5	10	7.5
F...............	5	5.0	5	5.0
	100	100.0	100	100.0

Expected Frequencies: _Joint_ $P(A \cap 1) = P(A) \cdot P(1)$ _Joint_ $P(A \cap 2) = P(A) \cdot P(2)$

$(A \cap 1) = \frac{25}{200} \times \frac{100}{200} \times 200 = 12.5$ $(A \cap 2) = \frac{25}{200} \times \frac{100}{200} \times 200 = 12.5$

$(B \cap 1) = \frac{40}{200} \times \frac{100}{200} \times 200 = 20.0$ $(B \cap 2) = \frac{40}{200} \times \frac{100}{200} \times 200 = 20.0$

$(C \cap 1) = \frac{110}{200} \times \frac{100}{200} \times 200 = 55.0$ $(C \cap 2) = \frac{110}{200} \times \frac{100}{200} \times 200 = 55.0$

$(D \cap 1) = \frac{15}{200} \times \frac{100}{200} \times 200 = 7.5$ $(D \cap 2) = \frac{15}{200} \times \frac{100}{200} \times 200 = 7.5$

$(F \cap 1) = \frac{10}{200} \times \frac{100}{200} \times 200 = 5.0$ $(F \cap 2) = \frac{10}{200} \times \frac{100}{200} \times 200 = 5.0$

$$\chi^2 = \frac{(15 - 12.5)^2}{12.5} + \frac{(25 - 20.0)^2}{20} + \frac{(50 - 55.0)^2}{55} + \frac{(5 - 7.5)^2}{7.5}$$

$$+ \frac{(5 - 5.0)^2}{5} + \frac{(10 - 12.5)^2}{12.5} + \frac{(15 - 20.0)^2}{20} + \frac{(60 - 55.0)^2}{55}$$

$$+ \frac{(10 - 7.5)^2}{7.5} + \frac{(5 - 5.0)^2}{5} = 0.50 + 1.25 + 0.45 + 0.83 + 0 + 0.50 + 1.25 + 0.45$$

$$+ 0.83 + 0 = 6.06$$

10.33   Hypotheses about the Equality of Two Population Proportions

Test for. Homogeneity

It is often useful to test hypotheses about the equality of two binomial population proportions. Although this hypothesis could have been introduced in Chapter 9 using the normal approximation to the binomial distribution, a test equivalent to that procedure may be accomplished in a simpler manner by using the chi-square distribution. This test is a test of homogeneity, which can be illustrated with an example.

A stock broker is investigating the effectiveness of two different procedures for securing new customers. In procedure A, a prospective customer was given an opportunity to have an analysis of an existing portfolio, while in procedure B a prospective customer was given an opportunity to

Figure 10.14

[handwritten] H_0: Two proportions are equal
H_a: " " " are not equal.

Test of Homogeneity: Equality of Two Population Proportions

Procedure \ Resulting Customer	Profitable	Not Profitable	Totals
A	34	166	200
B	73	227	300
Totals	107	393	500

Expected frequencies:

$$(\text{Profitable} \cap A) = \frac{107}{500} \cdot \frac{200}{500} \cdot 500 = 42.8$$

$$(\text{Profitable} \cap B) = \frac{107}{500} \cdot \frac{300}{500} \cdot 500 = 64.2$$

[handwritten] $\nu = (\text{column} - 1)(\text{rows} - 1)$
$= (2-1)(2-1)$
$= 1 \times 1 = 1$

$$(\text{Not Profitable} \cap A) = \frac{393}{500} \cdot \frac{200}{500} \cdot 500 = 157.2$$

$$(\text{Not Profitable} \cap B) = \frac{393}{500} \cdot \frac{300}{500} \cdot 500 = 235.8$$

$$\chi^2_{\nu=1} = \frac{(34 - 42.8)^2}{42.8} + \frac{(166 - 157.2)^2}{157.2} + \frac{(73 - 64.2)^2}{64.2} + \frac{(227 - 235.8)^2}{235.8}$$

$$\chi^2_{\nu=1} = 3.84$$

p-value is between 0.0513 and 0.0455, or about 0.0501

receive an extensive report about three securities of interest to the prospect. A simple random sample of 200 prospects from procedure A shows 34 have become profitable customers. A simple random sample of Procedure B prospects shows 73 of 300 prospects have become profitable customers. Is the proportion of prospects who have become profitable customers the same for each procedure? The test of homogeneity for this example is shown in Figure 10.14. With the p-value at 0.0501, the null hypothesis that the two proportions are equal will be rejected if α has been specified at, say, 0.10.

[handwritten] Rule of Thumb: for χ^2 test to be useful, expected freq. should be at least five.

10.4 SUMMARY

This chapter has considered statistical inferences for goodness of fit, independence, and homogeneity. As with any statistical hypothesis tests, the information from these tests is useful for conveying information about the results of the test from one person to another. One can never "prove" or "disprove" anything with these tests. One can only calculate the p-value, or the conditional probability of obtaining a particular sample

[handwritten] $\alpha > p$ reject H_0

[handwritten] $\alpha < p$ accept H_0

result, given the condition that the null hypothesis is true. If one obtains a "high" probability for this value, one tends to believe the null hypothesis; if a "low" probability value is obtained, one tends to doubt the hypothesis. By stating the p-value, it is possible to convey meaningful information about an experiment to a person who is conversant with statistical inference and has use for the information obtained in these analyses.

EXERCISES

* 10.1 A coin is flipped 100 times, resulting in 40 heads. Test the hypothesis that the coin is fair, and report the p-value for the test. Use a chi-square goodness of fit test.

* 10.2 For the coin experiment described in Problem 10.1, use the normal approximation to the binomial distribution to test the hypothesis that the coin is fair. Compare your results with the results in Exercise 10.1.

* 10.3 Extensive studies made several years ago indicated that three different methods of inventory evaluation were used by the following proportion of firms in the industry: Method A, 45 percent; Method B, 30 percent; Method C, 25 percent. To investigate whether this relationship still holds true, an accountant takes a random sample of 75 companies and ascertains their method of inventory evaluation. The results are: Method A, 39; Method B, 26; Method C, 10. Test the hypothesis that the proportion of firms using each method of inventory evaluation is the same as it was in the earlier studies. Find the p-value and explain its meaning.

  10.4 For the situation of Exercise 10.3, suppose the p-value can be shown to be 0.02. The accountant is attempting to formulate a statement to use in reporting the results of the experiment. Several possible statements are listed below. Comment on whether each of these statements is correct, and provide a correct statement if none of the statements is correct.
  a. There is a 0.02 probability that the proportion of inventory evaluation methods is the same as previously reported.
  b. There is a 0.98 probability that the proportion of inventory evaluation methods is the same as previously reported.
  c. The p-value, 0.02, is less than 0.05, which everybody knows is the correct level of significance. I know I am correct when I reject the hypothesis that the methods of inventory evaluation are the same as previously reported.

* 10.5 Many states have regulations describing the way in which public utilities (companies selling gas, electricity, communication services, etc.) may sell bonds. In some states, firms are required to use what is

---

* Answers to exercises marked with an asterisk (*) are in Appendix L.

called "competitive bidding" to select the underwriter for the bonds. Other states permit, under certain circumstances, the utility to sell bonds either with competitive bidding or with a "negotiated" placement. It has been hypothesized that, given a choice, a public utility company will always use the negotiated placement. To test this hypothesis, the year 1972 is selected. Some states which permitted a choice in the manner of selling bonds are also selected. In each case selected, the utility had a choice in the manner in which it placed the offering of bonds in 1972. For this year and these states, there were 14 competitive offerings, and 39 negotiated offerings.

a. What statistical inferences are appropriate in this case?

b. Suppose the hypothesis is that 80 percent of the firms will choose negotiated placement. For this situation, what statistical inferences may be made about the year 1972 and the states studied?

10.6 Go to the table of random numbers in the appendices and choose a random starting point. Then select the next 100 digits in the table. Keep track of the number of 0s, 1s, 2s, . . . , 9s. Perform a chi-square goodness of fit test for the randomness of these digits, using a level of significance, $\alpha = 0.10$. What does it mean if you reject the hypothesis? If 100 students perform this exercise, does it surprise you if about ten students report that the table of random numbers is not random?

* 10.7 A university switchboard keeps track of the number of telephone calls received between 10:00 AM and 10:10 AM, by each minute during that interval, for each of five days during a week. The results are:

Number of Calls in a Minute	f_o Frequency	hf
0	1	0
1	1 $\Big\} = 6$	1
2	4	8
3	8	24
4	8	32
5	11	36
6	6	21
7	3	12
8	4	18
9	2	0
10	0	11
11	1	12
12	1	
13 or more	0	0
	50	250

$\bar{X} = \frac{250}{50} = 5$

Use a chi-square goodness of fit test to report the p-value for the hypothesis that the Poisson distribution describes the arrival of telephone calls at the switchboard. Remember to group numbers of calls so that the expected frequency is at least five for each grouping.

* 10.8 For the telephone call experiment, the length of each of the 250 calls is also measured. The data are:

Call Length, Minutes	Frequency
0 < 1	80
1 < 2	56
2 < 3	42
3 < 4	30
4 < 5	21
5 < 6	7
6 < 7	5
7 < 8	3
8 < 9	0
9 < 10	3
10 < 11	2
11 < 12	1
12 or longer	0
	250

A misguided statistician hypothesizes that the length of telephone calls is described by the normal distribution. Use the chi-square goodness of fit test to test this hypothesis at the one percent level of significance.

* 10.9 Test the hypothesis that weight and income are independent, and report the p-value:

	Overweight	Not Overweight
High Income	200	100
Low or Average Income	100	100

The numbers in the cells represent the number of people, randomly selected from the population, who fall into each of the four categories.

* 10.10 A mail order firm keeps track of the orders it receives from three geographical regions: East, West, and Midwest. For each region, the number of customers ordering size small, size medium, and size large was observed. The data are:

	Size		
Region	Small	Medium	Large
East	80	160	100
West	60	140	100
Midwest	40	100	60

Test the hypothesis that size and region are independent. Use a level of significance, $\alpha = 0.10$.

* 10.11 Take the data from Exercise 10.10, and divide each combination count by four. Use the new data matrix to test the hypothesis of independence between region and size. How can you account for the difference in p-value obtained in these two experiments, when the sample proportions are identical?

* 10.12 A random sample of 100 men and 100 women were interrogated to find their views on presidential impeachment. Of the men, 30 percent favored, 40 percent opposed, and 30 percent were undecided. Of the women, 40 percent favored, 36 percent opposed, and 24 percent were

independence Test

undecided. Regarding impeachment, is there a significant difference in the opinions of men and women? Let $\alpha = 0.05$.

* 10.13   A statistics class was permitted to use electronic calculators on an exam. The exam grades, contingent upon calculator usage were:

	A	B	C	D or F
Used calculator..................	30	70	20	10
No calculator....................	18	38	8	4

a. Is grade independent of calculator use?

b. If you reject the hypothesis of independence and observe the data, it appears that the nonusers got higher grades. Does this mean the users should become nonusers to improve their grades? Discuss.

* 10.14   In a double-blind study of the effects of medication, neither the patient nor the physician knows whether a particular patient is receiving the medication being studied or a *placebo,* which is a "fake" inert substance that looks like the real thing. In a test of new medication using a double-blind study and a placebo, these results were observed:

	Condition		
Medication	Improved	Unchanged	Deteriorated
Real....................	37	16	10
Placebo................	29	29	5

Note that a substantial number of patients improved while receiving the placebo. This is due to many factors not controlled by the researchers. These factors might include weather, smog index, elapsed time, mental attitude, etc. What is the p-value for the test of the hypothesis that the two "medications" are equally effective?

* 10.15   The students enrolled in a MBA program were cross-classified by age and grade point:

do this

	Age		
Grade Point	24 and Under	25–27	Over 27
Under 3.0.................	6	9	5
3.0 < 3.5.................	18	19	8
3.5 ≤ 4.0.................	11	12	17

a. Viewing these data as a population (all students are included), what statistical inferences are in order?

b. Viewing the students actually enrolled as a random sample of all potential enrollees, test the hypothesis that age and grade point are independent.

REFERENCES

Cochran, W. G. "Some Methods for Strengthening the Common Chi-Square Tests," *Biometrics,* vol. 10 (1954), pp. 417–451.

Cochran, W. G. "The χ^2 Test of Goodness of Fit," *Annals of Mathematical Statistics,* vol. 23 (1952), pp. 315–345.

Richmond, S. B. *Statistical Analysis,* 2d ed. New York: Ronald Press, 1964.

Siegel, S. *Nonparametric Statistics.* New York: McGraw-Hill Book Co., Inc., 1956.

11

Analysis of Variance

equality of more than two pop. mean (handwritten)

Chapter 9 presented methods of testing hypotheses concerning the equality of the means of two populations. But questions involving the equality of population means need not be limited to just two populations. In order to address the larger field of the equality of more than two population means, this chapter introduces procedures generally called *analysis of variance.* More specifically, this chapter deals with one-factor analysis of variance.

11.1 EXCELLENT HEALTH FOOD COMPANY EXAMPLE

The owner of Excellent Health Food Company has three salespersons who sell to retail health food stores. The owner is interested in one factor, which is whether there is a difference in the average sales of the three salespersons. (A second factor, beyond the scope of this chapter, might be the season of the year.) A simple random sample of sales for each of four weeks (from the past two years) is selected for each salesperson. Since it is necessary for the observations for each salesperson to be selected independently of the other sample selections, a table of random numbers is used to simulate the following process: for each salesperson, the past two years of weekly sales are written on slips of paper, folded, and placed in three urns, one for each salesperson. Then four slips of paper are withdrawn from each urn, giving four observations for each salesperson. The data are shown in Figure 11.1.

Figure 11.1 *sample observations, random, independent* (handwritten)
Weekly Sales, Randomly Selected (in $1,000)

Observation	$j = 1$ Salesperson A	$j = 2$ Salesperson B	$j = 3$ Salesperson C
$i = 1$	9	5	16
$i = 2$	8	10	12
$i = 3$	7	9	14
$i = 4$	12	8	10

sample size $i = n$ (handwritten)

231

In Figure 11.1 the rows are denoted with the values $i = 1,2,3, \ldots n$, where n is the sample size for each salesperson. The columns are denoted with the values, $j = 1,2$, and 3, which represent the three salespersons. Thus, any sales value in Figure 11.1 can be located and described by the symbol, X_{ij}. Hence, the value of observation X_{32} (third observation, second salesperson) is 9. The data from Figure 11.1 are summarized as follows:

Average Sales for salesperson A:

$$\bar{X}_1 = \frac{\sum_{i=1}^{n} X_{i1}}{n} = \frac{9 + 8 + 7 + 12}{4} = \frac{36}{4} = 9$$

Variance of Sales for salesperson A:

$$s_1^2 = \frac{\sum_{i=1}^{n} (X_{i1} - \bar{X}_1)^2}{n-1} = \frac{(9-9)^2 + (8-9)^2 + (7-9)^2 + (12-9)^2}{4-1}$$
$$= \frac{0 + 1 + 4 + 9}{3} = \frac{14}{3} = 4.667$$

Average Sales for salesperson B:

$$\bar{X}_2 = \frac{\sum_{i=1}^{n} X_{i2}}{n} = \frac{5 + 10 + 9 + 8}{4} = \frac{32}{4} = 8$$

Variance of Sales for salesperson B:

$$s_2^2 = \frac{\sum_{i=1}^{n} (X_{i2} - \bar{X}_2)^2}{n-1} = \frac{(5-8)^2 + (10-8)^2 + (9-8)^2 + (8-8)^2}{4-1}$$
$$= \frac{9 + 4 + 1 + 0}{3} = \frac{14}{3} = 4.667$$

Average Sales for salesperson C:

$$\bar{X}_3 = \frac{\sum_{i=1}^{n} X_{i3}}{n} = \frac{16 + 12 + 14 + 10}{4} = \frac{52}{4} = 13$$

Variance of Sales for salesperson C:

$$s_3^2 = \frac{\sum_{i=1}^{n} (X_{i3} - \bar{X}_3)^2}{n-1} = \frac{(16-13)^2 + (12-13)^2 + (14-13)^2 + (10-13)^2}{4-1}$$

$$= \frac{9+1+1+9}{3} = \frac{20}{3} = 6.667$$

The overall mean for all weekly sales is given the symbol $\bar{\bar{X}}$:

$$\bar{\bar{X}} = \frac{\sum_{j=1}^{c} \sum_{i=1}^{n} X_{ij}}{nC}$$

$$= \frac{9+8+7+12+5+10+9+8+16+12+14+10}{4(3)} = \frac{120}{12} = 10$$

The symbol C has been used to note the number of columns (or salespersons), and nC is the total number of observations.

11.11 Null Hypothesis for Analysis of Variance

The owner of the company could judgmentally decide whether the sample means, 9, 8, and 13, are far enough apart to conclude there is a difference in the means of the populations of weekly sales for the three salespersons. However, the problem can also be approached statistically by hypothesizing:

$$H_N: \quad \mu_1 = \mu_2 = \mu_3$$

with the alternate:

$$H_A: \quad \text{Not all population means are equal} \quad \text{or at least one } \mu_{ij} \text{ is different}$$

11.12 Assumptions for Analysis of Variance

The procedure called *analysis of variance* (ANOVA) may be used to test this hypothesis of equality of population means when the following assumptions are met:

1. For each of the C columns (or *levels* of the *factor* being investigated), a simple random sample of size n is selected. In this example, there is one factor being investigated—salesperson. That factor has three levels (there are three salespersons). For more advanced work, the sample size need not be the same for each level.
2. The C populations from which the samples are selected are normally distributed.

3. The variance (or standard deviation) of each of the C populations is identical. Symbolically, this assumption is that $\sigma_1^2 = \sigma_2^2 = \ldots = \sigma_C^2$. Call this common variance σ^2.
4. Each of the C samples is independent of the other samples.

In terms of the Excellent Health Foods Company, the assumptions suggest that three populations exist. These are the populations of weekly sales for the three salespersons. The assumptions further require that each population have a normal distribution, and that all three populations have the same variance. A simple random sample has been selected from each of the three, as reported in Figure 11–1. Further, these samples must be independent of each other. The samples would *not* be independent of each other if, for example, the four weeks had been randomly selected and then these same four weeks had been used for all three salespersons.

$H_N = True$
The null hypothesis is that all three of these populations have the same mean. If the null hypothesis is true, then there is only *one* statistically identifiable population, because the three populations are identical in shape (normal) and parameters (μ and σ^2). If H_N is not true, then there

$H_N = false$
are several different populations.   *false*

11.13   Rationale for ANOVA

The rationale for analysis of variance requires two methods of estimating the variance, σ^2.

Method 1:   Whether H_N is true or false, there are now three unbiased point estimates of σ^2; these were calculated earlier in section 11.1:

$$s_1^2 = 4.667$$
$$s_2^2 = 4.667$$
$$s_3^2 = 6.667$$

These three estimates may be averaged (or pooled) to obtain one better estimate. This estimate is:

$$\frac{s_1^2 + s_2^2 + s_3^2}{3} = \frac{4.667 + 4.667 + 6.667}{3} = 5.333$$

Within
This can also be written generally as:

$$\frac{\sum_{j=1}^{c} [s_j^2]}{C} = \frac{\sum_{j=1}^{c} \left[\frac{\sum_{j=1}^{n}(X_{ij} - \bar{X}_j)^2}{n-1} \right]}{C} = \frac{\sum_{j=1}^{c} \sum_{i=1}^{n}(X_{ij} - \bar{X}_j)^2}{C(n-1)} = \frac{\sum_{j=1}^{c} s_j^2}{C}$$

This estimate is derived from the variation within each column, and is the *within-column* estimate of σ^2.

Method 2: If (and only if) H_N is true, one may view $\bar{X}_1$, $\bar{X}_2$ and $\bar{X}_3$ as three independent observations (with mean $\bar{\bar{X}}$) from the sampling distribution of $\bar{X}$ values for the combined population. From estimation procedures (Chapter 8) an unbiased estimator of $\sigma_{\bar{X}}^2$ is

$$\sigma_{\bar{X}}^2 = \frac{(\bar{X}_1 - \bar{\bar{X}})^2 + (\bar{X}_2 - \bar{\bar{X}})^2 + (\bar{X}_3 - \bar{\bar{X}})^2}{3 - 1}$$

BETWEEN
only if H_N True

But from sampling theory,

$$\sigma_{\bar{X}}^2 = \frac{\sigma^2}{n}$$

Each $\bar{X}$ is based on $n = 4$; hence, the variance of the three $\bar{X}$ observations

$$\frac{(\bar{X}_1 - \bar{\bar{X}})^2 + (\bar{X}_2 - \bar{\bar{X}})^2 + (\bar{X}_3 - \bar{\bar{X}})^2}{3 - 1} \text{ estimates } \frac{\sigma^2}{n} = \frac{\sigma^2}{4}$$

Numerically, this is

$$\frac{(9 - 10)^2 + (8 - 10)^2 + (13 - 10)^2}{3 - 1} = \frac{1 + 4 + 9}{2} = \frac{14}{2} = 7$$

which estimates $\sigma^2/4$. Thus, $7 \times 4 = 28$ is an estimate of σ^2. This estimate of σ^2 is based on the variation *between* the columns, or the variation *between* the three $\bar{X}$ values. Hence, if H_N is true, then 28 is a "between-columns" estimate of σ^2.

In more general terms, this between-columns estimate can be written:

$$\frac{(\bar{X}_1 - \bar{\bar{X}})^2 + (\bar{X}_2 - \bar{\bar{X}})^2 + (\bar{X}_3 - \bar{\bar{X}})^2}{C - 1}$$

estimates σ^2/n, or

$$n\frac{[(\bar{X}_1 - \bar{\bar{X}})^2 + (\bar{X}_2 - \bar{\bar{X}})^2 + (\bar{X}_3 - \bar{\bar{X}})^2]}{C - 1} = \frac{n\sum_{j=1}^{c}(\bar{X}_j - \bar{\bar{X}})^2}{C - 1}$$

estimates σ^2.

Methods 1 and 2 should give similar values if H_N is true. (Recall Method 2 works *only* if H_N is true.) The ratio of the between-columns estimate to the within-columns estimate should be near one if H_N is true. When H_N is not true, the within-columns term still estimates σ^2, but the between-columns term tends to be larger than σ^2. This happens because the $\bar{X}$ values are "spread out" if H_N is not true, because then the values of μ_1, μ_2, and μ_3 are also spread out. Hence, if H_N is false, the ratio of the two estimates is expected to be greater than one. This ratio is given the symbol F. Numerically,

$$F = \frac{\text{Between}}{\text{Within}} = \frac{28}{5.333} = 5.25$$

> 1 so H_0 is false

In general, this ratio is:

(handwritten, left margin)
$$\frac{n\sum_{j=1}^{c}\left(\bar{X}_i - \bar{\bar{X}}\right)^2 / v_1}{(n-1)\sum_{j=1}^{c} S_{jc}^2 / v_2}$$

(handwritten top right) v_1, degree of freed

$$F = \frac{n\sum_{j=1}^{c}(\bar{X}_i - \bar{\bar{X}})^2/(C-1)}{\sum_{j=1}^{c}\sum_{i=1}^{n}(X_{ij} - \bar{X}_i)^2/[C(n-1)]}$$

(handwritten, pointing to numerator) v_1
(handwritten, pointing to denominator) v_2 degree of freedoms

When H_N is true, this ratio is distributed according to what is called the *F* distribution.

11.2 *F* DISTRIBUTION   *Appendix K*

(handwritten, left margin) v_1
(handwritten, left margin) v_2

The *F* distribution has two parameters v_1 and v_2. These parameters are v_1, the degrees of freedom in the numerator, and v_2, the degrees of freedom in the denominator.

For every different pair of v_1 and v_2 there is a different *F* distribution. A comparison of several *F* distributions is shown in Figure 11.2.

The reader will note that for small values of v_1 and v_2, the *F* distribution is quite skewed to the right, and approaches normality as v_1 and v_2 increase.

Appendix K lists right-tail cumulative probabilities for various *F* distributions. A listing of values for several *F* distributions will facilitate use

Figure 11.2

F Distribution Curves (v_1, v_2)

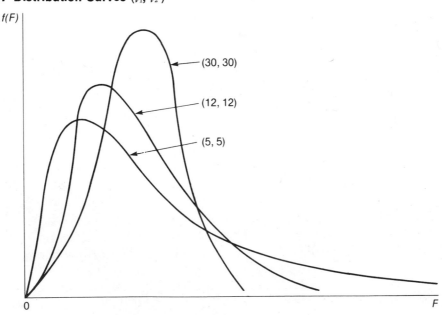

f(F)

(30, 30)
(12, 12)
(5, 5)

0   F

Degrees of Freedom	F	Right-Tail Probability
2,2	1.0	0.500
	5.0	0.167
	10.0	0.091
2,5	1.0	0.431
	5.0	0.064
	10.0	0.018
2,9	1.0	0.405
	5.0	0.035
	10.0	0.005
5,5	1.0	0.500
	5.0	0.051
	10.0	0.012

of the table; the reader should verify each of these values from Appendix K.

11.3   TEST OF THE HYPOTHESIS

The *p*-value for the hypothesis of equality of means is the area from the table of the F distribution to the right of the sample F statistic, which has a value of 5.25 for the example. The appropriate F table is determined by the values of v_1 and v_2. For problems of the type being discussed,

$$v_1 = C-1$$

and

$$v_2 = C(n-1)$$

As with any other hypothesis test, a prespecified α may be used. The procedure is:

> Do not reject H_N if *p*-value $> \alpha$
> Reject H_N if *p*-value $< \alpha$

As stated before the hypotheses are:

> H_N: $\mu_1 = \mu_2 = \mu_3$
> H_A: The null hypothesis is not true

For the sales example, $v_1 = 2$, $v_2 = 9$, $F = 5.25$, and the *p*-value is between 0.035 and 0.022, or about 0.032 (see Appendix K). For a prespecified value $\alpha = 0.05$, one would reject H_N. But if the person specifying α considered the cost of a Type I error to be very high and chose, say, $\alpha = 0.01$ (a one percent chance of rejecting a null hypothesis which is true), do not reject the null hypothesis that the means are equal.

No attempt was made to calculate the Type II error for our example for several important reasons. One is that the F distribution applies only

Type I error

No Type II error

when the null hypothesis is true. The second reason is the many alternate hypotheses which may be true. Appropriate statistical procedures exist for estimating the Type II error, but they are beyond the scope of this text.

11.4 ANALYSIS OF VARIANCE TABLE   *ANOVA TABLE*

Although the sample statistic which is used in analysis of variance,

$$F = \frac{n\sum_{j=1}^{c}(\bar{X}_i - \bar{\bar{X}})^2/(C-1)}{\sum_{j=1}^{c}\sum_{i=1}^{n}(X_{ij} - \bar{X}_j)^2/[C(n-1)]} \qquad = \frac{n\sum_{j=1}^{c}(\bar{X}_i - \bar{\bar{X}})^2/v_1}{(n-1)\sum_{j=1}^{c}\left(s_j^2/v_2\right)}$$

can be computed directly from its definition, it is usually more convenient to keep track of the computations by using an analysis of variance table. When this table is used, four components are used in computing the F statistic. These four components are:

Sum of squares, between columns (SSB). This term is the sum of squares of each of the sample means from their own mean $\bar{\bar{X}}$, multiplied by n. Computationally it is

$$SSB = n\sum_{j=1}^{c}(\bar{X}_j - \bar{\bar{X}})^2$$

Degrees of freedom, between columns (v_1). This is the divisor in the numerator of the F statistic, and its value is $C-1$.

Sum of squares, within columns (SSW). This term is the sum of squares of each observation from its own (column) mean. Computationally, it is

$$s_j^2 = \frac{\sum_{i=1}^{n}(X_{ij}-\bar{X}_j)^2}{(n-1)} \qquad SSW = \sum_{j=1}^{c}\sum_{i=1}^{n}(X_{ij}-\bar{X}_j)^2 = (n-1)\sum_{j=1}^{c}s_j^2$$

Degrees of freedom, within columns (v_2). This is the divisor in the denominator of the F statistic, and its value is $C(n-1)$.

The ratio of each of the sum of squares terms, SSB and SSW, to its own degrees of freedom, v_1 and v_2, is called a *mean square*. The first of the mean square terms is called the *mean square between columns* (MSB); the second is called the *mean square within columns* (MSW). The F statistic is then the ratio of the two mean squares, or

$$F = \frac{MSB}{MSW}$$

Figure 11.3

ANOVA Table, Excellent Health Foods Example

use these equations to be on the safe

Source of Variation	*Sum of Squares*	*Degrees of Freedom*	*Mean Sum of Squares*
Between salespersons (Columns)	$SSB = n \sum_{j=1}^{C} (\bar{X}_j - \bar{\bar{X}})^2 = 56$	$\nu_1 = C - 1 = 2$	$MSB = SSB/\nu_1 = 28$
Within salespersons (Columns)	$SSW = \sum_{j=1}^{C} \sum_{i=1}^{n} (X_{ij} - \bar{X}_j)^2 = 48$	$\nu_2 = C(n - 1) = 9$	$MSW = SSW/\nu_2 = 5.333$
Total (not used in computations; shown for reference only.) for Check only	$SST = \sum_{j=1}^{C} \sum_{i=1}^{n} (X_{ij} - \bar{\bar{X}})^2 = 104$ or $SST = SSB + SSW = 104$		

$$F = \frac{MSB}{MSW} = \frac{28}{5.33} = 5.25$$

Degrees of freedom $\nu_1 = 2$, $\nu_2 = 9$

Alternate Form

$$SSW = (n-1) \sum_{j=1}^{c} s_j^2$$

where $s_j^2 = \sum_{i=1}^{n} \frac{(X_{ij} - \bar{X}_{j})^2}{(n-1)}$

with degrees of freedom v_1 and v_2. The ANOVA Table is Figure 11.3 for the sales example.

11.5 EXAMPLE

Four different suppliers are being investigated for quality, measured by tensile strength of the steel in their output. The null hypothesis is that all four are equal, or

$$H_N: \quad \mu_1 = \mu_2 = \mu_3 = \mu_4 \qquad Ha: \text{ atleast one is not equal}$$

To investigate this hypothesis, a simple random sample of size $n = 2$ is taken from the latest batch of each supplier's output. The results of tensile strength, measured in thousands of pounds per square inch, are:

Observation	Supplier			
	$j = 1$	$j = 2$	$j = 3$	$j = 4$
$i = 1$....................	20	19	24	22
$i = 2$....................	18	24	24	25

Imp Assumptions To use ANOVA, one must assume:

1. Each of the four samples is a simple random sample.
2. Each of the four populations (tensile strength of items in the suppliers' batches) is normally distributed. (Modest deviations from normality are unimportant.)
3. Each of the four populations has the same variance. (Modest deviations from equal variance are unimportant.)
4. Each of the four samples is independent of the others. (This assumption is very important.)

Assumptions 1 and 4 reflect the way in which the samples are taken. Assumptions 2 and 3 require knowledge about the situation being studied.

Step 1: Calculate $\bar{X}_j$, for $j = 1, 2, \ldots, C$

$$\bar{X}_1 = \frac{20 + 18}{2} = 19$$

$$\bar{X}_2 = \frac{19 + 24}{2} = 21.5$$

$$\bar{X}_3 = \frac{24 + 24}{2} = 24$$

$$\bar{X}_4 = \frac{22 + 25}{2} = 23.5$$

Step 2:   Calculate $\bar{\bar{X}}$

$$\bar{\bar{X}} = \frac{\sum\limits_{j=1}^{c} \sum\limits_{i=1}^{n} X_{ij}}{nC} = \frac{20 + 18 + 19 + 24 + 24 + 24 + 22 + 25}{2(4)} = \frac{176}{8} = 22$$

Step 3:   Calculate SSB

$$= n \sum_{j=1}^{c} (\bar{X}_j - \bar{\bar{X}})^2$$

$$\text{SSB} = n[(19 - 22)^2 + (21.5 - 22)^2 + (24 - 22)^2 + (23.5 - 22)^2]$$
$$= 2[9 + 0.25 + 4 + 2.25] = 2(15.5) = 31$$

Step 4:   Calculate SSW

$$= \sum_{j=1}^{c} \sum_{i=1}^{n} (X_{ij} - \bar{X}_j)^2 \quad = \quad (n-1) \sum_{j=1}^{c} S_j^2$$

$$\text{SSW} = (20 - 19)^2 + (18 - 19)^2 + (19 - 21.5)^2 + (24 - 21.5)^2$$
$$+ (24 - 24)^2 + (24 - 24)^2 + (22 - 23.5)^2 + (25 - 23.5)^2$$
$$= 1 + 1 + 6.25 + 6.25 + 0 + 0 + 2.25 + 2.25$$
$$= 19$$

$$v_1 = c - 1$$
$$v_2 = c(n-1)$$

Step 5:   Calculate MSB, MSW

$$\text{MSB} = \frac{\text{SSB}}{v_1} = \frac{\text{SSB}}{C - 1} = \frac{31}{3} = 10.333$$

$$\text{MSW} = \frac{\text{SSW}}{v_2} = \frac{\text{SSW}}{C(n - 1)} = \frac{19}{4(2 - 1)} = \frac{19}{4} = 4.75$$

Step 6:   Calculate F, and report the p-value

$$F = \frac{\text{MSB}}{\text{MSW}} = \frac{10.333}{4.75} = 2.175$$

Using $v_1 = 3$, $v_2 = 4$, the p-value is between 0.256 and 0.199, or about 0.236, which should be reported or compared to α. The ANOVA Table is shown as Figure 11.4.

11.6 SEVERAL FACTOR ANALYSIS

In the example in this chapter, only one factor was investigated to explain the difference found in the sample means: the sales ability among the three salespersons, as reflected in their sales results. But there may be other factors that might explain these differences: the size of sales areas, the number of potential outlets for products, or ethnic differences in

Figure 11.4

ANOVA Table, Tensile Strength Example

Source of Variation	Sum of Squares	Degrees of Freedom	Mean Sum of Squares
Between Suppliers	SSB $= 31$	$\nu_1 = C - 1 = 3$	$31/3 = 10.333$
Within Suppliers	SSW $= 19$	$\nu_2 = C(n - 1) = 4$	$19/4 = 4.75$
Total (reference only)	SST $= 50$		

$$F = \frac{10.333}{4.75} = 2.175$$

$\nu_1 = 3; \nu_2 = 4$

p-value is between 0.256 and 0.199, or about 0.236

their areas' populations. These problems are two-factor analysis of variance examples, or three-factor, and so on. They are beyond the scope of this text.[1] However, the power of analysis of variance is enhanced by these many-factor capabilities. In addition, more general methods for one-factor ANOVA are available if the sample size is different for various levels (or columns).

11.7 MODEL FOR ANALYSIS OF VARIANCE: A SUMMARY

One useful way of viewing analysis of variance data is to segregate the various effects that generate differences in observations. For single-factor ANOVA these effects are:

1. An overall mean, for all observations of the population combined, given the symbol μ.
2. A column effect, arising from the fact that the columns differ from each other when H_N is false. For an individual column, j, this is given the symbol K_j. Thus, a column population mean is $\mu + K_j$.
3. An error term, showing the variation of each observation from its column population mean. This is given the symbol ϵ_{ij}, for population (or column) j. (ϵ is the Greek letter *epsilon*.)

The ANOVA assumptions are that the ϵ_{ij} terms are independent and normally distributed, with mean zero and a common variance σ^2. Thus, the model for simple-factor ANOVA is:

$$X_{ij} = \mu + K_j + \epsilon_{ij}$$

---

[1] See John Neter and William Wasserman, *Applied Linear Statistical Models,* Richard D. Irwin, Inc., 1974, pp. 549–604.

The null hypothesis is:

$$H_N: \quad \text{All } K_j = 0$$

This is equivalent to hypothesizing that the individual column means, μ_1, $\mu_2, \ldots, \mu_C$ are equal, since each column mean is $\mu + K_j$; if all K_j values are zero, $\mu = \mu_1 = \mu_2 = \ldots = \mu_C$.

The advantage of this statement of the model is that extensions to multi-factor ANOVA follow easily. If a second (row) factor is added, with only one observation for each row-column combination, the model is

$$X_{ij} = \mu + R_i + K_j + \epsilon_{ij}$$

where R_i indicates the effect of row i. The model may be extended as more factors are used, and as the number of observations for a row-column combination goes beyond one.

EXERCISES

11.1   Explain why you agree or disagree with this statement. "Analysis of variance tests the hypothesis that several populations have the same variance."

* 11.2   What is the null hypothesis investigated in analysis of variance? Ho: $\mu_1 = \mu_2 = \mu_3 =$

11.3   Which of the following is an assumption that must be made before the analysis of variance procedure is precise?
    a. There are at least two populations of interest.
    b. A simple random sample has been selected from each population.
    c. The sample size is the same for each population.
    d. Each population has the same variance.
    e. Each population has the same mean.
    f. Each population is normally distributed.

11.4   Three makes of cars were driven at 18 mph into a 27-inch diameter oak tree. Two cars of each make were used. The damage for each crash was:

Test \ Make	Guzzler	Poncho	Pizza
A	$1,800	$2,100	$1,400
B	$2,000	$2,500	$1,600

    a. What assumptions need to be made to use ANOVA?
    b. Making these assumptions, test the hypothesis that all makes of car tested are equally damaged by 18 mph crashes into a 27-inch diameter oak tree. Report the *p*-value.

* 11.5   In order to investigate whether verbal skills affect student performance

in statistics, a class of 728 students is divided into three populations according to verbal skills. The groups are the lower third, middle third, and upper third, as determined on a placement test. The semester score in the statistics course is determined for a random sample of five students from each group. The results are:

Lower Third	Middle Third	Upper Third
78	62	92
82	78	88
64	90	76
90	66	84
86	54	100

a. What is the null hypothesis, if analysis of variance is to be used?
b. What assumptions must be made about the three populations?
c. What assumptions must be made about the sampling procedure?
d. Test the hypothesis of part a, and report the p-value.

* 11.6   Four makes of automobiles are being considered for purchase by Hummingbird Seed Company. Since the firm will be buying about 400 cars to deliver seed, gasoline consumption is very important. Because of the prospects for the large order, each of the four dealers is willing to loan six cars for gasoline consumption tests. The results are:

Car \ Make	Canary	Bluebird	Hawk	Vulture
A	3.7	4.0	2.9	3.7
B	4.1	3.6	3.1	3.9
C	3.5	3.4	3.5	3.9
D	3.6	3.5	3.4	4.1
E	3.4	3.6	3.1	3.8
F	3.3	2.9	2.6	4.0

These figures represent gallons consumed for 100 miles of test driving under similar conditions. Test the hypothesis of equality of consumption for the four cars, and interpret the results of your test.

11.7   Suppose in Exercise 11.6 the first row of data represents the results when the cars are driven by Mr. Humming, the second row represents the cars driven by Mrs. Bird, the third row cars were driven by Ms. Seed, etc. Which assumption(s) of analysis of variance have been violated?

11.8   Test the hypothesis that the average defect rate is the same for machines A and B. Four days of output were randomly selected for machine A, and four for machine B. The results (number of defectives) are:

Machine A	Machine B
39	41
42	40
57	35
34	56

11.9 Discuss some pitfalls that might exist in the assumption of normality for the test of Exercise 11.8.

* **11.10** In an investigation of college major and initial salary at first job, a random sample of students from business, engineering, history, journalism, and pharmacy was taken. The initial monthly salary for those in the sample was:

Business....................	$ 900	$1,050	$1,050
Engineering.................	$1,000	$1,200	$1,100
History....................	$ 800	$ 700	$ 600
Journalism.................	$ 900	$ 900	$1,200
Pharmacy..................	$ 800	$1,000	$1,200

Test the hypothesis that the average initial salary is the same for all majors, and report your results.

* **11.11** A test of small-muscle nimbleness is conducted on left-handed people, right-handed people, and people who use both hands equally well. A high score indicates nimbleness; a low score represents clumsiness. The people tested are randomly selected from each of the three populations. The test scores are:

Left-handed	Right-handed	Either hand
94	27	90
107	82	80
132	36	148
148	59	70
119	96	62

Report the results of the test of the hypothesis that nimbleness is the same for all three groups. (Note to Latin scholars: Why did the left-handed author refuse to use the words dexterity and ambidextrous? Is there a sinister motive?)

* **11.12** The city of Rocktown is investigating three procedures for municipal garbage collection. The procedures are:

A: Three-person crew, consisting of a driver and two loaders.

B: Two-person crew, consisting of a driver and one loader.

C: One-person crew, with a special truck designed for right-hand drive and side loading directly behind the driver's seat.

For the same type neighborhood, each procedure is used for five days. The entire period has similar weather and season, so the trash-generation habits of residents are similar throughout the experiment. The trash collected (tons per person per day) is measured and reported as:

$$F = \frac{15}{.968} = 15.49 \qquad p\text{-value} < .003$$

Procedure		
A	B	C
7.2	6.7	10.3
6.8	5.0	8.2
5.1	7.0	9.7
5.9	4.9	8.8
5.0	6.4	8.0

Is there a statistically significant ($\alpha = 0.01$) difference in the three procedures?

* 11.13 Three computer programs use three different approaches to solve a problem in resource allocation. These are the only three programs of interest to the user. The programs are tested on the same problem (the only one of interest) on three _different_ computers. These are the only computers of interest to the user. The execution times (in minutes) are:

	Program		
Computer	A	B	C
X.....................	39.0	40.2	28.7
I.....................	3.9	4.7	2.9
D.....................	7.9	9.4	5.8

a. Is there a difference in average time for the three programs?
b. Is a statistical inference appropriate here? Why or why not?

REFERENCES

Eisenhart, C. "The Assumptions Underlying the Analysis of Variance," _Biometrics,_ vol. 3 (1947), pp. 1–21.

Guenther, W. C. _Analysis of Variance._ Englewood Cliffs, N.J.: Prentice-Hall, Inc., 1964.

Hicks, C. R. _Fundamental Concepts in the Design of Experiments._ New York: Holt, Rinehart and Winston, Inc., 1964.

Neter, John, and Wasserman, William. _Applied Linear Statistical Models._ Homewood, Ill.: Richard D. Irwin, Inc., 1974.

Richmond, S. B. _Statistical Analysis,_ 2d ed. New York: Ronald Press, 1964.

$p > \alpha$ accept Ho or do not reject

$p < \alpha$ reject Ho.

This is one tail test, so use α (& not $\frac{\alpha}{2}$)

12

Linear Regression

12.1 NATURE OF REGRESSION

Regression analysis may be useful for situations in which the value of one variable is known, and one wishes to forecast the value of an associated variable. For example, one might be interested in predicting a person's success in a given job when the score on a preemployment test is known. There might be interest in predicting the defect rate in a production process, knowing the number of years of experience the operator has with the equipment. As a final example, and the one to be used throughout most of this chapter, one might be interested in predicting how long it will take a taxicab to reach an address, when the distance from the taxi stand to the address is known. This information may be useful to a taxicab company in deciding where to locate taxi stands.

The last two chapters have dealt with relationships between two factors; in those chapters the primary focus has been in investigating the association between two factors when we measure at least one of those factors by *categories* rather than by *numerical data*. For example, in an analysis of variance investigation of the relationship between test scores and job success, there might be three categories of success: low, average, and high. Within each of these categories, the test scores of the randomly selected employees can be measured. In this situation, the factor "job success" is categorical. There is no numerical score for job success; an employee is judged and placed in one of three categories. The other factor, test score, has a numerical value and is a random variable.

In a linear regression model, there are *numerical* values for each of the two factors whose association is being investigated. To continue with the job success example, one might measure job success by annual salary while still using numerical test scores, thereby altering the example to yield not one but two numerically-valued variables: job success, as measured by income; and preemployment test scores. As shall be seen later in this chapter, it is possible to calculate descriptive measures of the apparent strength of the relationship (but not necessarily cause and effect) between two variables in a regression analysis. Thus, regression is useful for two primary purposes:

1. Regression analysis can be used to predict the value of one variable, when the value of the other related variable is known;
2. Regression analysis can be used to investigate whether there is a relationship between two variables, and can describe the apparent strength of that relationship.

In regression analysis the two variables being studied are traditionally labeled the *independent variable* and the *dependent variable;* they are denoted by the symbols X and Y.

> The *independent variable* (X) is the variable which is used as the basis of prediction. The *dependent variable* (Y) is the variable which is being predicted.

Some examples of associated independent and dependent variables are:

Independent Variable, X	Dependent Variable, Y
Score on preemployment test	Job success
Research expenditures	Profitability of firm
Experience of the operator	Defect rate in a production process
Floor space of stores	Total sales
Distance from taxi stand to address	Taxi response time
Number of salespersons	Number of units sold

A linear relationship between a dependent variable (Y) and an independent variable (X) is given by the equation

$$Y = a + bX$$

where a is the *intercept* (the value of Y when $X = 0$) and b is the *slope* (the amount of change in Y when X changes by one unit). In managerial situations, it is very unusual if the equation for a straight line predicts the value of Y exactly. Hence, as shall be illustrated in a later section, regression is used to predict the *average* value of Y for any given value of X. Thus, the regression line is usually expressed as

$$\bar{Y}_c = a + bX$$

The symbol $\bar{Y}$ indicates an average, while the subscript c indicates a value calculated from the equation.

The organization of this chapter is first to present regression as a descriptive device, using the method of least squares to fit a line to a set of values. Then the inferential uses of least squares lines will be described.

12.2 SCATTER DIAGRAMS AND FITTING LINES

A useful tool in regression analysis is the *scatter diagram,* which shows the plot of the values of X and Y on a sheet of graph paper. Since there are two variables, each member of the sample must yield two values—an X value and a Y value. Thus, each sample member produces a point on the scatter diagram. To see how a sample member can yield two values, think about the preemployment test and job success. For each person whose success is being considered, two things must be measured: success and preemployment test score. For the taxicab example, each taxicab run produces two measurements: distance traveled and response time.

Figure 12.1a

Scatter Diagram Showing an Apparent Linear Relationship

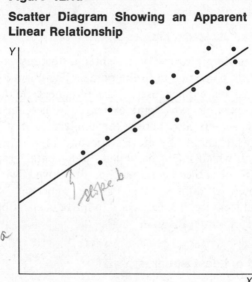

In many situations, these plotted points on the scatter diagram appear to lie near a straight line; such a situation is said to be *linear.* A scatter diagram exhibiting apparent linearity is shown in Figure 12.1a. The relationship between two variables of interest need not be a linear relationship. Figure 12.1b shows a scatter diagram for two variables which appear to have a nonlinear relationship. This chapter is concerned primarily with linear relationships.

After constructing the scatter diagram, the next step is to fit a line to the points. The easiest way of fitting a straight line to the points on a

Figure 12.1*b*

Scatter Diagram Showing an Apparent Nonlinear Relationship

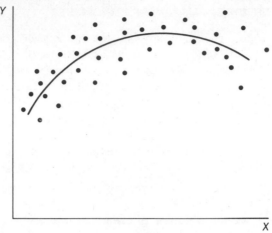

scatter diagram is simply to use a straightedge to draw a line that judgmentally appears to be a good fit to the points. There is a lot to be said for this method. It allows explicit use of the judgment of the analyst, who might know, for example, why some extreme points should be ignored in fitting a straight line. It also allows the analyst to pay more attention to some points which might be more important than other points. However, this method, which might be called "judgmental graphics," has the disadvantage of being subjective rather than objective. Two analysts would typically fit somewhat different lines to the same set of numbers. To overcome this subjectivity, it is necessary to introduce an objective criterion for fitting a line to a scatter diagram.

12.21   Method of Least Squares

We shall use the *method of least squares* to fit a straight line to the points on a scatter diagram. If it were possible to draw one straight line through every point on a scatter diagram, the fit would be perfect. This is rare; ordinarily most points do not fall directly on the line. The vertical distance from a point to the line is called the *deviation* of that point from the line, as seen in Figure 12.2. If this deviation (which may be positive or negative) is squared, a positive number results. If a line is chosen so that the sum of these squared deviations for all points on the scatter diagram is as small as possible, the method of least squares is being used.[1]

---

[1] Other criteria for a "good fit" could be chosen, such as the minimum of the summed absolute values of deviations, which has certain difficult mathematical properties.

Figure 12.2

Deviations of Points from a Line

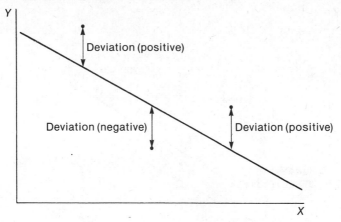

The equation for a straight line has the general equation:

$$Y = a + bx$$

where the sign of a and the sign of b can be positive or negative (b is negative in the case plotted above).

This method is chosen because it produces desirable statistical results, such as unbiased estimators. More formally, the least squares method may be stated:

The method of least squares requires that the line chosen to represent the points on a scatter diagram shall have a sum of squared deviations smaller than the sum of squared deviations for any other line.

To illustrate the method of least squares, consider the example of the time required for a taxi to travel various distances. Suppose three data points have been observed, representing three runs. The data for these three runs are shown in Figure 12.3, which also shows two possible straight lines that have been fitted to these three points. It is unrealistic to talk about fitting a straight line on the basis of only three data points; however, it is a useful illustration to demonstrate the least squares method for choosing a line. It is also unrealistic to have only two candidate lines to represent the data on the scatter diagram. But again, it is a useful teaching device.

Notice that the data at the bottom of Figure 12.3 show the observed time for each of the three runs, along with the time predicted by each of the two candidate straight lines. It is reasonable to use the vertical difference between the measured time and the time on the line as an input to

Figure 12.3

Scatter Diagram for Taxi Runs

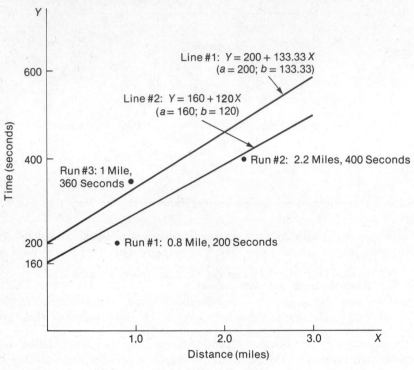

Observed Time in Seconds, Y	Distance, X	Time (Line 1)	Time (Line 2)
200	0.8	200 + 133.33 (0.8) = 306.66	160 + 120 (0.8) = 256
400	2.2	200 + 133.33 (2.2) = 493.33	160 + 120 (2.2) = 424
360	1.0	200 + 133.33 (1.0) = 333.33	160 + 120 (1.0) = 280

a measure of closeness of fit of the lines. According to the least squares criterion, choose a line on the basis of the square of the difference between the measured time and the time on a particular line, added for all points on the scatter diagram. As shown in Figure 12.4 for line 1, the first run was different by -106.66 seconds, the second run was different by -93.33 seconds, and the third was different by 26.67 seconds. Square each of these differences, and obtain $(-106.66)^2 + (-93.33)^2 + (26.67)^2 = 20,797$. Do the same for line 2, and obtain $(-56)^2 + (-24)^2 + (80)^2 = 10,112$. Line 2 is a better fit than line 1, according to the criterion of least squares, because it has the smaller total squared deviations of the points from the line. By repeating this process for all possible lines, eventually the line with the smallest sum of squared deviations can be found.

Figure 12.4

Squared Deviations for Two Lines

	Observed Time	Predicted Time	Difference	Square
Line 1..................	200	306.66	−106.66	11,376
	400	493.33	− 93.33	8,710
	360	333.33	26.67	711
			Total	20,797
Line 2..................	200	256	− 56	3,136
	400	424	− 24	576
	360	280	80	6,400
			Total	10,112

Fortunately, there is an easier approach than this to find the one line which produces the lowest sum of squared deviations.

In order to specify uniquely a straight line, it is only necessary to know two of its properties: its slope, and its intercept. The symbol a is used for the intercept and the symbol b for the slope of the regression line. The term *regression coefficient* is often used for b. It can be shown mathematically that the values of a and b which specify the straight line with the smallest total squared deviations is given by the solution of these two simultaneous equations, called the *normal equations:*

$$\Sigma Y = na + b\Sigma X$$
$$\Sigma XY = a\Sigma X + b\Sigma X^2$$

where n is the number of observations in the scatter diagram. Solving these equations simultaneously and performing some algebra, one can obtain:

$$b = \frac{n\Sigma XY - (\Sigma X)(\Sigma Y)}{n\Sigma X^2 - (\Sigma X)^2}$$
$$a = \frac{\Sigma Y}{n} - b\frac{\Sigma X}{n} = \bar{Y} - b\bar{X}$$

The normal equations and the equations for a and b are derived in Notes 12.21a and 12.21b following Chapter 17.

12.22   Computations for Finding Least Squares Line

To illustrate the method for finding the least squares line, expand the taxicab response time example to include eight runs. The data are shown in Figure 12.5, along with the computations required for the regression analysis. From Figure 12.5, the regression calculations result in this straight line equation:

$$\bar{Y}_c = a + bX = 92.220 + 169.616X$$

Suppose one wants a point estimate for the time required for a taxicab to respond two miles to pick up a passenger. Using the equation for the regression line shown above with $X = 2$ miles, the prediction is:

$$\bar{Y}_c = 92.220 + 169.616 \, (X)$$
$$= 92.220 + 169.616 \, (2.0) = 431.452 \text{ seconds}$$

which suggests that a two-mile response would take about 431 seconds, or 7 minutes and 11 seconds. When considering using a regression equation for prediction outside the range of X from data collection, one should question whether the linear relationship holds true in the unobserved range.

Figure 12.5

Regression Computations: Eight Taxi Runs

X Distance, Miles	Y Time, Seconds	X^2	XY	Y^2
0.8	200	0.64	160	40,000
2.2	400	4.84	880	160,000
1.0	160	1.00	160	25,600
0.6	120	0.36	72	14,400
1.0	360	1.00	360	129,600
1.4	280	1.96	392	78,400
2.2	560	4.84	1,232	313,600
0.6	320	0.36	192	102,400
$\Sigma X = 9.8$	$\Sigma Y = 2,400$	$\Sigma X^2 = 15.00$	$\Sigma XY = 3,448$	$\Sigma Y^2 = 864,000$

$$\bar{X} = \frac{\Sigma X}{n} = \frac{9.8}{8} = 1.225 \qquad \bar{Y} = \frac{\Sigma Y}{n} = \frac{2400}{8} = 300$$

$$b = \frac{n\Sigma XY - (\Sigma X)(\Sigma Y)}{n\Sigma X^2 - (\Sigma X)^2} = \frac{8(3,448) - (9.8)(2,400)}{8(15) - (9.8)^2} = 169.616$$

$$a = \bar{Y} - b\bar{X} = 300 - 169.616 \, (1.225) = 92.220$$

Regression Line: $\bar{Y}_c = 92.220 + 169.616X$

12.3 GOODNESS OF FIT

Now that a regression line has been computed to represent taxicab response times, it is appropriate to ask how well this regression line fits the observed data. A very easy and obvious approach is to observe the scatter diagram, shown in Figure 12.6. It is possible from such a scatter diagram to observe judgmentally that the line is either a "good" fit or a "bad" fit, depending on the use to be made of the regression line. However, one usually wants a more objective measure of the goodness of fit of the regression line to the observed data points.

Figure 12.6

Scatter Diagram for Eight Taxicab Runs

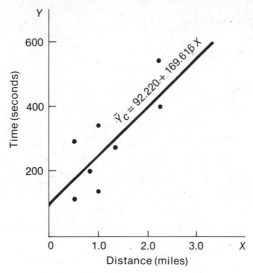

12.31 Standard Error of Estimate *for Goodness of fit*

One measure of the goodness of fit of a regression line to the data points is called the *standard error of estimate*. Continuing to use the symbol $\bar{Y}_c$ to denote the points on the regression line,

The *standard error of estimate* for a simple linear regression line is:

$$s_{YX} = \sqrt{\frac{\Sigma(Y - \bar{Y}_c)^2}{n - 2}}$$

← *deviation of data points about regression line $\bar{Y}_c$*

The denominator is $n - 2$, because two sample estimates (a and b) have been made. Recall that the standard deviation of Y, as estimated from the sample, is:

$$s_Y = \sqrt{\frac{\Sigma(Y - \bar{Y})^2}{n - 1}}$$

← *deviation of data points about mean line $\bar{Y}$*

The standard error of estimate deals with deviations of the data points about the regression line, while the standard deviation of Y deals with deviations of the data points about the horizontal line going through $\bar{Y}$. *Imp*

To calculate the standard error of estimate, the definition given above can be used. However, this requires calculation of the value of $\bar{Y}_c$ for each X value. This calculation, although straightforward, becomes tedious for large problems. Instead, an equivalent procedure, which is computationally superior, is used. In Figure 12.5, a column of Y^2 values was included which has not yet been used. These values will now be used in calculating the standard error of estimate.

To calculate s_{YX}, the standard error of estimate for the eight taxicab runs, an alternate equation is:

Note 12.31

$$s_{YX} = \sqrt{\frac{\Sigma Y^2 - a\Sigma Y - b\Sigma XY}{n - 2}}$$

$$= \sqrt{\frac{864{,}000 - 92.220(2{,}400) - 169.616(3{,}448)}{6}}$$

$$= \sqrt{9{,}639.3} = 98.18 \text{ seconds}$$

Notice that this equation does not require any summation calculations other than those already shown in Figure 12.5. This equation is derived in Note 12.31.

This standard error of estimate takes on an additional meaning when compared to the standard deviation of the observed Y values. To calculate the standard deviation of observed Y values for the eight taxicab runs:

$$s_Y = \sqrt{\frac{\Sigma(Y - \bar{Y})^2}{n - 1}} = \sqrt{\frac{\Sigma Y^2 - (\Sigma Y)^2/n}{n - 1}} = \sqrt{\frac{864{,}000 - (2{,}400)^2/8}{7}}$$

$$= \sqrt{20{,}571.4} = 143.4 \text{ seconds}$$

We now have two measures of dispersion: the standard error of estimate, which measures dispersion of the points about the regression line, and the standard deviation, which measures the dispersion of the Y values about their mean. The standard error of estimate is the smaller of these two measures. The standard error of estimate measures the dispersion that remains *after* using the regression line; the standard deviation measures the total dispersion of the Y values *before* a regression line was calculated. Mathematically, it can be shown that the ratio of the square of these two measures gives a meaningful estimate of the proportion of the variation that is "unexplained" by the regression line. For the example, the proportion of variation unexplained by the regression line is:

$$\frac{(s_{YX})^2}{(s_Y)^2} = \left(\frac{s_{YX}}{s_Y}\right)^2 = \left(\frac{98.18}{143.4}\right)^2 = 0.469$$

Thus, the regression analysis has left "unexplained" about 47 percent of the variation in response time. Therefore, the regression line has "explained" about 53 percent of variation in response time. Since the regression analysis dealt with distance as the single independent variable, factors other than distance account for about 47 percent of the variation in response time.

Note the use of quotation marks around "explained" and "unexplained" in the paragraph above. We do not mean to imply that distance and time are a cause and effect; it is only possible to say that the data of Y and X values make it appear they are related to each other. It is possible that there is some other factor which is the causal factor in the relationship. It seems doubtful that this would be the case for taxicab response times, because it is common sense that longer runs take more time. In other regression problems, however, such an obvious cause and effect relationship may not be present. For example, would a regression analysis between the income and weight of people have a common-sense basis to show a cause and effect relationship?

12.32   Coefficient of Determination

The paragraphs immediately above have discussed the proportion of the variation that was "unexplained" by the regression line. It is also useful to look again at the proportion of variation which is "explained" by the regression line. This is, of course, the complement of the proportion already calculated; this complement is called the *coefficient of determination*.[2]

The *coefficient of determination* in a regression model, r^2, is the proportion of the variation that is "explained" by the regression line. This is given by:

$$r^2 = 1 - \frac{s_{YX}^2}{s_Y^2} = 1 - \left(\frac{s_{YX}}{s_Y}\right)^2$$

For the taxicab example,

$$r^2 = 1 - \left(\frac{98.18}{143.4}\right)^2 = 1 - 0.469 = 0.531$$

The square root of the coefficient of determination, r, is called the *coefficient of correlation,* and for the taxicab example it is 0.729.

---

[2] To be a bit more precise, the coefficient of determination is more correctly called the "coefficient of determination, adjusted for degrees of freedom," or more simply, the "adjusted coefficient of determination." The unadjusted coefficient of determination does not take into account the different number of degrees of freedom, $n - 2$ for s_{YX} and $n - 1$ for s_Y. The unadjusted coefficient of determination is given by:

$$\hat{r}^2 = 1 - \frac{\Sigma(Y - \bar{Y}_c)^2}{\Sigma(Y - \bar{Y})^2}$$

When the sample size is large, the two are virtually the same. The relationship between the two is:

$$r^2 = 1 - \frac{\Sigma(Y - \bar{Y}_c)^2}{\Sigma(Y - \bar{Y})^2} \cdot \frac{(n-1)}{(n-2)} = 1 - (1 - \hat{r}^2)\left(\frac{n-1}{n-2}\right)$$

An alternate approach to the unadjusted coefficient of determination is given in Note 12.32.

The coefficient of determination, r^2, and to a lesser extent its square root, the coefficient of correlation, $r,$ are useful descriptive measures of the goodness of fit of a regression line to the observed data.

12.4 STATISTICAL INFERENCE IN LINEAR REGRESSION ANALYSIS: THE NECESSARY ASSUMPTIONS

The discussion of regression analysis up to this point has been primarily oriented toward fitting a linear regression line to observed data. However, regression analysis is a much more powerful tool than line fitting. With a proper definition of the population involved in a regression experiment, regression analysis becomes a powerful tool of inferential statistics.

The necessary assumptions for inference are illustrated by continuing the example of taxicab response time. It is much easier to understand and explain these assumptions in terms of a specific example; however, once the assumptions are understood, it is easy to generalize to other regression situations.

The first concept needed is the average response time for all taxicab runs of a given distance. For example, consider taxicab responses for a distance of one mile. A particular one-mile response may require a time anywhere from, say, 100 seconds to 600 seconds, depending on road and traffic conditions, detours, and many other factors. If instead of considering a *single* one-mile run, one considers the population of *all* one-mile runs that might occur under current operating conditions, this defines a population of one-mile runs. This population of one-mile runs has its own mean, standard deviation, and distribution shape. It is convenient to denote the mean of this population as $\mu_{Y|X\,=\,1}$. This is read, "The mean value of Y (time), given that X (distance) equals one mile." Using similar notation, the standard deviation of this population of Y values, when X is one mile, is denoted $\sigma_{Y|X\,=\,1}$.

There is a similar population of Y (time) for *every* value of X (distance). Each of these populations has its own mean, variance, and distribution shape. However, as shown below, the assumptions of linear regression analysis will be very specific about the mean, standard deviation, and distribution shape for these populations of response times (Y) for the various values of response distances (X).

12.41 Linearity

The first assumption of linear regression analysis involves the linear relationship between the population means, $\mu_{Y|X}$, and the X values. Specifically, this assumption is that these population means lie on a straight line when they are plotted against the independent variable, X.

Figure 12.7

Linearity

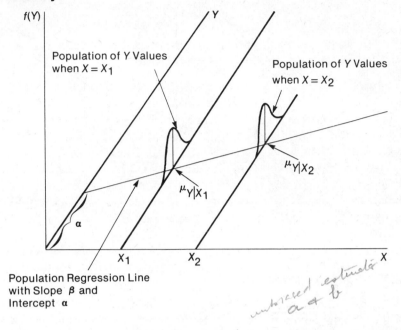

Population Regression Line
with Slope β and
Intercept α

The *assumption of linearity* of simple regression analysis is that

$$\mu_{Y|X} = \alpha + \beta X$$

where α and β are the population parameters, which the regression analysis estimates. The symbol α is the Greek letter *alpha*, and the symbol β is the Greek letter *beta*.[3]

It shall be seen after the assumptions are complete that the least squares values of a and b that have already been calculated are unbiased *estimators* of α and β.

A diagram of the assumption of linearity, along with two populations of Y values for corresponding X values, is shown in Figure 12.7. Two scatter diagrams showing when linearity may, and may not, be present are shown in Figure 12.8. The scatter diagram on the left of Figure 12.8 is a scatter diagram which appears the way one would expect if the linearity assumption is met. The right half of Figure 12.8 shows a scatter diagram in which there is an appearance of a curvilinear relationship between Y, the dependent variable, and X, the independent variable.

---

[3] Although the symbol α is also used for the level of significance, there should be no ambiguity that is not obviously resolved by context.

Figure 12.8

Assumption of Linearity

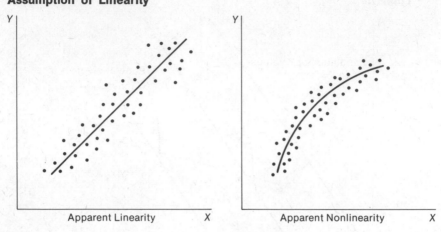

Apparent Linearity   X   Apparent Nonlinearity   X

assumption
②

12.42   Equal Variance

The second assumption of linear regression analysis is that the variance of the population of times (Y) is the same for all distances (X) of interest. Thus, regardless of the value of X, $\sigma_{Y|X}^2$ has the same value. This assumption is called the assumption of equal variance, or homoscedasticity.

> The *assumption of equal variance* states that for each value of X there is a population of Y values, and each of these populations has the same variance. The symbol $\sigma_{Y|X}^2$ is used for this variance.

A scatter diagram illustrating equal variance is shown in Figure 12.9. The scatter diagram on the left appears to meet the assumption of equal variance, while the scatter diagram on the right obviously has an increasing variance as the value of X increases.

assumption
③

12.43   Independence

The third assumption of regression analysis is the assumption of independence.

> The *assumption of independence* requires that the response time for a particular taxicab run is independent of the response time for any other taxicab run.

This assumption means that knowing the time for a particular run conveys no additional information about any other run.

Figure 12.9

Assumption of Equal Variance

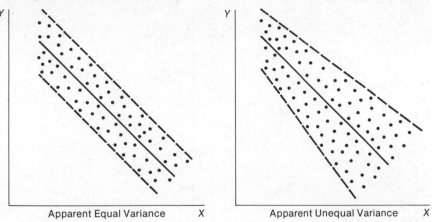

Apparent Equal Variance   X   Apparent Unequal Variance   X

The assumption of independence is somewhat more difficult to illustrate in terms of a scatter diagram. It is easy, however, to give examples of situations which cause independence to be violated. Returning to the taxi example, independence might be violated if nighttime runs are generally faster than daytime runs because of differences in traffic conditions. If taxicab runs are faster at night, one would expect a fast run to be followed by another fast run, where a fast run means a point below the regression line. A slow run would also be expected to be followed by another slow run. A slow run is more likely to happen during the daytime hours, and a daytime run is more likely to be followed by another daytime run rather than by a nighttime run.

12.44 Normality

The fourth assumption specifies the shape of the distribution of each of the response time (Y) populations.

> The *assumption of normality* requires that the Y populations, for each value of X, are described by the normal probability distribution.

Notice that the first two assumptions, linearity and equal variance, have specified the parameters (mean and variance) of the Y distributions, whereas this assumption specifies the shape of these Y distributions. The assumption of independence specifies that there is no relationship between the various populations, except the relationship of linearity.

The assumption of normality is illustrated informally in Figure 12.10.

Figure 12.10

Assumption of Normality

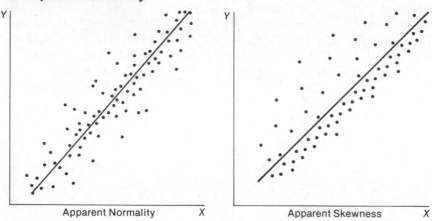

In the scatter diagram on the left, the density of points near the regression line is greater than the density of points that are relatively far away from the regression line; this is a characteristic of a normal distribution. Furthermore, it appears that this scatter diagram has about the same number of points above and below the regression line. This is the symmetry property of a normal distribution. The scatter diagram on the right appears to indicate some skewness of the populations of Y values. Note that in this case the Y observations above the regression line generally lie farther from the line than those below the regression line. It also appears that there are more observations below than above the regression line, or that the population of Y values is skewed.

12.45   Alternate Statement of the Assumptions

The four assumptions of linearity, equal variance, independence, and normality may be combined into one succinct statement:

$$Y_i = \alpha + \beta X_i + \epsilon_i \text{ for } i = 1, 2, 3, \ldots, n$$

where the ϵ values are independent and normally distributed random variables with a mean of zero and a variance of $\sigma_{Y|X}^2$. The ϵ values are called the *error terms*.

12.5   INFERENCE IN REGRESSION ANALYSIS

Now that assumptions of what is called the *general linear regression model* have been discussed, it is possible to make inferences using regression. When these assumptions are satisfied, the least squares method of

a → α estimator
b → β
s_{yx}^2 → $\sigma_{Y|X}^2$

estimation provides estimators of the three regression parameters: α, β, and $\sigma_{Y|X}^2$. Previous work has already calculated these estimators: *a* is an estimator of α, *b* is an estimator of β, and s_{YX}^2 is an estimator of $\sigma_{Y|X}^2$. These estimators possess a desirable property of estimation; they are unbiased estimators. If one is interested only in point estimation, it is necessary to make no other comments about inference and regression analysis. However, one is usually interested in other inferences, such as confidence intervals and tests of hypotheses. The unbiasedness of *a* and *b* is demonstrated in the Notes for section 12.5.

12.51   Confidence Intervals for β and α

In general terms, α is the intercept of the *population* linear regression line, and β is its slope. In terms of the taxicab example, it is assumed by linearity that a taxicab requires a period of time from the receipt of a call until the cab begins to move, and then it moves at a constant speed. Thus, α is the average time required for the cab to begin moving, and β is the average time required to travel an additional mile. The example at the beginning of this chapter (Figure 12.5) *estimated* α to be 92.220 seconds, and β to be 169.616 seconds per mile. To investigate the reliability of these estimators, one needs to know the variance of the sampling distribution of *a* and *b*. If one were to take another sample of taxicab runs with distances similar to those in the previous experiment, observing the distance (X) and times (Y) required for these other runs, one would anticipate getting different values of *a* and *b*. A measure of the variability of *a* in such repeated experimentation is the *standard error* of *a*, s_a. This standard error is an estimate of the standard deviation of the sampling distribution of *a*. Similarly, a measure of the variability of *b* is given by the standard error of *b*, s_b. This standard error is an estimate of the standard deviation of the sampling distribution of *b*. These values are calculated using Figure 12.5 data from these equations:

$$s_b = \frac{s_{YX}}{\sqrt{\Sigma X^2 - \frac{(\Sigma X)^2}{n}}}$$

$$s_a = s_b \sqrt{\frac{\Sigma X^2}{n}}$$

Standard errors
$\equiv \sqrt{\text{Stand. deviation}}$

These equations are derived in Notes 12.51*a* and 12.51*b*.

For the taxicab example, the standard errors are:

$$s_b = \frac{98.18}{\sqrt{15.00 - \frac{(9.8)^2}{8}}} = \frac{98.18}{\sqrt{2.995}} = 56.73$$

$$s_a = 56.73 \sqrt{\frac{15.00}{8}} = 77.68$$

small sample

$t_{\bar{v}-2}$ distribution

Using the t distribution with $v = n - 2 = 8 - 2 = 6$ degrees of freedom, calculate the confidence intervals for α and β using these relationships:

$\pm \tfrac{1}{2}\alpha$

$$\text{Confidence interval for } \alpha: \quad a \pm t(s_a)$$
$$\text{Confidence interval for } \beta: \quad b \pm t(s_b)$$

$t_{v, \frac{1}{2}\alpha}$

t is used because the sample is small. For the data being used, the 80 percent confidence intervals is:

80 percent confidence interval for α:

$$a \pm t(s_a) = 92.220 \pm 1.4398 \,(77.68) = -19.6 \text{ to } 204.1$$

80 percent confidence interval for β:

$$b \pm t(s_b) = 169.616 \pm 1.4398 \,(56.73) = 87.9 \text{ to } 251.3$$

The t value for these confidence intervals are from the t distribution (Appendix I) for an 80 percent confidence interval with six degrees of freedom. Note that the 80 percent confidence interval requires an 80 percent central area, leaving 10 percent of the area under the t distribution in each tail. For $n - 2 > 30$, use the standard normal (Z) to approximate t.

It is worthwhile to remember that these confidence intervals reflect only the information contained in this *single* sampling experiment on taxicab response times. They include no prior information that one may have about taxicabs and speed. For example, the lower confidence limit for b has a value of 87.9 seconds per mile. This implies a velocity of approximately 41 miles per hour ($3,600 \div 87.9 = 41$). The confidence interval procedure is not powerful enough to include a consideration of whether 41 miles per hour is a reasonable speed for a taxicab. If a 95 percent or 99 percent confidence interval for b had been used, an interval which is even more unreasonable would result. One can reduce the unreasonableness of the estimation procedures by making the sample size larger, and reducing the size of t, s_a and s_b.

12.52   Tests of Hypotheses about β and α

Now that the estimated values of standard errors of b and a are known, one can test hypotheses about the values of β and α. The general procedure which has been discussed at length in Chapter 9 is applicable here. The test statistic is t-distributed with $n - 2$ degrees of freedom, where n is the number of observations in the regression analysis, and $(n - 2) \leq 30$. For $n - 2 > 30$, use the standard normal (Z) to approximate t.

For example, suppose that an exhaustive study conducted several years ago indicated that an additional 180 seconds after getting started is required for a taxi to drive one mile. You are interested in testing the hypothesis that this incremental time for one mile is still 180 seconds. The formal test procedure is:

$$H_N: \quad \beta = 180$$
$$H_A: \quad \beta \neq 180$$

$$\text{Test statistic: } t = \frac{b - \beta}{s_b} = \frac{169.616 - 180}{56.73} = -0.183 \qquad \nu = n-2$$

where $\nu = n - 2 = 8 - 2 = 6$.

From Appendix I the p-value for this two-tailed test is found to be approximately 2×0.4304, or 0.8608. For a prespecified level of significance, of say, 20 percent, this leads to the conclusion that there is no significant difference in the incremental response time of 169.616 from the previous value of 180. The reader should note that the confidence interval for β computed at the 80 percent confidence level furnished this same conclusion concerning significance in that the value of 180 was included in the interval of 87.9 to 251.3.

The corresponding test statistic for tests about α is:

$$t = \frac{a - \alpha}{s_a} \qquad \nu = n-2$$

where $\nu = n - 2$.

12.53 Is There a Linear Relationship between X and Y?

Up to now the primary interest has been in investigating the regression line about two variables in order to predict the value of Y when a value of X is given. Regression analysis has power beyond this predictive device. One of the important aspects of much scientific investigation is simply determining whether or not a *relationship* exists between two variables. Thus, it is often interesting to inquire whether an observed relationship is one due to chance, or whether there is an underlying true relationship between the two variables. Regression analysis can be used to investigate (but not *prove*) the existence of a true linear relationship between two variables. If there is a true linear relationship between two variables, β is not zero. If one asserts in a scientific investigation that there is *no* linear relationship, this is accomplished by hypothesizing that $\beta = 0$. Hence, a test of the null hypothesis that $\beta = 0$ is a powerful tool of scientific investigation.

In the taxicab response time example, a skeptical researcher might suggest that variation in time is not caused by distance. The researcher would investigate this assertion by hypothesizing that β is zero. The formal test procedure would be:

$$H_0: \beta = 0 \qquad \text{no relationship}$$
$$H_a: \beta \neq 0 \qquad \text{yes} \qquad ''$$

$$\text{H}_\text{N}: \quad \beta = 0$$
$$\text{H}_\text{A}: \quad \beta \neq 0$$

— no relationship

$$\text{Test statistic: } t = \frac{b - \beta}{s_b} = \frac{169.616 - 0}{56.73} = 2.99$$

where $\nu = n - 2 = 6$

The skeptical investigator would then report that the p-value for the test is $2 \times (0.0122)$ or 0.0244. This is a concise way of reporting the results of the experimentation to determine whether a relationship exists between time and distance for a taxicab. If a prespecified level of significance had been set at 0.05, the investigator would reject the null hypothesis and accept that $\beta \neq 0$, which in this example would mean to accept that $\beta > 0$. Again, the reader is advised not to consider this test a *proof* of either hypothesis.

$\alpha = .05$
$> p = .024$
reject H₀

12.54   Confidence Intervals for Forecasting

The earlier discussions of regression, as a line fitting technique, have suggested that regression analysis may be useful for forecasts. Having the sample regression equation

$$\bar{Y}_c = a + bX$$

one can obtain a point estimate of the calculated value for any X value of interest. But how good are these estimates? One way of evaluating these estimators is to construct a *confidence interval* about these *point* estimates.

The first kind of confidence interval to be discussed is the estimate of the *average* value of Y for a given value of X, $\mu_{Y|X}$. For the taxi example this is the average response time for all runs of, say, two miles length. What is really estimated here is how closely the sample regression line $(\bar{Y}_c = a + bX)$ estimates the population regression line $(\mu_{Y|X} = \alpha + \beta X)$. If one were to take another sample of the same size, one would not necessarily obtain the same values of a and b that were obtained before; this indicates that the sample regression line varies for repeated regression samples. The confidence interval for the *average* value of the dependent variable, $\mu_{Y|X}$, for a given X value, X_o, is:

$$\text{Confidence interval for } \mu_{Y|X_o}: (a + bX_o) \pm t \cdot s_{YX} \sqrt{\frac{1}{n} + \frac{(X_o - \bar{X})^2}{\Sigma X^2 - \frac{(\Sigma X)^2}{n}}}$$

where $\nu = n - 2$ degrees of freedom, as demonstrated in Note 12.54*a*.

For the taxicab example, the 90 percent confidence interval for the average time for all two mile runs is:

$$X_o = 2 \text{ miles}$$

90 percent confidence interval for $\mu_{Y|X \,=\, 2}$:

$$92.220 + 169.616(2) \pm 1.9432 \,(98.18)\sqrt{\frac{1}{8} + \frac{(0.775)^2}{2.995}}$$

$$= 431.46 \pm 108.85, \text{ or } 322.61 \text{ to } 540.31$$

One might also be interested in a prediction interval for a *particular* two mile run. Notice that the confidence interval just above was for the *average time for all two mile runs.* An average hides variability; a confidence interval for a particular two mile run will have greater variability than the variability in the confidence interval for the average of all such runs. The confidence interval for a *particular* value of the dependent variable is:

Confidence interval for forecasting the value of Y corresponding to a given X, X_o:

$$(a + bX_o) \pm t \cdot s_{YX}\sqrt{1 + \frac{1}{n} + \frac{(X_o - \bar{X})^2}{\Sigma X^2 - \dfrac{(\Sigma X)^2}{n}}}$$

where $v = n - 2$ degrees of freedom. This demonstrated in Note 12.54*b*.

For taxi response times, the 90 percent confidence interval for the number of seconds required for a *particular* two mile run is:

$$92.220 + 169.616(2) \pm 1.9432 \,(98.18)\sqrt{1 + \frac{1}{8} + \frac{(0.775)^2}{2.995}}$$

$$= 431.46 \pm 219.65, \text{ or } 211.81 \text{ to } 651.11$$

12.55 How Important Is the Normality Assumption?

Up to this point in the discussion of inference in regression it has been assumed that the individual values of Y for a given value of X are normally distributed about their mean, $\mu_{Y|X}$. This assumption may be relaxed in certain instances, without affecting the validity of some of the inferential procedures. First of all, the estimators a, b, and s_{YX}^2, are always unbiased estimators of their respective population parameters, α, β, and $\sigma_{Y|X}^2$, even without the assumption of normality. The confidence intervals and tests of hypotheses on α, β, and $\mu_{Y|X}$ are also valid without the assumption of normality, if the sample size is sufficiently large. (Typically a sample of 30 or so is sufficiently large if the population shape is not too skewed.) The final inference, a confidence interval for forecasting a *particular* value of Y given a value of $\bar{X}$ *always* requires the assumption of normality regardless of the sample size.

12.6 ANOTHER EXAMPLE OF REGRESSION ANALYSIS

The ABC Company sells vacuum cleaners. It has sold the same basic cleaner for more than 15 years, using door-to-door salespersons and a small salesroom. Since 1960, when the firm started selling in Atlanta, the Atlanta sales have increased from 150 to 260, while the number of door-to-door salespersons has increased from one to three. The company is interested in investigating the effect of additional salespersons upon its sales of vacuum cleaners. The following data for the past years are all that are available:

X, Number of Salespersons	Y, Number of Cleaners Sold
1	150
1	170
2	230
2	200
3	220
3	260

The company is investigating these questions:

1. Is there a relationship between the number of salespersons and the number of cleaners sold?
2. What relationship would enable a prediction of the number of cleaners sold, knowing the number of salespersons?
3. Estimate (with a 90 percent confidence interval) the number of cleaners an additional salesperson would be expected to sell.
4. Estimate (with a 90 percent confidence interval) the number of cleaners the company would sell next year with four salespersons. (Are there any pitfalls in this estimate?)

The calculations to answer these questions are in Figure 12.11.

The answers are:

1. The existence of a relationship between number of salespersons and number of cleaners can be investigated by hypothesizing that $\beta = 0$:

$$H_N: \quad \beta = 0$$
$$H_A: \quad \beta \neq 0$$

Test statistic: $t = \dfrac{b - \beta}{s_b} = \dfrac{40 - 0}{10.46} = 3.82$

Using a t-table with $\nu = 4$, the p-value is $2(0.0094) = 0.0188$.

Figure 12.11

ABC Company Data and Calculations

X	Y	X^2	Y^2	XY
1	150	1	22,500	150
1	170	1	28,900	170
2	230	4	52,900	460
2	200	4	40,000	400
3	220	9	48,400	660
3	260	9	67,600	780
$\Sigma X = 12$	$\Sigma Y = 1{,}230$	$\Sigma X^2 = 28$	$\Sigma Y^2 = 260{,}300$	$\Sigma XY = 2{,}620$

$$\bar{X} = \frac{\Sigma X}{n} = \frac{12}{6} = 2$$

$$\bar{Y} = \frac{\Sigma Y}{n} = \frac{1{,}230}{6} = 205$$

$$b = \frac{n\Sigma XY - (\Sigma X)(\Sigma Y)}{n\Sigma X^2 - (\Sigma X)^2} = \frac{6(2{,}620) - 12(1{,}230)}{6(28) - (12)^2} = 40$$

$$a = \bar{Y} - b\bar{X} = 205 - 40(2) = 125$$

$$s_{YX} = \sqrt{\frac{\Sigma Y^2 - a\Sigma Y - b\Sigma XY}{n-2}} = \sqrt{\frac{260{,}300 - 125(1{,}230) - 40(2{,}620)}{4}} = 20.92$$

std. dev. about $\hat{Y}$ or std. error of estimate

$$s_Y = \sqrt{\frac{\Sigma Y^2 - \frac{(\Sigma Y)^2}{n}}{n-1}} = \sqrt{\frac{260{,}300 - \frac{(1{,}230)^2}{6}}{5}} = 40.37$$

← *std. dev. about $\bar{Y}$ to be used for r^2 calculation*

$$r^2 = 1 - \left(\frac{s_{YX}}{s_Y}\right)^2 = 1 - \left(\frac{20.92}{40.37}\right)^2 = 0.73$$

← *coeff. of determination*

$$s_b = \frac{s_{YX}}{\sqrt{\Sigma X^2 - \frac{(\Sigma X)^2}{n}}} = \frac{20.92}{\sqrt{28 - \frac{(12)^2}{6}}} = 10.46$$

← *std. error of b*

$$s_a = s_b\sqrt{\frac{\Sigma X^2}{n}} = 10.46\sqrt{\frac{28}{6}} = 22.60$$

← *std. error of a*

2. The regression line is:

$$\bar{Y}_c = 125 + 40X$$

The coefficient of determination is 0.73, and the standard error of estimate is 20.92. It is usually customary to write the standard errors of a and b, s_a and s_b, underneath the values of a and b and to note the value of r^2 alongside. This would appear as:

$$\bar{Y}_c = \underset{(22.60)}{125} + \underset{(10.46)}{40X} \text{ where } r^2 = 0.73$$

3. A 90 percent confidence interval for the incremental sales of a salesperson is the interval:

$v = (6-1) - 1 = 4$

$$b \pm ts_b = 40 \pm 2.1318(10.46)$$
$$= 40 \pm 22.30$$
$$= 17.70 \text{ to } 62.30$$

4. For next year with four salespersons it is necessary to be cautious of extrapolating beyond the observed data. If judgment indicates this is valid, the forecast for next year is:

$X_0 = 4$

$$a + bX_o \pm ts_{YX} \sqrt{1 + \frac{1}{n} + \frac{(X_o - \bar{X})^2}{\Sigma X^2 - \frac{(\Sigma X)^2}{n}}}$$

$$= 125 + 40(4) \pm 2.1318(20.92) \sqrt{1 + \frac{1}{6} + \frac{(4 - 2)^2}{28 - \frac{(12)^2}{6}}}$$

$$= 219.4 \text{ to } 350.7$$

Note that all of the inferences assume that everything that affects sales (other than salespersons) has been held constant over the years. Changes in advertising, for example, could make the analysis invalid.

12.7 CURVILINEAR REGRESSION

Some extensions of linear regression analysis will be introduced briefly here, so that the student will have some guide to reading more advanced literature, and also be aware that linear regression can have many pitfalls.

If the assumption of linearity for simple regression is not met, it may be possible to find some kind of transformation or change in either or both variables which will bring about a linear relationship. If the scatter diagram shows a possible curvilinear relationship, and if there is a physical reason or theory for so doing, it may be appropriate to consider taking, say, the square root or the logarithm of each Y observation. If a plot of the scatter diagram of X against the logarithm of Y shows an apparently linear relationship, such a transformed model may be used with the logarithm of Y replacing Y in the simple linear regression analysis discussed throughout this chapter.

12.71 EXAMPLE OF CURVILINEAR REGRESSION

A recording executive has decided that the sixth week of a "hit" record is the decision point for the final production lot. This production decision is crucial for profits on the record. Based on past experience (a single hit) the data are shown in Figure 12.12.

The scatter diagrams are shown in Figure 12.13 for Y versus X, and in Figure 12.14 for log Y versus X. Logarithmic values are found in Appendix B.

It is readily apparent that a linear regression analysis is inferior to a curvilinear analysis. The calculations for the goodness of fit to these data

Figure 12.12

Sales per Week (Y) ($1,000)	Log Y	Week since Introduction (X)
60........................	1.7782	1
90........................	1.9542	2
140........................	2.1461	3
225........................	2.3522	4
350........................	2.5441	5

Figure 12.13

Scatter Diagram for Record Sales

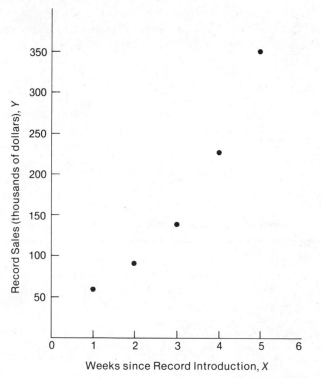

Weeks since Record Introduction, X

are given in Figure 12.15 for a linear straight line regression analysis ($r^2 = 0.911$), and in Figure 12.16 for a curvilinear regression analysis ($r^2 = 0.999$). These findings demonstrate that (1) linear regression can be misused for curvilinear relationships, despite a high value of the coefficient of determination, and (2) that curvilinear regression is an added tool of statistical analysis, but with constraints when dealing with data over time. Much more will be said on this subject in Chapter 14.

Figure 12.14

Logarithmic Scatter Diagram for Record Sales

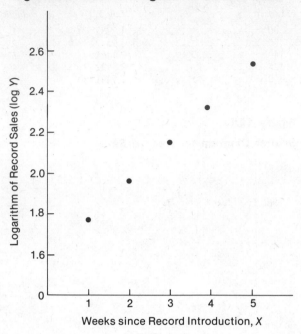

Figure 12.15

Regression Computations, Record Sales

X, Weeks since Introduction	Y, Sales ($1,000)	X^2	XY	Y^2
1...................	60	1	60	3,600
2...................	90	4	180	8,100
3...................	140	9	420	19,600
4...................	225	16	900	50,625
5...................	350	25	1,750	122,500
$\Sigma X = \overline{15}$	$\Sigma Y = \overline{865}$	$\Sigma X^2 = \overline{55}$	$\Sigma XY = \overline{3,310}$	$\Sigma Y^2 = \overline{204,425}$

$$\bar{X} = 3$$
$$\bar{Y} = 173$$
$$b = \frac{n\Sigma XY - (\Sigma X)(\Sigma Y)}{n\Sigma X^2 - (\Sigma X)^2} = \frac{5(3,310) - 15(865)}{5(55) - (15)^2} = \frac{3,575}{50} = 71.5$$
$$a = \bar{Y} - b\bar{X} = 173 - (71.5)3 = 173 - 214.5 = -41.5$$
$$s_{YX}^2 = \frac{\Sigma Y^2 - a\Sigma Y - b\Sigma XY}{n-2} = \frac{204,425 + 35,898 - 236,665}{5-2} = 1,219.3$$
$$s_Y^2 = \frac{\Sigma Y^2 - \frac{(\Sigma Y)^2}{n}}{n-1} = \frac{204,425 - \frac{748,225}{5}}{5-1} = \frac{204,425 - 149,645}{4} = 13,695$$
$$r^2 \text{(adjusted)} = 1 - \frac{s_{YX}^2}{s_Y^2} = 1 - \frac{1,219.3}{13,695} = 1 - 0.089 = 0.911$$
where $\bar{Y}_c = -41.5 + 71.5X$

Figure 12.16

Regression Computations, Record Sales

X, Weeks since Introduction	Y Sales ($1,000)	log Y	X²	X · log Y	(log Y)²
1.........	60	1.7782	1	1.7782	3.1620
2.........	90	1.9542	4	3.9084	3.8189
3.........	140	2.1461	9	6.4383	4.6057
4.........	225	2.3522	16	9.4088	5.5328
5.........	350	2.5441	25	12.7205	6.4724
$\Sigma X = 15$		$\Sigma \log Y = 10.7748$	$\Sigma X^2 = 55$	$\Sigma X \log Y = 34.2542$	$\Sigma (\log Y)^2 = 23.5918$

$$\bar{X} = 3$$
$$\overline{\log Y} = 2.1550$$
$$b = \frac{n \Sigma X \log Y - (\Sigma X)(\Sigma \log Y)}{n \Sigma X^2 - (\Sigma X)^2} = \frac{5(34.2542) - 15(10.7748)}{5(55) - (15)^2} = \frac{9.649}{50} = 0.19298$$
$$a = \frac{\Sigma \log Y}{n} - b\bar{X} = 2.15496 - 0.19298(3) = 1.57602$$
$$s_{YX}^2 = \frac{\Sigma (\log Y)^2 - a\Sigma \log Y - b\Sigma X \log Y}{n - 2} = \frac{23.5918 - 16.9813 - 6.6104}{3}$$
$$= 0.0001$$
$$s_Y^2 = \frac{\Sigma (\log Y)^2 - \frac{(\Sigma \log Y)^2}{n}}{n - 1} = \frac{23.5918 - \frac{(10.7748)^2}{5}}{4}$$
$$= \frac{23.5918 - 23.2193}{4} = 0.0931$$
$$r^2 (\text{adjusted}) = 1 - \frac{s_{YX}^2}{s_Y^2} = 1 - \frac{0.0001}{0.0931} = 1 - 0.001 = 0.999$$

where $\log \bar{Y}_c = 1.5760 + 0.1930 X$

The model for this curvilinear relationship is

$$\bar{Y}_c = c(1 + g)^X$$

Taking logarithms,

$$\log \bar{Y}_c = \log c + \log [(1 + g)^X]$$
$$= \log c + X \log (1 + g)$$

or

$$\log \bar{Y}_c = a + bX$$

where

$$a = \log c \text{ or } \qquad c = 10^a = \text{antilog } a$$
$$b = \log (1 + g) \text{ or } 1 + g = 10^b = \text{antilog } b$$

Thus, since the regression equation is

$$\log \bar{Y}_c = 1.5760 + 0.1930X$$

and

$$c = \text{antilog } (a) = \text{antilog } (1.5760) = 37.67$$
$$1 + g = \text{antilog } (b) = \text{antilog } (0.1930) = 1.5596$$

The equation for $\bar{Y}_c$ is

$$\bar{Y}_c = 37.67 \,(1.5596)^X$$

As X increases by one, the calculated value of $\bar{Y}_c$ increases by 55.96 percent.

12.8   REGRESSION ANALYSIS AND THE COMPUTER

It is apparent that the arithmetic may be somewhat tedious for some regression problems. It is very unusual to compute a regression analysis for a realistic problem "by hand." There are several alternatives; miniature calculators are available which compute some limited forms of regression analysis, and programmable calculators include some complete regression methods. Finally, and most important, the widespread use of digital computers, and access to these computers via time-sharing methods, makes the power of regression analyses available without arithmetic drudgery.

Most computer installations have rather powerful regression packages available, so that the student need not know computer programming to use these regression methodologies. We should caution, however, that it is always important to determine that there is a theoretical basis behind the regression analysis being performed. It may be dangerous to try all kinds of predictor variables attempting to find the highest value of the coefficient of determination. Such a procedure may lead to a very good fit for past data; if this is a fit which is observed by chance alone, and is not caused by some underlying physical mechanism, the regression model may be of no value for prediction.

12.9   SUMMARY

This chapter has investigated the least squares method of fitting straight lines to points on a scatter diagram. In general, there is an independent or X variable whose value must be known in order to predict the value of the dependent or Y variable. For this general situation, assumptions of linearity, equal variance, independence, and normality have been required; these permit inferences about regression situations. The use of computer techniques is often required to solve large-scale regression problems.

For ease in computational organization the formulas in this chapter are summarized here.

$$b = \frac{n\Sigma XY - (\Sigma X)(\Sigma Y)}{n\Sigma X^2 - (\Sigma X)^2}$$

$$a = \bar{Y} - b\bar{X}$$

$$s_{YX} = \sqrt{\frac{\Sigma Y^2 - a\Sigma Y - b\Sigma XY}{n - 2}}$$

$$s_Y = \sqrt{\frac{\Sigma Y^2 - \frac{(\Sigma Y)^2}{n}}{n - 1}}$$

$$r^2 = 1 - \left(\frac{s_{YX}}{s_Y}\right)^2$$

$$s_b = \frac{s_{YX}}{\sqrt{\Sigma X^2 - \frac{(\Sigma X)^2}{n}}}$$

$$s_a = s_b\sqrt{\frac{\Sigma X^2}{n}}$$

EXERCISES

12.1   Explain the criterion of least squares.

12.2   Regression analysis refers to a dependent variable (Y) and an independent variable (X). Explain the meaning of these terms.

12.3   An advertising agency is investigating the relationship between the number of 30-second TV ads for a detergent and the number of cases of the detergent sold at retail in the market area. Discuss the appropriateness of a linear model to predict cases sold, knowing the number of 30-second TV ads. In your discussion, be sure to include such ideas as a possible minimum number of ads necessary to attain brand recognition (a threshold effect) and a possible saturation effect which might cause displeasure with the product. Also consider using linear models for a limited range of number of ads.

12.4   From your own experience and education, comment upon the appropriateness of a linear assumption in each of these situations:
   a. Predicting (at the macro-economic level) personal savings when disposable personal income is known.
   b. Predicting your score on a statistics exam when you know the number of hours you have studied.
   c. Predicting the distance you will travel on an interstate highway when you know the number of hours you will be in the car and traveling.
   d. Predicting the time a drag racer will require to travel a known distance from a standing start.
   e. Predicting the first class domestic air fare when the distance is known.
   f. Predicting the number of standardized, uniform pieces manu-

factured in an eight-hour shift when the number of employees is known.

g. Predicting the price of a share of common stock for a nationally known firm in a specified industry, when the earnings per share are known.

12.5   Consider this set of regression data, scatter diagram, and regression computations:

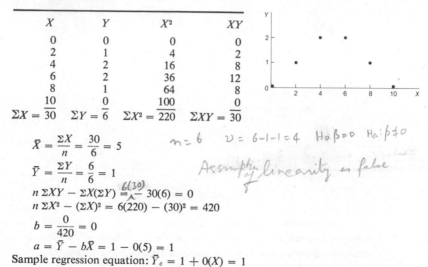

X	Y	X^2	XY
0	0	0	0
2	1	4	2
4	2	16	8
6	2	36	12
8	1	64	8
10	0	100	0
$\Sigma X = 30$	$\Sigma Y = 6$	$\Sigma X^2 = 220$	$\Sigma XY = 30$

$$\bar{X} = \frac{\Sigma X}{n} = \frac{30}{6} = 5$$

$$\bar{Y} = \frac{\Sigma Y}{n} = \frac{6}{6} = 1$$

$n\,\Sigma XY - \Sigma X(\Sigma Y) = \overset{6(30)}{} 30(6) = 0$

$n\,\Sigma X^2 - (\Sigma X)^2 = 6(220) - (30)^2 = 420$

$$b = \frac{0}{420} = 0$$

$a = \bar{Y} - b\bar{X} = 1 - 0(5) = 1$

Sample regression equation: $\bar{Y}_c = 1 + 0(X) = 1$

(handwritten: $n = 6$ $v = 6-1-1 = 4$ $H_0: \beta = 0$ $H_a: \beta \neq 0$)

(handwritten: Assumption of linearity is false)

According to the sample regression equation, what value of Y would you predict when $X = 1$? When $X = 3$? From looking at the scatter diagram, do you think that knowing the value of X would help you predict the value of Y? Why do you think the regression analysis indicated no relationship between X and Y, while the scatter diagram indicates an apparently orderly relationship? Which of the assumptions of regression analysis may have been violated?

* 12.6   A cheese factory manager is attempting to attain a better understanding of the cost structure of making cheese. He realized that he could point out several types of costs associated with making a batch of cheese: the cost of ingredients, which should be very closely determined by the number of pounds of cheese in the batch; the labor cost which are determined by the size of the batch; and the labor cost which occur because a batch is being processed, but which do not depend on the size of the batch. The records immediately available show only two items for the batches produced in the last ten days: the number of pounds of cheese in a batch, and the costs associated with producing that batch. From the data below, compute a least-squares regression line which will help the manager predict the cost of a batch of cheese when he knows its size, and which will also help separate costs into these two categories: the cost of setting up for and

---

* Answers to exercises marked with an asterisk (*) are in Appendix L.

producing a batch of cheese, and the incremental cost of a pound of cheese, given that a batch is being produced.

Batch Number	Y Total Cost	X Number of Pounds
1	$300	200
2	500	1,000
3	450	600
4	280	350
5	470	800
6	400	700
7	390	500
8	200	150
9	450	900
10	360	400

$\Sigma X = 5,600; \Sigma Y = 3,800; \Sigma X^2 = 3,895,000; \Sigma XY = 2,358,000;$
$\Sigma Y^2 = 1,526,000$

* 12.7 For the regression analysis of Exercise 12.6, compute and explain the meaning of the standard error of estimate and the coefficient of determination.

* 12.8 After the cheese factory manager of Exercise 12.6 has obtained the regression results, he obtains another study which claims the incremental cost of manufacturing a pound of cheese, given that a batch is being produced, is really $0.24. At what level of significance do the data of Exercise 12.6 refute the claim of an incremental cost of $0.24 per pound; i.e., what is the p-value?

* 12.9 Construct an 80 percent confidence interval for the cost of setting up to produce a batch of cheese.

* 12.10 Comment upon the relevance of a test of the hypothesis that $\beta = 0$ for Exercise 12.6, when it is known that the ingredients used in making cheese have economic value.

* 12.11 Construct a 90 percent confidence interval for the average cost of all 500-pound batches of cheese, using the data of Exercise 12.6.

* 12.12 The cheese factory manager of Exercise 12.6 needs to forecast the cost of producing a 500-pound batch in order to prepare a bid for a special order. To help in bidding strategy, he has asked for a 50 percent confidence interval for the cost of a 500 pound batch. Find the desired confidence interval.

12.13 The ten batches of cheese in the data for Exercise 12.6 were produced in the sequence indicated, batch one through batch ten. How would the assumption of independence possibly be violated by factors such as a few days when milk prices were unusually high, a three-day period when labor troubles were beginning to surface, and a three-day period immediately after the announcement of a very generous bonus to the workers.

* 12.14 A securities analyst is investigating the relationship between the number of shares of a stock traded on the New York Stock Exchange

and the percentage change in price for that stock, on a weekly basis. She has collected these data:

Stock Number	Shares Traded (hundreds)	Changes in Price, Percent
1.	4	1
2.	61	0
3.	31	2
4.	6	5
5.	17	3
6.	98	1
7.	31	5
8.	5	0
9.	56	5
10.	20	0
11.	33	5
12.	23	4
13.	73	3
14.	14	1
15.	14	4
16.	53	0
17.	90	1
18.	39	2
19.	71	0
20.	29	4

Compute the least squares regression line to determine the percentage change in price, knowing the number of shares traded during the week. How much variation in price change is accounted for by knowing the number of shares traded?

* 12.15 For the data of Exercise 12.14, test the hypothesis that change in price is not related to the weekly volume (number of shares traded). What is the p-value?

* 12.16 A real estate developer is investigating the relationship between the selling price and the size of lots in a mountain subdivision. All the lots are judged about equal in convenience, terrain, view, and other important factors; there is some variation in size. There is considerable bargaining between buyer and seller, so the original list or "asking" prices are seldom followed in making the transaction. The selling price and size of a sample of the lots in the subdivision are as follows:

Lot Number	Selling Price, ($1,000)	Lot Size, Acres
1.	10	0.8
2.	12	1.2
3.	8	0.7
4.	9	0.9
5.	13	1.1
6.	14	1.4
7.	10	0.9

Make a point estimate for the eventual selling price of a one-acre lot in the subdivision.

* 12.17 Construct an 80 percent confidence interval for the average selling price for all one-acre lots in the subdivision, for Exercise 12.16.

* 12.18 Construct an 80 percent confidence interval for the selling price for lot #108, which has an area of one acre, from the data of Exercise 12.16.

* 12.19 Construct an 80 percent confidence interval for the change in selling price brought about by adding an acre to a lot, for Exercise 12.16.

* 12.20 Calculate and interpret each of these statistics for Exercise 12.16: s_{YX}, r, r^2, a, and b.

* 12.21 For Exercise 12.16, what is the p-value for testing the hypothesis of a linear relationship between lot size and selling price?

12.22 Suppose it is pointed out to you that there is a very significant relationship between the number of new stork nests in Denmark and the number of babies born in New York City. Observations were taken over a 50-year period, one observation per year, ending in 1956. Comment upon the relevance of such information to a manufacturer of baby clothing who is planning 1975 inventories, and who is offered a "stork nest count" by a Danish firm at a very "reasonable rate."

REFERENCES

Draper, Norman R., and Smith, Harry. *Applied Regression Analysis*. New York: John Wiley & Sons, Inc., 1966.

Ezekiel, Mordecai, and Fox, Karl A. *Methods of Correlation and Regression Analysis*, 3d ed. New York: John Wiley & Sons, Inc., 1959.

Simon, Herbert A. *Models of Man*. New York: John Wiley & Sons, Inc., 1957.

Williams, E. J. *Regression Analysis*. New York: John Wiley & Sons, Inc., 1959.

13

Multiple Regression

Chapter 12 discussed simple linear and curvilinear regression and the calculation, by the method of least squares, of the mathematical relationship between *one* independent variable and *one* dependent variable. The coefficient of determination, which shows how well the mathematical equation "explains" the variation in the dependent variable, was also discussed. This chapter presents a more powerful analytical tool in dealing with the "explanation" of the variation of a dependent variable.

Most important dependent variables are influenced by more than one independent variable. For example, the time for taxi runs may be affected by traffic, driver, snow, and time of day, as well as distance. Thus, the more common situation is that a dependent variable is influenced by more than one independent variable.

There are very few new concepts in multiple regression; almost all the ideas of simple regression can be extended directly into multiple regression. In the most elementary situation, using regression as a line-fitting device, the concept of a least square line is extended to multiple regression to fit a least squares plane (or its higher-dimension extension, a hyperplane) to a set of data. In problems of inference, the concept of a true population regression line becomes a true population regression plane. The sample regression equation is used to estimate the (unknown) true population regression equation in both simple and multiple regression. Similarly, the descriptive measures (standard error of estimate, coefficient of determination) have direct analogies in multiple regression.

13.1 LINEAR MULTIPLE REGRESSION EQUATION

In simple regression (one independent variable) the linear model is:

$$\mu_{Y|X} = \alpha + \beta X$$

in which the parameters α and β are estimated by the least squares equation:

$$\bar{Y}_c = a + bX$$

In multiple regression (more than one independent variable) the linear model with *two* independent variables is:

$$\mu_{Y|X_1X_2} = \alpha + \beta_1 X_1 + \beta_2 X_2$$

and the parameters (α, β_1, β_2) are estimated by a least squares equation:

$$\bar{Y}_c = a + b_1 X_1 + b_2 X_2$$

For more independent variables, additional terms may be added to these expressions. The coefficients b_1 and b_2 are called *partial regression coefficients*.

13.2 LEAST SQUARES METHOD

The method used to calculate the multiple regression equation is similar to the simple (one independent variable) linear regression case in the previous chapter. The difference is that there are now three estimates (a, b_1, and b_2) to calculate instead of the previous two (a and b).

Exactly as in the simple linear regression case, the objective is to minimize the sum of the squared differences between the observed values of the dependent variable, Y, and those calculated, $\bar{Y}_c$, using the multiple regression equation. The least squares method states:

$$\text{Minimize } \Sigma(Y - \bar{Y}_c)^2$$

By using the calculus, the minimization eventually reduces to the following three normal equations:

$$\Sigma Y = n\,a + b_1\Sigma X_1 + b_2\Sigma X_2$$
$$\Sigma X_1 Y = a\Sigma X_1 + b_1\Sigma X_1^2 + b_2\Sigma X_1 X_2$$
$$\Sigma X_2 Y = a\Sigma X_2 + b_1\Sigma X_1 X_2 + b_2\Sigma X_2^2$$

13.21 Interpretation of Least Squares Equation
$\bar{Y}_c = a + b_1 X_1 + b_2 X_2$

The three normal equations can be reformulated into separate equations for a, b_1, and b_2. Because of the complexity of these equations (and similar equations for cases with four or even more variables), the typical and sensible procedure is to use a computer program to make these calculations.

Almost every major computing center has a package of statistical programs which contains programs for multiple linear-regression. Rather than attempt to explain any one (or several) of these programs, the remainder of this chapter is written as if a computer printout is available for the example problem being solved. The reader is advised to obtain such a printout from a local computer center, if possible. (However, the unavailability of a computer printout does not affect the understandability of what follows. By following this chapter with the printout available, the interpretation of the various measures which are reported in the printout will become clear. Thus, the purpose of this chapter is to explain uses and interpretations of multiple regression analysis; no emphasis is placed upon the computational aspects of the analysis, due to their burdensome nature. These calculations are almost never done manually. The emphasis is on interpretation and use of multiple linear regression.

13.22 Example of Two Independent Variables

The data for this example are found in Figure 13.1 (ignore the data for variables X_3, X_4, and X_5 for now). The data represent a sample of 48 students in an introductory statistics course. The data will be used to explore a simple question: Weight is a function of what? Or, weight $= f$ (what variables) Or, in the case of this example, weight $= f$ (height and age).

Limited to these *two* independent variables the least squares solution (Figure 13.2) is:

$$\text{Weight} = -215.290 + 5.088 \,(\text{Height}) + 0.789 \,(\text{Age})$$
$$\bar{Y}_c = -215.290 + 5.088X_1 + 0.789X_2$$

The interpretation of this equation is quite straightforward (except for the constant term, $a = -215.290$). The value of b_1 (5.088) indicates that for each added inch in height (while age remains constant) a person on the average would be predicted to weigh 5.088 pounds more. The value of b_2 (0.789) indicates that for each added year in age (while height remains constant) a person on the average would be predicted to weigh 0.789 pounds more. The coefficients b_1 and b_2 are called coefficients of partial regression.[1]

The meaning of the constant term ($a = -215.290$) is less obvious. Taken literally, it means that a person who is zero inches tall and is zero years old weighs minus 215.290 pounds. Obviously, this is meaningless. The proper interpretation of the constant term is that it is meaningful for values of X_1 and X_2 when X_1 and X_2 are in a relevant (observed) range of their values. Thus, the equation should not be taken literally unless the values of X_1 are between 59 to 76 inches (or near these values), and the

---

[1] These coefficients of partial regression should not be confused with the simple regression coefficients that can be obtained by two separate simple regression analyses (between weight and height, and between weight and age). The simple regression coefficients assume that variables not included in the model vary according to the makeup of the population, while the partial regression coefficients assume that other variables which are included in the equation are held constant. Thus, there is often a substantial difference between a simple regression coefficient and a corresponding partial regression coefficient.

Figure 13.1. Variables of 48 Students

Y Weight (lbs)	X_1 Height (inches)	X_2 Age (years)	X_3 Sex (Male = 1, Female = 0)	X_4 Telephone (last four digits)	X_5 Social Security (last four digits)
145	68	22	F = 0	1323	3181
170	71	31	M = 1	4797	2078
135	68	25	M = 1	6443	4471
180	74	32	M = 1	7120	3214
194	72	35	M = 1	7465	4452
190	72	24	M = 1	8586	8637
190	72	23	M = 1	7993	3699
162	75	19	M = 1	0220	9197
120	64	35	F = 0	3905	5170
130	68	19	F = 0	6456	8343
150	70	30	M = 1	8048	9872
175	74	20	M = 1	1236	2056
185	73	27	M = 1	0775	0806
162	68	28	M = 1	1385	9514
165	72	21	M = 1	4195	9548
102	63	21	F = 0	5526	6557
125	64	23	F = 0	3406	6769
155	68	44	M = 1	2079	6476
125	64	27	M = 1	3044	7722
210	76	54	M = 1	2644	6159
175	72	37	M = 1	2924	5183
120	69	22	M = 1	4685	1693
160	72	34	M = 1	8768	8733
185	74	42	M = 1	4551	9261
145	70	20	M = 1	1639	6385
142	59	28	M = 1	8467	5953
185	72	28	M = 1	7681	7947
145	67	27	M = 1	0596	0032
155	73	19	M = 1	5708	5013
195	71	46	M = 1	2196	0889
160	72	48	M = 1	1705	4775
175	71	24	M = 1	4501	4968
210	68	27	M = 1	8063	2585
140	68	42	M = 1	2069	3137
135	66	30	M = 1	2040	7720
142	66	50	F = 0	6698	1253
155	69	27	M = 1	5206	7170
165	71	26	M = 1	9174	7966
170	66	44	M = 1	2177	6097
160	69	21	M = 1	4672	7711
165	68	37	M = 1	6447	1561
230	71	55	M = 1	3894	8714
200	71	23	M = 1	8395	7271
195	70	19	M = 1	2491	9347
165	70	25	M = 1	3675	9232
117	66	20	F = 0	9116	0256
145	69	20	M = 1	0667	1587
128	64	25	F = 0	9422	1037

Average Weight = 161.125
    Standard Deviation = 27.777
Average Height = 69.375
    Standard Deviation = 3.480
Average Age = 29.708
    Standard Deviation = 9.944

Average Sex (?) = 0.833
    Standard Deviation = 0.377
Average Telephone Number = 4672.354
    Standard Deviation = 2791.699
Average Social Security Number = 5445.771
    Standard Deviation = 3002.858

Figure 13.2

Computer Printout for Two Independent Variable Solution (partial printout)

```
STANDARD ERROR OF ESTIMATE    19.5496
INTERCEPT        −215.28964
                 PARTIAL
VARIABLE         REG. COEF.
   1             5.08806
   2             0.78868
```

values of X_2 are between 19 to 55 years (or near these values). Used with these constraints, the constant, a, becomes understandable.

As a simple demonstration of the predictive use of the model, for the first student in the sample the following point estimate of the average weight for a person of that height and age is:

$$
\begin{aligned}
\bar{Y}_c &= -215.290 + 5.088X_1 + 0.789X_2 \\
&= -215.290 + 5.088(68) + 0.789(22) \\
&= -215.290 + 345.984 + 17.358 \\
&= 148.052 \text{ pounds}
\end{aligned}
$$

The actual weight of the student is 145 pounds; the estimate is about three pounds in error. Before hastily assuming that the regression equation is quite accurate, let us compute all 48 point estimates and compare these predictions with the actual weights. See Figure 13.3 and note several rather large errors.

13.3 STANDARD ERROR OF ESTIMATE

As in simple linear regression, there is an interest in describing the variability of the observed weights, Y, from the predictions of the regression equation, $\bar{Y}_c$. The standard error of estimate again provides this description of variability about $\bar{Y}_c$. It is calculated as:

$$
s_{Y12} = \sqrt{\frac{\Sigma(Y - \bar{Y}_c)^2}{n - 3}}
$$

where $Y12$ indicates Y to be the dependent variable and 1 and 2 as the two independent variables. The denominator is $n - 3$, because three sample estimates (a, b_1, b_2) have been made.

For the weight example, this value from (Figure 13.2) is:

$$
s_{Y12} = 19.5496 \text{ pounds}
$$

The value of 19.5496 pounds is viewed as the estimate of the standard deviation of Y values about the *true* (population) regression plane (equation).

Figure 13.3

Comparison of Predicted and Actual Weights

Student	Weight		Error
	Actual Y	Predicted $\bar{Y}_c$	$Y - \bar{Y}_c$
1............................	145	148.0	− 3.0
2............................	170	170.4	− 0.4
3............................	135	150.4	−15.4
4............................	180	186.5	− 6.5
5............................	194	178.7	15.3
6............................	190	170.0	20.0
7............................	190	169.2	20.8
8............................	162	181.3	−19.3
9............................	120	138.0	−18.0
10............................	130	145.7	−15.7
11............................	150	164.5	−14.5
12............................	175	177.0	− 2.0
13............................	185	177.4	7.6
14............................	162	152.8	9.2
15............................	165	167.6	− 2.6
16............................	102	121.8	−19.8
17............................	125	128.5	− 3.5
18............................	155	165.4	−10.4
19............................	125	131.6	− 6.6
20............................	210	214.0	− 4.0
21............................	175	180.2	− 5.2
22............................	120	153.1	−33.1
23............................	160	177.9	−17.9
24............................	185	194.4	− 9.4
25............................	145	156.6	−11.6
26............................	142	107.0	35.0
27............................	185	173.1	11.9
28............................	145	146.9	− 1.9
29............................	155	171.1	−16.1
30............................	195	182.2	12.8
31............................	160	188.9	−28.9
32............................	175	164.9	10.1
33............................	210	152.0	58.0
34............................	140	163.8	−23.8
35............................	135	144.2	− 9.2
36............................	142	160.0	−18.0
37............................	155	157.1	− 2.1
38............................	165	166.5	− 1.5
39............................	170	155.2	14.8
40............................	160	152.3	7.7
41............................	165	159.9	5.1
42............................	230	189.3	40.7
43............................	200	164.1	35.9
44............................	195	155.9	39.1
45............................	165	160.6	4.4
46............................	117	136.3	−19.3
47............................	145	151.6	− 6.6
48............................	128	130.1	− 2.1

13.4 COEFFICIENT OF MULTIPLE DETERMINATION

As in simple regression the question of how good does the equation "explain" the observed data can be answered by looking at the square of the ratio of the standard error of estimate to the standard deviation of Y. (The standard deviation of Y is equal to 27.78 as found in Figure 13.1). This ratio is:

Proportion of variation "unexplained" $=$

$$\frac{s_{Y12}^2}{s_Y^2} = \left(\frac{s_{Y12}}{s_Y}\right)^2 = \left(\frac{19.55}{27.78}\right)^2 = 0.4953$$

Thus, the proportion of variation "explained" $=$ *(1 - unexplained)* *coeff of multiple determination*

$$1 - 0.4953 = 0.5047 = R_{Y12}^2$$

This proportion of variation which is "explained" by the regression plane is called the *coefficient of multiple determination*. This coefficient of determination has been adjusted for degrees of freedom.[2]

13.5 INFERENCE IN MULTIPLE REGRESSION

By use of analysis of variance, which was introduced in Chapter 11, the hypothesis that $\beta_1 = \beta_2 = 0$ can be tested. For this test the F distribution is used. Computer programs typically perform the necessary calculations. For our example, the analysis of variance table, extracted from Figure 13.4, is:

Variation	Sum of Squares	÷ df =	Mean Squares
Regression	SSR = 19,066.636	2	MSR = 9,533.318
Error (Residual)	SSE = 17,196.614	45	MSE = 382.147
Total	SST = 36,263.250	47	

---

[2] The unadjusted coefficient of multiple determination, $\hat{R}^2$, is related to the adjusted coefficient in this way for two independent variables:

$$R_{Y12}^2 = 1 - (1 - \hat{R}_{Y12}^2)\left(\frac{n-1}{n-3}\right)$$

(handwritten: $R_y^2 = 1 - (1 - \bar{R}_{y,12}^2)\left(\frac{n-1}{n-k}\right)$ *)*

$$(1 - \hat{R}_{Y12}^2)\left(\frac{n-1}{n-3}\right) = 1 - R_{Y12}^2$$

$$1 - \hat{R}_{Y12}^2 = \frac{n-3}{n-1}(1 - R_{Y12}^2)$$

In the case of the weight example:

$$1 - \hat{R}_{Y12}^2 = \frac{45}{47}(0.4953) = 0.4742$$

Thus,

$$\hat{R}_{Y12}^2 = 0.5258$$

where SSR is the "explained" variation and SSE is the "unexplained" variation.

To test whether weights are related to height and age:

$$H_N: \quad \beta_1 = 0 \text{ and } \beta_2 = 0$$
$$H_A: \quad \text{Not both } \beta_1 \text{ and } \beta_2 = 0$$

Using the F statistic, obtain:

$$F = \frac{MSR}{MSE} = \frac{9,533.318}{382.147} = 24.947$$

From Appendix K for $v_1 = 2$ and $v_2 = 45$, the p-value $= 0.000$, or trivial. Typically, one would reject H_N with a p-value this small.

Note that in the analysis of variance table the total sum of squares, SST is the numerator of the expression for s_Y^2, and the error (residual) sum of squares, SSE, is the numerator of the expression for s_{Y12}^2, the square of the standard error of estimate.

Figure 13.4

Computer Printout for Two Independent Variable Solution (partial printout)

STANDARD ERROR OF ESTIMATE	19.5496			
INTERCEPT	−215.28964			

VARIABLE	PARTIAL REG. COEF.			
1	5.08806			
2	0.78868			

SOURCE OF VARIATION	D.F.	SUM OF SQ.	MEAN SQ.	F VALUE
EXPLAINED BY REGRESS.	2	19066.636	9533.318	24.947
DEVIATION FROM REGRESS.	45	17196.614	382.147	
TOTAL	47	36263.250		

MULTIPLE CORR. R	0.7251	ADJUSTED R	0.7104
COEF. OF DETERM.	0.5258	ADJUSTED R (SQD)	0.5047

13.51   Significance of Regression Coefficients

Just as in the case of simple linear regression, there is interest in whether b_1 and b_2 are statistically significantly different from zero. Again, hypothesis testing is used to answer this question. In order to conduct hypotheses tests for β_1 and β_2, it is necessary to obtain estimates of the standard error for b_1, s_{b_1}, and for b_2, s_{b_2}. From Figure 13.5 they are (rounded):

$$s_{b_1} = 0.8244$$
$$s_{b_2} = 0.2885$$

Figure 13.5

Computer Printout for Two Independent Variable Solution

STANDARD ERROR OF ESTIMATE   19.5486
INTERCEPT -215.28964

VARIABLE	PARTIAL REG. COEF.	STD. ERROR COEF.	COMPUTED T
1	5.08806	.82436	6.17
2	.78868	.28850	2.73

SOURCE OF VARIATION	D.F.	SUM OF SQ.	MEAN SQ.	F VALUE
EXPLAINED BY REGRESS.	2	19066.636	9533.318	24.947
DEVIATION FROM REGRESS.	45	17196.614	382.147	
TOTAL	47	36263.250		

MULTIPLE CORR. R 0.7251   ADJUSTED R   0.7104
COEF. OF DETERM. 0.5258   ADJUSTED R (SQD) 0.5047

(handwritten margin note: β_1 need not be $=0$ it could be any hypothesized value.)

The hypothesis tests are:[3]

$$H_N: \beta_1 = 0 \qquad\qquad H_N: \beta_2 = 0$$
$$H_A: \beta_1 \neq 0 \qquad\qquad H_A: \beta_2 \neq 0$$

$$t = \frac{b_1 - \beta_1}{s_{b_1}} = \frac{5.0881 - 0}{0.8244} = 6.17 \qquad t = \frac{b_2 - \beta_2}{s_{b_2}} = \frac{0.7886 - 0}{0.2885} = 2.73$$

p-value = negligibly small $\qquad\qquad$ p-value = 2(0.0032) = 0.0064

Thus, in both cases, if the analyst had prespecified a value of $\alpha = .01$, one would conclude that a statistically significant relationship exists between weight and height (holding age constant) and between weight and age (holding height constant). These same procedures may be used to test any other hypothesized value for β_1 and β_2.

13.6 BETA COEFFICIENTS

Although the regression coefficient for height has a larger value than the coefficient for age (5.0881 versus 0.7886), this does *not* mean that height is necessarily more important than age in weight determination. The basic problem is that b_1 and b_2 are in different units, pounds per inch versus pounds per year. In order to eliminate this problem of different units, each of these regression coefficients is converted to *beta coefficients*. This is accomplished as follows:

---

[3] The p-values were obtained from the standard normal table as the degrees of freedom $(48 - 3 = 45)$ is large. For degrees of freedom less than 30, values from the t distribution should be used.

$$\text{Beta (1)} = b_1\left(\frac{s_{X_1}}{s_Y}\right) = 5.0881\left(\frac{3.480}{27.777}\right) = 0.637$$

$$\text{Beta (2)} = b_2\left(\frac{s_{X_2}}{s_Y}\right) = 0.7886\left(\frac{9.944}{27.777}\right) = 0.282$$

These beta coefficients are the regression coefficients adjusted for both the variation (standard deviations) in the dependent and the appropriate independent variable. This adjustment eliminates the difference in units for b_1 and b_2 and places them on comparable levels. Note that if an independent variable has a very small standard deviation, its beta coefficient will tend to be small. This indicates that independent variable is of little importance for prediction, since its value is about the same for all observations.

13.7 DUMMY VARIABLES

By observing that R_{Y12}^2 is about 0.505, it is apparent that about 49.5 percent of the total variation in Y remains "unexplained." One possible reason for this is that the initial solution was computed treating males and females in the sample alike; i.e., having the same values for a, b_1, and b_2. The use of *dummy variables* is a technique designed to determine the different intercepts for males and females. Referring back to Figure 13.1, note that the sex of each student in the sample is identified. A new variable is created by assigning a value of $X_3 = 1$ for a male and $X_3 = 0$ for a female. The value of b_3 estimates the difference in intercept for males and females.

The question is whether the addition of a new variable for sex (X_3)

Figure 13.6

Computer Printout for Three Independent Variable Solution

STANDARD ERROR OF ESTIMATE   18.5597

INTERCEPT   −151.84123

VARIABLE	PARTIAL REG. COEF.	STD. ERROR COEF.	COMPUTED T
1	3.95082	0.91154	4.33
2	0.73234	0.27488	2.66
3	20.54613	8.44207	2.43

SOURCE OF VARIATION	D.F.	SUM OF SQ.	MEAN SQ.	F VALUE
EXPLAINED BY REGRESS.	3	21106.975	7035.658	20.425
DEVIATION FROM REGRESS.	44	15156.275	344.461	
TOTAL	47	36263.250		

MULTIPLE CORR. R	0.7629	ADJUSTED R	0.7444
COEF. OF DETERM.	0.5820	ADJUSTED R (SQD)	0.5535

improves the "explanation" of the (new) regression equation, whose print-out is shown in Figure 13.6.

The new regression equation is:

$$\bar{Y}_c = -151.841 + 3.951X_1 + 0.732X_2 + 20.546X_3$$

where $R_{Y123}^2 = 0.554$ (recall $R_{Y12}^2 = 0.505$) and b_3 is positive and shows that men weigh about 20.546 pounds more than women, given the same height and age.

Now that there are three coefficients for the independent variables, it may be pertinent to test the hypotheses concerning these *three* coefficients. The hypothesis tests are as follows:

$$H_N: \quad \beta_1 = 0$$
$$H_A: \quad \beta_1 \neq 0$$

$$t_1 = \frac{b_1 - \beta_1}{s_{b_1}} = \frac{3.951 - 0}{0.912} = 4.33$$
p-value = negligibly small

$$H_N: \quad \beta_2 = 0$$
$$H_A: \quad \beta_2 \neq 0$$

$$t_2 = \frac{b_2 - \beta_2}{s_{b_2}} = \frac{0.732 - 0}{0.275} = 2.66$$
p-value = 2(0.0039) = 0.0078

$$H_N: \quad \beta_3 = 0$$
$$H_A: \quad \beta_3 \neq 0$$

$$t_3 = \frac{b_3 - \beta_3}{s_{b_3}} = \frac{20.546 - 0}{8.442} = 2.43$$
p-value = 2(0.0075) = 0.0150

If a prespecified level of $\alpha = 0.05$ had been used, all three coefficients would be significant. The p-values for b_1 and b_2 are still significant for $\alpha = 0.01$, whereas for $\alpha = 0.01$ the p-value for b_3 is not quite significant, as $0.0150 > 0.01$.

As stated in the preceding section, the use of a dummy variable questions only whether the intercept, α, is the same for (in this example) males and females. Its use implicitly assumes that the other coefficients (β_1 and β_2) are the same for males and females. Thus, the use of β_3 merely shifts (upward for males in this example) the estimated value of the intercept, a. Therefore, it is apparent that the dummy variable approach is *not* proper when the partial regression coefficients differ for the two groups (in the example, for males and females). There are statistical methods to address this question, but they are beyond the scope of this text. In many situations the judgment of the analyst may be sufficient.

13.8 RANDOM CORRELATION

Earlier in this chapter the reader was asked to ignore the data in Figure 13.1 for X_4 and X_5. These variables are the last four digits of each student's telephone number, and the last four digits of each student's social security number. The multiple regression equation was again computed with X_4 (and later with both X_4 and X_5) as independent variables. The solution which includes X_4 shows the results in Figure 13.7. The resulting regression equation is:

$$\bar{Y}_c = -166.661 + 4.007X_1 + 0.783X_2 + 22.280X_3 + 0.00171X_4$$

We have previously discussed the meanings and uses of b_1, b_2, and b_3. But what is the meaning of b_4? It mathematically states that for each unit increase in the last four digits of a person's telephone number (holding height, age, and sex constant) a person will weigh 0.001711 pounds more. If this appears suspect, it is even stranger to note that (1) the standard error of estimate has *decreased* to 18.1269, (2) the computed t value for X_4 has a two-tailed p-value of 0.0784, and (3) the *adjusted* coefficient of determination has increased from 0.5535 to 0.5742. All these facts constitute fairly good evidence to support the assumption that weight is affected by a person's telephone number. But how can one rationally argue that there is a causal relationship between a person's weight and a person's telephone number? One scarcely can. All the above "evidence" is no doubt a random correlation that can occur anytime a sample is taken. The essence of this example is that, unless a causal relationship "makes sense," do not accept the relationship from statistical evidence alone.

A further example of such random correlation is seen in Figure 13.8

Figure 13.7

Computer Printout for Four Independent Variable Solution

STANDARD ERROR OF ESTIMATE   18.1269

INTERCEPT   −166.66113

VARIABLE	PARTIAL REG. COEF.	STD. ERROR COEF.	COMPUTED T
1	4.00680	0.89084	4.50
2	0.78275	0.26998	2.90
3	22.28025	8.30335	2.68
4	0.00171	0.00097	1.76

SOURCE OF VARIATION	D.F.	SUM OF SQ.	MEAN SQ.	F VALUE
EXPLAINED BY REGRESS.	4	22134.120	5533.530	16.841
DEVIATION FROM REGRESS.	43	14129.130	328.584	
TOTAL	47			

MULTIPLE CORR. R   0.7813   ADJUSTED R   0.7578
COEF. OF DETERM.   0.6104   ADJUSTED R (SQD)   0.5742

Figure 13.8

Computer Printout for Five Independent Variable Solution

STANDARD ERROR OF ESTIMATE   18.3254

INTERCEPT   −167.09377

VARIABLE	PARTIAL REG. COEF.	STD. ERROR COEF.	COMPUTED T
1	3.99703	0.90132	4.43
2	0.78921	0.27390	2.88
3	21.87001	8.52975	2.56
4	0.00169	0.00098	1.72
5	0.00025	0.00092	0.27

SOURCE OF VARIATION	D.F.	SUM OF SQ.	MEAN SQ.	F VALUE
EXPLAINED BY REGRESS.	5	22158.774	4431.755	13.197
DEVIATION FROM REGRESS.	42	14104.476	335.821	
TOTAL	47			

MULTIPLE CORR. R   0.7817   ADJUSTED R   0.7515

COEF. OF DETERM.   0.6111   ADJUSTED R (SQD)   0.5648

when both X_4 and X_5 (social security number) are used. The regression equation is:

$$\bar{Y}_c = -167.094 + 3.997X_1 + 0.789X_2 + 21.870X_3 + 0.00169X_4 + 0.00025X_5$$

In this case the *adjusted* coefficient of determination has decreased, the standard error of estimate has increased, and the *p*-value for X_5 is 0.7872. None of these factors indicates X_5 should be included.

The data in Figure 13.9 furnish several important insights into multiple regression analysis. The reader will note that, regardless of the computed *t* value, each additional independent variable entered into the equation has increased the *unadjusted* coefficient of determination. Also note that whenever the new variable made a reduction in the standard error of estimate the *adjusted* coefficient of determination increased. It can be proved that this will occur only if the *t*-value for this new variable exceeds one in the new model.[4] Thus, a user of multiple regression models should be aware of the difference in the unadjusted and adjusted measures of the coefficient of determination. The latter is a more reliable measure; however, it is not foolproof, as seen in the example of phone numbers. The analyst must always look beyond the numbers and ask if there is a "common sense" reason to believe there is a causal relationship between the dependent and independent variables.

---

[4] See Plane, Donald R. and Robert Taylor, "Choice of the Critical t-Value in Regression," *Proceedings,* 8th Annual Conference, American Institute for Decision Sciences, November 1976.

Figure 13.9

Summary of Weight Example

Independent Variables	Computed t Values	Unadjusted Coefficient of Determination	Standard Error of Estimate	Adjusted Coefficient of Determination
1,2	6.17, 2.73	0.5258	19.5486	0.5047
1,2,3	4.33, 2.66, 2.43	0.5820	18.5597	0.5535
1,2,3,4	4.50, 2.90, 2.68, 1.76	0.6104	18.1269	0.5742
1,2,3,4,5	4.43, 2.88, 2.56, 1.72, .27	0.6111	18.3254	0.5648

13.9 ASSUMPTIONS AND PROBLEMS IN MULTIPLE LINEAR REGRESSION

The proper use of multiple linear regression rests upon extension of the assumptions that were described in Chapter 12 for simple linear regression. In review, these are:

1. The regression relationship is linear in that

$$\mu_{Y|12} \ldots = \alpha + \beta_1 X_1 + \beta_2 X_2 + \cdots$$

2. The variance (and standard deviation) of Y values is the same for all values of $X_1, X_2, \ldots$
3. The values of Y are independent of each other.
4. The values of Y are normally distributed. (This assumption may be ignored for large samples.)

Several of the more common problems associated with multiple regression are directly the result of these assumptions not being met.

13.91   Serial Correlation

If the crucial assumption of the independence of Y values fails, the problem of *serial correlation* arises. This problem often arises when time series data are used. An example is a time series of values of gross national product (GNP) where a "high" value in one year tends to be followed by a "high" value in the following year. Serial correlation causes problems such as incorrect values for the standard errors for a, b_1, b_2, etc. Serial correlation also invalidates the t and F tests described in this chapter. Methods for measuring for serial correlation, such as the Durbin-Watson test,[5] are available with many computer programs.

---

[5] J. Durbin and G. S. Watson, "Testing for Serial Correlation in Least-squares Regression," parts 1 and 2, *Biometrika*, 1950 and 1951.

13.92 Equal Variance

When the assumption of the equal variance for values of Y for all values of X_1 and X_2 is violated, the problem of heteroscedasticity arises. The major effect of this problem is to invalidate the statistical inferences.

13.93 Multicollinearity

This term applies to the situation where there is a high degree of correlation between two (or more) independent variables. The result is that the regression model is unable to separate their individual effects, because the two independent variables behave in such a similar fashion. This causes the individual regression coefficients (and inferences from them) to be relatively meaningless. A useful solution is to delete one (or all but one) of the related variables.

13.10 SUMMARY

This chapter has extended the use of regression analysis to more than one independent variable. The assumptions of simple linear regression still apply. The problem of random correlation has been discussed and should be watched carefully. The basic rule is to question whether there is a "common sense" causal relationship.

EXERCISES

13.1   Explain the primary difference between simple linear regression and multiple linear regression.

13.2   One use of multiple regression is "appraisal models." These models are sometimes used to estimate valuations of residential properties as an aid in property tax assessment. Consider two regression models for single family homes in similar neighborhoods:

Model A
Dependent variable: Sales price
Independent variable: Usable square feet of interior space

Model B
Dependent variable: Sales price
Independent variables: 1. Usable square feet of interior space
2. Size of lot, square feet

Although both models are far simpler than the appraisal models being used, they are useful to develop an understanding of the models.
a. How would you go about collecting data for each of these models?
b. How or where would you obtain these data? Are these data publicly available?

    c. What substantial problem would arise if the data collected covered all sales in the neighborhood between 1965 and 1975?

* 13.3 For the appraisal models of Exercise 13.2, suppose the least squares regressions yielded these values:

Model A
$$Y = \$6,300 + \$29.40\ X$$
where X is the usable interior space in square feet.

Model B
$$Y = -\$320 + \$27.80\ X_1 + \$1.10\ X_2$$

where X_1 is the usable interior space in square feet and X_2 is the lot size in square feet

    a. Use each model to estimate the value of a home with 1,500 square feet of usable interior space and a lot of 8,000 square feet.

    b. Explain this interpretation of Model A: "The average lot is worth $6,300 and houses are worth an average of $29.40 per square foot." Do you agree with this interpretation?

    c. Develop a similar explanation for the coefficients in Model B. Why does it *not* make sense to say, "The existence of the property is worth $320?"

    d. Explain this statement more thoroughly: "In Model A, a square foot of living space is worth $29.40, while Model B values living space at $27.80. This is because Model A ignores lot size, and thereby mixes lot size with usable floor space. There is some indication that larger homes are built on larger lots."

    e. Would you feel comfortable using Model B on a three-room house, if the data used for the model had no houses with fewer than five rooms? Why or why not?

13.4 If you were constructing an appraisal model (see Exercise 13.2), what other variables would you consider for inclusion?

* 13.5 Holman Industrial Supply Company is interested in the profitability of customer accounts, so that its future marketing efforts might be shifted toward customers that might produce more profit. The following data were collected on existing customers.

Customer Number	X_1 No. of Customer's Employees	X_2 Customer's Annual Sales ($ millions)	X_3 Holman's Profit
1	200	4.2	$ 9,000
2	300	3.2	9,000
3	400	7.0	15,000
4	150	6.9	13,500
5	100	2.7	8,000
6	200	5.8	12,000

* Answers to exercises marked with an asterisk (*) are in Appendix L.

A computer printout for the multiple regression equation to predict Holman's profit is shown below:

VARIABLE	REG.COEF.	STD.ERROR COEF.	COMPUTED T
1	4.51927	2.93801 S_{b_1}	1.53821 t_{x_1}
2	1380.53576	170.65368 S_{b_2}	8.08969 t_{x_2}

INTERCEPT   3209.83659 S_a
MULTIPLE CORRELATION   0.98334 R
STD. ERROR OF ESTIMATE   665.49194 SEE

ANALYSIS OF VARIANCE FOR THE REGRESSION *ANOVA*

SOURCE OF VARIATION	D.F.	SUM OF SQ.	MEAN SQ.	F VALUE
ATTRIBUTABLE TO REGRESSION $v_1=2$	2	38879694.7481 SSB	19439847.3740 MSB	43.8942
DEVIATION FROM REGRESSION $v_2=3$	3	1328638.5852 SSW	442879.5284 MSW	
TOTAL	5	40208333.3333		

    a. Interpret every number in the printout.
    b. What is the predictive equation?
    c. Predict Holman's profit for a customer with 300 employees and sales of $5.8 million.

13.6   Explain the meaning and use of:
    a. Coefficient of multiple determination
    b. Coefficient of partial regression
    c. Standard error of a regression coefficient

13.7   After some sophisticated analysis of installment loan profitability, including a regression analysis of factors from a borrower's credit report, a bank officer discovers that the information from credit reports has no statistically apparent effect on profit. Hence, the officer recommends that credit reports no longer be obtained before passing on a loan application. Does this recommendation make sense? Consider what might happen to the quality of future applicants if this policy were to become publicly known.

13.8   HAPCO RecV Corporation makes ladders to be installed on recreational vehicles. These ladders, which give access to the vehicle roof, must be custom made for each order, due to the great variety of recreational vehicles. Cost estimation has been a costly (but important) aspect of HAPCO's bidding process. In order to simplify the procedure, the 500 most recent orders were investigated. For each order, the following factors were ascertained:

> Zip code of buyer
> Actual manufacturing cost per ladder
> Vehicle weight
> Vehicle height
> Whether vehicle has a rear bumper (step)
> Carrying capacity of ladder, pounds

    a. What is the dependent variable?
    b. Which variables do you think are reasonable for inclusion in the model as independent variables?

c. Which of the independent variables should be dummy $(0-1)$ variables?

13.9 For the HAPCO RecV Corporation in Exercise 13.8, would it be appropriate to use the number of ladders in the order as an independent variable if:

a. The order size ranges from 300 to 600 ladders?

b. The order size ranges from 1 to 1,000,000 ladders?

13.10 Explain the use of a dummy $(0-1)$ variable in multiple regression.

13.11 Rainbow Painting Contractors provided these data:

x_1 (1) Square Feet of Painted Area	x_2 (2) Linear Feet of Edge Trim	x_3 (3) Number of Colors	x_4 (4) Use of Scaffolding	(5) Labor Cost
10,000	8,000	1	0	$1,150
3,000	3,000	3	1	450
2,500	500	2	0	250
7,000	4,000	4	1	730
9,000	3,000	5	1	860
2,600	2,000	4	1	400
4,200	2,000	2	1	525
5,700	2,500	1	0	510
4,000	2,500	1	1	530
2,100	2,200	1	0	250
1,900	1,000	7	1	350
3,900	2,600	6	0	360
6,000	2,500	2	1	650
7,500	3,000	3	0	600
2,900	2,000	4	0	375

The first computer run used all of these variables, yielding this output:

VARIABLE	REG. COEF.	STD. ERROR COEF.	COMPUTED T
1	0.05877	0.00756	7.77188
2	0.05896	0.01196	4.93002
3	-2.12239	7.04050	-0.30145
4	105.89273	25.33568	4.17959

INTERCEPT   39.04846
MULTIPLE DETERMINATION   0.97296
STD. ERROR OF ESTIMATE   47.04616
ADJUSTED R SQ = 0.96213

After studying the output, the analyst discarded the variable X_3 (Number of Colors). The next output was:

VARIABLE	REG. COEF.	STD. ERROR COEF.	COMPUTED T
1	0.05866	0.00723	8.10899
2	0.05968	0.01122	5.31887
4	104.23616	23.68846	4.40029

INTERCEPT   32.02061
MULTIPLE DETERMINATION   0.97271
STD. ERROR OF ESTIMATE   45.06011
ADJUSTED R SQ = 0.96526

a. Why did the analyst make the second run? *small t << 2*

b. Explain the meaning of the output of the second run to Rainbow's manager, who is not a statistician. The manager is particularly interested in:

How to use the results in bidding for jobs.

How to use the results in preliminary scheduling of painters.

How much it costs to use scaffolding. *$ 104.236*

How much it costs to get set up for a job. — *$ 32.02061*

How much it costs for 100 square feet of painting. *$ 5.866*

How much it costs for 100 feet of edge trim. *$ 5.968*

13.12 What is multicollinearity? What precautions should the analyst take to avoid the problem?

* 13.13 The Huntley Mechanisms Corporation set up a multiple regression model to predict shipping weight of a finished product, when both the maximum length and the maximum height are known. The data are shown below. *dep — indep. — indep.*

X_1 Shipped Wt., Pounds	X_2 Maximum Length, Inches	X_3 Maximum Height, Inches
34	5.0	5.0
29	4.2	4.5
43	8.5	10.0
12	1.4	2.5
35	3.6	5.0
27	1.3	3.0

The computer output:

VARIABLE	REG. COEF.	STD. ERROR COEF.	COMPUTED T
2	1.11808	4.73554	0.23610
3	2.20141	4.73554	0.46487

INTERCEPT 14.52065

COEF. OF MULT. CORR. 0.71671

STD. ERROR OF ESTIMATE 7.27401

ADJUSTED R SQ = 0.51368

a. Explain the apparent meaning of the regression coefficients.

b. Test the hypothesis that maximum length does not affect shipping weight.

c. Test the hypothesis that maximum height does not affect shipping weight.

* 13.14 For the situation of Exercise 13.13, the analyst performed three simple regressions. The printouts gave the following information:

Dependent Variable: X_1

Independent Variable: X_2

Intercept 17.01972

Regression Coefficient 3.24507

Std. Error of Reg. Coef. 1.095

Computed T-Value	2.964
Correlation Coefficient (unadj)	0.829
Standard Error of Estimate	6.522

Dependent Variable: X_1
Independent Variable: X_3

Intercept	13.59155
Regression Coefficient	3.28169
Std. Error of Reg. Coef	1.067
Computed T-Value	3.075
Correlation Coefficient (unadj)	0.838
Standard Error of Estimate	6.358

Dependent Variable: X_2
Independent Variable: X_3

Intercept	−0.83099
Regression Coefficient	0.96621
Std. Error of Reg. Coef.	0.129
Computed T-Value	7.496
Correlation Coefficient (unadj)	0.966
Standard Error of Estimate	0.768

Discuss fully the meaning of the three printouts, including recommendations for a model to use for prediction.

REFERENCES

Bryant, Edward C. *Statistical Analysis,* rev. ed. New York: McGraw-Hill Book Co., Inc., 1966.

Cockrane, D. and Orcutt, G. H. "Applications of Least Square Regressions to Relationships Containing Auto-Correlated Error Terms," *Journal of the American Statistical Association,* vol. 44, no. 245 (March 1949), pp. 32–61.

Fox, Karl A. *Intermediate Economic Statistics.* New York: John Wiley & Sons, Inc., 1968.

Waugh, Frederick V. and Fox, Karl A. "Graphic Computation of $R_{1.23}$," *Journal of the American Statistical Association,"* vol. 52, no. 280 (Dec. 1957), pp. 479–81.

14

Time Series Analysis

14.1 WHAT IS A TIME SERIES?

Many useful data for business and economic analysis occur in *time series*. A time series is a set of observations, at various points in time, for some business or economic quantity of interest. Corporate data provide examples of time series; quarterly sales of a firm make up a time series, as do observations over time of profit, assets, liabilities, working capital, stock prices, profit margins, number of employees, and so on.

So many data are available in time series that it is useful to develop procedures for analyzing time series. There is one particular difficulty that arises in the analysis of time series which limits many of the techniques of statistical inference discussed earlier. The difficulty is that the individual observations in a time series often depend on previous observations. For example, an unusually high stock price in one week is more likely to be followed by a continued high price in the following week than it is to be followed by an unusually low price. This phenomenon, called *serial correlation,* causes most time series analyses to be descriptive rather than inferential. Although we will be using regression analysis, an inferential technique, its use will be descriptive rather than inferential.

The descriptive analysis of time series in this chapter is a discussion of a time series and its several components. These components may be classified as long-term influence, short-term influences, and other influences. The long-term influences are typically called *secular trends;* the short-term influences are typically called *seasonal factors;* other influences are typically called *cyclical* and *irregular* movements in the time series.

14.2 LONG-TERM INFLUENCES: SECULAR TREND

The basic underlying movement over a long period of time in a time series is called *secular trend*. Over long periods of time, there are usually

Figure 14.1

Population of A Town, 1901–1920

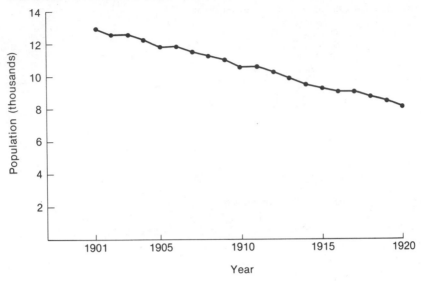

changes in economic and sociological factors which bring about changes of the values in time series. Increases in population cause some time series to have long-term growth. A long-term increase in productivity in agriculture has caused the number of people employed in agriculture to have a long-term decline. A newly introduced product may experience a long-term pattern of early rapid growth, then stable growth, then stability, and finally decline over its life cycle. The purpose of secular trend analysis is to develop a model characterizing these long-term patterns in a time series, while neglecting the short term influences. These short-term influences cause deviations from the long-term pattern on a daily, weekly, monthly, yearly, or perhaps even a longer period of time.

As an example of a time series with long-term trend, the population of A Town is plotted in Figure 14.1, for 1901–1920. Note a rather consistent decline in population, which can easily be approximated by a straight line.

As an example of a time series which exhibits a very pronounced long-term trend, Figure 14.2 shows a graph of state and local government purchases of goods and services. It is apparent from this graph that this particular time series has exhibited a very stable growth over the years shown, 1953–1975. This graph of state and local government purchases of goods and services is plotted on what is called a *ratio scale*. This ratio scale, which is used as the vertical axis, has the property that a constant *ratio* between two values is shown as a constant vertical distance on the graph. For example, 80 is twice as large as 40, and 200 is twice as large

Figure 14.2

Secular Trend: Government Purchases of Goods and Services (state and local governments; annual rate in billions of dollars)

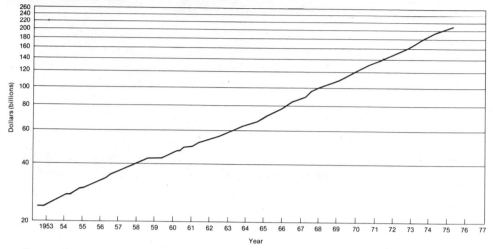

Source: *Business Conditions Digest,* U.S. Department of Commerce.

as 100. Hence, the distance between 80 and 40 is the same as the distance between 200 and 100. By marking a strip of paper with one of these distances, they can easily be compared to verify that this is true. A ratio scale is also called a *logarithmic scale,* because the same plot may be obtained by finding the logarithm of each time series value, and plotting that logarithm on ordinary (arithmetic) graph paper. This procedure was used previously in Figure 12.14. The use of ratio (logarithmic) graph paper simplifies the plotting chore, because it is not necessary to look up the logarithms of the time series values when ratio (logarithmic) graph paper is used.

If a time series exhibits a *percentage* growth from year to year which is approximately constant, the plot on logarithmic paper will approximate a straight line. If a time series exhibits a constant *amount* of growth (rather than a constant *percentage* growth) on a yearly basis, a plot of the time series on arithmetic paper will approximate a straight line. Probably the simplest method of determining whether a time series is better described by a constant amount of growth or a constant percentage growth (or perhaps by neither) is to plot the observations on both arithmetic and ratio paper to observe the closeness of fit to a straight line for each case.

It is not unusual to find a time series for which neither an arithmetic nor ratio scale is a good description of the secular trend in a time series. In these cases, one way to proceed is to use more complex models, or to simply use a freehand curve which judgmentally captures the essence of the secular trend for the time series.

14.21   Fitting a Straight Line Arithmetic Trend

If it is appropriate to fit a straight line secular trend, the equations for regression analysis (Chapter 12) may be used to find a predictive equation for future values of secular trend. If the arithmetic model is to be used to describe a straight line on ordinary (arithmetic) graph paper, the appropriate equation is

$$Y = a + bt$$

where Y is the value of the time series, and t is the independent variable in years (or some other time period such as days, weeks, months or quarters). It is usually convenient to change the origin (the "zero" year)

Figure 14.3

Calculations for Trend Line

Year	t	Population Y (in thousands)	tY	t^2
1901	1	13.0	13.0	1
1902	2	12.6	25.2	4
1903	3	12.6	37.8	9
1904	4	12.3	49.2	16
1905	5	11.9	59.5	25
1906	6	11.9	71.4	36
1907	7	11.5	80.5	49
1908	8	11.1	88.8	64
1909	9	11.0	99.0	81
1910	10	10.6	106.0	100
1911	11	10.7	117.7	121
1912	12	10.4	124.8	144
1913	13	9.9	128.7	169
1914	14	9.5	133.0	196
1915	15	9.2	138.0	225
1916	16	9.1	145.6	256
1917	17	9.0	153.0	289
1918	18	8.8	158.4	324
1919	19	8.4	159.6	361
1920	20	8.1	162.0	400
	$\Sigma t = 210$	$\Sigma Y = 211.6$	$\Sigma tY = 2{,}051.2$	$\Sigma t^2 = 2{,}870$

$$b = \frac{n\,\Sigma tY - (\Sigma t)(\Sigma Y)}{n\,\Sigma t^2 - (\Sigma t)^2} = \frac{20(2051.2) - (210)(211.6)}{20(2870) - (210)^2}$$

$$b = -0.2565$$

$$a = \frac{\Sigma Y}{n} - b\frac{\Sigma t}{n} = \frac{211.6}{20} - (-0.2565)\frac{210}{20} = 13.27$$

Trend equation: Population $= 13.27 - 0.2565t$ origin, 1900

from the actual AD 0 to a more recent year. For example, if the data begin in 1953, that year might be called year one; 1954 becomes year two, and so on. Thus, the origin or "zero" year is 1952 in this case. When the origin has been shifted in this fashion, the value of t to be used in a trend equation is the number of years (or other time period) from the origin year.

To fit a straight line arithmetic trend, the equations to find the slope and intercept are

$$b = \frac{n\Sigma tY - (\Sigma t)(\Sigma Y)}{n\Sigma t^2 - (\Sigma t)^2}$$

$$a = \frac{\Sigma Y}{n} - b\frac{\Sigma t}{n} = \bar{Y} - b\bar{t}$$

Since the symbol t is being used to indicate the time period measured from the origin (months, years, quarters, etc.), t replaces X in the regression equations in Section 12.21. The data and calculations for A Town are shown in Figure 14.3.

14.22 Fitting a Straight Line Logarithmic Trend

In order to fit a least squares line which will appear as a straight line on ratio (logarithmic) paper, it is necessary to find the logarithm of each value in the time series, and then find the regression line between t (independent variable) and the logarithm of Y (dependent variable). The appropriate regression equations are:

$$b = \frac{n\Sigma t \log Y - (\Sigma t)(\Sigma \log Y)}{n\Sigma t^2 - (\Sigma t)^2}$$

$$a = \frac{\Sigma \log Y}{n} - b\frac{\Sigma t}{n} = \frac{\Sigma \log Y}{n} - b\bar{t}$$

To illustrate the use of these equations to fit a logarithmic straight line trend, Figure 14.4 shows the annual data for state and local government purchases of goods and services. These data are plotted (on a quarterly basis) in Figure 14.2. It is apparent from this graph that a straight line on ratio (logarithmic) graph paper is a reasonable description of the data. Using the data from Figure 14.4, the slope and intercept of the trend equation (where the equation will gives the logarithm of Y) are:

$$b = \frac{23(549.815) - (276)(42.344)}{23(4,324) - (276)^2} = 0.04119$$

$$a = \frac{42.344}{23} - 0.04199\frac{276}{23} = 1.34676$$

Thus, the regression equation is

$$\log Y = 1.34676 + 0.04119t$$

where origin is 1952.

To use this equation to find the projected trend value for some year, say 1978, one first needs to find the value of t for 1978. Since the origin is 1952, $t = 1978 - 1952 = 26$. To find the projected value of Y, state and local government purchases of goods and services for 1978, it is necessary to find the number whose logarithm is $1.34676 + 0.04119(26) = 1.34676 + 1.07094 = 2.41770$, or $Y = 261.6$.

Figure 14.4

Data for Trend Analysis, Government Purchases of Goods and Services

Year	t	Purchases ($ billions), Y	log Y†	t log Y	t^2
1953..........	1	25.0	1.398	1.398	1
1954..........	2	27.8	1.444	2.888	4
1955..........	3	30.6	1.486	4.458	9
1956..........	4	33.5	1.525	6.100	16
1957..........	5	37.1	1.569	7.845	25
1958..........	6	41.1	1.614	9.684	36
1959..........	7	43.7	1.640	11.480	49
1960..........	8	46.5	1.667	13.336	64
1961..........	9	50.8	1.706	15.354	81
1962..........	10	54.3	1.735	17.350	100
1963..........	11	59.0	1.771	19.481	121
1964..........	12	64.6	1.810	21.720	144
1965..........	13	71.1	1.852	24.076	169
1966..........	14	79.8	1.902	26.628	196
1967..........	15	89.3	1.951	29.265	225
1968..........	16	100.7	2.003	32.048	256
1969..........	17	110.4	2.043	34.731	289
1970..........	18	123.2	2.091	37.638	324
1971..........	19	137.5	2.138	40.622	361
1972..........	20	151.0	2.179	43.580	400
1973..........	21	168.0	2.225	46.725	441
1974..........	22	189.4	2.277	50.094	484
1975..........	23	207.8	2.318	53.314	529
	276		42.344	549.815	4,324

† Logarithmic values are found in Appendix B.
Source: U.S. Department of Commerce.

Another way of expressing the secular trend is to find the annual percentage growth indicated by the regression line. To find this annual growth rate, g, use the expression from Section 12.71.

$$b = \log (1 + g)$$

or, for the data of this example,

$$0.04119 = \log (1 + g)$$
$$1 + g = \text{antilog} (0.04119) = 1.099$$
$$g = 0.099 = 9.9 \text{ percent annual growth}$$

14.23 Cautions in the Use of Trend Projections

There is nothing magic or sacred about the use of least squares trend equations. They may be useful, they may be misleading, or they may be downright wrong. A trend projection for sugar prices would have been painfully wrong in late 1974, when the price of sugar increased more than 300 percent in a period of several months. But, if the user of a trend equation has reason to believe that the underlying forces which determine the value of a time series will continue to behave much as they have in the past, it may be reasonable to use a least squares trend equation. But there is no substitute for the *judgment* of the analyst. The false precision of numbers is often mistakenly comfortable!

14.3 SHORT-TERM INFLUENCES: SEASONAL FACTORS

Perhaps the most common form of seasonal variation is brought about by changes in weather during a year. For example, sales of air conditioners are much greater in June than in December, while more skis are sold in December than in June. Many kinds of vacation expenditures are much heavier in summer months, when there is no school, than in other months of the year. Long-distance household moving is also seasonal in nature, with the peak months for moving occurring in the summer. There are many such climatic and economic factors which bring about similar kinds of seasonal behavior in many time series.

In using data from a time series for managerial purposes, it is usually advantageous to be able to separate the seasonal factors from other factors. A retail store manager, in examining the change in sales from the third quarter to the fourth quarter, would be interested in knowing whether the increase (which comes about during the Christmas season) is less than the usual seasonal increase, or is about the same, or perhaps more. To investigate important questions like this, a time series may be seasonally adjusted, so that these recurring seasonal forces may be separated from other movements in a time series.

> A *seasonal adjustment* is a statistical modification made to compensate for fluctuations in a time series which recur more or less regularly from year to year. By adjustment, the seasonal effect is removed from the basic data.

14.31 Simplified Example of Seasonal Adjustment

To understand the method of seasonal adjustment, first consider a hypothetical situation that is simpler than those usually encountered in the real world. In this hypothetical situation the time series has *no* trend. The major movement in the hypothetical time series is caused by seasonal

Figure 14.5

Hypothetical Time Series (no trend)

Year	Qtr.	Value	Value/Average
1900...............	1	80	1.231
	2	90	1.385
	3	40	0.615
	4	50	0.769
1901...............	1	82	1.262
	2	88	1.354
	3	41	0.631
	4	49	0.754
	Average:	65	

factors; the task in this situation is to remove these seasonal factors. These hypothetical data are shown in Figure 14.5. Note that the average for the eight quarters shown is 65. The final column of Figure 14.5 shows the ratio of each quarterly value to the quarterly average, 65. From these data it can be seen that the first quarter for 1900 is 1.231 times the average, and so on. In Figure 14.6, the hypothetical data are summarized by quarter. From this figure it is apparent that the first quarter is, on the average, 1.246 times the series average; the second quarter is 1.370 times the series average, and so on. This average ratio for each quarter, expressed as an index (an implied percentage) is a crude form of quarterly seasonal index.

The use of this seasonal index is shown in Figure 14.7 where the original time series (Figure 14.5) has been seasonally adjusted. This is done by dividing the original value by the seasonal index, and then multiplying by 100. From Column 3 in Figure 14.7, observe that the series has indeed fluctuated around its average of 65. In 1900, Quarters 1 and 3 were somewhat below average, while in 1901 Quarters 2 and 4 were somewhat below average. By this seasonal adjustment, it is possible to remove the recurring seasonal factors and to view statistically the changes that apparently would have occurred from quarter to quarter had there been no

Figure 14.6

Hypothetical Time Series (no trend), Ratio of Value to Series Average

	Quarter			
	1	*2*	*3*	*4*
1900...................	1.231	1.385	0.615	0.769
1901...................	1.262	1.354	0.631	0.754
Average...............	1.246	1.370	0.623	0.762
Seasonal Index..........	124.6	137.0	62.3	76.2

Figure 14.7

Seasonal Adjustment of Hypothetical Time Series

Year	Quarter	(1) Original Value	(2) Seasonal Index	(3) Seasonally Adjusted Series (1) ÷ (2) × 100
1900.............	1	80	124.6	64.2
	2	90	137.0	65.7
	3	40	62.3	64.2
	4	50	76.2	65.6
1901.............	1	82	124.6	65.8
	2	88	137.0	64.2
	3	41	62.3	65.8
	4	49	76.2	64.3

seasonal pattern. This hypothetical example is simplified by the absence of trend. Furthermore, it would often be poor practice to construct a seasonal index on the basis of only two years of data.

14.32   Example of Seasonal Adjustment of Sales

The Mercantile Stores Company, Inc., is a chain of retail department stores. To illustrate the process and meaning of seasonal adjustment, quarterly data for Mercantile Stores sales for 1966 to 1973 will be used. The user of the data wants to study changes in the physical volume of sales rather than in changes in the dollar value of sales. Therefore the sales are reported in constant (1967) dollars.[1]

The fiscal (or accounting) year for Mercantile Stores ends on January 31 of each year. Hence, the first quarter sales includes the months February, March, April; the second quarter includes May, June, July, and so on. The quarterly sales data are shown in Figure 14.8.

From these data it is obvious that there is a strong seasonal factor in the sales of Mercantile Stores: the fourth quarter, which includes the Christmas selling season, has substantially larger sales volume than any other quarter in each year. Without seasonal adjustment, what comparisons can be made when the next quarter of data is available? It would be

---

[1] In order to look at changes in the physical sales volume, it is necessary to deflate the dollar sales (which are reported in annual reports and other financial sources) with an appropriate price index. Since Mercantile Stores deals primarily in clothing, the apparel and upkeep component of the Consumer Price Index is a reasonable choice for this index. This index is inappropriate to the extent that Mercantile Stores does not deal in clothing upkeep, such as dry cleaning. However, this apparel and upkeep component of the Consumer Price Index is a readily available index number which is close to the actual activities of Mercantile Stores. The actual sales dollars for each quarter are deflated by dividing actual sales by the index for that quarter. This subject will be fully discussed in Chapter 15.

Figure 14.8

Mercantile Stores Quarterly Sales in 1967 Dollars

Year	Quarter	Sales in 1967 Dollars (millions)
1966	1 (Feb.–Apr.)	48.6
	2 (May–July)	54.2
	3 (Aug.–Oct)	59.8
	4 (Nov.–Jan.)	79.8
1967	1	49.5
	2	56.0
	3	63.5
	4	85.8
1968	1	54.7
	2	59.9
	3	65.0
	4	89.0
1969	1	57.0
	2	63.9
	3	68.6
	4	94.2
1970	1	58.7
	2	67.1
	3	74.2
	4	102.8
1971	1	65.3
	2	72.3
	3	78.3
	4	111.2
1972	1	72.1
	2	82.0
	3	91.6
	4	127.5
1973	1	82.3
	2	92.0
	3	96.7
	4	134.9

easy to compare the first quarter of 1974 (unadjusted) with the first quarter of 1973 (unadjusted). But this is a comparison with a number which is a year old. How does the first quarter of 1974 compare with the fourth quarter of 1973? Obviously, the first quarter of 1974 (unadjusted) will be lower than the fourth quarter of 1973 (unadjusted) because of the seasonal influence. Thus, without a seasonal adjustment to remove the recurring seasonal movement, there is no way to make a comparison of two consecutive quarters. Yet this kind of comparison may often be necessary to detect changes in sales patterns. The next task is to develop the seasonally adjusted data for Mercantile Stores sales.

Unfortunately, the Mercantile Stores data cannot be seasonally adjusted by the simplified procedure described earlier. The reason is that Mercantile Stores quarterly sales have a pronounced trend. When there are important movements other than seasonal ones, it is not legitimate to take the ratio of each quarterly observation to the average for the series. One way around this difficulty is to construct what is called a *moving average* for the data. If the first four quarterly observations, beginning February 1, 1966, are averaged, the result is a number representing the average sales for the point at the middle of this time period. This middle point is at the end of the second quarter or the beginning of the third quarter. By averaging the second, third, fourth, and fifth quarterly observations, the

Figure 14.9

Moving Averages for Mercantile Stores Sales

Year	Quarter	*1* Sales, 1967 $ (millions)	*2* Moving Average	*3* Centered Moving Average	*4* Ratio to Moving Average (1) ÷ (3)
1966	1	48.6			
	2	54.2			
	3	59.8	÷ 4 = 60.60	÷ 2 = 60.71	0.9850
	4	79.8	60.82	61.05	1.3071
1967	1	49.5	61.28	61.74	0.8017
	2	56.0	62.20	62.91	0.8806
	3	63.5	63.62	64.27	0.9880
	4	85.5	64.92	65.41	1.3071
1968	1	54.7	65.90	66.09	0.8276
	2	59.9	66.28	66.72	0.8978
	3	65.0	67.15	67.44	0.9638
	4	89.0	67.72	68.22	1.3046
1969	1	57.0	68.72	69.17	0.8240
	2	63.9	69.62	70.27	0.9093
	3	68.6	70.92	71.14	0.9643
	4	94.2	71.35	71.75	1.3129
1970	1	58.7	72.15	72.85	0.8058
	2	67.1	73.55	74.62	0.8992
	3	74.2	75.70	76.52	0.9697
	4	102.8	77.35	78.00	1.3179
1971	1	65.3	78.65	79.16	0.8249
	2	72.3	79.68	80.73	0.8956
	3	78.3	81.78	82.63	0.9476
	4	111.2	83.48	84.69	1.3130
1972	1	72.1	85.90	87.56	0.8234
	2	82.0	89.22	91.26	0.8985
	3	91.6	93.30	94.58	0.9685
	4	127.5	95.85	97.10	1.3131
1973	1	82.3	98.35	98.98	0.8315
	2	92.0	99.62	100.55	0.9150
	3	96.7	101.48		
	4	134.9			

result is an average for the middle of that time span. Moving along one quarter at a time and constructing an average, a moving average is obtained. This moving average is shown in Column 2 of Figure 14.9. Note that the column of the moving average is shown one-half line offset from the sales data, because the moving average represents the average value for the middle of the time span. Since each average is constructed over a one-year period, each value is two quarters from both the beginning and the end of that time span.

The moving average shown in Column 2 in Figure 14.9 is not a "typical" value for any quarter, so the next step is to center the moving average as in Column 3. This centering is accomplished by averaging two

Figure 14.10

Quarterly Ratios of Mercantile Sales to Centered Moving Average (from Figure 14.7, Column 4)

	Quarter			
Year	1	2	3	4
1966............			0.9850	1.3071
1967............	0.8017	0.8806	0.9880	1.3071
1968............	0.8276	0.8978	0.9638	1.3046
1969............	0.8240	0.9093	0.9643	1.3129
1970............	0.8058	0.8992	0.9697	1.3179
1971............	0.8249	0.8956	0.9476	1.3130
1972............	0.8234	0.8985	0.9685	1.3131
1973............	0.8315	0.9150		

adjacent averages in Column 2 in Figure 14.9. This centered moving average is shown in Column 3. The first value in this column represents the centered moving average for the third quarter of 1966. Note that the first period for which a centered moving average is available is not the first period for which raw data are available. When quarterly data are used, two quarters are lost at the beginning and again at the end of the data. Column 3 in Figure 14.9, the centered moving average, takes the place of the average used earlier in the hypothetical (no trend) example for seasonal adjustment. The centered moving average represents the "typical" value for each quarter in the data, just as in the hypothetical (no trend) example the overall average was the "typical" value for every quarter. Hence, the remaining procedures for seasonal adjustment are the same as those used for the hypothetical (no trend) data. Column 4 in Figure 14.9 shows the ratio of each quarterly value to the centered moving average. Figure 14.10 shows these ratios for each quarter. For this particular set of data, there appears to be a great deal of stability in the seasonal patterns.

Another way of investigating the stability of the seasonal patterns is to plot a *tier* chart, as shown in Figure 14.11. The horizontal scale for this

Figure 14.11

Tier Chart for Mercantile Stores Sales

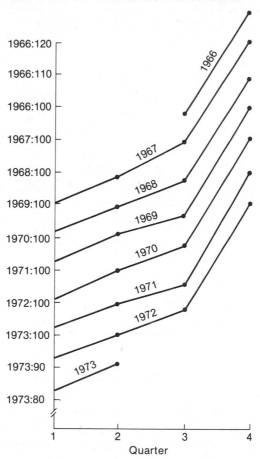

figure is the four quarters of each year, while the vertical scale is con-structed so that the value of 100 varies for each year on the plot. This "floating" vertical scale is used so that the quarterly ratios do not fall on top of each other, which might obscure the plot. From this tier chart for the Mercantile Stores sales, observe that the seasonal pattern seems to be very similar from year to year. In other sets of data, there might be con-siderably different seasonal patterns in some years, particularly if there are unusual forces such as strikes, unusual weather, or other factors which affect the seasonal pattern.

The next task is to find a typical value of the quarterly ratios which are shown in Figure 14.10. There are many ways to proceed in finding this value. For the case of Mercantile Stores, it might be appropriate simply to take the arithmetic mean of the ratios for each quarter. However, it is

Figure 14.12

Computation of Seasonal Index

Year	Quarter			
	1	2	3	4
1966........................			0.9850	1.3071
1967........................	0.8017	0.8806	0.9880	1.3071
1968........................	0.8276	0.8978	0.9638	1.3046
1969........................	0.8240	0.9093	0.9643	1.3129
1970........................	0.8058	0.8992	0.9697	1.3179
1971........................	0.8249	0.8956	0.9476	1.3130
1972........................	0.8234	0.8985	0.9685	1.3131
1973........................	0.8315	0.9150		
Modified Total.............	4.1057	4.5004	4.8513	6.5532
Modified Mean.............	0.82114	0.90008	0.97026	1.31064
Adjusted Modified Mean.....	0.821	0.900	0.970	1.310
Seasonal Index.............	82.1	90.0	97.0	131.0

Calculations:
Total of modified means $= 0.82114 + 0.90008 + 0.97026 + 1.31064 = 4.00212$
    Adjusted Modified Means

1: $0.82114 \times \dfrac{4.0}{4.00212} = 0.821$ 3: $0.97026 \times \dfrac{4.0}{4.00212} = 0.970$

2: $0.90008 \times \dfrac{4.0}{4.00212} = 0.900$ 4: $1.31064 \times \dfrac{4.0}{4.00212} = 1.310$

usually considered to be more reasonable to construct a *modified mean*. A modified mean is found by striking out the highest and lowest value for each quarter, and averaging the remaining values. This is done to remove the influences of any unusual quarter. It assumes that the unusual quarter is not typical and is not to be considered in the seasonal index. But when an unusually high (low) value is removed, it is necessary to remove the lowest (highest) value as well, so that the mean of the remaining values still represents a useful measure of central tendency. If the data are highly volatile, it might be desirable to strike out two or three low values and a similar number of high values for each quarter, depending on the number of years of data.

The modified mean for Mercantile Stores is constructed in Figure 14.12. For each column, the highest and lowest values are struck out. The remaining values are averaged. Since they do not total precisely four, they have next been adjusted so that their total is 4 (within the limits of rounding) by multiplying each modified mean by four and dividing by the actual total of the modified means. These adjusted modified means, expressed as seasonal indices, are shown in the last row of Figure 14.12.

The steps for constructing a seasonal index for a time series can now be summarized:

1. Construct a centered moving average using one year of data for each period. (Use four periods for quarterly data, 12 periods for monthly data, 52 periods for weekly data, and so on.) This centered moving average is constructed using these steps:

   a. Average the first four (or 12, or 52) values of the time series. This gives the first term in the moving average.

   b. Construct the second term in the moving average by dropping the first observation and including the next observation. For quarterly data, this means to average observations two through five; for monthly data, observations two through thirteen; for weekly data, observations two through 53.

   c. Construct the remaining terms in the moving average by moving down one period at a time, and constructing the average.

   d. Center the moving average by averaging the first and second terms in the moving average, then the second and third terms, then the third and fourth terms, and so on throughout all terms of the moving average.

2. Compute the ratio of each observation to the centered moving average for that observation. This ratio is computed only for observations after the first half-year, and before the last half-year, because the centered moving average does not exist for the first half-year or the last half-year.

3. For each quarter (or month or week) find the modified mean of the ratios computed in Step 2. The modified mean is computed by:

   a. Strike out the highest and lowest ratios for the first quarter (month, week), for the second quarter (month, week), and so on for the remaining quarters (months, weeks).

   b. Average the ratios that have not been struck out.

4. Adjust the modified means so they have an average equal to one. This adjustment is accomplished by:

   a. Find the total of the modified means. This total will be close to four (or 12, or 52).

   b. Adjust each modified mean by multiplying it by four (or 12, or 52) and dividing it by the total found in Step 4*a.*

5. Express this adjusted modified mean as an index, by multiplying by 100. This result is the seasonal index.

14.33 Using Seasonal Indices

Now that the seasonal indices are available, it is a simple matter to perform the seasonal adjustment for the original time series of quarterly sales in 1967 dollars for Mercantile Stores. Consider the seasonal index of 131.0 for the fourth quarter. This means that on the average the fourth quarter is 131.0 percent of the statistical estimate of what it would be if there were no seasonal factors in the data. Hence, in seasonal adjustment, the seasonally adjusted fourth quarter values must be lower than the actual values. The seasonal adjustment is accomplished by dividing the actual value for each quarter by the appropriate seasonal

Figure 14.13

Seasonal Adjustment of Mercantile Stores Sales

Year	Quarter	(1) Quarterly Sales 1967 Dollars (millions)	(2) Seasonal Index	(3) Seasonally Adjusted Quarterly Sales [(1) ÷ (2)] × 100
1966..........	1	48.6	82.1	59.2
	2	54.2	90.0	60.2
	3	59.8	97.0	61.6
	4	79.8	131.0	60.9
1967..........	1	49.5	82.1	60.3
	2	56.0	90.0	62.2
	3	63.5	97.0	65.5
	4	85.8	131.0	65.5
1968..........	1	54.7	82.1	66.6
	2	59.9	90.0	66.6
	3	65.0	97.0	67.0
	4	89.0	131.0	71.8
1969..........	1	57.0	82.1	69.4
	2	63.9	90.0	71.0
	3	68.6	97.0	70.7
	4	94.2	131.0	71.9
1970..........	1	58.7	82.1	71.5
	2	67.1	90.0	74.6
	3	74.2	97.0	76.5
	4	102.8	131.0	78.5
1971..........	1	65.3	82.1	79.5
	2	72.3	90.0	80.3
	3	78.3	97.0	80.7
	4	111.2	131.0	84.9
1972..........	1	72.1	82.1	87.8
	2	82.0	90.0	91.1
	3	91.6	97.0	94.4
	4	127.5	131.0	97.3
1973..........	1	82.3	82.1	100.2
	2	92.0	90.0	102.2
	3	96.7	97.0	99.7
	4	134.9	131.0	103.0

index, and multiplying by 100. The seasonally adjusted time series is shown in Figure 14.13.

The procedure used in Figure 14.13 to produce a seasonally adjusted time series can be summarized as:

$$Y_{SA} = \frac{Y}{S} \cdot 100$$

where

Y = Actual value of time series
S = Seasonal index
Y_{SA} = Seasonally adjusted value of time series

These seasonally adjusted data are also plotted in Figure 14.14. This plot of the seasonally adjusted data reveals far more informtion than would have been obtained from plotting the original series of Mercantile Sales in 1967 dollars. Furthermore, now that the seasonal indices are available, quarterly data may be compared with the previous quarter as they become available, after making an appropriate statistical adjustment for the seasonalities of the data.

As an example of using seasonally adjusted data to compare quarterly sales from one quarter to the next, the data for the next seven quarters became available after the seasonal indices had been computed. These data, presented as seasonally adjusted sales in millions of 1967 dollars, are shown in Figure 14.15, and added to Figure 14.14.

Notice that the increasing trend, which had been apparent for several years up through 1973, appears to have taken a sudden reversal in the third quarter of 1974. It is interesting to note that 1974 was a year in which an economic downtown became pronounced in the United States

Figure 14.14

Mercantile Stores Sales, Quarterly, Seasonally Adjusted (millions of 1967 dollars)

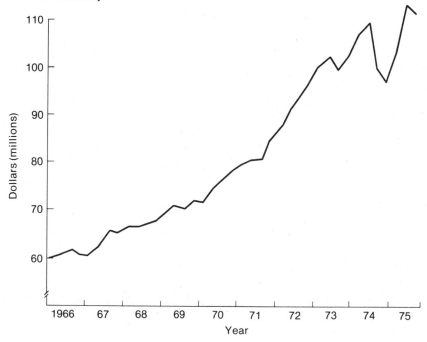

Figure 14.15

Recent Sales Data for Mercantile Stores

Year	Quarter	Sales, 1967 Dollars (millions)	Seasonal Index	Seasonally Adjusted Sales, 1967 Dollars (millions)
1974 1		87.9	82.1	107.1
	2	98.2	90.0	109.1
	3	97.1	97.0	100.1
	4	126.8	131.0	96.8
1975 1		84.4	82.1	102.8
	2	102.5	90.0	113.9
	3	108.4	97.0	111.8

economy. The unadjusted sales figures alone do not clearly show this rather pronounced decline.

There are other more sophisticated methods of seasonal adjustment. Almost all economic time series published by the United States Government are available in seasonally adjusted form. Although the basic concepts of seasonal adjustment in this chapter are used in seasonally adjusted government time series, additional features have been incorporated into their seasonal adjustment. In some cases there will be gradual changes in the pattern of seasonality. For example, as construction activity changes in character, the construction which is increasing may have a different seasonal pattern than that which is decreasing. This causes a change over time in the seasonal indices. If such a time series is encountered, a crude refinement for changing seasonal patterns may be accomplished by plotting the ratio of the time series value to the centered moving average (for a particular quarter or month) for the various years in the data. Then a trend line may be fitted either visually or by the method of least squares to aid in projecting future seasonal indices for that period. However, these procedures should be used with care; it may be very misleading to project a changing seasonal pattern for future periods of time, if the mechanism generating these changes in seasonal patterns is not understood by the analyst.

Seasonal adjustment may be performed for time series with monthly, weekly or even daily data, if desired. If monthly data are used, the procedures used in the Mercantile Stores example apply, except that it is necessary to use 12 months in place of four quarters as the basic period for constructing the centered moving average. Seasonal adjustment may also be performed for days of the week. When this is being done, it is not necessary to center the moving average, because the moving average for a seven-day period will be the average value for the middle day of that week.

There are other considerations which need to be applied to time series data. For example, in automobile sales the number of selling days is extremely important in evaluating sales data. Automobile sales data are typically reported for the first ten days of a month, second ten days of a month, and so on, so the number of Sundays (not a selling day) in each ten-day period is extremely important. When a situation such as this is encountered, it is usually considered good practice to express sales per selling day, instead of sales during the whole ten-day period. In some cases it is also advantageous to adjust for the number of days in the month. Although the typical monthly variation in days per month is reflected in the seasonal adjustment, it is more direct to express the value of a series as a daily rate. This also allows for a leap year to be accurately reflected.

There are still other editing changes which may be appropriate for time series data. Changes in population may be an important factor in some time series. In order to study residential use of electricity, it may be more useful to look at the *per capita* use, rather than total use. If population is changing, expressing electricity consumption on a per capita basis separates the increased electric use brought about by increased population from the increased electric usage brought about by changing patterns of living.

14.34   Forecasting Future Values for a Time Series

The procedures just described for analyzing the trend and seasonal components of a time series may be reversed in order to predict future values of the time series. As always, it is cautioned that any prediction is better thought of as a projection from past data. If the basic forces underlying the time series change, the future values of a time series may not reflect the behavior indicated by past values.

In order to predict annual values using a trend equation, the procedure is quite straightforward, as described in the earlier discussion of trend in a time series. If a projection is desired for a specific period, such as a quarter, the rate during that quarter is estimated as one fourth of the annual value that the trend equation would project for the middle of that quarter. The middle of the first quarter occurs one eighth of the year from the beginning of that year, and so on. In order to introduce the seasonal factors into the projection to produce a forecast which is *not* seasonally adjusted, it is necessary to *multiply* this trend value by the seasonal index for that quarter. This product of trend value and seasonal index is what is called *statistical normal*. It is the value that would be projected if there were no forces other than trend and seasonal.

An expression commonly used in economic data is the "seasonally adjusted quarterly value at annual rate." The difference between an annual rate and a quarterly rate is a factor of four. For example, a firm which has seasonally adjusted sales of $25 million in the first quarter is experiencing sales at an annual rate of $100 million per year. It is often more convenient to state quarterly values at annual rates to make them directly comparable to annual values.

These concepts will be illustrated by making a trend-seasonal (statistical normal) forecast for state and local government purchases of goods and services, for which a trend equation was developed in section 14.22. That trend equation is:

$$\log Y = 1.34676 + 0.04119\,t$$

where the origin is 1952.

The seasonal indices for state and local government purchases of goods and services can be found from data published by the U.S. Department of Commerce. Most GNP (gross national product) data are typically published as seasonally adjusted annual rates; however, GNP data are occasionally published without being seasonally adjusted. By taking the ratio of an unadjusted value to the corresponding seasonally adjusted value, the seasonal index for that period can be obtained. For state and local government purchases of goods and services, these seasonal indices for 1973 are:[2]

> Quarter 1:   97.2
> Quarter 2:   101.0
> Quarter 3:   102.3
> Quarter 4:   99.6

The first step in obtaining the trend-seasonal forecast for a quarter is to use the trend equation for that quarter. For 1977, the value of t (for the trend equation) is $t = 1977 - 1952 = 25$. But that value is for the *middle* of 1977. The beginning of 1977 has $t = 24.5$; the end is $t = 25.5$. The first quarter of 1977 begins at $t = 24.5$ and ends at $t = 24.75$; the middle of the first quarter is half way between these values, or $t = 24.625$. By similar reasoning: Quarter 2, $t = 24.875$; Quarter 3, $t = 25.125$; Quarter 4, $t = 25.375$. Using each of these values of t in the trend equation, the trend projection for each quarter, seasonally adjusted at annual rates, are shown in Figure 14.16.

To complete the trend-seasonal projection, each of the quarterly values from the trend equation must be multiplied by the seasonal index for that quarter, as shown in Figure 14.16. If it is desired to express each of these values at a quarterly rate (i.e., a projection of the actual dollar transactions for that quarter) instead of an annual rate, the values are divided by four (the number of quarters in a year), as shown in Figure 14.16. Note the distinction between trend projection (seasonally-adjusted; i.e., no seasonal factors are in the data) and trend-seasonal projection (*not* seasonally adjusted; i.e., there *are* seasonal factors in the data).

---

[2] From data in *Survey of Current Business,* July, 1974.

Figure 14.16

Trend-Seasonal Projection for State and Local Government Purchases of Goods and Services, 1977

Quarter	t	log Y	Trend Projection Y	Trend—Seasonal Projection, Annual Rate	Quarterly Rate = Annual Rate/4
1........	24.625	2.36106	229.6	229.6 × .972 = 223.2	55.8
2........	24.875	2.37136	235.2	235.2 × 1.010 = 237.5	59.4
3........	25.125	2.38166	240.8	240.8 × 1.023 = 246.3	61.6
4........	25.375	2.39196	246.6	246.6 × .996 = 245.6	61.4

Given: Trend equation: $\log Y = 1.34676 + 0.04119\,t$
  Origin: 1952
  Seasonal indices: 97.2, 101.0, 102.3, 99.6

14.4 CYCLICAL MOVEMENTS IN ECONOMIC TIME SERIES

In addition to the secular trend and seasonal movement in a time series, many economic time series exhibit cyclical movement. As general economic conditions change, time series exhibit changes. GNP may be declining during a period of recession, unemployment may be increasing during a recession, and so on. The most widely accepted definitions of *turning points* in economic activity are those defined by the National Bureau of Economic Research (NBER). This organization establishes *peaks* and *troughs* in economic activity. A peak is the point in time at which an economic downturn or recession begins; a trough is the point at which the recovery or economic upturn begins.

As an example of a time series which indicates a substantial amount of cyclical activity, Figure 14.17 shows the Index of Industrial Production[3] for 22 years, beginning in 1952. The vertical shaded regions on this plot are the periods of declining economic activity. The NBER has identified these turning points:

Peak:	July, 1953	Trough:	May, 1954
Peak:	August, 1957	Trough:	April, 1958
Peak:	April, 1960	Trough:	February, 1961
Peak:	December, 1969	Trough:	November, 1970

At the time this graph was constructed, the downturn which became pronounced in 1974 had not officially received a month for its peak.

Not all economic time series behave in this fashion. The index of industrial production is said to be a coincident time series, in that its

---

[3] The index of industrial production is a time series measuring output of manufacturing, mining, and utilities. It is discussed more fully in Chapter 15.

Figure 14.17

Index of Industrial Production

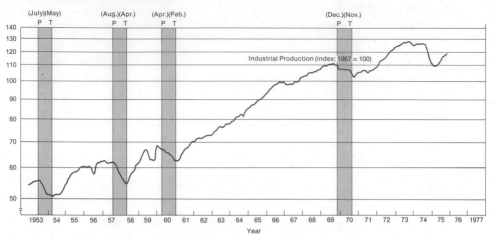

Source: *Business Conditions Digest,* U.S. Department of Commerce.

behavior and turning points typically coincide with the accepted turning points for the economy as a whole. Figure 14.18 shows the NBER short list of coincident time series, leading time series, and lagging time series. A *leading* time series is one which generally reaches its turning point ahead of the economy as a whole, while a *lagging* time series generally reaches its turning point after the economy as a whole. Although forecasting turning points in economic activity is not a statistical problem, the use of leading indicators may be of considerable value in gaining insight into the future behavior of the economy.

It is also useful to use the NBER turning points in the analysis of a particular time series. For the Mercantile Stores data presented earlier in this chapter, there was one period of general economic contraction from December, 1969, to November, 1970. In Figure 14.14, there is no obvious downturn in Mercantile Stores sales (1967 dollars) for the year 1970. This might suggest that the firm was not particularly sensitive to general economic conditions for that particular (relatively mild) period of recession. However, the data plotted in Figure 14.14 for 1974 suggest that the recession which was pronounced in 1974 had a substantial effect on Mercantile Stores.

A thorough understanding of cyclical behavior of time series is important before a secular trend analysis is performed. If the period of data for trend analysis begins at a cyclical trough and ends at a cyclical peak, a severe overstatement of growth may result. Similarly, using data from

Figure 14.18

NBER Short List of Leading, Coincident, and Lagging Indicators (1966)

Leading Indicators:
  Average workweek, production workers, manufacturing
  Average weekly initial claims, State unemployment insurance
  Net business formation
  New orders, durable goods industry
  Contracts and orders, plant and equipment
  New building permits, private housing units
  Change in book value, manufacturing and trade inventories
  Industrial materials prices
  Stock prices, 500 common stocks
  Corporate profits after taxes
  Ratio, price to unit labor cost
  Change in consumer installment debt

Roughly Coincident Indicators:
  Personal income
  GNP in current dollars
  GNP in 1958 dollars
  Industrial production
  Manufacturing and trade sales
  Sales of retail stores
  Employees on nonagricultural payrolls
  Unemployment rate, total

Lagging Indicators:
  Unemployment rate, persons unemployed 15 weeks and over
  Business expenditures, new plant and equipment
  Book value, manufacturing and trade inventories
  Labor cost per unit of output, manufacturing
  Commercial and industrial loans outstanding, weekly reporting large commercial
    banks
  Bank rates on short-term business loans

  Source: *Business Conditions Digest,* U.S. Department of Commerce.

peak to trough may cause a severe understatement of secular growth. Hence, in fitting a secular trend line, the period of time chosen should begin and end at times which display very little cyclical forces.

To illustrate the importance of the time period to estimate a rate of growth in a time series, the growth rate in the Index of Industrial Production will be computed for three time periods. From Figure 14.17, it is observed that the period from 1955 to 1973 should be fairly "typical;" there is no peak or trough in either year. In 1955, the Index value was 58.5; in 1973, 125.6. To determine the annual growth rate, g, for this 18-year period the calculations are:

$$58.5 \ (1 + g)^{18} = 125.6$$
$$\log 58.5 + 18 \log (1 + g) = \log 125.6$$
$$18 \log (1 + g) = \log (125.6) - \log (58.5) = 2.0990 - 1.7672$$
$$= 0.3318$$
$$\log (1 + g) = 0.3318/18 = 0.0184$$
$$1 + g = 1.043$$
$$g = 0.043 = 4.3 \text{ percent per year}$$

For the period 1957 to 1960, the index moved from 61.9 to 66.2; the annual growth rate during this period was 2.3 percent per year. By referring to Figure 14.17, it is apparent that this latter choice of time periods was poor. The year 1957 was a peak year, while 1960 was a year in which a decline took place. Another choice of time periods, 1961 to 1969, shows a higher annual growth rate of 6.5 percent (from 66.7 to 110.7 in eight years). This period was one of high and sustained growth; a growth rate based on this interval is substantially different from the growth rates calculated for other time periods.

14.5 IRREGULAR MOVEMENTS IN A TIME SERIES

Up to this point, three kinds of movement in economic time series have been described: secular trend, or movement that is typical of a long period of time; seasonal movements, which occur within a one-year period of time, and cyclical movements, which occur over a period of perhaps one to three years. Variations in the value of a time series which do not fit into one of these three categories are usually called *irregular* movements. To remove irregular movements in a time series, one procedure is to construct a moving average of perhaps three or more periods in order to smooth the irregularities in the data. Any moving average of more than three periods runs a substantial risk of losing current information. In general, an erratic time series requires a relatively large number of time periods in the average to smooth out the irregular movement, while a stable time series may not require any smoothing for analysis.

14.6 SUMMARY

The purpose of this chapter has been to describe the various kinds of movements that occur in a time series. Perhaps the concept of seasonal adjustment is the most widely used idea discussed in this chapter. Almost all economic data are better understood if they are published on a seasonally adjusted basis, which permits period-to-period comparison instead of more cumbersome comparisons with a similar period the previous year.

The use of trend equations for a long-term forecast may be particularly useful, or it may be particularly misleading. The blind use of a trend projection should be avoided. A projection of college enrollments for 1980 based on a trend established in the 1960's might be particularly misleading. But if the analyst is careful and uses these projections along with good sense, they may be particularly useful.

Cyclical movements in a time series are usually observed in relation to established turning points for the economy. This helps establish both the magnitude and timing of the cyclical behavior of a particular time series. Although cyclical movements can be identified statistically, their prediction requires more economics than statistics.

EXERCISES

14.1   What is a time series? Are all economic data collected as time series?

14.2   Give an example of a time series which has had a declining secular trend in the past ten years. Do you expect this trend to continue for the next several years? Do you expect it to continue indefinitely? Can statistical methodologies answer either of these questions?

14.3   Which of these time series, average workweek for hourly employees in a large commercial bank or average workweek for highway construction workers, would you expect to have more pronounced seasonal patterns? Why?

14.4   Distinguish between *secular trend, cyclical movement,* and *seasonal movement.* Can you generalize about which is most important?

14.5   If a time series has a growth pattern of approximately 9 percent per year, how would this be represented as a straight line on a graph?

14.6   If a time series has a growth pattern of approximately $1,000 per month, how would this be represented as a straight line on a graph?

* 14.7   If Robert Smith's annual salary was $14,000 in 1967 and $30,000 in 1975, what is the annual rate of growth in his salary?

* 14.8   The imported automobile dealer in Nuggetville reported these annual sales:

Year	Number of New Cars Sold
1974	709
1975	797
1976	883
1977	1,002
1978	1,111
1979	1,254

   a. Plot the annual sales on logarithmic (ratio) graph paper.
   b. Plot the annual sales on arithmetic graph paper.

---

* Answers to exercises marked with an asterisk (*) are in Appendix L.

c. Does your logarithmic or arithmetic plot appear to provide a better fit?

* 14.9   For the Nuggetville dealer in Exercise 14.8, fit the least squares line to the original data. For each of the six years, calculate the *residual* (the difference between the observed number of sales and the number of sales from the regression equation). Pay attention to sign in these calculations. What do you observe about the sequence of signs of the residuals? Can you generalize from this observation?

* 14.10   For the Nuggetville dealer in Exercise 14.8, fit the least squares line to the logarithm of the number of cars sold in each year. Use this equation to estimate the sales in 1981.

* 14.11   The Board of Governors of the Federal Reserve System reports the amount of savings within the U.S. Postal Savings System ($ billions), 1950–1962 as:

1950.................	2.9	1957.................	1.3
1951.................	2.7	1958.................	1.1
1952:................	2.5	1959.................	0.9
1953.................	2.4	1960.................	0.8
1954.................	2.1	1961.................	0.6
1955.................	1.9	1962.................	0.5
1956.................	1.6		

a. Plot the amount of Postal Savings for the end of each year on logarithmic (ratio) graph paper.
b. Plot the amount of postal savings for the end of each year on arithmetic graph paper.
c. Does your logarithmic or arithmetic plot appear to provide a better fit?

* 14.12   For the Postal Savings data in Exercise 14.11, fit the least squares line to the original data. Use this equation to estimate the amount of Postal Savings at the end of 1970. Does this prediction make sense? If not, is the statistical method correct? Is the logic correct?

14.13   For the Postal Savings data in Exercise 14.11, fit the least squares line to the logarithm of the amount of Postal Savings in each year. For each of the years, calculate the *residual* (or the difference between the observed value of Postal Savings and the value of Postal Savings from the least squares equation). Pay attention to sign in these calculations. What do you observe about the sequence of signs of the residuals?

* 14.14   Stepping Stones Corporation reported these quarterly sales for the past two years:

Year	Quarter	Sales (in 1,000)
1974.....................	1 (Jan–Mar)	81
	2 (Apr–June)	175
	3 (July–Sept)	159
	4 (Oct–Dec)	90
1975.....................	1	88
	2	190
	3	157
	4	110

From previous statistical analysis, the seasonal indices had already been calculated for the Corporation. The indices are:

Quarter	Seasonal Index
1	65
2	140
3	125
4	70

a. Calculate the seasonally adjusted quarterly sales for the Stepping Stones Corporation for 1974 and 1975. Explain the meaning of these data.

b. By observing the seasonal indices, would you be more inclined to guess that the Stepping Stones Corporation is primarily engaged in: repairing lawn mowers, providing lodging at a ski resort, selling college textbooks at a school on the semester system, or repairing dishwashers and other household appliances?

* 14.15 If the seasonally adjusted value of retail sales is $82.5 billion, and the unadjusted value is $103.6 billion, what is the seasonal index?

* 14.16 For a ten-day period, total new car sales were 179,000 cars. What is the seasonally adjusted annual rate if the seasonal index for the period is 87?

* 14.17 Seasonally adjust this time series of quarterly consumption of electricity for the residence of G. A. Jimson:

Year	Quarter	Electricity Consumed (kwh)
1970	1	3,000
	2	2,900
	3	2,400
	4	2,710
1971	1	3,120
	2	3,100
	3	2,720
	4	3,040
1972	1	3,200
	2	2,120
	3	2,760
	4	3,170
1973	1	3,460
	2	3,350
	3	3,050
	4	3,180

14.18 An oil embargo was imposed on the United States in the last quarter of 1973. Although Mr. Jimson's electricity consumption (see Exercise 14.17) increased from the third to the fourth quarter, do the seasonally adjusted data suggest that he might have practiced conservation during that quarter? Does a comparison of the fourth quarter of 1973 to the fourth quarter of 1972 yield the same conclusion?

14.19 Would Mr. Jimson's seasonal indices apply to his neighbor? Discuss.

14.20 Explain this statement to a nonstatistician: "Although actual unemployment increased from 6.6 million people to 6.7 million people, this represents a decline of 0.3 percentage points in the unemployment rate on a seasonally adjusted basis."

14.21   Explain the meaning of a "peak" and a "trough" in an economic time series.

14.22   Do all time series for an economy have the same peaks and troughs?

14.23   Is it true that a trend equation computed using the data from one peak to the next trough overstates growth, while a trend question computed using the data from one trough to the next peak understates growth? Explain your answer.

14.24   The Octo Manufacturing Company reported quarterly sales, from which a statistician reported:

"In order to analyze the sales of the Octo Manufacturing Company, it was necessary to develop a trend equation which produced a very good fit for the years 1960–1975, using annual data. This equation is:

$$Y = 9,735(1.09^t)$$

or

$$\log Y = \log (9,735) + t\log (1.09)$$

where Y is annual sales in thousands of dollars and t is the year $(1959 = 0)$.

The seasonal indices for Octo's sales are:

Quarter	Seasonal Index
1	91
2	93
3	104
4	112

These data should prove very useful to the Management of Octo."

a.   Use the appropriate equation to forecast 1976 sales for the Octo Manufacturing Company.

b.   Use the appropriate data to forecast quarterly sales for 1976 for the Octo Manufacturing Company.

c.   For the first quarter of 1976, Octo reported sales of $16,430,000. How would you interpret this figure, using the information from the statistician's report?

d.   If the reported sales for a quarter are below the figure calculated for that quarter in b, which of the following might account for the difference?

There are cyclical factors which have caused a cyclical decline in sales.

There were irregular factors (e.g., a strike) that affected Octo's output.

The trend equation is no longer an adequate representation of Octo's sales pattern.

The seasonal factors which the statistician computed have changed since they were calculated.

REFERENCES

Box, G. E. P., and Jenkins, G. M.   *Time Series Analysis, Forecasting and Control.* San Francisco: Holden-Day, 1970.

Brown, Robert G.   *Smoothing, Forecasting, and Prediction of Discrete Time Series.* Englewood Cliffs, N. J.: Prentice-Hall, Inc., 1963.

Bry, Gerhard, and Boschan, Charlotte.   "Interpretation and Analysis of Time-Series Scatters." *The American Statistician,* vol. 25, no. 2 (April 1971), pp. 29–33.

Zarnowitz, Victor (ed.)   *The Business Cycle Today.* New York: National Bureau of Economic Research, Columbia University Press, 1972.

15

Index Numbers

15.1 WHAT IS AN INDEX NUMBER?

Index numbers are a form of descriptive statistics. We are all aware that prices, for example, vary from time to time and from place to place. A price index number is useful to describe the way in which prices vary from one time period to another, or from one place to another. There are many other forms of index numbers besides price indices. Industrial output, farm output, unemployment, employment, and highway accidents vary from time to time and from place to place. Any of these can be measured and described with an appropriate index number.

Index numbers are used in many situations. A firm choosing a new plant location may be interested in the price of consumer goods, which might be an important factor in determining the wage rates necessary for a given location. An organization interested in promoting highway safety might be interested in an index of highway accidents to determine where a safety campaign should be instituted. Many labor contracts contain so-called "escalator clauses" which relate the rate of pay to the consumer price index, an index published by the United States Department of Labor which estimates the price levels of a well-defined set of consumer goods. A person seeking a retirement home might be interested in the price of consumer goods in various places, to aid in determining where to live after retirement. There are many other uses for index numbers.

15.2 ILLUSTRATION OF A PRICE INDEX

In preparing for labor negotiations, a structural steel fabricating firm is interested in constructing a price index for the primary inputs used in fabricating structural steel. A structural steel fabricator takes the output of a steel mill (large steel beams, etc.) and converts them into the steel "skeleton" that supports many large buildings. Although there are many

331

inputs required for this process, we shall consider only two: structural steel beams as delivered by the steel mill, and welders who convert the steel into pieces capable of being connected for the building skeleton.

15.21   Simple Price Index

The analyst for the steel firm has searched the firm's records and found the information shown in Figure 15.1. This figure shows the wage rate for structural steel welders and the delivered price for unfabricated structural steel beams, for each year from 1970 through 1974. In looking at the data, the analyst observes that the wage rate for a welder has changed from $5.00 to $6.10 per hour in these four years. This change of $1.10 compares with a change of $18.00 per ton (from $120.00 to $138.00) for

Figure 15.1

Price Data for a Steel Fabricator

Year	Wage Rate for Structural Steel Welder ($ per hour)	Delivered Price of Structural Steel Beams, Not Fabricated ($ per ton)
1970	$5.00	$120.00
1971	5.10	123.00
1972	5.60	126.00
1973	6.00	132.00
1974	6.10	138.00

structural steel beams. Does this mean that the change in the price of structural steel beams has been far greater than the change in the price of welding? Not necessarily, for the comparison may contain many fallacies. One of the fallacies is the difference in units. The price of welding is expressed in dollars per hour, while the price of steel beams is expressed in dollars per ton. It is not necessarily legitimate to compare two price changes which are measured in different units.

One way to make the price changes somewhat comparable is to construct a simple price index for each item for each year. In Figure 15.2, the price index for a structural steel welder is computed. For each year, the price index is constructed as the ratio of the price in that year to the price in the base year, multiplied by 100. In Figure 15.2, the base year has been selected (arbitrarily) as 1970. The factor of 100 indicates that the price index is a percentage figure, although it is common to omit the percentage symbol in index numbers. This index is called a *simple price index* for a structural steel welder. It is called a simple price index because only one item or commodity is included.

The interpretation of a simple price index is straightforward. The price

Figure 15.2

Price Index for Structural Steel Welder (1970 = 100)

Year	Price Index
1970	$5.00/5.00 \times 100 = 100$
1971	$5.10/5.00 \times 100 = 102$
1972	$5.60/5.00 \times 100 = 112$
1973	$6.00/5.00 \times 100 = 120$
1974	$6.10/5.00 \times 100 = 122$

Figure 15.3

Price Index for Structural Steel (not fabricated), (1970 = 100)

Year	Simple Price Index
1970	$\$120/120 \times 100 = 100.0$
1971	$123/120 \times 100 = 102.5$
1972	$126/120 \times 100 = 105.0$
1973	$132/120 \times 100 = 110.0$
1974	$138/120 \times 100 = 115.0$

index for 1974 is 122. This means that the 1974 price for a welder is 122 percent of the 1970 (base year) price for a welder.

The simple price index for structural steel is shown in Figure 15.3. The computations are identical to those already illustrated. From Figure 15.3, for example, the 1974 price of structural steel was 115 percent of the 1970 (base year) price.

15.22 Should Simple Indices Be Weighted for Combining?

Now that two simple price indices have been computed, one is closer to understanding the price behavior of inputs to fabricated structural steel. The price for welders has increased 22 percent over the base year, while the price for structural steel beams has increased 15 percent over the base year. The next step is to combine these two simple price indices into an *aggregate index* of prices for fabricated structural steel inputs. To construct the aggregate price index for 1973, for example, should one simply average the index value of 120 for a welder and 110 for structural steel? An unweighted average for these two simple index values implies that the two inputs, welders and structural steel, are of equal importance. If the analyst believes the two inputs are equally important, such an unweighted average is appropriate. However, the analyst is aware of the information

Figure 15.4

Amounts Paid (1970) for Welders and Structural Steel

Item	Quantity	Unit Price	Value
Welders.................	60,000 hrs.	$ 5.00/hr.	$ 300,000
Steel...................	5,833 tons	120.00/ton	700,000
			$1,000,000

shown in Figure 15.4, which shows the amounts paid in 1970 for welders and for structural steel beams. This information shows that the total cost of welders in 1970 was $300,000, while the total amount spent for steel beams was $700,000. This shows that a price change in steel beams is more important than a similar percentage price change for welders, because the firm spends more than twice as much for steel beams as it does for welders. These values, $300,000 and $700,000, are the appropriate weights that may be used to combine the two simple price indices already computed.

The two simple price indices are combined into an aggregate index of prices for fabricated structural steel inputs in Figure 15.5. The computations are quite straightforward; for each year the simple index for each item is weighted by the relative importance of that item, as measured by the amount spent in 1970 for that item. This aggregate price index shows that the 1974 price for fabricated structural steel inputs was 117.1 percent of the price of the same inputs in the base year, 1970. Also observe that the price index rose 2.4 percentage points from 1970 to 1971, 4.7 percentage points from 1971 to 1972, 5.9 percentage points from 1972 to 1973, and 4.1 percentage points from 1973 to 1974. It is important to note that these individual year changes in the index are stated as *percentage*

Figure 15.5

Price Index for Structural Steel Inputs (based on 1970 weights), 1970 = 100

Year	Welders	Steel	Aggregate Index
1970........	$100.0 \times \dfrac{300,000}{1,000,000}$	$+ \ 100.0 \times \dfrac{700,000}{1,000,000}$	$= \ 100.0$
1971	$102.0 \times \dfrac{300,000}{1,000,000}$	$+ \ 102.5 \times \dfrac{700,000}{1,000,000}$	$= \ 102.4$
1972	$112.0 \times \dfrac{300,000}{1,000,000}$	$+ \ 105.0 \times \dfrac{700,000}{1,000,000}$	$= \ 107.1$
1973........	$120.0 \times \dfrac{300,000}{1,000,000}$	$+ \ 110.0 \times \dfrac{700,000}{1,000,000}$	$= \ 113.0$
1974........	$122.0 \times \dfrac{300,000}{1,000,000}$	$+ \ 115.0 \times \dfrac{700,000}{1,000,000}$	$= \ 117.1$

point changes, and not as percentage changes. From 1973 to 1974, for example, the index changed 4.1 percentage points, from the base 113. Hence, the percentage change between 1973 and 1974 was

$$\frac{117.1 - 113.0}{113.0} = \frac{4.1}{113.0} = 3.6 \text{ percent}$$

This 3.6 percent increase is smaller than the 4.1 percentage point increase, because the basis for comparison is 113.0, which is larger than 100.

15.23 Other Weights for Combining Simple Indices

In the example to this point, the analyst has rather arbitrarily specified that the weights to be used in combining the two simple price indices are the values of each item, measured by 1970 purchases. The computed price index shows the price for each year to purchase the 1970 *market basket,* relative to the price of that market basket in 1970. If the relative importance of welders and steel changes from 1970 to 1974, such an index may be misleading. If there has been a drastic change in the technology of fabricating structural steel (e.g., the increased use of automatic welding machines), welders will be less important in 1974 than in 1970. Then it is appropriate to use weights other than the 1970 values in combining the simple price indices.

The weights to be used in combining indices depend largely on the questions to be answered by the index number. It has already been mentioned that the index computed in Figure 15.5 shows the relative price of the 1970 market basket of structural steel inputs. If we had used the 1974 values, the index would show the relative price for the 1974 market basket of inputs. It would also be possible to use as weights some average of the values for various years, or some judgmentally determined "typical" set of weights. There is not necessarily a right or wrong set of weights to be used in index number construction.

15.3 CONSTRUCTION OF INDEX NUMBERS

Now that an aggregate price index has been constructed, it may be helpful to state in symbols what has already been accomplished in the preceding section. Using the symbol p to stand for the price of a commodity, the subscript n to represent the year under consideration (called the *given* year), the subscript 0 to indicate the base year, and the symbol q to stand for the quantity of a commodity bought or sold, we can restate the index number calculations already accomplished.

The simple price index for a commodity for a given year is $\frac{p_n}{p_0} \times 100$.

To combine these simple price indices into an aggregate price index, using the base year value of transactions as weights, the index is constructed as:

$$\frac{\Sigma \frac{p_n}{p_0}(p_0 q_0)}{\Sigma p_0 q_0} \times 100$$

where the summation sign indicates a summation over all commodities included in the index. (For historical purposes, this particular form of price index is called the *Laspeyres price index*, named after the person influential in its development.) If the weights selected are the given year weights, the equation for computing a price index is:

$$\frac{\Sigma \frac{p_n}{p_0}(p_0 q_n)}{\Sigma p_0 q_n} \times 100$$

Note that in this index the weights change for each year, because the given year weights are always used. This index, called a *Paasche index*, always uses the market basket for the year for which the index is being computed. Although this is logically desirable in many situations, the data requirements are much greater for this type of index. In many situations, it is much easier to obtain information on prices than it is to obtain information on the quantity sold for a commodity.

If some typical market basket is selected for weighting the price relatives, the index number is computed as:

$$\frac{\Sigma \frac{p_n}{p_0}(p_0 q_t)}{\Sigma p_0 q_t} \times 100$$

where the subscript t denotes the typical quantity sold for that commodity.

15.31   Expanding the Commodities Included in an Index

The index constructed in the example above may or may not represent an adequate description of price changes for structural steel inputs, because the analyst has included only two commodities. If there are only two major input classes, steel and labor, the representation may be adequate. If all labor prices vary closely with the variation in welder wage rates, all steel inputs have price behavior similar to the structural steel beam price behavior shown, and if labor typically represents 30 percent of the value of inputs, then the price index constructed may be adequate.

If the two commodities already included are not typical indicators of price behavior for their class of inputs, or if there are factors other than labor and steel, it is necessary to expand the set of commodities to include the other inputs as well. In most index number construction, the choice of a set of commodities to be included is highly judgmental, rather than being determined by a random sampling procedure. This procedure often leads to a very useful index (the usefulness is determined by the skill of the analyst), although statistical inferences are not possible with a judgmentally determined set of commodities.

Another aspect of index number construction is the choice of a base period. Although there may be no such thing as a "normal" year, it is desirable to select as a base period a year which is not highly abnormal. The selection of a base year in which prices were unusually low makes future values appear high, while the selection of a base period in which prices were unusually high makes future values appear low.

15.4 VALUE, QUANTITY, AND GEOGRAPHICAL INDICES

The example to this point has dealt exclusively with the construction of an aggregate price index. There are other forms of useful indices. For example, consider a retail store which sells two products: cross-country skis and bicycles. The store is interested in looking at the changes in its volume of sales over the past several years. If prices have changed over this time period, a very important question is whether the firm is interested in looking at changes in the dollar value of sales, or in changes in the physical units sold. The first question, the change in dollar value of sales, is addressed by constructing a *value index*. The second question, changes in physical volume of sales, is addressed by constructing a *quantity index*. The firm's records yielded the information shown in Figure 15.6.

Figure 15.6

Sales of Skis and Bicycles

Year	Bicycles Sold	Price	Bicycle Sales	Pairs of Skis Sold	Price	Ski Sales	Total Sales
1970	300	$100	$30,000	50	$20	$1,000	$31,000
1971	320	110	35,200	80	25	2,000	37,200
1972	260	90	23,400	130	35	4,550	27,950
1973	200	105	21,000	140	30	4,200	25,200
1974	270	120	32,400	120	35	4,200	36,600

15.41 Value Index

A value index is nothing more than the ratio of the dollar volume of sales in the given year to the dollar volume of sales in the base year (with the usual factor of 100, arising because index numbers are im-

Figure 15.7

Value Index for a Ski and Bicycle Shop
(1970 = 100)

1970...................	31,000/31,000 × 100 = 100.0
1971...................	37,200/31,000 × 100 = 120.0
1972...................	27,950/31,000 × 100 = 90.2
1973...................	25,200/31,000 × 100 = 81.3
1974...................	36,600/31,000 × 100 = 118.1

plicitly stated as percentages). For the data given in Figure 15.6 the value index is computed in Figure 15.7. From Figure 15.7 it is apparent that 1972 sales, for example, were 90.2 percent of 1970 sales, and so on for other years.

In equation form, the value index is computed as

$$\frac{\Sigma p_n q_n}{\Sigma p_0 q_0} \times 100$$

It is important to note that a value index combines both changes in prices and quantity of transactions into one figure.

15.42   Quantity Index

If the owner of the bicycle and ski shop is interested in describing changes in the physical volume of sales, apart from the dollar volume of sales, a quantity index should be computed. The first step in computing this index is to compute the simple index of quantities for each of the individual commodities, bicycles and skis. This simple quantity index is computed in Figure 15.8.

Figure 15.8

Simple Quantity Indices: Bicycles and Skis (1970 = 100)

Year	Bicycles	Skis
1970...................	300/300 × 100 = 100.0	50/50 × 100 = 100.0
1971...................	320/300 × 100 = 106.7	80/50 × 100 = 160.0
1972...................	260/300 × 100 = 86.7	130/50 × 100 = 260.0
1973...................	200/300 × 100 = 66.7	140/50 × 100 = 280.0
1974...................	270/300 × 100 = 90.0	120/50 × 100 = 240.0

To combine these two simple quantity indices into one *aggregate quantity index,* it is necessary to weight each commodity by its importance. For this problem, the store owner (or the statistical analyst) must make a decision about the appropriate importance of bicycles and skis. In 1970, skis contributed only about 3 percent of dollar sales, while

Figure 15.9

Quantity Index for Bicycle–Ski Shop, Based on Judgmental Weights (1970 = 100)

Year	Bicycles		Skis		Aggregate Index
1970.......................	0.9×100.0	$+$	0.1×100.0	$=$	100.0
1971.......................	0.9×106.7	$+$	0.1×160.0	$=$	112.0
1972.......................	0.9×86.7	$+$	0.1×260.0	$=$	104.0
1973.......................	0.9×66.7	$+$	0.1×280.0	$=$	88.0
1974.......................	0.9×90.0	$+$	0.1×240.0	$=$	105.0

in 1973 skis amounted to nearly 17 percent of dollar sales. If the owner of the shop felt that typical sales figures for the store were 90 percent bicycles and 10 percent skis, these weights could be used in constructing the aggregate quantity index. Of course, it is possible to use any other set of weights, such as 1970 values, 1974 values, or some average of values for various years. Using the store owner's judgmentally determined 90 percent versus 10 percent weights, the aggregate quantity index is shown in Figure 15.9.

From this figure it is apparent that there has been a substantial decline in physical volume of sales from 1971 into 1972 and 1973. It is also apparent that the value index of 118.1 for 1974 does not represent changes in physical volume alone. Although the dollar volume in 1974 was 118.1 percent of the dollar volume in 1970 (from Figure 15.7), the physical quantity of merchandise passing through the doors increased only to an index of 105.0.

The formula for computing a quantity index may be expressed as

$$\Sigma \frac{q_n}{q_0} w \times 100$$

where the symbol w denotes the weight appropriate for a particular commodity, and the sum of the weights is one. If dollar values are used as weights, the quantity index using base year weights (a Laspeyres quantity index) is

$$\frac{\Sigma \frac{q_n}{q_0} (p_0 q_0)}{\Sigma (p_0 q_0)} \times 100$$

Values for other years could be used as weights.

15.43 Geographical Price Index

Price indices discussed so far reflect price changes over time at the same location. Prices may also vary from place to place at the same time.

For simplicity, let us consider price indices for two cities, A and B, for the year 1974. This simplified example will assume only three commodities: transportation, housing, and food. The example is further simplified by assuming that only one price exists for each commodity in each city. The raw data are shown in Figure 15.10.

Figure 15.10

Data for Price Index in the Cities (price per unit)

City	Transportation	Housing	Food
A	58.9¢	$195	$1.89
B	51.9¢	$235	$1.92

It is apparent by now that the construction of an index number requires weights. Suppose consumer expenditure studies in each city reveal the proportion of expenditures for each commodity in each city, as shown in Figure 15.11. Suppose a soon-to-retire worker is interested in whether

Figure 15.11

Proportion of Expenditures for Each Commodity

City	Transportation	Housing	Food
A	0.30	0.45	0.25
B	0.35	0.25	0.40

prices are higher in A or B. However, the worker needs to answer, "The price of what?" If the worker is interested in the price in city B of the "market basket" of city A, the expenditure proportions for city A are used to weight the price of city B relative to city A:

$$\text{Price index in city B for the market basket of city A} = \frac{\Sigma \frac{p_B}{p_A} w_A}{\Sigma w_A} \times 100$$

where w_A is the relative importance of a commodity in city A. A similar definition, with A and B reversed, gives the price index in city A for the market basket of city B. These indices are calculated below.

Price Index in city B for market basket of city A:

$$\left[\left(\frac{51.9}{58.9} \times 0.30\right) + \left(\frac{235}{195} \times 0.45\right) + \left(\frac{1.92}{1.89} \times 0.25\right)\right] \times 100 = 106.1$$

Price Index in city A for market basket of city B:

$$\left[\left(\frac{58.9}{51.9} \times 0.35\right) + \left(\frac{195}{235} \times 0.25\right) + \left(\frac{1.89}{1.92} \times 0.40\right)\right] \times 100 = 99.8$$

These calculations indicate that prices in city B are higher than prices in city A. More specifically, a resident of city A who went to city B and purchased the "A" market basket would pay 106.1 percent as much as for the same items in city A. However, a resident of city B who went to city A and purchased the "B" market basket would pay 99.8 percent as much as for the same items in city B. This seems to be saying that city B prices are about 6 percent higher than city A prices, but city A prices are about the same as city B prices! The apparent contradiction arises because the market basket differs from city to city.

This differing market basket makes geographical price indices particularly difficult to construct. A commodity which is very important in one city, such as home heating fuel in Fairbanks, is less important in another city. If the price of home heating fuel were tenfold higher in Hawaii than Alaska, a resident of Hawaii really is not concerned. One way around this dilemma is to compute costs for a specified "standard of living." These costs are calculated by including both the price of various commodities and the quantity of that commodity required for a given standard of living in each city.

15.5   IMPORTANT INDEX NUMBERS

Many economic research organizations publish statistical data about many aspects of our economy. Many of these data are expressed as index numbers. The most prolific publisher of economic data is the United States government. From a personal standpoint, the index number series which directly affects most of us is the consumer price index, which is often loosely called the "cost of living" index.

15.51   Consumer Price Index

The consumer price index (CPI) "is a statistical measure of changes in prices of goods and services bought by urban wage earners and clerical workers (families and single persons living alone)."[1] This index is broken down into several series, each of which represents a set of items customarily purchased for daily living. The 400 items in the series are grouped into individual areas of consumption, including food, housing, apparel and upkeep, transportation, and others. These commodity groupings are then weighted to form the overall index.

Figure 15.12 shows the consumer price index, and some of its components, for the years 1960–1975, with a base year of 1967.

One of the necessary evils of the construction of any index such as the CPI is maintaining its currency. As consumer tastes and preferences

---

[1] U.S. Department of Commerce, Office of Business Economics, *1971 Business Statistics, 18th Biannual Edition*, p. 40.

Figure 15.12

Consumer Price Index, by Selected Expenditure Classes (1967 = 100)

Year	Food	Housing	Apparel and Upkeep	Trans-portation	Medical Care	All Items
1960...............	88.0	90.2	89.6	89.6	79.1	88.7
1961...............	89.1	90.9	90.4	90.6	81.4	89.6
1962...............	89.9	91.7	90.9	92.5	83.5	90.6
1963...............	91.2	92.7	91.9	93.0	85.6	91.7
1964...............	92.4	93.8	92.7	94.3	87.3	92.9
1965...............	94.4	94.9	93.7	95.9	89.5	94.5
1966...............	99.1	97.2	96.1	97.2	93.4	97.2
1967...............	100.0	100.0	100.0	100.0	100.0	100.0
1968...............	103.6	104.2	105.4	103.2	106.1	104.2
1969...............	108.9	110.8	111.5	107.2	113.4	109.8
1970..:...........	114.9	118.9	116.1	112.7	120.6	116.3
1971...............	118.4	124.3	119.8	118.6	128.4	121.3
1972...............	123.5	129.2	122.3	119.9	132.5	125.3
1973...............	141.4	135.0	126.8	123.8	137.7	133.1
1974...............	161.7	150.6	136.2	137.7	150.5	147.7
1975...............	175.4	166.8	142.3	150.6	168.6	161.2

Source: Department of Labor, Bureau of Labor Statistics.

change, the commodities purchased change. The statistician, keeping such an index up to date, is faced with a dilemma: should the list of commodities be held constant, so that the index has the same meaning over all periods of time, or should the index be kept up to date by changing the "market basket" of commodities used in constructing the index? For the consumer price index, major revisions are made occasionally. A major revision was completed for the 1964 index values. The market basket was changed to include items which had increased in importance prior to 1964. Such things as between-meal snacks, hotel and motel rooms, garbage disposer units, moving expenses, college tuition, textbooks, and legal services, were added in the 1964 revision.

One aspect which the index number should incorporate, if possible, is changes in the quality of goods included in the index. Unfortunately, quality is a very difficult aspect to measure. Are 1977 automobiles "better" than 1967 automobiles? How are quality changes in gas mileage and safety features measured? The index statistician needs to be aware of such changes in product composition while the index is being compiled. One way of handling quality change is by calculating the proportion of a change in a price that is caused by the added (or reduced) cost of manufacturing the product. For example, if the price of an automobile increased from $5,000 to $5,400, but $300 of the increase represented the increased cost from added quality (such as safety equipment), the numerator of the price index for this commodity could be taken as $5,100.

It is important to note that the consumer price index measures *changes* in the prices of goods and services. Although indices for the various cities in which the data are collected are available, these data can be interpreted only to measure the changes of prices in the various cities. Individual city indices cannot be used to determine whether prices or living costs are higher or lower in one city than in another, because all city indices have the same base year (currently 1967) set at 100. Thus, the city indices measure changes, not relative costs, from one city to another.

15.52 Wholesale Price Index

The wholesale price index (WPI) is a second important index published by the United States Department of Labor, Bureau of Labor Statistics. "The index is designed to show the general rate and direction of the composite of price movements in primary markets. . . . It is designed to measure 'real' price changes between two periods of time, i.e., to measure price changes not influenced by changes in quality, quantity, terms of sale, or level of distribution. . . . The prices used in constructing the index represent the first important commercial transaction for each commodity."[2]

The wholesale price index is based on prices paid by wholesalers, while the consumer price index is based on prices paid by consumers. Hence, the WPI measures price changes at the beginning of the chain of transactions, while the CPI measures price changes at the final transaction. Like the CPI, the WPI is available as monthly and annual data.

There are several individual series for the WPI. Data are available by stage of processing (crude material for further processing, intermediate goods, finished goods) and by durability of product (durable goods, nondurable goods). A further breakdown is by farm products (which is broken into nine subcategories) and industrial commodities with more than 30 separate components.

With the WPI, a manufacturer can compare changes in the prices paid or received with the national average price changes for similar commodities. For example, there is a separate index available for the industrial commodity, "prepared paint." This index shows the prices (relative to the base year) for prepared paint at the first important commercial transaction after manufacture, the price paid to a paint manufacturer. A manufacturer of some other commodity, such as household furniture, might be interested in comparing its prices (relative to the same base year) for prepared paint with the national index. Thus, the prepared paint series represents a selling price for the paint manufacturing industry and a purchase price for the household furniture industry.

---

[2] U.S. Department of Commerce, Office of Business Economics, *1971 Business Statistics, 18th Biannual Edition*, p. 43.

15.53   Indices of Quantity Output

One of the more important indices of industrial output for the entire economy is the Federal Reserve Board index of quantity output, more commonly called the index of industrial production. This index "measures changes in the physical volume or quantity of output of manufacturers, minerals, and electric and gas utilities. . . . The index does not cover production on farms, in the construction industry, in transportation, or in the various trade and service industries."[3] The index reflects output changes at all stages of production.

As with other indices we have examined, the index of industrial production is broken into many components. For example, there are separate indices available for automotive products, which are further broken into subcategories. Output indices are also available for carpeting and furniture; appliances, TV, and furniture; primary metals, fabricated metal products; machinery; transportation equipment; lumber; and so on. With this kind of detailed information, a firm is able to compare its own output over time with the appropriate industry index of output, to determine how its own growth compares with the national average. From an investor's standpoint, the index also provides information about the relative growth of various product groups or industries. As with other indices, the index of industrial production is revised periodically to reflect changes in the economy. For example, a revision in 1971 incorporated information to match the index series to bench marks obtained in the *Annual Survey of Manufacturers*. A prior revision was completed in 1962.

Another useful index of output can be constructed from gross national product data. The GNP is "the market value of the output of goods and services produced by the nation's economy."[4] This series is one of the more widely used measures of the output of the entire economy. The time series of GNP can easily be expressed as an index, simply by dividing the value for each year by the value of GNP for the base year. This computation, showing 1967 as the base year, is shown in Figure 15.13. This index is a value index, rather than a measure of the aggregate physical output of the economy. As price levels change (inflation or deflation), the value index becomes a very poor measure of actual changes in output. To compensate for this deficiency, the GNP is also published in constant dollars. The series is currently in terms of 1972 dollars, which estimates the value that GNP would attain if there had been no change in price levels since 1972. This series may also be expressed as a simple index by dividing each yearly value by the value for the base year. This computation is demon-

---

[3] U.S. Department of Commerce, Office of Business Economics, *1971 Business Statistics, 18th Biannual Edition,* p. 16.

[4] Ibid, p. 1.

Figure 15.13

GNP as a Value Index (1967 = 100)

Year	(1) GNP ($ Billions)	Value Index (1) ÷ 796.3 × 100
1960	506.0	63.5
1961	523.3	65.7
1962	563.8	70.8
1963	594.7	74.8
1964	635.7	79.8
1965	688.1	86.4
1966	753.0	94.6
1967	796.3	100.0
1968	868.5	109.1
1969	935.5	117.5
1970	982.4	123.4
1971	1,063.4	133.5
1972	1,171.1	147.1
1973	1,306.3	164.0
1974	1,406.9	176.7
1975	1,499.0	188.2

Source: United States Department of Commerce, Office of Business Economics.

strated in Figure 15.14. With the GNP value index (Figure 15.13) and the GNP quantity index (Figure 15.14), a very broad-based price index for the entire economy can be computed. This index, called the *implicit GNP deflator,* is obtained by dividing the value index by the quantity index,

Figure 15.14

GNP as a Quantity Index (1967 = 100)

Year	(1) GNP in Constant Dollars (billions of 1972 dollars)	Quantity Index (1) ÷ 1,007.7 × 100
1960	736.8	73.1
1961	755.3	75.0
1962	799.1	79.3
1963	830.7	82.4
1964	874.4	86.8
1965	925.9	91.9
1966	981.0	97.4
1967	1,007.7	100.0
1968	1,051.8	104.4
1969	1,078.8	107.1
1970	1,075.3	106.7
1971	1,107.5	109.9
1972	1,171.1	116.2
1973	1,233.4	122.4
1974	1,210.7	120.2
1975	1,186.4	117.7

Source: United States Department of Commerce, Office of Business Economics.

Figure 15.15

Implicit GNP Deflator (1967 = 100)

Year	(1) GNP Value Index (from Figure 15.13)	(2) GNP Quantity Index (from Figure 15.14)	Implicit GNP Deflator (1) ÷ (2) × 100
1960	63.5	73.1	86.9
1961	65.7	75.0	87.6
1962	70.8	79.3	89.3
1963	74.8	82.4	90.8
1964	79.8	86.8	91.9
1965	86.4	91.9	94.0
1966	94.6	97.4	97.1
1967	100.0	100.0	100.0
1968	109.1	104.4	104.5
1969	117.5	107.1	109.7
1970	123.4	106.7	115.7
1971	133.5	109.9	121.5
1971	147.1	116.2	126.6
1973	164.0	122.4	134.0
1974	176.6	120.2	147.0
1975	188.2	117.7	159.9

Source: United States Department of Commerce, Office of Business Economics.

as shown in Figure 15.15. This index is very useful when a measure of changes in prices for the entire economy is desired.

Just as there were various price indices to measure various price changes, we have now seen two quantity indices to measure different kinds of output changes. The GNP in constant dollars expressed as an index is a much broader-based output index than the Federal Reserve Board index of industrial production. Two important sectors of the economy covered by GNP, but omitted in the Federal Reserve Board index, are agriculture and services.

15.54   Productivity Indices

The economic stabilization programs of the early 1970s placed great emphasis upon productivity as an important factor in evaluating proposed price increases. Labor productivity is really nothing more than output per man hour. If a measure of output is available, this output may be divided by the labor input (usually expressed in hours). This quotient, expressed as an index, is a measure of changes in labor productivity. The United States Department of Labor, Bureau of Labor Statistics, prepares an index of output per labor input hour for both the total private sector of the economy and the nonfarm private sector of the economy.

To construct a productivity index for a particular firm (or industry), it is necessary only to divide a measure of output for that industry (such

Figure 15.16

Labor Productivity for the Bicycle–Ski Shop (1970 = 100)

Year	(1) Output Index	(2) Labor Hours	(3) (1) ÷ (2)	Labor Productivity Index (3) ÷ 0.0200 × 100
1970	100.0	5,000	0.0200	100.0
1971	112.0	5,200	0.0215	107.5
1972	104.0	5,400	0.0193	96.5
1973	88.0	4,600	0.0191	95.5
1974	105.0	4,800	0.0219	109.5

as a quantity index) by the amount of input of the factor of production whose productivity is being computed. As an example, the owner of the bicycle-ski shop 15 could easily compute the productivity of the labor force of the shop by dividing the output index from Figure 15.9 by the number of labor hours used in each of the year. The output of the shop (see Figure 15.9) and the labor input are shown in Figure 15.16. This figure also shows the index of labor productivity for the five years for which data are available. This index could then be compared with published indices of labor productivity to provide information useful to the manager of the firm.

15.6 USE OF INDEX NUMBERS

In many index number uses, it is necessary to perform some very simple computations in order to obtain the desired information. The purpose of this section is to show some of the computations that may be required in using index numbers.

15.61 Changing the Base Period

In order to change the base period of an index, only a simple division is required. If an index is available with 1967 = 100, and the same index is desired with, say, 1970 = 100, it is necessary only to divide each value by the value of the index for 1970, and then re-express all values as an index by multiplying by 100. Figure 15.17 shows a change in the wholesale price index from 1967 = 100 to 1970 = 100.

15.62 Splicing Two Index Number Series

It has already been mentioned that two of the problems faced by an index number statistician are maintaining currency of the index and maintaining comparability with previous time periods. When a price index is

Figure 15.17

Changing the Base of the Wholesale Price Index

Year	(1) 1967 = 100	(2) 1970 Value	1970 = 100 (1) ÷ (2) × 100
1960.................	94.9	110.4	86.0
1961.................	94.5	110.4	85.6
1962.................	94.8	110.4	85.9
1963.................	94.5	110.4	85.6
1964.................	94.7	110.4	85.8
1965.................	96.6	110.4	87.5
1966.................	99.8	110.4	90.4
1967.................	100.0	110.4	90.6
1968.................	102.5	110.4	92.8
1969.................	106.5	110.4	96.5
1970.................	110.4	110.4	100.0
1971.................	113.9	110.4	103.2
1972.................	119.1	110.4	107.9
1973.................	134.7	110.4	122.0
1974.................	160.1	110.4	145.0
1975.................	174.9	110.4	158.4

Source: Department of Labor, Bureau of Labor Statistics.

Figure 15.18

Splicing Two Index Series

Year	(1) Old Index	(2) New Index	(3) (2) × 109.1 ÷ 97.2	(4) Spliced Series
1970.................	104.2			104.2
1971.................	107.3			107.3
1972.................	109.1	97.2	109.1	109.1
1973.................		99.1	111.2	111.2
1974.................		106.3	119.3	119.3

Note that the splicing can be made in the other direction by using 97.2 as the common number, and 97.2 ÷ 109.1 as the ratio applied to Column 1.

revised, for example, a typical change is a change in the "market basket" of commodities used in computing the index. Thus, the two index number series, before and after the change, are no longer strictly comparable with each other. A common procedure for linking the two series together is an operation called *splicing*. Splicing is accomplished by computing the index with both the old market basket and the new market basket for at least one time period (usually a year). Then the beginning value of the new series is chosen so that the two series have identical values in the year for which both series are computed. Figure 15.18 shows the splicing of two index number series.

15.63   Combining Two Index Number Series

Published indices may be used very easily to construct special purpose index series. Consider a large furniture dealer who buys almost all the merchandise directly from manufacturers. The dealer is interested in computing a price index for the merchandise bought, which will be useful both in setting salaries for employees and in setting prices. All sales fall either in the household appliances category or in the household furniture category; price indices for these commodities are available as part of the wholesale price index. Knowing the weights and proportion of the business which each of these represents, the dealer may use the published data to construct a special index. If 30 percent of the purchases are of household appliances, and the remaining 70 percent is household furniture, the special purpose index is computed in Figure 15.19. This index

Figure 15.19

Special Index Computed from the Wholesale Price Index (1967 = 100)

Year	(1) Household Appliances	(2) Household Furniture	Combined Index (1) × 0.3 + (2) × 0.7
1965	98.9	94.1	95.5
1966	98.8	96.6	97.3
1967	100.0	100.0	100.0
1968	101.8	103.9	103.3
1969	103.1	108.3	106.7

Source: Department of Labor, Bureau of Labor Statistics.

is simply a weighting of the two series, according to the proportion of business that each component represents.

15.64   Purchasing Power of a Dollar

If the price level increases by 5 percent it is also said that the purchasing power of a dollar declines by 5 percent. More formally, the purchasing power of a dollar is defined to be the reciprocal of the price index, with the base year of the index being the year in which the dollar is said to have a purchasing power of $1.00. Using the consumer price index, it is very easy to construct the purchasing power of $1.00 for urban wage earners and clerical workers. The value of the dollar at wholesale transactions can also be computed by taking the reciprocal of the wholesale price index. Using the consumer price index, the purchasing power of a dollar is shown in Figure 15.20. This concept is quite useful in many contractual

Figure 15.20

Purchasing Power of the Dollar (1967 = 100 or $1.00)

Year	(I) CPI	Purchasing Power 100 ÷ (I)
1960	88.7	$1.127
1961	89.6	1.116
1962	90.6	1.104
1963	91.7	1.091
1964	92.9	1.076
1965	94.5	1.058
1966	97.2	1.029
1967	100.0	1.000
1968	104.2	.960
1969	109.8	.911
1970	116.3	.860
1971	121.3	.824
1972	125.3	.798
1973	133.1	.751
1974	147.7	.677
1975	161.2	.620

Source: Department of Labor, Bureau of Labor Statistics.

agreements, including some labor contracts which require increased wage rates as the purchasing power of a dollar declines, or as the consumer price index increases.

15.7 DEFLATING A TIME SERIES

Recall the Mercantile Stores example introduced in section 14.32 with sales data displayed in Figure 14.6. These data were reported in constant (1967) dollars with a brief word description regarding the deflation of the actual sales to constant dollar sales.

Selecting a small series of quarterly sales figures for an example, the deflation of a part of this time series is demonstrated in Figure 15.21. The apparel and upkeep component of the CPI was used for the price index. This is not a perfect choice, because Mercantile does not deal in upkeep (dry cleaning, etc.). It also omits household furnishings (bedding, etc.) which are a part of Mercantile's business. Each index value used for deflation is the average of the index for the three months in that quarter.

The reader should note that sales in Column 1 are affected by changes in quantities *and* prices, whereas sales in Column 3 reflect changes in quantity only. The sales in Column 1 are measures of values (i.e. prices × quantities), whereas sales in Column 3 reflect quantities, but in dollar units. In general, sales in *current* dollars (as in Column 1) constitute a time series of *values,* and sales in constant dollars (as in Column 3) constitute a time series reflecting *physical sales,* not dollar sales.

Figure 15.21

Mercantile Stores Quarterly Sales and Apparel and Upkeep Price Index

Year	Quarter	(1) Reported Sales Current Dollars* (millions)	(2) Price Index† (1967 = 100)	(3) = (1) ÷ (2) × 100 Sales 1967 Dollars (millions)
1972...............	1	87.4	121.3	72.1
	2	100.0	121.9	82.0
	3	112.4	122.7	91.6
	4	158.5	124.3	127.5
1973...............	1	102.6	124.7	82.3
	2	116.3	126.4	92.0
	3	123.9	128.1	96.7
	4	175.3	129.9	134.9

Sources: * COMPUSTAT Primary Industrial File, Investors Management Sciences, Inc.
† Department of Labor, Bureau of Labor Statistics.

15.8   SUMMARY

Index numbers are very useful descriptive statistics. As the reader has observed, index number construction revolves around the art and common sense of number use, rather than around any formal probabilistic or statistical procedures. Decisions must always be made about what data are to be used in constructing an index. This question is answered by considering the question to be addressed by the index number. A similarly important consideration is the cost of data collection for the index, and the value of the index once it has been constructed.

Many published index number series are available for the statistical analyst. Several price indices and several quantity indices have been discussed in this chapter. All the published index numbers which have been discussed are quite carefully constructed. Nonetheless, difficulties always arise from changes in consumer tastes and preferences, changes in quality, new products being introduced which may not be reflected in the index, and old products being phased out which may be included in the index. However, index numbers are indeed very useful descriptive statistics.

EXERCISES

15.1   The price index for 1975 stood at 289.2. Does that necessarily mean there had been a recent price increase? Discuss.

* 15.2   Construct a population index for the United States, 1967 = 100, for the years 1965 to 1970.

---

* Answers to exercises marked with an asterisk (*) are in Appendix L.

Year	Population (*thousands*)
1965	194,303
1966	196,560
1967	198,712
1968	200,706
1969	202,677
1970	204,879

* 15.3   The population of the United States in 1929 was 121,767,000. Using the data from Exercise 15.2, construct a population index for the United States, 1929 = 100, for the years 1965 to 1970.

15.4   The population data given in Exercise 15.2 and 15.3 includes armed forces overseas beginning in 1940, and includes Alaska and Hawaii beginning in 1950. Consider the individual effects of each of these changes; does the change cause the population index constructed in Exercise 15.3 to overstate, understate, or leave unchanged the following:

   a.   The population of the United States.
   b.   The population of the 48 contiguous states.

* 15.5   Construct an index for the retail price (including taxes) for a U.S. gallon of gasoline for these three countries: (U.S.A. = 100)

Country	Price, *including taxes* (*U.S. currency*)
United States	$0.59/U.S. gallon
Canada	$0.79/Imperial gallon
West Germany	$0.41/Liter

An Imperial Gallon is five quarts; one liter is 1.06 quarts.

* 15.6   The RM Structural Steel Company published the following data about its yearly output of fabricated structural steel for the past four years:

Year	Output (*tons*)
1971	1,062,000
1972	1,174,000
1973	1,378,000
1974	937,000

   a.   Construct an index of output for the firm, using 1971 = 100.
   b.   The product mix was substantially different in 1974 for RM. Until 1974, the firm had a reasonably constant mix of light commercial buildings, highway bridges, and large structures (such as basketball stadia). However, in 1974, almost all RM's output was light commercial buildings, which have a relatively high labor content per ton of steel. What is the effect of this change on the output index you constructed in Part *a?* How might this effect be properly accounted for in constructing an index of output?

* 15.7   The wholesale price of a 40-lb. box of red delicious apples, 3-inch diameter, on February 1 of each year for five years was:

Year	Price
1970............................	$4.40
1971............................	3.20
1972............................	4.80
1973............................	6.20
1974............................	7.00

   a. Construct a price index for these apples, 1970 = 100.

   b. What additional information would you need to construct this same index with 1967 = 100?

   c. What possible changes in the product, its packaging, terms of sale, condition etc., could have occurred to introduce possible biases into this index?

15.8 A two-product firm reported these sales data:

	1975	1976
Surfboards............	15,000 @ $17 each	19,000 @ $14 each
Tennis shoes............	17,000 @ $11 each	6,000 @ $12 each

   a. Construct a 1976 aggregate price index, 1975 = 100, using 1975 values as weights.

   b. Construct a 1976 aggregate price index, 1975 = 100, using 1976 values as weights.

   c. Construct a 1976 aggregate price index, 1975 = 100, weighting each sample index equally.

   d. Construct 1976 aggregate quantity indices, 1975 = 100, for the weights of *a*, *b*, and *c*.

* 15.9 A manufacturer of specialty stainless steel produces three major grades of stainless steel. The price of each ($ per pound) and the quantity sold (tons) is shown below:

	1974		1975		1976	
Grade	Price	Quantity	Price	Quantity	Price	Quantity
1........	$1.34	3.86 tons	$1.41	4.71 tons	$1.26	8.31 tons
2........	0.34	41.81 tons	0.31	58.46 tons	0.27	51.22 tons
3........	0.21	9.80 tons	0.28	8.03 tons	0.31	11.41 tons

   a. For each product, construct a simple price index with 1974 = 100.

   b. For each product, construct a simple quantity index with 1974 = 100.

   c. Using 1974 values as weights, construct an aggregate price index, 1974 = 100.

   d. Using 1974 values as weights, construct an aggregate quantity index, 1974 = 100.

15.10 For the data of Exercise 15.9, construct an aggregate price index, 1976 = 100, using 1974 values as weights. Compare the percentage change in prices, using this index and the index from 15.9, for each pair of years. What do you observe? What generalizations can you make from this comparison?

* 15.11 Construct an index of the value of sales for the manufacturer of Exercise 15.9, 1974 = 100. What does this value index show?

* 15.12 For the purpose of comparing year-to-year percentage changes in aggregate prices, will changing the base year of the price index be of any importance?

15.13 A price index was constructed using 1975 values as weights, with 1975 = 100. The index was then reconstructed using 1975 values as weights, with 1972 = 100. Will the percentage change from 1972 to 1975 be identical for the two indices?

15.14 What is the difference between an increase of 6.1 percent and an increase of 6.1 percentage points?

* 15.15 An appliance manufacturer was satisfied that a price index the trade association published was useful. Using this index, express the manufacturer's sales in constant (1975) dollars. Are the sales gains apparently real or due to inflation?

Year	Reported Sales	Price Index
1973	$12,327,000	83.2
1974	15,883,000	91.4
1975	16,220,000	100.0
1976	19,148,000	104.7

* 15.16 For the manufacturer of Exercise 15.15, construct an index of output, 1973 = 100.

15.17 Differentiate between *current dollars* and *constant dollars*.

15.18 What does it mean to deflate a time series to account for price changes?

15.19 Consumer price indices are available for major cities in the United States. These are published with a common year (such as 1967) set equal to 100 for each city. What does it mean if the 1976 price index for City A is 187.3 (1967 = 100), and the 1976 price index for City B is 167.4 (1967 = 100)?

15.20 According to the Federal Reserve Board index of industrial production, 1967 = 100 for all components, the 1960 production index for manufacturing was 65.4 and for mining was 82.7. Does this mean that the amount of mining output in 1960 was greater than the amount of production output in 1960? If not, what is the meaning?

* 15.21 As Ajax Products Corporation expanded, it continued its practice of revising its price index for raw materials every five years. This revision was accomplished to reflect changing needs of the corporation. It was common practice to set the revised index of 100 for its first year, and to compute both indices for the year of change. Ajax provided the following data:
  a. Splice the index numbers into a useful combined index.
  b. Compute the raw material purchases in constant (1970) dollars.

Year	1965–1970 Index	1970–1975 Index	Invoice Totals for Raw Materials
1965	100.0		$ 837,000
1966	101.2		926,000
1967	98.3		938,000
1968	94.2		927,000
1969	100.8		983,000
1970	104.7	100.0	986,000
1971		103.3	1,002,000
1972		104.2	1,041,000
1973		108.4	1,052,000
1974		118.9	1,103,000
1975		127.3	1,108,000

    c. Construct a quantity index showing raw materials purchased by Ajax.

15.22 *a.* What is the consumer price index?

    b. How often is it published?

    c. Why is it necessary periodically to change the commodities and weights for the index?

15.23 It has been argued that the mix of consumer purchases has shifted toward a higher proportion of services, reducing the (relative) purchases of goods. If it is true that prices for services have risen more rapidly than the prices for goods, what would be the direction of the bias (if any) in the consumer price index, if the construction of the index remained unchanged?

15.24 What is the meaning of the implicit deflator for GNP? How is it constructed?

15.25 Explain the meaning of this statement: "For the average hourly worker in the United States this month, the wage rate went up 0.4 percent, but consumer prices rose 0.6 percent. This means that an hour of work brings more money but buys less. But workers averaged 0.2 more hours than last month, so they really buy more now." If the work week last month was 40.0 hours, what is the increase in purchasing power for a week of work?

15.26 Why might it be that the United States finds its diplomatic employees in another capital experiencing a higher cost of living than they would in Washington, and the nationals of that country living in Washington also experience a higher cost of living than they would in their own capitals? How does this phenomenon affect interpretation of geographical price indices constructed using a fixed market basket?

15.27 If greatly increased unionization caused higher wages for retail employees, how would you expect the wholesale price index and the commodities components of the consumer price index to behave relative to each other?

15.28 Why might a value index be more useful in planning cash requirements than in planning production levels?

REFERENCES

Doody, Francis S. *Introduction to the Use of Economic Indicators.* New York: Random House, Inc., 1965.

Fisher, Irving. *The Making of Index Numbers.* New York: Houghton Mifflin Co., 1923.

Moore, Geoffrey H., and Shishkin, Julius. *Indicators of Business Expansions and Contractions.* New York: National Bureau of Economic Research, Columbia University Press, 1967.

Mudgett, Bruce D. *Index Numbers.* New York: John Wiley & Sons, Inc., 1951.

16

Decision Analysis

Previous chapters of this book have built a background for the study of decision making. Ways of presenting data for analysis have been discussed. Probability theory, the language of uncertainty, has been discussed. Statistical inference has been discussed as a means of concisely reporting the probabilistic information contained in a sample. In this chapter and the next, probability theory and sampling theory will be combined into what is called *decision analysis*.

16.1 CLASSIFICATION OF DECISION PROBLEMS

A decision arises when a person (the decision maker) must select one of several courses of action. There are three different decision categories: decisions under certainty, decisions under uncertainty, and decisions under conflict. Unfortunately, the nomenclature of decision categories is not consistent in the literature, so the reader is warned that in studying other references one might find different names for the three decision categories described here.

16.11 Decisions under Certainty

The first category of decision problems is decision making under certainty. A decision is made under certainty if the decision maker knows what the result will be for each course of action that could be followed. This might appear to be a trivial type of decision. After all, there is really no problem if the decision maker knows what is going to occur. The difficulty of decision making under certainty is that there are often so many feasible courses of action that it may be impossible to consider each of them individually and then pick the best. Much of the emphasis of the discipline called *operations research* or *management science* deals with decision making under certainty. Decisions under certainty are not considered in this text.

16.12 Decisions under Uncertainty

The second category of decision problems is decision making under uncertainty. A decision is made under uncertainty if each course of action leads to an array of possible outcomes, each with its own probability of occurrence. The decision maker knows there is no opponent (other than chance or nature) to affect the outcome for a decision. For example, the decision whether to place a dollar on "red" in roulette is a decision problem under uncertainty. I know the probability of winning a dollar is 18/38 and the probability of losing a dollar is 20/38. Thus, if my selected course of action is to play the game, I do not know for certain what will happen. But I do know the probabilities for what might happen. A decision maker in almost any organization is very often faced with decisions under uncertainty. For example, the demand for a product with a specified price and performance is often not known with certainty. This is a decision problem under uncertainty. In such situations, the decision maker must assess (based on experience) the probabilities for the various events.

The discussions in this chapter and in Chapter 17 deal with decisions under uncertainty.

16.13 Decisions under Conflict

The final decision category is conflict. The previous types of decision problems (certainty and uncertainty) have assumed that there is only one decision maker, i.e., only one person or organization whose situation will be affected by the decision problem. If the decision problem is one under conflict or competition, there are two or more economic entities with opposing interests in the problem. If I am faced with a decision problem in which the outcome depends not only on what I do, but upon what you do as well, we are in a decision problem under conflict. *Game theory*, which is a quantitative discussion of decision making under conflict, is not considered in this text.

16.2 DECISIONS UNDER UNCERTAINTY: PAYOFF TABLES

There are several elements in any decision problem. These elements are illustrated by the problem faced by a building contractor who must decide whether to accept a contract on either a "fixed price" basis or a "cost plus percentage" basis. There is a set of two *acts* (or courses of action) available: "fixed price" or "cost plus." The set of acts represents the first element of the decision problem.

If the decision problem were made under certainty, it would be only an accounting problem (profit = revenue − cost) to determine which method of contracting to accept. (The real-world problem is more complex than this example.) However, in a world of changing prices and wages, the decision is made under uncertainty. The decision maker is uncertain about the amount of change in prices and wages. The various amounts by which prices and wages can change over the contract period represent the set of events which can occur. These events are the second element of the decision problem.

The economics of the decision problem for the contractor are simplified from reality to clarify the illustration. According to today's prices, the contract will cost $500,000 for material, and $100,000 for labor. The building contractor has a labor contract which will run throughout the entire period of the contract, and therefore assumes that labor costs will be exactly $100,000. However, the contractor is unable to obtain any long term commitment for materials. Material prices will be greater than today's prices by either 4 percent, 6 percent, or 8 percent. For signing a fixed price contract, the contractor will receive $635,000. For a cost plus contract, the revenue will be expenditures *plus* 1 percent. The costs and revenues (the third element of the problem) are:

Costs

If material prices increase 4 percent:
$500,000 + 0.04(500,000) + 100,000 = $620,000
If material prices increase 6 percent:
$500,000 + 0.06(500,000) + 100,000 = 630,000
If material prices increase 8 percent:
$500,000 + .08(500,000) + 100,000 = $640,000

Revenue

Fixed price contract: $635,000 regardless of the price of materials.
Cost plus contract: 101 percent of cost, or:
1.01 × 620,000 = 626,200 for 4 percent price increase of materials
1.01 × 630,000 = 636,300 for 6 percent price increase of materials
1.01 × 640,000 = 646,400 for 8 percent price increase of materials

The next step is to combine these *acts, events,* and their *payoffs* into a *payoff table.* A payoff table clearly describes each of the elements of the decision problem. The payoff table for this problem is shown in Figure 16.1. Notice that each *act* is one column of the payoff table, while each *event* is one row of the payoff table. At the intersection of each row and column the (final) figure shows the *payoff* (profit or loss) obtained by

Figure 16.1

Payoff Table for the Contractor's Problem

Events \ Acts	Fixed Price Contract	Cost Plus Contract
4% Increase	$635,000 − 620,000 = $15,000	$626,200 − 620,000 = $6,200
6% Increase	$635,000 − 630,000 = $ 5,000	$636,300 − 630,000 = $6,300
8% Increase	$635,000 − 640,000 = − $5,000	$646,400 − 640,000 = $6,400

the contractor for each *outcome,* or act-event combination. Thus, if the contractor chooses the fixed price contract (act) and a 6 percent increase (event) occurs, the profit will be $5,000. If the contractor chooses the cost plus contract (act) and the 8 percent increase (event) occurs, the profit will be $6,400.

16.3 PROBABILITY ASSESSMENT

In the contractor's problem probability values are needed for the various price increases before the contractor can choose an act. If, for example, the contractor is certain that a 4 percent increase will occur, the fixed price contract will be chosen. On the other hand, if the 8 percent increase is certain to occur, the contractor will choose the cost plus contract.

In Chapter 4, probability and its definition was discussed at some length. Recall that three approaches to probability were discussed: (1) an equally likely definition, (2) a relative frequency definition, and (3) a subjective (or personal) definition of probabilities. As in any probability problem, the decision maker must use the approach to probability which best fits the situation at hand. Unless there is some reason for the events to be equally likely (as in a gambling decision problem), the equally likely approach to probability is inadequate. Unless the decision is one for which there is a large amount of information about past repetitions of the identical situation, relative frequency probabilities may be inappropriate. Hence, many of the probabilities for decision problems will be subjective probabilities. (This is not to imply that other definitions of probability may not be used for decision analysis; on the contrary, all available information should be considered by the decision maker in assigning probabilities.)

How does the decision maker go about using judgment, experience, "hunch," intuition, and executive ability to assess probabilities? What is proposed in this section is a procedure which can be used by a decision maker to assist in assigning probability numbers to events in a decision problem. This is no magic scheme which makes "correct" probabilities appear out of nowhere. It is a procedure to help organize a decision maker's abilities to assess probabilities for a decision problem.

This probability assessment method is based primarily on the premise that a decision maker is able to decide which of two relatively simple situations is preferred. The decision maker must be asked repeated questions about these very simple probability situations.

For example, suppose someone offered you the choice of one of two bargains. Bargain A (called the "urn" bargain) is as follows:

An urn contains a large number of red and green balls. Except for color, the balls are identical. At the present time, the urn contains 10 percent red and 90 percent green balls; they are quite well mixed. A ball is to be selected without looking. If a red ball is drawn, you receive $10. If a green ball is drawn you receive $5. You have nothing to lose other than the few seconds required to participate in the game.

Bargain B (called "strawberry" bargain) is as follows:

A third person will call the Fifth St. Supermarket at the corner of Fifth and Broadway. If they have fresh strawberries available for sale at $0.69 a quart or less, you receive $10; if they do not, you receive $5. You have nothing to lose other than the few seconds required to participate in the game.

Most of us would be delighted to accept both of these bargains. However, it is a bit more difficult decision problem when you can choose only one of the two bargains. *The urn and strawberry bargains differ only in the probability of whether the $5 or $10 is received.* You know that the probability that a red ball will be selected is 0.10. Thus, if you prefer the urn to the strawberry bargain it must be because you believe the probability of strawberries at $0.69 a quart (or less) is less than 0.10. If you prefer the strawberry to the urn bargain, it must be because you believe the probability of cheap strawberries is greater than 0.10. If you are indifferent between the two bargains, you must be saying you believe the probability of finding cheap strawberries is exactly the same as the probability of a red ball, which is 0.10.

Suppose you choose the strawberry bargain. This states that you believe the probability that cheap strawberries are available is greater than 0.10. The question now arises, what probability would you assess for cheap strawberries? The answer is approached by using some mixture of red and green balls which has more red balls than before. Suppose you are asked about the same two bargains, except that there are 20 percent red balls (instead of the previous 10 percent). If you again say you prefer the strawberry bargain, go to a higher proportion of red balls—say, 30 percent. Continue this process until your decision shifts from the strawberry to the urn bargain. Once this switch happens, we would reduce the proportion of red balls, and continue back and forth until we found your point of indifference. Once we found the proportion of red balls which caused you to be indifferent between the strawberry and the urn bargains, the probability that you believe strawberries are available for $0.69 a quart (or less) at the supermarket has been found; it is the same as the proportion of red balls in the urn of indifference.

Now return to the building contractor. In order to assess the contractor's probabilities for various price increases of materials, simply change the bargain from strawberries to a cost increase in materials. Instead of asking about strawberries at $0.69 (or less), ask the contractor about a price change of 4 percent. After the point of indifference has been reached for a 4 percent price increase, question the contractor about a 6 percent price increase. After these two indifference probabilities have been established, the indifference probability of an 8 percent increase is determined, because the three probabilities must add to one.

This procedure for assessing probabilities is by no means foolproof. The analyst needs to be very careful to assist the decision maker in avoiding inconsistencies. It is also difficult for any decision maker to assess very small probabilities (say 0.01 or smaller). Special techniques are required for assessing small probabilities.

16.4 EXPECTATION AS A DECISION CRITERION

The four elements of a decision problem under uncertainty have now been described: the *acts* which are under the control of the decision maker, the *events* which are not under the control of the decision maker, a *payoff* for each outcome, and the *probabilities* that the decision maker assesses for each event. Continue the building contractor example by stating that the contractor assesses the probabilities to be:

$$P \text{ (4 percent price increase)} = 0.30$$
$$P \text{ (6 percent price increase)} = 0.50$$
$$P \text{ (8 percent price increase)} = \underline{0.20}$$
$$\overline{1.00}$$

16.41 Expected Monetary Value (EMV)

Chapter 4 described the calculation of the expected value (or mean) of a probability distribution. From the payoff table (Figure 16.1) the building contractor has a choice of one of two random variables as the payoff. By choosing the fixed price contract, the contractor will receive $15,000, $5,000, or −$5,000 as the payoff, with probabilities of 0.3, 0.5, and 0.2, respectively. The other set of payoffs, from a cost plus contract, are $6,200; $6,300; or $6,400, with probabilities of 0.3, 0.5, and 0.2, respectively. *The expected value of these payoffs may be used as a decision criterion to assist the decision maker in choosing the preferred act.* This expectation is referred to as the *expected monetary value* (*EMV*). The calculations for EMV are:

EMV(any act) $= \Sigma X_i P(X_i)$, for payoffs X_i with probabilities $P(X_i)$
EMV(fixed price) $= 0.3(15{,}000) + 0.5(5{,}000) + 0.2(-5{,}000)$
                 $= 4{,}500 + 2{,}500 - 1{,}000 = \$6{,}000$
EMV(cost plus) $= 0.3(6{,}200) + 0.5(6{,}300) = 0.2(6{,}400)$
                 $= 1{,}860 + 3{,}150 + 1{,}280 = \$6{,}290$

Based on EMV as a decision criterion, the contractor would choose the cost plus contract, because $6,290 is greater than $6,000.

How may EMV be justified as a decision criterion? If this decision problem is repeated many times, EMV is exactly the same thing as the (long run) average payoff the contractor would obtain in choosing this course of action many times. Thus, if this decision problem were repeated a large number of times, regardless of the outcome of each particular outcome of the decision problem, the contractor would average $6,290 per repetition, which is better than a long-run average of $6,000. By assumption, the long run average payoff is going to occur in this particular situation. There is no reason not to choose that course of action which will give the best average in this long run, if the long run is certain to occur. A difficulty with expected monetary value arises when the long run is not feasible. In most situations a decision problem is not repeated a large number of times. For example, bankruptcy may keep the decision from being repeated.

When dealing with a decision problem under uncertainty which is not repeated, an important factor in determining whether or not to use expected monetary value as the decision criterion is the economic consequence of an extreme negative payoff in the decision problem. In a business setting, a very large loss might lead to bankruptcy, which prohibits the long run from occurring. If, however, the payoffs are relatively small compared with the financial situation of the organization under consideration, it is reasonable to use expected monetary value as a legitimate decision criterion. This is because one particular decision does not affect the viability of the organization, and does not affect the organization's ability to exist in the future. Even though the particular decision is not being repeated, many other decisions will be made over time and by other parts of the organization. This enables the long run averaging process to work. To summarize, EMV is a legitimate decision criterion when payoffs are relatively small; thus, the payoffs of any particular decision do not affect the existence of the organization so that the long run averaging process can occur over many decisions.

When a decision has large economic consequences, a method of analysis called *utility analysis* or *risk preference analysis* may be used.

The general idea in utility analysis is to replace dollar payoffs with specially derived utility payoffs. These utilities are derived so that expected value, in this case expected utility, is a useful decision criterion. A further description of utility analysis is beyond the scope of this text.

16.42   Expected Value of Perfect Information (EVPI) or "Should I Hire a Clairvoyant?"

Under the assumption that the payoffs are relatively small compared with the financial situation, the contractor should be willing to use EMV as a criterion. Thus, the contractor would choose the cost plus contract because of its higher EMV. However, additional information might change the contractor's decision.

If the building contractor had an economic forecaster, should the contractor consider basing the decision on these forecasts? To answer this question, let us suppose that the contractor has an economic forecaster who is *clairvoyant* (one who can correctly predict the economic future in every situation). The economic forecaster is *only* clairvoyant; there are no powers of wizardry which enable the forecaster to *influence* the economic future.

If there will be a 4 percent price increase, a clairvoyant forecaster will state that there will be a 4 percent price increase. In this case, the contractor will choose the fixed price contract, because $15,000 is better than $6,200. Similarly, for a clairvoyant forecast of a 6 percent increase, the choice will be cost plus ($6,300 is better than $5,000), and for a clairvoyant forecast of an 8 percent price increase, the choice will be the cost plus contract ($6,400 profit is better than a loss of $5,000). The probability that the clairvoyant economic forecaster will say "4 percent increase" is 0.3, "6 percent increase" is 0.5, and "8 percent increase" is 0.2, given that these are the contractor's probabilities. Thus, if the contractor is making the decision based on perfect forecasts by the clairvoyant, the profit will be:

$15,000 with a probability of 0.3
6,300 with a probability of 0.5
6,400 with a probability of 0.2

The expected value of this probability distribution of payments is:

EMV with clairvoyance $= (15,000 \times 0.3) + (6,300 \times 0.5) + (6,400 \times 0.2) = \$8,930$

By using the forecasts of the clairvoyant, the contractor is able to increase the expected monetary value from $6,290 to $8,930, an increase of $2,640. This increase of $2,640 is called the *expected value of perfect information*, or EVPI.

EVPI is very useful because it sets an upper limit on the amount of money the contractor will be willing to pay for a perfect forecast about price behavior. If perfect information is worth $2,640, the contractor would be foolish to pay more than $2,640 for any forecast about material price behavior, regardless of the accuracy of the forecast. On the other hand, the contractor would be delighted to accept a *perfect* forecast for less than $2,640. In the next chapter, a method for calculating the expected value of less than perfect information is discussed.

The procedure used to calculate EVPI is:

1. Construct the payoff table and calculate EMV for each act.
2. Choose the act with the highest EMV. Use the symbol EMV* for the expected monetary value of this best act.
3. For each event find the best payoff; multiply this best payoff by the probability of that event.
4. Add these products. This total is the expected value with clairvoyance, or perfect information. This is also called *expected profit under certainty,* or EPC.
5. Calculate the expected value of perfect information as:

$$EVPI = EPC - EMV*$$

16.43 Expected Opportunity Loss (EOL)

An alternative way of analyzing a decision problem under uncertainty combines both the selection of the optimal act (best EMV) and the expected value of perfect information into one set of computations. The expected opportunity loss (EOL) is the measure which allows this combination. The opportunity loss for an outcome is the difference between the payoff for that outcome and the best payoff for that event. The opportunity loss table in the bottom part of Figure 16.2 corresponds to the contractor's payoff table repeated from Figure 16.1. To construct an opportunity loss table look at each event, one at a time. For the first event "4 percent increase" ask, "What is the best act for this event?" It is the fixed price contract and a payoff of $15,000, marked *. There is no opportunity loss for that particular outcome, so enter zero in that cell of the opportunity loss table. Choosing the cost plus contract when a 4 percent increase occurs yields a payoff of $6,200, when the contractor could have received a payoff of $15,000. The difference of $15,000 − $6,200 = $8,800 is the opportunity loss for the 4 percent increase and cost plus contract combination.

Going to the 6 percent increase event, the best act is now the cost plus contract. Hence, the contractor has a zero opportunity loss in that cell. If a 6 percent increase occurs, and the contractor picks the fixed price contract, opportunity loss will be $6,300 − $5,000 = $1,300. For the last event, 8 percent increase, the opportunity losses are $11,400 and $0.

The opportunity loss table can be used to calculate the expected op-

Figure 16.2

Contractor's Problem Payoff Table

Events \ Acts	Fixed Price Contract	Cost Plus Contract	Probabilities
4% Increase	$15,000*	$6,200	0.30
6% Increase	$ 5,000	$6,300*	0.50
8% Increase	− $ 5,000	$6,400*	0.20
EMV	$ 6,000	$6,290	1.00

Opportunity Loss Table

Events \ Acts	Fixed Price Contract	Cost Plus Contract	Probabilities
4% Increase	$0	$8,800	0.30
6% Increase	$ 1,300	$0	0.50
8% Increase	$11,400	$0	0.20
EOL	$ 2,930	$2,640	1.00

portunity loss for each act in the same way as the EMV for each act was calculated using the payoff table. For the fixed price contract the expected opportunity loss is:

$$\text{EOL (Fixed Price)} = (0 \times 0.3) + (\$1,300 \times 0.5) + (\$11,400 \times 0.2) = \$2,930$$

For the cost plus contract, the expected opportunity loss is:

$$\text{EOL (Cost Plus)} = (\$8,800 \times 0.3) + (0 \times 0.5) + (0 \times 0.2) = \$2,640$$

The contractor prefers to avoid opportunity loss, and therefore chooses the act with the lower EOL. Thus, the cost plus contract should be selected in order to minimize expected opportunity loss. It is important to note that this act with the lower EOL is the same as the act with the higher EMV. This is not coincidental; it is mathematically true that the act with best EMV will also have the lowest EOL. This is proved in Note 16.43 following Chapter 17.

There is another similarity between expected opportunity loss and other previous calculations. Notice that the value of EOL for the cost plus contract is $2,640. This is the same as the EVPI that was calculated earlier. Again, this is not coincidental; it is mathematically true that the lowest EOL is equal to EVPI. This is proved in Note 16.43.

In many decision problems, the decision maker can construct the opportunity loss table without the payoff table. To illustrate this, consider the problem faced by a Christmas tree merchant who can place only one order for Christmas trees during the pre-Christmas selling season. The merchant buys trees for $2 and sells them for $6, thus gaining a $4 profit on each tree sold and a $2 loss on each tree that is left over. Trees have no salvage value. Suppose the merchant assesses that only one, two, or three Chrismas trees will be sold, each with a probability of ⅓. The merchant can construct the opportunity loss table, Figure 16.3, without a payoff table.

Figure 16.3

Opportunity Loss Table for the Christmas Tree Problem

Events Acts	Stock 1	Stock 2	Stock 3	Probabilities
Demand is 1 tree	0	$2	$4	1/3
Demand is 2 trees	$4	0	$2	1/3
Demand is 3 trees	$8	$4	$0	1/3

The opportunity loss for an outcome is how much worse the merchant fares than if the best act for that event is selected. Using this concept, look at the "Demand is 1 tree" and "Stock 1 tree" cell in Figure 16.3. The decision maker asks, "If I stock one tree and one is demanded, how much worse off am I than I could have been for this demand?" Obviously, the best act was chosen; there is no opportunity loss for this cell. Continuing for a demand of one tree, if two trees had been stocked, the merchant is $2 worse off than he could have been; $2 represents the opportunity loss for stocking the tree which was not sold. If three trees are stocked and only one tree is demanded, the profit is $4 less than it would have been with the best act (stock 1) for this event. This $4 is the two trees purchased (at $2 each) which were left over.

Similarly, if demand is two trees, the optimal act is to stock two trees; this gives a zero opportunity loss. If the demand is two trees and the stock is one tree, the opportunity loss is $4. The second tree was demanded but not stocked; the merchant made no profit on the second tree, when a $4 profit could have been made. If the stock is three trees when demand is two trees, there is an opportunity loss of $2, which is the amount paid for the unsold tree.

If the demand is three trees, the best course of action is to stock three trees, as indicated by the zero opportunity loss in the lower right hand corner of the opportunity loss table. If the stock is one tree when the demand is three trees, no profit is made on the second and third trees. Hence, the merchant is $8 worse off than he could have been. If two trees are stocked and demand is three trees, he is $4 worse off, because of the unavailability of the third tree.

From the opportunity loss table:

$$EOL \ (Stock \ 1) \ = \frac{1}{3} \ (0) + \frac{1}{3} \ (4) + \frac{1}{3} \ (8) = \$4.00$$
$$EOL \ (Stock \ 2) \ = \frac{1}{3} \ (2) + \frac{1}{3} \ (0) + \frac{1}{3} \ (4) = \$2.00$$
$$EOL \ (Stock \ 3) \ = \frac{1}{3} \ (4) + \frac{1}{3} \ (2) + \frac{1}{3} \ (0) = \$2.00$$
$$EOL^* \qquad\qquad = \$2.00 \ for \ Stock \ 2 \ or \ 3$$
$$EVPI = EOL^* \quad = \$2.00$$

Hence, the merchant should stock either two or three trees.

16.5 DECISION TREES

Some decision problems are somewhat difficult to represent with a payoff table. If there is a sequence of decisions to be made, a *decision tree* is a useful way of depicting the sequence. One important aspect of a sequential decision problem is that it may be desirable to let the selection of some future act depend upon which of several events occurs before that act is (or is not) selected. Let us consider the building contractor's problem in terms of a decision tree. Although this is not a sequential problem, it is used to illustrate a decision tree.

16.51 Decision Tree Representation of a Payoff Table

For the reader's convenience, the building contractor's decision problem is repeated in Figure 16.4. To convert this payoff table to a decision

Figure 16.4

Payoff Table for the Contractor's Problem

Events \ Acts	Fixed Price Contract	Cost Plus Contract	Probabilities
4% Increase	$15,000	$6,200	0.3
6% Increase	$ 5,000	$6,300	0.5
8% Increase	−$ 5,000	$6,400	0.2
EMV	$ 6,000	$6,290*	1.0

tree, it is first necessary to determine the sequence of acts and events. Under uncertainty, the *act* always precedes the event in a problem. If this were not the case, the event would happen first and then one would select the best act, which is a decision problem under certainty.

The decision tree corresponding to the building contractor's payoff table is shown in Figure 16.5. A *square* node is used to indicate a decision point, where an act must be selected. A *circle* is used for a node where an event occurs. (For the moment, ignore the circled numbers.) Start at the

Figure 16.5

Decision Tree for the Contractor's Problem

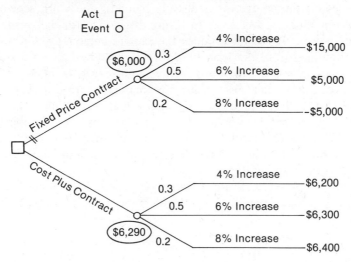

left, and observe that the contractor may elect either the fixed price or the cost plus contract. If the fixed price contract is chosen, the upper event node indicates there is a 0.3 chance of a 4 percent increase, a 0.5 chance of a 6 percent increase, and a 0.2 chance of an 8 percent increase. The payoffs for each of these end positions is also indicated: $15,000; $5,000; −$5,000. The lower event node depicts the events, probabilities, and pay-offs for the choice of a cost plus contract.

Given the decision tree, one can apply the criterion of EMV to deter-mine which should be selected. It is easy to replace the upper three-forked event node with an EMV. It has been shown (Section 16.41) that a 0.3 chance of receiving a $15,000, a 0.5 chance of receiving $5,000, and a 0.2 chance of receiving −$5,000 has an expectation of $6,000. Similarly, one can replace the lower three-forked event node following the selection of the cost plus contract with its EMV of $6,290. This leaves the very simple decision tree, choosing between $6,000 and $6,290. It is apparent that the cost plus contract should be selected, as $6,290 is greater than $6,000. The upper branch (which should *not* be selected) has been blocked off.

The basic ideas of decision trees have been illustrated in this simple example. However, decision trees are particularly useful when there is a sequence such as act, event, act, event, act, ... In this situation it is essential to depict accurately the sequence of acts and events as they would occur in the actual decision problem. This is illustrated with an example. T.H., the owner of a ski cabin in Colorado, needs to do some roof repair before the heavy snow season. T.H. is indifferent about doing the repairs personally. T.H. could hire a contractor to do the work, but it will cost $200. Because the contractor is already planning the work schedule for the next few months, any delay in hiring the contractor will result in an increase in price. If the owner does the repairs personally, the materials may be obtained from the local hardware store. The hardware store has the materials in stock now, but a delay might cause them to be out of stock. The owner can also order the materials from either of two catalogue firms, the "Stock-Out" Company and the "Well-Stock" Company. If T.H. orders from either catalogue company and the company is out of stock, and the hardware store is out of stock, the contractor will need to be hired at a higher price. Because of credit limitation, T.H. cannot order from both catalogue stores.

The specific dollar costs are: Contractor's price, $200 now, $220 after the owner has found out either catalogue store is out of stock, or $240 if

Figure 16.6

Decision Tree for Mountain Cabin Repair

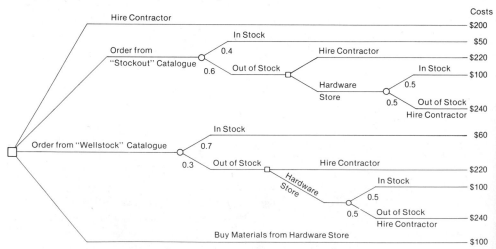

the owner finds out that both the selected catalogue store and the hardware store are out of stock. The "Stock-Out" catalogue price is $50; the "Well-Stock" catalogue price is $60, and the hardware store price is $100.

The probability that the "Stock-Out" Company will be out of stock is 0.6; the probability that the "Well-Stock" Company will be out of stock is 0.3; the probability that the hardware store will be out of stock (after the catalogue order has been placed) is 0.5. All of this information is included in the decision tree of Figure 16.6. To analyze this sequence of acts and events, one starts at the right hand end of the decision tree, and works to the left. Specifically, the analysis of a decision tree is as follows: Start at the extreme right branches; if the right-most node under consideration is an act, block off the acts from that node which would not be selected, and value that node with the best payoff for the acts available at that node. If the extreme right node under consideration is an event, one finds the EMV for that event. After this has been completed for all extreme right nodes, move one node to the left with the same procedures, until all nodes have been evaluated, and the left-most node has been reached.

For Figure 16.6, first make the calculations for the expected monetary values for the event nodes at the extreme right. In Figure 16.7, EMV's have been calculated for the two right-most nodes. These values enable one to block off two acts: the act of hiring a contractor after an out-of-stock notice from a catalogue store, as $220 is greater than $170 in both cases. Then place the best EMV near the next act (square node) to the left.

Continuing at the nodes following each catalogue order, replace these

Figure 16.7

Decision Tree for the Mountain Cabin Repair

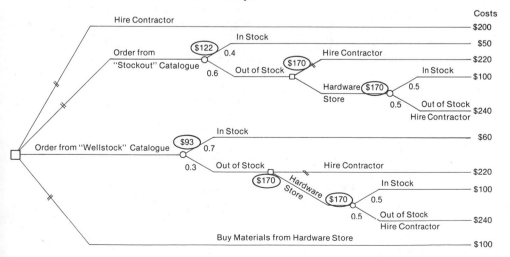

event nodes with their equivalent EMVs. These EMVs, $122 and $93, are shown circled in this figure. It is now a simple decision problem. The owner has acts with EMVs of $200, $122, $93, or $100. The act, order from "Well-Stock" Company, with an EMV of $93.00 is the best (lowest cost) of the four. The complete decision strategy, obtained by following the unblocked paths in Figure 16.7, is to place an initial order with the "Well-Stock" Company. If the items are available, the problem is solved. If the items are out of stock, the owner would then proceed to the hardware store. If the hardware store has the merchandise in stock, the problem is again solved. If the hardware store is out, the owner must then hire the contractor at a cost of $240.

16.6 SUMMARY

The purpose of this chapter has been to demonstrate the procedures for taking a complex decision problem and breaking it down into its simple elements. This procedure of decomposition greatly simplifies the thought processes involved in analyzing decision problems under uncertainty.

A decision problem under uncertainty has four basic elements: (1) acts which are under the control of the decision maker, (2) events which are the uncontrollable factors of the decision problem, (3) probabilities which are assessed by the decision maker, using any available information, and (4) dollar payoffs for each outcome. The elements of a decision problem may be shown in either a payoff table or a decision tree.

The procedure of finding an expected value is used to combine the four elements into a recommendation for a rational course of action to be followed by a decision maker. Expected value may be calculated for monetary payoffs, if EMV is a useful decision criterion. If the payoffs in the problem are too large to permit the use of EMV, risk preference analysis (which is beyond the scope of this text) may be used.

It is often found that a great deal of understanding may be obtained simply by structuring the problem into a table or a decision tree. Either of these methods may be quite useful in helping the decision maker analyze decision problems.

EXERCISES

16.1   Discuss: "A probability value can be established by a series of questions of the form, 'Which do you prefer, A or B?' "

16.2   Discuss: "All probabilities have some degree of subjectivity, in that a judgment must be made as to the relevance to the future of the period of data collection."

16.3   Discuss: "After flipping a fair coin, but before the outcome is known, the probability of a head can be only zero or one."

* 16.4   Calculate the expected monetary value for each course of action:

Events \ Acts	A_1	A_2	A_3	A_4	Probabilities
E_1	$100	10	10	−500	0.4
E_2	−50	20	10	1,000	0.5
E_3	−10	30	50	0	0.1

* 16.5   A machine manufacturing aircraft struts produces good struts and defective struts; the output of the machine conforms to the requirements of a Bernoulli process with probability π for a defective. If the machine is properly set up, the value of π is 0.1; if it is set up incorrectly, $\pi = 0.3$. When the machine is set up by an ordinary mechanic, the value of π is not known with certainty. Before a production run is made, a master mechanic can check the setup and adjust the machine if necessary, thereby guaranteeing that $\pi = 0.1$. The cost of having the master mechanic check and adjust the machine is $2,500. Experience has shown that 60 percent of the setups made by ordinary mechanics are correct, so that $\pi = 0.1$; 40 percent of the setups by ordinary mechanics are not correct, so that $\pi = 0.3$. A production run of 1,000 struts is to be made. Defective struts in the production run are to be rectified at a cost of $25 per piece. Should the master mechanic check the setup?

* 16.6   You must say either *Go* or *Stop* to a marketing proposal submitted to you by your staff. The desirability of the proposal depends on the rate of technological advance in the next two years, as the marketing proposal is highly dependent upon product technology. You have condensed the future technological advance possibilities into three categories, simply named *Much, Little,* and *None.* After much consternation, you have decided that you are willing to use the following payoff table and EMV for your decision. The table gives profits in millions of dollars:

Advance \ Decision	Go	Stop
Much	2	3
Little	5	2
None	−1	4

The probabilities are 0.2, 0.5, and 0.3 for *Much, Little,* and *None.* What should be done?

* 16.7   A small stationery store is planning its inventory for the Christmas

* Answers to exercises marked with an asterisk (*) are in Appendix L.

season. The owner must decide the allocation of the budget between expensive Christmas cards and inexpensive Christmas cards. Once the decision is made and the order placed, the order cannot be changed. In addition, the owner cannot reorder. The owner has $6 to spend for cards, and pays $1 for a box of inexpensive cards and $2 for a box of expensive cards. The entire $6 must be spent. The retail price for a box of inexpensive cards is $2, and the owner can sell at this price all the inexpensive cards stocked. The expensive cards retail for $5 a box before Christmas, or $2 a box after Christmas. The owner is willing to use the following experience-based probability distribution for before-Christmas demand for boxes of expensive cards:

X, Number of Expensive Boxes Demanded before Christmas at $5 per Box	P(X), Probability
0	0.1
1	0.3
2	0.5
3	0.1
	1.0

All boxes of expensive cards which are ordered but not demanded before Christmas can be sold after Christmas (at $2 per box). A customer is not displeased if no expensive cards are available.

a. Construct a payoff table showing the retailer's profit for the $6 outlay; consider ordering 0, 1, 2, or 3 boxes of expensive cards (along with enough inexpensive cards to spend $6) and the probability distribution for demand given above.

b. Find the expected profit of each act, and indicate the act which will maximize expected profit.

c. Construct the opportunity loss table corresponding to the payoff of Part a.

d. For a fee of $2, the owner can find out the actual demand before placing the order. Should the owner spend the $2 to obtain this perfect information? Expected monetary value is acceptable to the owner as the decision criterion.

* **16.8** A newsstand operator assigns probabilities to the demand for *Fox* magazine as follows:

Copies Demanded	Probability
1	0.4
2	0.2
3	0.3
4	0.1
	1.0

An issue sells for 70¢ and costs 30¢.

a. If the operator can return unsold copies for 20¢ each refund, what is the act (stock level) that will maximize EMV?

b. If the operator cannot return unsold copies, but must throw them away, what is the act (stock level) that will maximize EMV?

* **16.9** An engine repair shop for a trucking company performs two types of work on the company's engines: A major overhaul, costing $100, or a minor repair, costing $20. If the major overhaul is performed when the minor repair is needed, the engine is nonetheless "fixed" at the end of the operation. However, if an engine requiring a major overhaul is given a minor repair, the repair is wasted and the full $100 must then be expended to "fix" the engine. There is another strategy that can be followed. A master mechanic can spend an hour (cost $10) to fully diagnose the trouble. He can correctly classify the engine as one needing a $100 overhaul or a $20 repair. In the long run, 40 percent of the engines received require the major overhaul; 60 percent require only the minor repair.

    a. Recommend a course of action to minimize expected cost for the trucking company.

    b. Construct an opportunity loss table, and calculate the EOL of each act.

16.10 Build the opportunity loss table for the payoff table in Exercise 16.4.

* **16.11** Calculate the expected opportunity loss for each act in Exercise 16.10.

16.12 For the situation in Exercises 16.4, 16.10, and 16.11 show

$$EOL_i - EOL_j = EMV_j - EMV_i$$

for all pairs of acts, i and j.

* **16.13** You are concerned with the response rate from a new questionnaire to be used for market research. You will have a response rate of either 30 percent, 40 percent or 50 percent, with probabilities (based on all information you have to this time) of 0.5, 0.3, and 0.2 respectively. You face this opportunity loss table for the situation. What should be done?

Acts Response Rate	Use Old Form	Use New Form
30%	$ 0	$1,000
40%	1,000	0
50%	3,000	0

16.14 Use the probability assessment technique to assist a classmate in assessing the probability that the instructor of your statistics course had a $10 bill at the start of the previous statistics class. Recommend whether the classmate should be willing to pay $3 to receive one $10 bill if the instructor had at least one $10 bill at the start of the class.

* **16.15** The SNOBIRD ski products company is deciding which of two promotional campaigns to use for a new ski. Initially, they must decide whether to go "point of purchase" or "national ads" for their major thrust. If they elect to go "national ads," their first set of ads will be in magazines. Then they may elect to conclude the campaign with a continuation of the magazine ads, or it may be modified to emphasize television (with emphasis on stations which are carried into ski resorts on CATV systems). The decision to use "point of purchase" is a single-stage decision; that is, it does not permit modification during the season. There are two major sources of uncertainty: weather conditions in the ski areas (which we will simply call "glorious" or "yucky"), and the effectiveness of the TV ("good" or "bad"). The timing of the actions and the events, and the payoffs for each end point, are shown in the tree below. The probabilities of the events are also shown below.

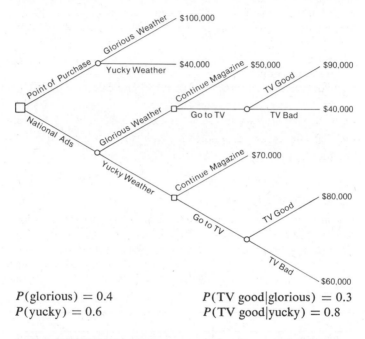

$P(\text{glorious}) = 0.4$
$P(\text{yucky}) = 0.6$

$P(\text{TV good}|\text{glorious}) = 0.3$
$P(\text{TV good}|\text{yucky}) = 0.8$

Assume SNOBIRD wants to maximize its expected monetary value (expected profit). Below are five strategies for SNOBIRD. Which of them is optimal?

a. Use point of purchase display.
b. Use national ads, continue the magazines regardless of weather.
c. Use national ads, continue the magazine for glorious weather, go to TV for yucky weather.
d. Use national ads, go to TV if the weather is glorious, continue the magazines if the weather is yucky.
e. Use national ads, switch to TV regardless of the weather.

What is the EMV or expected profit of the optimal strategy you selected above?

*   16.16   Using this notation:

□ = Act
○ = Event

Numbers *without* $ represent probabilities
Numbers *with* $ represent profit

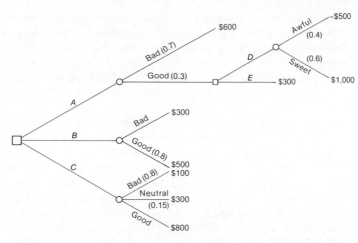

recommend a course of action to maximize EMV for this situation.

* **16.17**   A firm has received an order for 10 can openers. Its warehouse of can openers is known to have 5 percent defective can openers; to unpack a can opener, determine whether it is defective, and fix it if needed, costs $10; thus, profit for each *good* can opener shipped is $30 if it has been inspected, or $40 if it hasn't. However, the cost of shipping a bad can opener has been estimated at $60 for each bad one in the lot, in addition to the lost profit. Recommend a course of action.

* **16.18**   A distributor of transistors is contemplating the purchase of a supply of 100,000 transistors. She will purchase either from a new manufacturer, or from her regular manufacturer. The new manufacturer has an uncertain defect rate; it is known that the regular brand will have 5 percent defectives. The decision maker, Ms. Jones, has assessed this probability distribution for the proportion defective for the new transistors.

Proportion Defective	Probability
0.01	0.1
0.03	0.1
0.05	0.2
0.10	0.4
0.15	0.2
	1.0

The cost of having to replace defective transistors (including the replacement transistor and goodwill) is 50 cents per transistor. The new transistors are three cents cheaper to the distributor; they can be sold at the same price as the old transistors. What should she do?

* **16.19**   Mr. Weber, Contracts Manager, has just finished a cost and status review of the *Digger* project, a $500,000 cost-plus-fixed-fee government job. Three months remain to complete the final report required by the contract. He has requested an estimate of the cost to complete the final report, and, after several iterations during which the cost estimates are rethought and revised downward from $61,000, he re-

ceives what the engineering manager assures him is a "bare-bones" estimate of $42,000. This estimate is accompanied by a plan to complete the report in the remaining three months. It makes a convincing package.

At the same time, Mr. Weber has been informed by the accounting department that only $28,000 remains in the contract to complete the effort.

In an effort to better understand the problem, Mr. Weber has called a meeting of Marketing, Engineering, and Estimating to investigate the possible alternatives. Engineering and Estimating have established three possible target costs for the final report: the $42,000 estimated earlier, an estimate of $35,000 obtained by deleting those portions of the development that have been discussed in interim reports, and an estimate of $28,000 which is unsatisfactory to Engineering and (in their words) based upon, "If that's all you've got, that's all you get."

Engineering emphasizes that the $42,000 estimate represents a report the customer will like and accept, which is more than can be said for the other two estimates. Estimating points out that the historical median of the final report costs of this nature is between 10 percent and 12 percent of the total effort. Marketing asserts that the customer will insist on a satisfactory report, even if it requires additional funding, although no fee will be paid on any additional funds. Indeed, because some real costs of doing business are not allowed as costs on government contracts, work on overruns without fee not only hurts the firm's reputation but its pocketbook as well.

Engineering, with Marketing's concurrence, states that there is a 90 percent chance the $42,000 report will be accepted as is; but if it is not, there is an 80 percent chance that $700 of rework and travel will suffice. The maximum rework will be only $2,000, and the customer will be happy in any case.

Engineering is pessimistic about the $35,000 report and feels there is a 70 percent chance the customer will question the report. If they do, Engineering is 90 percent sure it will cost $9,000 to rework the final report; they believe there is only a 10 percent chance $2,000 will satisfy. In addition, Engineering does not like doing a poor job in the first place. Marketing agrees with the likelihood and the possible rework required, but does not feel the firm's reputation will be severely damaged.

All agree the firm's reputation will suffer if the customer does not accept the $28,000 final report. Engineering believes there is a 95 percent chance rework will be required, and further, because the customer will feel insulted, that there is a 90 percent chance it will cost $25,000 more and only a 10 percent chance they can get by with as little as $16,000. There is no middle ground, because the estimates are based on excluding certain portions of the $42,000 report.

According to the contract, Mr. Weber must immediately notify the customer of any anticipated overrun. To further complicate matters, Marketing is planning to submit a proposal for additional work in a month. While they do not want to have an overrun against them, they want even less to face the charge of unsatisfactory technical performance on the current job. What should they do to minimize expected cost?

* 16.20 Banhab Clothing company has received a letter from a supplier offering a lot of 5,000 men's neckties at an unusually attractive price of $1 each, or $5,000 for the lot. They must buy the entire lot or none of it; the supplier is unwilling to break the lot.

Banhab has a mailing list of 100,000 customers, and all its sales are by mail. The regular price of the ties will be $2 each; the customer pays any mailing and handling expense, so that the gross margin to Banhab is $1 for each tie sold. However, there is some uncertainty about the number of customers who will buy the ties at $2. If customers place orders for more than 5,000 ties, Banhab will be forced to buy ties at a premium price of $2.25 for each tie, which it will then sell for the advertised price of $2.00. On the other hand, if orders are received for fewer than 5,000 ties, Banhab will be forced to dispose of the lot by selling each remaining tie to Feline's Basement for $0.50/tie. Because of the structure of Banhab's direct mail advertising, it is not feasible to advertise these ties to only a portion of its customers; all 100,000 customers receive the same catalog. For simplicity, assume that each customer orders no more than one tie.

The decision analysis group at Banhab has discussed, at great length, the market acceptance of these ties with the vice president for sales. After quite a bit of interplay, the vice president accepts the following probability distribution for the numbers of orders received for these neckties in the regular all-customer catalog mailing:

Orders	Probability
1,000	0.05
2,000	0.10
3,000	0.40
4,000	0.30
5,000	0.10
10,000	0.05
	1.00

As head of the decision analysis group, write a report to the purchasing director recommending future actions to be taken regarding these neckties.

16.21 E-Z Personnel Training Consulting Firm has a client that is considering a change in its sales training program. The product being sold is highly technical, so it is important that the sales force be well trained. The two proposed training programs are:

Plan A: Send every salesperson through the same program, at a cost of $2,000 per salesperson. This program will result in every student "passing" the training program.

Plan B: Send every salesperson through an exploratory technical knowledge program at a cost of $150. This program will result in two categories: those whose training can be completed at a cost of an additional $1,250, and those whose training can be completed at an additional cost of $1,950. This program will also result in every student "passing" the training program.

The plan selected will remain in use for the training of 1,000 salespersons. However, it is uncertain just what proportion of this group will require the more expensive training if Plan B is selected. The client, in an interview of some three hours, gave these probabilities for the proportion requiring the less expensive ($150 + $1,250) program, if B is used:

Proportion	Probability
0.100	0.40
0.150	0.30
0.200	0.20
0.250	0.10
	1.00

Write a report, along with recommendation, that E-Z can send to its client.

* 16.22   A computer software firm has entered into an agreement to produce a simulation program by December 31. The current date is October 1. There are three primary development strategies for the simulation program: modify existing programs, assign junior programmers, or assign senior programmers. Modifying existing programs may not work; it will take a month of effort (costing $30,000) to find out whether it will work. The probability the modification will work is 0.60. A team of junior programmers costs $40,000 per month; after one month it will be known how long it will take the junior programmers to complete the simulation program. It will be completed in a total of one month, two months, or three months, with probability of 0.1, 0.5, and 0.4. Senior programmers, at a cost of $60,000 per month, will complete the project in one month or two months, with probabilities of 0.6 and 0.4. Recommend a course of action. Remember that it may be desirable to start on a course of action and abandon it when more information is obtained. Parallel efforts may *not* be undertaken.

* 16.23   A motorist traveling on an interstate highway knows there are three interchanges (each with a gas station) in the next ten miles. The first station is A, then B, then C. The motorist will buy gas at only one of these stations; he wants to design a purchase strategy that will minimize his expected cost per gallon of gas. There is uncertainty about the price at each gas station, but the motorist can observe the price at each station before he commits himself to purchase at that station. There are four possible prices at each station, and the probability of each price for each station is:

Price \ Station	A	B	C
$0.40	0.0	0.0·	0.1
$0.44	0.1	0.2	0.2
$0.48	0.9	0.6	0.2
$0.52	0.0	0.2	0.5

Recommend a course of action that will minimize the expected cost per gallon. What is the minimum expected cost per gallon?

* 16.24   The purchaser for a margarine manufacturer is faced with the uncertainties of the market for salad oil. She must buy a quantity of oil either Monday, Tuesday, or Wednesday. For Monday, she believes the oil will be obtainable at the following probability distribution of prices:

Price	Probability
$2.00	0.4
$2.02	0.4
$2.04	0.2
	1.0

If she does not buy Monday, the probability distribution of prices for Tuesday depends upon the price Monday, according to this table:

Price Monday \ Price Tuesday	$1.98	$2.00	$2.02	$2.04
$2.00	0.1	0.8	0.1	0.0
$2.02	0.0	0.2	0.7	0.1
$2.04	0.0	0.0	0.6	0.4

The price on Wednesday depends in a rather complicated way on the price on Tuesday, which the decision maker is willing to simplify as follows: the probability of a decline of $0.02 is 0.2; the probability of the price remaining the same is 0.5; the probability of the price increasing $0.02 is 0.3. These increases and decreases refer to changes from Tuesday's price. Write instructions for the purchaser to follow in order to minimize the expected cost per unit of salad oil.

REFERENCES

Dyckman, T. R.; Smidt, S.; and McAdams, A. K. *Managerial Decision Making Under Uncertainty.* New York: MacMillan, 1969.

Hadley, G. *Introduction to Probability and Statistical Decision Theory.* San Francisco: Holden-Day, 1967.

Raiffa, Howard. *Decision Analysis, Introductory Lectures on Choices Under Uncertainty.* Reading, Mass.: Addison-Wesley Publishing Co., Inc., 1968.

Schlaifer, Robert. *Introduction to Statistics for Business Decisions.* New York: McGraw-Hill Book Co., 1961.

Winkler, R. L. *An Introduction to Bayesian Inference and Decision.* New York: Holt, Rinehart & Winston, 1972.

17

Sampling, Imperfect Information, and Decision Making

In the previous chapter, analysis of a decision under uncertainty was discussed. One of the important concepts is perfect information, or clairvoyance. The concept of perfect information is important because it often serves as a guide to answer the question, "Should I get more information before I decide?"

In this chapter, the concept of additional information is broadened from perfect information to imperfect information. Imperfect information includes forecasts, samples, and experiments. The approach of this chapter is to illustrate the concepts of imperfect information using the building contractor's example from Chapter 16, then broadening the consideration to include sampling. The goal is to answer the question, "For this decision problem, how large a sample should I take?"

17.1 FORECAST AS IMPERFECT INFORMATION

To illustrate the concept of a forecast as imperfect information, we continue with the example of the contractor deciding between a fixed price contract and a cost plus contract. This example was developed at some length in Chapter 16. Figure 17.1 summarizes this decision problem; the contractor must choose one of two contracting schemes, fixed price or cost plus. Profit then depends on whether the price increases 4 percent, or 6 percent or 8 percent. The profit outcomes are shown at the end points of the decision tree in Figure 17.1. The contractor maximizes expected profit by choosing the cost plus contract with an EMV of $6,290; the fixed price contract has an EMV of $6,000.

Now suppose a firm of economic consultants approaches the contractor. The consultants suggest that they can give the contractor some insight into price behavior for the period covered by the contracting situation;

Figure 17.1

Decision Tree for the Contractor's Problem

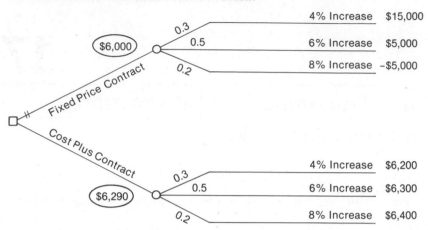

however, the economists are not willing to go very far out on a limb. Their proposal is that they will submit a one-word forecast about the price situation. This forecast consists of either the word "high" or the word "low." These two possible reports constitute the *information* (forecast) *results*. So that this one word forecast will have some meaning to the contractor, they propose putting some probabilities on the reliability of their forecast. Later in this chapter we will discuss interpreting history to arrive at these probabilities. The economists make the following statements about the reliability of the forecast:

If there is to be a 4 percent price increase, there is a 0.1 probability of a "high" forecast and a 0.9 probability of a "low" forecast.

If there is to be a 6 percent price increase, there is a 0.6 probability of a "high" forecast and a 0.4 probability of a "low" forecast.

If there is to be an 8 percent price increase, there is a 0.8 probability of a "high" forecast and a 0.2 probability of a "low" forecast.

These forecasts are conditional probability statements. In probability terms, the equivalent statements are:

$$\left.\begin{array}{l} P(\text{high} \mid 4\%) = 0.10 \\ P(\text{low} \mid 4\%) = 0.90 \end{array}\right\} 1.00$$

$$\left.\begin{array}{l} P(\text{high} \mid 6\%) = 0.60 \\ P(\text{low} \mid 6\%) = 0.40 \end{array}\right\} 1.00$$

$$\left.\begin{array}{l} P(\text{high} \mid 8\%) = 0.80 \\ P(\text{low} \mid 8\%) = 0.20 \end{array}\right\} 1.00$$

Note that each of these probabilities is represented as: $P($Information result $\mid$ Event$)$. Such a probability is called a *likelihood*.

A *likelihood* is a conditional probability of the form:

P (Information result | Event)

Given these conditional probability statements, the reader should observe that this forecast is not the same thing as perfect information. If the information were perfect, the "forecaster" would be clairvoyant, and the report would be one of three possibilities, 4 percent, 6 percent or 8 percent, instead of the more vague "high" or "low." However, this forecast does contain information useful to the contractor. Hence, it is reasonable to view this forecast as imperfect information. We need to study probability revisions to put a dollar value on imperfect information.

17.11 Revising the Probabilities

Prior to the appearance of the forecast, the contractor assessed these probabilities:

$$P(4\%) = 0.30$$
$$P(6\%) = 0.50$$
$$P(8\%) = 0.20$$
$$\overline{1.00}$$

These are called *prior* probabilities because they are the probabilities assessed by the contractor prior to receiving the information (forecast) result. If, however, the contractor has just been told "high" by the economic consultant, one can expect a change in probabilities to reflect the new information. For example, given the forecast of "high," the probability of an 8 percent increase now seems to be higher than the 0.20 prior probability. The task now is to demonstrate how the rules of probabilities (from Chapter 4) can be used to *revise* the prior probabilities to account for this new information from the economic consultants.

> **The process of *revising* probabilities combines the prior probabilities with the added imperfect information, yielding *revised* or *posterior* probabilities. *Prior* means before an information result is received, and *posterior* means after an information result is received. A posterior probability is in the form:**

P (Event | Information result)

The first step in revising the probabilities is to return to Chapter 4 and study the second example in Section 4.6 (about bus ridership). The procedures illustrated in that example demonstrate a probability revision, although the terms, "prior probability," "revised probability," and "probability revision," were not used in that example.

The next step is to construct a table of joint probabilities, as shown in the top part of Figure 17.2. Note that the prior probabilities for the right-most column were given in the statement of the problem; the

Figure 17.2

Probability Revision for the Contractor's Problem

Table of Joint Probabilities
P (Event $\cap$ Information Result)

Event \ Information Result	*High*	*Low*	*Prior Probabilities*
4%	$P(\text{high} \mid 4\%)P(4\%) = P(\text{high} \cap 4\%)$ $0.1 \times 0.3 = 0.03$	$P(\text{low} \mid 4\%)P(4\%) = P(\text{low} \cap 4\%)$ $0.9 \times 0.3 = 0.27$	$P(4\%) = 0.30$ (given)
6%	$P(\text{high} \mid 6\%)P(6\%) = P(\text{high} \cap 6\%)$ $0.6 \times 0.5 = 0.30$	$P(\text{low} \mid 6\%)P(6\%) = P(\text{low} \cap 6\%)$ $0.4 \times 0.5 = 0.20$	$P(6\%) = 0.50$ (given)
8%	$P(\text{high} \mid 8\%)P(8\%) = P(\text{high} \cap 8\%)$ $0.8 \times 0.2 = 0.16$	$P(\text{low} \mid 8\%)P(8\%) = P(\text{low} \cap 8\%)$ $0.2 \times 0.2 = 0.04$	$P(8\%) = 0.20$ (given)
	$P(\text{high}) = 0.03 + 0.30 + 0.16 = 0.49$	$P(\text{low}) = 0.27 + 0.20 + 0.04 = 0.51$	

Posterior Probabilities
P (Event | Information Result)

Information Result / Event	High	Low
4%	$\dfrac{P(\text{high} \cap 4\%)}{P(\text{high})} = P(4\% \mid \text{high})$ $\dfrac{0.03}{0.49} = 0.0612$	$\dfrac{P(\text{low} \cap 4\%)}{P(\text{low})} = P(4\% \mid \text{low})$ $\dfrac{0.27}{0.51} = 0.5294$
6%	$\dfrac{P(\text{high} \cap 6\%)}{P(\text{high})} = P(6\% \mid \text{high})$ $\dfrac{0.30}{0.49} = 0.6122$	$\dfrac{P(\text{low} \cap 6\%)}{P(\text{low})} = P(6\% \mid \text{low})$ $\dfrac{0.20}{0.51} = 0.3922$
8%	$\dfrac{P(\text{high} \cap 8\%)}{P(\text{high})} = P(8\% \mid \text{high})$ $\dfrac{0.16}{0.49} = 0.3266$	$\dfrac{P(\text{low} \cap 8\%)}{P(\text{low})} = P(8\% \mid \text{low})$ $\dfrac{0.04}{0.51} = 0.0784$
Totals	1.0000	1.000

likelihoods—i.e., the probability of an information (forecast) result given an event—are also given in the problem. Appropriate products of a likelihood and a prior probability are joint probabilities, shown in the body of the table. A column total is the probability of an information (forecast) result, such as $P(\text{high}) = 0.49$ and $P(\text{low}) = 0.51$. Notice that this joint probability table has been constructed using the multiplicative law of probabilities and the additive law for three mutually exclusive events.

The final steps in the probability revision process are shown in the bottom part of Figure 17.2. Each cell in the body of the table uses the definition of conditional probability to find a posterior probability, based on probabilities which were calculated in the joint probability table shown in the top part of Figure 17.2.

This probability revision process is often given the name *Bayes'* *theorem*. This theorem, which is nothing more than a usage of conditional probability, was introduced in the 18th century by the English clergyman, Thomas Bayes. Because of this theorem, much of the material from this Chapter and Chapter 16 is often given the names *Bayesian statistics*.

The procedure just demonstrated for revising probabilities is quite general. However, a more formal definition of Bayes' theorem is also possible. Using these symbols:

Events are labelled $E_1, E_2, \ldots E_n$
Information results are labelled $I_1, I_2, \ldots$

Then a posterior probability of Event k, given that information result i has been observed, is:

$$P(E_k|I_i) = \frac{P(I_i|E_k)P(E_k)}{\sum_{j=1}^{n} P(I_i|E_j)P(E_j)}$$

Applying this statement of Bayes' theorem to find $P(6\% \mid \text{high})$:

$$P(6\% \mid \text{high}) = \frac{P(\text{high} \mid 6\%)P(6\%)}{P(\text{high} \mid 4\%)P(4\%) + P(\text{high} \mid 6\%)P(6\%) + P(\text{high} \mid 8\%)P(8\%)}$$

$$= \frac{0.60(0.50)}{0.10(0.30) + 0.60(0.50) + 0.80(0.20)}$$

$$= \frac{0.30}{0.03 + 0.30 + 0.16}$$

$$= \frac{0.30}{0.49}$$

$$= 0.6122$$

Notice that the numerator is found in the joint probability table, and the denominator is the total of a column in the joint probability table.

17.12 Decision Tree with Revised Probabilities

These revised probability distributions have been calculated because they are very useful in decision making. Suppose the contractor has retained the services of the economic consultants, and has just received the report saying "high." The contractor must decide whether to choose the fixed price or cost plus contract. However, the decision tree shown in Figure 17.1 is no longer relevant; the (prior) probabilities shown on that tree are no longer applicable, because additional information has been received. The revised (posterior) probabilities including this additional information have already been calculated. After receiving the "high" report, the contractor is in the situation depicted in Figure 17.3, which incorporates the posterior probabilities.

Figure 17.3

Contractor's Problem after a "High" Report

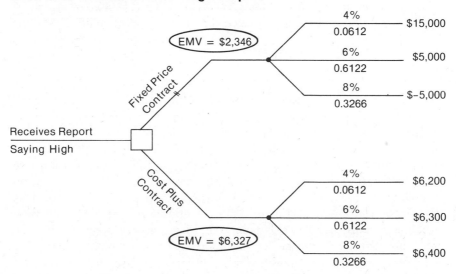

This decision tree can easily be used for analysis, as discussed in the previous chapter. Calculating the expected monetary value at each event node, the fixed price contract leads to an EMV of $2,346, while the cost plus contract leads to an EMV of $6,327. Thus, after receiving the report of "high," the contractor should choose the cost plus contract to maximize EMV.

If the contractor had received the report saying "low," the situation would be as depicted in Figure 17.4. From this figure, it is obvious that the contractor should elect the fixed price contract if the forecast is a

Figure 17.4

Contractor's Problem after a "Low" Report

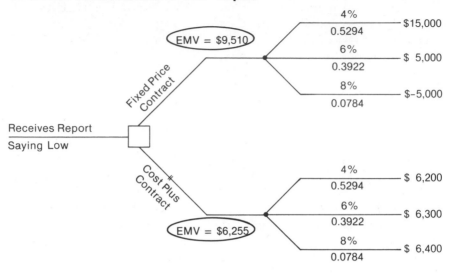

report of "low." Up to this time, it has been assumed that the forecast of the economic consultants is free. However, it is more realistic if the forecast has a cost, given as $1,000. This cost can be taken into account by lowering the end point values on the decision trees by $1,000, but it is much simpler to show this cost by indicating a "toll" on a decision tree which shows the purchase of the forecast as an explicit act. Such a decision tree can be produced by combining Figures 17.1, 17.3, and 17.4. This combined decision tree, Figure 17.5, recapitulates the entire decision problem as constructed to this point. The decision tree indicates that the cost plus contract should be selected after receiving a "high" report, and the fixed price contract should be selected after receiving a "low" report.

Now address the question of whether the contractor should obtain the forecast. On the decision tree, a 0.49 probability of receiving a "high" report and a 0.51 probability of receiving a "low" report are indicated. These probabilities are calculated in Figure 17.2. The tree indicates that there is a 0.49 probability of reaching a position with an EMV of $6,327 with a "high" forecast, and a 0.51 probability of reaching a position with an EMV of $9,510 with a "low" forecast. Taking the expected value for this situation, or $0.49(6,327) + 0.51(9,510) = \$7,950$, which is the EMV of the decision problem after receiving the forecast. In the decision tree, a "toll" of $1,000 is shown immediately before the $7,950 figure; therefore, $6,950 is the expected profit after buying the forecast, and is better

Figure 17.5

Decision Tree with Additional Information

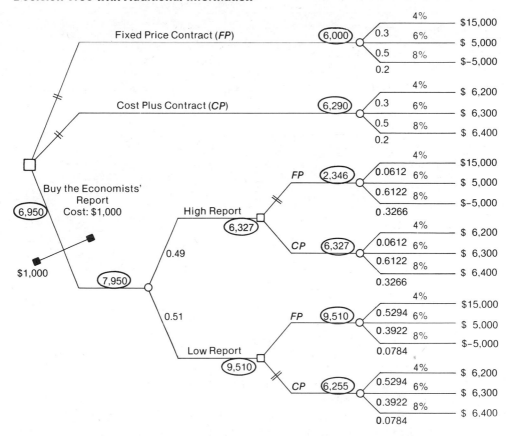

than the $6,290 from the cost plus contract without the forecast. Thus, in order to maximize EMV, the contractor should buy the forecast, use the cost plus contract after receiving a "high" forecast, and the fixed price contract after receiving a "low" forecast. The net gain in EMV from buying the additional information in the report is the difference between $6,950 with the report and $6,290 without the report, or $660. The contractor is given the opportunity to buy a forecast worth $1,660 for a price of $1,000, which is a gain of $660.

17.13 Interpreting History Correctly

Earlier in this chapter, the likelihoods for the economists' forecast were stated without much explanation. One would usually expect to find some historical information available to assist in this probability assessment;

Figure 17.6

Economists' History of Forecasts

Forecast \ State of Nature	4%	6%	8%	Totals
"high"	1	3	4	8
"low"	9	2	1	12
Totals	10	5	5	20

$$P(\text{high} \mid 4\%) = 1/10 = 0.10 \atop P(\text{low} \mid 4\%) = 9/10 = 0.90 \Big\} \; 1.00$$

$$P(\text{high} \mid 6\%) = 3/5 = 0.60 \atop P(\text{low} \mid 6\%) = 2/5 = 0.40 \Big\} \; 1.00$$

$$P(\text{high} \mid 8\%) = 4/5 = 0.80 \atop P(\text{low} \mid 8\%) = 1/5 = 0.20 \Big\} \; 1.00$$

one would want to modify the historical information to account for changing conditions in order to obtain useful probabilities. But it is necessary to be able to interpret past information correctly.

Suppose the economists had prepared 20 forecasts, with results indicated in Figure 17.6. This table shows that the economists have issued a total of eight "high" reports and 12 "low" reports. Of these, they issued ten reports when the true event was a 4 percent increase, five for a 6 percent increase, and five for an 8 percent increase. Looking at the individual columns in this report, it is apparent that their "batting average" suggests that the probability of a "high" forecast given a 4 percent increase is 0.10, of a "low" forecast given a 4 percent increase is 0.90, of a "high" forecast given a 6 percent increase is 0.60, etc. These are the same probabilities given in Figure 17.1

There is a pitfall in Figure 17.6 for the unwary. It is very tempting to read the table in rows, rather than in columns. For example, it is very tempting to say that there were eight "high" forecasts issued, and four of these were for an 8 percent price increase. Thus, it is tempting to say that the probability of an 8 percent increase, given a "high" report, is 4/8 = 0.50. This is wrong! It is wrong because it is based on the assumption that a 4 percent increase will occur 10/20, or half, the time; a 6 percent increase will occur 5/20, or one-fourth, the time; and an 8 percent increase will occur 5/20, or one-fourth, the time. These assumptions are contrary to the prior probability beliefs held by the contractor, as indicated in the probability assessments that 0.3, 0.5, and 0.2 were the probabilities for a 4 percent, 6 percent, and 8 percent price increase. One is able to use history in assessing the conditional probability of an information result (forecast) given an event, because this holds the event constant. It is a mistake, however, to use the economists' forecast history to estimate directly the conditional probability of an event given an information (forecast) result, because this ignores the judgmental input of the contractor's prior probabilities.

As seen in the next section, there are more direct ways of using sampling theory to obtain these likelihoods in many decision problems.

17.2 SAMPLE AS IMPERFECT INFORMATION

Now that the logic of evaluating the decision to buy imperfect information has been completed, we extend the concept of imperfect information to include sampling. In many decision problems, the event is a population parameter. In this situation, sampling provides additional information which can be incorporated in the decision process in exactly the same way we incorporated the economists' report. These concepts are illustrated with a quality control example.

A manufacturer of electronics equipment manufactures some of its own components. Because of the advanced state of technology, the production process normally turns out a particular component with a defect rate of 10 percent. However, the process sometimes goes out of control, perhaps when a new worker starts operating the machine. When the process is out of control, it produces components with a defect rate of 40 percent. Thursday morning, a new worker starts operating the machine. The line supervisor is suspicious of the output, so that day's output is sent to quality control for inspection. The line supervisor, after watching the new worker, felt there was a 0.7 chance that the process was operating normally (10 percent defect rate). Quality control must make the decision of whether to use or destroy these components. Furthermore, quality control can test a sample of this very large batch in order to obtain additional information. This additional information is called an *information result* or a *sample result;* the sample result is completely analogous to the forecast result in the previous problem. The information (sample) result can be none defective ($X = 0$), one defective ($X = 1$), two defective ($X = 2$), and so on.

If the batch is destroyed, there is no further cost associated with that batch; neither is there any profit. If the batch is used, and the process was in control, the profit on the batch of components is $1,000. If the batch is used and the process was out of control, there is a loss of $2,000 arising from difficulties in subsequent production processes. The quality control analysis, neglecting the possibility of further testing, is shown in the decision tree of Figure 17.7. This tree indicates that the decision should be made to use the batch, if an immediate decision must be made. However, the possibility of obtaining additional sample information must be considered.

Figure 17.7

Quality Control Decision Tree

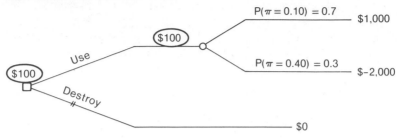

If quality control takes a random sample of components from this batch, and counts the number of defectives in the sample, a binomial probability distribution will describe the sampling distribution. It is assumed that the batch is sufficiently large that a binomial distribution is applicable. But this is different from previous sampling situations, because the proportion defective in the binomial population being sampled is not known. However, it is known that π has a value of 0.1 or 0.4. It is also known that the prior probabilities are $P(\pi = 0.1) = 0.7$ and $P(\pi = 0.4) = 0.3$.

17.21   Using Sample Information

In answering the question of whether or not it is economical to take a sample in this situation, the discussion flows more easily if one first considers how to use such sample information. Suppose that while the quality control manager is mulling over the courses of action for this batch of components, the assistant walks in and says, "Boss, I just drew a random sample of two components. I tested them; one is defective." How should the quality control manager incorporate this additional information into the decision process? The decision tree now faced is shown in Figure 17.8. In order to calculate the probability values for this decision tree, the probabilities revision shown in Figure 17.9 is necessary. The reader should note that the likelihoods in the top part of Figure 17.9—such as $P(X = 0 \mid \pi = 0.1) = 0.81$—are obtained from the table of binomial probabilities. The reader should also be sure to understand that Figure 17.7 and 17.8 have different probability values for the upper-right events, because sample information is available in Figure 17.8 and the revised probabilities are relevant. The prior probabilities were relevant in Figure 17.7, because no information (sample) result was known. From Figure 17.8, after a sample of size $n = 2$ shows that $X = 1$, the batch should be destroyed.

The decision tree in Figure 17.8 assumes that a sample size of two has been taken, with the sample result $X = 1$, meaning one of the two in the

Figure 17.8

Quality Control Decision Tree after a Sample of Two Has One Defective

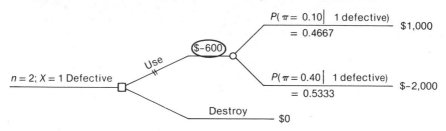

sample is defective. The broader question is to ask whether a sample of size $n = 2$ should have been selected in the first place. If $n = 2$ is not a good sample size, what sample size should have been taken? To answer this broad question of the best sample size, it is necessary to understand the evaluation of economic gain from a sample of size $n = 2$.

The decision tree of Figure 17.10 shows the quality control problem with a sample of size $n = 2$. Notice that there are three information (sample) results: $X = 0$, $X = 1$, and $X = 2$. After each of these results is known, a decision must be made: should the batch be destroyed or used? If the decision is to destroy the batch, the additional profit from the batch is $0. If the decision is to use the batch, an event occurs: the machine was operating normally ($\pi = 0.1$) or the machine was out of control ($\pi = 0.4$). The probabilities shown on these event branches are the posterior probabilities calculated in Figure 17.9; a different set of posterior probabilities applies to each of the three different sample result branches, because each branch represents a different information result.

From the decision tree in Figure 17.10, it is seen that the following decision should be adopted. If one or two defectives occur, destroy the components; the payoff is $0. If zero defectives occur, use the components; the payoff is $520. Then EMV(sample) $= 0.6750(520) + 0.2700(0) + 0.0550(0) = \$351$. Hence, the use of a sample of size two has an EMV of $351. If the sample were free, it would certainly be advantageous to take this sample. Before sampling, the EMV of the decision problem was $100 (see Figure 17.7). With a sample of $n = 2$, the EMV is $351, an increase of $251.

The reader should note that there is no difference between the logic of the calculations shown in this example and the logic of the calculations shown in the contractor example earlier in this chapter. The only detail in which they differ is the manner of obtaining the likelihoods. In the contractor example, the likelihoods were obtained by considering the forecaster's history. In the quality control example, the likelihoods were obtained from a binomial probability distribution.

Figure 17.9
Probability Revision for Quality Control Problems

Table of Joint Probabilities
$P(\text{Event } [\pi] \cap \text{Information Result } [X])$
Binomial Sampling, $n = 2$

Event	Information (Sample) Result			Prior Probabilities
	$X = 0$	$X = 1$	$X = 2$	
$\pi = 0.1$	$P(X = 0 \mid \pi = 0.1)P(\pi = 0.1)$ $= P(X = 0 \cap \pi = 0.1)$ $0.81 \times 0.7 = 0.5670$	$P(X = 1 \mid \pi = 0.1)P(\pi = 0.1)$ $= P(X = 1 \cap \pi = 0.1)$ $0.1800 \times 0.7 = 0.1260$	$P(X = 2 \mid \pi = 0.1)P(\pi = 0.1)$ $= P(X = 2 \cap \pi = 0.1)$ $0.0100 \times 0.7 = 0.0070$	0.7 (given)
$\pi = 0.4$	$P(X = 0 \mid \pi = 0.4)P(\pi = 0.4)$ $= P(X = 0 \cap \pi = 0.4)$ $0.36 \times 0.3 = 0.1080$	$P(X = 1 \mid \pi = 0.4)P(\pi = 0.4)$ $= P(X = 1 \cap \pi = 0.4)$ $0.48 \times 0.3 = 0.1440$	$P(X = 2 \mid \pi = 0.4)P(\pi = 0.4)$ $= P(X = 2 \cap \pi = 0.4)$ $0.1600 \times 0.3 = 0.0480$	0.3 (given)
Totals	$P(X = 0) = 0.5670$ $+ 0.1080 = 0.6750$	$P(X = 1) = 0.1260$ $+ 0.1440 = 0.2700$	$P(X = 2) = 0.0070$ $+ 0.0480 = 0.0550$	

Posterior Probabilities
P(Event | Information Result)

Event	*Information (Sample) Result*		
	$X = 0$	$X = 1$	$X = 2$
$\pi = 0.1$	$\dfrac{P(X = 0 \cap \pi = 0.1)}{P = (X = 0)} = P(\pi = 0.1 \mid X = 0)$ $\dfrac{0.5670}{0.6750} = 0.8400$	$\dfrac{P(X = 1 \cap \pi = 0.1)}{P(X = 1)} = P(\pi = 0.1 \mid X = 1)$ $\dfrac{0.1260}{0.2700} = 0.4667$	$\dfrac{P(X = 2 \cap \pi = 0.1)}{P(X = 2)} = P(\pi = 0.1 \mid X = 2)$ $\dfrac{0.0070}{0.0550} = 0.1273$
$\pi = 0.4$	$\dfrac{P(X = 0 \cap \pi = 0.4)}{P(X = 0)} = P(\pi = 0.4 \mid X = 0)$ $\dfrac{0.1080}{0.6750} = 0.1600$	$\dfrac{P(X = 1 \cap \pi = 0.4)}{P(X = 1)} = P(\pi = 0.4 \mid X = 1)$ $\dfrac{0.1440}{0.2700} = 0.5333$	$\dfrac{P(X = 2 \cap \pi = 0.4)}{P(X = 2)} = P(\pi = 0.4 \mid X = 2)$ $\dfrac{0.0480}{0.0550} = 0.8727$
Totals	1.000	1.000	1.000

Figure 17.10

Partial Decision Tree for Quality Control Problem, $n = 2$

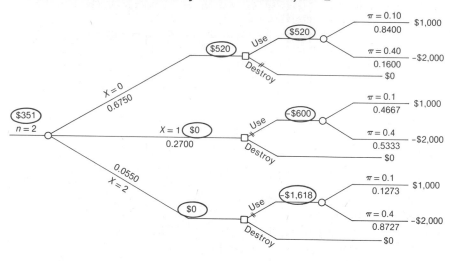

17.22   What Size Sample Should Be Taken?

This quality control problem has an EMV of $351 with a sample of size two, and $100 without sampling. Thus, a sample of size two is worth $251 to the electronics manufacturer. If a sample of size two were the only feasible sample size, and this sample of size two could be obtained for any amount up to $251, expected profit would be maximized by taking this sample. However, a more relevant question is: what is the optimal sample size?

At this point, it is helpful to introduce some additional terminology. The dollar amount by which EMV is increased by sampling is the *expected value of sample information* (EVSI) for that sample size. For a sample of two, it has already been calculated that EVSI = $251. Now assume that a sample costs $50 for each observation; a sample of size two would cost $100. The difference between EVSI and the cost of the sample is called the *expected net gain from sampling* (ENGS) for that sample size. For $n = 2$, ENGS = $251 − $100 = $151. The expected net gain from sampling for a given sample size is the increased profit that results from taking the sample. In order to maximize profits, one would choose that sample size which makes ENGS as large as possible.

These definitions and relationships may be summarized as:

EMV (prior)   = Expected monetary value prior to sampling
EMV (posterior) = Expected monetary value after considering all possible sample results. This value is calculated

before a sample is taken, but it requires the use
of all of the posterior (revised) probabilities,
because all potential sample results must be
considered

EVSI   = Expected value of sample information
         = EMV(posterior) — EMV(prior)
C   = Cost of sample
ENGS   = Expected net gain from sampling
         = EVSI — C

In rather general terms, the relationship among sample size, expected value of sample information (EVSI), cost of sample (C), and expected net gain from sampling (ENGS) is shown graphically in Figure 17.11. Note that both C and EVSI increase as n increases, but their difference, ENGS = EVSI − C, may reach some maximum value and then fall off. In Figure 17.11(a), ENGS has a positive value for some values of n; the largest value for ENGS indicates the optimal sample size. This need not always happen, as suggested by Figure 17.11b. If ENGS is never positive, it means that sampling is too costly relative to the benefits, and should not be undertaken. Figure 17.11c illustrates a pattern of "scallops" that sometimes occurs. In this figure, EVSI is zero for small samples, suggesting there is not enough information in a small sample to change a decision. As larger samples are considered, the EVSI curve increases, but not like the smooth curve shown in the other illustrations. The ENGS curve also takes on a scalloped appearance.

In order to find the information to plot curves, such as Figure 17.11, to determine the sample size that makes ENGS as large as possible, one could draw a decision tree for each sample size in interest. However, such a process becomes quite tedious. There is nothing new in the way of logic or probability manipulation required to do this, but the arithmetic becomes exhausting rather quickly if calculations are done by hand. Fortunately, calculations may be done by a computer, so it is relatively easy to calculate ENGS for many sample sizes.

When one is determining the optimal sample size, a simplification is very easy. If one calculates the expected value of perfect information, one never wants to spend more for a sample (imperfect information) than for perfect information. For the quality control example, EVPI (calculated in Figure 17.12) is $600. For a cost of $50 per observation, one would never take a sample of 12 or more because that would be paying as much as the expected value of perfect information for information which is less than perfect. Figure 17.13 summarizes the results of the calculations (not shown) of EVSI and ENGS for sample sizes from one to eleven for the quality control problem. These data are also plotted in Figure 17.14. Notice that ENGS increases from samples of zero and one to a sample of size two, and then begins to decrease for three and four. However, it

Figure 17.11

Several Possible Situations for Determining Optimal Sample Size

a. Illustration of Optimal Sample Size

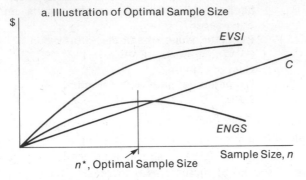

b. Illustration of Situation Where It Is Optimal Not to Sample

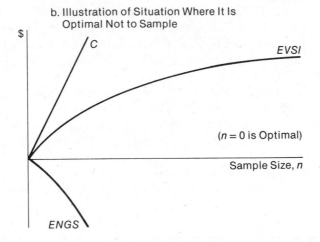

c. Illustration of Scallops

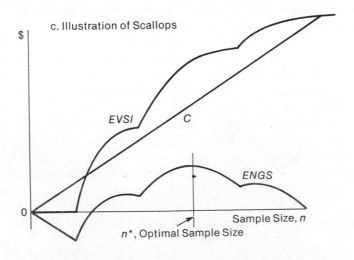

Figure 17.12

Opportunity Loss for the Quality Control Problem

Events \ Acts	Use	Destroy	Probabilities
$\pi = 0.1$	$0	$1,000	0.7
$\pi = 0.4$	$2,000	$0	0.3
EVPI	$600*	$700	

EOL* = EVPI = $600

Figure 17.13

Value of Sample Information for the Quality Control Problem

n	EVSI	Cost of Sample	ENGS
1	$170	$ 50	$ 120
2	251	100	151*
3	281	150	131
4	282	200	82
5	341	250	91
6	380	300	80
7	400	350	50
8	405	400	5
9	424	450	−26
10	450	500	−50
11	466	550	−84

again increases for five, and then begins to decrease again. When calculating ENGS for various sample sizes in order to find the optimal value, one should be careful to explore a large enough range of sample sizes.

17.3 SUMMARY

The purpose of this chapter has been to demonstrate how imperfect information can be incorporated into a decision process, and how the decision of whether to buy imperfect information can be made on economic grounds. Imperfect information includes both forecasts and sample information.

Sample information has been considered for the situation in which a binomial probability distribution was used. However, the same principles

Figure 17.14

ENGS versus *n* for the Quality Control Problem

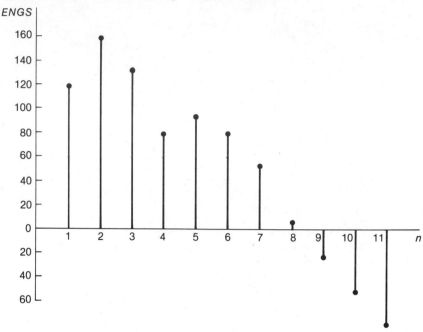

that have been applied can be used if some other sampling distribution, such as the Poisson distribution, is appropriate. In the example using binomial sampling, the reader may have felt it somewhat absurd to allow for only two states of nature. There is nothing in the method that limits the approach to only two states of nature; as many as necessary can be incorporated. In fact, more advanced procedures consider situations in which the prior probability distribution for values of π is described by a continuous probability distribution. It is also possible to consider situations in which the likelihoods are obtained by a continuous probability distribution, such as the normal distribution. Although these methods are not explicitly considered in this text, all of the logic described here is applicable. The use of computers to perform the extensive calculations necessary in these situations is making this economic evaluation of sampling a very useful tool.

EXERCISES

17.1   What is imperfect information? How does it differ from perfect information?

17.2   What is a *prior* probability? Why is the word *prior* (meaning *before*) used?

17.3   What is a revised probability?

17.4   What is a *posterior* probability? Why is the word *posterior* (meaning *after*) used?

17.5   Comment on this statement: "Bayes' theorem is really a 'mixer' of probabilities. It mixes prior information with imperfect information and yields revised information."

17.6   Is it true that a sample provides imperfect information and a census provides perfect information? Discuss.

17.7   Discuss: "Bayes theorem reverses the direction of a conditional probability."

* 17.8   A racing greyhound named JT is known to win with probability 0.3 if the track is fast, and 0.4 if the track is slow. For Wednesday, there is a 0.8 probability of a fast track and a 0.2 probability of a slow track. What is the probability JT will win Wednesday?

* 17.9   You just read in Thursday's paper that the racing greyhound named JT (from Exercise 17.8) won on Wednesday. What is the probability that the track was fast? What is the probability that the track was slow?

* 17.10   Relate each of these concepts to the probabilities for the racing greyhound named JT from Exercises 17.8 and 17.9:
a.   Prior probabilities
b.   Likelihoods
c.   Revised probabilities

* 17.11   "My Old Car" has three ways of breaking down: engine, transmission, and fuel system. The probability that My Old Car will break down from engine trouble is 0.7; from transmission, 0.2; from fuel system, 0.1. The mechanic for My Old Car had been overheard saying: "If My Old Car is going to suffer in the engine, the chances are one in three there will be a grinding noise. If she is going to break down from transmission ailments, the chances are five in seven there will be a grinding noise. If a fuel system problem will do her in, the chances are one in ten she will emit that grinding noise."
a.   What is the probability that the next breakdown for My Old Car will be accompanied by a grinding noise?
b.   If there is no grinding noise, what is the probability that the ailment is the engine? Transmission? Fuel system?
c.   If there is a grinding noise, what is the probability that the ailment is the engine? Transmission? Fuel system?
d.   For My Old Car and her ailments, identify the prior probabilities, the likelihoods, and the revised probabilities.

* 17.12   "My Old Car" (Exercise 17.11) has just been towed into the garage after a breakdown. The mechanic must decide what to investigate

---

* Answers to exercises marked with an asterisk (*) are in Appendix L.

first—the engine, the transmission, or the fuel system. Examining the engine costs $40, the transmission $15, and the fuel system $5. After this first examination, the mechanic will know what the trouble is (an unrealistic assumption, but it surely makes the problem easier). The added costs of repair are as follows: A repair of the engine costs $100 if the engine has already been examined, and $140 if not; repair of the transmission costs $75 if the transmission has been examined, and $90 if not; repair of the fuel system costs $20 if the fuel system has been examined, and $25 if not.

a.   Construct the payoff table showing the costs, the acts, the events, and the prior probabilities for this problem.

b.   Construct a tree for this problem showing the same information shown in the payoff table.

c.   Based on the prior probabilities (i.e., before the mechanic has been able to find out whether a grinding noise occurred with the break-down), which part of the car should the mechanic examine first to minimize the expected cost of repairing My Old Car.

d.   If the owner of the car walked in and said, "Hey Joe, there was no noise when she died this time," what should the mechanic examine first?

e.   If the owner of the car walked in and said, "Hey Joe, that grinding noise really sounded off this time," what should the mechanic examine first?

f.   What is the expected repair cost saving if the mechanic is able to find out whether there was a grinding noise before performing the first examination?

*   17.13   An applicant for a job has applied after seeing an ad either in the morning newspaper or on TV. The applicants split 30 percent newspaper and 70 percent TV. Half the newspaper applicants pass the screening test; one third of the TV applicants pass the screening test.

a.   What is the probability that the applicant will pass the screening test?

b.   If the applicant passes, what is the probability that he or she saw the newspaper ad?

c.   If the applicant fails, what is the probability that he or she saw the TV ad?

d.   For this situation, identify the prior probabilities, the likelihoods, and the revised probabilities.

*   17.14   A batch of integrated circuit chips has arrived from one of three suppliers. For supplier A, it is known that 1 percent of the chips are bad. For supplier B it is known that 3 percent of the chips are bad. For supplier C, it is known that 8 percent of the chips are bad. The chips are unlabelled; it is not clear who made the chips. However, it is known that 70 percent of the batches come from A, 20 percent from B and 10 percent from C.

a.   One chip is randomly selected from the batch. What is the probability it will be bad?

b. If one chip is randomly selected and it is bad, what is the probability the batch was supplied by A? B? C?

c. If two chips are randomly selected from the batch, what is the probability that both will be good?

d. If two chips are randomly selected and both are good, what is the probability the batch was supplied by A? B? C?

e. If two chips are randomly selected from the batch, what is the probability that one will be good and one will be bad?

f. If two chips are randomly selected and one is good and one is bad, what is the probability that batch was supplied by A? B? C?

* 17.15   It is time for you to reorder tulip bulbs for your nursery. You have been purchasing bulbs from an old reliable supplier; you know you will make $2,000 if you purchase the next batch from the old supplier. However, a new supplier has approached you with a more advantageous price. If you buy from the new supplier, and the bulbs are "good," you will make a profit of $3,000 on the next batch of bulbs. However, if the new supplier supplies bulbs which are considered "bad," you will make $1,000 profit on the batch. A good batch is defined to be one in which 80 percent of the bulbs bloom; a bad batch is defined to one in which 30 percent of the bulbs bloom. (For simplicity, assume the batch is either 80 percent or 30 percent bloomers—there is nothing in between.) You believe, after talking to the new supplier, that there is a 60 percent chance the batch will be "good" (80 percent bloomers), and a 40 percent chance that the batch will be "bad" (30 percent bloomers). For a fee, you can randomly sample one bulb from the batch the new supplier will supply to you, and have it tested to see if it is a "bloomer." This laboratory test is completely reliable for the bulb tested; any inferences are at the risk of the statistician. How much (at most) would you pay for this laboratory inspection of one bulb, knowing that you will get the results of the inspection before you determine whether to order from the old or new supplier?

* 17.16   This exercise is an extension of Exercise 16.9. In addition to the information already given in Exercise 16.9, there is an additional opportunity which the trucking firm might wish to exploit to reduce its expected cost of engine repair. A modified compression test is available for these engines. Although not a perfect test, it does give an indication of the work needed to "fix" the engine. When the test is applied, the needle on the testing machine will point to one of three positions on the dial: purple, yellow, or green. The manufacturer of the tester has stated these performance characteristics: If the tester is used on an engine known to need a major overhaul, the needle will point to purple, yellow, or green with probabilities 0.6, 0.3, and 0.1 respectively. If the tester is used on an engine known to need a minor repair, the needle will point to purple, yellow or green with probabilities of 0.05, 0.15 and 0.80 respectively. How much would the company expect to save on each engine it tested before trying to "fix"?

* 17.17   This exercise is an extension of Exercise 16.18. In addition to the information given in Exercise 16.18, the following is also applicable. The distributor of the transistors is able to take a sample of the output from the new manufacturer. If a random sample selection and testing (to ascertain whether the selected transistors are defective) costs $2 per transistor, what is the expected net gain (or loss) to the distributor from taking a sample of three transistors before making a decision?

17.18   This exercise is an extension of Exercise 16.21. In addition to the information given in that exercise, the following is also applicable. The question arises about the desirability of sending one randomly selected salesperson through the program, in order to gain more information. How much is this worth?

* 17.19   This exercise is an extension of Exercise 16.13. In addition to the information given in Exercise 16.13 the following is also applicable. A pretest of the new form can be conducted to find the response rate in this pretest sample. If a pretest of ten users of the questionnaire is used, and two of the ten respond, which form should be used? Before the pretest was conducted, how should the size of the pretest be determined?

17.20   This exercise is an extension of Exercise 16.5. For the scenario of Exercise 16.5, what constitutes sample information? Explain how the optimal sample size should be determined, if the cost of obtaining sample information is known.

17.21   (This exercise requires extensive computations.) If a pilot production run of the machine from Exercise 16.5 can be accomplished at a cost of $10 per item, what is the optimal size of the pilot run? Assume the pilot run is not a part of the regular production run of 1,000 struts, and that only multiples of five are feasible for pilot production.

REFERENCES

See references for Chapter 16.

Optional Notes for the Student

NOTE 3.34

Alternative Formula for Population Variance

$$\sigma_X^2 = \frac{\Sigma(X - \mu_X)^2}{N} = \frac{1}{N}\Sigma(X - \mu_X)^2$$

$$= \frac{1}{N}[\Sigma(X^2 - 2X\mu_X + \mu_X^2)]$$

$$= \frac{1}{N}[\Sigma X^2 - 2\Sigma X\mu_X + \Sigma\mu_X^2]$$

$$= \frac{1}{N}[\Sigma X^2 - 2\mu_X\Sigma X + \Sigma\mu_X^2]$$

$$= \frac{1}{N}[\Sigma X^2 - 2\mu_X N\mu_X + N\mu_X^2]$$

$$= \frac{1}{N}[\Sigma X^2 - 2N\mu_X^2 + N\mu_X^2]$$

$$= \frac{1}{N}[\Sigma X^2 - N\mu_X^2]$$

$$= \frac{1}{N}\left[\Sigma X^2 - N\left(\frac{\Sigma X}{N}\right)^2\right]$$

$$= \frac{1}{N}\left[\Sigma X^2 - \frac{(\Sigma X)^2}{N}\right]$$

$$\sigma_X^2 = \frac{\Sigma X^2 - \dfrac{(\Sigma X)^2}{N}}{N}$$

408   Statistics for Management Decisions

NOTE 5.32A (REQUIRED FOR 5.32C)

Proof that $E(aX) = aE(X)$

Where a is a constant
    X is a random variable with N distinct values
By definition of expectation:

$$E(aX) = \sum_{i=1}^{N} (aX_i) P(X_i)$$

$$E(aX) = a \sum_{i=1}^{N} X_i \cdot P(X_i)$$

$$E(aX) = aE(X)$$

NOTE 5.32B (REQUIRED FOR NOTE 5.32C)

Proof that $E(X + Y) = E(X) + E(Y)$

Where X is a random variable
    Y is a random variable

By definition of expectation:

$$E(X + Y) = \sum_{i=1}^{N} \sum_{j=1}^{N} (X_i + Y_j) P(X_i, Y_j)$$

$$= \sum_{i=1}^{N} \sum_{j=1}^{N} X_i \cdot P(X_i, Y_j) + \sum_{i=1}^{N} \sum_{j=1}^{N} Y_j \cdot P(X_i, Y_j)$$

$$= \sum_{i=1}^{N} X_i \left[\sum_{j=1}^{N} P(X_i, Y_j) \right] + \sum_{j=1}^{N} Y_j \left[\sum_{i=1}^{N} P(X_i, Y_j) \right]$$

$$= \sum_{i=1}^{N} X_i P(X_i) + \sum_{j=1}^{N} Y_j P(Y_j)$$

$$E(X + Y) = E(X) + E(Y)$$

By repeated application for random variables $X_1, X_2, X_3, \ldots, X_i$ it follows that

$$E(\Sigma X_i) = \Sigma E(X_i)$$

NOTE 5.32C

Proof that $\mu_{\bar{X}} = \mu_X$

From Chapter 3

$$E(X) = \mu_X = \frac{1}{N} \sum_{i=1}^{N} X_i$$

Now, for a sample of n:

$$\mu_{\bar{X}} = E(\bar{X}) = E\left[\frac{1}{n} \sum_{i=1}^{n} X_i\right]$$

$$\mu_{\bar{X}} = \frac{1}{n}\left[E \sum_{i=1}^{n} X_i\right] \qquad E \text{ and } \Sigma \text{ are interchangeable}$$

$$\mu_{\bar{X}} = \frac{1}{n} \sum_{i=1}^{n} [E(X_i)]$$

$$\mu_{\bar{X}} = \frac{1}{n} \sum_{i=1}^{n} (\mu_X)$$

$$\mu_{\bar{X}} = \frac{1}{n} (n\mu_X)$$

Thus

$$\mu_{\bar{X}} = E(\bar{X}) = \mu_X$$

or

$$\mu_{\bar{X}} = \mu_X$$

NOTE 5.32D (REQUIRED FOR 5.32F)

Proof that Var$(X + Y)$ = Var(X) + Var(Y)   For X, Y independent

Where

X is a random variable
Y is a random variable
X and Y are independent

$$\begin{aligned}
\text{Var}(X+Y) &= E[(X+Y) - (\mu_X + \mu_Y)]^2 \\
\text{Var}(X+Y) &= E[(X - \mu_X) + (Y - \mu_Y)]^2 \qquad (1) \\
\text{Var}(X+Y) &= E(X - \mu_X)^2 + E(Y - \mu_Y)^2 \\
&\quad + 2E(X - \mu_X)(Y - \mu_Y)
\end{aligned}$$

covariance

Let us examine the last term:

$$E(X - \mu_X)(Y - \mu_Y) = E(XY - \mu_X Y - \mu_Y X + \mu_Y \mu_X) \tag{2}$$
$$= E(XY) - \mu_X E(Y) - \mu_Y E(X) + \mu_Y \mu_X$$
$$= E(XY) - \mu_X \mu_Y - \mu_Y \mu_X + \mu_Y \mu_X$$
$$= E(XY) - \mu_X \mu_Y$$

However,

$$E(XY) = \sum_X \sum_Y (XY)\, P(X,Y)$$

But since X and Y are independent,

$$E(XY) = \sum_X \sum_Y (XY)\, P(X)\, P(Y)$$

$$= \sum_X X \cdot P(X) \left[\sum_Y Y \cdot P(Y) \right]$$

$$= \sum_X X \cdot P(X) \cdot E(Y)$$

$$= E(Y) \sum_X X \cdot P(X)$$

$$= E(Y) \cdot E(X)$$

$$E(XY) = \mu_Y \mu_X$$

Hence the expression in (2) is equal to zero, so that the expression in (1) is

$$\text{Var}\,(X + Y) = E(X - \mu_X)^2 + E(Y - \mu_Y)^2 + 0$$
or
$$\text{Var}\,(X + Y) = \text{Var}\,(X) + \text{Var}\,(Y)$$

By repeated application for independent random variables $X_1, X_2, X_3, \ldots, X_i$ it follows that

$$\text{Var}\left(\sum_{i=1}^{N} X_i \right) = \sum_{i=1}^{N} \text{Var}\,(X_i)$$

NOTE 5.32E

Proof that Var(aX) = a^2Var(X)

By definition of expectation

$$\text{Var}\,(X) = E(X - \mu_X)^2$$

Now let a random variable be defined as

$$Y = aX$$

where a is a constant

$$\text{Var}\,(Y) = E(Y - \mu_Y)^2 \tag{1}$$

But since

$$Y = aX$$

then
$$E(Y) = E(aX) = aE(X)$$
or
$$\mu_Y = a\mu_X$$

Thus (1) becomes

$$\begin{aligned}
\text{Var }(Y) &= E(aX - a\mu_X)^2 \qquad\qquad (2)\\
&= E[a^2(X - \mu_X)^2]\\
&= a^2\,E(X - \mu_X)^2\\
\text{Var }(Y) &= a^2\,\text{Var }(X)
\end{aligned}$$

or
$$\text{Var }(aX) = a^2\,\text{Var }(X)$$

NOTE 5.32F

Proof that $\sigma_{\bar{X}}^2 = \sigma_X^2/n$

$$\text{Var }(\bar{X}) = \frac{\text{Var }(X)}{n} \text{ or } \sigma_{\bar{X}}^2 = \frac{\sigma_X^2}{n} \qquad\qquad \bar{X} = \frac{\sum_{i=1}^{n} X_i}{n}$$

$$\text{Var }(\bar{X}) = \text{Var }\left(\frac{\Sigma X_i}{n}\right)$$

$$= \frac{1}{n^2}\,\text{Var }(\Sigma X_i)$$

$$= \frac{1}{n^2}\sum_{i=1}^{n}\text{Var }(X_i) \qquad \Sigma \text{ \& Var can be interchanged}$$
$$\qquad\qquad\qquad\qquad\qquad\qquad \text{if } X \text{ are independent}$$

$$= \frac{1}{n^2}\sum_{i=1}^{n}(\sigma_X)^2 \qquad\qquad n\cdot(\sigma_X)^2$$

$$= \frac{1}{n^2}(n\sigma_X^2)$$

$$\text{Var }(\bar{X}) = \frac{\sigma_X^2}{n}$$

or
$$\sigma_{\bar{X}}^2 = \frac{\sigma_X^2}{n}$$

or
$$\sigma_{\bar{X}} = \frac{\sigma_X}{\sqrt{n}}$$

NOTE 6.3

Hypergeometric Distribution

A binomial random variable is the sum of n independent Bernoulli random variables, where each Bernoulli random variable has an identical value of π. If the population from which a sample is being taken has N elements, of which N_1 are successes and N_2 are failures (and $N_1 + N_2 = N$), and the sample is selected without replacement, the Bernoulli process corresponding to each observation is not independent of the previous observations. Thus, when a sample is taken without replacement from a finite population of successes and failures, the resulting random variable number of successes is not described by the binomial probability distribution, but is described by the *hypergeometric* probability distribution.

The hypergeometric distribution is derived from the definition of simple random sampling, in which each combination of n elements has an equal chance of being selected. If there are N elements in the population, the probability of any specific set of n elements in that sample is

$$1 \left/ \left(\frac{N!}{n!(N-n)!} \right) \right.$$

We next find the number of samples which have X successes (and, of course, $n - X$ failures). Of the N_1 successes in the population, the number of ways of selecting X of N_1 is

$$\frac{N_1!}{X!(N_1 - X)!}$$

Similarly, the number of ways $n - X$ failures can be selected from N_2 failures is:

$$\frac{N_2!}{(n-X)!(N_2 - n + X)!}$$

The number of ways of selecting X successes *and* $n - X$ failures is:

$$\frac{N_1!}{X!(N_1 - X)!} \cdot \frac{N_2!}{(n-X)!(N_2 - n + X)!}$$

Since the probability of each of these is

$$\frac{1}{\left(\dfrac{N!}{n!(N-n)!} \right)}$$

then

$$P(X|n, N_1, N_2) = \frac{\dfrac{N_1!}{X!\,(N_1 - X)!} \cdot \dfrac{N_2!}{(n-X)!\,(N_2 - n + X)!}}{\dfrac{N!}{n!\,(N-n)!}}$$

which is the hypergeometric distribution.

NOTE 6.32A

Proof that $\mu_X = n\pi$

As with any Bernoulli process, we know that the binomial random variable is

$$X = \sum_{i=1}^{n} Y_i$$

where Y is the Bernoulli random variable.

In Figure 6.1 it was shown that:

$$E(Y) = \pi \tag{1}$$

Then

$$\mu_X = E(X) = E\left[\sum_{i=1}^{n} Y\right] \tag{2}$$

$$\mu_X = \sum_{i=1}^{n} E(Y)$$

And from (1):

$$\mu_X = \sum_{i=1}^{n} \pi \tag{3}$$

Thus

$$\mu_X = n\pi \tag{4}$$

NOTE 6.32B

Proof that $\sigma_X^2 = n\pi(1 - \pi)$

Letting Y be a Bernoulli random variable, it is shown in Chapter 6 that:

$$\sigma_{Y2} = \pi(1 - \pi)$$

A binomial random variable is

$$X = \sum_{i=1}^{n} Y_i$$

From Note 5.32d

$$\sigma_X^2 = \sum_{i=1}^{n} \sigma_Y^2$$

Or

$$\sigma_X^2 = \sum_{i=1}^{n} \pi(1 - \pi)$$

Thus

$$\sigma_X^2 = n\pi(1 - \pi)$$

NOTE 6.41A

Proof that $\mu_p = \pi$

$$\mu_p = E(p) = E\left(\frac{X}{n}\right) = \sum_{X=0}^{n} \left(\frac{X}{n}\right) P(X) \tag{1}$$

$$= \frac{1}{n} \sum_{X=0}^{n} XP(X)$$

$$= \frac{1}{n} (\mu x)$$

$$= \frac{1}{n} (n\pi)$$

$$\mu_p = \pi \qquad (2)$$

NOTE 6.41*B*

Proof that $\sigma_p^2 = \dfrac{\pi(1 - \pi)}{n}$

$$p = \frac{X}{n}$$

Thus
$$\sigma_p^2 = \text{Var}(p) = \text{Var}\left(\frac{X}{n}\right)$$

From Note 5.31e:

$$\text{Var}\left(\frac{X}{n}\right) = \left(\frac{1}{n}\right)^2 \text{Var}(X)$$

From Note 6.32c
$$\text{Var}(p) = \frac{1}{n^2}(n\pi[1 - \pi])$$

$$\sigma_p^2 = \frac{\pi(1 - \pi)}{n}$$

NOTE 6.5*A*

For the next three notes, the following properties of *e* are required:

$$e \equiv \lim_{X \to 0} (1 - X)^{-\frac{1}{x}} \qquad (1)$$

$$e^a = \sum_{X=1}^{\infty} \frac{a^{X-1}}{(X - 1)!} \qquad (2)$$

NOTE 6.5*B*

Proof that $P(X) = \dfrac{e^{-\mu}\mu^X}{X!}$ **for a Poisson Distribution**

Let us start with the Binomial distribution

$$P(X|n, \pi) = \frac{n!}{X! \, (n - X)!} \, \pi^X (1 - \pi)^{n-X} \tag{1}$$

$$= \frac{n(n - 1)(n - 2) \ldots (1)}{(n - X)! \, X!} \, \pi^X (1 - \pi)^{n-X}$$

$$= \frac{n(n - 1)(n - 2) \ldots (n - X + 1)}{X!} \, \pi^X (1 - \pi)^{n-X}$$

$$= \frac{n(n - 1)(n - 2) \ldots (n - X + 1)}{X! \, n^X} \, (n\pi)^X (1 - \pi)^{n-X}$$

But $n\pi = \mu$

$$P(X|n, \pi) = \frac{n(n - 1)(n - 2) \ldots (n - X + 1)}{X! \, n^X} \, \mu^X (1 - \pi)^{n-X}$$

Multiplying by $\dfrac{(1 - \pi)^X}{(1 - \pi)^X}$

$$P(X|n, \pi) = \frac{n(n - 1)(n - 2) \ldots (n - X + 1)(1 - \pi)^n}{(1 - \pi)^X \, n^X} \cdot \frac{\mu^X}{X!}$$

Dividing numerator and denominator by n^X

$$P(X|n, \pi) = \frac{1\left(1 - \dfrac{1}{n}\right)\left(1 - \dfrac{2}{n}\right) \ldots \left(1 - \dfrac{X+1}{n}\right)}{(1 - \pi)^X} \cdot (1 - \pi)^n \cdot \frac{\mu^X}{X!} \tag{2}$$

Now let $n \to \infty$ such that $n\pi$ remains constant. In this manner, the mean number of successes stays constant, while the number of opportunities for a success approaches infinity. Then:

$$\frac{1}{n}, \frac{2}{n}, \ldots \frac{X+1}{n} \text{ all approach zero} \tag{a}$$

π approaches zero as $n\pi = \mu$ which is constant; thus $(1 - \pi)^X$ approaches one. (b)

As

$$n = \left(-\frac{1}{\pi}\right)(-n\pi) = \left(-\frac{1}{\pi}\right)(-\mu) \tag{c}$$

we can rewrite

$$(1 - \pi)^n = [(1 - \pi)^{-\frac{1}{\pi}}]^{-\mu}$$

and as π approaches zero, the value in brackets approaches e.

Hence, we can rewrite (2) as $n \to \infty$

$$P(X) = \frac{e^{-\mu}\mu^X}{X!} \tag{3}$$

NOTE 6.51*A*

Proof that $\mu_X = E(X) = \mu$ for the Poisson Distribution

$$\mu_X = E(X) = \sum_{X=0}^{\infty} X\,P(X) = \sum_{X=0}^{\infty} \frac{X\,e^{-\mu}\mu^X}{X!}$$

$$= e^{-\mu} \sum_{X=0}^{\infty} \frac{X\mu^X}{X!}$$

$$= e^{-\mu} \sum_{X=1}^{\infty} \frac{\mu^X}{(X-1)!}$$

$$= e^{-\mu} \sum_{X=1}^{\infty} \frac{\mu^{X-1}\mu}{(X-1)!}$$

$$= e^{-\mu}\mu \sum_{X=1}^{\infty} \frac{\mu^{X-1}}{(X-1!)}$$

$$= e^{-\mu} \cdot \mu \cdot e^{\mu}$$
$$= e^0 \cdot \mu \qquad \text{where } e^0 = 1$$
$$\mu_X = \mu$$

NOTE 6.51*B* (REQUIRED FOR 6.51*C*)

The variance of a random variable has been defined as:

$$\sigma_X^2 = E(X - \mu)^2$$
$$= E(X^2 - 2\mu X + \mu^2)$$
$$= E(X^2) - 2\mu E(X) + \mu^2$$
$$\sigma_X^2 = E(X^2) - 2\mu^2 + \mu^2$$

Or

$$\sigma_X^2 = E(X^2) - \mu^2$$

NOTE 6.51*C*

Proof that $\sigma_X^2 = \mu$ for the Poisson Distribution

$$\sigma_X^2 = E(X - \mu)^2 = \sum_{X=0}^{\infty} (X - \mu)^2 P(X) \qquad (1)$$

$$= \sum_{X=0}^{\infty} X^2 P(X) - \mu^2$$

$$= \sum_{X=0}^{\infty} \frac{e^{-\mu}\mu^{X}}{X!} X^2 - \mu^2$$

$$= e^{-\mu} \sum_{X=1}^{\infty} \frac{\mu^{X}X}{(X-1)!} - \mu^2$$

$$= e^{-\mu} \sum_{X=1}^{\infty} \frac{\mu^{X}(X+1-1)}{(X-1)!} - \mu^2$$

$$= e^{-\mu}\mu \sum_{X=1}^{\infty} \frac{\mu^{X-1}(X+1-1)}{(X-1)!} - \mu^2$$

$$= e^{-\mu}\mu \sum_{X=1}^{\infty} \frac{\mu^{X-1}(X-1)+\mu^{X-1}}{(X-1)!} - \mu^2$$

$$= e^{-\mu}\mu \left[\sum_{X=1}^{\infty} \frac{\mu^{X-1}}{(X-1)!} + \sum_{X=2}^{\infty} \frac{\mu^{X-1}}{(X-2)!} \right] - \mu^2$$

$$= e^{-\mu}\mu(e^{\mu} + \mu e^{\mu}) - \mu^2$$

$$= \mu + \mu^2 - \mu^2$$

$$\sigma_X^2 = \mu$$

NOTE 7.1A

Probability from a Density Function

Given a continuous random variable, X, and its density function, $f(X)$, these properties must hold by definition of a density function:

$$f(X) \geq 0 \quad \text{everywhere}$$

$$\int_{-\infty}^{+\infty} f(X)dX = 1 \tag{2}$$

To use the density function to find probabilities:

$$P(X \geq X_1) \quad = \int_{X_1}^{+\infty} f(X)dX$$

$$P(X_1 \leq X \leq X_2) = \int_{X_1}^{X_2} f(X)dX$$

$$P(X \leq X_1) \quad = \int_{-\infty}^{X_1} f(X)dX$$

NOTE 7.1*B*

Mean and Variance of a Continuous Random Variable

For a continuous random variable, X, and its density function, $f(X)$, these definitions apply:

$$\mu_X = E(X) = \int_{-\infty}^{+\infty} Xf(X)dX$$

$$\sigma_X^2 = E(X - \mu_X)^2 = \int_{-\infty}^{+\infty} (X - \mu_X)^2 f(X)dX$$

1. Show that

$$\sigma_X^2 = \int_{-\infty}^{+\infty} X^2 f(X)dX - \mu_X^2$$

follows from the definition of σ_X^2.

2. Let

$$f(X) = 2X \quad 0 \le X \le |$$
$$f(X) = 0 \quad X < 0, X > |$$

   a. Show that $\int_{-\infty}^{+\infty} f(X)dX = 1$

   b. Show that $E(X) = \frac{2}{3}$

   c. Show that $\sigma_X^2 = \frac{1}{18}$

3. Let

$$f(X) = \frac{1}{4}X^2, 0 \le X \le a$$
$$f(X) = 0\ X, < 0, X > a$$

Find the value of a.

NOTE 7.22A

Proof that $\mu_Z = 0$

We define the values of the standard normal random variable as:

$$Z = \frac{X - \mu_X}{\sigma_X} \qquad (1)$$

Hence
$$\mu_z = E\left(\frac{X - \mu_X}{\sigma_X}\right)$$

Or
$$\mu_z = E\left(\frac{X}{\sigma_X}\right) - \frac{\mu_X}{\sigma_X}$$

$$\mu_z = \frac{1}{\sigma_X} E(X) - \frac{\mu_X}{\sigma_X}$$

But
$$E(X) = \mu_X$$

Hence
$$\mu_z = \frac{\mu_X}{\sigma_X} - \frac{\mu_X}{\sigma_X}$$

Thus
$$u_z = 0 \qquad (2)$$

NOTE 7.22B

Proof that $\sigma_Z = 1$

As
$$Z = \frac{X - \mu_X}{\sigma_X}$$

Then
$$\sigma_z^2 = E\left[\left(\frac{X - \mu_X}{\sigma_X}\right) - \mu_z\right]^2 \qquad (1)$$

But we know $\mu_z = 0$ (Note 7.23a)
Thus
$$\sigma_z^2 = E\left(\frac{X - \mu_X}{\sigma_X}\right)^2 \qquad (2)$$

Or
$$\sigma_z^2 = \left(\frac{1}{\sigma_X^2}\right) E(X - \mu_X)^2 \qquad (3)$$

Which is
$$\sigma_z^2 = \frac{1}{\sigma_X^2}(\sigma_X^2) \qquad (4)$$

Thus
$$\sigma_z^2 = 1 \qquad (5)$$

And
$$\sigma_z = 1 \qquad (6)$$

NOTE 7.44

Exponential Distribution

The exponential distribution (sometimes called the negative exponential distribution) is closely related to the Poisson distribution. For example, in a large electronic communications network, the number of failures is Poisson distributed, with an average of μ_X per day. Thus, the probability of X failures in one day is

$$P(X) = \frac{e^{-\mu_z} \mu_X^X}{X!}$$

For a period which is T(days) long, the probability of X failures in the period is

$$P(X) = \frac{e^{-\mu_z T} (\mu_X T)^X}{X!}$$

Thus, the probability that there will be no failures ($X = 0$) is a period of length T is:

Or
$$P(0) = \frac{e^{-\mu_z T} (\mu_X T)^0}{0!} = e^{-\mu_z T}$$

$$P(\text{no failures in a period of length } T) = e^{-\mu_z T}$$

It does not matter when the period T begins. If the time period begins with a failure,

$$P(\text{next failure occurs later than } T \text{ from previous failure}) = e^{-\mu_z T}$$

If we let s be the random variable "time between failures" then

$$P(s > T) = e^{-\mu_z T}$$

is the expression for the time between failures. This is the expression for the right tail of the exponential distribution, which describes time between events if the number of events is described by the Poisson distribution.

The density function for the exponential distribution is:

$$f(s) = \mu_X e^{-\mu_z s}$$

which has this appearance:

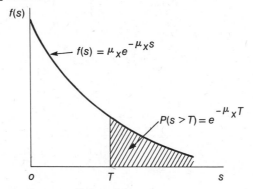

The mean time between events (failures) is:

$$\mu_s = \frac{1}{\mu_X}$$

Thus, if the average is two failures per day, the average time between failures is half a day.

NOTE 8.24

The reader will have noted that the equation for the sample variance was

$$s_X^2 = \frac{1}{n-1} \sum_{i=1}^{n} (X - \bar{X})^2 \tag{1}$$

and not

$$\hat{s}_X{}^2 = \frac{1}{n} \sum_{i=1}^{n} (X - \bar{X})^2 \tag{2}$$

This is because the estimate of $\sigma_X{}^2$ based on Equation 2 is a biased estimate of $\sigma_X{}^2$; i.e, for equation (2)

$$E(\hat{s}_X{}^2) \neq \sigma_X{}^2$$

whereas for Equation 1

$$E(\hat{s}_X{}^2) = \sigma_X{}^2$$

Simply stated, this is caused by the fact that the dispersion found in a sample, as in Equation 2, will tend to be smaller than that found in the population, i.e., it is a biased estimate unless stated as in Equation 1. To demonstrate:

$$\hat{s}_X{}^2 = \frac{1}{n} \sum_{i=1}^{n} (X - \bar{X})^2$$

$$E(\hat{s}_X{}^2) = E\left[\frac{1}{n} \sum_{i=1}^{n} (X - \bar{X})^2 \right]$$

Subtracting and adding a μ_X:

$$E(\hat{s}_X{}^2) = E\left(\frac{1}{n} \sum_{i=1}^{n} [(X - \mu_X) - (\bar{X} - \mu_X)]^2 \right)$$

$$E(\hat{s}_X{}^2) = E\left(\frac{1}{n} \sum_{i=1}^{n} [(X - \mu_X)^2 - 2(X - \mu_X)(\bar{X} - \mu_X) + (\bar{X} - \mu_X)^2] \right)$$

$$E(\hat{s}_X{}^2) = \frac{1}{n}\left[E\sum_{i=1}^{n} (X - \mu_X)^2 - 2E\sum_{i=1}^{n}(X\bar{X} - X\mu_X - \bar{X}\mu_X + \mu_X{}^2) \right.$$

$$\left. + E\sum_{i=1}^{n} (\bar{X} - \mu_X)^2 \right]$$

$$E(\hat{s}_X{}^2) = \frac{1}{n}\left[E\sum_{i=1}^{n} (X - \mu_X)^2 - 2E\sum_{i=1}^{n}X\bar{X} + 2E\sum_{i=1}^{n}X\mu_X + 2E\sum_{i=1}^{n}\bar{X}\mu_X \right.$$

$$\left. - 2E\sum_{i=1}^{n}\mu_X{}^2 + E\sum_{i=1}^{n}(\bar{X} - \mu_X)^2 \right]$$

$$E(\hat{s}_X{}^2) = \frac{1}{n}\left[E\sum_{i=1}^{n} (X - \mu_X)^2 - 2E(n\bar{X}^2) + 2E(n\bar{X}\mu_X) + 2E(n\bar{X}\mu_X) \right.$$

$$\left. - 2E(n\mu_X{}^2) + E\sum_{i=1}^{n}(\bar{X} - \mu_X)^2 \right]$$

$$E(\hat{s}_X^2) = \frac{1}{n}\left[E\sum_{i=1}^{n}(X - \mu_X)^2 - 2E(n\bar{X}^2) + 4E(n\bar{X}\mu_X) - 2E(n\mu_X^2) \right.$$
$$\left. + E\sum_{i=1}^{n}(\bar{X} - \mu_X)^2 \right]$$

$$E(\hat{s}_X^2) = \frac{1}{n}\left(E\sum_{i=1}^{n}(X - \mu_X)^2 - E[2n(\bar{X}^2 - 2\bar{X}\mu_X + \mu_X^2)] \right.$$
$$\left. + E\sum_{i=1}^{n}(\bar{X} - \mu_X)^2 \right)$$

$$E(\hat{s}_X^2) = \frac{1}{n}\left(E\sum_{i=1}^{n}(X - \mu_X)^2 - 2\left[E\sum_{i=1}^{n}(\bar{X} - \mu_X)^2 \right] \right.$$
$$\left. + E\sum_{i=1}^{n}(\bar{X} - \mu_X)^2 \right)$$

$$E(\hat{s}_X^2) = \frac{1}{n}\left[E\sum_{i=1}^{n}(X - \mu_X)^2 - E\sum_{i=1}^{n}(\bar{X} - \mu_X)^2 \right]$$

Assuming an infinite population,

$$E(\hat{s}_X^2) = \frac{1}{n}\left(\sum_{i=1}^{n}\sigma_X^2 - \sum_{i=1}^{n}\sigma_{\bar{X}}^2 \right)$$

$$E(\hat{s}_X^2) = \frac{1}{n}(n\sigma_X^2 - n\sigma_{\bar{X}}^2)$$

$$E(\hat{s}_X^2) = \sigma_X^2 - \sigma_{\bar{X}}^2$$

Where

$$\sigma_{\bar{X}}^2 = \frac{\sigma_X^2}{n}$$

$$E(\hat{s}_X^2) = \sigma_X^2 - \frac{\sigma_X^2}{n}$$

$$E(\hat{s}_X^2) = \frac{n\sigma_X^2 - \sigma_X^2}{n}$$

$$E(\hat{s}_X^2) = \left(\frac{n-1}{n}\right)\sigma_X^2$$

But since

$$s_X^2 = \left(\frac{n}{n-1}\right)\hat{s}_X^2$$

$$E(s_X^2) = E\left[\left(\frac{n}{n-1}\right)\hat{s}_X^2\right]$$

$$= \left(\frac{n}{n-1}\right)E(\hat{s}_X^2)$$

$$= \left(\frac{n}{n-1}\right) \cdot \left(\frac{n-1}{n}\right) \sigma_X{}^2$$

or

$$E(s_X{}^2) = \sigma_X{}^2$$

Thus

$$s_X{}^2 = \frac{\sum_{i=1}^{n} (X - \bar{X})^2}{n-1}$$

is an unbiased estimator of $\sigma_X{}^2$ while

$$\hat{s}_X{}^2 = \frac{\sum_{i=1}^{n} (X - \bar{X})^2}{n}$$

is a biased estimator of $\sigma_X{}^2$

NOTE 8.38A

Proof that $\mu_{\bar{X}_1 - \bar{X}_2} = \mu_{X_1} - \mu_{X_2}$

$$\begin{aligned}
E(\bar{X}_1 - \bar{X}_2) &= E(\bar{X}_1 + [-1]\bar{X}^2) \\
&= E(\bar{X}_1) + E(-1)(\bar{X}_2) \\
&= E(\bar{X}_1) + (-1)E(\bar{X}_2) \\
&= E(\bar{X}_1) - E(\bar{X}_2)
\end{aligned}$$

Thus $\qquad \mu_{\bar{X}_1 - \bar{X}_2} = E(\bar{X}_1 - \bar{X}_2) = \mu_{X_1} - \mu_{X_2}$

NOTE 8.38B

Proof that $\sigma_{\bar{X}_1 - \bar{X}_2}{}^2 = \dfrac{\sigma_{X_1}{}^2}{n_1} + \dfrac{\sigma_{X_2}{}^2}{n_2}$ **X_1, X_2 Independent**

$$\begin{aligned}
\text{Var}(\bar{X}_1 - \bar{X}_2) &= \text{Var}(\bar{X}_1 + [-1]\bar{X}_2) \\
&= \text{Var}(\bar{X}_1) + \text{Var}([-1]\bar{X}_2) \\
&= \text{Var}(\bar{X}_1) + (-1)^2 \text{Var}(\bar{X}_2) \\
&= \frac{\sigma_{X_1}{}^2}{n_1} + \frac{\sigma_{X_2}{}^2}{n_2}
\end{aligned}$$

NOTE 11

Partition of Sum of Squares in ANOVA

Define *total* deviation of an observation as:

$$X_{ij} - \bar{\bar{X}} \tag{1}$$

The total sum of squares is

$$SST = \sum_{j=1}^{c} \sum_{i=1}^{n} (X_{ij} - \bar{\bar{X}})^2$$

It is algebraically true that

$$(X_{ij} - \bar{\bar{X}}) = (\bar{X}_j - \bar{\bar{X}}) + (X_{ij} - \bar{X}_j) \qquad (2)$$

Now if we square both sides of Equation 2 and sum over both i and j, there is:

$$\sum_{j=1}^{c} \sum_{i=1}^{n} (X_{ij} - \bar{\bar{X}})^2 = \sum_{j=1}^{c} \sum_{i=1}^{n} (\bar{X}_j - \bar{\bar{X}})^2 + \sum_{j=1}^{c} \sum_{i=1}^{n} (X_{ij} - \bar{X}_j)^2$$

$$+ 2 \sum_{j=1}^{c} \sum_{i=1}^{n} (\bar{X}_j - \bar{\bar{X}})(X_{ij} - \bar{X}_j) \qquad (3)$$

But

$$\sum_{j=1}^{c} \sum_{i=1}^{n} (\bar{X}_j - \bar{\bar{X}})^2 = n \sum_{j=1}^{c} (\bar{X}_j - \bar{\bar{X}})^2 = SSB \qquad (a)$$

as $(\bar{X}_j - \bar{\bar{X}})^2$ is constant for all values of i, and

$$\sum_{j=1}^{c} \sum_{i=1}^{n} (X_{ij} - \bar{X}_j)^2 = SSW \qquad (b)$$

and

$$2 \sum_{j=1}^{c} \sum_{i=1}^{n} (\bar{X}_j - \bar{\bar{X}})(X_{ij} - \bar{X}_j) = 2 \sum_{j=1}^{c} \left[(\bar{X}_j - \bar{\bar{X}}) \sum_{i=1}^{n} (X_{ij} - \bar{X}_j) \right] = 0 \qquad (c)$$

as

$$\sum_{i=1}^{n} (X_{ij} - \bar{X}_j) \equiv 0$$

Hence:

$$SST = SSB + SSW + 0$$

NOTE 12.21A

Derivation of Normal Equations

Let

Y = Actual (observed) dependent variable data
X = Actual (observed) independent variable data
$\bar{Y}_c$ = Dependent variable values computed from the least squares
derived regression line where:
$\bar{Y}_c = a + bX$

Let

$$Y - \bar{Y}_c = \text{error} = \epsilon$$

Thus, the least squares criterion can be stated as:

$$\min \Sigma \epsilon^2 = \min \Sigma (Y - \bar{Y}_c)^2$$

for all n values in the sample, or

$$\min \Sigma \epsilon^2 = \min \Sigma (Y - a - bX)^2$$

Now take the partial derivatives of the error function with respect to a and b and, in order to minimize, set them equal to zero:

$$\frac{\delta \Sigma \epsilon^2}{\delta a} = -2\Sigma (Y - a - bX) \quad = 0$$

$$\frac{\delta \Sigma \epsilon^2}{\delta b} = -2\Sigma [(Y - a - bX)(X)] = 0$$

which can be restated as:

$$\Sigma (Y - a - bX) \quad = 0$$

and

$$\Sigma (XY - aX - bX^2) = 0$$

or as

$$\Sigma Y = \Sigma a + \Sigma bX$$

and

$$\Sigma XY = \Sigma aX + \Sigma bX^2$$

or as

$$\Sigma Y = na + b\Sigma X \tag{1}$$
$$\Sigma XY = a\Sigma X + b\Sigma X^2 \tag{2}$$

A few further comments are of value. From Equation 1 it is noted that

$$n\bar{Y} = na + bn\bar{X}$$
$$\bar{Y} = a + b\bar{X}$$

Hence, when $X = \bar{X}$, then $\bar{Y}_c = \bar{Y}$. This is to say that the regression line passes through the point of means, $\bar{X}, \bar{Y}$.

Another useful relationship is:

$$\Sigma \bar{Y}_c = \Sigma Y$$

Proof:
$$\Sigma \bar{Y}_c = \Sigma (a + bX)$$
$$\Sigma \bar{Y}_c = \Sigma a + \Sigma bX$$
$$\Sigma \bar{Y}_c = na + b\Sigma X$$

But from the first normal equation,

$$\Sigma Y = na + b\Sigma X$$

Hence:

$$\Sigma \bar{Y}_c = \Sigma Y$$

because both are equal to the same quantity.

NOTE 12.21*B*

Equations for Constant Term *a* and Slope of Line *b*

We begin with the normal equations:

$$\Sigma Y = na + b\Sigma X \tag{1}$$
$$\Sigma XY = a\Sigma X + b\Sigma X^2 \tag{2}$$

or

$$na = -b\Sigma X + \Sigma Y \tag{3}$$
$$a\Sigma X = \Sigma XY - b\Sigma X^2 \tag{4}$$

Multiplying Equation 3 by $\bar{X}$, we have

$$na\bar{X} = -b\Sigma X(\bar{X}) + \Sigma Y(\bar{X}) \tag{5}$$

Solving as simultaneous equations, we subtract Equation 4 from Equation 5 and find:

$$-b\Sigma X(\bar{X}) + \Sigma Y(\bar{X}) - \Sigma XY + b\Sigma X^2 = an\bar{X} - a\Sigma X = 0$$

or

$$-b\Sigma X(\bar{X}) + b\Sigma X^2 = -\Sigma Y(\bar{X}) + \Sigma XY$$

or

$$b\Sigma X^2 - b\Sigma X(\bar{X}) = \Sigma XY - \Sigma Y(\bar{X})$$

or

$$b[\Sigma X^2 - \Sigma X(\bar{X})] = \Sigma XY - \Sigma Y(\bar{X})$$

or

$$b = \frac{\Sigma XY - \Sigma Y(\bar{X})}{\Sigma X^2 = \Sigma X(\bar{X})}$$

or

$$b = \frac{\Sigma XY - \Sigma Y\left(\dfrac{\Sigma X}{n}\right)}{\Sigma X^2 - \Sigma X\left(\dfrac{\Sigma X}{n}\right)}$$

After we multiply the numerator and the denominator by *n*, we have:

$$b = \frac{n\Sigma XY - (\Sigma X)(\Sigma Y)}{n\Sigma X^2 - (\Sigma X)^2}$$

Returning to the Equation 1 we have:

$$\Sigma Y = na + b\Sigma X$$

or

$$n\bar{Y} = na + bn\bar{X}$$

or

$$\bar{Y} = a + b\bar{X}$$

Thus, we have (after solving for the value of b above):

$$a = \bar{Y} - b\bar{X}$$

NOTE 12.31

Derivation of Calculation Form for S_{YX}

$$S_{YX}{}^2 = \frac{1}{n-2} \Sigma(Y - \bar{Y}_C)^2$$

$$= \frac{1}{n-2} \Sigma(Y - a - bX)^2$$

$$= \frac{1}{n-2} \Sigma(Y^2 - 2aY - 2bXY + 2abX + a^2 + b^2X^2)$$

$$S_{YX}{}^2 = \frac{1}{n-2} [\Sigma Y^2 - 2a\Sigma Y - 2b\Sigma XY + 2ab\Sigma X + \Sigma a^2 + b^2\Sigma X^2]$$

But, from the second normal equation:

$$b\Sigma X^2 = \Sigma XY - a\Sigma X$$

Thus

$$S_{YX}{}^2 = \frac{1}{n-2} [\Sigma Y^2 - 2a\Sigma Y - 2b\Sigma XY + 2ab\Sigma X + na^2 + b\Sigma XY - ab\Sigma X]$$

or

$$S_{YX}{}^2 = \frac{1}{n-2} [\Sigma Y^2 - 2a\Sigma Y - b\Sigma XY + ab\Sigma X + na^2]$$

From the first normal equation:

$$b\Sigma X = \Sigma Y - na$$

Thus

$$S_{YX}{}^2 = \frac{1}{n-2} [\Sigma Y^2 - 2a\Sigma Y - b\Sigma XY + a\Sigma Y - na^2 + na^2]$$

or $\qquad S_{YX}{}^2 = \frac{1}{n-2} [\Sigma Y^2 - a\Sigma Y - b\Sigma XY]$

Thus $\qquad S_{YX} = \sqrt{\dfrac{\Sigma Y^2 - a\Sigma Y - b\Sigma XY}{n-2}}$

NOTE 12.32A

Derivation of Coefficient of Determination

Any observed value of our dependent variable, Y, can be described in terms of deviations, as follows:

$$\text{Total Deviation} = Y - \bar{Y} \qquad\qquad (a)$$

This is the total vertical distance or deviation between this individual value of Y and the mean value of Y.

$$\text{"Explained" Deviation} = \bar{Y}_c - \bar{Y} \qquad\qquad (b)$$

This is the amount of the total deviation that is "explained," or removed, by the use of the regression line. The fact that it is not zero means that the regression line at least appears to be better than the horizontal $\bar{Y}$ line.

$$\text{"Unexplained" Deviation} = Y - \bar{Y}_c \qquad\qquad (c)$$

This is the remaining deviation even after we apply the regression line. The fact that it is not zero means that the regression line fails to "explain" all the original deviation; however, the use of the least squares criterion assures that the regression line is better than the horizontal $\bar{Y}$ line in "explaining Y values.

It is apparent that the total deviation (distance) between Y and $\bar{Y}$ must be such that

$$\text{"Total"} = \text{"Explained"} + \text{"Unexplained"}$$

or $\qquad Y - \bar{Y} = (\bar{Y}_c - \bar{Y}) + (Y - \bar{Y}_c)$

or $\qquad Y - \bar{Y} = \bar{Y}_c - \bar{Y} + Y - \bar{Y}_c = Y - \bar{Y}$

But in regression analysis we do not use deviations as above. Instead, we speak of the summations of squared deviations. Hence, our expression

$$(Y - \bar{Y}) = (\bar{Y}_c - \bar{Y}) + (Y - \bar{Y}_c)$$

is restated as

$$\text{Total Variation} = \text{Explained Variation} + \text{Unexplained Variation}$$

or $\qquad \Sigma(Y - \bar{Y})^2 = \Sigma(\bar{Y}_c - \bar{Y})^2 + \Sigma(Y - \bar{Y}_c)^2$

Thus, since the coefficient of determination is defined as the percentage of total variability that is "explained" by the regression line, we can state $\hat{r}^2$ in several ways:

$$\hat{r}^2 = \frac{\text{Explained Variation}}{\text{Total Variation}} = \frac{\Sigma(\bar{Y}_c - \bar{Y})^2}{\Sigma(Y - \bar{Y})^2} \qquad\qquad (1)$$

or $\qquad \hat{r}^2 = \dfrac{\text{Total Variation} - \text{Unexplained Variation}}{\text{Total Variation}} \qquad\qquad (2)$

$$= \frac{\Sigma(Y - \bar{Y})^2 - \Sigma(Y - \bar{Y}_c)^2}{\Sigma(Y - \bar{Y})^2}$$

$$= \frac{\Sigma(Y - \bar{Y})^2}{\Sigma(Y - \bar{Y})^2} - \frac{\Sigma(Y - \bar{Y}_c)^2}{\Sigma(Y - \bar{Y})^2}$$

$$\hat{r}^2 = 1 - \frac{\Sigma(Y - \bar{Y}_c)^2}{\Sigma(Y - \bar{Y})^2}$$

But the careful reader will have noted that:

$$(Y - \bar{Y}) = (\bar{Y}_c - \bar{Y}) + (Y - \bar{Y}_c)$$

is obviously true. However, it needs to be proved that:

$$\Sigma(Y - \bar{Y})^2 = \Sigma(\bar{Y}_c - \bar{Y})^2 + \Sigma(Y - \bar{Y}_c)^2$$

Begin with:

$$(Y - \bar{Y}) = (\bar{Y}_c - \bar{Y}) + (Y - \bar{Y}_c)$$

Squaring both sides:

$$(Y - \bar{Y})^2 = (\bar{Y}_c - \bar{Y})^2 + (Y - \bar{Y}_c)^2 + 2(\bar{Y}_c - \bar{Y})(Y - \bar{Y}_c)$$

Then summing both sides over all observations

$$\Sigma(Y - \bar{Y})^2 = \Sigma(\bar{Y}_c - \bar{Y})^2 + \Sigma(Y - \bar{Y}_c)^2 + 2\Sigma(\bar{Y}_c - \bar{Y})(Y - \bar{Y}_c)$$

But the last term on the right is:

$$2\Sigma(a + bX - \bar{Y})(Y - a - bX)$$

or $$2a\Sigma(Y - a - bX) + 2b\Sigma X(Y - a - bX) - 2\bar{Y}\Sigma(Y - a - bX)$$

However, from the first normal equation we know that

$$\Sigma(Y - a - bX) = 0$$

And from the second that

$$\Sigma X(Y - a - bX) = 0$$

Hence, this last term on the right is zero, and:

$$\Sigma(Y - \bar{Y})^2 = \Sigma(\bar{Y}_c - \bar{Y})^2 + \Sigma(Y - \bar{Y}_c)^2$$

NOTE 12.5

Inference in Regression Analysis

The purpose of this series of notes is to show that various estimators used in regression analysis are unbiased, and to derive the variance of these estimators. In regression analysis, the values of X are selected by the researcher; they are not random variables. The values of Y *are* random variables, obtained from:

$$Y_i = \alpha + \beta X_i + \epsilon$$

where ϵ is a random variable with

$$E(\epsilon) = \mu_\epsilon = 0$$
$$\text{var }(\epsilon) = \sigma_\epsilon^2 = \sigma_{Y/X}^2$$

For convenience, $\sigma_{Y/X}^2$ will be noted σ^2 throughout the remaining notes for Chapter 12.

Several expressions which arise frequently are:

$$\Sigma(X_i - \bar{X})^2 = \Sigma X_i^2 - \frac{(\Sigma X)^2}{n} = \Sigma X_i^2 - n\bar{X}^2$$

which is similar to that developed in Note 3.34.

$$E(aX) = aE(X) \tag{2}$$

as developed in Note 5.32a.

$$E(X + Y) = E(X) + E(Y) \tag{3}$$

as developed in Note 5.32b.

$$\text{Var} (\Sigma X) = \Sigma \text{ Var } X \qquad (4)$$

if all X are independent, as developed in Note 5.32d.

$$\text{Var} (aX) = a^2 \text{ Var} (X) \qquad (5)$$

as developed in Note 5.32e.

$$\text{Var} (\Sigma aX) = a^2 \Sigma \text{ Var } X \qquad (6)$$

if all X are independent.

Substitution of any of the above expressions will be frequently encountered in this series of notes.

NOTE 12.5A

Show that a and b are *linear estimators*. A linear estimator is one which may be expressed as a linear function of the actual observations of Y.

From an intermediate result in Note 12.21b:

$$b = \frac{\Sigma X_i Y_i - \Sigma Y_i \bar{X}}{\Sigma X_i^2 - \Sigma X_i \bar{X}} = \frac{\Sigma (X_i - \bar{X}) Y_i}{\Sigma X_i^2 - \dfrac{\Sigma X_i}{n} \Sigma X_i} = \Sigma \left[\frac{X_i - \bar{X}}{\Sigma (X_i - \bar{X})^2} \right] Y_i$$

Since the terms $\left[\dfrac{X_i - \bar{X}}{\Sigma (X_i - \bar{X})^2} \right]$ are constants once the values of X are specified,

$$b = \Sigma C_i Y_i$$

where

$$C_i = \frac{X_i - X}{\Sigma (X_i - \bar{X})^2}$$

which is a linear function of the values of Y. Hence, b is a linear estimator.

To show that a is a linear estimator:

$$a = \bar{Y} - b\bar{X} = \bar{Y} - (\Sigma C_i Y_i)\bar{X} = \Sigma \frac{Y_i}{n} - \bar{X} \Sigma C_i Y_i$$

$$= \Sigma \left(\frac{Y_i}{n} - \bar{X} C_i Y_i \right) = \Sigma \left[\frac{1}{n} - \bar{X} C_i \right] Y_i$$

or

$$a = \Sigma d_i Y_i$$

where

$$d_i = \frac{1}{n} - \bar{X} C_i$$

which demonstrates that a is also a linear estimator. These definitions of C_i and d_i are used throughout this series of notes.

For use in future notes, we next develop some useful properties of the set of constants, C_i.

$$\Sigma C_i = \Sigma \left[\frac{X_i - \bar{X}}{\Sigma (X_i - \bar{X})^2} \right] = \frac{\Sigma (X_i - \bar{X})}{\Sigma (X_i - \bar{X})^2} = \frac{\Sigma X_i - \Sigma \bar{X}}{\Sigma (X_i - \bar{X})^2} = \frac{n\bar{X} - n\bar{X}}{\Sigma (X_i - \bar{X})^2}$$

or $\Sigma C_i = 0$

$$\Sigma C_i{}^2 = \Sigma \left[\frac{X_i - \bar{X}}{\Sigma(X_i - \bar{X})^2}\right]^2 = \frac{\Sigma(X_i - \bar{X})^2}{[\Sigma(X_i - \bar{X})^2]^2} = \frac{1}{\Sigma(\bar{X}_i - \bar{X})^2}$$

$$\Sigma C_i X_i = \Sigma \left[\frac{X_i - \bar{X}}{\Sigma(X_i - \bar{X})^2}\right] X_i = \frac{\Sigma X_i{}^2 - \bar{X}\Sigma X_i}{\Sigma(X_i - \bar{X})^2} = \frac{\Sigma X_i{}^2 - \dfrac{(\Sigma X)^2}{n}}{\Sigma(X_i - \bar{X})^2}$$

or $$\Sigma C_i X_i = \frac{\Sigma(X_i - \bar{X})^2}{\Sigma(X_i - \bar{X})^2} = 1$$

NOTE 12.5B

Show that b is an unbiased estimator of β.

$$b = \Sigma C_i Y_i$$
$$E(b) = E(\Sigma C_i Y_i) = \Sigma C_i E(Y_i) = \Sigma C_i(\alpha + \beta X_i)$$
$$= \alpha \Sigma C_i + \beta \Sigma C_i X_i = \alpha(0) + \beta(1)$$
or $$E(b) = \beta$$

Showing that b is an unbiased estimator of β.

NOTE 12.5C

Show that a is an unbiased estimator of α.

$$a = \Sigma d_i Y_i = \Sigma \left(\frac{1}{n} - \bar{X}C_i\right)(\alpha + \beta X_i + \epsilon)$$

$$= \Sigma \left(\frac{\alpha}{n} + \frac{\beta X_i}{n} + \frac{\epsilon}{n} - \bar{X}C_i\alpha - \bar{X}C_i\beta X_i - \bar{X}C_i\epsilon\right)$$

$$= \frac{\Sigma \alpha}{n} + \beta \frac{\Sigma X_i}{n} + \frac{\Sigma \epsilon}{n} - \bar{X}\alpha \Sigma C_i - \beta \bar{X}\Sigma C_i X_i - \bar{X}\Sigma C_i\epsilon$$

$$= \alpha + \beta \bar{X} + \frac{\Sigma \epsilon}{n} - \bar{X}\alpha(0) - \beta \bar{X}(1) - \bar{X}\Sigma C_i\epsilon$$

$$= \alpha + \frac{\Sigma \epsilon}{n} - \bar{X}\Sigma C_i\epsilon$$

$$E(a) = E\left(\alpha + \frac{\Sigma \epsilon}{n} - \bar{X}\Sigma C_i\epsilon\right) = \alpha + \frac{\Sigma E(\epsilon)}{n} - \bar{X}\Sigma C_i E(\epsilon)$$

But since $E(\epsilon) = 0$,

$$E(a) = \alpha + 0 + 0 = \alpha$$

and a is an unbiased estimator of α

NOTE 12.51A

Variance of b

$$b = \Sigma C_i Y_i$$
$$\text{var } b = \text{var } (\Sigma C_i Y_i) = \Sigma \text{ var } (C_i Y_i)$$

$$= \Sigma C_i^2 \, \text{var} \, (Y_i) = \Sigma C_i^2 \, \text{var} \, (\alpha + \beta X_i + \epsilon)$$
$$= \Sigma C_i^2 \, [\text{var} \, (\alpha) + \text{var} \, (\beta X_i) + \text{var} \, (\epsilon)]$$
$$= \Sigma C_i^2 (0 + 0 + \sigma^2) = \sigma^2 \Sigma C_i^2$$

or
$$\text{var} \, (b) = \sigma_b^2 = \sigma^2 \left(\frac{1}{\Sigma(X_i - \bar{X})^2} \right)$$

Since
$$\Sigma C_i^2 = \frac{1}{\Sigma(X_i - \bar{X})^2}$$

Alternatively,

$$\sigma_b^2 = \frac{\sigma^2}{\Sigma X_i^2 - \dfrac{(\Sigma X_i)^2}{n}}$$

which is estimated by

$$S_b^2 = \frac{S_{YX}^2}{\Sigma X_i^2 - \dfrac{(\Sigma X_i)^2}{n}}$$

NOTE 12.51B

Variance of a

$$a = \Sigma d_i Y_i = \Sigma \left(\frac{1}{n} - \bar{X} C_i \right) Y_i$$

$$\text{var} \, (a) = \text{var} \left[\Sigma \left(\frac{1}{n} - \bar{X} C_i \right) Y_i \right] = \Sigma \left(\frac{1}{n} - \bar{X} C_i \right)^2 \text{var} \, Y_i$$

$$= \Sigma \left(\frac{1}{n^2} - \frac{2\bar{X} C_i}{n} + C_i^2 \bar{X}^2 \right) \sigma^2$$

$$= \sigma^2 \left(\frac{n}{n^2} - 2 \frac{\bar{X}}{n} \Sigma C_i + \bar{X}^2 \Sigma C_i^2 \right)$$

$$= \sigma^2 \left(\frac{1}{n} - 0 + \frac{\bar{X}^2}{\Sigma(X_i - \bar{X})^2} \right) = \frac{\sigma^2}{n} + \frac{\sigma^2 \bar{X}^2}{\Sigma(X_i - \bar{X})^2}$$

Substituting

$$\text{var} \, (b) = \frac{\sigma^2}{\Sigma(X_i - \bar{X})^2}$$

$$\text{var} \, (a) = \frac{\sigma^2}{n} + \bar{X}^2 \, \text{var} \, (b)$$

$$= \left(\frac{\Sigma(X_i - \bar{X})^2}{n} + \bar{X}^2 \right) \text{var} \, (b)$$

$$= \left(\frac{\Sigma X_i^2 - \dfrac{(\Sigma X_i)^2}{n} + \dfrac{(\Sigma X_i)^2}{n^2}}{n} \right) \text{var} \, (b)$$

$$= \sigma_b^2 \left(\frac{\Sigma X_i^2}{n} \right)$$

which is estimated by

$$s_a{}^2 = s_b{}^2 \left(\frac{\Sigma X_i{}^2}{n}\right)$$

NOTE 12.54A

Variance for Average Value of Y

When the value of X is known to be X_0 and one is making inferences about the average value of Y for the given X_0, the expression

$$Y_{c0} = a + bX_0$$

is used to estimate

$$\mu_Y|_{X0} = \alpha + \beta X_0$$

The error is the difference

$$\bar{Y}_{c0} - \mu_Y|_{X0} = a + bX_0 - (\alpha + \beta X_0)$$

The variance of this error is

$$\text{var}(\bar{Y}_{c0} - \mu_Y|_{X0}) = \text{var}(\bar{Y}_{c0}) + \text{var}(\mu_Y|_{X0})$$

but since $\mu_Y|_{X0}$ is the population constant,

$$\text{var}(\bar{Y}_{c0} - \mu_Y|_{X0}) = \text{var}(\bar{Y}_{c0})$$

$$
\begin{aligned}
\text{var}(\bar{Y}_{c0}) &= \text{var}(a + bX_0) = \text{var}(\Sigma d_i Y_i + \Sigma C_i Y_i X_0) \\
&= \text{var}[\Sigma(d_i + C_i X_0)Y_i] = \Sigma(d_i + C_i X_0)^2 \text{ var}(Y_i) \\
&= \sigma^2 \Sigma(d_i + C_i X_0)^2 \\
&= \sigma^2 \Sigma(d_i{}^2 + 2d_i C_i X_0 + C_i{}^2 X_0{}^2) \\
&= \sigma^2 \Sigma \left(\left[\frac{1}{n} - \bar{X}C_i\right]^2 + 2\left[\frac{1}{n} - \bar{X}C_i\right]C_i X_0 + C_i{}^2 X_0{}^2 \right) \\
&= \sigma^2 \Sigma \left(\frac{1}{n^2} - \frac{2\bar{X}C_i}{n} + \bar{X}^2 C_i{}^2 + 2\frac{C_i X_0}{n} - 2\bar{X}C_i{}^2 - X_0 + C_i{}^2 X_0{}^2 \right) \\
&= \sigma^2 \left(\frac{\Sigma 1}{n^2} - \frac{2\bar{X}\Sigma C_i}{n} + \bar{X}^2 \Sigma C_i{}^2 + \frac{2X_0}{n}\Sigma C_i - 2\bar{X}X_0 \Sigma C_i{}^2 + X_0{}^2 \Sigma C_i{}^2 \right) \\
&= \sigma^2 \left[\frac{n}{n^2} - \frac{2\bar{X}}{n}(0) + \frac{\bar{X}^2}{\Sigma(X_i - \bar{X})^2} + 2\frac{X_0}{n}(0) - \frac{2\bar{X}X_0}{\Sigma(X_i - \bar{X})^2} + \frac{X_0{}^2}{\Sigma(X_i - \bar{X})^2} \right] \\
&= \sigma^2 \left[\frac{1}{n} + \frac{1}{\Sigma(X_i - \bar{X})^2}(\bar{X}^2 - 2\bar{X}X_0 + X_0{}^2) \right] \\
&= \sigma^2 \left[\frac{1}{n} + \frac{(X_0 - \bar{X})^2}{\Sigma(X_0 - \bar{X})^2} \right]
\end{aligned}
$$

NOTE 12.54B

Variance for a Forecast of Y

When the value of X is known to be X_0 and one is making inferences about the forecast value of Y for the given X_0, the expression

$$\bar{Y}_{c0} = a + bX_0$$

is used to estimate

$$Y_0 = \alpha + \beta X_0 + \epsilon$$

The error is the difference

$$\bar{Y}_{c0} - Y_0 = a + bX_0 - (\alpha + \beta X_0 + \epsilon)$$
$$\text{var}(\bar{Y}_{c0} - Y_0) = \text{var}(a + bX_0) + \text{var}(\alpha + \beta X_0 + \epsilon)$$

because $(a + bX_0)$ and $(\alpha + \beta X_0 + \epsilon)$ are independent, because $(a + bX_0)$ depends upon the n observations, and $(\alpha + \beta X_0 + \epsilon)$ depends upon the future observation.

Thus,

$$\text{var}(\bar{Y}_{c0} - Y_0) = \text{var}(\bar{Y}_{c0}) + \sigma^2$$
$$= \sigma^2 \left(\frac{1}{n} + \frac{(X_0 - \bar{X})^2}{\Sigma(X_i - \bar{X})^2}\right) + \sigma^2$$
$$= \sigma^2 \left(1 + \frac{1}{n} + \frac{(X_0 - \bar{X})^2}{\Sigma(X_i - \bar{X})^2}\right)$$

It is useful to recognize that the variance for the *average* value of Y reflects the variation in the sample regression line if one were to take repeated samples of size n. The variance for a forecast of Y includes the variance in the regression line, and also the variance of an individual Y value about its mean. This second variance accounts for the "1" in the variance expression for forecast.

NOTE 16.43

To demonstrate that the act with the best (assumed to be highest) EMV is the same act that has the lowest EOL, we first show that, for any act,

$$\text{EPC} = \text{EMV}_j + \text{EOL}_j$$

We use these symbols:

EPC = Expected Profit Under Certainty
EMV_j = Expected Monetary Value of Act j
EOL_j = Expected Opportunity Loss of Act j
X_{ij} = Payoff if event i occurs and act j is selected
$\hat{X}_i$ = Best payoff for event i
P_i = Probability of event i

Then:

$$\text{EMV}_j = \sum_i X_{ij} P_i \quad \text{by definition}$$

$$\text{EPC} = \sum_i \hat{X}_i P_i \quad \text{by definition}$$

Since the opportunity loss corresponding to X_{ij} is $(\hat{X}_i - X_{ij})$:

$$\text{EOL}_j = \sum_i (\hat{X}_i - X_{ij})P_i = \sum_i \hat{X}_i P_i - \sum_i X_{ij} P_i$$

or

$$EOL_j = EPC - EMV_j$$

and

$$EPC = EMV_j + EOL_j$$

Hence, the sum of EMV_j and EOL_j is constant for all acts. It follows that the act with the best (highest) EMV must have the best (lowest) EOL.

This also implies that the value of EOL^*, the best EOL, is equal to EVPI, which was defined as:

$$EVPI = EPC - EMV^*$$

but since $EPC = EMV^* + EOL^*$ it follows that $EOL^* = EPC - EMV^*$ and $EOL^* = EVPI$.

Squares, Square Roots, and Reciprocals

TO FIND THE SQUARE ROOT OF A NUMBER

1. If the number is in the table (whole numbers from 1 to 1,000), the number may be read directly from the table.
2. If the number is ten times larger than a number shown in the table, use the column headed $\sqrt{10N}$ and read the square root directly from the table. For example, the square root of 990 is 31.46427, which is found by reading the $\sqrt{10N}$ column across from 99.
3. For numbers larger than those shown in the table, the following rules may be used:

$$\sqrt{100\ N} = 10\sqrt{N} \qquad \text{Example:} \quad \sqrt{24,900} = \sqrt{100(249)} = 10\sqrt{249}$$
$$= 10(15.77973) = 157.7973$$

$$\sqrt{10,000\ N} = 100\sqrt{N} \qquad \text{Example:} \ \sqrt{3,150,000} = 100\sqrt{315} = 1,774.824$$

4. For numbers smaller than those shown in the table, the following rules may be used:

$$\sqrt{(0.01)\ N} = 0.1\sqrt{N} \qquad \text{Example:} \quad \sqrt{0.83} = \sqrt{(0.01)(83)} = 0.1\sqrt{83}$$
$$= 0.9110434$$

$$\sqrt{(0.0001)\ N} = 0.01\sqrt{N} \qquad \text{Example:} \ \sqrt{0.0960} = \sqrt{(0.0001)(960)}$$
$$= 0.3098387$$

5. For numbers within the range of the table, the rules may also be used for fractional values.

$$\sqrt{3.76} = \sqrt{(.01)(376)} = 0.1\sqrt{376} = 1.939072$$

Squares, Square Roots, and Reciprocals 1–1,000*

N	N²	√N	√10N	1/N
1	1	1.000 000	3.162 278	1.0000000
2	4	1.414 214	4.472 136	.5000000
3	9	1.732 051	5.477 226	.3333333
4	16	2.000 000	6.324 555	.2500000
5	25	2.236 068	7.071 068	.2000000
6	36	2.449 490	7.745 967	.1666667
7	49	2.645 751	8.366 600	.1428571
8	64	2.828 427	8.944 272	.1250000
9	81	3.000 000	9.486 833	.1111111
10	100	3.162 278	10.00000	.1000000
11	121	3.316 625	10.48809	.09090909
12	144	3.464 102	10.95445	.08333333
13	169	3.605 551	11.40175	.07692308
14	196	3.741 657	11.83216	.07142857
15	225	3.872 983	12.24745	.06666667
16	256	4.000 000	12.64911	.06250000
17	289	4.123 106	13.03840	.05882353
18	324	4.242 641	13.41641	.05555556
19	361	4.358 899	13.78405	.05263158
20	400	4.472 136	14.14214	.05000000
21	441	4.582 576	14.49138	.04761905
22	484	4.690 416	14.83240	.04545455
23	529	4.795 832	15.16575	.04347826
24	576	4.898 979	15.49193	.04166667
25	625	5.000 000	15.81139	.04000000
26	676	5.099 020	16.12452	.03846154
27	729	5.196 152	16.43168	.03703704
28	784	5.291 503	16.73320	.03571429
29	841	5.385 165	17.02939	.03448276
30	900	5.477 226	17.32051	.03333333
31	961	5.567 764	17.60682	.03225806
32	1 024	5.656 854	17.88854	.03125000
33	1 089	5.744 563	18.16590	.03030303
34	1 156	5.830 952	18.43909	.02941176
35	1 225	5.916 080	18.70829	.02857143
36	1 296	6.000 000	18.97367	.02777778
37	1 369	6.082 763	19.23538	.02702703
38	1 444	6.164 414	19.49359	.02631579
39	1 521	6.244 998	19.74842	.02564103
40	1 600	6.324 555	20.00000	.02500000
41	1 681	6.403 124	20.24846	.02439024
42	1 764	6.480 741	20.49390	.02380952
43	1 849	6.557 439	20.73644	.02325581
44	1 936	6.633 250	20.97618	.02272727
45	2 025	6.708 204	21.21320	.02222222
46	2 116	6.782 330	21.44761	.02173913
47	2 209	6.855 655	21.67948	.02127660
48	2 304	6.928 203	21.90890	.02083333
49	2 401	7.000 000	22.13594	.02040816
50	2 500	7.071 068	22.36068	.02000000

N	N²	√N	√10N	1/N .0
50	2 500	7.071 068	22.36068	2000000
51	2 601	7.141 428	22.58318	1960784
52	2 704	7.211 103	22.80351	1923077
53	2 809	7.280 110	23.02173	1886792
54	2 916	7.348 469	23.23790	1851852
55	3 025	7.416 198	23.45208	1818182
56	3 136	7.483 315	23.66432	1785714
57	3 249	7.549 834	23.87467	1754386
58	3 364	7.615 773	24.08319	1724138
59	3 481	7.681 146	24.28992	1694915
60	3 600	7.745 967	24.49490	1666667
61	3 721	7.810 250	24.69818	1639344
62	3 844	7.874 008	24.89980	1612903
63	3 969	7.937 254	25.09980	1587302
64	4 096	8.000 000	25.29822	1562500
65	4 225	8.062 258	25.49510	1538462
66	4 356	8.124 038	25.69047	1515152
67	4 489	8.185 353	25.88436	1492537
68	4 624	8.246 211	26.07681	1470588
69	4 761	8.306 624	26.26785	1449275
70	4 900	8.366 600	26.45751	1428571
71	5 041	8.426 150	26.64583	1408451
72	5 184	8.485 281	26.83282	1388889
73	5 329	8.544 004	27.01851	1369863
74	5 476	8.602 325	27.20294	1351351
75	5 625	8.660 254	27.38613	1333333
76	5 776	8.717 798	27.56810	1315789
77	5 929	8.774 964	27.74887	1298701
78	6 084	8.831 761	27.92848	1282051
79	6 241	8.888 194	28.10694	1265823
80	6 400	8.944 272	28.28427	1250000
81	6 561	9.000 000	28.46050	1234568
82	6 724	9.055 385	28.63564	1219512
83	6 889	9.110 434	28.80972	1204819
84	7 056	9.165 151	28.98275	1190476
85	7 225	9.219 544	29.15476	1176471
86	7 396	9.273 618	29.32576	1162791
87	7 569	9.327 379	29.49576	1149425
88	7 744	9.380 832	29.66479	1136364
89	7 921	9.433 981	29.83287	1123596
90	8 100	9.486 833	30.00000	1111111
91	8 281	9.539 392	30.16621	1098901
92	8 464	9.591 663	30.33150	1086957
93	8 649	9.643 651	30.49590	1075269
94	8 836	9.695 360	30.65942	1063830
95	9 025	9.746 794	30.82207	1052632
96	9 216	9.797 959	30.98387	1041667
97	9 409	9.848 858	31.14482	1030928
98	9 604	9.899 495	31.30495	1020408
99	9 801	9.949 874	31.46427	1010101
100	10 000	10.00000	31.62278	1000000

* From Frederick E. Croxton, Dudley J. Cowden, and Ben W. Bolch, *Practical Business Statistics,* 4th Ed. © 1969, pp. 415–29. Reprinted by permission of Prentice-Hall, Inc., Englewood Cliffs, N.J.

Squares, Square Roots, and Reciprocals 1–1,000 (*continued*)

N	N^2	$\sqrt{N}$	$\sqrt{10N}$	$1/N$ .0	N	N^2	$\sqrt{N}$	$\sqrt{10N}$	$1/N$ .00
100	10 000	10.00000	31.62278	10000000	150	22 500	12.24745	38.72983	6666667
101	10 201	10.04988	31.78050	09900990	151	22 801	12.28821	38.85872	6622517
102	10 404	10.09950	31.93744	09803922	152	23 104	12.32883	38.98718	6578947
103	10 609	10.14889	32.09361	09708738	153	23 409	12.36932	39.11521	6535948
104	10 816	10.19804	32.24903	09615385	154	23 716	12.40967	39.24283	6493506
105	11 025	10.24695	32.40370	09523810	155	24 025	12.44990	39.37004	6451613
106	11 236	10.29563	32.55764	09433962	156	24 336	12.49000	39.49684	6410256
107	11 449	10.34408	32.71085	09345794	157	24 649	12.52996	39.62323	6369427
108	11 664	10.39230	32.86335	09259259	158	24 964	12.56981	39.74921	6329114
109	11 881	10.44031	33.01515	09174312	159	25 281	12.60952	39.87480	6289308
110	12 100	10.48809	33.16625	09090909	160	25 600	12.64911	40.00000	6250000
111	12 321	10.53565	33.31666	09009009	161	25 921	12.68858	40.12481	6211180
112	12 544	10.58301	33.46640	08928571	162	26 244	12.72792	40.24922	6172840
113	12 769	10.63015	33.61547	08849558	163	26 569	12.76715	40.37326	6134969
114	12 996	10.67708	33.76389	08771930	164	26 896	12.80625	40.49691	6097561
115	13 225	10.72381	33.91165	08695652	165	27 225	12.84523	40.62019	6060606
116	13 456	10.77033	34.05877	08620690	166	27 556	12.88410	40.74310	6024096
117	13 689	10.81665	34.20526	08547009	167	27 889	12.92285	40.86563	5988024
118	13 924	10.86278	34.35113	08474576	168	28 224	12.96148	40.98780	5952381
119	14 161	10.90871	34.49638	08403361	169	28 561	13.00000	41.10961	5917160
120	14 400	10.95445	34.64102	08333333	170	28 900	13.03840	41.23106	5882353
121	14 641	11.00000	34.78505	08264463	171	29 241	13.07670	41.35215	5847953
122	14 884	11.04536	34.92850	08196721	172	29 584	13.11488	41.47288	5813953
123	15 129	11.09054	35.07136	08130081	173	29 929	13.15295	41.59327	5780347
124	15 376	11.13553	35.21363	08064516	174	30 276	13.19091	41.71331	5747126
125	15 625	11.18034	35.35534	08000000	175	30 625	13.22876	41.83300	5714286
126	15 876	11.22497	35.49648	07936508	176	30 976	13.26650	41.95235	5681818
127	16 129	11.26943	35.63706	07874016	177	31 329	13.30413	42.07137	5649718
128	16 384	11.31371	35.77709	07812500	178	31 684	13.34166	42.19005	5617978
129	16 641	11.35782	35.91657	07751938	179	32 041	13.37909	42.30839	5586592
130	16 900	11.40175	36.05551	07692308	180	32 400	13.41641	42.42641	5555556
131	17 161	11.44552	36.19392	07633588	181	32 761	13.45362	42.54409	5524862
132	17 424	11.48913	36.33180	07575758	182	33 124	13.49074	42.66146	5494505
133	17 689	11.53256	36.46917	07518797	183	33 489	13.52775	42.77850	5464481
134	17 956	11.57584	36.60601	07462687	184	33 856	13.56466	42.89522	5434783
135	18 225	11.61895	36.74235	07407407	185	34 225	13.60147	43.01163	5405405
136	18 496	11.66190	36.87818	07352941	186	34 596	13.63818	43.12772	5376344
137	18 769	11.70470	37.01351	07299270	187	34 969	13.67479	43.24350	5347594
138	19 044	11.74734	37.14835	07246377	188	35 344	13.71131	43.35897	5319149
139	19 321	11.78983	37.28270	07194245	189	35 721	13.74773	43.47413	5291005
140	19 600	11.83216	37.41657	07142857	190	36 100	13.78405	43.58899	5263158
141	19 881	11.87434	37.54997	07092199	191	36 481	13.82027	43.70355	5235602
142	20 164	11.91638	37.68289	07042254	192	36 864	13.85641	43.81780	5208333
143	20 449	11.95826	37.81534	06993007	193	37 249	13.89244	43.93177	5181347
144	20 736	12.00000	37.94733	06944444	194	37 636	13.92839	44.04543	5154639
145	21 025	12.04159	38.07887	06896552	195	38 025	13.96424	44.15880	5128205
146	21 316	12.08305	38.20995	06849315	196	38 416	14.00000	44.27189	5102041
147	21 609	12.12436	38.34058	06802721	197	38 809	14.03567	44.38468	5076142
148	21 904	12.16553	38.47077	06756757	198	39 204	14.07125	44.49719	5050505
149	22 201	12.20656	38.60052	06711409	199	39 601	14.10674	44.60942	5025126
150	22 500	12.24745	38.72983	06666667	200	40 000	14.14214	44.72136	5000000

Squares, Square Roots, and Reciprocals 1–1,000 (*continued*)

N	N²	√N	√10N	1/N .00	N	N²	√N	√10N	1/N .00
200	40 000	14.14214	44.72136	5000000	250	62 500	15.81139	50.00000	4000000
201	40 401	14.17745	44.83302	4975124	251	63 001	15.84298	50.09990	3984064
202	40 804	14.21267	44.94441	4950495	252	63 504	15.87451	50.19960	3968254
203	41 209	14.24781	45.05552	4926108	253	64 009	15.90597	50.29911	3952569
204	41 616	14.28286	45.16636	4901961	254	64 516	15.93738	50.39841	3937008
205	42 025	14.31782	45.27693	4878049	255	65 025	15.96872	50.49752	3921569
206	42 436	14.35270	45.38722	4854369	256	65 536	16.00000	50.59644	3906250
207	42 849	14.38749	45.49725	4830918	257	66 049	16.03122	50.69517	3891051
208	43 264	14.42221	45.60702	4807692	258	66 564	16.06238	50.79370	3875969
209	43 681	14.45683	45.71652	4784689	259	67 081	16.09348	50.89204	3861004
210	44 100	14.49138	45.82576	4761905	260	67 600	16.12452	50.99020	3846154
211	44 521	14.52584	45.93474	4739336	261	68 121	16.15549	51.08816	3831418
212	44 944	14.56022	46.04346	4716981	262	68 644	16.18641	51.18594	3816794
213	45 369	14.59452	46.15192	4694836	263	69 169	16.21727	51.28353	3802281
214	45 796	14.62874	46.26013	4672897	264	69 696	16.24808	51.38093	3787879
215	46 225	14.66288	46.36809	4651163	265	70 225	16.27882	51.47815	3773585
216	46 656	14.69694	46.47580	4629630	266	70 756	16.30951	51.57519	3759398
217	47 089	14.73092	46.58326	4608295	267	71 289	16.34013	51.67204	3745318
218	47 524	14.76482	46.69047	4587156	268	71 824	16.37071	51.76872	3731343
219	47 961	14.79865	46.79744	4566210	269	72 361	16.40122	51.86521	3717472
220	48 400	14.83240	46.90416	4545455	270	72 900	16.43168	51.96152	3703704
221	48 841	14.86607	47.01064	4524887	271	73 441	16.46208	52.05766	3690037
222	49 284	14.89966	47.11688	4504505	272	73 984	16.49242	52.15362	3676471
223	49 729	14.93318	47.22288	4484305	273	74 529	16.52271	52.24940	3663004
224	50 176	14.96663	47.32864	4464286	274	75 076	16.55295	52.34501	3649635
225	50 625	15.00000	47.43416	4444444	275	75 625	16.58312	52.44044	3636364
226	51 076	15.03330	47.53946	4424779	276	76 176	16.61325	52.53570	3623188
227	51 529	15.06652	47.64452	4405286	277	76 729	16.64332	52.63079	3610108
228	51 984	15.09967	47.74935	4385965	278	77 284	16.67333	52.72571	3597122
229	52 441	15.13275	47.85394	4366812	279	77 841	16.70329	52.82045	3584229
230	52 900	15.16575	47.95832	4347826	280	78 400	16.73320	52.91503	3571429
231	53 361	15.19868	48.06246	4329004	281	78 961	16.76305	53.00943	3558719
232	53 824	15.23155	48.16638	4310345	282	79 524	16.79286	53.10367	3546099
233	54 289	15.26434	48.27007	4291845	283	80 089	16.82260	53.19774	3533569
234	54 756	15.29706	48.37355	4273504	284	80 656	16.85230	53.29165	3521127
235	55 225	15.32971	48.47680	4255319	285	81 225	16.88194	53.38539	3508772
236	55 696	15.36229	48.57983	4237288	286	81 796	16.91153	53.47897	3496503
237	56 169	15.39480	48.68265	4219409	287	82 369	16.94107	53.57238	3484321
238	56 644	15.42725	48.78524	4201681	288	82 944	16.97056	53.66563	3472222
239	57 121	15.45962	48.88763	4184100	289	83 521	17.00000	53.75872	3460208
240	57 600	15.49193	48.98979	4166667	290	84 100	17.02939	53.85165	3448276
241	58 081	15.52417	49.09175	4149378	291	84 681	17.05872	53.94442	3436426
242	58 564	15.55635	49.19350	4132231	292	85 264	17.08801	54.03702	3424658
243	59 049	15.58846	49.29503	4115226	293	85 849	17.11724	54.12947	3412969
244	59 536	15.62050	49.39636	4098361	294	86 436	17.14643	54.22177	3401361
245	60 025	15.65248	49.49747	4081633	295	87 025	17.17556	54.31390	3389831
246	60 516	15.68439	49.59839	4065041	296	87 616	17.20465	54.40588	3378378
247	61 009	15.71623	49.69909	4048583	297	88 209	17.23369	54.49771	3367003
248	61 504	15.74802	49.79960	4032258	298	88 804	17.26268	54.58938	3355705
249	62 001	15.77973	49.89990	4016064	299	89 401	17.29162	54.68089	3344482
250	62 500	15.81139	50.00000	4000000	300	90 000	17.32051	54.77226	3333333

Squares, Square Roots, and Reciprocals 1–1,000 (continued)

N	N²	√N	√10N	1/N .00	N	N²	√N	√10N	1/N .00
300	90 000	17.32051	54.77226	3333333	350	122 500	18.70829	59.16080	2857143
301	90 601	17.34935	54.86347	3322259	351	123 201	18.73499	59.24525	2849003
302	91 204	17.37815	54.95453	3311258	352	123 904	18.76166	59.32959	2840909
303	91 809	17.40690	55.04544	3300330	353	124 609	18.78829	59.41380	2832861
304	92 416	17.43560	55.13620	3289474	354	125 316	18.81489	59.49790	2824859
305	93 025	17.46425	55.22681	3278689	355	126 025	18.84144	59.58188	2816901
306	93 636	17.49286	55.31727	3267974	356	126 736	18.86796	59.66574	2808989
307	94 249	17.52142	55.40758	3257329	357	127 449	18.89444	59.74948	2801120
308	94 864	17.54993	55.49775	3246753	358	128 164	18.92089	59.83310	2793296
309	95 481	17.57840	55.58777	3236246	359	128 881	18.94730	59.91661	2785515
310	96 100	17.60682	55.67764	3225806	360	129 600	18.97367	60.00000	2777778
311	96 721	17.63519	55.76737	3215434	361	130 321	19.00000	60.08328	2770083
312	97 344	17.66352	55.85696	3205128	362	131 044	19.02630	60.16644	2762431
313	97 969	17.69181	55.94640	3194888	363	131 769	19.05256	60.24948	2754821
314	98 596	17.72005	56.03570	3184713	364	132 496	19.07878	60.33241	2747253
315	99 225	17.74824	56.12486	3174603	365	133 225	19.10497	60.41523	2739726
316	99 856	17.77639	56.21388	3164557	366	133 956	19.13113	60.49793	2732240
317	100 489	17.80449	56.30275	3154574	367	134 689	19.15724	60.58052	2724796
318	101 124	17.83255	56.39149	3144654	368	135 424	19.18333	60.66300	2717391
319	101 761	17.86057	56.48008	3134796	369	136 161	19.20937	60.74537	2710027
320	102 400	17.88854	56.56854	3125000	370	136 900	19.23538	60.82763	2702703
321	103 041	17.91647	56.65686	3115265	371	137 641	19.26136	60.90977	2695418
322	103 684	17.94436	56.74504	3105590	372	138 384	19.28730	60.99180	2688172
323	104 329	17.97220	56.83309	3095975	373	139 129	19.31321	61.07373	2680965
324	104 976	18.00000	56.92100	3086420	374	139 876	19.33908	61.15554	2673797
325	105 625	18.02776	57.00877	3076923	375	140 625	19.36492	61.23724	2666667
326	106 276	18.05547	57.09641	3067485	376	141 376	19.39072	61.31884	2659574
327	106 929	18.08314	57.18391	3058104	377	142 129	19.41649	61.40033	2652520
328	107 584	18.11077	57.27128	3048780	378	142 884	19.44222	61.48170	2645503
329	108 241	18.13836	57.35852	3039514	379	143 641	19.46792	61.56298	2638522
330	108 900	18.16590	57.44563	3030303	380	144 400	19.49359	61.64414	2631579
331	109 561	18.19341	57.53260	3021148	381	145 161	19.51922	61.72520	2624672
332	110 224	18 22087	57.61944	3012048	382	145 924	19.54483	61.80615	2617801
333	110 889	18.24829	57.70615	3003003	383	146 689	19.57039	61.88699	2610966
334	111 556	18.27567	57.79273	2994012	384	147 456	19.59592	61.96773	2604167
335	112 225	18.30301	57.87918	2985075	385	148 225	19.62142	62.04837	2597403
336	112 896	18.33030	57.96551	2976190	386	148 996	19.64688	62.12890	2590674
337	113 569	18.35756	58.05170	2967359	387	149 769	19.67232	62.20932	2583979
338	114 244	18.38478	58.13777	2958580	388	150 544	19.69772	62.28965	2577320
339	114 921	18.41195	58.22371	2949853	389	151 321	19.72308	62.36986	2570694
340	115 600	18.43909	58.30952	2941176	390	152 100	19.74842	62.44998	2564103
341	116 281	18.46619	58.39521	2932551	391	152 881	19.77372	62.52999	2557545
342	116 964	18.49324	58.48077	2923977	392	153 664	19.79899	62.60990	2551020
343	117 649	18.52026	58.56620	2915452	393	154 449	19.82423	62.68971	2544529
344	118 336	18.54724	58.65151	2906977	394	155 236	19.84943	62.76942	2538071
345	119 025	18.57418	58.73670	2898551	395	156 025	19.87461	62.84903	2531646
346	119 716	18.60108	58.82176	2890173	396	156 816	19.89975	62.92853	2525253
347	120 409	18.62794	58.90671	2881844	397	157 609	19.92486	63.00794	2518892
348	121 104	18.65476	58.99152	2873563	398	158 404	19.94994	63.08724	2512563
349	121 801	18.68154	59.07622	2865330	399	159 201	19.97498	63.16645	2506266
350	122 500	18.70829	59.16080	2857143	400	160 000	20.00000	63.24555	2500000

Squares, Square Roots, and Reciprocals 1–1,000 (continued)

N	N²	$\sqrt{N}$	$\sqrt{10N}$	1/N .00	N	N²	$\sqrt{N}$	$\sqrt{10N}$	1/N .00
400	160 000	20.00000	63.24555	2500000	450	202 500	21.21320	67.08204	2222222
401	160 801	20.02498	63.32456	2493766	451	203 401	21.23676	67.15653	2217295
402	161 604	20.04994	63.40347	2487562	452	204 304	21.26029	67.23095	2212389
403	162 409	20.07486	63.48228	2481390	453	205 209	21.28380	67.30527	2207506
404	163 216	20.09975	63.56099	2475248	454	206 116	21.30728	67.37952	2202643
405	164 025	20.12461	63.63961	2469136	455	207 025	21.33073	67.45369	2197802
406	164 836	20.14944	63.71813	2463054	456	207 936	21.35416	67.52777	2192982
407	165 649	20.17424	63.79655	2457002	457	208 849	21.37756	67.60178	2188184
408	166 464	20.19901	63.87488	2450980	458	209 764	21.40093	67.67570	2183406
409	167 281	20.22375	63.95311	2444988	459	210 681	21.42429	67.74954	2178649
410	168 100	20.24846	64.03124	2439024	460	211 600	21.44761	67.82330	2173913
411	168 921	20.27313	64.10928	2433090	461	212 521	21.47091	67.89698	2169197
412	169 744	20.29778	64.18723	2427184	462	213 444	21.49419	67.97058	2164502
413	170 569	20.32240	64.26508	2421308	463	214 369	21.51743	68.04410	2159827
414	171 396	20.34699	64.34283	2415459	464	215 296	21.54066	68.11755	2155172
415	172 225	20.37155	64.42049	2409639	465	216 225	21.56386	68.19091	2150538
416	173 056	20.39608	64.49806	2403846	466	217 156	21.58703	68.26419	2145923
417	173 889	20.42058	64.57554	2398082	467	218 089	21.61018	68.33740	2141328
418	174 724	20.44505	64.65292	2392344	468	219 024	21.63331	68.41053	2136752
419	175 561	20.46949	64.73021	2386635	469	219 961	21.65641	68.48357	2132196
420	176 400	20.49390	64.80741	2380952	470	220 900	21.67948	68.55655	2127660
421	177 241	20.51828	64.88451	2375297	471	221 841	21.70253	68.62944	2123142
422	178 084	20.54264	64.96153	2369668	472	222 784	21.72556	68.70226	2118644
423	178 929	20.56696	65.03845	2364066	473	223 729	21.74856	68.77500	2114165
424	179 776	20.59126	65.11528	2358491	474	224 676	21.77154	68.84766	2109705
425	180 625	20.61553	65.19202	2352941	475	225 625	21.79449	68.92024	2105263
426	181 476	20.63977	65.26868	2347418	476	226 576	21.81742	68.99275	2100840
427	182 329	20.66398	65.34524	2341920	477	227 529	21.84033	69.06519	2096436
428	183 184	20.68816	65.42171	2336449	478	228 484	21.86321	69.13754	2092050
429	184 041	20.71232	65.49809	2331002	479	229 441	21.88607	69.20983	2087683
430	184 900	20.73644	65.57439	2325581	480	230 400	21.90890	69.28203	2083333
431	185 761	20.76054	65.65059	2320186	481	231 361	21.93171	69.35416	2079002
432	186 624	20.78461	65.72671	2314815	482	232 324	21.95450	69.42622	2074689
433	187 489	20.80865	65.80274	2309469	483	233 289	21.97726	69.49820	2070393
434	188 356	20.83267	65.87868	2304147	484	234 256	22.00000	69.57011	2066116
435	189 225	20.85665	65.95453	2298851	485	235 225	22.02272	69.64194	2061856
436	190 096	20.88061	66.03030	2293578	486	236 196	22.04541	69.71370	2057613
437	190 969	20.90454	66.10598	2288330	487	237 169	22.06808	69.78539	2053388
438	191 844	20.92845	66.18157	2283105	488	238 144	22.09072	69.85700	2049180
439	192 721	20.95233	66.25708	2277904	489	239 121	22.11334	69.92853	2044990
440	193 600	20.97618	66.33250	2272727	490	240 100	22.13594	70.00000	2040816
441	194 481	21.00000	66.40783	2267574	491	241 081	22.15852	70.07139	2036660
442	195 364	21.02380	66.48308	2262443	492	242 064	22.18107	70.14271	2032520
443	196 249	21.04757	66.55825	2257336	493	243 049	22.20360	70.21396	2028398
444	197 136	21.07131	66.63332	2252252	494	244 036	22.22611	70.28513	2024291
445	198 025	21.09502	66.70832	2247191	495	245 025	22.24860	70.35624	2020202
446	198 916	21.11871	66.78323	2242152	496	246 016	22.27106	70.42727	2016129
447	199 809	21.14237	66.85806	2237136	497	247 009	22.29350	70.49823	2012072
448	200 704	21.16601	66.93280	2232143	498	248 004	22.31591	70.56912	2008032
449	201 601	21.18962	67.00746	2227171	499	249 001	22.33831	70.63993	2004008
450	202 500	21.21320	67.08204	2222222	500	250 000	22.36068	70.71068	2000000

Squares, Square Roots, and Reciprocals 1–1,000 (*continued*)

N	N^2	$\sqrt{N}$	$\sqrt{10N}$	$1/N$ .00	N	N^2	$\sqrt{N}$	$\sqrt{10N}$	$1/N$ .00
500	250 000	22.36068	70.71068	2000000	550	302 500	23.45208	74.16198	1818182
501	251 001	22.38303	70.78135	1996008	551	303 601	23.47339	74.22937	1814882
502	252 004	22.40536	70.85196	1992032	552	304 704	23.49468	74.29670	1811594
503	253 009	22.42766	70.92249	1988072	553	305 809	23.51595	74.36397	1808318
504	254 016	22.44994	70.99296	1984127	554	306 916	23.53720	74.43118	1805054
505	255 025	22.47221	71.06335	1980198	555	308 025	23.55844	74.49832	1801802
506	256 036	22.49444	71.13368	1976285	556	309 136	23.57965	74.56541	1798561
507	257 049	22.51666	71.20393	1972387	557	310 249	23.60085	74.63243	1795332
508	258 064	22.53886	71.27412	1968504	558	311 364	23.62202	74.69940	1792115
509	259 081	22.56103	71.34424	1964637	559	312 481	23.64318	74.76630	1788909
510	260 100	22.58318	71.41428	1960784	560	313 600	23.66432	74.83315	1785714
511	261 121	22.60531	71.48426	1956947	561	314 721	23.68544	74.89993	1782531
512	262 144	22.62742	71.55418	1953125	562	315 844	23.70654	74.96666	1779359
513	263 169	22.64950	71.62402	1949318	563	316 969	23.72762	75.03333	1776199
514	264 196	22.67157	71.69379	1945525	564	318 096	23.74868	75.09993	1773050
515	265 225	22.69361	71.76350	1941748	565	319 225	23.76973	75.16648	1769912
516	266 256	22.71563	71.83314	1937984	566	320 356	23.79075	75.23297	1766784
517	267 289	22.73763	71.90271	1934236	567	321 489	23.81176	75.29940	1763668
518	268 324	22.75961	71.97222	1930502	568	322 624	23.83275	75.36577	1760563
519	269 361	22.78157	72.04165	1926782	569	323 761	23.85372	75.43209	1757469
520	270 400	22.80351	72.11103	1923077	570	324 900	23.87467	75.49834	1754386
521	271 441	22.82542	72.18033	1919386	571	326 041	23.89561	75.56454	1751313
522	272 484	22.84732	72.24957	1915709	572	327 184	23.91652	75.63068	1748252
523	273 529	22.86919	72.31874	1912046	573	328 329	23.93742	75.69676	1745201
524	274 576	22.89105	72.38784	1908397	574	329 476	23.95830	75.76279	1742160
525	275 625	22.91288	72.45688	1904762	575	330 625	23.97916	75.82875	1739130
526	276 676	22.93469	72.52586	1901141	576	331 776	24.00000	75.89466	1736111
527	277 729	22.95648	72.59477	1897533	577	332 929	24.02082	75.96052	1733102
528	278 784	22.97825	72.66361	1893939	578	334 084	24.04163	76.02631	1730104
529	279 841	23.00000	72.73239	1890359	579	335 241	24.06242	76.09205	1727116
530	280 900	23.02173	72.80110	1886792	580	336 400	24.08319	76.15773	1724138
531	281 961	23.04344	72.86975	1883239	581	337 561	24.10394	76.22336	1721170
532	283 024	23.06513	72.93833	1879699	582	338 724	24.12468	76.28892	1718213
533	284 089	23.08679	73.00685	1876173	583	339 889	24.14539	76.35444	1715266
534	285 156	23.10844	73.07530	1872659	584	341 056	24.16609	76.41989	1712329
535	286 225	23.13007	73.14369	1869159	585	342 225	24.18677	76.48529	1709402
536	287 296	23.15167	73.21202	1865672	586	343 396	24.20744	76.55064	1706485
537	288 369	23.17326	73.28028	1862197	587	344 569	24.22808	76.61593	1703578
538	289 444	23.19483	73.34848	1858736	588	345 744	24.24871	76.68116	1700680
539	290 521	23.21637	73.41662	1855288	589	346 921	24.26932	76.74634	1697793
540	291 600	23.23790	73.48469	1851852	590	348 100	24.28992	76.81146	1694915
541	292 681	23.25941	73.55270	1848429	591	349 281	24.31049	76.87652	1692047
542	293 764	23.28089	73.62065	1845018	592	350 464	24.33105	76.94154	1689189
543	294 849	23.30236	73.68853	1841621	593	351 649	24.35159	77.00649	1686341
544	295 936	23.32381	73.75636	1838235	594	352 836	24.37212	77.07140	1683502
545	297 025	23.34524	73.82412	1834862	595	354 025	24.39262	77.13624	1680672
546	298 116	23.36664	73.89181	1831502	596	355 216	24.41311	77.20104	1677852
547	299 209	23.38803	73.95945	1828154	597	356 409	24.43358	77.26578	1675042
548	300 304	23.40940	74.02702	1824818	598	357 604	24.45404	77.33046	1672241
549	301 401	23.43075	74.09453	1821494	599	358 801	24.47448	77.39509	1669449
550	302 500	23.45208	74.16198	1818182	600	360 000	24.49490	77.45967	1666667

Squares, Square Roots, and Reciprocals 1–1,000 (*continued*)

N	N^2	$\sqrt{N}$	$\sqrt{10N}$	$1/N$ .00	N	N^2	$\sqrt{N}$	$\sqrt{10N}$	$1/N$ .00
600	360 000	24.49490	77.45967	1666667	650	422 500	25.49510	80.62258	1538462
601	361 201	24.51530	77.52419	1663894	651	423 801	25.51470	80.68457	1536098
602	362 404	24.53569	77.58866	1661130	652	425 104	25.53429	80.74652	1533742
603	363 609	24.55606	77.65307	1658375	653	426 409	25.55386	80.80842	1531394
604	364 816	24.57641	77.71744	1655629	654	427 716	25.57342	80.87027	1529052
605	366 025	24.59675	77.78175	1652893	655	429 025	25.59297	80.93207	1526718
606	367 236	24.61707	77.84600	1650165	656	430 336	25.61250	80.99383	1524390
607	368 449	24.63737	77.91020	1647446	657	431 649	25.63201	81.05554	1522070
608	369 664	24.65766	77.97435	1644737	658	432 964	25.65151	81.11720	1519757
609	370 881	24.67793	78.03845	1642036	659	434 281	25.67100	81.17881	1517451
610	372 100	24.69818	78.10250	1639344	660	435 600	25.69047	81.24038	1515152
611	373 321	24.71841	78.16649	1636661	661	436 921	25.70992	81.30191	1512859
612	374 544	24.73863	78.23043	1633987	662	438 244	25.72936	81.36338	1510574
613	375 769	24.75884	78.29432	1631321	663	439 569	25.74879	81.42481	1508296
614	376 996	24.77902	78.35815	1628664	664	440 896	25.76820	81.48620	1506024
615	378 225	24.79919	78.42194	1626016	665	442 225	25.78759	81.54753	1503759
616	379 456	24.81935	78.48567	1623377	666	443 556	25.80698	81.60882	1501502
617	380 689	24.83948	78.54935	1620746	667	444 889	25.82634	81.67007	1499250
618	381 924	24.85961	78.61298	1618123	668	446 224	25.84570	81.73127	1497006
619	383 161	24.87971	78.67655	1615509	669	447 561	25.86503	81.79242	1494768
620	384 400	24.89980	78.74008	1612903	670	448 900	25.88436	81.85353	1492537
621	385 641	24.91987	78.80355	1610306	671	450 241	25.90367	81.91459	1490313
622	386 884	24.93993	78.86698	1607717	672	451 584	25.92296	81.97561	1488095
623	388 129	24.95997	78.93035	1605136	673	452 929	25.94224	82.03658	1485884
624	389 376	24.97999	78.99367	1602564	674	454 276	25.96151	82.09750	1483680
625	390 625	25.00000	79.05694	1600000	675	455 625	25.98076	82.15838	1481481
626	391 876	25.01999	79.12016	1597444	676	456 976	26.00000	82.21922	1479290
627	393 129	25.03997	79.18333	1594896	677	458 329	26.01922	82.28001	1477105
628	394 384	25.05993	79.24645	1592357	678	459 684	26.03843	82.34076	1474926
629	395 641	25.07987	79.30952	1589825	679	461 041	26.05763	82.40146	1472754
630	396 900	25.09980	79.37254	1587302	680	462 400	26.07681	82.46211	1470588
631	398 161	25.11971	79.43551	1584786	681	463 761	26.09598	82.52272	1468429
632	399 424	25.13961	79.49843	1582278	682	465 124	26.11513	82.58329	1466276
633	400 689	25.15949	79.56130	1579779	683	466 489	26.13427	82.64381	1464129
634	401 956	25.17936	79.62412	1577287	684	467 856	26.15339	82.70429	1461988
635	403 225	25.19921	79.68689	1574803	685	469 225	26.17250	82.76473	1459854
636	404 496	25.21904	79.74961	1572327	686	470 596	26.19160	82.82512	1457726
637	405 769	25.23886	79.81228	1569859	687	471 969	26.21068	82.88546	1455604
638	407 044	25.25866	79.87490	1567398	688	473 344	26.22975	82.94577	1453488
639	408 321	25.27845	79.93748	1564945	689	474 721	26.24881	83.00602	1451379
640	409 600	25.29822	80.00000	1562500	690	476 100	26.26785	83.06624	1449275
641	410 881	25.31798	80.06248	1560062	691	477 481	26.28688	83.12641	1447178
642	412 164	25.33772	80.12490	1557632	692	478 864	26.30589	83.18654	1445087
643	413 449	25.35744	80.18728	1555210	693	480 249	26.32489	83.24662	1443001
644	414 736	25.37716	80.24961	1552795	694	481 636	26.34388	83.30666	1440922
645	416 025	25.39685	80.31189	1550388	695	483 025	26.36285	83.36666	1438849
646	417 316	25.41653	80.37413	1547988	696	484 416	26.38181	83.42661	1436782
647	418 609	25.43619	80.43631	1545595	697	485 809	26.40076	83.48653	1434720
648	419 904	25.45584	80.49845	1543210	698	487 204	26.41969	83.54639	1432665
649	421 201	25.47548	80.56054	1540832	699	488 601	26.43861	83.60622	1430615
650	422 500	25.49510	80.62258	1538462	700	490 000	26.45751	83.66600	1428571

Squares, Square Roots, and Reciprocals 1–1,000 (*continued*)

N	N²	√N	√10N	1/N .00	N	N²	√N	√10N	1/N .00
700	490 000	26.45751	83.66600	1428571	750	562 500	27.38613	86.60254	1333333
701	491 401	26.47640	83.72574	1426534	751	564 001	27.40438	86.66026	1331558
702	492 804	26.49528	83.78544	1424501	752	565 504	27.42262	86.71793	1329787
703	494 209	26.51415	83.84510	1422475	753	567 009	27.44085	86.77557	1328021
704	495 616	26.53300	83.90471	1420455	754	568 516	27.45906	86.83317	1326260
705	497 025	26.55184	83.96428	1418440	755	570 025	27.47726	86.89074	1324503
706	498 436	26.57066	84.02381	1416431	756	571 536	27.49545	86.94826	1322751
707	499 849	26.58947	84.08329	1414427	757	573 049	27.51363	87.00575	1321004
708	501 264	26.60827	84.14274	1412429	758	574 564	27.53180	87.06320	1319261
709	502 681	26.62705	84.20214	1410437	759	576 081	27.54995	87.12061	1317523
710	504 100	26.64583	84.26150	1408451	760	577 600	27.56810	87.17798	1315789
711	505 521	26.66458	84.32082	1406470	761	579 121	27.58623	87.23531	1314060
712	506 944	26.68333	84.38009	1404494	762	580 644	27.60435	87.29261	1312336
713	508 369	26.70206	84.43933	1402525	763	582 169	27.62245	87.34987	1310616
714	509 796	26.72078	84.49852	1400560	764	583 696	27.64055	87.40709	1308901
715	511 225	26.73948	84.55767	1398601	765	585 225	27.65863	87.46428	1307190
716	512 656	26.75818	84.61678	1396648	766	586 756	27.67671	87.52143	1305483
717	514 089	26.77686	84.67585	1394700	767	588 289	27.69476	87.57854	1303781
718	515 524	26.79552	84.73488	1392758	768	589 824	27.71281	87.63561	1302083
719	516 961	26.81418	84.79387	1390821	769	591 361	27.73085	87.69265	1300390
720	518 400	26.83282	84.85281	1388889	770	592 900	27.74887	87.74964	1298701
721	519 841	26.85144	84.91172	1386963	771	594 441	27.76689	87.80661	1297017
722	521 284	26.87006	84.97058	1385042	772	595 984	27.78489	87.86353	1295337
723	522 729	26.88866	85.02941	1383126	773	597 529	27.80288	87.92042	1293661
724	524 176	26.90725	85.08819	1381215	774	599 076	27.82086	87.97727	1291990
725	525 625	26.92582	85.14693	1379310	775	600 625	27.83882	88.03408	1290323
726	527 076	26.94439	85.20563	1377410	776	602 176	27.85678	88.09086	1288660
727	528 529	26.96294	85.26429	1375516	777	603 729	27.87472	88.14760	1287001
728	529 984	26.98148	85.32292	1373626	778	605 284	27.89265	88.20431	1285347
729	531 441	27.00000	85.38150	1371742	779	606 841	27.91057	88.26098	1283697
730	532 900	27.01851	85.44004	1369863	780	608 400	27.92848	88.31761	1282051
731	534 361	27.03701	85.49854	1367989	781	609 961	27.94638	88.37420	1280410
732	535 824	27.05550	85.55700	1366120	782	611 524	27.96426	88.43076	1278772
733	537 289	27.07397	85.61542	1364256	783	613 089	27.98214	88.48729	1277139
734	538 756	27.09243	85.67380	1362398	784	614 656	28.00000	88.54377	1275510
735	540 225	27.11088	85.73214	1360544	785	616 225	28.01785	88.60023	1273885
736	541 696	27.12932	85.79044	1358696	786	617 796	28.03569	88.65664	1272265
737	543 169	27.14774	85.84870	1356852	787	619 369	28.05352	88.71302	1270648
738	544 644	27.16616	85.90693	1355014	788	620 944	28.07134	88.76936	1269036
739	546 121	27.18455	85.96511	1353180	789	622 521	28.08914	88.82567	1267427
740	547 600	27.20294	86.02325	1351351	790	624 100	28.10694	88.88194	1265823
741	549 081	27.22132	86.08136	1349528	791	625 681	28.12472	88.93818	1264223
742	550 564	27.23968	86.13942	1347709	792	627 264	28.14249	88.99438	1262626
743	552 049	27.25803	86.19745	1345895	793	628 849	28.16026	89.05055	1261034
744	553 536	27.27636	86.25543	1344086	794	630 436	28.17801	89.10668	1259446
745	555 025	27.29469	86.31338	1342282	795	632 025	28.19574	89.16277	1257862
746	556 516	27.31300	86.37129	1340483	796	633 616	28.21347	89.21883	1256281
747	558 009	27.33130	86.42916	1338688	797	635 209	28.23119	89.27486	1254705
748	559 504	27.34959	86.48699	1336898	798	636 804	28.24889	89.33085	1253133
749	561 001	27.36786	86.54479	1335113	799	638 401	28.26659	89.38680	1251564
750	562 500	27.38613	86.60254	1333333	800	640 000	28.28427	89.44272	1250000

Squares, Square Roots, and Reciprocals 1–1,000 (continued)

N	N²	$\sqrt{N}$	$\sqrt{10N}$	1/N .00	N	N²	$\sqrt{N}$	$\sqrt{10N}$	1/N .00
800	640 000	28.28427	89.44272	1250000	850	722 500	29.15476	92.19544	1176471
801	641 601	28.30194	89.49860	1248439	851	724 201	29.17190	92.24966	1175088
802	643 204	28.31960	89.55445	1246883	852	725 904	29.18904	92.30385	1173709
803	644 809	28.33725	89.61027	1245330	853	727 609	29.20616	92.35800	1172333
804	646 416	28.35489	89.66605	1243781	854	729 316	29.22328	92.41212	1170960
805	648 025	28.37252	89.72179	1242236	855	731 025	29.24038	92.46621	1169591
806	649 636	28.39014	89.77750	1240695	856	732 736	29.25748	92.52027	1168224
807	651 249	28.40775	89.83318	1239157	857	734 449	29.27456	92.57429	1166861
808	652 864	28.42534	89.88882	1237624	858	736 164	29.29164	92.62829	1165501
809	654 481	28.44293	89.94443	1236094	859	737 881	29.30870	92.68225	1164144
810	656 100	28.46050	90.00000	1234568	860	739 600	29.32576	92.73618	1162791
811	657 721	28.47806	90.05554	1233046	861	741 321	29.34280	92.79009	1161440
812	659 344	28.49561	90.11104	1231527	862	743 044	29.35984	92.84396	1160093
813	660 969	28.51315	90.16651	1230012	863	744 769	29.37686	92.89779	1158749
814	662 596	28.53069	90.22195	1228501	864	746 496	29.39388	92.95160	1157407
815	664 225	28.54820	90.27735	1226994	865	748 225	29.41088	93.00538	1156069
816	665 856	28.56571	90.33272	1225490	866	749 956	29.42788	93.05912	1154734
817	667 489	28.58321	90.38805	1223990	867	751 689	29.44486	93.11283	1153403
818	669 124	28.60070	90.44335	1222494	868	753 424	29.46184	93.16652	1152074
819	670 761	28.61818	90.49862	1221001	869	755 161	29.47881	93.22017	1150748
820	672 400	28.63564	90.55385	1219512	870	756 900	29.49576	93.27379	1149425
821	674 041	28.65310	90.60905	1218027	871	758 641	29.51271	93.32738	1148106
822	675 684	28.67054	90.66422	1216545	872	760 384	29.52965	93.38094	1146789
823	677 329	28.68798	90.71935	1215067	873	762 129	29.54657	93.43447	1145475
824	678 976	28.70540	90.77445	1213592	874	763 876	29.56349	93.48797	1144165
825	680 625	28.72281	90.82951	1212121	875	765 625	29.58040	93.54143	1142857
826	682 276	28.74022	90.88454	1210654	876	767 376	29.59730	93.59487	1141553
827	683 929	28.75761	90.93954	1209190	877	769 129	29.61419	93.64828	1140251
828	685 584	28.77499	90.99451	1207729	878	770 884	29.63106	93.70165	1138952
829	687 241	28.79236	91.04944	1206273	879	772 641	29.64793	93.75500	1137656
830	688 900	28.80972	91.10434	1204819	880	774 400	29.66479	93.80832	1136364
831	690 561	28.82707	91.15920	1203369	881	776 161	29.68164	93.86160	1135074
832	692 224	28.84441	91.21403	1201923	882	777 924	29.69848	93.91486	1133787
833	693 889	28.86174	91.26883	1200480	883	779 689	29.71532	93.96808	1132503
834	695 556	28.87906	91.32360	1199041	884	781 456	29.73214	94.02127	1131222
835	697 225	28.89637	91.37833	1197605	885	783 225	29.74895	94.07444	1129944
836	698 896	28.91366	91.43304	1196172	886	784 996	29.76575	94.12757	1128668
837	700 569	28.93095	91.48770	1194743	887	786 769	29.78255	94.18068	1127396
838	702 244	28.94823	91.54234	1193317	888	788 544	29.79933	94.23375	1126126
839	703 921	28.96550	91.59694	1191895	889	790 321	29.81610	94.28680	1124859
840	705 600	28.98275	91.65151	1190476	890	792 100	29.83287	94.33981	1123596
841	707 281	29.00000	91.70605	1189061	891	793 881	29.84962	94.39280	1122334
842	708 964	29.01724	91.76056	1187648	892	795 664	29.86637	94.44575	1121076
843	710 649	29.03446	91.81503	1186240	893	797 449	29.88311	94.49868	1119821
844	712 336	29.05168	91.86947	1184834	894	799 236	29.89983	94.55157	1118568
845	714 025	29.06888	91.92388	1183432	895	801 025	29.91655	94.60444	1117318
846	715 716	29.08608	91.97826	1182033	896	802 816	29.93326	94.65728	1116071
847	717 409	29.10326	92.03260	1180638	897	804 609	29.94996	94.71008	1114827
848	719 104	29.12044	92.08692	1179245	898	806 404	29.96665	94.76286	1113586
849	720 801	29.13760	92.14120	1177856	899	808 201	29.98333	94.81561	1112347
850	722 500	29.15476	92.19544	1176471	900	810 000	30.00000	94.86833	1111111

Squares, Square Roots, and Reciprocals 1–1,000 (concluded)

N	N^2	$\sqrt{N}$	$\sqrt{10N}$	$1/N$ .00	N	N^2	$\sqrt{N}$	$\sqrt{10N}$	$1/N$ .00
900	810 000	30.00000	94.86833	1111111	950	902 500	30.82207	97.46794	1052632
901	811 801	30.01666	94.92102	1109878	951	904 401	30.83829	97.51923	1051525
902	813 604	30.03331	94.97368	1108647	952	906 304	30.85450	97.57049	1050420
903	815 409	30.04996	95.02631	1107420	953	908 209	30.87070	97.62172	1049318
904	817 216	30.06659	95.07891	1106195	954	910.116	30.88689	97.67292	1048218
905	819 025	30.08322	95.13149	1104972	955	912 025	30.90307	97.72410	1047120
906	820 836	30.09983	95.18403	1103753	956	913 936	30.91925	97.77525	1046025
907	822 649	30.11644	95.23655	1102536	957	915 849	30.93542	97.82638	1044932
908	824 464	30.13304	95.28903	1101322	958	917 764	30.95158	97.87747	1043841
909	826 281	30.14963	95.34149	1100110	959	919 681	30.96773	97.92855	1042753
910	828 100	30.16621	95.39392	1098901	960	921 600	30.98387	97.97959	1041667
911	829 921	30.18278	95.44632	1097695	961	923 521	31.00000	98.03061	1040583
912	831 744	30.19934	95.49869	1096491	962	925 444	31.01612	98.08160	1039501
913	833 569	30.21589	95.55103	1095290	963	927 369	31.03224	98.13256	1038422
914	835 396	30.23243	95.60335	1094092	964	929 296	31.04835	98.18350	1037344
915	837 225	30.24897	95.65563	1092896	965	931 225	31.06445	98.23441	1036269
916	839 056	30.26549	95.70789	1091703	966	933 156	31.08054	98.28530	1035197
917	840 889	30.28201	95.76012	1090513	967	935 089	31.09662	98.33616	1034126
918	842 724	30.29851	95.81232	1089325	968	937 024	31.11270	98.38699	1033058
919	844 561	30.31501	95.86449	1088139	969	938 961	31.12876	98.43780	1031992
920	846 400	30.33150	95.91663	1086957	970	940 900	31.14482	98.48858	1030928
921	848 241	30.34798	95.96874	1085776	971	942 841	31.16087	98.53933	1029866
922	850 084	30.36445	96.02083	1084599	972	944 784	31.17691	98.59006	1028807
923	851 929	30.38092	96.07289	1083424	973	946 729	31.19295	98.64076	1027749
924	853 776	30.39737	96.12492	1082251	974	948 676	31.20897	98.69144	1026694
925	855 625	30.41381	96.17692	1081081	975	950 625	31.22499	98.74209	1025641
926	857 476	30.43025	96.22889	1079914	976	952 576	31.24100	98.79271	1024590
927	859 329	30.44667	96.28084	1078749	977	954 529	31.25700	98.84331	1023541
928	861 184	30.46309	96.33276	1077586	978	956 484	31.27299	98.89388	1022495
929	863 041	30.47950	96.38465	1076426	979	958 441	31.28898	98.94443	1021450
930	864 900	30.49590	96.43651	1075269	980	960 400	31.30495	98.99495	1020408
931	866 761	30.51229	96.48834	1074114	981	962 361	31.32092	99.04544	1019368
932	868 624	30.52868	96.54015	1072961	982	964 324	31.33688	99.09591	1018330
933	870 489	30.54505	96.59193	1071811	983	966 289	31.35283	99.14636	1017294
934	872 356	30.56141	96.64368	1070664	984	968 256	31.36877	99.19677	1016260
935	874 225	30.57777	96.69540	1069519	985	970 225	31.38471	99.24717	1015228
936	876 096	30.59412	96.74709	1068376	986	972 196	31.40064	99.29753	1014199
937	877 969	30.61046	96.79876	1067236	987	974 169	31.41656	99.34787	1013171
938	879 844	30.62679	96.85040	1066098	988	976 144	31.43247	99.39819	1012146
939	881 721	30.64311	96.90201	1064963	989	978 121	31.44837	99.44848	1011122
940	883 600	30.65942	96.95360	1063830	990	980 100	31.46427	99.49874	1010101
941	885 481	30.67572	97.00515	1062699	991	982 081	31.48015	99.54898	1009082
942	887 364	30.69202	97.05668	1061571	992	984 064	31.49603	99.59920	1008065
943	889 249	30.70831	97.10819	1060445	993	986 049	31.51190	99.64939	1007049
944	891 136	30.72458	97.15966	1059322	994	988 036	31.52777	99.69955	1006036
945	893 025	30.74085	97.21111	1058201	995	990 025	31.54362	99.74969	1005025
946	894 916	30.75711	97.26253	1057082	996	992 016	31.55947	99.79980	1004016
947	896 809	30.77337	97.31393	1055966	997	994 009	31.57531	99.84989	1003009
948	898 704	30.78961	97.36529	1054852	998	996 004	31.59114	99.89995	1002004
949	900 601	30.80584	97.41663	1053741	999	998 001	31.60696	99.94999	1001001
950	902 500	30.82207	97.46794	1052632	1000	1 000 000	31.62278	100.00000	1000000

Appendix B

Logarithms

The logarithm of a number consists of two parts, the part to the right of the decimal point (called the *mantissa*) and the part to the left of the decimal point (called the *characteristic*). The mantissas of the logarithms of numbers are contained in this table. Only positive numbers have logarithms; zero and negative numbers do not have logarithms.

To determine the characteristic of the logarithm:

1. The characteristic of all numbers one or greater is one less than the number of digits (not counting zero) to the left of the decimal point in the number. For example, the characteristic of 132 is 2; there are three digits left of the (unstated) decimal point; one less than three is two. The characteristic of 4.82 is 0; there is one digit left of the decimal point; one less than one is zero. The characteristic of 9,350,000.000 is 6; there are seven digits left of the decimal point; one less than seven is six.

2. The characteristic of all numbers between zero and one has a numerical value that is one greater than the number of zeros between the decimal point and the first nonzero digit of the number itself. *The characteristic of a number between zero and one is always negative.* This is usually indicated by a negative sign written above the characteristic, or by a positive number followed by -10. The characteristic of 0.032 is $\bar{2}$ or $8 - 10$; the characteristic of 0.48 is $\bar{1}$ or $9 - 10$.

Examples. The logarithm of 132 is 2.1206; the characteristic 2 is determined from Rule 1, and the mantissa is found in the table across from 13 and down from 2. The logarithm of 0.132 is $\bar{1}.1206$; the characteristic $\bar{1}$ is found from rule 2, and the mantissa is found in the table. This logarithm may also be stated as $9.1206 - 10$. For use in computations, the mantissa is always positive, as indicated in these examples. However, for use in curvilinear regression or trend fitting, a logarithm such as $9.1206 - 10$ must be restated as -0.8794 by performing the indicated arithmetic $(9.1206 - 10)$.

449

Four-Place Logarithms

N	0	1	2	3	4	5	6	7	8	9
10	0000	0043	0086	0128	0170	0212	0253	0294	0334	0374
11	0414	0453	0492	0531	0569	0607	0645	0682	0719	0755
12	0792	0828	0864	0899	0934	0969	1004	1038	1072	1106
13	1139	1173	1206	1239	1271	1303	1335	1367	1399	1430
14	1461	1492	1523	1553	1584	1614	1644	1673	1703	1732
15	1761	1790	1818	1847	1875	1903	1931	1959	1987	2014
16	2041	2068	2095	2122	2148	2175	2201	2227	2253	2279
17	2304	2330	2355	2380	2405	2430	2455	2480	2504	2529
18	2553	2577	2601	2625	2648	2672	2695	2718	2742	2765
19	2788	2810	2833	2856	2878	2900	2923	2945	2967	2989
20	3010	3032	3054	3075	3096	3118	3139	3160	3181	3201
21	3222	3243	3263	3284	3304	3324	3345	3365	3385	3404
22	3424	3444	3464	3483	3502	3522	3541	3560	3579	3598
23	3617	3636	3655	3674	3692	3711	3729	3747	3766	3784
24	3802	3820	3838	3856	3874	3892	3909	3927	3945	3962
25	3979	3997	4014	4031	4048	4065	4082	4099	4116	4133
26	4150	4166	4183	4200	4216	4232	4249	4265	4281	4298
27	4314	4330	4346	4362	4378	4393	4409	4425	4440	4456
28	4472	4487	4502	4518	4533	4548	4564	4579	4594	4609
29	4624	4639	4654	4669	4683	4698	4713	4728	4742	4757
30	4771	4786	4800	4814	4829	4843	4857	4871	4886	4900
31	4914	4928	4942	4955	4969	4983	4997	5011	5024	5038
32	5051	5065	5079	5092	5105	5119	5132	5145	5159	5172
33	5185	5198	5211	5224	5237	5250	5263	5276	5289	5302
34	5315	5328	5340	5353	5366	5378	5391	5403	5416	5428
35	5441	5453	5465	5478	5490	5502	5514	5527	5539	5551
36	5563	5575	5587	5599	5611	5623	5635	5647	5658	5670
37	5682	5694	5705	5717	5729	5740	5752	5763	5775	5786
38	5798	5809	5821	5832	5843	5855	5866	5877	5888	5899
39	5911	5922	5933	5944	5955	5966	5977	5988	5999	6010
40	6021	6031	6042	6053	6064	6075	6085	6096	6107	6117
41	6128	6138	6149	6160	6170	6180	6191	6201	6212	6222
42	6232	6243	6253	6263	6274	6284	6294	6304	6314	6325
43	6336	6345	6355	6365	6375	6385	6395	6405	6415	6425
44	6435	6444	6454	6464	6474	6484	6493	6503	6513	6522
45	6532	6542	6551	6561	6571	6580	6590	6599	6609	6618
46	6628	6637	6646	6656	6665	6675	6684	6693	6702	6712
47	6721	6730	6739	6749	6758	6767	6776	6785	6794	6803
48	6812	6821	6830	6839	6848	6857	6866	6875	6884	6893
49	6902	6911	6920	6928	6937	6946	6955	6964	6972	6981
50	6990	6998	7007	7016	7024	7033	7042	7050	7059	7067
51	7076	7084	7093	7101	7110	7118	7126	7135	7143	7152
52	7160	7168	7177	7185	7193	7202	7210	7218	7226	7235
53	7243	7251	7259	7267	7275	7284	7292	7300	7308	7316
54	7324	7332	7340	7348	7356	7364	7372	7380	7388	7396

Four-Place Logarithms (*continued*)

N	0	1	2	3	4	5	6	7	8	9
55	7404	7412	7419	7427	7435	7443	7451	7459	7466	7474
56	7482	7490	7497	7505	7513	7520	7528	7536	7543	7551
57	7559	7566	7574	7582	7589	7597	7604	7612	7619	7627
58	7634	7642	7649	7657	7664	7672	7679	7686	7694	7701
59	7709	7716	7723	7731	7738	7745	7752	7760	7767	7774
60	7782	7789	7796	7803	7810	7818	7825	7832	7839	7846
61	7853	7860	7868	7875	7882	7889	7896	7903	7910	7917
62	7924	7931	7938	7945	7952	7959	7966	7973	7980	7987
63	7993	8000	8007	8014	8021	8028	8035	8041	8048	8055
64	8062	8069	8075	8082	8089	8096	8102	8109	8116	8122
65	8129	8136	8142	8149	8156	8162	8169	8176	8182	8189
66	8195	8202	8209	8215	8222	8228	8235	8241	8248	8254
67	8261	8267	8274	8280	8287	8293	8299	8306	8312	8319
68	8325	8331	8338	8344	8351	8357	8363	8370	8376	8382
69	8388	8395	8401	8407	8414	8420	8426	8432	8439	8445
70	8451	8457	8463	8470	8476	8482	8488	8494	8500	8506
71	8513	8519	8525	8531	8537	8543	8549	8555	8561	8567
72	8573	8579	8585	8591	8597	8603	8609	8615	8621	8627
73	8633	8639	8645	8651	8657	8663	8669	8675	8681	8686
74	8692	8698	8704	8710	8716	8722	8727	8733	8739	8745
75	8751	8756	8762	8768	8774	8779	8785	8791	8797	8802
76	8808	8814	8820	8825	8831	8837	8842	8848	8854	8859
77	8865	8871	8876	8882	8887	8893	8899	8904	8910	8915
78	8921	8927	8932	8938	8943	8949	8954	8960	8965	8971
79	8976	8982	8987	8993	8998	9004	9009	9015	9020	9025
80	9031	9036	9042	9047	9053	9058	9063	9069	9074	9079
81	9085	9090	9096	9101	9106	9112	9117	9122	9128	9133
82	9138	9143	9149	9154	9159	9165	9170	9175	9180	9186
83	9191	9196	9201	9206	9212	9217	9222	9227	9232	9238
84	9243	9248	9253	9258	9263	9269	9274	9279	9284	9289
85	9294	9299	9304	9309	9315	9320	9325	9330	9335	9340
86	9345	9350	9355	9360	9365	9370	9375	9380	9385	9390
87	9395	9400	9405	9410	9415	9420	9425	9430	9435	9440
88	9445	9450	9455	9460	9465	9469	9474	9479	9484	9489
89	9494	9499	9504	9509	9513	9518	9523	9528	9533	9538
90	9542	9547	9552	9557	9562	9566	9571	9576	9581	9586
91	9590	9595	9600	9605	9609	9614	9619	9624	9628	9633
92	9638	9643	9647	9652	9657	9661	9666	9671	9675	9680
93	9685	9689	9694	9699	9703	9708	9713	9717	9722	9727
94	9731	9736	9741	9745	9750	9754	9759	9763	9768	9773
95	9777	9782	9786	9791	9795	9800	9805	9809	9814	9818
96	9823	9827	9832	9836	9841	9845	9850	9854	9859	9863
97	9868	9872	9877	9881	9886	9890	9894	9899	9903	9908
98	9912	9917	9921	9926	9930	9934	9939	9943	9948	9952
99	9956	9961	9965	9969	9974	9978	9983	9987	9991	9996

Appendix C

Table of Random Numbers

54941	72711	39406	94620	27963	96478	21559	19246	88097	44026
02349	71389	45608	60947	60775	73181	43264	56895	04232	59604
98210	44546	27174	27499	53523	63110	57106	20865	91683	80688
11826	91326	29664	01603	23156	89223	43429	95353	44662	59433
96810	17100	35066	00815	01552	06392	31437	70385	45863	75971
81060	33449	68055	83844	90942	74857	52419	68723	47830	63010
56135	80647	51404	06626	10042	93629	37609	57215	08409	81906
57361	65304	93258	56760	63348	24949	11839	29793	37457	59377
24548	56415	61927	64416	29934	00755	09418	14230	62887	92683
66504	02036	02922	63569	17906	38076	32135	19096	96970	75917
45068	05520	56321	22693	35089	07694	04252	23791	60249	83010
99717	01542	72990	43413	59744	44595	71326	91382	45114	20245
05394	61840	83089	09224	78530	33996	49965	04851	18280	14039
38155	42661	02363	67625	34683	95372	74733	63558	09665	22610
74319	04318	99387	86874	12549	38369	54952	91579	26023	81076
18134	90062	10761	54548	49505	52685	63903	13193	33905	66936
92012	42710	34650	73236	66167	21788	03581	40699	10396	81827
78101	44392	53767	15220	66319	72953	14071	59148	95154	72852
23469	42846	94810	16151	08029	50554	03891	38313	34016	18671
35342	56119	97190	43635	84249	61254	80993	55431	90793	62603
55846	18076	12415	30193	42777	85611	57635	51362	79907	77364
22184	33998	87436	37430	45246	11400	20986	43996	73112	88474
83668	66236	79665	88312	93047	12088	86937	70794	01041	74867
50083	70696	13558	98995	58159	04700	90443	13168	31553	67891
97765	27552	49617	51734	20849	70198	67906	00880	82899	66065
49988	13176	94219	88698	41755	56216	66832	17748	04963	54859
78257	86249	46134	51865	09836	73966	65711	41699	11732	17173
30946	22210	79302	40300	08852	27528	84648	79589	95295	72895
19468	76358	69203	02760	28625	70476	76410	32988	10194	94917
30806	80857	84383	78450	26245	91763	73117	33047	03577	62599
42163	69332	98851	50252	56911	62693	73817	98693	18728	94741
39249	51463	95963	07929	66728	47761	81472	44806	15592	71357
88712	29289	77360	09030	39605	87507	85446	51257	89555	75520
16767	57345	42285	56670	88445	85799	76200	21795	38894	58070
77516	98648	51868	48140	13583	94911	13318	64741	64336	95103
87192	66483	55649	36764	86132	12463	28385	94242	32063	45233
74078	64120	04643	14351	71381	28133	68269	65145	28152	39087
94119	20108	78101	81276	00835	63835	87174	42446	08882	27067
62180	27453	18567	55524	86088	00069	59254	24654	77371	26409
56199	05993	71201	78852	65889	32719	13758	23937	90740	16866
04994	09879	70337	11861	69032	51915	23510	32050	52052	24004
21725	43827	78862	67699	01009	07050	73324	06732	27510	33761
24305	37661	18956	50064	39500	17450	18030	63124	48061	59412
14762	69734	89150	93126	17700	94400	76075	08317	27324	72723
28387	99781	52977	01657	92602	41043	05686	15650	29970	95877

Source: Extracted from "Table of 105,000 Random Decimal Digits," Statement No. 4914, File No. 261-A (Washington, D.C.: Interstate Commerce Commission, 1949).

Binomial Distribution—
Individual Terms

The table presents individual binomial probabilities for the number of successes, X, for selected values of n and π.

$$P(X) = \frac{n!}{X!(n-X)!} \pi^X (1 - \pi)^{n-X}$$

Binomial Distribution—Individual Terms

Prob. of success = π

# of trial = n

X = random var. Binomial

n	X	.01	.02	.03	.04	.05	.10	.15	.20	.25	.30	.35	.40	.45
1	0	.9900	.9800	.9700	.9600	.9500	.9000	.8500	.8000	.7500	.7000	.6500	.6000	.5500
	1	.0100	.0200	.0300	.0400	.0500	.1000	.1500	.2000	.2500	.3000	.3500	.4000	.4500

n	X	.01	.02	.03	.04	.05	.10	.15	.20	.25	.30	.35	.40	.45
2	0	.9801	.9604	.9409	.9216	.9025	.8100	.7225	.6400	.5625	.4900	.4225	.3600	.3025
	1	.0198	.0392	.0582	.0768	.0950	.1800	.2550	.3200	.3750	.4200	.4550	.4800	.4950
	2	.0001	.0004	.0009	.0016	.0025	.0100	.0225	.0400	.0625	.0900	.1225	.1600	.2025

n	X	.01	.02	.03	.04	.05	.10	.15	.20	.25	.30	.35	.40	.45
3	0	.9703	.9412	.9127	.8847	.8574	.7290	.6141	.5120	.4219	.3430	.2746	.2160	.1664
	1	.0294	.0576	.0847	.1106	.1354	.2430	.3251	.3840	.4219	.4410	.4436	.4320	.4084
	2	.0003	.0012	.0026	.0046	.0071	.0270	.0574	.0960	.1406	.1890	.2389	.2880	.3341
	3	.0000	.0000	.0000	.0001	.0001	.0010	.0034	.0080	.0156	.0270	.0429	.0640	.0911

n	X	.01	.02	.03	.04	.05	.10	.15	.20	.25	.30	.35	.40	.45
4	0	.9606	.9224	.8853	.8493	.8145	.6561	.5220	.4096	.3164	.2401	.1785	.1296	.0915
	1	.0388	.0753	.1095	.1416	.1715	.2916	.3685	.4096	.4219	.4116	.3845	.3456	.2995
	2	.0006	.0023	.0051	.0088	.0135	.0486	.0975	.1536	.2109	.2646	.3105	.3456	.3675
	3	.0000	.0000	.0001	.0002	.0005	.0036	.0115	.0256	.0469	.0756	.1115	.1536	.2005
	4	.0000	.0000	.0000	.0000	.0000	.0001	.0005	.0016	.0039	.0081	.0150	.0256	.0410

n	X	.01	.02	.03	.04	.05	.10	.15	.20	.25	.30	.35	.40	.45
5	0	.9510	.9039	.8587	.8154	.7738	.5905	.4437	.3277	.2373	.1681	.1160	.0778	.0503
	1	.0480	.0922	.1328	.1699	.2036	.3280	.3915	.4096	.3955	.3601	.3124	.2592	.2059
	2	.0010	.0038	.0082	.0142	.0214	.0729	.1382	.2048	.2637	.3087	.3364	.3456	.3369
	3	.0000	.0001	.0003	.0006	.0011	.0081	.0244	.0512	.0879	.1323	.1811	.2304	.2757
	4	.0000	.0000	.0000	.0000	.0000	.0004	.0022	.0064	.0146	.0283	.0488	.0768	.1128
	5	.0000	.0000	.0000	.0000	.0000	.0000	.0001	.0003	.0010	.0024	.0053	.0102	.0185

n	X	.01	.02	.03	.04	.05	.10	.15	.20	.25	.30	.35	.40	.45
6	0	.9415	.8858	.8330	.7828	.7351	.5314	.3771	.2621	.1780	.1176	.0754	.0467	.0277
	1	.0571	.1085	.1546	.1957	.2321	.3543	.3993	.3932	.3560	.3025	.2437	.1866	.1359
	2	.0014	.0055	.0120	.0204	.0305	.0984	.1762	.2458	.2966	.3241	.3280	.3110	.2780
	3	.0000	.0002	.0005	.0011	.0021	.0146	.0415	.0819	.1318	.1852	.2355	.2765	.3032
	4	.0000	.0000	.0000	.0000	.0001	.0012	.0055	.0154	.0330	.0595	.0951	.1382	.1861
	5	.0000	.0000	.0000	.0000	.0000	.0001	.0004	.0015	.0044	.0102	.0205	.0369	.0609
	6	.0000	.0000	.0000	.0000	.0000	.0000	.0000	.0001	.0002	.0007	.0018	.0041	.0083

n	X	.01	.02	.03	.04	.05	.10	.15	.20	.25	.30	.35	.40	.45
7	0	.9321	.8681	.8080	.7514	.6983	.4783	.3206	.2097	.1335	.0824	.0490	.0280	.0152
	1	.0659	.1240	.1749	.2192	.2573	.3720	.3960	.3670	.3115	.2471	.1848	.1306	.0872
	2	.0020	.0076	.0162	.0274	.0406	.1240	.2097	.2753	.3115	.3177	.2985	.2613	.2140
	3	.0000	.0003	.0008	.0019	.0036	.0230	.0617	.1147	.1730	.2269	.2679	.2903	.2918
	4	.0000	.0000	.0000	.0001	.0002	.0026	.0109	.0287	.0577	.0972	.1442	.1935	.2388
	5	.0000	.0000	.0000	.0000	.0000	.0002	.0012	.0043	.0115	.0250	.0466	.0774	.1172
	6	.0000	.0000	.0000	.0000	.0000	.0000	.0001	.0004	.0013	.0036	.0084	.0172	.0320
	7	.0000	.0000	.0000	.0000	.0000	.0000	.0000	.0000	.0001	.0002	.0006	.0016	.0037

π

.50	.55	.60	.65	.70	.75	.80	.85	.90	.95	.96	.97	.98	.99	X	n
.5000	.4500	.4000	.3500	.3000	.2500	.2000	.1500	.1000	.0500	.0400	.0300	.0200	.0100	0	1
.5000	.5500	.6000	.6500	.7000	.7500	.8000	.8500	.9000	.9500	.9600	.9700	.9800	.9900	1	

.50	.55	.60	.65	.70	.75	.80	.85	.90	.95	.96	.97	.98	.99	X	n
.2500	.2025	.1600	.1225	.0900	.0625	.0400	.0225	.0100	.0025	.0016	.0009	.0004	.0001	0	2
.5000	.4950	.4800	.4550	.4200	.3750	.3200	.2550	.1800	.0950	.0768	.0582	.0392	.0198	1	
.2500	.3025	.3600	.4225	.4900	.5625	.6400	.7225	.8100	.9025	.9216	.9409	.9604	.9801	2	

.50	.55	.60	.65	.70	.75	.80	.85	.90	.95	.96	.97	.98	.99	X	n
.1250	.0911	.0640	.0429	.0270	.0156	.0080	.0034	.0010	.0001	.0001	.0000	.0000	.0000	0	3
.3750	.3341	.2880	.2389	.1890	.1406	.0960	.0574	.0270	.0071	.0046	.0026	.0012	.0003	1	
.3750	.4084	.4320	.4436	.4410	.4219	.3840	.3251	.2430	.1354	.1106	.0847	.0576	.0294	2	
.1250	.1664	.2160	.2746	.3430	.4219	.5120	.6141	.7290	.8574	.8847	.9127	.9412	.9703	3	

.50	.55	.60	.65	.70	.75	.80	.85	.90	.95	.96	.97	.98	.99	X	n
.0625	.0410	.0256	.0150	.0081	.0039	.0016	.0005	.0001	.0000	.0000	.0000	.0000	.0000	0	4
.2500	.2005	.1536	.1115	.0756	.0469	.0256	.0115	.0036	.0005	.0002	.0001	.0000	.0000	1	
.3750	.3675	.3456	.3105	.2646	.2109	.1536	.0975	.0486	.0135	.0088	.0051	.0023	.0006	2	
.2500	.2995	.3456	.3845	.4116	.4219	.4096	.3685	.2916	.1715	.1416	.1095	.0753	.0388	3	
.0625	.0915	.1296	.1785	.2401	.3164	.4096	.5220	.6561	.8145	.8493	.8853	.9224	.9606	4	

.50	.55	.60	.65	.70	.75	.80	.85	.90	.95	.96	.97	.98	.99	X	n
.0313	.0185	.0102	.0053	.0024	.0010	.0003	.0001	.0000	.0000	.0000	.0000	.0000	.0000	0	5
.1563	.1128	.0768	.0488	.0283	.0146	.0064	.0022	.0005	.0000	.0000	.0000	.0000	.0000	1	
.3125	.2757	.2304	.1811	.1323	.0879	.0512	.0244	.0081	.0011	.0006	.0003	.0001	.0000	2	
.3125	.3369	.3456	.3364	.3087	.2637	.2048	.1382	.0729	.0214	.0142	.0082	.0038	.0010	3	
.1563	.2059	.2592	.3124	.3601	.3955	.4096	.3915	.3280	.2036	.1699	.1328	.0922	.0480	4	
.0313	.0503	.0778	.1160	.1681	.2373	.3277	.4437	.5905	.7738	.8154	.8587	.9039	.9510	5	

.50	.55	.60	.65	.70	.75	.80	.85	.90	.95	.96	.97	.98	.99	X	n
.0156	.0083	.0041	.0018	.0007	.0002	.0001	.0000	.0000	.0000	.0000	.0000	.0000	.0000	0	6
.0938	.0609	.0369	.0205	.0102	.0044	.0015	.0004	.0001	.0000	.0000	.0000	.0000	.0000	1	
.2344	.1861	.1382	.0951	.0595	.0330	.0154	.0055	.0012	.0001	.0000	.0000	.0000	.0000	2	
.3125	.3032	.2765	.2355	.1852	.1318	.0819	.0415	.0146	.0021	.0011	.0005	.0002	.0000	3	
.2344	.2780	.3110	.3280	.3241	.2965	.2458	.1762	.0984	.0305	.0204	.0120	.0055	.0014	4	
.0938	.1359	.1866	.2437	.3025	.3560	.3932	.3993	.3543	.2321	.1957	.1546	.1085	.0571	5	
.0156	.0277	.0467	.0754	.1176	.1780	.2621	.3771	.5314	.7351	.7828	.8330	.8858	.9415	6	

.50	.55	.60	.65	.70	.75	.80	.85	.90	.95	.96	.97	.98	.99	X	n
.0078	.0037	.0016	.0006	.0002	.0001	.0000	.0000	.0000	.0000	.0000	.0000	.0000	.0000	0	7
.0547	.0320	.0172	.0084	.0036	.0013	.0004	.0001	.0000	.0000	.0000	.0000	.0000	.0000	1	
.1641	.1172	.0774	.0466	.0250	.0115	.0043	.0012	.0002	.0000	.0000	.0000	.0000	.0000	2	
.2734	.2388	.1935	.1442	.0972	.0577	.0287	.0109	.0026	.0002	.0001	.0000	.0000	.0000	3	
.2734	.2918	.2903	.2679	.2269	.1730	.1147	.0617	.0230	.0036	.0019	.0008	.0003	.0000	4	
.1641	.2140	.2613	.2985	.3177	.3115	.2753	.2097	.1240	.0406	.0274	.0162	.0076	.0020	5	
.0547	.0872	.1306	.1848	.2471	.3115	.3670	.3960	.3720	.2573	.2192	.1749	.1240	.0659	6	
.0078	.0152	.0280	.0490	.0824	.1335	.2097	.3206	.4783	.6983	.7514	.8080	.8681	.9321	7	

Binomial Distribution—Individual Terms (*continued*)

π

n	X	.01	.02	.03	.04	.05	.10	.15	.20	.25	.30	.35	.40	.45
8	0	.9227	.8508	.7837	.7214	.6634	.4305	.2725	.1678	.1001	.0576	.0319	.0168	.0084
	1	.0746	.1389	.1939	.2405	.2793	.3826	.3847	.3355	.2670	.1977	.1373	.0896	.0548
	2	.0026	.0099	.0210	.0351	.0515	.1488	.2376	.2936	.3115	.2965	.2587	.2090	.1569
	3	.0001	.0004	.0013	.0029	.0054	.0331	.0839	.1468	.2076	.2541	.2786	.2787	.2568
	4	.0000	.0000	.0001	.0002	.0004	.0046	.0185	.0459	.0865	.1361	.1875	.2322	.2627
	5	.0000	.0000	.0000	.0000	.0000	.0004	.0026	.0092	.0231	.0467	.0808	.1239	.1719
	6	.0000	.0000	.0000	.0000	.0000	.0000	.0002	.0011	.0038	.0100	.0217	.0413	.0703
	7	.0000	.0000	.0000	.0000	.0000	.0000	.0000	.0001	.0004	.0012	.0033	.0079	.0164
	8	.0000	.0000	.0000	.0000	.0000	.0000	.0000	.0000	.0000	.0001	.0002	.0007	.0017

n	X	.01	.02	.03	.04	.05	.10	.15	.20	.25	.30	.35	.40	.45
9	0	.9135	.8337	.7602	.6925	.6302	.3874	.2316	.1342	.0751	.0404	.0207	.0101	.0046
	1	.0830	.1531	.2116	.2597	.2985	.3874	.3679	.3020	.2253	.1556	.1004	.0605	.0339
	2	.0034	.0125	.0262	.0433	.0629	.1722	.2597	.3020	.3003	.2668	.2162	.1612	.1110
	3	.0001	.0006	.0019	.0042	.0077	.0446	.1069	.1762	.2336	.2668	.2716	.2508	.2119
	4	.0000	.0000	.0001	.0003	.0006	.0074	.0283	.0661	.1168	.1715	.2194	.2508	.2600
	5	.0000	.0000	.0000	.0000	.0000	.0008	.0050	.0165	.0389	.0735	.1181	.1672	.2128
	6	.0000	.0000	.0000	.0000	.0000	.0001	.0006	.0028	.0087	.0210	.0424	.0743	.1160
	7	.0000	.0000	.0000	.0000	.0000	.0000	.0000	.0003	.0012	.0039	.0098	.0212	.0407
	8	.0000	.0000	.0000	.0000	.0000	.0000	.0000	.0000	.0001	.0004	.0013	.0035	.0083
	9	.0000	.0000	.0000	.0000	.0000	.0000	.0000	.0000	.0000	.0000	.0001	.0003	.0008

n	X	.01	.02	.03	.04	.05	.10	.15	.20	.25	.30	.35	.40	.45
10	0	.9044	.8171	.7374	.6648	.5987	.3487	.1969	.1074	.0563	.0282	.0135	.0060	.0025
	1	.0914	.1667	.2281	.2770	.3151	.3874	.3474	.2684	.1877	.1211	.0725	.0403	.0207
	2	.0042	.0153	.0317	.0519	.0746	.1937	.2759	.3020	.2816	.2335	.1757	.1209	.0763
	3	.0001	.0008	.0026	.0058	.0105	.0574	.1298	.2013	.2503	.2668	.2522	.2150	.1665
	4	.0000	.0000	.0001	.0004	.0010	.0112	.0401	.0881	.1460	.2001	.2377	.2508	.2384
	5	.0000	.0000	.0000	.0000	.0001	.0015	.0085	.0264	.0584	.1029	.1536	.2007	.2340
	6	.0000	.0000	.0000	.0000	.0000	.0001	.0012	.0055	.0162	.0368	.0689	.1115	.1596
	7	.0000	.0000	.0000	.0000	.0000	.0000	.0001	.0008	.0031	.0090	.0212	.0425	.0746
	8	.0000	.0000	.0000	.0000	.0000	.0000	.0000	.0001	.0004	.0014	.0043	.0106	.0229
	9	.0000	.0000	.0000	.0000	.0000	.0000	.0000	.0000	.0000	.0001	.0005	.0016	.0042
	10	.0000	.0000	.0000	.0000	.0000	.0000	.0000	.0000	.0000	.0000	.0000	.0001	.0003

n	X	.01	.02	.03	.04	.05	.10	.15	.20	.25	.30	.35	.40	.45
11	0	.8953	.8007	.7153	.6382	.5688	.3138	.1673	.0859	.0422	.0198	.0088	.0036	.0014
	1	.0995	.1798	.2433	.2925	.3293	.3835	.3248	.2362	.1549	.0932	.0518	.0266	.0125
	2	.0050	.0183	.0376	.0609	.0867	.2131	.2866	.2953	.2581	.1998	.1395	.0887	.0513
	3	.0002	.0011	.0035	.0076	.0137	.0710	.1517	.2215	.2581	.2568	.2254	.1774	.1259
	4	.0000	.0000	.0002	.0006	.0014	.0158	.0536	.1107	.1721	.2201	.2428	.2365	.2060
	5	.0000	.0000	.0000	.0000	.0001	.0025	.0132	.0388	.0803	.1321	.1830	.2207	.2360
	6	.0000	.0000	.0000	.0000	.0000	.0003	.0023	.0097	.0268	.0566	.0985	.1471	.1931
	7	.0000	.0000	.0000	.0000	.0000	.0000	.0003	.0017	.0064	.0173	.0379	.0701	.1128
	8	.0000	.0000	.0000	.0000	.0000	.0000	.0000	.0002	.0011	.0037	.0102	.0234	.0462
	9	.0000	.0000	.0000	.0000	.0000	.0000	.0000	.0000	.0001	.0005	.0018	.0052	.0126
	10	.0000	.0000	.0000	.0000	.0000	.0000	.0000	.0000	.0000	.0000	.0002	.0007	.0021
	11	.0000	.0000	.0000	.0000	.0000	.0000	.0000	.0000	.0000	.0000	.0000	.0000	.0002

n	X	.01	.02	.03	.04	.05	.10	.15	.20	.25	.30	.35	.40	.45
12	0	.8864	.7847	.6938	.6127	.5404	.2824	.1422	.0687	.0317	.0138	.0057	.0022	.0008
	1	.1074	.1922	.2575	.3064	.3413	.3766	.3012	.2062	.1267	.0712	.0368	.0174	.0075
	2	.0060	.0216	.0438	.0702	.0988	.2301	.2924	.2835	.2323	.1678	.1088	.0639	.0339
	3	.0002	.0015	.0045	.0098	.0173	.0852	.1720	.2362	.2581	.2397	.1954	.1419	.0923
	4	.0000	.0001	.0003	.0009	.0021	.0213	.0683	.1329	.1936	.2311	.2367	.2128	.1700
	5	.0000	.0000	.0000	.0001	.0002	.0038	.0193	.0532	.1032	.1585	.2039	.2270	.2225
	6	.0000	.0000	.0000	.0000	.0000	.0005	.0040	.0155	.0401	.0792	.1281	.1766	.2124
	7	.0000	.0000	.0000	.0000	.0000	.0000	.0006	.0033	.0115	.0291	.0591	.1009	.1489
	8	.0000	.0000	.0000	.0000	.0000	.0000	.0001	.0005	.0024	.0078	.0199	.0420	.0762
	9	.0000	.0000	.0000	.0000	.0000	.0000	.0000	.0001	.0004	.0015	.0048	.0125	.0277
	10	.0000	.0000	.0000	.0000	.0000	.0000	.0000	.0000	.0000	.0002	.0008	.0025	.0068
	11	.0000	.0000	.0000	.0000	.0000	.0000	.0000	.0000	.0000	.0000	.0001	.0003	.0010
	12	.0000	.0000	.0000	.0000	.0000	.0000	.0000	.0000	.0000	.0000	.0000	.0000	.0001

π

.50	.55	.60	.65	.70	.75	.80	.85	.90	.95	.96	.97	.98	.99	X	n
.0039	.0017	.0007	.0002	.0001	.0000	.0000	.0000	.0000	.0000	.0000	.0000	.0000	.0000	0	8
.0313	.0164	.0079	.0033	.0012	.0004	.0001	.0000	.0000	.0000	.0000	.0000	.0000	.0000	1	
.1094	.0703	.0413	.0217	.0100	.0038	.0011	.0002	.0000	.0000	.0000	.0000	.0000	.0000	2	
.2188	.1719	.1239	.0808	.0467	.0231	.0092	.0026	.0004	.0000	.0000	.0000	.0000	.0000	3	
.2734	.2627	.2322	.1875	.1361	.0865	.0459	.0185	.0046	.0004	.0002	.0001	.0000	.0000	4	
.2188	.2568	.2787	.2786	.2541	.2076	.1468	.0839	.0331	.0054	.0029	.0013	.0004	.0001	5	
.1094	.1569	.2090	.2587	.2965	.3115	.2936	.2376	.1488	.0515	.0351	.0210	.0099	.0026	6	
.0313	.0548	.0896	.1373	.1977	.2670	.3355	.3847	.3826	.2793	.2405	.1939	.1389	.0746	7	
.0039	.0084	.0168	.0319	.0576	.1001	.1678	.2725	.4305	.6634	.7214	.7837	.8508	.9227	8	

.50	.55	.60	.65	.70	.75	.80	.85	.90	.95	.96	.97	.98	.99	X	n
.0020	.0008	.0003	.0001	.0000	.0000	.0000	.0000	.0000	.0000	.0000	.0000	.0000	.0000	0	9
.0176	.0083	.0035	.0013	.0004	.0001	.0000	.0000	.0000	.0000	.0000	.0000	.0000	.0000	1	
.0703	.0407	.0212	.0098	.0039	.0012	.0003	.0000	.0000	.0000	.0000	.0000	.0000	.0000	2	
.1641	.1160	.0743	.0424	.0210	.0087	.0028	.0006	.0001	.0000	.0000	.0000	.0000	.0000	3	
.2461	.2128	.1672	.1181	.0735	.0389	.0165	.0050	.0008	.0000	.0000	.0000	.0000	.0000	4	
.2461	.2600	.2508	.2194	.1715	.1168	.0661	.0283	.0074	.0006	.0003	.0001	.0000	.0000	5	
.1641	.2119	.2508	.2716	.2668	.2336	.1762	.1069	.0446	.0077	.0042	.0019	.0006	.0001	6	
.0703	.1110	.1612	.2162	.2668	.3003	.3020	.2597	.1722	.0629	.0433	.0262	.0125	.0034	7	
.0176	.0339	.0605	.1004	.1556	.2253	.3020	.3679	.3874	.2985	.2597	.2116	.1531	.0830	8	
.0020	.0046	.0101	.0207	.0404	.0751	.1342	.2316	.3874	.6302	.6925	.7602	.8337	.9135	9	

.50	.55	.60	.65	.70	.75	.80	.85	.90	.95	.96	.97	.98	.99	X	n
.0010	.0003	.0001	.0000	.0000	.0000	.0000	.0000	.0000	.0000	.0000	.0000	.0000	.0000	0	10
.0098	.0042	.0016	.0005	.0001	.0000	.0000	.0000	.0000	.0000	.0000	.0000	.0000	.0000	1	
.0439	.0229	.0106	.0043	.0014	.0004	.0001	.0000	.0000	.0000	.0000	.0000	.0000	.0000	2	
.1172	.0746	.0425	.0212	.0090	.0031	.0008	.0001	.0000	.0000	.0000	.0000	.0000	.0000	3	
.2051	.1596	.1115	.0689	.0368	.0162	.0055	.0012	.0001	.0000	.0000	.0000	.0000	.0000	4	
.2461	.2340	.2007	.1536	.1029	.0584	.0264	.0085	.0015	.0001	.0000	.0000	.0000	.0000	5	
.2051	.2384	.2508	.2377	.2001	.1460	.0881	.0401	.0112	.0010	.0004	.0001	.0000	.0000	6	
.1172	.1665	.2150	.2522	.2668	.2503	.2013	.1298	.0574	.0105	.0058	.0026	.0008	.0001	7	
.0439	.0763	.1209	.1757	.2335	.2816	.3020	.2759	.1937	.0746	.0519	.0317	.0153	.0042	8	
.0098	.0207	.0403	.0725	.1211	.1877	.2684	.3474	.3874	.3151	.2770	.2281	.1667	.0914	9	
.0010	.0025	.0060	.0135	.0282	.0563	.1074	.1969	.3487	.5987	.6648	.7374	.8171	.9044	10	

.50	.55	.60	.65	.70	.75	.80	.85	.90	.95	.96	.97	.98	.99	X	n
.0005	.0002	.0000	.0000	.0000	.0000	.0000	.0000	.0000	.0000	.0000	.0000	.0000	.0000	0	11
.0054	.0021	.0007	.0002	.0000	.0000	.0000	.0000	.0000	.0000	.0000	.0000	.0000	.0000	1	
.0269	.0126	.0052	.0018	.0005	.0001	.0000	.0000	.0000	.0000	.0000	.0000	.0000	.0000	2	
.0806	.0462	.0234	.0102	.0037	.0011	.0002	.0000	.0000	.0000	.0000	.0000	.0000	.0000	3	
.1611	.1128	.0701	.0379	.0173	.0064	.0017	.0003	.0000	.0000	.0000	.0000	.0000	.0000	4	
.2256	.1931	.1471	.0985	.0566	.0268	.0097	.0023	.0003	.0000	.0000	.0000	.0000	.0000	5	
.2256	.2360	.2207	.1830	.1321	.0803	.0388	.0132	.0025	.0001	.0000	.0000	.0000	.0000	6	
.1611	.2060	.2365	.2428	.2201	.1721	.1107	.0536	.0158	.0014	.0006	.0002	.0000	.0000	7	
.0806	.1259	.1774	.2254	.2568	.2581	.2215	.1517	.0710	.0137	.0076	.0035	.0011	.0002	8	
.0269	.0513	.0887	.1395	.1998	.2581	.2953	.2866	.2131	.0867	.0609	.0376	.0183	.0050	9	
.0054	.0125	.0266	.0518	.0932	.1549	.2362	.3248	.3835	.3293	.2925	.2433	.1798	.0995	10	
.0005	.0014	.0036	.0088	.0198	.0422	.0859	.1673	.3138	.5688	.6382	.7153	.8007	.8953	11	

.50	.55	.60	.65	.70	.75	.80	.85	.90	.95	.96	.97	.98	.99	X	n
.0002	.0001	.0000	.0000	.0000	.0000	.0000	.0000	.0000	.0000	.0000	.0000	.0000	.0000	0	12
.0029	.0010	.0003	.0001	.0000	.0000	.0000	.0000	.0000	.0000	.0000	.0000	.0000	.0000	1	
.0161	.0068	.0025	.0008	.0002	.0000	.0000	.0000	.0000	.0000	.0000	.0000	.0000	.0000	2	
.0537	.0277	.0125	.0048	.0015	.0004	.0001	.0000	.0000	.0000	.0000	.0000	.0000	.0000	3	
.1208	.0762	.0420	.0199	.0078	.0024	.0005	.0001	.0000	.0000	.0000	.0000	.0000	.0000	4	
.1934	.1489	.1009	.0591	.0291	.0115	.0033	.0006	.0000	.0000	.0000	.0000	.0000	.0000	5	
.2256	.2124	.1766	.1281	.0792	.0401	.0155	.0040	.0005	.0000	.0000	.0000	.0000	.0000	6	
.1934	.2225	.2270	.2039	.1585	.1032	.0532	.0193	.0038	.0002	.0001	.0000	.0000	.0000	7	
.1208	.1700	.2128	.2367	.2311	.1936	.1329	.0683	.0213	.0021	.0009	.0003	.0001	.0000	8	
.0537	.0923	.1419	.1954	.2397	.2581	.2362	.1720	.0852	.0173	.0098	.0045	.0015	.0002	9	
.0161	.0339	.0639	.1088	.1678	.2323	.2835	.2924	.2301	.0988	.0702	.0438	.0216	.0060	10	
.0029	.0075	.0174	.0368	.0712	.1267	.2062	.3012	.3766	.3413	.3064	.2575	.1922	.1074	11	
.0002	.0008	.0022	.0057	.0138	.0317	.0687	.1422	.2824	.5404	.6127	.6938	.7847	.8864	12	

Binomial Distribution—Individual Terms (*continued*)

π

n	X	.01	.02	.03	.04	.05	.10	.15	.20	.25	.30	.35	.40	.45
13	0	.8775	.7690	.6730	.5882	.5133	.2542	.1209	.0550	.0238	.0097	.0037	.0013	.0004
	1	.1152	.2040	.2706	.3186	.3512	.3672	.2774	.1787	.1029	.0540	.0259	.0113	.0045
	2	.0070	.0250	.0502	.0797	.1109	.2448	.2937	.2680	.2059	.1388	.0836	.0453	.0220
	3	.0003	.0019	.0057	.0122	.0214	.0997	.1900	.2457	.2517	.2181	.1651	.1107	.0660
	4	.0000	.0001	.0004	.0013	.0028	.0277	.0838	.1535	.2097	.2337	.2222	.1845	.1350
	5	.0000	.0000	.0000	.0001	.0003	.0055	.0266	.0691	.1258	.1803	.2154	.2214	.1989
	6	.0000	.0000	.0000	.0000	.0000	.0008	.0063	.0230	.0559	.1030	.1546	.1968	.2169
	7	.0000	.0000	.0000	.0000	.0001	.0001	.0011	.0058	.0186	.0442	.0833	.1312	.1775
	8	.0000	.0000	.0000	.0000	.0000	.0000	.0001	.0011	.0047	.0142	.0336	.0656	.1089
	9	.0000	.0000	.0000	.0000	.0000	.0000	.0000	.0001	.0009	.0034	.0101	.0243	.0495
	10	.0000	.0000	.0000	.0000	.0000	.0000	.0000	.0000	.0001	.0006	.0022	.0065	.0162
	11	.0000	.0000	.0000	.0000	.0000	.0000	.0000	.0000	.0000	.0001	.0003	.0012	.0036
	12	.0000	.0000	.0000	.0000	.0000	.0000	.0000	.0000	.0000	.0000	.0000	.0001	.0005
	13	.0000	.0000	.0000	.0000	.0000	.0000	.0000	.0000	.0000	.0000	.0000	.0000	.0000

n	X	.01	.02	.03	.04	.05	.10	.15	.20	.25	.30	.35	.40	.45
14	0	.8687	.7536	.6528	.5647	.4877	.2288	.1028	.0440	.0178	.0068	.0024	.0008	.0002
	1	.1229	.2153	.2827	.3294	.3593	.3559	.2539	.1539	.0832	.0407	.0181	.0073	.0027
	2	.0081	.0286	.0568	.0892	.1229	.2570	.2912	.2501	.1802	.1134	.0634	.0317	.0141
	3	.0003	.0023	.0070	.0149	.0259	.1142	.2056	.2501	.2402	.1943	.1366	.0845	.0462
	4	.0000	.0001	.0006	.0017	.0037	.0349	.0998	.1720	.2202	.2290	.2022	.1549	.1040
	5	.0000	.0000	.0000	.0001	.0004	.0078	.0352	.0860	.1468	.1963	.2178	.2066	.1701
	6	.0000	.0000	.0000	.0000	.0000	.0013	.0093	.0322	.0734	.1262	.1759	.2066	.2088
	7	.0000	.0000	.0000	.0000	.0000	.0002	.0019	.0092	.0280	.0618	.1082	.1574	.1952
	8	.0000	.0000	.0000	.0000	.0000	.0000	.0003	.0020	.0082	.0232	.0510	.0918	.1398
	9	.0000	.0000	.0000	.0000	.0000	.0000	.0000	.0003	.0018	.0066	.0183	.0408	.0762
	10	.0000	.0000	.0000	.0000	.0000	.0000	.0000	.0000	.0003	.0014	.0049	.0136	.0312
	11	.0000	.0000	.0000	.0000	.0000	.0000	.0000	.0000	.0000	.0002	.0010	.0033	.0093
	12	.0000	.0000	.0000	.0000	.0000	.0000	.0000	.0000	.0000	.0000	.0001	.0005	.0019
	13	.0000	.0000	.0000	.0000	.0000	.0000	.0000	.0000	.0000	.0000	.0000	.0001	.0002
	14	.0000	.0000	.0000	.0000	.0000	.0000	.0000	.0000	.0000	.0000	.0000	.0000	.0000

n	X	.01	.02	.03	.04	.05	.10	.15	.20	.25	.30	.35	.40	.45
15	0	.8601	.7386	.6333	.5421	.4633	.2059	.0874	.0352	.0134	.0047	.0016	.0005	.0001
	1	.1303	.2261	.2938	.3388	.3658	.3432	.2312	.1319	.0668	.0305	.0126	.0047	.0016
	2	.0092	.0323	.0636	.0988	.1348	.2669	.2856	.2309	.1559	.0916	.0476	.0219	.0090
	3	.0004	.0029	.0085	.0178	.0307	.1285	.2184	.2501	.2252	.1700	.1110	.0634	.0318
	4	.0000	.0002	.0008	.0022	.0049	.0428	.1156	.1876	.2252	.2186	.1792	.1268	.0780
	5	.0000	.0000	.0001	.0002	.0006	.0105	.0449	.1032	.1651	.2061	.2123	.1859	.1404
	6	.0000	.0000	.0000	.0000	.0000	.0019	.0132	.0430	.0917	.1472	.1906	.2066	.1914
	7	.0000	.0000	.0000	.0000	.0000	.0003	.0030	.0138	.0393	.0811	.1319	.1771	.2013
	8	.0000	.0000	.0000	.0000	.0000	.0000	.0005	.0035	.0131	.0348	.0710	.1181	.1647
	9	.0000	.0000	.0000	.0000	.0000	.0000	.0001	.0007	.0034	.0116	.0298	.0612	.1048
	10	.0000	.0000	.0000	.0000	.0000	.0000	.0000	.0001	.0007	.0030	.0096	.0245	.0515
	11	.0000	.0000	.0000	.0000	.0000	.0000	.0000	.0000	.0001	.0006	.0024	.0074	.0191
	12	.0000	.0000	.0000	.0000	.0000	.0000	.0000	.0000	.0000	.0001	.0004	.0016	.0052
	13	.0000	.0000	.0000	.0000	.0000	.0000	.0000	.0000	.0000	.0000	.0001	.0003	.0010
	14	.0000	.0000	.0000	.0000	.0000	.0000	.0000	.0000	.0000	.0000	.0000	.0001	.0001
	15	.0000	.0000	.0000	.0000	.0000	.0000	.0000	.0000	.0000	.0000	.0000	.0000	.0000

π

.50	.55	.60	.65	.70	.75	.80	.85	.90	.95	.96	.97	.98	.99	X	n
.0001	.0000	.0000	.0000	.0000	.0000	.0000	.0000	.0000	.0000	.0000	.0000	.0000	.0000	0	13
.0016	.0005	.0001	.0000	.0000	.0000	.0000	.0000	.0000	.0000	.0000	.0000	.0000	.0000	1	
.0095	.0036	.0012	.0003	.0001	.0000	.0000	.0000	.0000	.0000	.0000	.0000	.0000	.0000	2	
.0349	.0162	.0065	.0022	.0006	.0001	.0000	.0000	.0000	.0000	.0000	.0000	.0000	.0000	3	
.0873	.0495	.0243	.0101	.0034	.0009	.0001	.0000	.0000	.0000	.0000	.0000	.0000	.0000	4	
.1571	.1089	.0656	.0336	.0142	.0047	.0011	.0001	.0000	.0000	.0000	.0000	.0000	.0000	5	
.2095	.1775	.1312	.0833	.0442	.0186	.0058	.0011	.0001	.0000	.0000	.0000	.0000	.0000	6	
.2095	.2169	.1968	.1546	.1030	.0559	.0230	.0063	.0008	.0000	.0000	.0000	.0000	.0000	7	
.1571	.1989	.2214	.2154	.1803	.1258	.0691	.0266	.0055	.0003	.0001	.0000	.0000	.0000	8	
.0873	.1350	.1845	.2222	.2337	.2097	.1535	.0838	.0277	.0028	.0013	.0004	.0001	.0000	9	
.0349	.0660	.1107	.1651	.2181	.2517	.2457	.1900	.0997	.0214	.0122	.0057	.0019	.0003	10	
.0095	.0220	.0453	.0836	.1388	.2059	.2680	.2937	.2448	.1109	.0797	.0502	.0250	.0070	11	
.0016	.0045	.0113	.0259	.0540	.1029	.1787	.2774	.3672	.3512	.3186	.2706	.2040	.1152	12	
.0001	.0004	.0013	.0037	.0097	.0238	.0550	.1209	.2542	.5133	.5882	.6730	.7690	.8775	13	

.50	.55	.60	.65	.70	.75	.80	.85	.90	.95	.96	.97	.98	.99	X	n
.0001	.0000	.0000	.0000	.0000	.0000	.0000	.0000	.0000	.0000	.0000	.0000	.0000	.0000	0	14
.0009	.0002	.0001	.0000	.0000	.0000	.0000	.0000	.0000	.0000	.0000	.0000	.0000	.0000	1	
.0056	.0019	.0005	.0001	.0000	.0000	.0000	.0000	.0000	.0000	.0000	.0000	.0000	.0000	2	
.0222	.0093	.0033	.0010	.0002	.0000	.0000	.0000	.0000	.0000	.0000	.0000	.0000	.0000	3	
.0611	.0312	.0136	.0049	.0014	.0003	.0000	.0000	.0000	.0000	.0000	.0000	.0000	.0000	4	
.1222	.0762	.0408	.0183	.0066	.0018	.0003	.0000	.0000	.0000	.0000	.0000	.0000	.0000	5	
.1833	.1398	.0918	.0510	.0232	.0082	.0020	.0003	.0000	.0000	.0000	.0000	.0000	.0000	6	
.2095	.1952	.1574	.1082	.0618	.0280	.0092	.0019	.0002	.0000	.0000	.0000	.0000	.0000	7	
.1833	.2088	.2066	.1759	.1262	.0734	.0322	.0093	.0013	.0000	.0000	.0000	.0000	.0000	8	
.1222	.1701	.2066	.2178	.1963	.1468	.0860	.0352	.0078	.0004	.0001	.0000	.0000	.0000	9	
.0611	.1040	.1549	.2022	.2202	.2202	.1720	.0998	.0349	.0037	.0017	.0006	.0001	.0000	10	
.0222	.0462	.0845	.1366	.1943	.2402	.2501	.2056	.1142	.0259	.0149	.0070	.0023	.0003	11	
.0056	.0141	.0317	.0634	.1134	.1802	.2501	.2912	.2570	.1229	.0892	.0568	.0286	.0081	12	
.0009	.0027	.0073	.0181	.0407	.0832	.1539	.2539	.3559	.3593	.3294	.2827	.2153	.1229	13	
.0001	.0002	.0008	.0024	.0068	.0178	.0440	.1028	.2288	.4877	.5647	.6528	.7536	.8687	14	

.50	.55	.60	.65	.70	.75	.80	.85	.90	.95	.96	.97	.98	.99	X	n
.0000	.0000	.0000	.0000	.0000	.0000	.0000	.0000	.0000	.0000	.0000	.0000	.0000	.0000	0	15
.0005	.0001	.0000	.0000	.0000	.0000	.0000	.0000	.0000	.0000	.0000	.0000	.0000	.0000	1	
.0032	.0010	.0003	.0001	.0000	.0000	.0000	.0000	.0000	.0000	.0000	.0000	.0000	.0000	2	
.0139	.0052	.0016	.0004	.0001	.0000	.0000	.0000	.0000	.0000	.0000	.0000	.0000	.0000	3	
.0417	.0191	.0074	.0024	.0006	.0001	.0000	.0000	.0000	.0000	.0000	.0000	.0000	.0000	4	
.0916	.0515	.0245	.0096	.0030	.0007	.0001	.0000	.0000	.0000	.0000	.0000	.0000	.0000	5	
.1527	.1048	.0612	.0298	.0116	.0034	.0007	.0001	.0000	.0000	.0000	.0000	.0000	.0000	6	
.1964	.1647	.1181	.0710	.0348	.0131	.0035	.0005	.0000	.0000	.0000	.0000	.0000	.0000	7	
.1964	.2013	.1771	.1319	.0811	.0393	.0138	.0030	.0003	.0000	.0000	.0000	.0000	.0000	8	
.1527	.1914	.2066	.1906	.1472	.0917	.0430	.0132	.0019	.0000	.0000	.0000	.0000	.0000	9	
.0916	.1404	.1859	.2123	.2061	.1651	.1032	.0449	.0105	.0006	.0002	.0001	.0000	.0000	10	
.0417	.0780	.1268	.1792	.2186	.2252	.1876	.1156	.0428	.0049	.0022	.0008	.0002	.0000	11	
.0139	.0318	.0634	.1110	.1700	.2252	.2501	.2184	.1285	.0307	.0178	.0085	.0029	.0004	12	
.0032	.0090	.0219	.0476	.0916	.1559	.2309	.2856	.2669	.1348	.0988	.0636	.0323	.0092	13	
.0005	.0016	.0047	.0126	.0305	.0668	.1319	.2312	.3432	.3658	.3388	.2938	.2261	.1303	14	
.0000	.0001	.0005	.0016	.0047	.0134	.0352	.0874	.2059	.4633	.5421	.6333	.7386	.8601	15	

Binomial Distribution—Individual Terms (continued)

n	X	.01	.02	.03	.04	.05	.10	.15 (π)	.20	.25	.30	.35	.40	.45
20	0	.8179	.6676	.5438	.4420	.3585	.1216	.0388	.0115	.0032	.0008	.0002	.0000	.0000
	1	.1652	.2725	.3364	.3683	.3774	.2702	.1368	.0576	.0211	.0068	.0020	.0005	.0001
	2	.0159	.0528	.0988	.1458	.1887	.2852	.2293	.1369	.0669	.0278	.0100	.0031	.0008
	3	.0010	.0065	.0183	.0364	.0596	.1901	.2428	.2054	.1339	.0716	.0323	.0123	.0040
	4	.0000	.0006	.0024	.0065	.0133	.0898	.1821	.2182	.1897	.1304	.0738	.0350	.0139
	5	.0000	.0000	.0002	.0009	.0022	.0319	.1028	.1746	.2023	.1789	.1272	.0746	.0365
	6	.0000	.0000	.0000	.0001	.0003	.0089	.0454	.1091	.1686	.1916	.1712	.1244	.0746
	7	.0000	.0000	.0000	.0000	.0000	.0020	.0160	.0545	.1124	.1643	.1844	.1659	.1221
	8	.0000	.0000	.0000	.0000	.0000	.0004	.0046	.0222	.0609	.1144	.1614	.1797	.1623
	9	.0000	.0000	.0000	.0000	.0000	.0001	.0011	.0074	.0271	.0654	.1158	.1597	.1771
	10	.0000	.0000	.0000	.0000	.0000	.0000	.0002	.0020	.0099	.0308	.0686	.1171	.1593
	11	.0000	.0000	.0000	.0000	.0000	.0000	.0000	.0005	.0030	.0120	.0336	.0710	.1185
	12	.0000	.0000	.0000	.0000	.0000	.0000	.0000	.0001	.0008	.0039	.0136	.0355	.0727
	13	.0000	.0000	.0000	.0000	.0000	.0000	.0000	.0000	.0002	.0010	.0045	.0146	.0366
	14	.0000	.0000	.0000	.0000	.0000	.0000	.0000	.0000	.0000	.0002	.0012	.0049	.0150
	15	.0000	.0000	.0000	.0000	.0000	.0000	.0000	.0000	.0000	.0000	.0003	.0013	.0049
	16	.0000	.0000	.0000	.0000	.0000	.0000	.0000	.0000	.0000	.0000	.0000	.0003	.0013
	17	.0000	.0000	.0000	.0000	.0000	.0000	.0000	.0000	.0000	.0000	.0000	.0000	.0002
	18	.0000	.0000	.0000	.0000	.0000	.0000	.0000	.0000	.0000	.0000	.0000	.0000	.0000
	19	.0000	.0000	.0000	.0000	.0000	.0000	.0000	.0000	.0000	.0000	.0000	.0000	.0000
	20	.0000	.0000	.0000	.0000	.0000	.0000	.0000	.0000	.0000	.0000	.0000	.0000	.0000

n	X	.01	.02	.03	.04	.05	.10	.15	.20	.25	.30	.35	.40	.45
25	0	.7778	.6035	.4670	.3604	.2774	.0718	.0172	.0038	.0008	.0001	.0000	.0000	.0000
	1	.1964	.3079	.3611	.3754	.3650	.1994	.0759	.0236	.0063	.0014	.0003	.0000	.0000
	2	.0238	.0754	.1340	.1877	.2305	.2659	.1607	.0708	.0251	.0074	.0018	.0004	.0001
	3	.0018	.0118	.0318	.0600	.0930	.2265	.2174	.1358	.0641	.0243	.0076	.0019	.0004
	4	.0001	.0013	.0054	.0137	.0269	.1384	.2110	.1867	.1175	.0572	.0224	.0071	.0018
	5	.0000	.0001	.0007	.0024	.0060	.0646	.1564	.1960	.1645	.1030	.0506	.0199	.0063
	6	.0000	.0000	.0001	.0003	.0010	.0239	.0920	.1633	.1828	.1472	.0908	.0442	.0172
	7	.0000	.0000	.0000	.0000	.0001	.0072	.0441	.1108	.1654	.1712	.1327	.0800	.0381
	8	.0000	.0000	.0000	.0000	.0000	.0018	.0175	.0623	.1241	.1651	.1607	.1200	.0701
	9	.0000	.0000	.0000	.0000	.0000	.0004	.0058	.0294	.0781	.1336	.1635	.1511	.1084
	10	.0000	.0000	.0000	.0000	.0000	.0001	.0016	.0118	.0417	.0916	.1409	.1612	.1419
	11	.0000	.0000	.0000	.0000	.0000	.0000	.0004	.0040	.0189	.0536	.1034	.1465	.1583
	12	.0000	.0000	.0000	.0000	.0000	.0000	.0001	.0012	.0074	.0268	.0650	.1140	.1511
	13	.0000	.0000	.0000	.0000	.0000	.0000	.0000	.0003	.0025	.0115	.0350	.0760	.1236
	14	.0000	.0000	.0000	.0000	.0000	.0000	.0000	.0001	.0007	.0042	.0161	.0434	.0867
	15	.0000	.0000	.0000	.0000	.0000	.0000	.0000	.0000	.0002	.0013	.0064	.0212	.0520
	16	.0000	.0000	.0000	.0000	.0000	.0000	.0000	.0000	.0000	.0004	.0021	.0088	.0266
	17	.0000	.0000	.0000	.0000	.0000	.0000	.0000	.0000	.0000	.0001	.0006	.0031	.0115
	18	.0000	.0000	.0000	.0000	.0000	.0000	.0000	.0000	.0000	.0000	.0001	.0009	.0042
	19	.0000	.0000	.0000	.0000	.0000	.0000	.0000	.0000	.0000	.0000	.0000	.0002	.0013
	20	.0000	.0000	.0000	.0000	.0000	.0000	.0000	.0000	.0000	.0000	.0000	.0000	.0003
	21	.0000	.0000	.0000	.0000	.0000	.0000	.0000	.0000	.0000	.0000	.0000	.0000	.0001
	22	.0000	.0000	.0000	.0000	.0000	.0000	.0000	.0000	.0000	.0000	.0000	.0000	.0000
	23	.0000	.0000	.0000	.0000	.0000	.0000	.0000	.0000	.0000	.0000	.0000	.0000	.0000
	24	.0000	.0000	.0000	.0000	.0000	.0000	.0000	.0000	.0000	.0000	.0000	.0000	.0000
	25	.0000	.0000	.0000	.0000	.0000	.0000	.0000	.0000	.0000	.0000	.0000	.0000	.0000

π

.50	.55	.60	.65	.70	.75	.80	.85	.90	.95	.96	.97	.98	.99	X	n
.0000	.0000	.0000	.0000	.0000	.0000	.0000	.0000	.0000	.0000	.0000	.0000	.0000	.0000	0	20
.0000	.0000	.0000	.0000	.0000	.0000	.0000	.0000	.0000	.0000	.0000	.0000	.0000	.0000	1	
.0002	.0000	.0000	.0000	.0000	.0000	.0000	.0000	.0000	.0000	.0000	.0000	.0000	.0000	2	
.0011	.0002	.0000	.0000	.0000	.0000	.0000	.0000	.0000	.0000	.0000	.0000	.0000	.0000	3	
.0046	.0013	.0003	.0000	.0000	.0000	.0000	.0000	.0000	.0000	.0000	.0000	.0000	.0000	4	
.0148	.0049	.0013	.0003	.0000	.0000	.0000	.0000	.0000	.0000	.0000	.0000	.0000	.0000	5	
.0370	.0150	.0049	.0012	.0002	.0000	.0000	.0000	.0000	.0000	.0000	.0000	.0000	.0000	6	
.0739	.0366	.0146	.0045	.0010	.0002	.0000	.0000	.0000	.0000	.0000	.0000	.0000	.0000	7	
.1201	.0727	.0355	.0136	.0039	.0008	.0001	.0000	.0000	.0000	.0000	.0000	.0000	.0000	8	
.1602	.1185	.0710	.0336	.0120	.0030	.0005	.0000	.0000	.0000	.0000	.0000	.0000	.0000	9	
.1762	.1593	.1171	.0686	.0308	.0099	.0020	.0002	.0000	.0000	.0000	.0000	.0000	.0000	10	
.1602	.1771	.1597	.1158	.0654	.0271	.0074	.0011	.0001	.0000	.0000	.0000	.0000	.0000	11	
.1201	.1623	.1797	.1614	.1144	.0609	.0222	.0046	.0004	.0000	.0000	.0000	.0000	.0000	12	
.0739	.1221	.1659	.1844	.1643	.1124	.0545	.0160	.0020	.0000	.0000	.0000	.0000	.0000	13	
.0370	.0746	.1244	.1712	.1916	.1686	.1091	.0454	.0089	.0003	.0001	.0000	.0000	.0000	14	
.0148	.0365	.0746	.1272	.1789	.2023	.1746	.1028	.0319	.0022	.0009	.0002	.0000	.0000	15	
.0046	.0139	.0350	.0738	.1304	.1897	.2182	.1821	.0898	.0133	.0065	.0024	.0006	.0000	16	
.0011	.0040	.0123	.0323	.0716	.1339	.2054	.2428	.1901	.0596	.0364	.0183	.0065	.0010	17	
.0002	.0008	.0031	.0100	.0278	.0669	.1369	.2293	.2852	.1887	.1458	.0988	.0528	.0159	18	
.0000	.0001	.0005	.0020	.0068	.0211	.0576	.1368	.2702	.3774	.3683	.3364	.2725	.1652	19	
.0000	.0000	.0000	.0002	.0008	.0032	.0115	.0388	.1216	.3585	.4420	.5438	.6676	.8179	20	

.50	.55	.60	.65	.70	.75	.80	.85	.90	.95	.96	.97	.98	.99		
.0000	.0000	.0000	.0000	.0000	.0000	.0000	.0000	.0000	.0000	.0000	.0000	.0000	.0000	0	25
.0000	.0000	.0000	.0000	.0000	.0000	.0000	.0000	.0000	.0000	.0000	.0000	.0000	.0000	1	
.0000	.0000	.0000	.0000	.0000	.0000	.0000	.0000	.0000	.0000	.0000	.0000	.0000	.0000	2	
.0001	.0000	.0000	.0000	.0000	.0000	.0000	.0000	.0000	.0000	.0000	.0000	.0000	.0000	3	
.0004	.0001	.0000	.0000	.0000	.0000	.0000	.0000	.0000	.0000	.0000	.0000	.0000	.0000	4	
.0016	.0003	.0000	.0000	.0000	.0000	.0000	.0000	.0000	.0000	.0000	.0000	.0000	.0000	5	
.0053	.0013	.0002	.0000	.0000	.0000	.0000	.0000	.0000	.0000	.0000	.0000	.0000	.0000	6	
.0143	.0042	.0009	.0001	.0000	.0000	.0000	.0000	.0000	.0000	.0000	.0000	.0000	.0000	7	
.0322	.0115	.0031	.0006	.0001	.0000	.0000	.0000	.0000	.0000	.0000	.0000	.0000	.0000	8	
.0609	.0266	.0088	.0021	.0004	.0000	.0000	.0000	.0000	.0000	.0000	.0000	.0000	.0000	9	
.0974	.0520	.0212	.0064	.0013	.0002	.0000	.0000	.0000	.0000	.0000	.0000	.0000	.0000	10	
.1328	.0867	.0434	.0161	.0042	.0007	.0001	.0000	.0000	.0000	.0000	.0000	.0000	.0000	11	
.1550	.1236	.0760	.0350	.0115	.0025	.0003	.0000	.0000	.0000	.0000	.0000	.0000	.0000	12	
.1550	.1511	.1140	.0650	.0268	.0074	.0012	.0001	.0000	.0000	.0000	.0000	.0000	.0000	13	
.1328	.1583	.1465	.1034	.0536	.0189	.0040	.0004	.0000	.0000	.0000	.0000	.0000	.0000	14	
.0974	.1419	.1612	.1409	.0916	.0417	.0118	.0016	.0001	.0000	.0000	.0000	.0000	.0000	15	
.0609	.1084	.1511	.1635	.1336	.0781	.0294	.0058	.0004	.0000	.0000	.0000	.0000	.0000	16	
.0322	.0701	.1200	.1607	.1651	.1241	.0623	.0175	.0018	.0000	.0000	.0000	.0000	.0000	17	
.0143	.0381	.0800	.1327	.1712	.1654	.1108	.0441	.0072	.0001	.0000	.0000	.0000	.0000	18	
.0053	.0172	.0442	.0908	.1472	.1828	.1633	.0920	.0239	.0010	.0003	.0001	.0000	.0000	19	
.0016	.0063	.0199	.0506	.1030	.1645	.1960	.1564	.0646	.0060	.0024	.0007	.0001	.0000	20	
.0004	.0018	.0071	.0224	.0572	.1175	.1867	.2110	.1384	.0269	.0137	.0054	.0013	.0001	21	
.0001	.0004	.0019	.0076	.0243	.0641	.1358	.2174	.2265	.0930	.0600	.0318	.0118	.0018	22	
.0000	.0001	.0004	.0018	.0074	.0251	.0708	.1607	.2659	.2305	.1877	.1340	.0754	.0238	23	
.0000	.0000	.0000	.0003	.0014	.0063	.0236	.0759	.1994	.3650	.3754	.3611	.3079	.1964	24	
.0000	.0000	.0000	.0000	.0001	.0008	.0038	.0172	.0718	.2774	.3604	.4670	.6035	.7778	25	

Binomial Distribution—Individual Terms (continued)

n = 30

X	π=.01	.02	.03	.04	.05	.10	.15	.20	.25	.30	.35	.40	.45
0	.7397	.5455	.4010	.2939	.2146	.0424	.0076	.0012	.0002	.0000	.0000	.0000	.0000
1	.2242	.3340	.3721	.3673	.3389	.1413	.0404	.0093	.0018	.0003	.0000	.0000	.0000
2	.0328	.0988	.1669	.2219	.2586	.2277	.1034	.0337	.0086	.0018	.0003	.0000	.0000
3	.0031	.0188	.0482	.0863	.1270	.2361	.1703	.0785	.0269	.0072	.0015	.0003	.0000
4	.0002	.0026	.0101	.0243	.0451	.1771	.2028	.1325	.0604	.0208	.0056	.0012	.0002
5	.0000	.0003	.0016	.0053	.0124	.1023	.1861	.1723	.1047	.0464	.0157	.0041	.0008
6	.0000	.0000	.0002	.0009	.0027	.0474	.1368	.1795	.1455	.0829	.0353	.0115	.0029
7	.0000	.0000	.0000	.0001	.0005	.0180	.0828	.1538	.1662	.1219	.0652	.0263	.0081
8	.0000	.0000	.0000	.0000	.0001	.0058	.0420	.1106	.1593	.1501	.1009	.0505	.0191
9	.0000	.0000	.0000	.0000	.0000	.0016	.0181	.0676	.1298	.1573	.1328	.0823	.0382
10	.0000	.0000	.0000	.0000	.0000	.0004	.0067	.0355	.0909	.1416	.1502	.1152	.0656
11	.0000	.0000	.0000	.0000	.0000	.0001	.0022	.0161	.0551	.1103	.1471	.1396	.0976
12	.0000	.0000	.0000	.0000	.0000	.0000	.0006	.0064	.0291	.0749	.1254	.1474	.1265
13	.0000	.0000	.0000	.0000	.0000	.0000	.0001	.0022	.0134	.0444	.0935	.1360	.1433
14	.0000	.0000	.0000	.0000	.0000	.0000	.0000	.0007	.0054	.0231	.0611	.1101	.1424
15	.0000	.0000	.0000	.0000	.0000	.0000	.0000	.0002	.0019	.0105	.0351	.0783	.1242
16	.0000	.0000	.0000	.0000	.0000	.0000	.0000	.0000	.0006	.0042	.0177	.0489	.0953
17	.0000	.0000	.0000	.0000	.0000	.0000	.0000	.0000	.0002	.0015	.0079	.0269	.0642
18	.0000	.0000	.0000	.0000	.0000	.0000	.0000	.0000	.0000	.0005	.0031	.0129	.0379
19	.0000	.0000	.0000	.0000	.0000	.0000	.0000	.0000	.0000	.0001	.0010	.0054	.0196
20	.0000	.0000	.0000	.0000	.0000	.0000	.0000	.0000	.0000	.0000	.0003	.0020	.0088
21	.0000	.0000	.0000	.0000	.0000	.0000	.0000	.0000	.0000	.0000	.0001	.0006	.0034
22	.0000	.0000	.0000	.0000	.0000	.0000	.0000	.0000	.0000	.0000	.0000	.0002	.0012
23	.0000	.0000	.0000	.0000	.0000	.0000	.0000	.0000	.0000	.0000	.0000	.0000	.0003
24	.0000	.0000	.0000	.0000	.0000	.0000	.0000	.0000	.0000	.0000	.0000	.0000	.0001
25	.0000	.0000	.0000	.0000	.0000	.0000	.0000	.0000	.0000	.0000	.0000	.0000	.0000
26	.0000	.0000	.0000	.0000	.0000	.0000	.0000	.0000	.0000	.0000	.0000	.0000	.0000
27	.0000	.0000	.0000	.0000	.0000	.0000	.0000	.0000	.0000	.0000	.0000	.0000	.0000
28	.0000	.0000	.0000	.0000	.0000	.0000	.0000	.0000	.0000	.0000	.0000	.0000	.0000
29	.0000	.0000	.0000	.0000	.0000	.0000	.0000	.0000	.0000	.0000	.0000	.0000	.0000
30	.0000	.0000	.0000	.0000	.0000	.0000	.0000	.0000	.0000	.0000	.0000	.0000	.0000

n = 40

X	π=.01	.02	.03	.04	.05	.10	.15	.20	.25	.30	.35	.40	.45
0	.6690	.4457	.2957	.1954	.1285	.0148	.0015	.0001	.0000	.0000	.0000	.0000	.0000
1	.2703	.3638	.3658	.3256	.2706	.0657	.0106	.0013	.0001	.0000	.0000	.0000	.0000
2	.0532	.1448	.2206	.2646	.2777	.1423	.0365	.0065	.0009	.0001	.0000	.0000	.0000
3	.0068	.0374	.0864	.1396	.1851	.2003	.0816	.0205	.0037	.0005	.0001	.0000	.0000
4	.0006	.0071	.0247	.0538	.0901	.2059	.1332	.0475	.0113	.0020	.0003	.0000	.0000
5	.0000	.0010	.0055	.0161	.0342	.1647	.1692	.0854	.0272	.0061	.0010	.0001	.0000
6	.0000	.0001	.0010	.0039	.0105	.1068	.1742	.1246	.0530	.0151	.0031	.0005	.0000
7	.0000	.0000	.0001	.0008	.0027	.0576	.1493	.1513	.0857	.0315	.0080	.0015	.0002
8	.0000	.0000	.0000	.0001	.0006	.0264	.1087	.1560	.1179	.0557	.0179	.0040	.0006
9	.0000	.0000	.0000	.0000	.0001	.0104	.0682	.1386	.1397	.0849	.0342	.0095	.0018
10	.0000	.0000	.0000	.0000	.0000	.0036	.0373	.1075	.1444	.1128	.0571	.0196	.0047
11	.0000	.0000	.0000	.0000	.0000	.0011	.0180	.0733	.1312	.1319	.0838	.0357	.0105
12	.0000	.0000	.0000	.0000	.0000	.0003	.0077	.0443	.1057	.1366	.1090	.0576	.0207
13	.0000	.0000	.0000	.0000	.0000	.0001	.0029	.0238	.0759	.1261	.1265	.0827	.0365
14	.0000	.0000	.0000	.0000	.0000	.0000	.0010	.0115	.0488	.1042	.1313	.1063	.0575
15	.0000	.0000	.0000	.0000	.0000	.0000	.0003	.0050	.0282	.0774	.1226	.1228	.0816
16	.0000	.0000	.0000	.0000	.0000	.0000	.0001	.0019	.0147	.0518	.1031	.1279	.1043
17	.0000	.0000	.0000	.0000	.0000	.0000	.0000	.0007	.0069	.0314	.0784	.1204	.1205
18	.0000	.0000	.0000	.0000	.0000	.0000	.0000	.0002	.0029	.0172	.0539	.1026	.1260
19	.0000	.0000	.0000	.0000	.0000	.0000	.0000	.0001	.0011	.0085	.0336	.0792	.1194
20	.0000	.0000	.0000	.0000	.0000	.0000	.0000	.0000	.0004	.0038	.0190	.0554	.1025
21	.0000	.0000	.0000	.0000	.0000	.0000	.0000	.0000	.0001	.0016	.0097	.0352	.0799
22	.0000	.0000	.0000	.0000	.0000	.0000	.0000	.0000	.0000	.0006	.0045	.0203	.0565
23	.0000	.0000	.0000	.0000	.0000	.0000	.0000	.0000	.0000	.0002	.0019	.0106	.0362
24	.0000	.0000	.0000	.0000	.0000	.0000	.0000	.0000	.0000	.0001	.0007	.0050	.0210
25	.0000	.0000	.0000	.0000	.0000	.0000	.0000	.0000	.0000	.0000	.0003	.0021	.0110
26	.0000	.0000	.0000	.0000	.0000	.0000	.0000	.0000	.0000	.0000	.0001	.0008	.0052
27	.0000	.0000	.0000	.0000	.0000	.0000	.0000	.0000	.0000	.0000	.0000	.0003	.0022
28	.0000	.0000	.0000	.0000	.0000	.0000	.0000	.0000	.0000	.0000	.0000	.0001	.0008
29	.0000	.0000	.0000	.0000	.0000	.0000	.0000	.0000	.0000	.0000	.0000	.0000	.0003
30	.0000	.0000	.0000	.0000	.0000	.0000	.0000	.0000	.0000	.0000	.0000	.0000	.0001
31	.0000	.0000	.0000	.0000	.0000	.0000	.0000	.0000	.0000	.0000	.0000	.0000	.0000
32	.0000	.0000	.0000	.0000	.0000	.0000	.0000	.0000	.0000	.0000	.0000	.0000	.0000
33	.0000	.0000	.0000	.0000	.0000	.0000	.0000	.0000	.0000	.0000	.0000	.0000	.0000
34	.0000	.0000	.0000	.0000	.0000	.0000	.0000	.0000	.0000	.0000	.0000	.0000	.0000
35	.0000	.0000	.0000	.0000	.0000	.0000	.0000	.0000	.0000	.0000	.0000	.0000	.0000
36	.0000	.0000	.0000	.0000	.0000	.0000	.0000	.0000	.0000	.0000	.0000	.0000	.0000
37	.0000	.0000	.0000	.0000	.0000	.0000	.0000	.0000	.0000	.0000	.0000	.0000	.0000
38	.0000	.0000	.0000	.0000	.0000	.0000	.0000	.0000	.0000	.0000	.0000	.0000	.0000
39	.0000	.0000	.0000	.0000	.0000	.0000	.0000	.0000	.0000	.0000	.0000	.0000	.0000
40	.0000	.0000	.0000	.0000	.0000	.0000	.0000	.0000	.0000	.0000	.0000	.0000	.0000

π

n = 30

.50	.55	.60	.65	.70	.75	.80	.85	.90	.95	.96	.97	.98	.99	X	n
.0000	.0000	.0000	.0000	.0000	.0000	.0000	.0000	.0000	.0000	.0000	.0000	.0000	.0000	0	30
.0000	.0000	.0000	.0000	.0000	.0000	.0000	.0000	.0000	.0000	.0000	.0000	.0000	.0000	1	
.0000	.0000	.0000	.0000	.0000	.0000	.0000	.0000	.0000	.0000	.0000	.0000	.0000	.0000	2	
.0000	.0000	.0000	.0000	.0000	.0000	.0000	.0000	.0000	.0000	.0000	.0000	.0000	.0000	3	
.0000	.0000	.0000	.0000	.0000	.0000	.0000	.0000	.0000	.0000	.0000	.0000	.0000	.0000	4	
.0001	.0000	.0000	.0000	.0000	.0000	.0000	.0000	.0000	.0000	.0000	.0000	.0000	.0000	5	
.0006	.0001	.0000	.0000	.0000	.0000	.0000	.0000	.0000	.0000	.0000	.0000	.0000	.0000	6	
.0019	.0003	.0000	.0000	.0000	.0000	.0000	.0000	.0000	.0000	.0000	.0000	.0000	.0000	7	
.0055	.0012	.0002	.0000	.0000	.0000	.0000	.0000	.0000	.0000	.0000	.0000	.0000	.0000	8	
.0133	.0034	.0006	.0001	.0000	.0000	.0000	.0000	.0000	.0000	.0000	.0000	.0000	.0000	9	
.0280	.0088	.0020	.0003	.0000	.0000	.0000	.0000	.0000	.0000	.0000	.0000	.0000	.0000	10	
.0509	.0196	.0054	.0010	.0001	.0000	.0000	.0000	.0000	.0000	.0000	.0000	.0000	.0000	11	
.0806	.0379	.0129	.0031	.0005	.0000	.0000	.0000	.0000	.0000	.0000	.0000	.0000	.0000	12	
.1115	.0642	.0269	.0079	.0015	.0002	.0000	.0000	.0000	.0000	.0000	.0000	.0000	.0000	13	
.1354	.0953	.0489	.0177	.0042	.0006	.0000	.0000	.0000	.0000	.0000	.0000	.0000	.0000	14	
.1445	.1242	.0783	.0351	.0106	.0019	.0002	.0000	.0000	.0000	.0000	.0000	.0000	.0000	15	
.1354	.1424	.1101	.0611	.0231	.0054	.0007	.0000	.0000	.0000	.0000	.0000	.0000	.0000	16	
.1115	.1433	.1360	.0935	.0444	.0134	.0022	.0001	.0000	.0000	.0000	.0000	.0000	.0000	17	
.0806	.1265	.1474	.1254	.0749	.0291	.0064	.0006	.0000	.0000	.0000	.0000	.0000	.0000	18	
.0509	.0976	.1396	.1471	.1103	.0551	.0161	.0022	.0001	.0000	.0000	.0000	.0000	.0000	19	
.0280	.0656	.1152	.1502	.1416	.0909	.0355	.0067	.0004	.0000	.0000	.0000	.0000	.0000	20	
.0133	.0382	.0823	.1328	.1573	.1298	.0676	.0181	.0016	.0000	.0000	.0000	.0000	.0000	21	
.0055	.0191	.0505	.1009	.1501	.1593	.1106	.0420	.0058	.0001	.0000	.0000	.0000	.0000	22	
.0019	.0081	.0263	.0652	.1219	.1662	.1538	.0828	.0180	.0005	.0001	.0000	.0000	.0000	23	
.0006	.0029	.0115	.0353	.0829	.1455	.1795	.1368	.0474	.0027	.0009	.0002	.0000	.0000	24	
.0001	.0008	.0041	.0157	.0464	.1047	.1723	.1861	.1023	.0124	.0053	.0016	.0003	.0000	25	
.0000	.0002	.0012	.0056	.0208	.0604	.1325	.2028	.1771	.0451	.0243	.0101	.0026	.0002	26	
.0000	.0000	.0003	.0015	.0072	.0269	.0785	.1703	.2361	.1270	.0863	.0482	.0188	.0031	27	
.0000	.0000	.0000	.0003	.0018	.0086	.0337	.1034	.2277	.2586	.2219	.1669	.0988	.0328	28	
.0000	.0000	.0000	.0000	.0003	.0018	.0093	.0404	.1413	.3389	.3673	.3721	.3340	.2242	29	
.0000	.0000	.0000	.0000	.0000	.0002	.0012	.0076	.0424	.2146	.2939	.4010	.5455	.7397	30	

n = 40

.50	.55	.60	.65	.70	.75	.80	.85	.90	.95	.96	.97	.98	.99	X	n
.0000	.0000	.0000	.0000	.0000	.0000	.0000	.0000	.0000	.0000	.0000	.0000	.0000	.0000	0	40
.0000	.0000	.0000	.0000	.0000	.0000	.0000	.0000	.0000	.0000	.0000	.0000	.0000	.0000	1	
.0000	.0000	.0000	.0000	.0000	.0000	.0000	.0000	.0000	.0000	.0000	.0000	.0000	.0000	2	
.0000	.0000	.0000	.0000	.0000	.0000	.0000	.0000	.0000	.0000	.0000	.0000	.0000	.0000	3	
.0000	.0000	.0000	.0000	.0000	.0000	.0000	.0000	.0000	.0000	.0000	.0000	.0000	.0000	4	
.0000	.0000	.0000	.0000	.0000	.0000	.0000	.0000	.0000	.0000	.0000	.0000	.0000	.0000	5	
.0000	.0000	.0000	.0000	.0000	.0000	.0000	.0000	.0000	.0000	.0000	.0000	.0000	.0000	6	
.0000	.0000	.0000	.0000	.0000	.0000	.0000	.0000	.0000	.0000	.0000	.0000	.0000	.0000	7	
.0001	.0000	.0000	.0000	.0000	.0000	.0000	.0000	.0000	.0000	.0000	.0000	.0000	.0000	8	
.0002	.0000	.0000	.0000	.0000	.0000	.0000	.0000	.0000	.0000	.0000	.0000	.0000	.0000	9	
.0008	.0001	.0000	.0000	.0000	.0000	.0000	.0000	.0000	.0000	.0000	.0000	.0000	.0000	10	
.0021	.0003	.0000	.0000	.0000	.0000	.0000	.0000	.0000	.0000	.0000	.0000	.0000	.0000	11	
.0051	.0008	.0001	.0000	.0000	.0000	.0000	.0000	.0000	.0000	.0000	.0000	.0000	.0000	12	
.0109	.0022	.0003	.0000	.0000	.0000	.0000	.0000	.0000	.0000	.0000	.0000	.0000	.0000	13	
.0211	.0052	.0008	.0001	.0000	.0000	.0000	.0000	.0000	.0000	.0000	.0000	.0000	.0000	14	
.0366	.0110	.0021	.0003	.0000	.0000	.0000	.0000	.0000	.0000	.0000	.0000	.0000	.0000	15	
.0572	.0210	.0050	.0007	.0001	.0000	.0000	.0000	.0000	.0000	.0000	.0000	.0000	.0000	16	
.0807	.0362	.0106	.0019	.0002	.0000	.0000	.0000	.0000	.0000	.0000	.0000	.0000	.0000	17	
.1031	.0565	.0203	.0045	.0006	.0000	.0000	.0000	.0000	.0000	.0000	.0000	.0000	.0000	18	
.1194	.0799	.0352	.0097	.0016	.0001	.0000	.0000	.0000	.0000	.0000	.0000	.0000	.0000	19	
.1254	.1025	.0554	.0190	.0038	.0004	.0000	.0000	.0000	.0000	.0000	.0000	.0000	.0000	20	
.1194	.1194	.0792	.0336	.0085	.0011	.0001	.0000	.0000	.0000	.0000	.0000	.0000	.0000	21	
.1031	.1260	.1026	.0539	.0172	.0029	.0002	.0000	.0000	.0000	.0000	.0000	.0000	.0000	22	
.0807	.1205	.1204	.0784	.0314	.0069	.0007	.0000	.0000	.0000	.0000	.0000	.0000	.0000	23	
.0572	.1043	.1279	.1031	.0518	.0147	.0019	.0001	.0000	.0000	.0000	.0000	.0000	.0000	24	
.0366	.0816	.1228	.1226	.0774	.0282	.0050	.0003	.0000	.0000	.0000	.0000	.0000	.0000	25	
.0211	.0575	.1063	.1313	.1042	.0488	.0115	.0010	.0000	.0000	.0000	.0000	.0000	.0000	26	
.0109	.0365	.0827	.1265	.1261	.0759	.0238	.0029	.0001	.0000	.0000	.0000	.0000	.0000	27	
.0051	.0207	.0576	.1090	.1366	.1057	.0443	.0077	.0003	.0000	.0000	.0000	.0000	.0000	28	
.0021	.0105	.0357	.0838	.1319	.1312	.0733	.0180	.0011	.0000	.0000	.0000	.0000	.0000	29	
.0008	.0047	.0196	.0571	.1128	.1444	.1075	.0373	.0036	.0000	.0000	.0000	.0000	.0000	30	
.0002	.0018	.0095	.0342	.0849	.1397	.1386	.0682	.0104	.0001	.0000	.0000	.0000	.0000	31	
.0001	.0006	.0040	.0179	.0557	.1179	.1560	.1087	.0264	.0006	.0001	.0000	.0000	.0000	32	
.0000	.0002	.0015	.0080	.0315	.0857	.1513	.1493	.0576	.0027	.0008	.0001	.0000	.0000	33	
.0000	.0000	.0005	.0031	.0151	.0530	.1246	.1742	.1068	.0105	.0039	.0010	.0001	.0000	34	
.0000	.0000	.0001	.0010	.0061	.0272	.0854	.1692	.1647	.0342	.0161	.0055	.0010	.0000	35	
.0000	.0000	.0000	.0003	.0020	.0113	.0475	.1332	.2059	.0901	.0538	.0247	.0071	.0006	36	
.0000	.0000	.0000	.0001	.0005	.0037	.0205	.0816	.2003	.1851	.1396	.0864	.0374	.0068	37	
.0000	.0000	.0000	.0000	.0001	.0009	.0065	.0365	.1423	.2777	.2646	.2206	.1448	.0532	38	
.0000	.0000	.0000	.0000	.0000	.0001	.0013	.0106	.0657	.2706	.3256	.3658	.3638	.2703	39	
.0000	.0000	.0000	.0000	.0000	.0000	.0001	.0015	.0148	.1285	.1954	.2957	.4457	.6690	40	

Binomial Distribution—Individual Terms (concluded)

n	X	.01	.02	.03	.04	.05	.10	.15	.20	.25	.30	.35	.40	.45
50	0	.6050	.3642	.2181	.1299	.0769	.0052	.0003	.0000	.0000	.0000	.0000	.0000	.0000
	1	.3056	.3716	.3372	.2706	.2025	.0286	.0026	.0002	.0000	.0000	.0000	.0000	.0000
	2	.0756	.1858	.2555	.2762	.2611	.0779	.0113	.0011	.0001	.0000	.0000	.0000	.0000
	3	.0122	.0607	.1264	.1842	.2199	.1386	.0319	.0044	.0004	.0000	.0000	.0000	.0000
	4	.0015	.0145	.0459	.0902	.1360	.1809	.0661	.0128	.0016	.0001	.0000	.0000	.0000
	5	.0001	.0027	.0131	.0346	.0658	.1849	.1072	.0295	.0049	.0006	.0000	.0000	.0000
	6	.0000	.0004	.0030	.0108	.0260	.1541	.1419	.0554	.0123	.0018	.0002	.0000	.0000
	7	.0000	.0001	.0006	.0028	.0086	.1076	.1575	.0870	.0259	.0048	.0006	.0000	.0000
	8	.0000	.0000	.0001	.0006	.0024	.0643	.1493	.1169	.0463	.0110	.0017	.0002	.0000
	9	.0000	.0000	.0000	.0001	.0006	.0333	.1230	.1364	.0721	.0220	.0042	.0005	.0000
	10	.0000	.0000	.0000	.0000	.0001	.0152	.0890	.1398	.0985	.0386	.0093	.0014	.0001
	11	.0000	.0000	.0000	.0000	.0000	.0061	.0571	.1271	.1194	.0602	.0182	.0035	.0004
	12	.0000	.0000	.0000	.0000	.0000	.0022	.0328	.1033	.1294	.0838	.0319	.0076	.0011
	13	.0000	.0000	.0000	.0000	.0000	.0007	.0169	.0755	.1261	.1050	.0502	.0147	.0027
	14	.0000	.0000	.0000	.0000	.0000	.0002	.0079	.0499	.1110	.1189	.0714	.0260	.0059
	15	.0000	.0000	.0000	.0000	.0000	.0001	.0033	.0299	.0888	.1223	.0923	.0415	.0116
	16	.0000	.0000	.0000	.0000	.0000	.0000	.0013	.0164	.0648	.1088	.1088	.0606	.0207
	17	.0000	.0000	.0000	.0000	.0000	.0000	.0005	.0082	.0432	.0983	.1171	.0808	.0339
	18	.0000	.0000	.0000	.0000	.0000	.0000	.0001	.0037	.0264	.0772	.1156	.0987	.0508
	19	.0000	.0000	.0000	.0000	.0000	.0000	.0000	.0016	.0148	.0558	.1048	.1109	.0700
	20	.0000	.0000	.0000	.0000	.0000	.0000	.0000	.0006	.0077	.0370	.0875	.1146	.0888
	21	.0000	.0000	.0000	.0000	.0000	.0000	.0000	.0002	.0036	.0227	.0673	.1091	.1038
	22	.0000	.0000	.0000	.0000	.0000	.0000	.0000	.0001	.0016	.0128	.0478	.0959	.1119
	23	.0000	.0000	.0000	.0000	.0000	.0000	.0000	.0000	.0006	.0067	.0313	.0778	.1115
	24	.0000	.0000	.0000	.0000	.0000	.0000	.0000	.0000	.0002	.0032	.0190	.0584	.1026
	25	.0000	.0000	.0000	.0000	.0000	.0000	.0000	.0000	.0001	.0014	.0106	.0405	.0873
	26	.0000	.0000	.0000	.0000	.0000	.0000	.0000	.0000	.0000	.0006	.0055	.0259	.0687
	27	.0000	.0000	.0000	.0000	.0000	.0000	.0000	.0000	.0000	.0002	.0026	.0154	.0500
	28	.0000	.0000	.0000	.0000	.0000	.0000	.0000	.0000	.0000	.0001	.0012	.0084	.0336
	29	.0000	.0000	.0000	.0000	.0000	.0000	.0000	.0000	.0000	.0000	.0005	.0043	.0208
	30	.0000	.0000	.0000	.0000	.0000	.0000	.0000	.0000	.0000	.0000	.0002	.0020	.0119
	31	.0000	.0000	.0000	.0000	.0000	.0000	.0000	.0000	.0000	.0000	.0001	.0009	.0063
	32	.0000	.0000	.0000	.0000	.0000	.0000	.0000	.0000	.0000	.0000	.0000	.0003	.0031
	33	.0000	.0000	.0000	.0000	.0000	.0000	.0000	.0000	.0000	.0000	.0000	.0001	.0014
	34	.0000	.0000	.0000	.0000	.0000	.0000	.0000	.0000	.0000	.0000	.0000	.0000	.0006
	35	.0000	.0000	.0000	.0000	.0000	.0000	.0000	.0000	.0000	.0000	.0000	.0000	.0002
	36	.0000	.0000	.0000	.0000	.0000	.0000	.0000	.0000	.0000	.0000	.0000	.0000	.0001
	37	.0000	.0000	.0000	.0000	.0000	.0000	.0000	.0000	.0000	.0000	.0000	.0000	.0000
	38	.0000	.0000	.0000	.0000	.0000	.0000	.0000	.0000	.0000	.0000	.0000	.0000	.0000
	39	.0000	.0000	.0000	.0000	.0000	.0000	.0000	.0000	.0000	.0000	.0000	.0000	.0000
	40	.0000	.0000	.0000	.0000	.0000	.0000	.0000	.0000	.0000	.0000	.0000	.0000	.0000
	41	.0000	.0000	.0000	.0000	.0000	.0000	.0000	.0000	.0000	.0000	.0000	.0000	.0000
	42	.0000	.0000	.0000	.0000	.0000	.0000	.0000	.0000	.0000	.0000	.0000	.0000	.0000
	43	.0000	.0000	.0000	.0000	.0000	.0000	.0000	.0000	.0000	.0000	.0000	.0000	.0000
	44	.0000	.0000	.0000	.0000	.0000	.0000	.0000	.0000	.0000	.0000	.0000	.0000	.0000
	45	.0000	.0000	.0000	.0000	.0000	.0000	.0000	.0000	.0000	.0000	.0000	.0000	.0000
	46	.0000	.0000	.0000	.0000	.0000	.0000	.0000	.0000	.0000	.0000	.0000	.0000	.0000
	47	.0000	.0000	.0000	.0000	.0000	.0000	.0000	.0000	.0000	.0000	.0000	.0000	.0000
	48	.0000	.0000	.0000	.0000	.0000	.0000	.0000	.0000	.0000	.0000	.0000	.0000	.0000
	49	.0000	.0000	.0000	.0000	.0000	.0000	.0000	.0000	.0000	.0000	.0000	.0000	.0000
	50	.0000	.0000	.0000	.0000	.0000	.0000	.0000	.0000	.0000	.0000	.0000	.0000	.0000

π

.50	.55	.60	.65	.70	.75	.80	.85	.90	.95	.96	.97	.98	.99	X	n
.0000	.0000	.0000	.0000	.0000	.0000	.0000	.0000	.0000	.0000	.0000	.0000	.0000	.0000	0	50
.0000	.0000	.0000	.0000	.0000	.0000	.0000	.0000	.0000	.0000	.0000	.0000	.0000	.0000	1	
.0000	.0000	.0000	.0000	.0000	.0000	.0000	.0000	.0000	.0000	.0000	.0000	.0000	.0000	2	
.0000	.0000	.0000	.0000	.0000	.0000	.0000	.0000	.0000	.0000	.0000	.0000	.0000	.0000	3	
.0000	.0000	.0000	.0000	.0000	.0000	.0000	.0000	.0000	.0000	.0000	.0000	.0000	.0000	4	
.0000	.0000	.0000	.0000	.0000	.0000	.0000	.0000	.0000	.0000	.0000	.0000	.0000	.0000	5	
.0000	.0000	.0000	.0000	.0000	.0000	.0000	.0000	.0000	.0000	.0000	.0000	.0000	.0000	6	
.0000	.0000	.0000	.0000	.0000	.0000	.0000	.0000	.0000	.0000	.0000	.0000	.0000	.0000	7	
.0000	.0000	.0000	.0000	.0000	.0000	.0000	.0000	.0000	.0000	.0000	.0000	.0000	.0000	8	
.0000	.0000	.0000	.0000	.0000	.0000	.0000	.0000	.0000	.0000	.0000	.0000	.0000	.0000	9	
.0000	.0000	.0000	.0000	.0000	.0000	.0000	.0000	.0000	.0000	.0000	.0000	.0000	.0000	10	
.0000	.0000	.0000	.0000	.0000	.0000	.0000	.0000	.0000	.0000	.0000	.0000	.0000	.0000	11	
.0001	.0000	.0000	.0000	.0000	.0000	.0000	.0000	.0000	.0000	.0000	.0000	.0000	.0000	12	
.0003	.0000	.0000	.0000	.0000	.0000	.0000	.0000	.0000	.0000	.0000	.0000	.0000	.0000	13	
.0008	.0001	.0000	.0000	.0000	.0000	.0000	.0000	.0000	.0000	.0000	.0000	.0000	.0000	14	
.0020	.0002	.0000	.0000	.0000	.0000	.0000	.0000	.0000	.0000	.0000	.0000	.0000	.0000	15	
.0044	.0006	.0000	.0000	.0000	.0000	.0000	.0000	.0000	.0000	.0000	.0000	.0000	.0000	16	
.0087	.0014	.0001	.0000	.0000	.0000	.0000	.0000	.0000	.0000	.0000	.0000	.0000	.0000	17	
.0160	.0031	.0003	.0000	.0000	.0000	.0000	.0000	.0000	.0000	.0000	.0000	.0000	.0000	18	
.0270	.0063	.0009	.0001	.0000	.0000	.0000	.0000	.0000	.0000	.0000	.0000	.0000	.0000	19	
.0419	.0119	.0020	.0002	.0000	.0000	.0000	.0000	.0000	.0000	.0000	.0000	.0000	.0000	20	
.0598	.0208	.0043	.0005	.0000	.0000	.0000	.0000	.0000	.0000	.0000	.0000	.0000	.0000	21	
.0788	.0336	.0084	.0012	.0001	.0000	.0000	.0000	.0000	.0000	.0000	.0000	.0000	.0000	22	
.0960	.0500	.0154	.0026	.0002	.0000	.0000	.0000	.0000	.0000	.0000	.0000	.0000	.0000	23	
.1080	.0687	.0259	.0055	.0006	.0000	.0000	.0000	.0000	.0000	.0000	.0000	.0000	.0000	24	
.1123	.0873	.0405	.0106	.0014	.0001	.0000	.0000	.0000	.0000	.0000	.0000	.0000	.0000	25	
.1080	.1026	.0584	.0190	.0032	.0002	.0000	.0000	.0000	.0000	.0000	.0000	.0000	.0000	26	
.0960	.1115	.0778	.0313	.0067	.0006	.0000	.0000	.0000	.0000	.0000	.0000	.0000	.0000	27	
.0788	.1119	.0959	.0478	.0128	.0016	.0001	.0000	.0000	.0000	.0000	.0000	.0000	.0000	28	
.0598	.1038	.1091	.0673	.0227	.0036	.0002	.0000	.0000	.0000	.0000	.0000	.0000	.0000	29	
.0419	.0888	.1146	.0875	.0370	.0077	.0006	.0000	.0000	.0000	.0000	.0000	.0000	.0000	30	
.0270	.0700	.1109	.1048	.0558	.0148	.0016	.0000	.0000	.0000	.0000	.0000	.0000	.0000	31	
.0160	.0508	.0987	.1156	.0772	.0264	.0037	.0001	.0000	.0000	.0000	.0000	.0000	.0000	32	
.0087	.0339	.0808	.1171	.0983	.0432	.0082	.0005	.0000	.0000	.0000	.0000	.0000	.0000	33	
.0044	.0207	.0606	.1088	.1147	.0648	.0164	.0013	.0000	.0000	.0000	.0000	.0000	.0000	34	
.0020	.0116	.0415	.0923	.1223	.0888	.0299	.0033	.0001	.0000	.0000	.0000	.0000	.0000	35	
.0008	.0059	.0260	.0714	.1189	.1110	.0499	.0079	.0002	.0000	.0000	.0000	.0000	.0000	36	
.0003	.0027	.0147	.0502	.1050	.1261	.0755	.0169	.0007	.0000	.0000	.0000	.0000	.0000	37	
.0001	.0011	.0076	.0319	.0838	.1294	.1033	.0328	.0022	.0000	.0000	.0000	.0000	.0000	38	
.0000	.0004	.0035	.0182	.0602	.1194	.1271	.0571	.0061	.0000	.0000	.0000	.0000	.0000	39	
.0000	.0001	.0014	.0093	.0386	.0985	.1398	.0890	.0152	.0001	.0000	.0000	.0000	.0000	40	
.0000	.0000	.0005	.0042	.0220	.0721	.1364	.1230	.0333	.0006	.0001	.0000	.0000	.0000	41	
.0000	.0000	.0002	.0017	.0110	.0463	.1169	.1493	.0643	.0024	.0006	.0001	.0000	.0000	42	
.0000	.0000	.0000	.0006	.0048	.0259	.0870	.1575	.1076	.0086	.0028	.0006	.0001	.0000	43	
.0000	.0000	.0000	.0002	.0018	.0123	.0554	.1419	.1541	.0260	.0108	.0030	.0004	.0000	44	
.0000	.0000	.0000	.0000	.0006	.0049	.0295	.1072	.1849	.0658	.0346	.0131	.0027	.0001	45	
.0000	.0000	.0000	.0000	.0001	.0016	.0128	.0661	.1809	.1360	.0902	.0459	.0145	.0015	46	
.0000	.0000	.0000	.0000	.0000	.0004	.0044	.0319	.1386	.2199	.1842	.1264	.0607	.0122	47	
.0000	.0000	.0000	.0000	.0000	.0001	.0011	.0113	.0779	.2611	.2762	.2555	.1858	.0756	48	
.0000	.0000	.0000	.0000	.0000	.0000	.0002	.0026	.0286	.2025	.2706	.3372	.3716	.3056	49	
.0000	.0000	.0000	.0000	.0000	.0000	.0000	.0003	.0052	.0769	.1299	.2181	.3642	.6050	50	

Appendix E

Binomial Distribution—Right Tail (cumulative) Terms

The table presents cumulative right tail binomial probabilities for X or more successes, for selected values of n and π.

$$\sum_{X}^{n} \frac{n!}{X!(n-X)!} \pi^X (1-\pi)^{n-X}$$

Binomial Distribution—Right Tail (cumulative) Terms

π

n	X	.01	.02	.03	.04	.05	.10	.15	.20	.25	.30	.35	.40	.45
1	1	.0100	.0200	.0300	.0400	.0500	.1000	.1500	.2000	.2500	.3000	.3500	.4000	.4500

n	X	.01	.02	.03	.04	.05	.10	.15	.20	.25	.30	.35	.40	.45
2	1	.0199	.0396	.0591	.0784	.0975	.1900	.2775	.3600	.4375	.5100	.5775	.6400	.6975
	2	.0001	.0004	.0009	.0016	.0025	.0100	.0225	.0400	.0625	.0900	.1225	.1600	.2025

n	X	.01	.02	.03	.04	.05	.10	.15	.20	.25	.30	.35	.40	.45
3	1	.0297	.0588	.0873	.1153	.1426	.2710	.3859	.4880	.5781	.6570	.7254	.7840	.8336
	2	.0003	.0012	.0026	.0047	.0073	.0280	.0608	.1040	.1563	.2150	.2818	.3520	.4253
	3	.0000	.0000	.0000	.0001	.0001	.0010	.0034	.0080	.0156	.0270	.0429	.0640	.0911

n	X	.01	.02	.03	.04	.05	.10	.15	.20	.25	.30	.35	.40	.45
4	1	.0394	.0776	.1147	.1507	.1855	.3439	.4780	.5904	.6836	.7599	.8215	.8704	.9085
	2	.0006	.0023	.0052	.0091	.0140	.0523	.1095	.1808	.2617	.3483	.4370	.5248	.6090
	3	.0000	.0000	.0001	.0002	.0005	.0037	.0120	.0272	.0508	.0837	.1265	.1792	.2415
	4	.0000	.0000	.0000	.0000	.0000	.0001	.0005	.0016	.0039	.0081	.0150	.0256	.0410

n	X	.01	.02	.03	.04	.05	.10	.15	.20	.25	.30	.35	.40	.45
5	1	.0490	.0961	.1413	.1846	.2262	.4095	.5563	.6723	.7627	.8319	.8840	.9222	.9497
	2	.0010	.0038	.0085	.0148	.0226	.0815	.1648	.2627	.3672	.4718	.5716	.6630	.7438
	3	.0000	.0001	.0003	.0006	.0012	.0086	.0266	.0579	.1035	.1631	.2352	.3174	.4069
	4	.0000	.0000	.0000	.0000	.0000	.0005	.0022	.0067	.0156	.0308	.0540	.0870	.1312
	5	.0000	.0000	.0000	.0000	.0000	.0000	.0001	.0003	.0010	.0024	.0053	.0102	.0185

n	X	.01	.02	.03	.04	.05	.10	.15	.20	.25	.30	.35	.40	.45
6	1	.0585	.1142	.1670	.2172	.2649	.4686	.6229	.7379	.8220	.8824	.9246	.9533	.9723
	2	.0015	.0057	.0125	.0216	.0328	.1143	.2235	.3446	.4661	.5798	.6809	.7667	.8364
	3	.0000	.0002	.0005	.0012	.0022	.0159	.0473	.0989	.1694	.2557	.3529	.4557	.5585
	4	.0000	.0000	.0000	.0000	.0001	.0013	.0059	.0170	.0376	.0705	.1174	.1792	.2553
	5	.0000	.0000	.0000	.0000	.0000	.0001	.0004	.0016	.0046	.0109	.0223	.0410	.0692
	6	.0000	.0000	.0000	.0000	.0000	.0000	.0000	.0001	.0002	.0007	.0018	.0041	.0083

n	X	.01	.02	.03	.04	.05	.10	.15	.20	.25	.30	.35	.40	.45
7	1	.0679	.1319	.1920	.2486	.3017	.5217	.6794	.7903	.8665	.9176	.9510	.9720	.9848
	2	.0020	.0079	.0171	.0294	.0444	.1497	.2834	.4233	.5551	.6706	.7662	.8414	.8976
	3	.0000	.0003	.0009	.0020	.0038	.0257	.0738	.1480	.2436	.3529	.4677	.5801	.6836
	4	.0000	.0000	.0000	.0001	.0002	.0027	.0121	.0333	.0706	.1260	.1998	.2898	.3917
	5	.0000	.0000	.0000	.0000	.0000	.0002	.0012	.0047	.0129	.0288	.0556	.0963	.1529
	6	.0000	.0000	.0000	.0000	.0000	.0000	.0001	.0004	.0013	.0038	.0090	.0188	.0357
	7	.0000	.0000	.0000	.0000	.0000	.0000	.0000	.0000	.0001	.0002	.0006	.0016	.0037

.50	.55	.60	.65	.70	.75	.80	π .85	.90	.95	.96	.97	.98	.99	X	n
.5000	.5500	.6000	.6500	.7000	.7500	.8000	.8500	.9000	.9500	.9600	.9700	.9800	.9900	1	1

.50	.55	.60	.65	.70	.75	.80	.85	.90	.95	.96	.97	.98	.99		
.7500	.7975	.8400	.8775	.9100	.9375	.9600	.9775	.9900	.9975	.9984	.9991	.9996	.9999	1	2
.2500	.3025	.3600	.4225	.4900	.5625	.6400	.7225	.8100	.9025	.9216	.9409	.9604	.9801	2	

.50	.55	.60	.65	.70	.75	.80	.85	.90	.95	.96	.97	.98	.99		
.8750	.9089	.9360	.9571	.9730	.9844	.9920	.9966	.9990	.9999	.9999	1.0000	1.0000	1.0000	1	3
.5000	.5748	.6480	.7182	.7840	.8437	.8960	.9392	.9720	.9927	.9953	.9974	.9988	.9997	2	
.1250	.1664	.2160	.2746	.3430	.4219	.5120	.6141	.7290	.8574	.8847	.9127	.9412	.9703	3	

.50	.55	.60	.65	.70	.75	.80	.85	.90	.95	.96	.97	.98	.99		
.9375	.9590	.9744	.9850	.9919	.9961	.9984	.9995	.9999	1.0000	1.0000	1.0000	1.0000	1.0000	1	4
.6875	.7585	.8208	.8735	.9163	.9492	.9728	.9880	.9963	.9995	.9998	.9999	1.0000	1.0000	2	
.3125	.3910	.4752	.5630	.6517	.7383	.8192	.8905	.9477	.9860	.9909	.9948	.9977	.9994	3	
.0625	.0915	.1296	.1785	.2401	.3164	.4096	.5220	.6561	.8145	.8493	.8853	.9224	.9606	4	

.50	.55	.60	.65	.70	.75	.80	.85	.90	.95	.96	.97	.98	.99		
.9687	.9815	.9898	.9947	.9976	.9990	.9997	.9999	1.0000	1.0000	1.0000	1.0000	1.0000	1.0000	1	5
.8125	.8688	.9130	.9460	.9692	.9844	.9933	.9978	.9995	1.0000	1.0000	1.0000	1.0000	1.0000	2	
.5000	.5931	.6826	.7648	.8369	.8965	.9421	.9734	.9914	.9988	.9994	.9997	.9999	1.0000	3	
.1875	.2562	.3370	.4284	.5282	.6328	.7373	.8352	.9185	.9774	.9852	.9915	.9962	.9990	4	
.0313	.0503	.0778	.1160	.1681	.2373	.3277	.4437	.5905	.7738	.8154	.8587	.9039	.9510	5	

.50	.55	.60	.65	.70	.75	.80	.85	.90	.95	.96	.97	.98	.99		
.9844	.9917	.9959	.9982	.9993	.9998	.9999	1.0000	1.0000	1.0000	1.0000	1.0000	1.0000	1.0000	1	6
.8906	.9308	.9590	.9777	.9891	.9954	.9984	.9996	.9999	1.0000	1.0000	1.0000	1.0000	1.0000	2	
.6562	.7447	.8208	.8826	.9295	.9624	.9830	.9941	.9987	.9999	1.0000	1.0000	1.0000	1.0000	3	
.3437	.4415	.5443	.6471	.7443	.8306	.9011	.9527	.9841	.9978	.9988	.9995	.9998	1.0000	4	
.1094	.1636	.2333	.3191	.4202	.5339	.6554	.7765	.8857	.9672	.9784	.9875	.9943	.9985	5	
.0156	.0277	.0467	.0754	.1176	.1780	.2621	.3771	.5314	.7351	.7828	.8330	.8858	.9415	6	

.50	.55	.60	.65	.70	.75	.80	.85	.90	.95	.96	.97	.98	.99		
.9922	.9963	.9984	.9994	.9998	.9999	1.0000	1.0000	1.0000	1.0000	1.0000	1.0000	1.0000	1.0000	1	7
.9375	.9643	.9812	.9910	.9962	.9987	.9996	.9999	1.0000	1.0000	1.0000	1.0000	1.0000	1.0000	2	
.7734	.8471	.9037	.9444	.9712	.9871	.9953	.9988	.9998	1.0000	1.0000	1.0000	1.0000	1.0000	3	
.5000	.6083	.7102	.8002	.8740	.9294	.9667	.9879	.9973	.9998	.9999	1.0000	1.0000	1.0000	4	
.2266	.3164	.4199	.5323	.6471	.7564	.8520	.9262	.9743	.9962	.9980	.9991	.9997	1.0000	5	
.0625	.1024	.1586	.2338	.3294	.4449	.5767	.7166	.8503	.9556	.9706	.9829	.9921	.9980	6	
.0078	.0152	.0280	.0490	.0824	.1335	.2097	.3206	.4783	.6983	.7514	.8080	.8681	.9321	7	

Binomial Distribution—Right Tail (cumulative) Terms (*continued*)

n	X	.01	.02	.03	.04	.05	.10	π .15	.20	.25	.30	.35	.40	.45
8	1	.0773	.1492	.2163	.2786	.3366	.5695	.7275	.8322	.8999	.9424	.9681	.9832	.9916
	2	.0027	.0103	.0223	.0381	.0572	.1869	.3428	.4967	.6329	.7447	.8309	.8936	.9368
	3	.0001	.0004	.0013	.0031	.0058	.0381	.1052	.2031	.3215	.4482	.5722	.6846	.7799
	4	.0000	.0000	.0001	.0002	.0004	.0050	.0214	.0563	.1138	.1941	.2936	.4059	.5230
	5	.0000	.0000	.0000	.0000	.0000	.0004	.0029	.0104	.0273	.0580	.1061	.1737	.2604
	6	.0000	.0000	.0000	.0000	.0000	.0000	.0002	.0012	.0042	.0113	.0253	.0498	.0885
	7	.0000	.0000	.0000	.0000	.0000	.0000	.0000	.0001	.0004	.0013	.0036	.0085	.0181
	8	.0000	.0000	.0000	.0000	.0000	.0000	.0000	.0000	.0000	.0001	.0002	.0007	.0017

n	X	.01	.02	.03	.04	.05	.10	.15	.20	.25	.30	.35	.40	.45
9	1	.0865	.1663	.2398	.3075	.3698	.6126	.7684	.8658	.9249	.9596	.9793	.9899	.9954
	2	.0034	.0131	.0282	.0478	.0712	.2252	.4005	.5638	.6997	.8040	.8789	.9295	.9615
	3	.0001	.0006	.0020	.0045	.0084	.0530	.1409	.2618	.3993	.5372	.6627	.7682	.8505
	4	.0000	.0000	.0001	.0003	.0006	.0083	.0339	.0856	.1657	.2703	.3911	.5174	.6386
	5	.0000	.0000	.0000	.0000	.0000	.0009	.0056	.0196	.0489	.0988	.1717	.2666	.3786
	6	.0000	.0000	.0000	.0000	.0000	.0001	.0006	.0031	.0100	.0253	.0536	.0994	.1658
	7	.0000	.0000	.0000	.0000	.0000	.0000	.0000	.0003	.0013	.0043	.0112	.0250	.0498
	8	.0000	.0000	.0000	.0000	.0000	.0000	.0000	.0000	.0001	.0004	.0014	.0038	.0091
	9	.0000	.0000	.0000	.0000	.0000	.0000	.0000	.0000	.0000	.0000	.0001	.0003	.0008

n	X	.01	.02	.03	.04	.05	.10	.15	.20	.25	.30	.35	.40	.45
10	1	.0956	.1829	.2626	.3352	.4013	.6513	.8031	.8926	.9437	.9718	.9865	.9940	.9975
	2	.0043	.0162	.0345	.0582	.0861	.2639	.4557	.6242	.7560	.8507	.9140	.9536	.9767
	3	.0001	.0009	.0028	.0062	.0115	.0702	.1798	.3222	.4744	.6172	.7384	.8327	.9004
	4	.0000	.0000	.0001	.0004	.0010	.0128	.0500	.1209	.2241	.3504	.4862	.6177	.7340
	5	.0000	.0000	.0000	.0000	.0001	.0016	.0099	.0328	.0781	.1503	.2485	.3669	.4956
	6	.0000	.0000	.0000	.0000	.0000	.0001	.0014	.0064	.0197	.0473	.0949	.1662	.2616
	7	.0000	.0000	.0000	.0000	.0000	.0000	.0001	.0009	.0035	.0106	.0260	.0548	.1020
	8	.0000	.0000	.0000	.0000	.0000	.0000	.0000	.0001	.0004	.0016	.0048	.0123	.0274
	9	.0000	.0000	.0000	.0000	.0000	.0000	.0000	.0000	.0000	.0001	.0005	.0017	.0045
	10	.0000	.0000	.0000	.0000	.0000	.0000	.0000	.0000	.0000	.0000	.0000	.0001	.0003

n	X	.01	.02	.03	.04	.05	.10	.15	.20	.25	.30	.35	.40	.45
11	1	.1047	.1993	.2847	.3618	.4312	.6862	.8327	.9141	.9578	.9802	.9912	.9964	.9986
	2	.0052	.0195	.0413	.0692	.1019	.3026	.5078	.6779	.8029	.8870	.9394	.9698	.9861
	3	.0002	.0012	.0037	.0083	.0152	.0896	.2212	.3826	.5448	.6873	.7999	.8811	.9348
	4	.0000	.0000	.0002	.0007	.0016	.0185	.0694	.1611	.2867	.4304	.5744	.7037	.8089
	5	.0000	.0000	.0000	.0000	.0001	.0028	.0159	.0504	.1146	.2103	.3317	.4672	.6029
	6	.0000	.0000	.0000	.0000	.0000	.0003	.0027	.0117	.0343	.0782	.1487	.2465	.3669
	7	.0000	.0000	.0000	.0000	.0000	.0000	.0003	.0020	.0076	.0216	.0501	.0994	.1738
	8	.0000	.0000	.0000	.0000	.0000	.0000	.0000	.0002	.0012	.0043	.0122	.0293	.0610
	9	.0000	.0000	.0000	.0000	.0000	.0000	.0000	.0000	.0001	.0006	.0020	.0059	.0148
	10	.0000	.0000	.0000	.0000	.0000	.0000	.0000	.0000	.0000	.0000	.0002	.0007	.0022
	11	.0000	.0000	.0000	.0000	.0000	.0000	.0000	.0000	.0000	.0000	.0000	.0000	.0002

n	X	.01	.02	.03	.04	.05	.10	.15	.20	.25	.30	.35	.40	.45
12	1	.1136	.2153	.3062	.3873	.4596	.7176	.8578	.9313	.9683	.9862	.9943	.9978	.9992
	2	.0062	.0231	.0486	.0809	.1184	.3410	.5565	.7251	.8416	.9150	.9576	.9804	.9917
	3	.0002	.0015	.0048	.0107	.0196	.1109	.2642	.4417	.6093	.7472	.8487	.9166	.9579
	4	.0000	.0001	.0003	.0010	.0022	.0256	.0922	.2054	.3512	.5075	.6533	.7747	.8655
	5	.0000	.0000	.0000	.0001	.0002	.0043	.0239	.0726	.1576	.2763	.4167	.5618	.6956
	6	.0000	.0000	.0000	.0000	.0000	.0005	.0046	.0194	.0544	.1178	.2127	.3348	.4731
	7	.0000	.0000	.0000	.0000	.0000	.0001	.0007	.0039	.0143	.0386	.0846	.1582	.2607
	8	.0000	.0000	.0000	.0000	.0000	.0000	.0001	.0006	.0028	.0095	.0255	.0573	.1117
	9	.0000	.0000	.0000	.0000	.0000	.0000	.0000	.0001	.0004	.0017	.0056	.0153	.0356
	10	.0000	.0000	.0000	.0000	.0000	.0000	.0000	.0000	.0000	.0002	.0008	.0028	.0079
	11	.0000	.0000	.0000	.0000	.0000	.0000	.0000	.0000	.0000	.0000	.0001	.0003	.0011
	12	.0000	.0000	.0000	.0000	.0000	.0000	.0000	.0000	.0000	.0000	.0000	.0000	.0001

π

.50	.55	.60	.65	.70	.75	.80	.85	.90	.95	.96	.97	.98	.99	X	n
.9961	.9983	.9993	.9998	.9999	1.0000	1.0000	1.0000	1.0000	1.0000	1.0000	1.0000	1.0000	1.0000	1	8
.9648	.9819	.9915	.9964	.9987	.9996	.9999	1.0000	1.0000	1.0000	1.0000	1.0000	1.0000	1.0000	2	
.8555	.9115	.9502	.9747	.9887	.9958	.9988	.9998	1.0000	1.0000	1.0000	1.0000	1.0000	1.0000	3	
.6367	.7396	.8263	.8939	.9420	.9727	.9896	.9971	.9996	1.0000	1.0000	1.0000	1.0000	1.0000	4	
.3633	.4770	.5941	.7064	.8059	.8862	.9437	.9786	.9950	.9996	.9998	.9999	1.0000	1.0000	5	
.1445	.2201	.3154	.4278	.5518	.6785	.7969	.8948	.9619	.9942	.9969	.9987	.9996	.9999	6	
.0352	.0632	.1064	.1691	.2553	.3671	.5033	.6572	.8131	.9428	.9619	.9777	.9897	.9973	7	
.0039	.0084	.0168	.0319	.0576	.1001	.1678	.2725	.4305	.6634	.7214	.7837	.8508	.9227	8	

.50	.55	.60	.65	.70	.75	.80	.85	.90	.95	.96	.97	.98	.99	X	n
.9980	.9992	.9997	.9999	1.0000	1.0000	1.0000	1.0000	1.0000	1.0000	1.0000	1.0000	1.0000	1.0000	1	9
.9805	.9909	.9962	.9986	.9996	.9999	1.0000	1.0000	1.0000	1.0000	1.0000	1.0000	1.0000	1.0000	2	
.9102	.9502	.9750	.9888	.9957	.9987	.9997	1.0000	1.0000	1.0000	1.0000	1.0000	1.0000	1.0000	3	
.7461	.8342	.9006	.9464	.9747	.9900	.9969	.9994	.9999	1.0000	1.0000	1.0000	1.0000	1.0000	4	
.5000	.6214	.7334	.8283	.9012	.9511	.9804	.9944	.9991	1.0000	1.0000	1.0000	1.0000	1.0000	5	
.2539	.3614	.4826	.6089	.7297	.8343	.9144	.9661	.9917	.9994	.9997	.9999	1.0000	1.0000	6	
.0898	.1495	.2318	.3373	.4628	.6007	.7382	.8591	.9470	.9916	.9955	.9980	.9994	.9999	7	
.0195	.0385	.0705	.1211	.1960	.3003	.4362	.5995	.7748	.9288	.9522	.9718	.9869	.9966	8	
.0020	.0046	.0101	.0207	.0404	.0751	.1342	.2316	.3874	.6302	.6925	.7602	.8337	.9135	9	

.50	.55	.60	.65	.70	.75	.80	.85	.90	.95	.96	.97	.98	.99	X	n
.9990	.9997	.9999	1.0000	1.0000	1.0000	1.0000	1.0000	1.0000	1.0000	1.0000	1.0000	1.0000	1.0000	1	10
.9893	.9955	.9983	.9995	.9999	1.0000	1.0000	1.0000	1.0000	1.0000	1.0000	1.0000	1.0000	1.0000	2	
.9453	.9726	.9877	.9952	.9984	.9996	.9999	1.0000	1.0000	1.0000	1.0000	1.0000	1.0000	1.0000	3	
.8281	.8980	.9452	.9740	.9894	.9965	.9991	.9999	1.0000	1.0000	1.0000	1.0000	1.0000	1.0000	4	
.6230	.7384	.8338	.9051	.9527	.9803	.9936	.9986	.9999	1.0000	1.0000	1.0000	1.0000	1.0000	5	
.3770	.5044	.6331	.7515	.8497	.9219	.9672	.9901	.9984	.9999	1.0000	1.0000	1.0000	1.0000	6	
.1719	.2660	.3823	.5138	.6496	.7759	.8791	.9500	.9872	.9990	.9996	.9999	1.0000	1.0000	7	
.0547	.0996	.1673	.2616	.3828	.5256	.6778	.8202	.9298	.9885	.9938	.9972	.9991	.9999	8	
.0107	.0233	.0464	.0860	.1493	.2440	.3758	.5443	.7361	.9139	.9418	.9655	.9838	.9957	9	
.0010	.0025	.0060	.0135	.0282	.0563	.1074	.1969	.3487	.5987	.6648	.7374	.8171	.9044	10	

.50	.55	.60	.65	.70	.75	.80	.85	.90	.95	.96	.97	.98	.99	X	n
.9995	.9998	1.0000	1.0000	1.0000	1.0000	1.0000	1.0000	1.0000	1.0000	1.0000	1.0000	1.0000	1.0000	1	11
.9941	.9978	.9993	.9998	1.0000	1.0000	1.0000	1.0000	1.0000	1.0000	1.0000	1.0000	1.0000	1.0000	2	
.9673	.9852	.9941	.9980	.9994	.9999	1.0000	1.0000	1.0000	1.0000	1.0000	1.0000	1.0000	1.0000	3	
.8867	.9390	.9707	.9878	.9957	.9988	.9998	1.0000	1.0000	1.0000	1.0000	1.0000	1.0000	1.0000	4	
.7256	.8262	.9006	.9499	.9784	.9924	.9980	.9997	1.0000	1.0000	1.0000	1.0000	1.0000	1.0000	5	
.5000	.6331	.7535	.8513	.9218	.9657	.9883	.9973	.9997	1.0000	1.0000	1.0000	1.0000	1.0000	6	
.2744	.3971	.5328	.6683	.7897	.8854	.9496	.9841	.9972	.9999	1.0000	1.0000	1.0000	1.0000	7	
.1133	.1911	.2963	.4256	.5696	.7133	.8389	.9306	.9815	.9984	.9993	.9998	1.0000	1.0000	8	
.0327	.0652	.1189	.2001	.3127	.4552	.6174	.7788	.9104	.9848	.9917	.9963	.9988	.9998	9	
.0059	.0139	.0302	.0606	.1130	.1971	.3221	.4922	.6974	.8981	.9308	.9587	.9805	.9948	10	
.0005	.0014	.0036	.0088	.0198	.0422	.0859	.1673	.3138	.5688	.6382	.7153	.8007	.8953	11	

.50	.55	.60	.65	.70	.75	.80	.85	.90	.95	.96	.97	.98	.99	X	n
.9998	.9999	1.0000	1.0000	1.0000	1.0000	1.0000	1.0000	1.0000	1.0000	1.0000	1.0000	1.0000	1.0000	1	12
.9968	.9989	.9997	.9999	1.0000	1.0000	1.0000	1.0000	1.0000	1.0000	1.0000	1.0000	1.0000	1.0000	2	
.9807	.9921	.9972	.9992	.9998	1.0000	1.0000	1.0000	1.0000	1.0000	1.0000	1.0000	1.0000	1.0000	3	
.9270	.9644	.9847	.9944	.9983	.9996	.9999	1.0000	1.0000	1.0000	1.0000	1.0000	1.0000	1.0000	4	
.8062	.8883	.9427	.9745	.9905	.9972	.9994	.9999	1.0000	1.0000	1.0000	1.0000	1.0000	1.0000	5	
.6128	.7393	.8418	.9154	.9614	.9857	.9961	.9993	.9999	1.0000	1.0000	1.0000	1.0000	1.0000	6	
.3872	.5269	.6652	.7873	.8822	.9456	.9806	.9954	.9995	1.0000	1.0000	1.0000	1.0000	1.0000	7	
.1938	.3044	.4382	.5833	.7237	.8424	.9274	.9761	.9957	.9998	.9999	1.0000	1.0000	1.0000	8	
.0730	.1345	.2253	.3467	.4925	.6488	.7946	.9078	.9744	.9978	.9990	.9997	.9999	1.0000	9	
.0193	.0421	.0834	.1513	.2528	.3907	.5583	.7358	.8891	.9804	.9893	.9952	.9985	.9998	10	
.0032	.0083	.0196	.0424	.0850	.1584	.2749	.4435	.6590	.8816	.9191	.9514	.9769	.9938	11	
.0002	.0008	.0022	.0057	.0138	.0317	.0687	.1422	.2824	.5404	.6127	.6938	.7847	.8864	12	

Binomial Distribution—Right Tail (cumulative) Terms (*continued*)

n	X	.01	.02	.03	.04	.05	.10	π .15	.20	.25	.30	.35	.40	.45
13	1	.1225	.2310	.3270	.4118	.4867	.7458	.8791	.9450	.9762	.9903	.9963	.9987	.9996
	2	.0072	.0270	.0564	.0932	.1354	.3787	.6017	.7664	.8733	.9363	.9704	.9874	.9951
	3	.0003	.0020	.0062	.0135	.0245	.1339	.3080	.4983	.6674	.7975	.8868	.9421	.9731
	4	.0000	.0001	.0005	.0014	.0031	.0342	.1180	.2527	.4157	.5794	.7217	.8314	.9071
	5	.0000	.0000	.0000	.0001	.0003	.0065	.0342	.0991	.2060	.3457	.4995	.6470	.7721
	6	.0000	.0000	.0000	.0000	.0000	.0009	.0075	.0300	.0802	.1654	.2841	.4256	.5732
	7	.0000	.0000	.0000	.0000	.0000	.0001	.0013	.0070	.0243	.0624	.1295	.2288	.3563
	8	.0000	.0000	.0000	.0000	.0000	.0000	.0002	.0012	.0056	.0192	.0462	.0977	.1788
	9	.0000	.0000	.0000	.0000	.0000	.0000	.0000	.0002	.0010	.0040	.0126	.0321	.0698
	10	.0000	.0000	.0000	.0000	.0000	.0000	.0000	.0000	.0001	.0007	.0025	.0078	.0203
	11	.0000	.0000	.0000	.0000	.0000	.0000	.0000	.0000	.0000	.0001	.0003	.0013	.0041
	12	.0000	.0000	.0000	.0000	.0000	.0000	.0000	.0000	.0000	.0000	.0000	.0001	.0005
	13	.0000	.0000	.0000	.0000	.0000	.0000	.0000	.0000	.0000	.0000	.0000	.0000	.0000

n	X	.01	.02	.03	.04	.05	.10	.15	.20	.25	.30	.35	.40	.45
14	1	.1313	.2464	.3472	.4353	.5123	.7712	.8972	.9560	.9822	.9932	.9976	.9992	.9998
	2	.0084	.0310	.0645	.1059	.1530	.4154	.6433	.8021	.8990	.9525	.9795	.9919	.9971
	3	.0003	.0025	.0077	.0167	.0301	.1584	.3521	.5519	.7189	.8392	.9161	.9602	.9830
	4	.0000	.0001	.0006	.0019	.0042	.0441	.1465	.3018	.4787	.6448	.7795	.8757	.9368
	5	.0000	.0000	.0000	.0002	.0004	.0092	.0467	.1298	.2585	.4158	.5773	.7207	.8328
	6	.0000	.0000	.0000	.0000	.0000	.0015	.0115	.0439	.1117	.2195	.3595	.5141	.6627
	7	.0000	.0000	.0000	.0000	.0000	.0002	.0022	.0116	.0383	.0933	.1836	.3075	.4539
	8	.0000	.0000	.0000	.0000	.0000	.0000	.0003	.0024	.0103	.0315	.0753	.1501	.2586
	9	.0000	.0000	.0000	.0000	.0000	.0000	.0000	.0004	.0022	.0083	.0243	.0583	.1189
	10	.0000	.0000	.0000	.0000	.0000	.0000	.0000	.0000	.0003	.0017	.0060	.0175	.0426
	11	.0000	.0000	.0000	.0000	.0000	.0000	.0000	.0000	.0000	.0002	.0011	.0039	.0114
	12	.0000	.0000	.0000	.0000	.0000	.0000	.0000	.0000	.0000	.0000	.0001	.0006	.0022
	13	.0000	.0000	.0000	.0000	.0000	.0000	.0000	.0000	.0000	.0000	.0000	.0001	.0003
	14	.0000	.0000	.0000	.0000	.0000	.0000	.0000	.0000	.0000	.0000	.0000	.0000	.0000

n	X	.01	.02	.03	.04	.05	.10	.15	.20	.25	.30	.35	.40	.45
15	1	.1399	.2614	.3667	.4579	.5367	.7941	.9126	.9648	.9866	.9953	.9984	.9995	.9999
	2	.0096	.0353	.0730	.1191	.1710	.4510	.6814	.8329	.9198	.9647	.9858	.9948	.9983
	3	.0004	.0030	.0094	.0203	.0362	.1841	.3958	.6020	.7639	.8732	.9383	.9729	.9893
	4	.0000	.0002	.0008	.0024	.0055	.0556	.1773	.3518	.5387	.7031	.8273	.9095	.9576
	5	.0000	.0000	.0001	.0002	.0006	.0127	.0617	.1642	.3135	.4845	.6481	.7827	.8796
	6	.0000	.0000	.0000	.0000	.0001	.0022	.0168	.0611	.1484	.2784	.4357	.5968	.7392
	7	.0000	.0000	.0000	.0000	.0000	.0003	.0036	.0181	.0566	.1311	.2452	.3902	.5478
	8	.0000	.0000	.0000	.0000	.0000	.0000	.0006	.0042	.0173	.0500	.1132	.2131	.3465
	9	.0000	.0000	.0000	.0000	.0000	.0000	.0001	.0008	.0042	.0152	.0422	.0950	.1818
	10	.0000	.0000	.0000	.0000	.0000	.0000	.0000	.0001	.0008	.0037	.0124	.0338	.0769
	11	.0000	.0000	.0000	.0000	.0000	.0000	.0000	.0000	.0001	.0007	.0028	.0093	.0255
	12	.0000	.0000	.0000	.0000	.0000	.0000	.0000	.0000	.0000	.0001	.0005	.0019	.0063
	13	.0000	.0000	.0000	.0000	.0000	.0000	.0000	.0000	.0000	.0000	.0001	.0003	.0011
	14	.0000	.0000	.0000	.0000	.0000	.0000	.0000	.0000	.0000	.0000	.0000	.0000	.0001
	15	0.0000	.0000	.0000	.0000	.0000	.0000	.0000	.0000	.0000	.0000	.0000	.0000	.0000

π

.50	.55	.60	.65	.70	.75	.80	.85	.90	.95	.96	.97	.98	.99	X	n
.9999	1.0000	1.0000	1.0000	1.0000	1.0000	1.0000	1.0000	1.0000	1.0000	1.0000	1.0000	1.0000	1.0000	1	13
.9983	.9995	.9999	1.0000	1.0000	1.0000	1.0000	1.0000	1.0000	1.0000	1.0000	1.0000	1.0000	1.0000	2	
.9888	.9959	.9987	.9997	.9999	1.0000	1.0000	1.0000	1.0000	1.0000	1.0000	1.0000	1.0000	1.0000	3	
.9539	.9797	.9922	.9975	.9993	.9999	1.0000	1.0000	1.0000	1.0000	1.0000	1.0000	1.0000	1.0000	4	
.8666	.9302	.9679	.9874	.9960	.9990	.9998	1.0000	1.0000	1.0000	1.0000	1.0000	1.0000	1.0000	5	
.7095	.8212	.9023	.9538	.9818	.9944	.9988	.9998	1.0000	1.0000	1.0000	1.0000	1.0000	1.0000	6	
.5000	.6437	.7712	.8705	.9376	.9757	.9930	.9987	.9999	1.0000	1.0000	1.0000	1.0000	1.0000	7	
.2905	.4268	.5744	.7159	.8346	.9198	.9700	.9925	.9991	1.0000	1.0000	1.0000	1.0000	1.0000	8	
.1334	.2279	.3530	.5005	.6543	.7940	.9009	.9658	.9935	.9997	.9999	1.0000	1.0000	1.0000	9	
.0461	.0929	.1686	.2783	.4206	.5843	.7473	.8820	.9658	.9969	.9986	.9995	.9999	1.0000	10	
.0112	.0269	.0579	.1132	.2025	.3326	.5017	.6920	.8661	.9755	.9865	.9938	.9980	.9997	11	
.0017	.0049	.0126	.0296	.0637	.1267	.2336	.3983	.6213	.8646	.9068	.9436	.9730	.9928	12	
.0001	.0004	.0013	.0037	.0097	.0238	.0550	.1209	.2542	.5133	.5882	.6730	.7690	.8775	13	

.50	.55	.60	.65	.70	.75	.80	.85	.90	.95	.96	.97	.98	.99	X	n
.9999	1.0000	1.0000	1.0000	1.0000	1.0000	1.0000	1.0000	1.0000	1.0000	1.0000	1.0000	1.0000	1.0000	1	14
.9991	.9997	.9999	1.0000	1.0000	1.0000	1.0000	1.0000	1.0000	1.0000	1.0000	1.0000	1.0000	1.0000	2	
.9935	.9978	.9994	.9999	1.0000	1.0000	1.0000	1.0000	1.0000	1.0000	1.0000	1.0000	1.0000	1.0000	3	
.9713	.9886	.9961	.9989	.9998	1.0000	1.0000	1.0000	1.0000	1.0000	1.0000	1.0000	1.0000	1.0000	4	
.9102	.9574	.9825	.9940	.9983	.9997	1.0000	1.0000	1.0000	1.0000	1.0000	1.0000	1.0000	1.0000	5	
.7880	.8811	.9417	.9757	.9917	.9978	.9996	1.0000	1.0000	1.0000	1.0000	1.0000	1.0000	1.0000	6	
.6047	.7414	.8499	.9247	.9685	.9897	.9976	.9997	1.0000	1.0000	1.0000	1.0000	1.0000	1.0000	7	
.3953	.5461	.6925	.8164	.9067	.9617	.9884	.9978	.9998	1.0000	1.0000	1.0000	1.0000	1.0000	8	
.2120	.3373	.4859	.6405	.7805	.8883	.9561	.9885	.9985	1.0000	1.0000	1.0000	1.0000	1.0000	9	
.0898	.1672	.2793	.4227	.5842	.7415	.8702	.9533	.9908	.9996	.9998	1.0000	1.0000	1.0000	10	
.0287	.0632	.1243	.2205	.3552	.5213	.6982	.8535	.9559	.9958	.9981	.9994	.9999	1.0000	11	
.0065	.0170	.0398	.0839	.1608	.2811	.4481	.6479	.8416	.9699	.9833	.9923	.9975	.9997	12	
.0009	.0029	.0081	.0205	.0475	.1010	.1979	.3567	.5846	.8470	.8941	.9355	.9690	.9916	13	
.0001	.0002	.0008	.0024	.0068	.0178	.0440	.1028	.2288	.4877	.5647	.6528	.7536	.8687	14	

.50	.55	.60	.65	.70	.75	.80	.85	.90	.95	.96	.97	.98	.99	X	n
1.0000	1.0000	1.0000	1.0000	1.0000	1.0000	1.0000	1.0000	1.0000	1.0000	1.0000	1.0000	1.0000	1.0000	1	15
.9995	.9999	1.0000	1.0000	1.0000	1.0000	1.0000	1.0000	1.0000	1.0000	1.0000	1.0000	1.0000	1.0000	2	
.9963	.9989	.9997	.9999	1.0000	1.0000	1.0000	1.0000	1.0000	1.0000	1.0000	1.0000	1.0000	1.0000	3	
.9824	.9937	.9981	.9995	.9999	1.0000	1.0000	1.0000	1.0000	1.0000	1.0000	1.0000	1.0000	1.0000	4	
.9408	.9745	.9907	.9972	.9993	.9999	1.0000	1.0000	1.0000	1.0000	1.0000	1.0000	1.0000	1.0000	5	
.8491	.9231	.9662	.9876	.9963	.9992	.9999	1.0000	1.0000	1.0000	1.0000	1.0000	1.0000	1.0000	6	
.6964	.8182	.9050	.9578	.9848	.9958	.9992	.9999	1.0000	1.0000	1.0000	1.0000	1.0000	1.0000	7	
.5000	.6535	.7869	.8868	.9500	.9827	.9958	.9994	1.0000	1.0000	1.0000	1.0000	1.0000	1.0000	8	
.3036	.4522	.6098	.7548	.8689	.9434	.9819	.9964	.9997	1.0000	1.0000	1.0000	1.0000	1.0000	9	
.1509	.2608	.4032	.5643	.7216	.8516	.9389	.9832	.9978	.9999	1.0000	1.0000	1.0000	1.0000	10	
.0592	.1204	.2173	.3519	.5155	.6865	.8358	.9383	.9873	.9994	.9998	.9999	1.0000	1.0000	11	
.0176	.0424	.0905	.1727	.2969	.4613	.6482	.8227	.9444	.9945	.9976	.9992	.9998	1.0000	12	
.0037	.0107	.0271	.0617	.1268	.2361	.3980	.6042	.8159	.9638	.9797	.9906	.9970	.9996	13	
.0005	.0017	.0052	.0142	.0353	.0802	.1671	.3186	.5490	.8290	.8809	.9270	.9647	.9904	14	
.0000	.0001	.0005	.0016	.0047	.0134	.0352	.0874	.2059	.4633	.5421	.6333	.7386	.8601	15	

Binomial Distribution—Right Tail (cumulative) Terms (*continued*)

n	X	π .01	.02	.03	.04	.05	.10	.15	.20	.25	.30	.35	.40	.45
20	1	.1821	.3324	.4562	.5580	.6415	.8784	.9612	.9885	.9968	.9992	.9998	1.0000	1.0000
	2	.0169	.0599	.1198	.1897	.2642	.6083	.8244	.9308	.9757	.9924	.9979	.9995	.9999
	3	.0010	.0071	.0210	.0439	.0755	.3231	.5951	.7939	.9087	.9645	.9879	.9964	.9991
	4	.0000	.0006	.0027	.0074	.0159	.1330	.3523	.5886	.7748	.8929	.9556	.9840	.9951
	5	.0000	.0000	.0003	.0010	.0026	.0432	.1702	.3704	.5852	.7625	.8818	.9490	.9811
	6	.0000	.0000	.0000	.0001	.0003	.0113	.0673	.1958	.3828	.5836	.7546	.8744	.9447
	7	.0000	.0000	.0000	.0000	.0000	.0024	.0219	.0867	.2142	.3920	.5834	.7500	.8701
	8	.0000	.0000	.0000	.0000	.0000	.0004	.0059	.0321	.1018	.2277	.3990	.5841	.7480
	9	.0000	.0000	.0000	.0000	.0000	.0001	.0013	.0100	.0409	.1133	.2376	.4044	.5857
	10	.0000	.0000	.0000	.0000	.0000	.0000	.0002	.0026	.0139	.0480	.1218	.2447	.4086
	11	.0000	.0000	.0000	.0000	.0000	.0000	.0000	.0006	.0039	.0171	.0532	.1275	.2493
	12	.0000	.0000	.0000	.0000	.0000	.0000	.0000	.0001	.0009	.0051	.0196	.0565	.1308
	13	.0000	.0000	.0000	.0000	.0000	.0000	.0000	.0000	.0002	.0013	.0060	.0210	.0580
	14	.0000	.0000	.0000	.0000	.0000	.0000	.0000	.0000	.0000	.0003	.0015	.0065	.0214
	15	.0000	.0000	.0000	.0000	.0000	.0000	.0000	.0000	.0000	.0000	.0003	.0016	.0064
	16	.0000	.0000	.0000	.0000	.0000	.0000	.0000	.0000	.0000	.0000	.0000	.0003	.0015
	17	0.0000	.0000	.0000	.0000	.0000	.0000	.0000	.0000	.0000	.0000	.0000	.0000	.0003
	18	0.0000	.0000	.0000	.0000	.0000	.0000	.0000	.0000	.0000	.0000	.0000	.0000	.0000
	19	0.0000	0.0000	.0000	.0000	.0000	.0000	.0000	.0000	.0000	.0000	.0000	.0000	.0000
	20	0.0000	0.0000	0.0000	.0000	.0000	.0000	.0000	.0000	.0000	.0000	.0000	.0000	.0000

n	X	.01	.02	.03	.04	.05	.10	.15	.20	.25	.30	.35	.40	.45
25	1	.2222	.3965	.5330	.6396	.7226	.9282	.9828	.9962	.9992	.9999	1.0000	1.0000	1.0000
	2	.0258	.0886	.1720	.2642	.3576	.7288	.9069	.9726	.9930	.9984	.9997	.9999	1.0000
	3	.0020	.0132	.0380	.0765	.1271	.4629	.7463	.9018	.9679	.9910	.9979	.9996	.9999
	4	.0001	.0014	.0062	.0165	.0341	.2364	.5289	.7660	.9038	.9668	.9903	.9976	.9995
	5	.0000	.0001	.0008	.0028	.0072	.0980	.3179	.5793	.7863	.9095	.9680	.9905	.9977
	6	.0000	.0000	.0001	.0004	.0012	.0334	.1615	.3833	.6217	.8065	.9174	.9706	.9914
	7	.0000	.0000	.0000	.0000	.0002	.0095	.0695	.2200	.4389	.6593	.8266	.9264	.9742
	8	.0000	.0000	.0000	.0000	.0000	.0023	.0255	.1091	.2735	.4882	.6939	.8464	.9361
	9	.0000	.0000	.0000	.0000	.0000	.0005	.0080	.0468	.1494	.3231	.5332	.7265	.8660
	10	.0000	.0000	.0000	.0000	.0000	.0001	.0021	.0173	.0713	.1894	.3697	.5754	.7576
	11	.0000	.0000	.0000	.0000	.0000	.0000	.0005	.0056	.0297	.0978	.2288	.4142	.6157
	12	.0000	.0000	.0000	.0000	.0000	.0000	.0001	.0015	.0107	.0442	.1254	.2677	.4574
	13	.0000	.0000	.0000	.0000	.0000	.0000	.0000	.0004	.0034	.0175	.0604	.1538	.3063
	14	.0000	.0000	.0000	.0000	.0000	.0000	.0000	.0001	.0009	.0060	.0255	.0778	.1827
	15	.0000	.0000	.0000	.0000	.0000	.0000	.0000	.0000	.0002	.0018	.0093	.0344	.0960
	16	.0000	.0000	.0000	.0000	.0000	.0000	.0000	.0000	.0000	.0005	.0029	.0132	.0440
	17	.0000	.0000	.0000	.0000	.0000	.0000	.0000	.0000	.0000	.0001	.0008	.0043	.0174
	18	0.0000	.0000	.0000	.0000	.0000	.0000	.0000	.0000	.0000	.0000	.0002	.0012	.0058
	19	0.0000	.0000	.0000	.0000	.0000	.0000	.0000	.0000	.0000	.0000	.0000	.0003	.0016
	20	0.0000	0.0000	.0000	.0000	.0000	.0000	.0000	.0000	.0000	.0000	.0000	.0001	.0004
	21	0.0000	0.0000	.0000	.0000	.0000	.0000	.0000	.0000	.0000	.0000	.0000	.0000	.0001
	22	0.0000	0.0000	0.0000	.0000	.0000	.0000	.0000	.0000	.0000	.0000	.0000	.0000	.0000
	23	0.0000	0.0000	0.0000	0.0000	.0000	.0000	.0000	.0000	.0000	.0000	.0000	.0000	.0000
	24	0.0000	0.0000	0.0000	0.0000	0.0000	.0000	.0000	.0000	.0000	.0000	.0000	.0000	.0000
	25	0.0000	0.0000	0.0000	0.0000	0.0000	.0000	.0000	.0000	.0000	.0000	.0000	.0000	.0000

π

.50	.55	.60	.65	.70	.75	.80	.85	.90	.95	.96	.97	.98	.99	X	n
1.0000	1.0000	1.0000	1.0000	1.0000	1.0000	1.0000	1.0000	1.0000	1.0000	1.0000	1.0000	1.0000	1.0000	1	20
1.0000	1.0000	1.0000	1.0000	1.0000	1.0000	1.0000	1.0000	1.0000	1.0000	1.0000	1.0000	1.0000	1.0000	2	
.9998	1.0000	1.0000	1.0000	1.0000	1.0000	1.0000	1.0000	1.0000	1.0000	1.0000	1.0000	1.0000	1.0000	3	
.9997	.9997	1.0000	1.0000	1.0000	1.0000	1.0000	1.0000	1.0000	1.0000	1.0000	1.0000	1.0000	1.0000	4	
.9941	.9985	.9997	1.0000	1.0000	1.0000	1.0000	1.0000	1.0000	1.0000	1.0000	1.0000	1.0000	1.0000	5	
.9793	.9936	.9984	.9997	1.0000	1.0000	1.0000	1.0000	1.0000	1.0000	1.0000	1.0000	1.0000	1.0000	6	
.9423	.9786	.9935	.9985	.9997	1.0000	1.0000	1.0000	1.0000	1.0000	1.0000	1.0000	1.0000	1.0000	7	
.8684	.9420	.9790	.9940	.9987	.9998	1.0000	1.0000	1.0000	1.0000	1.0000	1.0000	1.0000	1.0000	8	
.7483	.8692	.9435	.9804	.9949	.9991	.9999	1.0000	1.0000	1.0000	1.0000	1.0000	1.0000	1.0000	9	
.5881	.7507	.8725	.9468	.9829	.9961	.9994	1.0000	1.0000	1.0000	1.0000	1.0000	1.0000	1.0000	10	
.4119	.5914	.7553	.8782	.9520	.9861	.9974	.9998	1.0000	1.0000	1.0000	1.0000	1.0000	1.0000	11	
.2517	.4143	.5956	.7624	.8867	.9591	.9900	.9987	.9999	1.0000	1.0000	1.0000	1.0000	1.0000	12	
.1316	.2520	.4159	.6010	.7723	.8982	.9679	.9941	.9996	1.0000	1.0000	1.0000	1.0000	1.0000	13	
.0577	.1299	.2500	.4166	.6080	.7858	.9133	.9781	.9976	1.0000	1.0000	1.0000	1.0000	1.0000	14	
.0207	.0553	.1256	.2454	.4164	.6172	.8042	.9327	.9887	.9997	.9999	1.0000	1.0000	1.0000	15	
.0059	.0189	.0510	.1182	.2375	.4148	.6296	.8298	.9568	.9974	.9990	.9997	1.0000	1.0000	16	
.0013	.0049	.0160	.0444	.1071	.2252	.4114	.6477	.8670	.9841	.9926	.9973	.9994	1.0000	17	
.0002	.0009	.0036	.0121	.0355	.0913	.2061	.4049	.6769	.9245	.9561	.9790	.9929	.9990	18	
.0000	.0001	.0005	.0021	.0076	.0243	.0692	.1756	.3917	.7358	.8103	.8802	.9401	.9831	19	
.0000	.0000	.0000	.0002	.0008	.0032	.0115	.0388	.1216	.3585	.4420	.5438	.6676	.8179	20	

.50	.55	.60	.65	.70	.75	.80	.85	.90	.95	.96	.97	.98	.99	X	n
1.0000	1.0000	1.0000	1.0000	1.0000	1.0000	1.0000	1.0000	1.0000	1.0000	1.0000	1.0000	1.0000	1.0000	1	25
1.0000	1.0000	1.0000	1.0000	1.0000	1.0000	1.0000	1.0000	1.0000	1.0000	1.0000	1.0000	1.0000	1.0000	2	
1.0000	1.0000	1.0000	1.0000	1.0000	1.0000	1.0000	1.0000	1.0000	1.0000	1.0000	1.0000	1.0000	1.0000	3	
.9999	1.0000	1.0000	1.0000	1.0000	1.0000	1.0000	1.0000	1.0000	1.0000	1.0000	1.0000	1.0000	1.0000	4	
.9995	.9999	1.0000	1.0000	1.0000	1.0000	1.0000	1.0000	1.0000	1.0000	1.0000	1.0000	1.0000	1.0000	5	
.9980	.9996	.9999	1.0000	1.0000	1.0000	1.0000	1.0000	1.0000	1.0000	1.0000	1.0000	1.0000	1.0000	6	
.9927	.9984	.9997	1.0000	1.0000	1.0000	1.0000	1.0000	1.0000	1.0000	1.0000	1.0000	1.0000	1.0000	7	
.9784	.9942	.9988	.9998	1.0000	1.0000	1.0000	1.0000	1.0000	1.0000	1.0000	1.0000	1.0000	1.0000	8	
.9461	.9826	.9957	.9992	.9999	1.0000	1.0000	1.0000	1.0000	1.0000	1.0000	1.0000	1.0000	1.0000	9	
.8852	.9560	.9868	.9971	.9995	1.0000	1.0000	1.0000	1.0000	1.0000	1.0000	1.0000	1.0000	1.0000	10	
.7878	.9040	.9656	.9907	.9982	.9998	1.0000	1.0000	1.0000	1.0000	1.0000	1.0000	1.0000	1.0000	11	
.6550	.8173	.9222	.9745	.9940	.9991	.9999	1.0000	1.0000	1.0000	1.0000	1.0000	1.0000	1.0000	12	
.5000	.6937	.8462	.9396	.9825	.9966	.9996	1.0000	1.0000	1.0000	1.0000	1.0000	1.0000	1.0000	13	
.3450	.5426	.7323	.8746	.9558	.9893	.9985	.9999	1.0000	1.0000	1.0000	1.0000	1.0000	1.0000	14	
.2122	.3843	.5858	.7712	.9022	.9703	.9944	.9995	1.0000	1.0000	1.0000	1.0000	1.0000	1.0000	15	
.1148	.2424	.4246	.6303	.8106	.9287	.9827	.9979	.9999	1.0000	1.0000	1.0000	1.0000	1.0000	16	
.0539	.1340	.2735	.4668	.6769	.8506	.9532	.9920	.9995	1.0000	1.0000	1.0000	1.0000	1.0000	17	
.0216	.0639	.1536	.3061	.5118	.7265	.8909	.9745	.9977	1.0000	1.0000	1.0000	1.0000	1.0000	18	
.0073	.0258	.0736	.1734	.3407	.5611	.7800	.9305	.9905	.9998	1.0000	1.0000	1.0000	1.0000	19	
.0020	.0086	.0294	.0826	.1935	.3783	.6167	.8385	.9666	.9988	.9996	.9999	1.0000	1.0000	20	
.0005	.0023	.0095	.0320	.0905	.2137	.4207	.6821	.9020	.9928	.9972	.9992	.9999	1.0000	21	
.0001	.0005	.0024	.0097	.0332	.0962	.2340	.4711	.7636	.9659	.9835	.9938	.9986	.9999	22	
.0000	.0001	.0004	.0021	.0090	.0321	.0982	.2537	.5371	.8729	.9235	.9620	.9868	.9980	23	
.0000	.0000	.0001	.0003	.0016	.0070	.0274	.0931	.2712	.6424	.7358	.8280	.9114	.9742	24	
.0000	.0000	.0000	.0000	.0001	.0008	.0038	.0172	.0718	.2774	.3604	.4670	.6035	.7778	25	

Binomial Distribution—Right Tail (cumulative) Terms (*continued*)

π

n	X	.01	.02	.03	.04	.05	.10	.15	.20	.25	.30	.35	.40	.45
30	1	.2603	.4545	.5990	.7061	.7854	.9576	.9924	.9988	.9998	1.0000	1.0000	1.0000	1.0000
	2	.0361	.1205	.2269	.3388	.4465	.8163	.9520	.9895	.9980	.9997	1.0000	1.0000	1.0000
	3	.0033	.0217	.0601	.1169	.1878	.5886	.8486	.9558	.9894	.9979	.9997	1.0000	1.0000
	4	.0002	.0029	.0119	.0306	.0608	.3526	.6783	.8773	.9626	.9907	.9981	.9997	1.0000
	5	.0000	.0003	.0018	.0063	.0156	.1755	.4755	.7448	.9021	.9698	.9925	.9985	.9998
	6	.0000	.0000	.0002	.0011	.0033	.0732	.2894	.5725	.7974	.9234	.9767	.9943	.9989
	7	.0000	.0000	.0000	.0001	.0006	.0258	.1526	.3930	.6519	.8405	.9414	.9828	.9960
	8	.0000	.0000	.0000	.0000	.0001	.0078	.0698	.2392	.4857	.7186	.8762	.9565	.9879
	9	.0000	.0000	.0000	.0000	.0000	.0020	.0278	.1287	.3264	.5685	.7753	.9060	.9688
	10	.0000	.0000	.0000	.0000	.0000	.0005	.0097	.0611	.1966	.4112	.6425	.8237	.9306
	11	.0000	.0000	.0000	.0000	.0000	.0001	.0029	.0256	.1057	.2696	.4922	.7085	.8650
	12	.0000	.0000	.0000	.0000	.0000	.0000	.0008	.0095	.0507	.1593	.3452	.5689	.7673
	13	.0000	.0000	.0000	.0000	.0000	.0000	.0002	.0031	.0216	.0845	.2198	.4215	.6408
	14	.0000	.0000	.0000	.0000	.0000	.0000	.0000	.0009	.0082	.0401	.1263	.2855	.4975
	15	.0000	.0000	.0000	.0000	.0000	.0000	.0000	.0002	.0027	.0169	.0652	.1754	.3552
	16	.0000	.0000	.0000	.0000	.0000	.0000	.0000	.0001	.0008	.0064	.0301	.0971	.2309
	17	.0000	.0000	.0000	.0000	.0000	.0000	.0000	.0000	.0002	.0021	.0124	.0481	.1356
	18	.0000	.0000	.0000	.0000	.0000	.0000	.0000	.0000	.0001	.0006	.0045	.0212	.0714
	19	0.0000	.0000	.0000	.0000	.0000	.0000	.0000	.0000	.0000	.0002	.0014	.0083	.0334
	20	0.0000	.0000	.0000	.0000	.0000	.0000	.0000	.0000	.0000	.0000	.0004	.0029	.0138
	21	0.0000	0.0000	.0000	.0000	.0000	.0000	.0000	.0000	.0000	.0000	.0001	.0009	.0050
	22	0.0000	0.0000	.0000	.0000	.0000	.0000	.0000	.0000	.0000	.0000	.0000	.0002	.0016
	23	0.0000	0.0000	0.0000	.0000	.0000	.0000	.0000	.0000	.0000	.0000	.0000	.0000	.0004
	24	0.0000	0.0000	0.0000	.0000	.0000	.0000	.0000	.0000	.0000	.0000	.0000	.0000	.0001
	25	0.0000	0.0000	0.0000	0.0000	.0000	.0000	.0000	.0000	.0000	.0000	.0000	.0000	.0000
	26	0.0000	0.0000	0.0000	0.0000	0.0000	.0000	.0000	.0000	.0000	.0000	.0000	.0000	.0000
	27	0.0000	0.0000	0.0000	0.0000	0.0000	.0000	.0000	.0000	.0000	.0000	.0000	.0000	.0000
	28	0.0000	0.0000	0.0000	0.0000	0.0000	.0000	.0000	.0000	.0000	.0000	.0000	.0000	.0000
	29	0.0000	0.0000	0.0000	0.0000	0.0000	.0000	.0000	.0000	.0000	.0000	.0000	.0000	.0000
	30	0.0000	0.0000	0.0000	0.0000	0.0000	0.0000	.0000	.0000	.0000	.0000	.0000	.0000	.0000

n	X	.01	.02	.03	.04	.05	.10	.15	.20	.25	.30	.35	.40	.45
40	1	.3310	.5543	.7043	.8046	.8715	.9852	.9985	.9999	1.0000	1.0000	1.0000	1.0000	1.0000
	2	.0607	.1905	.3385	.4790	.6009	.9195	.9879	.9985	.9999	1.0000	1.0000	1.0000	1.0000
	3	.0075	.0457	.1178	.2145	.3233	.7772	.9514	.9921	.9990	.9999	1.0000	1.0000	1.0000
	4	.0007	.0082	.0314	.0748	.1381	.5769	.8698	.9715	.9953	.9994	.9999	1.0000	1.0000
	5	.0000	.0012	.0067	.0210	.0480	.3710	.7367	.9241	.9840	.9974	.9997	1.0000	1.0000
	6	.0000	.0001	.0012	.0049	.0139	.2063	.5675	.8387	.9567	.9914	.9987	.9999	1.0000
	7	.0000	.0000	.0002	.0010	.0034	.0995	.3933	.7141	.9038	.9762	.9956	.9994	.9999
	8	.0000	.0000	.0000	.0002	.0007	.0419	.2441	.5629	.8180	.9447	.9876	.9979	.9998
	9	.0000	.0000	.0000	.0000	.0001	.0155	.1354	.4069	.7002	.8890	.9697	.9939	.9991
	10	.0000	.0000	.0000	.0000	.0000	.0051	.0672	.2682	.5605	.8041	.9356	.9844	.9973
	11	.0000	.0000	.0000	.0000	.0000	.0015	.0299	.1608	.4161	.6913	.8785	.9648	.9926
	12	.0000	.0000	.0000	.0000	.0000	.0004	.0120	.0875	.2849	.5594	.7947	.9291	.9821
	13	.0000	.0000	.0000	.0000	.0000	.0001	.0043	.0432	.1791	.4228	.6857	.8715	.9614
	14	.0000	.0000	.0000	.0000	.0000	.0000	.0014	.0194	.1032	.2968	.5592	.7888	.9249
	15	.0000	.0000	.0000	.0000	.0000	.0000	.0004	.0079	.0544	.1926	.4279	.6826	.8674
	16	.0000	.0000	.0000	.0000	.0000	.0000	.0001	.0029	.0262	.1151	.3054	.5598	.7858
	17	.0000	.0000	.0000	.0000	.0000	.0000	.0000	.0010	.0116	.0633	.2022	.4319	.6815
	18	.0000	.0000	.0000	.0000	.0000	.0000	.0000	.0003	.0047	.0320	.1239	.3115	.5609
	19	.0000	.0000	.0000	.0000	.0000	.0000	.0000	.0001	.0017	.0148	.0699	.2089	.4349
	20	0.0000	.0000	.0000	.0000	.0000	.0000	.0000	.0000	.0006	.0063	.0363	.1298	.3156
	21	0.0000	.0000	.0000	.0000	.0000	.0000	.0000	.0000	.0002	.0024	.0173	.0744	.2130
	22	0.0000	.0000	.0000	.0000	.0000	.0000	.0000	.0000	.0000	.0009	.0075	.0392	.1331
	23	0.0000	.0000	.0000	.0000	.0000	.0000	.0000	.0000	.0000	.0003	.0030	.0189	.0767
	24	0.0000	0.0000	.0000	.0000	.0000	.0000	.0000	.0000	.0000	.0001	.0011	.0083	.0405
	25	0.0000	0.0000	.0000	.0000	.0000	.0000	.0000	.0000	.0000	.0000	.0004	.0034	.0196
	26	0.0000	0.0000	0.0000	.0000	.0000	.0000	.0000	.0000	.0000	.0000	.0001	.0012	.0086
	27	0.0000	0.0000	0.0000	.0000	.0000	.0000	.0000	.0000	.0000	.0000	.0000	.0004	.0034
	28	0.0000	0.0000	0.0000	0.0000	.0000	.0000	.0000	.0000	.0000	.0000	.0000	.0001	.0012
	29	0.0000	0.0000	0.0000	0.0000	0.0000	.0000	.0000	.0000	.0000	.0000	.0000	.0000	.0004
	30	0.0000	0.0000	0.0000	0.0000	0.0000	.0000	.0000	.0000	.0000	.0000	.0000	.0000	.0001
	31	0.0000	0.0000	0.0000	0.0000	0.0000	.0000	.0000	.0000	.0000	.0000	.0000	.0000	.0000
	32	0.0000	0.0000	0.0000	0.0000	0.0000	.0000	.0000	.0000	.0000	.0000	.0000	.0000	.0000
	33	0.0000	0.0000	0.0000	0.0000	0.0000	.0000	.0000	.0000	.0000	.0000	.0000	.0000	.0000
	34	0.0000	0.0000	0.0000	0.0000	0.0000	.0000	.0000	.0000	.0000	.0000	.0000	.0000	.0000
	35	0.0000	0.0000	0.0000	0.0000	0.0000	.0000	.0000	.0000	.0000	.0000	.0000	.0000	.0000
	36	0.0000	0.0000	0.0000	0.0000	0.0000	.0000	.0000	.0000	.0000	.0000	.0000	.0000	.0000
	37	0.0000	0.0000	0.0000	0.0000	0.0000	.0000	.0000	.0000	.0000	.0000	.0000	.0000	.0000
	38	0.0000	0.0000	0.0000	0.0000	0.0000	.0000	.0000	.0000	.0000	.0000	.0000	.0000	.0000
	39	0.0000	0.0000	0.0000	0.0000	0.0000	0.0000	.0000	.0000	.0000	.0000	.0000	.0000	.0000
	40	0.0000	0.0000	0.0000	0.0000	0.0000	0.0000	0.0000	.0000	.0000	.0000	.0000	.0000	.0000

π

.50	.55	.60	.65	.70	.75	.80	.85	.90	.95	.96	.97	.98	.99	X	n
1.0000	1.0000	1.0000	1.0000	1.0000	1.0000	1.0000	1.0000	1.0000	1.0000	1.0000	1.0000	1.0000	1.0000	1	30
1.0000	1.0000	1.0000	1.0000	1.0000	1.0000	1.0000	1.0000	1.0000	1.0000	1.0000	1.0000	1.0000	1.0000	2	
1.0000	1.0000	1.0000	1.0000	1.0000	1.0000	1.0000	1.0000	1.0000	1.0000	1.0000	1.0000	1.0000	1.0000	3	
1.0000	1.0000	1.0000	1.0000	1.0000	1.0000	1.0000	1.0000	1.0000	1.0000	1.0000	1.0000	1.0000	1.0000	4	
1.0000	1.0000	1.0000	1.0000	1.0000	1.0000	1.0000	1.0000	1.0000	1.0000	1.0000	1.0000	1.0000	1.0000	5	
.9998	1.0000	1.0000	1.0000	1.0000	1.0000	1.0000	1.0000	1.0000	1.0000	1.0000	1.0000	1.0000	1.0000	6	
.9993	.9999	1.0000	1.0000	1.0000	1.0000	1.0000	1.0000	1.0000	1.0000	1.0000	1.0000	1.0000	1.0000	7	
.9974	.9996	1.0000	1.0000	1.0000	1.0000	1.0000	1.0000	1.0000	1.0000	1.0000	1.0000	1.0000	1.0000	8	
.9919	.9984	.9998	1.0000	1.0000	1.0000	1.0000	1.0000	1.0000	1.0000	1.0000	1.0000	1.0000	1.0000	9	
.9786	.9950	.9991	.9999	1.0000	1.0000	1.0000	1.0000	1.0000	1.0000	1.0000	1.0000	1.0000	1.0000	10	
.9506	.9862	.9971	.9996	1.0000	1.0000	1.0000	1.0000	1.0000	1.0000	1.0000	1.0000	1.0000	1.0000	11	
.8998	.9666	.9917	.9986	.9998	1.0000	1.0000	1.0000	1.0000	1.0000	1.0000	1.0000	1.0000	1.0000	12	
.8192	.9286	.9788	.9955	.9994	.9999	1.0000	1.0000	1.0000	1.0000	1.0000	1.0000	1.0000	1.0000	13	
.7077	.8644	.9519	.9876	.9979	.9998	1.0000	1.0000	1.0000	1.0000	1.0000	1.0000	1.0000	1.0000	14	
.5722	.7691	.9029	.9699	.9936	.9992	.9999	1.0000	1.0000	1.0000	1.0000	1.0000	1.0000	1.0000	15	
.4278	.6448	.8246	.9348	.9831	.9973	.9998	1.0000	1.0000	1.0000	1.0000	1.0000	1.0000	1.0000	16	
.2923	.5025	.7145	.8737	.9599	.9918	.9991	1.0000	1.0000	1.0000	1.0000	1.0000	1.0000	1.0000	17	
.1808	.3592	.5785	.7802	.9155	.9784	.9969	.9998	1.0000	1.0000	1.0000	1.0000	1.0000	1.0000	18	
.1002	.2327	.4311	.6548	.8407	.9493	.9905	.9992	1.0000	1.0000	1.0000	1.0000	1.0000	1.0000	19	
.0494	.1350	.2915	.5078	.7304	.8943	.9744	.9971	.9999	1.0000	1.0000	1.0000	1.0000	1.0000	20	
.0214	.0694	.1763	.3575	.5888	.8034	.9389	.9903	.9995	1.0000	1.0000	1.0000	1.0000	1.0000	21	
.0081	.0312	.0940	.2247	.4315	.6736	.8713	.9722	.9980	1.0000	1.0000	1.0000	1.0000	1.0000	22	
.0026	.0121	.0435	.1238	.2814	.5143	.7608	.9302	.9922	.9999	1.0000	1.0000	1.0000	1.0000	23	
.0007	.0040	.0172	.0586	.1595	.3481	.6070	.8474	.9742	.9994	.9999	1.0000	1.0000	1.0000	24	
.0002	.0011	.0057	.0233	.0766	.2026	.4275	.7106	.9268	.9967	.9989	.9998	1.0000	1.0000	25	
.0000	.0002	.0015	.0075	.0302	.0979	.2552	.5245	.8245	.9844	.9937	.9982	.9997	1.0000	26	
.0000	.0000	.0003	.0019	.0093	.0374	.1227	.3217	.6474	.9392	.9694	.9881	.9971	.9998	27	
.0000	.0000	.0000	.0003	.0021	.0106	.0442	.1514	.4114	.8122	.8831	.9399	.9783	.9967	28	
.0000	.0000	.0000	.0000	.0003	.0020	.0105	.0480	.1837	.5535	.6612	.7731	.8795	.9639	29	
.0000	.0000	.0000	.0000	.0000	.0002	.0012	.0076	.0424	.2146	.2939	.4010	.5455	.7397	30	

.50	.55	.60	.65	.70	.75	.80	.85	.90	.95	.96	.97	.98	.99	X	n
1.0000	1.0000	1.0000	1.0000	1.0000	1.0000	1.0000	1.0000	1.0000	1.0000	1.0000	1.0000	1.0000	1.0000	1	40
1.0000	1.0000	1.0000	1.0000	1.0000	1.0000	1.0000	1.0000	1.0000	1.0000	1.0000	1.0000	1.0000	1.0000	2	
1.0000	1.0000	1.0000	1.0000	1.0000	1.0000	1.0000	1.0000	1.0000	1.0000	1.0000	1.0000	1.0000	1.0000	3	
1.0000	1.0000	1.0000	1.0000	1.0000	1.0000	1.0000	1.0000	1.0000	1.0000	1.0000	1.0000	1.0000	1.0000	4	
1.0000	1.0000	1.0000	1.0000	1.0000	1.0000	1.0000	1.0000	1.0000	1.0000	1.0000	1.0000	1.0000	1.0000	5	
1.0000	1.0000	1.0000	1.0000	1.0000	1.0000	1.0000	1.0000	1.0000	1.0000	1.0000	1.0000	1.0000	1.0000	6	
1.0000	1.0000	1.0000	1.0000	1.0000	1.0000	1.0000	1.0000	1.0000	1.0000	1.0000	1.0000	1.0000	1.0000	7	
1.0000	1.0000	1.0000	1.0000	1.0000	1.0000	1.0000	1.0000	1.0000	1.0000	1.0000	1.0000	1.0000	1.0000	8	
.9999	1.0000	1.0000	1.0000	1.0000	1.0000	1.0000	1.0000	1.0000	1.0000	1.0000	1.0000	1.0000	1.0000	9	
.9997	1.0000	1.0000	1.0000	1.0000	1.0000	1.0000	1.0000	1.0000	1.0000	1.0000	1.0000	1.0000	1.0000	10	
.9989	.9999	1.0000	1.0000	1.0000	1.0000	1.0000	1.0000	1.0000	1.0000	1.0000	1.0000	1.0000	1.0000	11	
.9968	.9996	1.0000	1.0000	1.0000	1.0000	1.0000	1.0000	1.0000	1.0000	1.0000	1.0000	1.0000	1.0000	12	
.9917	.9988	.9999	1.0000	1.0000	1.0000	1.0000	1.0000	1.0000	1.0000	1.0000	1.0000	1.0000	1.0000	13	
.9808	.9966	.9996	1.0000	1.0000	1.0000	1.0000	1.0000	1.0000	1.0000	1.0000	1.0000	1.0000	1.0000	14	
.9597	.9914	.9988	.9999	1.0000	1.0000	1.0000	1.0000	1.0000	1.0000	1.0000	1.0000	1.0000	1.0000	15	
.9231	.9804	.9966	.9996	1.0000	1.0000	1.0000	1.0000	1.0000	1.0000	1.0000	1.0000	1.0000	1.0000	16	
.8659	.9595	.9917	.9989	.9999	1.0000	1.0000	1.0000	1.0000	1.0000	1.0000	1.0000	1.0000	1.0000	17	
.7852	.9233	.9811	.9970	.9997	1.0000	1.0000	1.0000	1.0000	1.0000	1.0000	1.0000	1.0000	1.0000	18	
.6821	.8669	.9608	.9925	.9991	1.0000	1.0000	1.0000	1.0000	1.0000	1.0000	1.0000	1.0000	1.0000	19	
.5627	.7870	.9256	.9827	.9976	.9998	1.0000	1.0000	1.0000	1.0000	1.0000	1.0000	1.0000	1.0000	20	
.4373	.6844	.8702	.9637	.9937	.9994	1.0000	1.0000	1.0000	1.0000	1.0000	1.0000	1.0000	1.0000	21	
.3179	.5651	.7911	.9301	.9852	.9983	.9999	1.0000	1.0000	1.0000	1.0000	1.0000	1.0000	1.0000	22	
.2148	.4391	.6885	.8761	.9680	.9953	.9997	1.0000	1.0000	1.0000	1.0000	1.0000	1.0000	1.0000	23	
.1341	.3185	.5681	.7978	.9367	.9884	.9990	1.0000	1.0000	1.0000	1.0000	1.0000	1.0000	1.0000	24	
.0769	.2142	.4402	.6946	.8849	.9738	.9971	.9999	1.0000	1.0000	1.0000	1.0000	1.0000	1.0000	25	
.0403	.1326	.3174	.5721	.8074	.9456	.9921	.9996	1.0000	1.0000	1.0000	1.0000	1.0000	1.0000	26	
.0192	.0751	.2112	.4408	.7032	.8968	.9806	.9986	1.0000	1.0000	1.0000	1.0000	1.0000	1.0000	27	
.0083	.0386	.1285	.3143	.5772	.8209	.9568	.9957	.9999	1.0000	1.0000	1.0000	1.0000	1.0000	28	
.0032	.0179	.0709	.2053	.4406	.7151	.9125	.9880	.9996	1.0000	1.0000	1.0000	1.0000	1.0000	29	
.0011	.0074	.0352	.1215	.3087	.5839	.8392	.9701	.9985	1.0000	1.0000	1.0000	1.0000	1.0000	30	
.0003	.0027	.0156	.0644	.1959	.4395	.7318	.9328	.9949	1.0000	1.0000	1.0000	1.0000	1.0000	31	
.0001	.0009	.0061	.0303	.1110	.2998	.5931	.8646	.9845	.9999	1.0000	1.0000	1.0000	1.0000	32	
.0000	.0002	.0021	.0124	.0553	.1820	.4371	.7559	.9581	.9993	.9998	1.0000	1.0000	1.0000	33	
.0000	.0001	.0006	.0044	.0238	.0962	.2859	.6067	.9005	.9966	.9990	.9998	1.0000	1.0000	34	
.0000	.0000	.0001	.0013	.0086	.0433	.1613	.4325	.7937	.9861	.9951	.9988	.9999	1.0000	35	
.0000	.0000	.0000	.0003	.0026	.0160	.0759	.2633	.6290	.9520	.9790	.9933	.9988	1.0000	36	
.0000	.0000	.0000	.0001	.0006	.0047	.0285	.1302	.4231	.8619	.9252	.9686	.9918	.9993	37	
.0000	.0000	.0000	.0000	.0001	.0010	.0079	.0486	.2228	.6767	.7855	.8822	.9543	.9925	38	
.0000	.0000	.0000	.0000	.0000	.0001	.0015	.0121	.0805	.3991	.5210	.6615	.8095	.9393	39	
.0000	.0000	.0000	.0000	.0000	.0000	.0001	.0015	.0148	.1285	.1954	.2957	.4457	.6690	40	

Binomial Distribution—Right Tail (cumulative) Terms (*concluded*)

n	X	.01	.02	.03	.04	.05	.10	.15	.20	.25	.30	.35	.40	.45
50	1	.3950	.6358	.7819	.8701	.9231	.9948	.9997	1.0000	1.0000	1.0000	1.0000	1.0000	1.0000
	2	.0894	.2642	.4447	.5995	.7206	.9662	.9971	.9998	1.0000	1.0000	1.0000	1.0000	1.0000
	3	.0138	.0784	.1892	.3233	.4595	.8883	.9858	.9987	.9999	1.0000	1.0000	1.0000	1.0000
	4	.0016	.0178	.0628	.1391	.2396	.7497	.9540	.9943	.9995	1.0000	1.0000	1.0000	1.0000
	5	.0001	.0032	.0168	.0490	.1036	.5688	.8879	.9815	.9979	.9998	1.0000	1.0000	1.0000
	6	.0000	.0005	.0037	.0144	.0378	.3839	.7806	.9520	.9930	.9993	.9999	1.0000	1.0000
	7	.0000	.0001	.0007	.0036	.0118	.2298	.6387	.8966	.9806	.9975	.9998	1.0000	1.0000
	8	.0000	.0000	.0001	.0008	.0032	.1221	.4812	.8096	.9547	.9927	.9992	.9999	1.0000
	9	.0000	.0000	.0000	.0001	.0008	.0579	.3319	.6927	.9084	.9817	.9975	.9998	1.0000
	10	.0000	.0000	.0000	.0000	.0002	.0245	.2089	.5563	.8363	.9598	.9933	.9992	.9999
	11	.0000	.0000	.0000	.0000	.0000	.0094	.1199	.4164	.7378	.9211	.9840	.9978	.9998
	12	.0000	.0000	.0000	.0000	.0000	.0032	.0628	.2893	.6184	.8610	.9658	.9943	.9994
	13	.0000	.0000	.0000	.0000	.0000	.0010	.0301	.1861	.4890	.7771	.9339	.9867	.9982
	14	.0000	.0000	.0000	.0000	.0000	.0003	.0132	.1106	.3630	.6721	.8837	.9720	.9955
	15	.0000	.0000	.0000	.0000	.0000	.0001	.0053	.0607	.2519	.5532	.8122	.9460	.9896
	16	.0000	.0000	.0000	.0000	.0000	.0000	.0019	.0308	.1631	.4308	.7199	.9045	.9780
	17	.0000	.0000	.0000	.0000	.0000	.0000	.0007	.0144	.0983	.3161	.6111	.8439	.9573
	18	.0000	.0000	.0000	.0000	.0000	.0000	.0002	.0063	.0551	.2178	.4940	.7631	.9235
	19	.0000	.0000	.0000	.0000	.0000	.0000	.0001	.0025	.0287	.1406	.3784	.6644	.8727
	20	.0000	.0000	.0000	.0000	.0000	.0000	.0000	.0009	.0139	.0848	.2736	.5535	.8026
	21	.0000	.0000	.0000	.0000	.0000	.0000	.0000	.0003	.0063	.0478	.1861	.4390	.7138
	22	0.0000	.0000	.0000	.0000	.0000	.0000	.0000	.0001	.0026	.0251	.1187	.3299	.6100
	23	0.0000	.0000	.0000	.0000	.0000	.0000	.0000	.0000	.0010	.0123	.0710	.2340	.4981
	24	0.0000	.0000	.0000	.0000	.0000	.0000	.0000	.0000	.0004	.0056	.0396	.1562	.3866
	25	0.0000	0.0000	.0000	.0000	.0000	.0000	.0000	.0000	.0001	.0024	.0207	.0978	.2840
	26	0.0000	0.0000	.0000	.0000	.0000	.0000	.0000	.0000	.0000	.0009	.0100	.0573	.1966
	27	0.0000	0.0000	.0000	.0000	.0000	.0000	.0000	.0000	.0000	.0003	.0045	.0314	.1279
	28	0.0000	0.0000	0.0000	.0000	.0000	.0000	.0000	.0000	.0000	.0001	.0019	.0160	.0780
	29	0.0000	0.0000	0.0000	.0000	.0000	.0000	.0000	.0000	.0000	.0000	.0007	.0076	.0444
	30	0.0000	0.0000	0.0000	0.0000	.0000	.0000	.0000	.0000	.0000	.0000	.0003	.0034	.0235
	31	0.0000	0.0000	0.0000	0.0000	.0000	.0000	.0000	.0000	.0000	.0000	.0001	.0014	.0116
	32	0.0000	0.0000	0.0000	0.0000	0.0000	.0000	.0000	.0000	.0000	.0000	.0000	.0005	.0053
	33	0.0000	0.0000	0.0000	0.0000	0.0000	.0000	.0000	.0000	.0000	.0000	.0000	.0002	.0022
	34	0.0000	0.0000	0.0000	0.0000	0.0000	.0000	.0000	.0000	.0000	.0000	.0000	.0001	.0009
	35	0.0000	0.0000	0.0000	0.0000	0.0000	.0000	.0000	.0000	.0000	.0000	.0000	.0000	.0003
	36	0.0000	0.0000	0.0000	0.0000	0.0000	.0000	.0000	.0000	.0000	.0000	.0000	.0000	.0001
	37	0.0000	0.0000	0.0000	0.0000	.0000	.0000	.0000	.0000	.0000	.0000	.0000	.0000	.0000
	38	0.0000	0.0000	0.0000	0.0000	0.0000	.0000	.0000	.0000	.0000	.0000	.0000	.0000	.0000
	39	0.0000	0.0000	0.0000	0.0000	0.0000	0.0000	.0000	.0000	.0000	.0000	.0000	.0000	.0000
	40	0.0000	0.0000	0.0000	0.0000	0.0000	0.0000	.0000	.0000	.0000	.0000	.0000	.0000	.0000
	41	0.0000	0.0000	0.0000	0.0000	0.0000	0.0000	.0000	.0000	.0000	.0000	.0000	.0000	.0000
	42	0.0000	0.0000	0.0000	0.0000	0.0000	0.0000	.0000	.0000	.0000	.0000	.0000	.0000	.0000
	43	0.0000	0.0000	0.0000	0.0000	0.0000	0.0000	.0000	.0000	.0000	.0000	.0000	.0000	.0000
	44	0.0000	0.0000	0.0000	0.0000	0.0000	0.0000	0.0000	.0000	.0000	.0000	.0000	.0000	.0000
	45	0.0000	0.0000	0.0000	0.0000	0.0000	0.0000	0.0000	.0000	.0000	.0000	.0000	.0000	.0000
	46	0.0000	0.0000	0.0000	0.0000	0.0000	0.0000	0.0000	.0000	.0000	.0000	.0000	.0000	.0000
	47	0.0000	0.0000	0.0000	0.0000	0.0000	0.0000	0.0000	.0000	.0000	.0000	.0000	.0000	.0000
	48	0.0000	0.0000	0.0000	0.0000	0.0000	0.0000	0.0000	0.0000	.0000	.0000	.0000	.0000	.0000
	49	0.0000	0.0000	0.0000	0.0000	0.0000	0.0000	0.0000	0.0000	.0000	.0000	.0000	.0000	.0000
	50	0.0000	0.0000	0.0000	0.0000	0.0000	0.0000	0.0000	0.0000	0.0000	.0000	.0000	.0000	.0000

π

.50	.55	.60	.65	.70	.75	.80	.85	.90	.95	.96	.97	.98	.99	X	n
1.0000	1.0000	1.0000	1.0000	1.0000	1.0000	1.0000	1.0000	1.0000	1.0000	1.0000	1.0000	1.0000	1.0000	1	50
1.0000	1.0000	1.0000	1.0000	1.0000	1.0000	1.0000	1.0000	1.0000	1.0000	1.0000	1.0000	1.0000	1.0000	2	
1.0000	1.0000	1.0000	1.0000	1.0000	1.0000	1.0000	1.0000	1.0000	1.0000	1.0000	1.0000	1.0000	1.0000	3	
1.0000	1.0000	1.0000	1.0000	1.0000	1.0000	1.0000	1.0000	1.0000	1.0000	1.0000	1.0000	1.0000	1.0000	4	
1.0000	1.0000	1.0000	1.0000	1.0000	1.0000	1.0000	1.0000	1.0000	1.0000	1.0000	1.0000	1.0000	1.0000	5	
1.0000	1.0000	1.0000	1.0000	1.0000	1.0000	1.0000	1.0000	1.0000	1.0000	1.0000	1.0000	1.0000	1.0000	6	
1.0000	1.0000	1.0000	1.0000	1.0000	1.0000	1.0000	1.0000	1.0000	1.0000	1.0000	1.0000	1.0000	1.0000	7	
1.0000	1.0000	1.0000	1.0000	1.0000	1.0000	1.0000	1.0000	1.0000	1.0000	1.0000	1.0000	1.0000	1.0000	8	
1.0000	1.0000	1.0000	1.0000	1.0000	1.0000	1.0000	1.0000	1.0000	1.0000	1.0000	1.0000	1.0000	1.0000	9	
1.0000	1.0000	1.0000	1.0000	1.0000	1.0000	1.0000	1.0000	1.0000	1.0000	1.0000	1.0000	1.0000	1.0000	10	
1.0000	1.0000	1.0000	1.0000	1.0000	1.0000	1.0000	1.0000	1.0000	1.0000	1.0000	1.0000	1.0000	1.0000	11	
1.0000	1.0000	1.0000	1.0000	1.0000	1.0000	1.0000	1.0000	1.0000	1.0000	1.0000	1.0000	1.0000	1.0000	12	
.9998	1.0000	1.0000	1.0000	1.0000	1.0000	1.0000	1.0000	1.0000	1.0000	1.0000	1.0000	1.0000	1.0000	13	
.9995	1.0000	1.0000	1.0000	1.0000	1.0000	1.0000	1.0000	1.0000	1.0000	1.0000	1.0000	1.0000	1.0000	14	
.9987	.9999	1.0000	1.0000	1.0000	1.0000	1.0000	1.0000	1.0000	1.0000	1.0000	1.0000	1.0000	1.0000	15	
.9967	.9997	1.0000	1.0000	1.0000	1.0000	1.0000	1.0000	1.0000	1.0000	1.0000	1.0000	1.0000	1.0000	16	
.9923	.9991	.9999	1.0000	1.0000	1.0000	1.0000	1.0000	1.0000	1.0000	1.0000	1.0000	1.0000	1.0000	17	
.9836	.9978	.9998	1.0000	1.0000	1.0000	1.0000	1.0000	1.0000	1.0000	1.0000	1.0000	1.0000	1.0000	18	
.9675	.9947	.9995	1.0000	1.0000	1.0000	1.0000	1.0000	1.0000	1.0000	1.0000	1.0000	1.0000	1.0000	19	
.9405	.9884	.9986	.9999	1.0000	1.0000	1.0000	1.0000	1.0000	1.0000	1.0000	1.0000	1.0000	1.0000	20	
.8987	.9765	.9966	.9997	1.0000	1.0000	1.0000	1.0000	1.0000	1.0000	1.0000	1.0000	1.0000	1.0000	21	
.8389	.9556	.9924	.9993	1.0000	1.0000	1.0000	1.0000	1.0000	1.0000	1.0000	1.0000	1.0000	1.0000	22	
.7601	.9220	.9840	.9981	.9999	1.0000	1.0000	1.0000	1.0000	1.0000	1.0000	1.0000	1.0000	1.0000	23	
.6641	.8721	.9686	.9955	.9997	1.0000	1.0000	1.0000	1.0000	1.0000	1.0000	1.0000	1.0000	1.0000	24	
.5561	.8034	.9427	.9900	.9991	1.0000	1.0000	1.0000	1.0000	1.0000	1.0000	1.0000	1.0000	1.0000	25	
.4439	.7160	.9022	.9793	.9976	.9999	1.0000	1.0000	1.0000	1.0000	1.0000	1.0000	1.0000	1.0000	26	
.3359	.6134	.8438	.9604	.9944	.9996	1.0000	1.0000	1.0000	1.0000	1.0000	1.0000	1.0000	1.0000	27	
.2399	.5019	.7660	.9290	.9877	.9990	1.0000	1.0000	1.0000	1.0000	1.0000	1.0000	1.0000	1.0000	28	
.1611	.3900	.6701	.8813	.9749	.9974	.9999	1.0000	1.0000	1.0000	1.0000	1.0000	1.0000	1.0000	29	
.1013	.2862	.5610	.8139	.9522	.9937	.9997	1.0000	1.0000	1.0000	1.0000	1.0000	1.0000	1.0000	30	
.0595	.1974	.4465	.7264	.9152	.9861	.9991	1.0000	1.0000	1.0000	1.0000	1.0000	1.0000	1.0000	31	
.0325	.1273	.3356	.6216	.8594	.9713	.9975	.9999	1.0000	1.0000	1.0000	1.0000	1.0000	1.0000	32	
.0164	.0765	.2369	.5060	.7822	.9449	.9937	.9998	1.0000	1.0000	1.0000	1.0000	1.0000	1.0000	33	
.0077	.0427	.1561	.3889	.6839	.9017	.9856	.9993	1.0000	1.0000	1.0000	1.0000	1.0000	1.0000	34	
.0033	.0220	.0955	.2801	.5692	.8369	.9692	.9981	1.0000	1.0000	1.0000	1.0000	1.0000	1.0000	35	
.0013	.0104	.0540	.1878	.4468	.7481	.9393	.9947	.9999	1.0000	1.0000	1.0000	1.0000	1.0000	36	
.0005	.0045	.0280	.1163	.3279	.6370	.8894	.9868	.9997	1.0000	1.0000	1.0000	1.0000	1.0000	37	
.0002	.0018	.0133	.0661	.2229	.5110	.8139	.9699	.9990	1.0000	1.0000	1.0000	1.0000	1.0000	38	
.0000	.0006	.0057	.0342	.1390	.3816	.7107	.9372	.9968	1.0000	1.0000	1.0000	1.0000	1.0000	39	
.0000	.0002	.0022	.0160	.0789	.2622	.5836	.8801	.9906	1.0000	1.0000	1.0000	1.0000	1.0000	40	
.0000	.0001	.0008	.0067	.0402	.1637	.4437	.7911	.9755	.9998	1.0000	1.0000	1.0000	1.0000	41	
.0000	.0000	.0002	.0025	.0183	.0916	.3073	.6681	.9421	.9992	.9999	1.0000	1.0000	1.0000	42	
.0000	.0000	.0001	.0008	.0073	.0453	.1904	.5188	.8779	.9968	.9992	.9999	1.0000	1.0000	43	
.0000	.0000	.0000	.0002	.0025	.0194	.1034	.3613	.7702	.9882	.9964	.9993	.9999	1.0000	44	
.0000	.0000	.0000	.0001	.0007	.0070	.0480	.2194	.6161	.9622	.9856	.9963	.9995	1.0000	45	
.0000	.0000	.0000	.0000	.0002	.0021	.0185	.1121	.4312	.8964	.9510	.9832	.9968	.9999	46	
.0000	.0000	.0000	.0000	.0000	.0005	.0057	.0460	.2503	.7604	.8609	.9372	.9822	.9984	47	
.0000	.0000	.0000	.0000	.0000	.0001	.0013	.0142	.1117	.5405	.6767	.8108	.9216	.9862	48	
.0000	.0000	.0000	.0000	.0000	.0000	.0002	.0029	.0338	.2794	.4005	.5553	.7358	.9106	49	
.0000	.0000	.0000	.0000	.0000	.0000	.0000	.0003	.0052	.0769	.1299	.2181	.3642	.6050	50	

Poisson Distribution—
Individual Terms

The table presents individual Poisson probabilities for the number of occurrences X for selected values of μ_X, the mean number of occurrences.

$$P(X|\mu_X) = e^{-\mu_X}\frac{(\mu_X)^X}{X!}$$

$$\text{mean} = E(x) = \mu_X$$

$$\text{also} \quad \sigma^2(x) = \mu_X$$

handwritten: $n\pi = \mu_x = .080$

Poisson Distribution—Individual Terms

μ

X	.001	.002	.003	.004	.005	.006	.007	.008	.009	.010	.020	.030	.040	.050	.060	.070	.080	.090	.100	.150	
0	.999	.998	.997	.996	.995	.994	.993	.992	.991	.990	.980	.970	.961	.951	.942	.932	.923	.914	.905	.861	0
1	.001	.002	.003	.004	.005	.006	.007	.008	.009	.010	.020	.029	.038	.048	.057	.065	.074	.082	.090	.129	1
2												.001	.001	.002	.002	.003	.004	.005	.010		2

μ

X	.20	.25	.30	.40	.50	.60	.70	.80	.90	1.00	1.10	1.20	1.30	1.40	1.50	1.60	1.70	1.80	1.90	2.00	
0	.819	.779	.741	.670	.607	.549	.497	.449	.407	.368	.333	.301	.273	.247	.223	.202	.183	.165	.150	.135	0
1	.164	.195	.222	.268	.303	.329	.348	.359	.366	.368	.366	.361	.354	.345	.335	.323	.311	.298	.284	.271	1
2	.016	.024	.033	.054	.076	.099	.122	.144	.165	.184	.201	.217	.230	.242	.251	.258	.264	.268	.270	.271	2
3	.001	.002	.003	.007	.013	.020	.028	.038	.049	.061	.074	.087	.100	.113	.126	.138	.150	.161	.171	.180	3
4			.001	.002	.003	.005	.008	.011	.015	.020	.026	.032	.039	.047	.055	.064	.072	.081	.090	4
5					.001	.001	.002	.003	.004	.006	.008	.011	.014	.018	.022	.026	.031	.036	5
6						.001	.001	.001	.002	.003	.004	.005	.006	.008	.010	.012	6
7								.001	.001	.001	.001	.002	.003	.003	7
8												.001	.001	8

μ

X	2.10	2.20	2.30	2.40	2.50	2.60	2.70	2.80	2.90	3.00	3.10	3.20	3.30	3.40	3.50	3.60	3.70	3.80	3.90	4.00	
0	.122	.111	.100	.091	.082	.074	.067	.061	.055	.050	.045	.041	.037	.033	.030	.027	.025	.022	.020	.018	0
1	.257	.244	.231	.218	.205	.193	.181	.170	.160	.149	.140	.130	.122	.113	.106	.098	.091	.085	.079	.073	1
2	.270	.268	.265	.261	.257	.251	.245	.238	.231	.224	.216	.209	.201	.185	.177	.169	.162	.154	.147	2
3	.189	.197	.203	.209	.214	.218	.220	.222	.224	.224	.224	.223	.221	.219	.216	.212	.209	.205	.200	.195	3
4	.099	.108	.117	.125	.134	.141	.149	.156	.162	.168	.173	.178	.182	.186	.189	.191	.193	.194	.195	.195	4
5	.042	.048	.054	.060	.067	.074	.080	.087	.094	.101	.107	.114	.120	.126	.132	.138	.143	.148	.152	.156	5
6	.015	.017	.021	.024	.028	.032	.036	.041	.045	.050	.056	.061	.066	.072	.077	.083	.088	.094	.099	.104	6
7	.004	.005	.007	.008	.010	.012	.014	.016	.019	.022	.025	.028	.031	.035	.039	.042	.047	.051	.055	.060	7
8	.001	.002	.002	.002	.003	.004	.005	.006	.007	.008	.010	.011	.013	.015	.017	.019	.022	.024	.027	.030	8
9			.001	.001	.001	.001	.002	.002	.003	.003	.004	.005	.006	.007	.008	.009	.010	.012	.013	9
10						.001	.001	.001	.001	.002	.002	.002	.003	.003	.004	.005	.005	10
11									.001	.001	.001	.001	.001	.001	.002	.002	11
12													.001	.001	12

Poisson Distribution—Individual Terms (*continued*)

μ

X	4.10	4.20	4.30	4.40	4.50	4.60	4.70	4.80	4.90	5.00	5.10	5.20	5.30	5.40	5.50	5.60	5.70	5.80	5.90	6.00	X
0	.017	.015	.014	.012	.011	.010	.009	.008	.007	.007	.006	.006	.005	.005	.004	.004	.003	.003	.003	.002	0
1	.068	.063	.058	.054	.050	.046	.043	.040	.036	.034	.031	.029	.026	.024	.022	.021	.019	.018	.016	.015	1
2	.139	.132	.125	.119	.112	.106	.100	.095	.089	.084	.079	.075	.070	.066	.062	.058	.054	.051	.048	.045	2
3	.190	.185	.180	.174	.169	.163	.157	.152	.145	.140	.135	.129	.124	.119	.113	.108	.103	.098	.094	.089	3
4	.195	.194	.193	.192	.190	.188	.185	.182	.179	.175	.172	.168	.164	.160	.156	.152	.147	.143	.138	.134	4
5	.160	.163	.166	.169	.171	.173	.174	.175	.175	.175	.175	.174	.173	.171	.170	.168	.166	.163	.161		5
6	.109	.114	.119	.124	.128	.132	.136	.140	.143	.146	.149	.151	.154	.156	.157	.158	.159	.160	.160	.161	6
7	.064	.069	.073	.078	.082	.087	.091	.096	.100	.104	.109	.113	.116	.120	.123	.127	.130	.133	.135	.138	7
8	.033	.036	.039	.043	.046	.050	.054	.058	.061	.065	.069	.073	.077	.081	.085	.089	.092	.096	.100	.103	8
9	.015	.017	.019	.021	.023	.026	.028	.031	.033	.036	.039	.042	.045	.049	.052	.055	.059	.062	.065	.069	9
10	.006	.007	.008	.009	.010	.012	.013	.015	.016	.018	.020	.022	.024	.026	.029	.031	.033	.036	.039	.041	10
11	.002	.003	.003	.004	.004	.005	.006	.006	.007	.008	.009	.010	.012	.013	.014	.016	.017	.019	.021	.023	11
12	.001	.001	.001	.001	.002	.002	.002	.003	.003	.003	.004	.005	.005	.006	.007	.007	.008	.009	.010	.011	12
13					.001	.001	.001	.001	.001	.001	.002	.002	.002	.002	.003	.003	.004	.004	.005	.005	13
14										.001	.001	.001	.001	.001	.001	.001	.002	.002	.002		14
15																	.001	.001	.001	.001	15

μ

X	6.10	6.20	6.30	6.40	6.50	6.60	6.70	6.80	6.90	7.00	7.10	7.20	7.30	7.40	7.50	7.60	7.70	7.80	7.90	8.00	X
0	.002	.002	.002	.002	.002	.001	.001	.001	.001	.001	.001	.001	.001	.001	.001	.001	.000	.000	.000	.000	0
1	.014	.013	.012	.011	.010	.009	.008	.008	.007	.006	.006	.005	.005	.005	.004	.004	.003	.003	.003	.003	1
2	.042	.039	.036	.034	.032	.030	.028	.026	.024	.022	.021	.019	.018	.017	.016	.014	.013	.012	.012	.011	2
3	.085	.081	.077	.073	.069	.065	.062	.058	.055	.052	.049	.046	.044	.041	.039	.037	.034	.032	.030	.029	3
4	.129	.125	.121	.116	.112	.108	.103	.099	.095	.091	.087	.084	.080	.076	.073	.070	.066	.063	.060	.057	4
5	.158	.155	.152	.149	.145	.142	.138	.135	.131	.128	.124	.120	.117	.113	.109	.106	.102	.099	.095	.092	5
6	.160	.160	.159	.159	.157	.156	.155	.153	.151	.149	.147	.144	.142	.139	.137	.134	.131	.128	.125	.122	6
7	.140	.142	.144	.145	.146	.147	.148	.149	.149	.149	.149	.148	.147	.146	.145	.144	.143	.141	.140	.140	7
8	.107	.110	.113	.116	.119	.121	.124	.126	.128	.130	.132	.134	.135	.136	.137	.138	.139	.139	.139	.140	8
9	.072	.076	.079	.082	.086	.089	.092	.095	.098	.101	.104	.107	.110	.112	.114	.117	.119	.121	.122	.124	9
10	.044	.047	.050	.053	.056	.059	.062	.065	.068	.071	.074	.077	.080	.083	.086	.089	.091	.094	.097	.099	10
11	.024	.026	.029	.031	.033	.035	.038	.040	.043	.045	.048	.050	.053	.056	.059	.061	.064	.067	.069	.072	11
12	.012	.014	.015	.016	.018	.019	.021	.023	.025	.026	.028	.030	.032	.034	.037	.039	.041	.043	.046	.048	12
13	.006	.007	.007	.008	.009	.010	.011	.012	.013	.014	.015	.017	.018	.020	.021	.023	.024	.026	.028	.030	13
14	.003	.003	.003	.004	.004	.005	.005	.006	.006	.007	.008	.009	.009	.010	.011	.012	.013	.015	.016	.017	14
15	.001	.001	.001	.002	.002	.002	.002	.003	.003	.003	.004	.004	.005	.005	.006	.006	.007	.008	.008	.009	15
16			.001	.001	.001	.001	.001	.001	.001	.001	.002	.002	.002	.002	.003	.003	.003	.004	.004	.005	16
17											.001	.001	.001	.001	.001	.001	.001	.002	.002	.002	17
18																.001	.001	.001	.001	.001	18

μ

X	8.10	8.20	8.30	8.40	8.50	8.60	8.70	8.80	8.90	9.00	9.10	9.20	9.30	9.40	9.50	9.60	9.70	9.80	9.90	10.0	X
0	.000	.000	.000	.000	.000	.000	.000	.000	.000	.000	.000	.000	.000	.000	.000	.000	.000	.000	.000	.000	0
1	.002	.002	.002	.002	.002	.002	.001	.001	.001	.001	.001	.001	.001	.001	.001	.001	.001	.001	.000	.000	1
2	.010	.009	.009	.008	.007	.007	.006	.006	.005	.005	.005	.004	.004	.004	.003	.003	.003	.003	.002	.002	2
3	.027	.025	.024	.022	.021	.020	.018	.017	.016	.015	.014	.013	.012	.011	.011	.010	.009	.009	.008	.008	3
4	.054	.052	.049	.047	.044	.042	.040	.038	.036	.034	.032	.030	.028	.027	.025	.024	.023	.021	.020	.019	4
5	.088	.085	.082	.078	.075	.072	.069	.066	.063	.061	.058	.055	.053	.051	.048	.046	.044	.042	.040	.038	5
6	.119	.116	.113	.110	.107	.103	.100	.097	.094	.091	.088	.085	.082	.079	.076	.074	.071	.068	.066	.063	6
7	.138	.136	.134	.132	.129	.127	.125	.122	.120	.117	.114	.112	.109	.106	.104	.101	.098	.096	.093	.090	7
8	.140	.139	.139	.138	.138	.137	.136	.134	.133	.132	.130	.129	.127	.125	.123	.121	.119	.117	.115	.113	8
9	.126	.127	.128	.129	.130	.131	.131	.131	.132	.132	.132	.131	.131	.131	.130	.129	.128	.127	.126	.125	9
10	.102	.104	.106	.108	.110	.112	.114	.116	.117	.119	.120	.121	.122	.123	.124	.124	.125	.125	.125	.125	10
11	.075	.078	.080	.083	.085	.088	.090	.093	.095	.097	.099	.101	.103	.105	.107	.108	.110	.111	.113	.114	11
12	.051	.053	.055	.058	.060	.063	.065	.068	.070	.073	.075	.078	.080	.082	.084	.087	.089	.091	.093	.095	12
13	.031	.033	.035	.037	.040	.042	.044	.046	.048	.050	.053	.055	.057	.059	.062	.064	.066	.068	.071	.073	13
14	.018	.020	.021	.022	.024	.026	.027	.029	.031	.032	.034	.036	.038	.040	.042	.044	.046	.048	.050	.052	14
15	.010	.011	.012	.013	.014	.015	.016	.017	.018	.019	.021	.022	.024	.025	.027	.028	.030	.031	.033	.035	15
16	.005	.005	.006	.007	.007	.008	.009	.009	.010	.011	.012	.013	.014	.015	.016	.017	.018	.019	.020	.022	16
17	.002	.003	.003	.003	.004	.004	.004	.005	.005	.006	.006	.007	.007	.008	.009	.010	.010	.011	.012	.013	17
18	.001	.001	.001	.002	.002	.002	.002	.002	.003	.003	.003	.004	.004	.004	.005	.005	.006	.006	.007	.007	18
19		.001	.001	.001	.001	.001	.001	.001	.001	.001	.002	.002	.002	.002	.002	.003	.003	.003	.003	.004	19
20									.001	.001	.001	.001	.001	.001	.001	.001	.001	.002	.002	.002	20
21																.001	.001	.001	.001	.001	21

Poisson Distribution—Right Tail (cumulative) Terms

The table presents the Poisson probabilities of X or more occurrences for selected values of μ_X the mean number of occurrences.

$$\sum_{X=0}^{\infty} \frac{e^{-\mu_X}(\mu_X)^X}{X!}$$

Poisson Distribution—Right Tail (cumulative) Terms

μ

X	.001	.002	.003	.004	.005	.006	.007	.008	.009	.010	.020	.030	.040	.050	.060	.070	.080	.090	.100	.150	
1	.001	.002	.003	.004	.005	.006	.007	.008	.009	.010	.020	.030	.039	.049	.058	.068	.077	.086	.095	.139	1
2													.001	.001	.002	.002	.003	.004	.005	.010	2
3																				.001	3

μ

X	.20	.25	.30	.40	.50	.60	.70	.80	.90	1.00	1.10	1.20	1.30	1.40	1.50	1.60	1.70	1.80	1.90	2.00	
1	.181	.221	.259	.330	.393	.451	.503	.551	.593	.632	.667	.699	.727	.753	.777	.798	.817	.835	.850	.865	1
2	.018	.026	.037	.062	.090	.122	.156	.191	.228	.264	.301	.337	.373	.408	.442	.475	.507	.537	.566	.594	2
3	.001	.002	.004	.008	.014	.023	.034	.047	.063	.080	.100	.121	.143	.167	.191	.217	.243	.269	.296	.323	3
4				.001	.002	.003	.006	.009	.013	.019	.026	.034	.043	.054	.066	.079	.093	.109	.125	.143	4
5							.001	.001	.002	.004	.005	.008	.011	.014	.019	.024	.030	.036	.044	.053	5
6										.001	.001	.002	.002	.003	.004	.006	.008	.010	.013	.017	6
7														.001	.001	.001	.002	.003	.003	.005	7
8																		.001	.001	.001	8

(handwritten note: M+=26; value .053 circled)

μ

X	2.10	2.20	2.30	2.40	2.50	2.60	2.70	2.80	2.90	3.00	3.10	3.20	3.30	3.40	3.50	3.60	3.70	3.80	3.90	4.00	
1	.878	.889	.900	.909	.918	.926	.933	.939	.945	.950	.955	.959	.963	.967	.970	.973	.975	.978	.980	.982	1
2	.620	.645	.669	.692	.713	.733	.751	.769	.785	.801	.815	.829	.841	.853	.864	.874	.884	.893	.901	.908	2
3	.350	.377	.404	.430	.456	.482	.506	.531	.554	.577	.599	.620	.641	.660	.679	.697	.715	.731	.747	.762	3
4	.161	.181	.201	.221	.242	.264	.286	.308	.330	.353	.375	.397	.420	.442	.463	.485	.506	.527	.547	.567	4
5	.062	.072	.084	.096	.109	.123	.137	.152	.168	.185	.202	.219	.237	.256	.275	.294	.313	.332	.352	.371	5
6	.020	.025	.030	.036	.042	.049	.057	.065	.074	.084	.094	.105	.117	.129	.142	.156	.170	.184	.199	.215	6
7	.006	.007	.009	.012	.014	.017	.021	.024	.029	.034	.039	.045	.051	.058	.065	.073	.082	.091	.101	.111	7
8	.001	.002	.003	.003	.004	.005	.007	.008	.010	.012	.014	.017	.020	.023	.027	.031	.035	.040	.045	.051	8
9			.001	.001	.001	.001	.002	.002	.003	.004	.005	.006	.007	.008	.010	.012	.014	.016	.019	.021	9
10							.001	.001	.001	.001	.001	.002	.002	.003	.003	.004	.005	.006	.007	.008	10
11													.001	.001	.001	.001	.002	.002	.002	.003	11
12																		.001	.001	.001	12

Poisson Distribution—Right Tail (cumulative) Terms (*continued*)

μ

X	4.10	4.20	4.30	4.40	4.50	4.60	4.70	4.80	4.90	5.00	5.10	5.20	5.30	5.40	5.50	5.60	5.70	5.80	5.90	6.00	X
1	.983	.985	.986	.988	.989	.990	.991	.992	.993	.993	.994	.994	.995	.995	.996	.996	.997	.997	.997	.998	1
2	.915	.922	.928	.934	.939	.944	.948	.952	.956	.960	.963	.966	.969	.971	.973	.976	.978	.979	.981	.983	2
3	.776	.790	.803	.815	.826	.837	.848	.857	.867	.875	.884	.891	.898	.905	.912	.918	.923	.928	.933	.938	3
4	.586	.605	.623	.641	.658	.674	.690	.706	.721	.735	.749	.762	.775	.787	.798	.809	.820	.830	.840	.849	4
5	.391	.410	.430	.449	.468	.487	.505	.524	.542	.560	.577	.594	.610	.627	.642	.658	.673	.687	.701	.715	5
6	.231	.247	.263	.280	.297	.314	.332	.349	.366	.384	.402	.419	.437	.454	.471	.488	.505	.522	.538	.554	6
7	.121	.133	.144	.156	.169	.182	.195	.209	.223	.238	.253	.268	.283	.298	.314	.330	.346	.362	.378	.394	7
8	.057	.064	.071	.079	.087	.095	.104	.113	.123	.133	.144	.155	.167	.178	.191	.203	.215	.229	.242	.256	8
9	.024	.028	.032	.036	.040	.045	.050	.056	.062	.068	.075	.082	.089	.097	.105	.114	.123	.133	.143	.153	9
10	.010	.011	.013	.015	.017	.020	.022	.025	.028	.032	.036	.040	.044	.049	.054	.059	.065	.071	.077	.084	10
11	.003	.004	.005	.006	.007	.008	.009	.010	.012	.014	.016	.018	.020	.023	.025	.028	.031	.035	.039	.043	11
12	.001	.001	.002	.002	.002	.003	.003	.004	.005	.005	.006	.007	.008	.010	.011	.012	.014	.016	.018	.020	12
13			.001	.001	.001	.001	.001	.001	.002	.002	.002	.003	.003	.004	.004	.005	.006	.007	.008	.009	13
14									.001	.001	.001	.001	.001	.001	.002	.002	.002	.003	.003	.004	14
15															.001	.001	.001	.001	.001	.001	15
16																				.001	16

μ

X	6.10	6.20	6.30	6.40	6.50	6.60	6.70	6.80	6.90	7.00	7.10	7.20	7.30	7.40	7.50	7.60	7.70	7.80	7.90	8.00	X
1	.998	.998	.998	.998	.998	.999	.999	.999	.999	.999	.999	.999	.999	.999	.999	.999	1.0	1.0	1.0	1.0	1
2	.984	.985	.987	.988	.988	.989	.990	.991	.992	.993	.993	.994	.994	.995	.995	.995	.996	.996	.996	.997	2
3	.942	.946	.950	.954	.957	.960	.963	.966	.968	.970	.973	.975	.976	.978	.980	.981	.983	.984	.985	.986	3
4	.857	.866	.874	.881	.888	.895	.901	.907	.913	.918	.923	.928	.933	.937	.941	.945	.948	.952	.955	.958	4
5	.728	.741	.753	.765	.776	.787	.798	.809	.818	.827	.836	.844	.853	.860	.868	.875	.882	.888	.894	.900	5
6	.570	.586	.601	.616	.631	.645	.659	.673	.686	.699	.712	.724	.736	.747	.759	.769	.780	.790	.799	.809	6
7	.410	.426	.442	.458	.473	.489	.505	.520	.535	.550	.565	.580	.594	.608	.622	.635	.649	.662	.674	.687	7
8	.270	.284	.298	.313	.327	.342	.357	.372	.386	.401	.416	.431	.446	.461	.475	.490	.504	.519	.533	.547	8
9	.163	.174	.185	.197	.208	.220	.233	.245	.258	.271	.284	.297	.311	.324	.338	.352	.366	.380	.393	.407	9
10	.091	.098	.106	.114	.123	.131	.140	.150	.160	.170	.180	.190	.201	.212	.224	.235	.247	.259	.271	.283	10
11	.047	.051	.056	.061	.067	.073	.079	.085	.092	.099	.106	.113	.121	.129	.138	.146	.155	.165	.174	.184	11
12	.022	.025	.028	.031	.034	.037	.041	.045	.049	.053	.058	.063	.068	.074	.079	.085	.091	.098	.105	.112	12
13	.010	.011	.013	.014	.016	.018	.020	.022	.024	.027	.030	.033	.036	.039	.043	.046	.050	.055	.059	.064	13
14	.004	.005	.005	.006	.007	.008	.009	.010	.011	.013	.014	.016	.018	.020	.022	.024	.026	.029	.031	.034	14
15	.002	.002	.002	.003	.003	.003	.004	.004	.005	.006	.006	.007	.008	.009	.010	.011	.013	.014	.016	.017	15
16	.001	.001	.001	.001	.001	.001	.002	.002	.002	.002	.003	.003	.004	.004	.005	.005	.006	.007	.007	.008	16
17							.001	.001	.001	.001	.001	.001	.001	.002	.002	.002	.003	.003	.003	.004	17
18													.001	.001	.001	.001	.001	.001	.001	.002	18
19																			.001	.001	19

μ

X	8.10	8.20	8.30	8.40	8.50	8.60	8.70	8.80	8.90	9.00	9.10	9.20	9.30	9.40	9.50	9.60	9.70	9.80	9.90	10.0	X
1	1.0	1.0	1.0	1.0	1.0	1.0	1.0	1.0	1.0	1.0	1.0	1.0	1.0	1.0	1.0	1.0	1.0	1.0	1.0	1.0	1
2	.997	.997	.998	.998	.998	.998	.998	.999	.999	.999	.999	.999	.999	.999	.999	.999	.999	.999	.999	1.0	2
3	.987	.988	.989	.990	.991	.991	.992	.993	.993	.994	.994	.995	.995	.995	.996	.996	.996	.997	.997	.997	3
4	.960	.963	.965	.968	.970	.972	.974	.976	.977	.979	.980	.982	.983	.984	.985	.986	.987	.988	.989	.990	4
5	.906	.911	.916	.921	.926	.930	.934	.938	.942	.945	.948	.951	.954	.957	.960	.962	.965	.967	.969	.971	5
6	.818	.826	.835	.843	.850	.858	.865	.872	.878	.884	.890	.896	.901	.907	.911	.916	.921	.925	.929	.933	6
7	.699	.710	.722	.733	.744	.754	.765	.774	.784	.793	.802	.811	.819	.827	.835	.843	.850	.857	.863	.870	7
8	.561	.575	.588	.601	.614	.627	.640	.652	.664	.676	.688	.699	.710	.721	.731	.742	.752	.761	.771	.780	8
9	.421	.435	.449	.463	.477	.491	.504	.518	.531	.544	.557	.570	.583	.596	.608	.620	.632	.644	.656	.667	9
10	.296	.308	.321	.334	.347	.360	.373	.386	.399	.413	.426	.439	.452	.465	.478	.491	.504	.517	.529	.542	10
11	.194	.204	.215	.226	.237	.248	.259	.271	.282	.294	.306	.318	.330	.342	.355	.367	.379	.392	.404	.417	11
12	.119	.127	.135	.143	.151	.160	.169	.178	.187	.197	.207	.217	.227	.237	.248	.259	.270	.281	.292	.303	12
13	.069	.074	.079	.085	.091	.097	.103	.110	.117	.124	.132	.139	.147	.155	.164	.172	.181	.190	.199	.208	13
14	.037	.040	.044	.048	.051	.055	.060	.064	.069	.074	.079	.084	.090	.096	.102	.108	.115	.121	.128	.136	14
15	.019	.021	.023	.025	.027	.030	.033	.035	.038	.041	.045	.048	.052	.056	.060	.064	.069	.073	.078	.083	15
16	.009	.010	.011	.013	.014	.015	.017	.018	.020	.022	.024	.026	.028	.031	.033	.036	.039	.042	.045	.049	16
17	.004	.005	.005	.006	.007	.007	.008	.009	.010	.011	.012	.013	.015	.016	.018	.019	.021	.023	.025	.027	17
18			.002	.002	.002	.003	.003	.003	.004	.004	.005	.005	.006	.007	.008	.009	.011	.012	.013	.014	18
19			.001	.001	.001	.001	.001	.001	.002	.002	.002	.003	.003	.003	.004	.004	.005	.006	.007	.007	19
20						.001	.001	.001	.001	.001	.001	.001	.002	.002	.002	.002	.002	.003	.003	.003	20
21											.001	.001	.001	.001	.001	.001	.001	.001	.001	.002	21
22																		.001	.001	.001	22

Right-Tail Areas under the Standard Normal Density Function

Z is a standardized normal random variable ($\mu = 0$, $\sigma = 1$)

Right-Tail Areas under the Standard Normal Density Function

Z' table

$f(Z)$

$\mu_x = 0$

← 0.1230 $\frac{1}{2}\alpha$ = Prob. of being in the right tail

Z

$Z = 1.16$

Z	.00	.01	.02	.03	.04	.05	.06	.07	.08	.09
0.0	.5000	.4960	.4920	.4880	.4840	.4801	.4761	.4721	.4681	.4641
.1	.4602	.4562	.4522	.4483	.4443	.4404	.4364	.4325	.4286	.4247
.2	.4207	.4168	.4129	.4090	.4052	.4013	.3974	.3936	.3897	.3859
.3	.3821	.3783	.3745	.3707	.3669	.3632	.3594	.3557	.3520	.3483
.4	.3446	.3409	.3372	.3336	.3300	.3264	.3228	.3192	.3156	.3121
.5	.3085	.3050	.3015	.2981	.2946	.2912	.2877	.2843	.2810	.2776
.6	.2743	.2709	.2676	.2643	.2611	.2578	.2546	.2514	.2483	.2451
.7	.2420	.2389	.2358	.2327	.2296	.2266	.2236	.2206	.2177	.2148
.8	.2119	.2090	.2061	.2033	.2005	.1977	.1949	.1922	.1894	.1867
.9	.1841	.1814	.1788	.1762	.1736	.1711	.1685	.1660	.1635	.1611
1.0	.1587	.1562	.1539	.1515	.1492	.1469	.1446	.1423	.1401	.1379
1.1	.1357	.1335	.1314	.1292	.1271	.1251	.1230	.1210	.1190	.1170
1.2	.1151	.1131	.1112	.1093	.1075	.1056	.1038	.1020	.1003	.0985
1.3	.0968	.0951	.0934	.0918	.0901	.0885	.0869	.0853	.0838	.0823
1.4	.0808	.0793	.0778	.0764	.0749	.0735	.0721	.0708	.0694	.0681
1.5	.0668	.0655	.0643	.0630	.0618	.0606	.0594	.0582	.0571	.0559
1.6	.0548	.0537	.0526	.0516	.0505	.0495	.0485	.0475	.0465	.0455
1.7	.0446	.0436	.0427	.0418	.0409	.0401	.0392	.0384	.0375	.0367
1.8	.0359	.0351	.0344	.0336	.0329	.0322	.0314	.0307	.0301	.0294
1.9	.0287	.0281	.0274	.0268	.0262	.0256	.0250	.0244	.0239	.0233
2.0	.0228	.0222	.0217	.0212	.0207	.0202	.0197	.0192	.0188	.0183
2.1	.0179	.0174	.0170	.0166	.0162	.0158	.0154	.0150	.0146	.0143
2.2	.0139	.0136	.0132	.0129	.0125	.0122	.0119	.0116	.0113	.0110
2.3	.0107	.0104	.0102	.0099	.0096	.0094	.0091	.0089	.0087	.0084
2.4	.0082	.0080	.0078	.0075	.0073	.0071	.0069	.0068	.0066	.0064
2.5	.0062	.0060	.0059	.0057	.0055	.0054	.0052	.0051	.0049	.0048
2.6	.0047	.0045	.0044	.0043	.0041	.0040	.0039	.0038	.0037	.0036
2.7	.0035	.0034	.0033	.0032	.0031	.0030	.0029	.0028	.0027	.0026
2.8	.0026	.0025	.0024	.0023	.0023	.0022	.0021	.0021	.0020	.0019
2.9	.0019	.0018	.0018	.0017	.0016	.0016	.0015	.0015	.0014	.0014
3.0	.0013	.0013	.0013	.0012	.0012	.0011	.0011	.0011	.0010	.0010
3.1	.0010	.0009	.0009	.0009	.0008	.0008	.0008	.0008	.0007	.0007
3.2	.0007	.0007	.0006	.0006	.0006	.0006	.0006	.0005	.0005	.0005
3.3	.0005	.0005	.0005	.0004	.0004	.0004	.0004	.0004	.0004	.0003
3.4	.0003	.0003	.0003	.0003	.0003	.0003	.0003	.0003	.0003	.0002
3.5	.0002	.0002	.0002	.0002	.0002	.0002	.0002	.0002	.0002	.0002
3.6	.0002	.0002	.0001	.0001	.0001	.0001	.0001	.0001	.0001	.0001
3.7	.0001	.0001	.0001	.0001	.0001	.0001	.0001	.0001	.0001	.0001
3.8	.0001	.0001	.0001	.0001	.0001	.0001	.0001	.0001	.0001	.0001
3.9	.0000	.0000	.0000	.0000	.0000	.0000	.0000	.0000	.0000	.0000

Prob. $\frac{1}{2}\alpha$

Appendix ▌

Right-Tail Areas under the *t* Density Function

Right-Tail Areas under the t Density Function

$f(t), v = 4$

←0.0731

t

$t=1.80$

	DEGREES OF FREEDOM, v				
t	1	2	3	4	5
0.0000	.5000	.5000	.5000	.5000	.5000
.1000	.4683	.4647	.4633	.4626	.4621
.2000	.4372	.4300	.4271	.4256	.4247
.3000	.4072	.3962	.3919	.3896	.3881
.4000	.3789	.3639	.3580	.3548	.3528
.5000	.3524	.3333	.3257	.3217	.3191
.6000	.3280	.3047	.2954	.2904	.2873
.7000	.3056	.2782	.2672	.2613	.2576
.8000	.2852	.2538	.2411	.2343	.2300
.9000	.2667	.2316	.2172	.2095	.2047
1.0000	.2500	.2113	.1955	.1870	.1816
1.1000	.2349	.1930	.1758	.1665	.1607
1.2000	.2211	.1765	.1581	.1482	.1419
1.3000	.2087	.1616	.1422	.1317	.1252
1.4000	.1974	.1482	.1280	.1171	.1102
1.4759					.1000
1.5000	.1872	.1362	.1153	.1040	.0970
1.5332				.1000	
1.6000	.1778	.1254	.1040	.0924	.0852
1.6377			.1000		
1.7000	.1693	.1156	.0938	.0822	.0749
1.8000	.1614	.1068	.0848	.0731	.0659
1.8856		.1000			
1.9000	.1542	.0989	.0768	.0651	.0579
2.0000	.1476	.0918	.0697	.0581	.0510
2.0150					.0500
2.1000	.1415	.0853	.0633	.0518	.0449
2.1318				.0500	
2.2000	.1358	.0794	.0576	.0463	.0395
2.3000	.1305	.0741	.0525	.0415	.0349
2.3534			.0500		
2.4000	.1257	.0692	.0479	.0372	.0308
2.5000	.1211	.0648	.0439	.0334	.0272
2.5706					.0250
2.6000	.1169	.0608	.0402	.0300	.0241
2.7000	.1129	.0571	.0369	.0270	.0214
2.7764				.0250	
2.8000	.1092	.0537	.0339	.0244	.0190
2.9000	.1057	.0506	.0313	.0221	.0169
2.9200		.0500			
3.0000	.1024	.0477	.0288	.0200	.0150
3.0777	.1000				

½ α values

Right-Tail Areas under the *t* Density Function (*continued*)

t	1	2	3	4	5
3.1000	.0993	.0451	.0266	.0181	.0134
3.1824			.0250		
3.2000	.0964	.0427	.0247	.0165	.0120
3.3000	.0937	.0404	.0229	.0150	.0107
3.4000	.0911	.0383	.0212	.0136	.0096
3.5000	.0886	.0364	.0197	.0124	.0086
3.6000	.0862	.0346	.0184	.0114	.0078
3.7000	.0840	.0330	.0171	.0104	.0070
3.8000	.0819	.0314	.0160	.0096	.0063
3.9000	.0799	.0299	.0150	.0088	.0057
4.0000	.0780	.0286	.0140	.0081	.0052
4.0322					.0050
4.1000	.0761	.0273	.0131	.0074	.0047
4.2000	.0744	.0261	.0123	.0068	.0042
4.3000	.0727	.0250	.0116	.0063	.0039
4.3027		.0250			
4.4000	.0711	.0240	.0109	.0058	.0035
4.5000	.0696	.0230	.0102	.0054	.0032
4.6000	.0681	.0221	.0097	.0050	.0029
4.6041				.0050	
4.7000	.0667	.0212	.0091	.0047	.0027
4.8000	.0654	.0204	.0086	.0043	.0024
4.9000	.0641	.0196	.0081	.0040	.0022
5.0000	.0628	.0189	.0077	.0037	.0021
5.1000	.0616	.0182	.0073	.0035	.0019
5.2000	.0605	.0175	.0069	.0033	.0017
5.3000	.0594	.0169	.0066	.0030	.0016
5.4000	.0583	.0163	.0062	.0028	.0015
5.5000	.0572	.0158	.0059	.0027	.0014
5.6000	.0562	.0152	.0056	.0025	.0013
5.7000	.0553	.0147	.0054	.0023	.0012
5.8000	.0543	.0142	.0051	.0022	.0011
5.8409			.0050		
5.9000	.0534	.0138	.0049	.0021	.0010
6.0000	.0526	.0133	.0046	.0019	.0009
6.1000	.0517	.0129	.0044	.0018	.0009
6.2000	.0509	.0125	.0042	.0017	.0008
6.3000	.0501	.0121	.0040	.0016	.0007
6.3138	.0500				
6.4000	.0493	.0118	.0039	.0015	.0007
6.5000	.0486	.0114	.0037	.0014	.0006
6.6000	.0479	.0111	.0035	.0014	.0006
6.7000	.0472	.0108	.0034	.0013	.0006
6.8000	.0465	.0105	.0033	.0012	.0005
6.9000	.0458	.0102	.0031	.0012	.0005
7.0000	.0452	.0099	.0030	.0011	.0005
9.9248		.0050			
12.7062	.0250				
63.6567	.0050				

Right-Tail Areas under the *t* Density Function (*continued*)

0 t	6	7	8	9	10
DEGREES OF FREEDOM, ν					
0.0000	.5000	.5000	.5000	.5000	.5000
.1000	.4618	.4616	.4614	.4613	.4612
.2000	.4240	.4236	.4232	.4230	.4227
.3000	.3871	.3864	.3859	.3855	.3852
.4000	.3515	.3505	.3498	.3492	.3488
.5000	.3174	.3162	.3153	.3145	.3139
.4000	.3515	.3505	.3498	.3492	.3488
.5000	.3174	.3162	.3153	.3145	.3139
.6000	.2852	.2837	.2826	.2817	.2809
.7000	.2551	.2533	.2519	.2508	.2499
.8000	.2271	.2250	.2234	.2222	.2212
.9000	.2014	.1990	.1972	.1958	.1946
1.0000	.1780	.1753	.1733	.1717	.1704
1.1000	.1567	.1539	.1517	.1499	.1486
1.2000	.1377	.1346	.1322	.1304	.1289
1.3000	.1207	.1174	.1149	.1130	.1114
1.3722					.1000
1.3830				.1000	
1.3968			.1000		
1.4000	.1055	.1021	.0995	.0975	.0959
1.4149		.1000			
1.4398	.1000				
1.5000	.0921	.0886	.0860	.0839	.0823
1.6000	.0804	.0768	.0741	.0720	.0703
1.7000	.0700	.0665	.0638	.0617	.0600
1.8000	.0610	.0574	.0548	.0527	.0510
1.8125					.0500
1.8331				.0500	
1.8595			.0500		
1.8946		.0500			
1.9000	.0531	.0496	.0470	.0449	.0433
1.9432	.0500				
2.0000	.0462	.0428	.0403	.0383	.0367
2.1000	.0402	.0369	.0345	.0326	.0310
2.2000	.0351	.0319	.0295	.0277	.0262
2.2281					.0250
2.2622				.0250	
2.3000	.0306	.0275	.0252	.0235	.0221
2.3060			.0250		
2.3646		.0250			
2.4000	.0266	.0237	.0216	.0199	.0187
2.4469	.0250				
2.5000	.0233	.0205	.0185	.0169	.0157
2.6000	.0203	.0177	.0158	.0144	.0132
2.7000	.0178	.0153	.0135	.0122	.0112
2.8000	.0156	.0133	.0116	.0104	.0094
2.9000	.0137	.0115	.0099	.0088	.0079
3.0000	.0120	.0100	.0085	.0075	.0067
3.1000	.0106	.0087	.0073	.0064	.0056
3.1693					.0050

Right-Tail Areas under the *t* Density Function (*continued*)

t	6	7	8	9	10
3.2000	.0093	.0075	.0063	.0054	.0047
3.2498				.0050	
3.3000	.0082	.0066	.0054	.0046	.0040
3.3554			.0050		
3.4000	.0072	.0057	.0047	.0039	.0034
3.4995		.0050			
3.5000	.0064	.0050	.0040	.0034	.0029
3.6000	.0057	.0044	.0035	.0029	.0024
3.7000	.0050	.0038	.0030	.0025	.0021
3.7074	.0050				
3.8000	.0045	.0034	.0026	.0021	.0017
3.9000	.0040	.0029	.0023	.0018	.0015
4.0000	.0036	.0026	.0020	.0016	.0013
4.1000	.0032	.0023	.0017	.0013	.0011
4.2000	.0028	.0020	.0015	.0012	.0009
4.3000	.0025	.0018	.0013	.0010	.0008
4.4000	.0023	.0016	.0011	.0009	.0007
4.5000	.0021	.0014	.0010	.0007	.0006
4.6000	.0018	.0012	.0009	.0006	.0005
4.7000	.0017	.0011	.0008	.0006	.0004
4.8000	.0015	.0010	.0007	.0005	.0004
4.9000	.0014	.0009	.0006	.0004	.0003
5.0000	.0012	.0008	.0005	.0004	.0003

DEGREES OF FREEDOM, v

t	11	12	13	14	15
0.0000	.5000	.5000	.5000	.5000	.5000
.1000	.4611	.4610	.4609	.4609	.4608
.2000	.4226	.4224	.4223	.4222	.4221
.3000	.3849	.3847	.3845	.3843	.3841
.4000	.3484	.3481	.3478	.3476	.3474
.5000	.3135	.3131	.3127	.3124	.3122
.6000	.2803	.2798	.2794	.2790	.2787
.7000	.2492	.2486	.2481	.2477	.2473
.8000	.2203	.2196	.2190	.2185	.2181
.9000	.1937	.1929	.1922	.1917	.1912
1.0000	.1694	.1685	.1678	.1671	.1666
1.1000	.1474	.1465	.1456	.1449	.1443
1.2000	.1277	.1266	.1258	.1250	.1244
1.3000	.1101	.1090	.1081	.1073	.1066
1.3406					.1000
1.3450				.1000	
1.3502			.1000		
1.3562		.1000			
1.3634	.1000				
1.4000	.0945	.0934	.0925	.0916	.0909
1.5000	.0809	.0797	.0788	.0779	.0772
1.6000	.0690	.0678	.0668	.0660	.0652
1.7000	.0586	.0574	.0565	.0556	.0549
1.7531					.0500
1.7613				.0500	
1.7709			.0500		
1.7823		.0500			
1.7959	.0500				
1.8000	.0497	.0485	.0475	.0467	.0460
1.9000	.0420	.0409	.0399	.0391	.0384
2.0000	.0354	.0343	.0334	.0326	.0320

Right-Tail Areas under the *t* Density Function
(continued)

t	11	12	13	14	15
				ν	
2.1000	.0298	.0288	.0279	.0272	.0265
2.1314					.0250
2.1448				.0250	
2.1604			.0250		
2.1788		.0250			
2.2000	.0250	.0241	.0232	.0226	.0219
2.2010	.0250				
2.3000	.0210	.0201	.0193	.0187	.0181
2.4000	.0176	.0168	.0160	.0154	.0149
2.5000	.0148	.0140	.0133	.0127	.0123
2.6000	.0123	.0116	.0110	.0105	.0100
2.7000	.0103	.0097	.0091	.0086	.0082
2.8000	.0086	.0080	.0075	.0071	.0067
2.9000	.0072	.0067	.0062	.0058	.0055
2.9467					.0050
2.9768				.0050	
3.0000	.0060	.0055	.0051	.0048	.0045
3.0123			.0050		
3.0545		.0050			
3.1000	.0051	.0046	.0042	.0039	.0037
3.1058	.0050				
3.2000	.0042	.0038	.0035	.0032	.0030
3.3000	.0035	.0032	.0029	.0026	.0024
3.4000	.0030	.0026	.0024	.0022	.0020
3.5000	.0025	.0022	.0020	.0018	.0016
3.6000	.0021	.0018	.0016	.0014	.0013
3.7000	.0018	.0015	.0013	.0012	.0011
3.8000	.0015	.0013	.0011	.0010	.0009
3.9000	.0012	.0011	.0009	.0008	.0007
4.0000	.0010	.0009	.0008	.0007	.0006

		DEGREES OF FREEDOM, ν			
0 t	16	17	18	19	20
0.0000	.5000	.5000	.5000	.5000	.5000
.1000	.4608	.4608	.4607	.4607	.4607
.2000	.4220	.4219	.4219	.4218	.4218
.3000	.3840	.3839	.3838	.3837	.3836
.4000	.3472	.3471	.3469	.3468	.3467
.5000	.3119	.3117	.3116	.3114	.3113
.6000	.2785	.2782	.2780	.2778	.2776
.7000	.2470	.2467	.2464	.2462	.2460
.8000	.2177	.2174	.2171	.2168	.2166
.9000	.1907	.1903	.1900	.1897	.1894
1.0000	.1661	.1657	.1653	.1649	.1646
1.1000	.1438	.1433	.1429	.1425	.1422
1.2000	.1238	.1233	.1228	.1224	.1221
1.3000	.1060	.1055	.1050	.1046	.1042
1.3253					.1000
1.3277				.1000	
1.3304			.1000		
1.3334		.1000			
1.3368	.1000				

Right-Tail Areas under the t Density Function (*continued*)

			ν		
t	16	17	18	19	20
1.4000	.0903	.0897	.0893	.0888	.0884
1.5000	.0765	.0760	.0755	.0750	.0746
1.6000	.0646	.0640	.0635	.0630	.0626
1.7000	.0542	.0537	.0532	.0527	.0523
1.7247					.0500
1.7291				.0500	
1.7341			.0500		
1.7396		.0500			
1.7459	.0500				
1.8000	.0454	.0448	.0443	.0439	.0435
1.9000	.0378	.0373	.0368	.0364	.0360
2.0000	.0314	.0309	.0304	.0300	.0296
2.0860					.0250
2.0930				.0250	
2.1000	.0260	.0255	.0250	.0247	.0243
2.1009			.0250		
2.1098		.0250			
2.1199	.0250				
2.2000	.0214	.0210	.0206	.0202	.0199
2.3000	.0176	.0172	.0168	.0165	.0162
2.4000	.0145	.0141	.0137	.0134	.0131
2.5000	.0118	.0115	.0112	.0109	.0106
2.6000	.0097	.0093	.0090	.0088	.0086
2.7000	.0079	.0076	.0073	.0071	.0069
2.8000	.0064	.0062	.0059	.0057	.0055
2.8453					.0050
2.8609				.0050	
2.8784			.0050		
2.8982		.0050			
2.9000	.0052	.0050	.0048	.0046	.0044
2.9208	.0050				
3.0000	.0042	.0040	.0038	.0037	.0035
3.1000	.0034	.0033	.0031	.0029	.0028
3.2000	.0028	.0026	.0025	.0024	.0022
3.3000	.0023	.0021	.0020	.0019	.0018
3.4000	.0018	.0017	.0016	.0015	.0014
3.5000	.0015	.0014	.0013	.0012	.0011
3.6000	.0012	.0011	.0010	.0010	.0009
3.7000	.0010	.0009	.0008	.0008	.0007
3.8000	.0008	.0007	.0007	.0006	.0006
3.9000	.0006	.0006	.0005	.0005	.0004
4.0000	.0005	.0005	.0004	.0004	.0004

	DEGREES OF FREEDOM, ν				
t	21	22	23	24	25
0.0000	.5000	.5000	.5000	.5000	.5000
.1000	.4606	.4606	.4606	.4606	.4606
.2000	.4217	.4217	.4216	.4216	.4215
.3000	.3836	.3835	.3834	.3834	.3833
.4000	.3466	.3465	.3464	.3463	.3463
.5000	.3111	.3110	.3109	.3108	.3107
.6000	.2775	.2773	.2772	.2771	.2770
.7000	.2458	.2456	.2455	.2453	.2452
.8000	.2163	.2161	.2159	.2158	.2156
.9000	.1892	.1889	.1887	.1885	.1884
1.0000	.1643	.1641	.1639	.1636	.1634
1.1000	.1419	.1416	.1414	.1411	.1409
1.2000	.1218	.1215	.1212	.1209	.1207
1.3000	.1038	.1035	.1032	.1030	.1027

0

Right-Tail Areas under the t Density Function (continued)

t	21	22	23	24	25
				ν	
1.3163					.1000
1.3178				.1000	
1.3195			.1000		
1.3212		.1000			
1.3232	.1000				
1.4000	.0881	.0877	.0874	.0872	.0869
1.5000	.0742	.0739	.0736	.0733	.0731
1.6000	.0623	.0619	.0616	.0613	.0611
1.7000	.0519	.0516	.0513	.0510	.0508
1.7081					.0500
1.7109				.0500	
1.7139			.0500		
1.7171		.0500			
1.7207	.0500				
1.8000	.0431	.0428	.0425	.0422	.0420
1.9000	.0356	.0353	.0350	.0348	.0345
2.0000	.0293	.0290	.0287	.0285	.0282
2.0595					.0250
2.0639				.0250	
2.0687			.0250		
2.0739		.0250			
2.0796	.0250				
2.1000	.0240	.0237	.0234	.0232	.0230
2.2000	.0196	.0193	.0191	.0188	.0186
2.3000	.0159	.0157	.0154	.0152	.0150
2.4000	.0129	.0126	.0124	.0123	.0121
2.5000	.0104	.0102	.0100	.0098	.0097
2.6000	.0084	.0082	.0080	.0079	.0077
2.7000	.0067	.0065	.0064	.0063	.0061
2.7874					.0050
2.7969				.0050	
2.8000	.0054	.0052	.0051	.0050	.0049
2.8073			.0050		
2.8188		.0050			
2.8314	.0050				
2.9000	.0043	.0042	.0040	.0039	.0038
3.0000	.0034	.0033	.0032	.0031	.0030

DEGREES OF FREEDOM, ν

t	26	27	28	29	30
0.0000	.5000	.5000	.5000	.5000	.5000
.1000	.4606	.4605	.4605	.4605	.4605
.2000	.4215	.4215	.4215	.4214	.4214
.3000	.3833	.3832	.3832	.3832	.3831
.4000	.3462	.3462	.3461	.3460	.3460
.5000	.3106	.3106	.3105	.3104	.3104
.6000	.2769	.2768	.2767	.2766	.2765
.7000	.2451	.2450	.2449	.2448	.2447
.8000	.2155	.2153	.2152	.2151	.2150
.9000	.1882	.1880	.1879	.1878	.1876
1.0000	.1633	.1631	.1629	.1628	.1627
1.1000	.1407	.1405	.1403	.1402	.1400
1.2000	.1205	.1203	.1201	.1199	.1198
1.3000	.1025	.1023	.1021	.1019	.1018
1.3104					.1000
1.3114				.1000	
1.3125			.1000		
1.3137		.1000			
1.3150	.1000				

Right-Tail Areas under the *t* Density Function (*concluded*)

t	26	27	28	29	30
			ν		
1.4000	.0867	.0864	.0862	.0861	.0859
1.5000	.0728	.0726	.0724	.0722	.0720
1.6000	.0608	.0606	.0604	.0602	.0600
1.6973					.0500
1.6991				.0500	
1.7000	.0505	.0503	.0501	.0499	.0497
1.7011			.0500		
1.7033		.0500			
1.7056	.0500				
1.8000	.0417	.0415	.0413	.0411	.0410
1.9000	.0343	.0341	.0339	.0337	.0335
2.0000	.0280	.0278	.0276	.0275	.0273
2.0423					.0250
2.0452				.0250	
2.0484			.0250		
2.0516		.0250			
2.0555	.0250				
2.1000	.0228	.0226	.0224	.0223	.0221
2.2000	.0184	.0183	.0181	.0180	.0178
2.3000	.0149	.0147	.0146	.0144	.0143
2.4000	.0119	.0118	.0116	.0115	.0114
2.5000	.0095	.0094	.0093	.0092	.0091
2.6000	.0076	.0075	.0074	.0073	.0072
2.7000	.0060	.0059	.0058	.0057	.0056
2.7500					.0050
2.7564				.0050	
2.7633			.0050		
2.7707		.0050			
2.7787	.0050				
2.8000	.0048	.0047	.0046	.0045	.0044
2.9000	.0037	.0037	.0036	.0035	.0035
3.0000	.0029	.0029	.0028	.0027	.0027

Appendix J

Right-Tail Areas under the Chi-Square Density Function

Right-Tail Areas under the Chi-Square Density Function

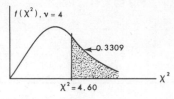

$f(X^2), v = 4$

0.3309

X^2

$X^2 = 4.60$

DEGREES OF FREEDOM, v

X^2	1	2	3	4	5	6
.20	.6547	.9048	.9776	.9953	.9991	.9998
.40	.5271	.8187	.9402	.9825	.9953	.9989
.60	.4386	.7408	.8964	.9631	.9880	.9964
.80	.3711	.6703	.8495	.9384	.9770	.9921
1.00	.3173	.6065	.8013	.9098	.9626	.9856
1.20	.2733	.5488	.7530	.8781	.9449	.9769
1.40	.2367	.4966	.7055	.8442	.9243	.9659
1.60	.2059	.4493	.6594	.8088	.9012	.9526
1.80	.1797	.4066	.6149	.7725	.8761	.9371
2.00	.1573	.3679	.5724	.7358	.8491	.9197
2.20	.1380	.3329	.5319	.6990	.8208	.9004
2.40	.1213	.3012	.4936	.6626	.7915	.8795
2.60	.1069	.2725	.4575	.6268	.7614	.8571
2.80	.0943	.2466	.4235	.5918	.7308	.8335
3.00	.0833	.2231	.3916	.5578	.7000	.8088
3.20	.0736	.2019	.3618	.5249	.6692	.7834
3.40	.0652	.1827	.3340	.4932	.6386	.7572
3.60	.0578	.1653	.3080	.4628	.6083	.7306
3.80	.0513	.1496	.2839	.4337	.5786	.7037
4.00	.0455	.1353	.2615	.4060	.5494	.6767
4.20	.0404	.1225	.2407	.3796	.5210	.6496
4.40	.0359	.1108	.2214	.3546	.4934	.6227
4.60	.0320	.1003	.2035	.3309	.4666	.5960
4.80	.0285	.0907	.1870	.3084	.4408	.5697
5.00	.0253	.0821	.1718	.2873	.4159	.5438
5.20	.0226	.0743	.1577	.2674	.3920	.5184
5.40	.0201	.0672	.1447	.2487	.3690	.4936
5.60	.0180	.0608	.1328	.2311	.3471	.4695
5.80	.0160	.0550	.1218	.2146	.3262	.4460
6.00	.0143	.0498	.1116	.1991	.3062	.4232
6.20	.0128	.0450	.1023	.1847	.2872	.4012
6.40	.0114	.0408	.0937	.1712	.2692	.3799
6.60	.0102	.0369	.0858	.1586	.2521	.3594
6.80	.0091	.0334	.0786	.1468	.2359	.3397
7.00	.0082	.0302	.0719	.1359	.2206	.3208
7.20	.0073	.0273	.0658	.1257	.2062	.3027
7.40	.0065	.0247	.0602	.1162	.1926	.2854
7.60	.0058	.0224	.0550	.1074	.1797	.2689
7.80	.0052	.0202	.0503	.0992	.1676	.2531
8.00	.0047	.0183	.0460	.0916	.1562	.2381
8.20	.0042	.0166	.0421	.0845	.1456	.2238
8.40	.0038	.0150	.0384	.0780	.1355	.2102
8.60	.0034	.0136	.0351	.0719	.1261	.1974
8.80	.0030	.0123	.0321	.0663	.1173	.1851
9.00	.0027	.0111	.0293	.0611	.1091	.1736
9.20	.0024	.0101	.0267	.0563	.1013	.1626
9.40	.0022	.0091	.0244	.0518	.0941	.1523
9.60	.0019	.0082	.0223	.0477	.0874	.1425
9.80	.0017	.0074	.0203	.0439	.0811	.1333
10.00	.0016	.0067	.0186	.0404	.0752	.1247

Right-Tail Areas under the Chi-Square Density Function (*continued*)

DEGREES OF FREEDOM, ν

χ^2	1	2	3	4	5	6
10.20	.0014	.0061	.0169	.0372	.0698	.1165
10.40	.0013	.0055	.0155	.0342	.0647	.1088
10.60	.0011	.0050	.0141	.0314	.0599	.1016
10.80	.0010	.0045	.0129	.0289	.0555	.0948
11.00	.0009	.0041	.0117	.0266	.0514	.0884
11.20	.0008	.0037	.0107	.0244	.0476	.0824
11.40	.0007	.0033	.0097	.0224	.0440	.0768
11.60	.0007	.0030	.0089	.0206	.0407	.0715
11.80	.0006	.0027	.0081	.0189	.0376	.0666
12.00	.0005	.0025	.0074	.0174	.0348	.0620
12.20	.0005	.0022	.0067	.0159	.0321	.0577
12.40	.0004	.0020	.0061	.0146	.0297	.0536
12.60	.0004	.0018	.0056	.0134	.0274	.0498
12.80	.0003	.0017	.0051	.0123	.0253	.0463
13.00	.0003	.0015	.0046	.0113	.0234	.0430
13.20	.0003	.0014	.0042	.0103	.0216	.0400
13.40	.0003	.0012	.0038	.0095	.0199	.0371
13.60	.0002	.0011	.0035	.0087	.0184	.0344
13.80	.0002	.0010	.0032	.0080	.0169	.0320
14.00	.0002	.0009	.0029	.0073	.0156	.0296
14.20	.0002	.0008	.0026	.0067	.0144	.0275
14.40	.0001	.0007	.0024	.0061	.0133	.0255
14.60	.0001	.0007	.0022	.0056	.0122	.0236
14.80	.0001	.0006	.0020	.0051	.0113	.0219
15.00	.0001	.0006	.0018	.0047	.0104	.0203
15.20	.0001	.0005	.0017	.0043	.0095	.0188
15.40	.0001	.0005	.0015	.0039	.0088	.0174
15.60	.0001	.0004	.0014	.0036	.0081	.0161
15.80	.0001	.0004	.0012	.0033	.0074	.0149
16.00	.0001	.0003	.0011	.0030	.0068	.0138
16.20	.0001	.0003	.0010	.0028	.0063	.0127
16.40	.0001	.0003	.0009	.0025	.0058	.0118
16.60	.0000	.0002	.0009	.0023	.0053	.0109
16.80	.0000	.0002	.0008	.0021	.0049	.0100
17.00	.0000	.0002	.0007	.0019	.0045	.0093
17.20	.0000	.0002	.0006	.0018	.0041	.0086
17.40	.0000	.0002	.0006	.0016	.0038	.0079
17.60	.0000	.0002	.0005	.0015	.0035	.0073
17.80	.0000	.0001	.0005	.0014	.0032	.0068
18.00	.0000	.0001	.0004	.0012	.0029	.0062
18.20	.0000	.0001	.0004	.0011	.0027	.0058
18.40	.0000	.0001	.0004	.0010	.0025	.0053
18.60	.0000	.0001	.0003	.0009	.0023	.0049
18.80	.0000	.0001	.0003	.0009	.0021	.0045
19.00	.0000	.0001	.0003	.0008	.0019	.0042
19.20	.0000	.0001	.0002	.0007	.0018	.0038
19.40	.0000	.0001	.0002	.0007	.0016	.0035
19.60	.0000	.0001	.0002	.0006	.0015	.0033
19.80	.0000	.0001	.0002	.0005	.0014	.0030
20.00	.0000	.0000	.0002	.0005	.0012	.0028

Right-Tail Areas under the Chi-Square Density Function (*continued*)

DEGREES OF FREEDOM, ν

χ^2	7	8	9	10	11	12	13	14	15
.50	.9994	.9999	1.0000	1.0000	1.0000	1.0000	1.0000	1.0000	1.0000
1.00	.9948	.9982	.9994	.9998	.9999	1.0000	1.0000	1.0000	1.0000
1.50	.9823	.9927	.9971	.9989	.9996	.9999	1.0000	1.0000	1.0000
2.00	.9598	.9810	.9915	.9963	.9985	.9994	.9998	.9999	1.0000
2.50	.9271	.9617	.9809	.9909	.9958	.9982	.9992	.9997	.9999
3.00	.8850	.9344	.9643	.9814	.9907	.9955	.9979	.9991	.9996
3.50	.8352	.8992	.9411	.9671	.9823	.9909	.9954	.9978	.9990
4.00	.7798	.8571	.9114	.9473	.9699	.9834	.9912	.9955	.9977
4.50	.7207	.8094	.8755	.9220	.9529	.9726	.9846	.9916	.9956
5.00	.6600	.7576	.8343	.8912	.9312	.9580	.9752	.9858	.9921
5.50	.5992	.7030	.7887	.8554	.9046	.9392	.9625	.9776	.9870
6.00	.5397	.6472	.7399	.8153	.8734	.9161	.9462	.9665	.9797
6.50	.4827	.5914	.6890	.7717	.8380	.8888	.9261	.9523	.9701
7.00	.4289	.5366	.6371	.7254	.7991	.8576	.9022	.9347	.9576
7.50	.3787	.4838	.5852	.6775	.7573	.8229	.8746	.9137	.9423
8.00	.3326	.4335	.5341	.6288	.7133	.7851	.8436	.8893	.9238
8.50	.2906	.3862	.4846	.5801	.6679	.7449	.8096	.8617	.9022
9.00	.2527	.3423	.4373	.5321	.6219	.7029	.7729	.8311	.8775
9.50	.2187	.3019	.3925	.4854	.5758	.6597	.7342	.7978	.8500
10.00	.1886	.2650	.3505	.4405	.5304	.6160	.6939	.7622	.8197
10.50	.1620	.2317	.3115	.3978	.4860	.5722	.6526	.7248	.7872
11.00	.1386	.2017	.2757	.3575	.4433	.5289	.6108	.6860	.7526
11.50	.1182	.1749	.2430	.3199	.4024	.4866	.5690	.6464	.7164
12.00	.1006	.1512	.2133	.2851	.3636	.4457	.5276	.6063	.6790
12.50	.0853	.1303	.1866	.2530	.3273	.4064	.4871	.5662	.6409
13.00	.0721	.1118	.1626	.2237	.2933	.3690	.4478	.5265	.6023
13.50	.0608	.0958	.1413	.1970	.2619	.3338	.4100	.4876	.5637
14.00	.0512	.0818	.1223	.1730	.2330	.3007	.3738	.4497	.5255
14.50	.0430	.0696	.1056	.1514	.2065	.2699	.3396	.4132	.4880
15.00	.0360	.0591	.0909	.1321	.1825	.2414	.3074	.3782	.4514
15.50	.0301	.0501	.0781	.1149	.1607	.2152	.2772	.3449	.4160
16.00	.0251	.0424	.0669	.0996	.1411	.1912	.2491	.3134	.3821
16.50	.0209	.0358	.0571	.0862	.1236	.1694	.2232	.2838	.3496
17.00	.0174	.0301	.0487	.0744	.1079	.1496	.1993	.2562	.3189
17.50	.0144	.0253	.0414	.0640	.0939	.1317	.1774	.2305	.2899
18.00	.0120	.0212	.0352	.0550	.0816	.1157	.1575	.2068	.2627
18.50	.0099	.0178	.0298	.0471	.0707	.1013	.1394	.1849	.2373
19.00	.0082	.0149	.0252	.0403	.0611	.0885	.1231	.1649	.2137
19.50	.0068	.0124	.0213	.0344	.0527	.0772	.1084	.1467	.1920
20.00	.0056	.0103	.0179	.0293	.0453	.0671	.0952	.1301	.1719

Right-Tail Areas under the Chi-Square Density Function (*continued*)

DEGREES OF FREEDOM, ν

χ^2	7	8	9	10	11	12	13	14	15
20.50	.0046	.0086	.0151	.0249	.0389	.0582	.0834	.1151	.1536
21.00	.0038	.0071	.0127	.0211	.0334	.0504	.0729	.1016	.1368
21.50	.0031	.0059	.0106	.0179	.0285	.0435	.0636	.0895	.1216
22.00	.0025	.0049	.0089	.0151	.0244	.0375	.0554	.0786	.1078
22.50	.0021	.0041	.0074	.0128	.0208	.0323	.0481	.0689	.0953
23.00	.0017	.0034	.0062	.0107	.0177	.0277	.0417	.0603	.0841
23.50	.0014	.0028	.0052	.0090	.0150	.0238	.0361	.0526	.0741
24.00	.0011	.0023	.0043	.0076	.0127	.0203	.0311	.0458	.0651
24.50	.0009	.0019	.0036	.0064	.0108	.0174	.0268	.0398	.0571
25.00	.0008	.0016	.0030	.0053	.0091	.0148	.0231	.0346	.0499
25.50	.0006	.0013	.0025	.0045	.0077	.0126	.0198	.0299	.0436
26.00	.0005	.0011	.0020	.0037	.0065	.0107	.0170	.0259	.0380
26.50	.0004	.0009	.0017	.0031	.0055	.0091	.0146	.0223	.0331
27.00	.0003	.0007	.0014	.0026	.0046	.0077	.0124	.0193	.0287
27.50	.0003	.0006	.0012	.0022	.0039	.0065	.0106	.0166	.0249
28.00	.0002	.0005	.0010	.0018	.0032	.0055	.0090	.0142	.0216
28.50	.0002	.0004	.0008	.0015	.0027	.0047	.0077	.0122	.0186
29.00	.0001	.0003	.0006	.0012	.0023	.0039	.0065	.0105	.0161
29.50	.0001	.0003	.0005	.0010	.0019	.0033	.0056	.0089	.0139
30.00	.0001	.0002	.0004	.0009	.0016	.0028	.0047	.0076	.0119
30.50	.0001	.0002	.0004	.0007	.0013	.0023	.0040	.0065	.0102
31.00	.0001	.0001	.0003	.0006	.0011	.0020	.0034	.0055	.0088
31.50	.0001	.0001	.0002	.0005	.0009	.0017	.0028	.0047	.0075
32.00	.0000	.0001	.0002	.0004	.0008	.0014	.0024	.0040	.0064
32.50	.0000	.0001	.0002	.0003	.0006	.0012	.0020	.0034	.0055
33.00	.0000	.0001	.0001	.0003	.0005	.0010	.0017	.0029	.0047
33.50	.0000	.0001	.0001	.0002	.0004	.0008	.0014	.0024	.0040
34.00	.0000	.0000	.0001	.0002	.0004	.0007	.0012	.0021	.0034
34.50	.0000	.0000	.0001	.0002	.0003	.0006	.0010	.0017	.0029
35.00	.0000	.0000	.0001	.0001	.0002	.0005	.0008	.0015	.0025

Right-Tail Areas under the Chi-Square Density Function (*continued*)

DEGREES OF FREEDOM, v

χ^2	16	17	18	19	20	21	22	23	24	25
1.00	1.0000	1.0000	1.0000	1.0000	1.0000	1.0000	1.0000	1.0000	1.0000	1.0000
2.00	1.0000	1.0000	1.0000	1.0000	1.0000	1.0000	1.0000	1.0000	1.0000	1.0000
3.00	.9998	.9999	1.0000	1.0000	1.0000	1.0000	1.0000	1.0000	1.0000	1.0000
4.00	.9989	.9995	.9998	.9999	1.0000	1.0000	1.0000	1.0000	1.0000	1.0000
5.00	.9958	.9978	.9989	.9994	.9997	.9999	.9999	1.0000	1.0000	1.0000
6.00	.9881	.9932	.9962	.9979	.9989	.9994	.9997	.9999	.9999	1.0000
7.00	.9733	.9835	.9901	.9942	.9967	.9981	.9990	.9995	.9997	.9999
8.00	.9489	.9665	.9786	.9867	.9919	.9951	.9972	.9984	.9991	.9995
9.00	.9134	.9403	.9597	.9735	.9829	.9892	.9933	.9960	.9976	.9986
10.00	.8666	.9036	.9319	.9529	.9682	.9789	.9863	.9913	.9945	.9967
11.00	.8095	.8566	.8944	.9238	.9462	.9628	.9747	.9832	.9890	.9929
12.00	.7440	.8001	.8472	.8856	.9161	.9396	.9574	.9705	.9799	.9866
13.00	.6728	.7362	.7916	.8386	.8774	.9086	.9332	.9520	.9661	.9765
14.00	.5987	.6671	.7291	.7837	.8305	.8696	.9015	.9269	.9467	.9617
15.00	.5246	.5955	.6620	.7226	.7764	.8230	.8622	.8946	.9208	.9414
16.00	.4530	.5238	.5925	.6573	.7166	.7697	.8159	.8553	.8881	.9148
17.00	.3856	.4544	.5231	.5899	.6530	.7111	.7634	.8093	.8487	.8818
18.00	.3239	.3888	.4557	.5224	.5874	.6490	.7060	.7575	.8030	.8424
19.00	.2687	.3285	.3918	.4568	.5218	.5851	.6453	.7012	.7520	.7971
20.00	.2202	.2742	.3328	.3946	.4579	.5213	.5830	.6419	.6968	.7468
21.00	.1785	.2263	.2794	.3368	.3971	.4589	.5207	.5811	.6387	.6926
22.00	.1432	.1847	.2320	.2843	.3405	.3995	.4599	.5203	.5793	.6357
23.00	.1137	.1493	.1906	.2373	.2888	.3440	.4017	.4608	.5198	.5776
24.00	.0895	.1194	.1550	.1962	.2424	.2931	.3472	.4038	.4616	.5194
25.00	.0698	.0947	.1249	.1605	.2014	.2472	.2971	.3503	.4058	.4624
26.00	.0540	.0745	.0998	.1302	.1658	.2064	.2517	.3009	.3532	.4076
27.00	.0415	.0581	.0790	.1047	.1353	.1709	.2112	.2560	.3045	.3559
28.00	.0316	.0449	.0621	.0834	.1094	.1402	.1757	.2158	.2600	.3079
29.00	.0239	.0345	.0484	.0660	.0878	.1140	.1449	.1803	.2201	.2639
30.00	.0180	.0263	.0374	.0518	.0699	.0920	.1185	.1494	.1848	.2243
31.00	.0135	.0200	.0288	.0404	.0552	.0737	.0961	.1228	.1538	.1890
32.00	.0100	.0150	.0220	.0313	.0433	.0586	.0774	.1001	.1270	.1580
33.00	.0074	.0113	.0167	.0240	.0337	.0462	.0619	.0811	.1041	.1311
34.00	.0054	.0084	.0126	.0184	.0261	.0362	.0491	.0652	.0847	.1079
35.00	.0040	.0062	.0095	.0140	.0201	.0282	.0387	.0520	.0684	.0882
36.00	.0029	.0046	.0071	.0106	.0154	.0219	.0304	.0413	.0549	.0716
37.00	.0021	.0034	.0052	.0079	.0117	.0168	.0237	.0325	.0438	.0577
38.00	.0015	.0025	.0039	.0059	.0089	.0129	.0183	.0255	.0347	.0463
39.00	.0011	.0018	.0028	.0044	.0067	.0098	.0141	.0198	.0273	.0368
40.00	.0008	.0013	.0021	.0033	.0050	.0074	.0108	.0154	.0214	.0292
41.00	.0006	.0009	.0015	.0024	.0037	.0056	.0082	.0118	.0167	.0230
42.00	.0004	.0007	.0011	.0018	.0028	.0042	.0063	.0091	.0129	.0180
43.00	.0003	.0005	.0008	.0013	.0020	.0031	.0047	.0069	.0099	.0140
44.00	.0002	.0003	.0006	.0009	.0015	.0023	.0035	.0053	.0076	.0108
45.00	.0001	.0002	.0004	.0007	.0011	.0017	.0027	.0040	.0058	.0084
46.00	.0001	.0002	.0003	.0005	.0008	.0013	.0020	.0030	.0044	.0064
47.00	.0001	.0001	.0002	.0004	.0006	.0009	.0015	.0022	.0033	.0049
48.00	.0000	.0001	.0002	.0003	.0004	.0007	.0011	.0017	.0025	.0037
49.00	.0000	.0001	.0001	.0002	.0003	.0005	.0008	.0012	.0019	.0028
50.00	.0000	.0000	.0001	.0001	.0002	.0004	.0006	.0009	.0014	.0021

Right-Tail Areas under the Chi-Square Density Function *(concluded)*

DEGREES OF FREEDOM, ν

χ^2	26	27	28	29	30	31	32	33	34	35
1.00	1.0000	1.0000	1.0000	1.0000	1.0000	1.0000	1.0000	1.0000	1.0000	1.0000
2.00	1.0000	1.0000	1.0000	1.0000	1.0000	1.0000	1.0000	1.0000	1.0000	1.0000
3.00	1.0000	1.0000	1.0000	1.0000	1.0000	1.0000	1.0000	1.0000	1.0000	1.0000
4.00	1.0000	1.0000	1.0000	1.0000	1.0000	1.0000	1.0000	1.0000	1.0000	1.0000
5.00	1.0000	1.0000	1.0000	1.0000	1.0000	1.0000	1.0000	1.0000	1.0000	1.0000
6.00	1.0000	1.0000	1.0000	1.0000	1.0000	1.0000	1.0000	1.0000	1.0000	1.0000
7.00	.9999	1.0000	1.0000	1.0000	1.0000	1.0000	1.0000	1.0000	1.0000	1.0000
8.00	.9997	.9999	.9999	1.0000	1.0000	1.0000	1.0000	1.0000	1.0000	1.0000
9.00	.9992	.9995	.9997	.9999	.9999	1.0000	1.0000	1.0000	1.0000	1.0000
10.00	.9980	.9988	.9993	.9996	.9998	.9999	.9999	1.0000	1.0000	1.0000
11.00	.9955	.9972	.9983	.9990	.9994	.9997	.9998	.9999	.9999	1.0000
12.00	.9912	.9943	.9964	.9977	.9986	.9991	.9995	.9997	.9998	.9999
13.00	.9840	.9892	.9929	.9954	.9970	.9981	.9988	.9993	.9996	.9997
14.00	.9730	.9813	.9872	.9914	.9943	.9963	.9976	.9985	.9990	.9994
15.00	.9573	.9694	.9784	.9850	.9897	.9931	.9954	.9970	.9980	.9987
16.00	.9362	.9529	.9658	.9755	.9827	.9880	.9918	.9944	.9963	.9975
17.00	.9091	.9311	.9486	.9622	.9726	.9804	.9862	.9904	.9934	.9955
18.00	.8758	.9035	.9261	.9443	.9585	.9696	.9780	.9843	.9889	.9923
19.00	.8364	.8700	.8981	.9213	.9400	.9549	.9665	.9755	.9823	.9873
20.00	.7916	.8308	.8645	.8929	.9165	.9358	.9513	.9635	.9730	.9802
21.00	.7420	.7863	.8253	.8591	.8879	.9119	.9317	.9477	.9604	.9704
22.00	.6887	.7374	.7813	.8202	.8540	.8830	.9074	.9276	.9441	.9573
23.00	.6329	.6850	.7330	.7765	.8153	.8491	.8783	.9030	.9236	.9405
24.00	.5760	.6303	.6815	.7289	.7720	.8105	.8444	.8737	.8987	.9197
25.00	.5190	.5745	.6278	.6782	.7250	.7677	.8060	.8399	.8693	.8945
26.00	.4631	.5186	.5730	.6255	.6751	.7213	.7636	.8017	.8355	.8650
27.00	.4093	.4638	.5182	.5717	.6233	.6722	.7178	.7597	.7975	.8313
28.00	.3585	.4110	.4644	.5179	.5704	.6212	.6694	.7144	.7559	.7936
29.00	.3111	.3609	.4125	.4651	.5176	.5692	.6192	.6667	.7112	.7523
30.00	.2676	.3142	.3632	.4140	.4657	.5173	.5681	.6173	.6641	.7081
31.00	.2283	.2711	.3171	.3654	.4154	.4662	.5170	.5670	.6154	.6617
32.00	.1931	.2321	.2745	.3199	.3675	.4167	.4667	.5167	.5660	.6137
33.00	.1621	.1971	.2357	.2777	.3225	.3695	.4180	.4673	.5165	.5650
34.00	.1350	.1660	.2009	.2393	.2808	.3251	.3715	.4192	.4677	.5162
35.00	.1116	.1389	.1699	.2045	.2426	.2838	.3275	.3733	.4204	.4682
36.00	.0917	.1153	.1426	.1736	.2081	.2459	.2867	.3299	.3751	.4215
37.00	.0748	.0951	.1189	.1462	.1771	.2115	.2490	.2894	.3321	.3767
38.00	.0606	.0779	.0984	.1223	.1497	.1806	.2148	.2520	.2920	.3343
39.00	.0488	.0634	.0809	.1017	.1257	.1532	.1840	.2180	.2550	.2946
40.00	.0390	.0512	.0661	.0839	.1049	.1290	.1565	.1872	.2211	.2578
41.00	.0310	.0412	.0537	.0689	.0869	.1080	.1323	.1598	.1904	.2241
42.00	.0245	.0329	.0434	.0562	.0716	.0898	.1111	.1354	.1629	.1935
43.00	.0193	.0262	.0348	.0455	.0586	.0742	.0927	.1141	.1385	.1660
44.00	.0151	.0207	.0278	.0367	.0477	.0610	.0769	.0955	.1170	.1415
45.00	.0118	.0163	.0221	.0294	.0386	.0499	.0634	.0795	.0983	.1199
46.00	.0091	.0127	.0174	.0235	.0311	.0405	.0520	.0658	.0821	.1010
47.00	.0070	.0099	.0137	.0186	.0249	.0327	.0424	.0541	.0681	.0846
48.00	.0054	.0077	.0107	.0147	.0198	.0263	.0344	.0443	.0563	.0705
49.00	.0041	.0059	.0083	.0115	.0157	.0211	.0278	.0361	.0462	.0584
50.00	.0031	.0046	.0065	.0090	.0124	.0168	.0223	.0292	.0377	.0481

Right-Tail Areas under the *F* Density Function

Right-Tail Areas under the *F* Density Function

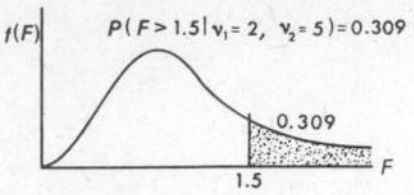

DEGREES OF FREEDOM, NUMERATOR (1) = 1

DEGREES OF FREEDOM, DENOMINATOR(2)

F	1	2	3	4	5	6	7	8	9
1.0	.500	.423	.391	.374	.363	.356	.351	.347	.343
1.5	.436	.345	.308	.288	.275	.267	.260	.256	.252
2.0	.392	.293	.252	.230	.216	.207	.200	.195	.191
2.5	.359	.255	.212	.189	.175	.165	.158	.153	.148
3.0	.333	.225	.182	.158	.144	.134	.127	.122	.117
3.5	.313	.202	.158	.135	.120	.111	.104	.098	.094
4.0	.295	.184	.139	.116	.102	.092	.086	.081	.077
5.0	.268	.155	.111	.089	.076	.067	.060	.056	.052
6.0	.247	.134	.092	.070	.058	.050	.044	.040	.037
7.0	.230	.118	.077	.057	.046	.038	.033	.029	.027
8.0	.216	.106	.066	.047	.037	.030	.025	.022	.020
9.0	.205	.095	.058	.040	.030	.024	.020	.017	.015
10.0	.195	.087	.051	.034	.025	.020	.016	.013	.012
15.0	.161	.061	.030	.018	.012	.008	.006	.005	.004
20.0	.140	.047	.021	.011	.007	.004	.003	.002	.002
30.0	.115	.032	.012	.005	.003	.002	.001	.001	.000
40.0	.100	.024	.008	.003	.001	.001	.000	.000	.000
50.0	.089	.019	.006	.002	.001	.000	.000	.000	.000
100.0	.063	.010	.002	.001	.000	.000	.000	.000	.000
500.0	.028	.002	.000	.000	.000	.000	.000	.000	.000

DEGREES OF FREEDOM, NUMERATOR (1) = 1

DEGREES OF FREEDOM, DENOMINATOR(2)

F	10	12	14	16	18	20	30	40	50	100	200	300
1.0	.341	.337	.334	.332	.331	.329	.325	.323	.322	.320	.319	.318
1.2	.299	.295	.292	.290	.288	.286	.282	.280	.279	.276	.275	.274
1.4	.264	.260	.256	.254	.252	.251	.246	.244	.242	.240	.238	.238
1.6	.235	.230	.227	.224	.222	.220	.216	.213	.212	.209	.207	.207
1.8	.209	.205	.201	.198	.196	.195	.190	.187	.186	.183	.181	.181
2.0	.188	.183	.179	.176	.174	.173	.168	.165	.163	.160	.159	.158
2.2	.169	.164	.160	.157	.155	.154	.148	.146	.144	.141	.140	.139
2.4	.152	.147	.144	.141	.139	.137	.132	.129	.128	.124	.123	.122
2.6	.138	.133	.129	.126	.124	.123	.117	.115	.113	.110	.108	.108
2.8	.125	.120	.116	.114	.112	.110	.105	.102	.101	.097	.096	.095
3.0	.114	.109	.105	.102	.100	.099	.094	.091	.089	.086	.085	.084
3.5	.091	.086	.082	.080	.078	.076	.071	.069	.067	.064	.063	.062
4.0	.073	.069	.065	.063	.061	.059	.055	.052	.051	.048	.047	.046
4.5	.060	.055	.052	.050	.048	.047	.042	.040	.039	.036	.035	.035
5.0	.049	.045	.042	.040	.038	.037	.033	.031	.030	.028	.026	.026
6.0	.034	.031	.028	.026	.025	.024	.020	.019	.018	.016	.015	.015
7.0	.024	.021	.019	.018	.016	.016	.013	.012	.011	.009	.009	.009
8.0	.018	.015	.013	.012	.011	.010	.008	.007	.007	.006	.005	.005
9.0	.013	.011	.010	.008	.008	.007	.005	.005	.004	.003	.003	.003
10.0	.010	.008	.007	.006	.005	.005	.004	.003	.003	.002	.002	.002

DEGREES OF FREEDOM, NUMERATOR (1) = 2

DEGREES OF FREEDOM, DENOMINATOR(2)

F	1	2	3	4	5	6	7	8	9
1.0	.577	.500	.465	.444	.431	.422	.415	.410	.405
1.5	.500	.400	.354	.327	.309	.296	.287	.280	.274
2.0	.447	.333	.281	.250	.230	.216	.206	.198	.191
2.5	.408	.286	.230	.198	.177	.162	.152	.143	.137
3.0	.378	.250	.192	.160	.139	.125	.115	.107	.100
3.5	.354	.222	.164	.132	.112	.098	.088	.081	.075
4.0	.333	.200	.142	.111	.092	.079	.069	.063	.057
5.0	.302	.167	.111	.082	.064	.053	.045	.039	.035
6.0	.277	.143	.089	.063	.047	.037	.030	.026	.022
7.0	.258	.125	.074	.049	.036	.027	.021	.017	.015
8.0	.243	.111	.063	.040	.028	.020	.016	.012	.010
9.0	.229	.100	.054	.033	.022	.016	.012	.009	.007
10.0	.218	.091	.047	.028	.018	.012	.009	.007	.005
15.0	.180	.063	.027	.014	.008	.005	.003	.002	.001
20.0	.156	.048	.018	.008	.004	.002	.001	.001	.000
30.0	.128	.032	.010	.004	.002	.001	.000	.000	.000
40.0	.111	.024	.007	.002	.001	.000	.000	.000	.000
50.0	.100	.020	.005	.001	.000	.000	.000	.000	.000
100.0	.071	.010	.002	.000	.000	.000	.000	.000	.000
500.0	.032	.002	.000	.000	.000	.000	.000	.000	.000

DEGREES OF FREEDOM, NUMERATOR (1) = 2

DEGREES OF FREEDOM, DENOMINATOR(2)

F	10	12	14	16	18	20	30	40	50	100	200	300
1.0	.402	.397	.393	.390	.387	.386	.380	.377	.375	.372	.370	.369
1.2	.341	.335	.330	.327	.324	.322	.315	.312	.310	.305	.303	.303
1.4	.291	.284	.279	.275	.272	.270	.262	.258	.256	.251	.249	.248
1.6	.250	.242	.237	.233	.229	.227	.219	.215	.212	.207	.204	.204
1.8	.215	.207	.202	.197	.194	.191	.183	.178	.176	.171	.168	.167
2.0	.186	.178	.172	.168	.164	.162	.153	.149	.146	.141	.138	.137
2.2	.162	.153	.148	.143	.140	.137	.128	.124	.121	.116	.113	.113
2.4	.141	.133	.127	.123	.119	.116	.108	.104	.101	.096	.093	.092
2.6	.123	.115	.110	.105	.102	.099	.091	.087	.084	.079	.077	.076
2.8	.108	.100	.095	.091	.087	.085	.077	.073	.070	.066	.063	.062
3.0	.095	.088	.082	.078	.075	.073	.065	.061	.059	.054	.052	.051
3.5	.070	.063	.059	.055	.052	.050	.043	.040	.038	.034	.032	.031
4.0	.053	.047	.042	.039	.037	.035	.029	.026	.024	.021	.020	.019
4.5	.040	.035	.031	.028	.026	.024	.020	.017	.016	.013	.012	.012
5.0	.031	.026	.023	.021	.019	.017	.013	.012	.010	.009	.008	.007
6.0	.019	.016	.013	.011	.010	.009	.006	.005	.005	.003	.003	.003
7.0	.013	.010	.008	.007	.006	.005	.003	.002	.002	.001	.001	.001
8.0	.008	.006	.005	.004	.003	.003	.002	.001	.001	.001	.000	.000
9.0	.006	.004	.003	.002	.002	.002	.001	.001	.000	.000	.000	.000
10.0	.004	.003	.002	.002	.001	.001	.000	.000	.000	.000	.000	.000

DEGREES OF FREEDOM, NUMERATOR (1) = 3

DEGREES OF FREEDOM, DENOMINATOR(2)

F	1	2	3	4	5	6	7	8	9
1.0	.609	.535	.500	.479	.465	.455	.447	.441	.436
1.5	.526	.424	.374	.343	.322	.307	.296	.287	.280
2.0	.470	.350	.292	.256	.233	.216	.203	.193	.185
2.5	.428	.299	.236	.199	.174	.156	.144	.133	.126
3.0	.396	.260	.196	.158	.134	.117	.105	.095	.088
3.5	.370	.230	.165	.129	.106	.090	.078	.069	.063
4.0	.349	.206	.142	.107	.085	.070	.060	.052	.046
5.0	.315	.171	.110	.077	.058	.045	.037	.031	.026
6.0	.290	.146	.088	.058	.041	.031	.024	.019	.016
7.0	.269	.128	.072	.045	.031	.022	.016	.013	.010
8.0	.253	.113	.061	.036	.024	.016	.012	.009	.007
9.0	.239	.102	.052	.030	.019	.012	.008	.006	.005
10.0	.227	.092	.045	.025	.015	.009	.006	.004	.003
15.0	.187	.063	.026	.012	.006	.003	.002	.001	.001
20.0	.163	.048	.017	.007	.003	.002	.001	.000	.000
30.0	.133	.032	.010	.003	.001	.001	.000	.000	.000
40.0	.116	.024	.006	.002	.001	.000	.000	.000	.000
50.0	.104	.020	.005	.001	.000	.000	.000	.000	.000
100.0	.073	.010	.002	.000	.000	.000	.000	.000	.000
500.0	.033	.002	.000	.000	.000	.000	.000	.000	.000

DEGREES OF FREEDOM, NUMERATOR (1) = 3

DEGREES OF FREEDOM, DENOMINATOR(2)

F	10	12	14	16	18	20	30	40	50	100	200	300
1.0	.432	.426	.422	.418	.415	.413	.406	.403	.401	.396	.394	.393
1.2	.359	.352	.346	.342	.338	.335	.327	.322	.319	.314	.311	.310
1.4	.299	.291	.284	.279	.275	.272	.262	.257	.254	.247	.244	.243
1.6	.251	.241	.234	.229	.224	.221	.210	.205	.201	.194	.191	.189
1.8	.211	.201	.193	.188	.183	.180	.168	.163	.159	.152	.148	.147
2.0	.178	.168	.160	.155	.150	.146	.135	.129	.126	.119	.115	.114
2.2	.151	.141	.133	.128	.123	.120	.109	.103	.100	.093	.089	.088
2.4	.129	.119	.111	.106	.102	.098	.087	.082	.079	.072	.069	.068
2.6	.110	.100	.093	.088	.084	.081	.070	.065	.062	.056	.053	.052
2.8	.095	.085	.079	.074	.070	.066	.057	.052	.049	.044	.041	.040
3.0	.082	.073	.066	.062	.058	.055	.046	.042	.039	.034	.032	.031
3.5	.058	.050	.044	.040	.037	.034	.027	.024	.022	.018	.016	.016
4.0	.041	.035	.030	.027	.024	.022	.017	.014	.013	.010	.009	.008
4.5	.030	.025	.021	.018	.016	.014	.010	.008	.007	.005	.004	.004
5.0	.023	.018	.015	.012	.011	.010	.006	.005	.004	.003	.002	.002
6.0	.013	.010	.008	.006	.005	.004	.002	.002	.001	.001	.001	.001
7.0	.008	.006	.004	.003	.003	.002	.001	.001	.001	.000	.000	.000
8.0	.005	.003	.002	.002	.001	.001	.000	.000	.000	.000	.000	.000
9.0	.003	.002	.001	.001	.001	.001	.000	.000	.000	.000	.000	.000
10.0	.002	.001	.001	.001	.000	.000	.000	.000	.000	.000	.000	.000

DEGREES OF FREEDOM, NUMERATOR (1) = 4

DEGREES OF FREEDOM, DENOMINATOR(2)

F	1	2	3	4	5	6	7	8	9
1.0	.626	.556	.521	.500	.486	.475	.467	.461	.456
1.5	.540	.438	.385	.352	.329	.313	.300	.289	.281
2.0	.481	.360	.298	.259	.233	.214	.199	.188	.178
2.5	.439	.306	.239	.198	.171	.152	.137	.126	.117
3.0	.405	.265	.197	.156	.130	.111	.097	.087	.079
3.5	.379	.234	.166	.126	.101	.084	.071	.062	.055
4.0	.357	.210	.142	.104	.080	.065	.053	.045	.039
5.0	.322	.174	.109	.074	.054	.041	.032	.026	.021
6.0	.296	.148	.086	.055	.038	.027	.020	.016	.012
7.0	.275	.129	.071	.043	.028	.019	.014	.010	.008
8.0	.258	.114	.060	.034	.021	.014	.009	.007	.005
9.0	.244	.102	.051	.028	.017	.010	.007	.005	.003
10.0	.232	.093	.044	.023	.013	.008	.005	.003	.002
15.0	.191	.063	.025	.011	.005	.003	.002	.001	.001
20.0	.166	.048	.017	.007	.003	.001	.001	.000	.000
30.0	.136	.033	.009	.003	.001	.000	.000	.000	.000
40.0	.118	.025	.006	.002	.001	.000	.000	.000	.000
50.0	.106	.020	.004	.001	.000	.000	.000	.000	.000
100.0	.075	.010	.002	.000	.000	.000	.000	.000	.000
500.0	.034	.002	.000	.000	.000	.000	.000	.000	.000

DEGREES OF FREEDOM, NUMERATOR (1) = 4

DEGREES OF FREEDOM, DENOMINATOR(2)

F	10	12	14	16	18	20	30	40	50	100	200	300
1.0	.452	.445	.440	.436	.433	.431	.423	.419	.416	.411	.409	.408
1.2	.369	.360	.354	.349	.345	.342	.331	.326	.322	.316	.312	.311
1.4	.303	.292	.285	.279	.274	.270	.258	.251	.248	.239	.235	.234
1.6	.249	.238	.229	.223	.217	.213	.200	.193	.189	.180	.176	.174
1.8	.205	.194	.185	.178	.173	.168	.155	.148	.144	.135	.130	.129
2.0	.171	.159	.150	.143	.138	.133	.120	.113	.109	.100	.096	.094
2.2	.142	.130	.122	.115	.110	.106	.093	.086	.082	.074	.070	.069
2.4	.119	.108	.099	.093	.088	.084	.072	.066	.062	.055	.051	.050
2.6	.100	.089	.082	.076	.071	.067	.056	.050	.047	.041	.037	.036
2.8	.085	.075	.067	.062	.057	.054	.044	.039	.036	.030	.027	.026
3.0	.072	.063	.056	.050	.046	.043	.034	.030	.027	.022	.020	.019
3.5	.049	.041	.035	.031	.028	.025	.018	.015	.014	.010	.009	.008
4.0	.034	.027	.023	.020	.017	.015	.010	.008	.007	.005	.004	.004
4.5	.024	.019	.015	.013	.011	.009	.006	.004	.003	.002	.002	.002
5.0	.018	.013	.010	.008	.007	.006	.003	.002	.002	.001	.001	.001
6.0	.010	.007	.005	.004	.003	.002	.001	.001	.001	.000	.000	.000
7.0	.006	.004	.003	.002	.001	.001	.000	.000	.000	.000	.000	.000
8.0	.004	.002	.001	.001	.001	.001	.000	.000	.000	.000	.000	.000
9.0	.002	.001	.001	.001	.000	.000	.000	.000	.000	.000	.000	.000
10.0	.002	.001	.000	.000	.000	.000	.000	.000	.000	.000	.000	.000

Right-Tail Areas under the *F* Density Function (*continued*)

DEGREES OF FREEDOM, NUMERATOR (1) = 5

DEGREES OF FREEDOM, DENOMINATOR(2)

F	1	2	3	4	5	6	7	8	9
1.0	.637	.569	.535	.514	.500	.489	.481	.475	.470
1.5	.549	.446	.392	.358	.334	.316	.301	.290	.281
2.0	.489	.366	.302	.261	.233	.212	.196	.183	.173
2.5	.445	.310	.241	.198	.169	.148	.132	.120	.110
3.0	.411	.269	.197	.155	.127	.107	.092	.081	.072
3.5	.384	.237	.166	.124	.098	.080	.066	.057	.049
4.0	.362	.212	.142	.102	.077	.061	.049	.041	.035
5.0	.327	.175	.108	.072	.051	.038	.029	.023	.018
6.0	.300	.149	.086	.054	.036	.025	.018	.013	.010
7.0	.279	.130	.070	.041	.026	.017	.012	.008	.006
8.0	.262	.115	.059	.033	.020	.012	.008	.006	.004
9.0	.248	.103	.050	.027	.015	.009	.006	.004	.003
10.0	.235	.093	.043	.022	.012	.007	.004	.003	.002
15.0	.193	.064	.025	.011	.005	.002	.001	.001	.000
20.0	.168	.048	.016	.006	.003	.001	.001	.000	.000
30.0	.138	.033	.009	.003	.001	.000	.000	.000	.000
40.0	.119	.025	.006	.002	.000	.000	.000	.000	.000
50.0	.107	.020	.004	.001	.000	.000	.000	.000	.000
100.0	.076	.010	.002	.000	.000	.000	.000	.000	.000
500.0	.034	.002	.000	.000	.000	.000	.000	.000	.000

DEGREES OF FREEDOM, NUMERATOR (1) = 5

DEGREES OF FREEDOM, DENOMINATOR(2)

F	10	12	14	16	18	20	30	40	50	100	200	300
1.0	.465	.458	.453	.449	.446	.443	.435	.430	.427	.422	.419	.418
1.2	.376	.366	.359	.353	.349	.345	.333	.327	.323	.315	.311	.309
1.4	.304	.292	.283	.277	.271	.267	.253	.245	.240	.231	.226	.224
1.6	.246	.234	.224	.217	.211	.206	.190	.182	.177	.167	.162	.160
1.8	.201	.187	.177	.170	.164	.159	.143	.135	.130	.120	.114	.113
2.0	.164	.151	.141	.133	.127	.123	.107	.100	.095	.085	.080	.079
2.2	.135	.122	.113	.105	.099	.095	.081	.073	.069	.060	.056	.054
2.4	.112	.099	.090	.083	.078	.074	.060	.054	.050	.042	.039	.037
2.6	.093	.081	.073	.066	.061	.057	.045	.040	.036	.030	.026	.025
2.8	.078	.067	.059	.053	.048	.045	.034	.029	.026	.021	.018	.017
3.0	.066	.055	.048	.043	.038	.035	.026	.022	.019	.014	.012	.012
3.5	.043	.035	.029	.025	.022	.020	.013	.010	.009	.006	.005	.004
4.0	.030	.023	.018	.015	.013	.011	.007	.005	.004	.002	.002	.002
4.5	.021	.015	.012	.009	.008	.007	.004	.002	.002	.001	.001	.001
5.0	.015	.010	.008	.006	.005	.004	.002	.001	.001	.000	.000	.000
6.0	.008	.005	.004	.003	.002	.002	.001	.000	.000	.000	.000	.000
7.0	.005	.003	.002	.001	.001	.001	.000	.000	.000	.000	.000	.000
8.0	.003	.002	.001	.001	.000	.000	.000	.000	.000	.000	.000	.000
9.0	.002	.001	.001	.000	.000	.000	.000	.000	.000	.000	.000	.000
10.0	.001	.001	.000	.000	.000	.000	.000	.000	.000	.000	.000	.000

DEGREES OF FREEDOM, NUMERATOR (1) = 6

DEGREES OF FREEDOM, DENOMINATOR(2)

F	1	2	3	4	5	6	7	8	9
1.0	.644	.578	.545	.525	.511	.500	.492	.485	.480
1.5	.555	.452	.397	.362	.337	.317	.302	.290	.280
2.0	.494	.370	.304	.262	.232	.210	.193	.179	.168
2.5	.450	.313	.242	.197	.167	.145	.128	.115	.105
3.0	.415	.271	.198	.154	.124	.104	.088	.077	.068
3.5	.388	.239	.166	.123	.095	.076	.063	.053	.045
4.0	.365	.213	.141	.100	.075	.058	.046	.038	.031
5.0	.330	.176	.107	.071	.049	.035	.027	.020	.016
6.0	.303	.150	.085	.052	.034	.023	.016	.012	.009
7.0	.282	.130	.069	.040	.025	.016	.011	.007	.005
8.0	.264	.115	.058	.032	.019	.012	.007	.005	.003
9.0	.250	.103	.050	.026	.015	.009	.005	.003	.002
10.0	.237	.094	.043	.022	.012	.007	.004	.002	.001
15.0	.195	.064	.024	.010	.005	.002	.001	.001	.000
20.0	.170	.048	.016	.006	.002	.001	.000	.000	.000
30.0	.139	.033	.009	.003	.001	.000	.000	.000	.000
40.0	.120	.025	.006	.002	.000	.000	.000	.000	.000
50.0	.108	.020	.004	.001	.000	.000	.000	.000	.000
100.0	.076	.010	.002	.000	.000	.000	.000	.000	.000
500.0	.034	.002	.000	.000	.000	.000	.000	.000	.000

DEGREES OF FREEDOM, NUMERATOR (1) = 6

DEGREES OF FREEDOM, DENOMINATOR(2)

F	10	12	14	16	18	20	30	40	50	100	200	300
1.0	.475	.468	.463	.459	.455	.452	.444	.439	.436	.430	.426	.425
1.2	.380	.370	.362	.356	.351	.347	.333	.326	.322	.313	.308	.306
1.4	.304	.291	.282	.274	.268	.263	.247	.239	.233	.222	.216	.214
1.6	.244	.230	.219	.211	.204	.199	.182	.172	.167	.155	.149	.147
1.8	.196	.182	.171	.163	.156	.150	.133	.124	.118	.107	.101	.099
2.0	.159	.145	.134	.126	.119	.114	.097	.088	.083	.073	.067	.066
2.2	.129	.115	.105	.097	.091	.086	.071	.063	.058	.049	.044	.043
2.4	.106	.093	.083	.076	.070	.065	.052	.045	.041	.033	.029	.028
2.6	.087	.075	.066	.059	.054	.050	.038	.032	.029	.022	.019	.018
2.8	.073	.061	.053	.047	.042	.038	.028	.023	.020	.015	.012	.012
3.0	.061	.050	.042	.037	.033	.029	.020	.016	.014	.010	.008	.007
3.5	.039	.031	.025	.021	.018	.016	.010	.007	.006	.003	.003	.002
4.0	.026	.020	.015	.012	.010	.009	.005	.003	.002	.001	.001	.001
4.5	.018	.013	.010	.007	.006	.005	.002	.001	.001	.000	.000	.000
5.0	.013	.009	.006	.005	.004	.003	.001	.001	.000	.000	.000	.000
6.0	.007	.004	.003	.002	.001	.001	.000	.000	.000	.000	.000	.000
7.0	.004	.002	.001	.001	.001	.000	.000	.000	.000	.000	.000	.000
8.0	.002	.001	.001	.000	.000	.000	.000	.000	.000	.000	.000	.000
9.0	.001	.001	.000	.000	.000	.000	.000	.000	.000	.000	.000	.000
10.0	.001	.000	.000	.000	.000	.000	.000	.000	.000	.000	.000	.000

DEGREES OF FREEDOM, NUMERATOR (1) = 7

DEGREES OF FREEDOM, DENOMINATOR(2)

F	1	2	3	4	5	6	7	8	9
1.0	.649	.585	.553	.533	.519	.508	.500	.493	.488
1.5	.559	.457	.401	.365	.339	.319	.303	.290	.280
2.0	.498	.373	.306	.262	.231	.208	.190	.176	.164
2.5	.453	.315	.242	.197	.165	.142	.125	.111	.101
3.0	.418	.273	.198	.153	.122	.101	.085	.073	.064
3.5	.390	.240	.166	.122	.093	.074	.060	.050	.042
4.0	.368	.215	.141	.099	.073	.056	.044	.035	.029
5.0	.332	.177	.107	.069	.048	.034	.025	.019	.015
6.0	.305	.150	.084	.051	.033	.022	.015	.011	.008
7.0	.283	.131	.069	.039	.024	.015	.010	.007	.005
8.0	.266	.116	.058	.031	.018	.011	.007	.004	.003
9.0	.251	.104	.049	.025	.014	.008	.005	.003	.002
10.0	.239	.094	.043	.021	.011	.006	.004	.002	.001
15.0	.196	.064	.024	.010	.004	.002	.001	.001	.000
20.0	.171	.048	.016	.006	.002	.001	.000	.000	.000
30.0	.140	.033	.009	.003	.001	.000	.000	.000	.000
40.0	.121	.025	.006	.002	.000	.000	.000	.000	.000
50.0	.108	.020	.004	.001	.000	.000	.000	.000	.000
100.0	.077	.010	.002	.000	.000	.000	.000	.000	.000
500.0	.034	.002	.000	.000	.000	.000	.000	.000	.000

DEGREES OF FREEDOM, NUMERATOR (1) = 7

DEGREES OF FREEDOM, DENOMINATOR(2)

F	10	12	14	16	18	20	30	40	50	100	200	300
1.0	.483	.476	.471	.466	.463	.460	.451	.446	.442	.436	.432	.431
1.2	.383	.372	.364	.357	.352	.347	.333	.325	.320	.310	.304	.302
1.4	.304	.290	.280	.272	.265	.259	.242	.232	.226	.214	.207	.205
1.6	.241	.226	.215	.206	.199	.193	.174	.164	.157	.144	.137	.135
1.8	.193	.177	.165	.156	.149	.143	.124	.114	.108	.095	.089	.087
2.0	.155	.139	.128	.119	.112	.106	.088	.079	.074	.062	.057	.055
2.2	.125	.110	.099	.091	.084	.079	.063	.055	.050	.040	.036	.034
2.4	.101	.088	.077	.070	.064	.059	.045	.038	.034	.026	.022	.021
2.6	.083	.070	.061	.054	.048	.044	.032	.026	.023	.017	.014	.013
2.8	.068	.056	.048	.042	.037	.033	.023	.018	.015	.011	.008	.008
3.0	.057	.046	.038	.033	.028	.025	.016	.013	.010	.007	.005	.005
3.5	.036	.028	.022	.018	.015	.013	.007	.005	.004	.002	.001	.001
4.0	.024	.017	.013	.010	.008	.007	.003	.002	.002	.001	.000	.000
4.5	.016	.011	.008	.006	.005	.004	.002	.001	.001	.000	.000	.000
5.0	.011	.007	.005	.004	.003	.002	.001	.000	.000	.000	.000	.000
6.0	.006	.004	.002	.001	.001	.001	.000	.000	.000	.000	.000	.000
7.0	.003	.002	.001	.001	.000	.000	.000	.000	.000	.000	.000	.000
8.0	.002	.001	.001	.000	.000	.000	.000	.000	.000	.000	.000	.000
9.0	.001	.001	.000	.000	.000	.000	.000	.000	.000	.000	.000	.000
10.0	.001	.000	.000	.000	.000	.000	.000	.000	.000	.000	.000	.000

DEGREES OF FREEDOM, NUMERATOR (1) = 8

DEGREES OF FREEDOM, DENOMINATOR(2)

F	1	2	3	4	5	6	7	8	9
1.0	.653	.590	.559	.539	.525	.515	.507	.500	.495
1.5	.562	.460	.404	.367	.340	.320	.303	.290	.279
2.0	.500	.376	.307	.263	.231	.207	.188	.173	.161
2.5	.455	.317	.243	.196	.164	.140	.122	.108	.097
3.0	.420	.274	.198	.152	.121	.099	.083	.071	.061
3.5	.392	.241	.165	.121	.092	.072	.058	.048	.040
4.0	.369	.215	.141	.098	.072	.054	.042	.033	.027
5.0	.333	.177	.106	.069	.046	.033	.024	.018	.013
6.0	.306	.151	.084	.051	.032	.021	.014	.010	.007
7.0	.285	.131	.069	.039	.023	.014	.009	.006	.004
8.0	.267	.116	.057	.031	.017	.010	.006	.004	.003
9.0	.253	.104	.049	.025	.013	.008	.004	.003	.002
10.0	.240	.094	.042	.021	.011	.006	.003	.002	.001
15.0	.197	.064	.024	.010	.004	.002	.001	.000	.000
20.0	.171	.048	.016	.006	.002	.001	.000	.000	.000
30.0	.140	.033	.009	.003	.001	.000	.000	.000	.000
40.0	.122	.025	.006	.001	.000	.000	.000	.000	.000
50.0	.109	.020	.004	.001	.000	.000	.000	.000	.000
100.0	.077	.010	.001	.000	.000	.000	.000	.000	.000
500.0	.035	.002	.000	.000	.000	.000	.000	.000	.000

DEGREES OF FREEDOM, NUMERATOR (1) = 8

DEGREES OF FREEDOM, DENOMINATOR(2)

F	10	12	14	16	18	20	30	40	50	100	200	300
1.0	.490	.483	.477	.473	.469	.466	.456	.451	.448	.441	.437	.436
1.2	.386	.374	.365	.358	.353	.348	.332	.324	.318	.307	.301	.299
1.4	.303	.289	.278	.269	.262	.256	.237	.226	.220	.206	.198	.196
1.6	.239	.223	.211	.201	.194	.187	.167	.156	.149	.134	.127	.124
1.8	.189	.173	.161	.151	.143	.137	.116	.106	.099	.086	.079	.077
2.0	.151	.135	.123	.113	.106	.100	.081	.071	.066	.054	.048	.046
2.2	.121	.106	.094	.085	.078	.073	.056	.048	.043	.034	.029	.027
2.4	.098	.083	.073	.065	.059	.054	.039	.032	.028	.021	.017	.016
2.6	.079	.066	.056	.049	.044	.040	.027	.022	.018	.013	.010	.009
2.8	.065	.053	.044	.038	.033	.029	.019	.015	.012	.008	.006	.005
3.0	.054	.042	.035	.029	.025	.022	.013	.010	.008	.005	.003	.003
3.5	.034	.025	.020	.016	.013	.011	.006	.004	.003	.001	.001	.001
4.0	.022	.016	.012	.009	.007	.006	.003	.001	.001	.000	.000	.000
4.5	.015	.010	.007	.005	.004	.003	.001	.001	.000	.000	.000	.000
5.0	.010	.007	.004	.003	.002	.002	.001	.000	.000	.000	.000	.000
6.0	.005	.003	.002	.001	.001	.001	.000	.000	.000	.000	.000	.000
7.0	.003	.002	.001	.001	.000	.000	.000	.000	.000	.000	.000	.000
8.0	.002	.001	.000	.000	.000	.000	.000	.000	.000	.000	.000	.000
9.0	.001	.000	.000	.000	.000	.000	.000	.000	.000	.000	.000	.000
10.0	.001	.000	.000	.000	.000	.000	.000	.000	.000	.000	.000	.000

Right-Tail Areas under the *F* Density Function (*continued*)

DEGREES OF FREEDOM, NUMERATOR (1) = 9

DEGREES OF FREEDOM, DENOMINATOR(2)

F	1	2	3	4	5	6	7	8	9
1.0	.657	.595	.564	.544	.530	.520	.512	.505	.500
1.5	.565	.463	.407	.369	.341	.320	.303	.289	.278
2.0	.503	.378	.308	.263	.230	.206	.186	.171	.158
2.5	.457	.318	.244	.196	.163	.139	.120	.106	.094
3.0	.422	.275	.198	.151	.120	.097	.081	.068	.059
3.5	.394	.242	.165	.120	.091	.071	.056	.046	.038
4.0	.371	.216	.141	.097	.071	.053	.041	.032	.026
5.0	.335	.178	.106	.068	.046	.032	.023	.017	.013
6.0	.307	.151	.084	.050	.031	.020	.014	.010	.007
7.0	.286	.131	.068	.038	.023	.014	.009	.006	.004
8.0	.268	.116	.057	.030	.017	.010	.006	.004	.002
9.0	.253	.104	.049	.025	.013	.007	.004	.003	.002
10.0	.241	.094	.042	.020	.010	.006	.003	.002	.001
15.0	.198	.064	.024	.010	.004	.002	.001	.000	.000
20.0	.172	.049	.016	.006	.002	.001	.000	.000	.000
30.0	.141	.033	.009	.003	.001	.000	.000	.000	.000
40.0	.122	.025	.006	.001	.000	.000	.000	.000	.000
50.0	.109	.020	.004	.001	.000	.000	.000	.000	.000
100.0	.077	.010	.001	.000	.000	.000	.000	.000	.000
500.0	.035	.002	.000	.000	.000	.000	.000	.000	.000

DEGREES OF FREEDOM, NUMERATOR (1) = 9

DEGREES OF FREEDOM, DENOMINATOR(2)

F	10	12	14	16	18	20	30	40	50	100	200	300
1.0	.495	.488	.482	.478	.474	.471	.461	.456	.452	.445	.441	.440
1.2	.388	.376	.366	.359	.353	.348	.331	.322	.316	.304	.297	.294
1.4	.303	.288	.276	.267	.259	.253	.232	.221	.214	.198	.190	.187
1.6	.237	.220	.208	.197	.189	.182	.160	.148	.141	.125	.117	.114
1.8	.186	.169	.156	.146	.138	.131	.110	.099	.092	.077	.070	.068
2.0	.148	.131	.118	.109	.101	.094	.075	.065	.059	.047	.041	.039
2.2	.118	.102	.090	.081	.074	.068	.051	.043	.038	.028	.023	.022
2.4	.094	.080	.069	.061	.054	.049	.035	.028	.024	.017	.013	.012
2.6	.076	.063	.053	.046	.040	.036	.024	.018	.015	.010	.007	.007
2.8	.062	.050	.041	.035	.030	.026	.016	.012	.010	.006	.004	.004
3.0	.051	.040	.032	.027	.023	.020	.011	.008	.006	.003	.002	.002
3.5	.032	.023	.018	.014	.011	.009	.005	.003	.002	.001	.000	.000
4.0	.021	.014	.010	.008	.006	.005	.002	.001	.001	.000	.000	.000
4.5	.014	.009	.006	.004	.003	.002	.001	.000	.000	.000	.000	.000
5.0	.010	.006	.004	.003	.002	.001	.000	.000	.000	.000	.000	.000
6.0	.005	.003	.002	.001	.001	.000	.000	.000	.000	.000	.000	.000
7.0	.003	.001	.001	.000	.000	.000	.000	.000	.000	.000	.000	.000
8.0	.002	.001	.000	.000	.000	.000	.000	.000	.000	.000	.000	.000
9.0	.001	.000	.000	.000	.000	.000	.000	.000	.000	.000	.000	.000
10.0	.001	.000	.000	.000	.000	.000	.000	.000	.000	.000	.000	.000

DEGREES OF FREEDOM, NUMERATOR (1) = 10

DEGREES OF FREEDOM, DENOMINATOR(2)

F	1	2	3	4	5	6	7	8	9
1.0	.659	.598	.568	.548	.535	.525	.517	.510	.505
1.5	.567	.465	.409	.370	.342	.321	.303	.289	.277
2.0	.504	.379	.309	.263	.230	.205	.185	.169	.156
2.5	.459	.319	.244	.196	.162	.137	.118	.104	.092
3.0	.424	.276	.198	.151	.118	.096	.079	.066	.057
3.5	.395	.243	.165	.119	.090	.069	.055	.044	.036
4.0	.372	.216	.140	.097	.070	.052	.039	.031	.024
5.0	.336	.178	.106	.067	.045	.031	.022	.016	.012
6.0	.308	.151	.084	.049	.031	.020	.013	.009	.006
7.0	.287	.131	.068	.038	.022	.014	.009	.006	.004
8.0	.269	.116	.057	.030	.017	.010	.006	.004	.002
9.0	.254	.104	.048	.024	.013	.007	.004	.002	.001
10.0	.242	.094	.042	.020	.010	.005	.003	.002	.001
15.0	.199	.064	.024	.009	.004	.002	.001	.000	.000
20.0	.172	.049	.016	.005	.002	.001	.000	.000	.000
30.0	.141	.033	.009	.003	.001	.000	.000	.000	.000
40.0	.122	.025	.006	.001	.000	.000	.000	.000	.000
50.0	.110	.020	.004	.001	.000	.000	.000	.000	.000
100.0	.078	.010	.001	.000	.000	.000	.000	.000	.000
500.0	.035	.002	.000	.000	.000	.000	.000	.000	.000

DEGREES OF FREEDOM, NUMERATOR (1) = 10

DEGREES OF FREEDOM, DENOMINATOR(2)

F	10	12	14	16	18	20	30	40	50	100	200	300
1.0	.500	.493	.487	.482	.479	.476	.465	.460	.456	.449	.445	.443
1.2	.389	.377	.367	.359	.353	.348	.330	.320	.314	.300	.293	.290
1.4	.302	.287	.274	.265	.257	.250	.228	.216	.208	.191	.182	.179
1.6	.235	.218	.205	.194	.185	.178	.155	.142	.134	.117	.109	.106
1.8	.184	.166	.153	.142	.133	.126	.104	.092	.085	.070	.063	.060
2.0	.145	.128	.114	.104	.096	.090	.070	.059	.053	.041	.035	.033
2.2	.115	.098	.086	.077	.070	.064	.047	.038	.033	.024	.019	.018
2.4	.092	.077	.066	.057	.051	.046	.031	.024	.020	.013	.010	.009
2.6	.074	.060	.050	.043	.037	.033	.021	.016	.013	.008	.005	.005
2.8	.060	.047	.039	.032	.028	.024	.014	.010	.008	.004	.003	.002
3.0	.049	.038	.030	.025	.021	.018	.010	.006	.005	.002	.001	.001
3.5	.030	.022	.016	.013	.010	.008	.004	.002	.001	.001	.000	.000
4.0	.020	.013	.009	.007	.005	.004	.002	.001	.000	.000	.000	.000
4.5	.013	.008	.006	.004	.003	.002	.001	.000	.000	.000	.000	.000
5.0	.009	.005	.003	.002	.002	.001	.000	.000	.000	.000	.000	.000
6.0	.005	.002	.001	.001	.001	.000	.000	.000	.000	.000	.000	.000
7.0	.002	.001	.001	.000	.000	.000	.000	.000	.000	.000	.000	.000
8.0	.001	.001	.000	.000	.000	.000	.000	.000	.000	.000	.000	.000
9.0	.001	.000	.000	.000	.000	.000	.000	.000	.000	.000	.000	.000
10.0	.001	.000	.000	.000	.000	.000	.000	.000	.000	.000	.000	.000

DEGREES OF FREEDOM, NUMERATOR (1) = 15

DEGREES OF FREEDOM, DENOMINATOR(2)

F	1	2	3	4	5	6	7	8	9
1.0	.667	.609	.580	.562	.549	.539	.532	.525	.520
1.5	.573	.472	.415	.375	.345	.322	.303	.287	.273
2.0	.510	.384	.312	.264	.228	.201	.180	.162	.148
2.5	.463	.323	.245	.194	.159	.132	.112	.097	.084
3.0	.428	.278	.199	.149	.115	.091	.074	.060	.050
3.5	.399	.245	.165	.117	.086	.065	.050	.040	.032
4.0	.376	.218	.140	.095	.067	.048	.036	.027	.021
5.0	.339	.179	.105	.066	.042	.028	.019	.014	.010
6.0	.311	.152	.083	.048	.029	.018	.012	.008	.005
7.0	.289	.132	.067	.037	.021	.012	.007	.005	.003
8.0	.271	.117	.056	.029	.015	.009	.005	.003	.002
9.0	.257	.104	.048	.023	.012	.006	.003	.002	.001
10.0	.244	.095	.041	.019	.009	.005	.002	.001	.001
15.0	.200	.064	.023	.009	.004	.002	.001	.000	.000
20.0	.174	.049	.015	.005	.002	.001	.000	.000	.000
30.0	.142	.033	.009	.002	.001	.000	.000	.000	.000
40.0	.124	.025	.006	.001	.000	.000	.000	.000	.000
50.0	.111	.020	.004	.001	.000	.000	.000	.000	.000
100.0	.078	.010	.001	.000	.000	.000	.000	.000	.000
500.0	.035	.002	.000	.000	.000	.000	.000	.000	.000

DEGREES OF FREEDOM, NUMERATOR (1) = 15

DEGREES OF FREEDOM, DENOMINATOR(2)

F	10	12	14	16	18	20	30	40	50	100	200	300
1.0	.516	.508	.502	.498	.494	.491	.480	.474	.470	.461	.457	.455
1.2	.394	.380	.369	.360	.352	.346	.324	.311	.303	.284	.274	.270
1.4	.300	.282	.267	.256	.246	.238	.210	.194	.184	.162	.150	.146
1.6	.229	.209	.193	.180	.170	.161	.133	.118	.108	.087	.076	.073
1.8	.175	.155	.140	.127	.117	.109	.083	.070	.061	.045	.037	.034
2.0	.135	.116	.102	.090	.081	.074	.052	.041	.034	.022	.017	.015
2.2	.105	.088	.074	.064	.057	.050	.032	.024	.019	.011	.007	.006
2.4	.083	.067	.055	.046	.040	.034	.020	.014	.011	.005	.003	.003
2.6	.066	.051	.041	.034	.028	.024	.013	.008	.006	.002	.001	.001
2.8	.053	.040	.031	.025	.020	.017	.008	.005	.003	.001	.001	.000
3.0	.042	.031	.023	.018	.014	.012	.005	.003	.002	.001	.000	.000
3.5	.026	.017	.012	.009	.007	.005	.002	.001	.000	.000	.000	.000
4.0	.016	.010	.007	.005	.003	.002	.001	.000	.000	.000	.000	.000
4.5	.010	.006	.004	.002	.002	.001	.000	.000	.000	.000	.000	.000
5.0	.007	.004	.002	.001	.001	.001	.000	.000	.000	.000	.000	.000
6.0	.003	.002	.001	.000	.000	.000	.000	.000	.000	.000	.000	.000
7.0	.002	.001	.000	.000	.000	.000	.000	.000	.000	.000	.000	.000
8.0	.001	.000	.000	.000	.000	.000	.000	.000	.000	.000	.000	.000
9.0	.001	.000	.000	.000	.000	.000	.000	.000	.000	.000	.000	.000
10.0	.000	.000	.000	.000	.000	.000	.000	.000	.000	.000	.000	.000

DEGREES OF FREEDOM, NUMERATOR (1) = 20

DEGREES OF FREEDOM, DENOMINATOR(2)

F	1	2	3	4	5	6	7	8	9
1.0	.671	.614	.587	.569	.557	.548	.540	.534	.529
1.5	.576	.476	.418	.377	.347	.323	.303	.286	.271
2.0	.512	.386	.313	.264	.227	.199	.177	.158	.143
2.5	.466	.324	.246	.194	.157	.130	.109	.093	.080
3.0	.430	.280	.199	.148	.113	.089	.071	.057	.047
3.5	.401	.246	.165	.116	.085	.063	.048	.037	.029
4.0	.377	.219	.140	.094	.065	.046	.034	.025	.019
5.0	.340	.180	.105	.065	.041	.027	.018	.012	.009
6.0	.313	.152	.082	.047	.028	.017	.011	.007	.005
7.0	.291	.132	.067	.036	.020	.012	.007	.004	.003
8.0	.273	.117	.056	.028	.015	.008	.005	.003	.002
9.0	.258	.105	.047	.023	.011	.006	.003	.002	.001
10.0	.245	.095	.041	.019	.009	.004	.002	.001	.001
15.0	.201	.064	.023	.009	.004	.001	.001	.000	.000
20.0	.175	.049	.015	.005	.002	.001	.000	.000	.000
30.0	.143	.033	.008	.002	.001	.000	.000	.000	.000
40.0	.124	.025	.006	.001	.000	.000	.000	.000	.000
50.0	.111	.020	.004	.001	.000	.000	.000	.000	.000
100.0	.079	.010	.001	.000	.000	.000	.000	.000	.000
500.0	.035	.002	.000	.000	.000	.000	.000	.000	.000

DEGREES OF FREEDOM, NUMERATOR (1) = 20

DEGREES OF FREEDOM, DENOMINATOR(2)

F	10	12	14	16	18	20	30	40	50	100	200	300
1.0	.524	.517	.512	.507	.503	.500	.489	.483	.479	.469	.464	.462
1.2	.397	.382	.370	.359	.351	.344	.319	.304	.293	.271	.257	.252
1.4	.298	.278	.263	.250	.239	.229	.198	.179	.167	.140	.125	.120
1.6	.224	.203	.186	.172	.160	.151	.119	.102	.090	.067	.055	.051
1.8	.170	.148	.132	.118	.108	.099	.071	.056	.047	.030	.023	.020
2.0	.130	.109	.094	.082	.072	.065	.042	.031	.024	.013	.009	.007
2.2	.100	.081	.068	.057	.049	.043	.025	.017	.012	.006	.003	.003
2.4	.078	.061	.049	.040	.034	.028	.015	.009	.006	.002	.001	.001
2.6	.061	.046	.036	.029	.023	.019	.009	.005	.003	.001	.000	.000
2.8	.049	.035	.027	.021	.016	.013	.005	.003	.002	.000	.000	.000
3.0	.039	.027	.020	.015	.011	.009	.003	.002	.001	.000	.000	.000
3.5	.023	.015	.010	.007	.005	.004	.001	.000	.000	.000	.000	.000
4.0	.014	.009	.005	.003	.002	.002	.000	.000	.000	.000	.000	.000
4.5	.009	.005	.003	.002	.001	.001	.000	.000	.000	.000	.000	.000
5.0	.006	.003	.002	.001	.001	.000	.000	.000	.000	.000	.000	.000
6.0	.003	.001	.001	.000	.000	.000	.000	.000	.000	.000	.000	.000
7.0	.002	.001	.000	.000	.000	.000	.000	.000	.000	.000	.000	.000
8.0	.001	.000	.000	.000	.000	.000	.000	.000	.000	.000	.000	.000
9.0	.001	.000	.000	.000	.000	.000	.000	.000	.000	.000	.000	.000
10.0	.000	.000	.000	.000	.000	.000	.000	.000	.000	.000	.000	.000

Right-Tail Areas under the F Density Function (concluded)

DEGREES OF FREEDOM, DENOMINATOR(2)

F	1	2	3	4	5	6	7	8	9
1.0	.673	.618	.591	.574	.562	.553	.546	.540	.535
1.5	.578	.478	.420	.379	.348	.323	.302	.285	.269
2.0	.514	.388	.314	.264	.227	.198	.174	.155	.140
2.5	.467	.325	.246	.193	.156	.128	.107	.090	.077
3.0	.431	.280	.199	.147	.112	.087	.069	.055	.045
3.5	.402	.246	.165	.116	.084	.062	.046	.036	.027
4.0	.379	.219	.139	.093	.064	.045	.033	.024	.018
5.0	.341	.180	.105	.064	.041	.026	.017	.012	.008
6.0	.313	.153	.082	.047	.027	.017	.010	.006	.004
7.0	.291	.132	.067	.036	.020	.011	.006	.004	.002
8.0	.273	.117	.056	.028	.015	.008	.004	.002	.001
9.0	.258	.105	.047	.023	.011	.006	.003	.001	.001
10.0	.246	.095	.041	.019	.009	.004	.002	.001	.001
15.0	.202	.064	.023	.009	.003	.001	.001	.000	.000
20.0	.175	.049	.015	.005	.002	.001	.000	.000	.000
30.0	.143	.033	.008	.002	.001	.000	.000	.000	.000
40.0	.124	.025	.005	.001	.000	.000	.000	.000	.000
50.0	.111	.020	.004	.001	.000	.000	.000	.000	.000
100.0	.079	.010	.001	.000	.000	.000	.000	.000	.000
500.0	.035	.002	.000	.000	.000	.000	.000	.000	.000

DEGREES OF FREEDOM, DENOMINATOR(2)

F	10	12	14	16	18	20	30	40	50	100	200	300
1.0	.530	.523	.518	.513	.510	.506	.495	.489	.485	.475	.469	.467
1.2	.398	.382	.370	.359	.350	.342	.314	.297	.286	.259	.243	.237
1.4	.297	.276	.259	.245	.233	.223	.188	.168	.154	.124	.107	.101
1.6	.221	.199	.181	.166	.154	.143	.109	.090	.078	.054	.041	.037
1.8	.166	.144	.126	.112	.101	.092	.062	.047	.039	.022	.015	.012
2.0	.126	.105	.089	.077	.067	.059	.035	.025	.019	.008	.005	.004
2.2	.097	.077	.063	.053	.044	.038	.020	.013	.009	.003	.001	.001
2.4	.075	.058	.045	.036	.030	.025	.012	.007	.004	.001	.000	.000
2.6	.058	.043	.033	.026	.020	.016	.007	.003	.002	.000	.000	.000
2.8	.046	.033	.024	.018	.014	.011	.004	.002	.001	.000	.000	.000
3.0	.037	.025	.018	.013	.010	.007	.002	.001	.000	.000	.000	.000
3.5	.022	.014	.009	.006	.004	.003	.001	.000	.000	.000	.000	.000
4.0	.013	.008	.005	.003	.002	.001	.000	.000	.000	.000	.000	.000
4.5	.008	.005	.003	.001	.001	.001	.000	.000	.000	.000	.000	.000
5.0	.006	.003	.001	.001	.000	.000	.000	.000	.000	.000	.000	.000
6.0	.003	.001	.001	.000	.000	.000	.000	.000	.000	.000	.000	.000
7.0	.001	.001	.000	.000	.000	.000	.000	.000	.000	.000	.000	.000
8.0	.001	.000	.000	.000	.000	.000	.000	.000	.000	.000	.000-.000	
9.0	.000	.000	.000	.000	.000	.000	.000	.000	.000	.0000	.000	.000
10.0	.000	.000	.000	.000	.000	.000	.000	.000	.000	.000	.000	.000

DEGREES OF FREEDOM, DENOMINATOR(2)

F	1	2	3	4	5	6	7	8	9
1.0	.675	.620	.594	.577	.565	.556	.549	.544	.539
1.5	.579	.479	.421	.380	.348	.323	.302	.284	.268
2.0	.515	.389	.315	.264	.226	.197	.173	.154	.137
2.5	.468	.326	.246	.193	.155	.127	.105	.088	.075
3.0	.432	.281	.199	.147	.111	.086	.068	.054	.043
3.5	.403	.247	.165	.115	.083	.061	.045	.034	.026
4.0	.379	.220	.139	.093	.063	.045	.032	.023	.017
5.0	.342	.180	.104	.064	.040	.026	.017	.011	.008
6.0	.314	.153	.082	.046	.027	.016	.010	.006	.004
7.0	.292	.133	.067	.035	.019	.011	.006	.004	.002
8.0	.274	.117	.055	.028	.014	.008	.004	.002	.001
9.0	.259	.105	.047	.022	.011	.006	.003	.002	.001
10.0	.246	.095	.041	.018	.009	.004	.002	.001	.001
15.0	.202	.064	.023	.009	.003	.001	.001	.000	.000
20.0	.175	.049	.015	.005	.002	.001	.000	.000	.000
30.0	.144	.033	.008	.002	.001	.000	.000	.000	.000
40.0	.125	.025	.005	.001	.000	.000	.000	.000	.000
50.0	.112	.020	.004	.001	.000	.000	.000	.000	.000
100.0	.079	.010	.001	.000	.000	.000	.000	.000	.000
500.0	.035	.002	.000	.000	.000	.000	.000	.000	.000

DEGREES OF FREEDOM, DENOMINATOR(2)

F	10	12	14	16	18	20	30	40	50	100	200	300
1.0	.535	.528	.522	.518	.514	.511	.500	.493	.489	.479	.473	.471
1.2	.399	.383	.370	.358	.349	.340	.310	.292	.279	.248	.230	.223
1.4	.296	.274	.256	.242	.229	.218	.181	.159	.144	.110	.092	.085
1.6	.219	.196	.177	.162	.149	.138	.102	.082	.070	.044	.031	.027
1.8	.164	.141	.122	.108	.096	.087	.056	.041	.032	.016	.010	.008
2.0	.124	.102	.085	.073	.063	.055	.031	.020	.015	.006	.003	.002
2.2	.094	.075	.060	.049	.041	.035	.017	.010	.007	.002	.001	.000
2.4	.073	.055	.043	.034	.027	.022	.010	.005	.003	.001	.000	.000
2.6	.056	.041	.031	.024	.018	.015	.005	.003	.001	.000	.000	.000
2.8	.044	.031	.022	.017	.012	.010	.003	.001	.001	.000	.000	.000
3.0	.035	.024	.017	.012	.009	.006	.002	.001	.000	.000	.000	.000
3.5	.021	.013	.008	.005	.004	.002	.001	.000	.000	.000	.000	.000
4.0	.013	.007	.004	.003	.002	.001	.000	.000	.000	.000	.000	.000
4.5	.008	.004	.002	.001	.001	.000	.000	.000	.000	.000	.000	.000
5.0	.005	.003	.001	.001	.000	.000	.000	.000	.000	.000	.000	.000
6.0	.003	.001	.000	.000	.000	.000	.000	.000	.000	.000	.000	.000
7.0	.001	.000	.000	.000	.000	.000	.000	.000	.000	.000	.000	.000
8.0	.001	.000	.000	.000	.000	.000	.000	.000	.000	.000	.000	.000
9.0	.000	.000	.000	.000	.000	.000	.000	.000	.000	.000	.000	.000
10.0	.000	.000	.000	.000	.000	.000	.000	.000	.000	.0000.000		

DEGREES OF FREEDOM, DENOMINATOR(2)

F	1	2	3	4	5	6	7	8	9
1.0	.678	.625	.599	.583	.573	.564	.558	.552	.548
1.5	.582	.482	.424	.382	.350	.323	.301	.282	.265
2.0	.517	.390	.316	.264	.225	.195	.170	.150	.133
2.5	.470	.328	.246	.192	.153	.124	.102	.085	.071
3.0	.434	.282	.199	.146	.110	.084	.065	.051	.040
3.5	.405	.247	.165	.114	.081	.059	.043	.032	.024
4.0	.381	.220	.139	.092	.062	.043	.030	.021	.015
5.0	.343	.181	.104	.063	.039	.025	.016	.010	.007
6.0	.315	.153	.082	.046	.026	.016	.009	.006	.003
7.0	.293	.133	.066	.035	.019	.010	.006	.003	.002
8.0	.275	.117	.055	.027	.014	.007	.004	.002	.001
9.0	.260	.105	.047	.022	.011	.005	.003	.001	.001
10.0	.247	.095	.040	.018	.008	.004	.002	.001	.000
15.0	.203	.064	.023	.008	.003	.001	.001	.000	.000
20.0	.176	.049	.015	.005	.002	.001	.000	.000	.000
30.0	.144	.033	.008	.002	.001	.000	.000	.000	.000
40.0	.125	.025	.005	.001	.000	.000	.000	.000	.000
50.0	.112	.020	.004	.001	.000	.000	.000	.000	.000
100.0	.079	.010	.001	.000	.000	.000	.000	.000	.000
500.0	.035	.002	.000	.000	.000	.000	.000	.000	.000

DEGREES OF FREEDOM, DENOMINATOR(2)

F	10	12	14	16	18	20	30	40	50	100	200	300
1.0	.544	.537	.532	.528	.524	.521	.511	.504	.500	.489	.482	.479
1.2	.401	.384	.369	.357	.346	.336	.301	.277	.261	.219	.191	.181
1.4	.293	.270	.250	.234	.220	.207	.164	.137	.119	.078	.055	.048
1.6	.215	.189	.169	.152	.137	.125	.085	.063	.050	.024	.013	.010
1.8	.158	.134	.114	.099	.046	.076	.044	.028	.020	.007	.002	.002
2.0	.118	.095	.078	.065	.054	.046	.022	.013	.008	.002	.000	.000
2.2	.089	.069	.054	.043	.035	.028	.012	.006	.003	.000	.000	.000
2.4	.068	.050	.038	.029	.022	.017	.006	.003	.001	.000	.000	.000
2.6	.052	.037	.027	.020	.015	.011	.003	.001	.000	.000	.000	.000
2.8	.041	.028	.019	.014	.010	.007	.002	.001	.000	.000	.000	.000
3.0	.032	.021	.014	.009	.007	.005	.001	.000	.000	.000	.000	.000
3.5	.018	.011	.007	.004	.003	.002	.000	.000	.000	.000	.000	.000
4.0	.011	.006	.003	.002	.001	.001	.000	.000	.000	.000	.000	.000
4.5	.007	.003	.002	.001	.001	.000	.000	.000	.000	.000	.000	.000
5.0	.005	.002	.001	.000	.000	.000	.000	.000	.000	.000	.000	.000
6.0	.002	.001	.000	.000	.000	.000	.000	.000	.000	.000	.000	.000
7.0	.001	.000	.000	.000	.000	.000	.000	.000	.000	.000	.000	.000
8.0	.001	.000	.000	.000	.000	.000	.000	.000	.000	.000	.000	.000
9.0	.000	.000	.000	.000	.000	.000	.000	.000	.000	.0000.0000.000		
10.0	.000	.000	.000	.000	.000	.000	.000	.000	.000	.0000.0000.000		

Appendix L

Answers to Selected Exercises

CHAPTER 2

2.1 *a.* External
     b. Internal
     c. Internal
     d. External
     e. Internal
     f. External
     g. Internal

2.2 *a.* Time series
     b. Cross section
     c. Time series
     d. Cross section
     e. Cross section
     f. Cross section
     g. Time series

2.5 *b.*

Class Size	Absolute Frequency	Relative Frequency
0–9	1	0.025
10–19	4	0.100
20–29	4	0.100
30–39	4	0.100
40–49	6	0.150
50–59	3	0.075
60–69	2	0.050
70–79	7	0.175
80–89	4	0.100
90–99	2	0.050
100–109	3	0.075
	40	1.000

2.7 *a.*

Frequency Distribution

Number of Rooms	Number of Houses
1	0
2	0
3	0
4	0
5	8
6	312
7	383
8	206
9	33
10	7
11	0
12	1

b.

Number of Rooms	Number of Houses
5	8
6	320
7	703
8	909
9	942
10	949
11	949
12	950

2.9 Answer *h* is probably best.

CHAPTER 3

3.5 $\mu_x = 7.44$ years
3.6 Median $= 7$ years

3.7   Bimodal with modes of 3 and 7 years

3.8   Range $= 17$ years

3.9 $\sigma_x{}^2 = 20.12$ (years)^2

3.10 $\sigma_x = 4.49$ years

3.11 13, 15, 16

3.15 $\overline{X} = 3$ minutes
      $s_x{}^2 = 3$ (minutes)^2
      $s_x = 1.732$ minutes

3.16 $\overline{X} = 3.08$ minutes
      $s_x = 1.22$ minutes

3.17 $\mu_x = 6.6$ years
      $\sigma_x = 5.24$ years

3.18 $\overline{X} = 6.6$ years
      $s_x = 5.86$ years

3.20 $\overline{X} = 55.28$ students
      $s_x = 28.1$ students

3.23 *a.* $\mu_x = 14.02\%$
      b.

Stuffed dog	$ 49.80
Stuffed cat	104.00
Back pack	7.50
Doll	648.00
Doll House	345.60

      c. Total profit $1,154.90
      d. Total sales $12,430.00
      e. Total profit margin 9.29%

3.24 13.33 mpg

CHAPTER 4

4.12 *a.* $\frac{4}{6}$, $\frac{3}{6}$
      b. $\frac{1}{6}$
      c. 1
      d. $\frac{1}{3}$, $\frac{1}{4}$
      e. No
      f. No

4.14 Zero

4.15 *a* and *d; e* and *f*

4.16 0.6

4.17 0.35

4.18 0.09

4.19 *a.* 0.72
      b. 0.55
      c. Some read more than one.
      d. 0.65

4.20 *a.* 0.75
      b. 0.95
      c. 0.40
      d. 0.76
      e. 0.27
      f. 0.08
      g. 0
      h. 0
      i. 0
      j. 0.83
      k. 0.52
      l. 0.70
      m. 0.067

4.23 0.7

4.24 *a.* 3.05
      b. 1.5961
      c. 0.20

4.25 *a.* 0.055
      b. 0.0775

4.26 0.60

4.27 *a.* 0.96
      b. 0.8
      c. 0.04
      d. 0.008
      e. 5
      f. First machine

4.28 $\frac{5}{6}$

4.31 *a.* 0.6
      b. $\frac{5}{9}$
      c. No

4.32 *b.* 0.36 orders
      c. 0.36 orders
      d. 0.6904
      e. 0.8309

4.35 No

CHAPTER 5

5.3   No

5.8   3.015

5.13 *a.*

X	$P(X)$
100	$\frac{1}{2}$
200	$\frac{1}{2}$

      b. $\mu_x = 150$ $\sigma_x{}^2 = 2{,}500$

d.

$\bar{X}$	$P(\bar{X})$
100	$\frac{1}{6}$
150	$\frac{4}{6}$
200	$\frac{1}{6}$

e. $\mu_{\bar{x}} = 150 \quad \sigma_{\bar{x}}^2 = 833.33$

f. $\mu_x = \mu_{\bar{x}} = 150$

$\sigma_{\bar{x}}^2 = \sigma_x^2 \cdot \dfrac{N-n}{n} = \dfrac{N-n}{N-1} =$

833.33

5.14

$\bar{X}$	$P(\bar{X})$
0.0	0.09
0.5	0.24
1.0	0.28
1.5	0.22
2.0	0.12
2.5	0.04
3.0	0.01
	1.00

5.15 $\mu_{\bar{x}} = 1.1 \quad \sigma_{\bar{x}}^2 = 0.445$

5.16   0.86

5.17   a. $\mu_{\bar{x}} = 500 \quad \sigma_{\bar{x}}^2 = 156.25$

b. $\mu_{\bar{x}} = 500 \quad \sigma_{\bar{x}}^2 = 56.82$

5.18 $P(9{,}000 < \bar{X} < 15{,}000) \geq$
88.89%, a contradiction.

CHAPTER 6

6.2   b.   0.3, 0.7

c.

X	$P(X)$
0.............	0.7
1:............	0.3

d. $\mu_x = 0.3 \quad \sigma_x^2 = 0.210$

e.   Yes

6.5 $P(0) = \frac{1}{8} \quad P(1) = \frac{3}{8}$
$P(2) = \frac{3}{8} \quad P(3) = \frac{1}{8}$

6.6 $P(0) = 0.1296 \quad P(1) =$
0.3456 $P(2) = 0.3456$
$P(3) = 0.1536 \quad P(4) =$
0.0256

6.7 $\mu_x = 1.6 \quad \sigma_x^2 = 0.96$

6.9   a.   0.2269

b.   0.1935

c.   0.2461

d.   0.8327

e.   0.1673

f.   0.3823

g.   0.8327

6.10   a.   0.4482

b.   0.5518

c.   0.7000

d.   0.0000

e.   0.0256

f.   0.1641

g.   0.2618

6.11   a.   0.8906

b.   0.3604

c.   0.0000

d.   0.0000

6.12   a.   0.113

b.   0.143

c.   0.195

d.   0.090

6.13   0.05518, 0.9136

6.14   0.3456

6.15   No, because of population size.

6.16   No

6.17 $6.25

6.18   a.   0.0153

6.21   0.3456

6.22   a.   0.2965

b.   0.7447

c.   0.5518

d.   0.7447

e.   0.0000

f.   0.2553

6.23 $\mu_p = 0.8 \quad \sigma_p^2 = 0.0016$

6.24 $\mu_x = 80 \quad \sigma_x^2 = 16$

6.25 $P(X = 5) = 0.175$
$P(X \geq 3) = 0.875$

6.27 $P(X = 3) = 0.214$

6.28   a.   0.368

b.   0.368

c.   0.135

d.   0.135

e.   0.271

6.29   a.   0.164

b.   0.268

c.   0.323

CHAPTER 7

7.7   a.   1

b.   0.5

	c.	0.6
	d.	0
7.9	a.	T
	b.	T
	c.	T
	d.	F
	e.	T
	f.	T
	g.	T
	h.	F
	i.	F
	j.	T
7.14	a.	no.
	b.	yes.
	c.	no.
	d.	no.
	e.	yes.
	f.	yes.
	g.	yes.
	h.	yes.
	i.	no.
	j.	yes.
7.16	$X = 17.5$	
7.17	$Z = -1.8$	
7.18	$Z = 0.2$	
7.19	a.	0.5000
	b.	0.5000
	c.	0.1587
	d.	0.0062
	e.	0.1056
	f.	0.3413
	g.	0.5328
	h.	0.1747
	i.	0.1026
	j.	0.0000
	k.	0.1056
	l.	0.5987
	m.	~ 0

7.20

Size	Number
XS	1
S	18
M	82
L	95
XL	5
KS	0

7.21 0.7340
0.9696

0.2660
0.4680
7.22 0.2902
7.23 a. 345
b. 1.0125
c. No
7.24 0.3413   0.5468
7.25 0.0559
7.26 0.5934
7.27 $n = 877$
7.28 If *both* n_π and $n(1-\pi) \geq 5$
7.30 a. 0.0796
b. 0.1841
c. 0.9192
d. 1.000
7.31 a. 0.0003
b. 0.9997
c. 0.1093

CHAPTER 8

8.6   15.82 to 18.58
8.7   a. 29.45
b. 46.44
c. 29.45 ± 1.12
d. 29.45 ± 1.75
8.8 $41 \pm .74$
8.10 0.1733
8.11 a. 0.1872
b. 0.0970
c. 0.0823
d. 0.0746
e. 0.0668
8.12 a. 3.0777
b. 1.4759
c. 1.3722
d. 1.3253
e. 1.28
8.13 a. −3.0777
b. −1.4759
c. −1.3722
d. −1.3253
e. −1.28
8.15 d. $995.67 to $1,870.99
8.16 a. $\bar{X} = 74.6$
b. $s_x = 13.30$
c. $\bar{X} = 74.6$
d. $s_x^2 = 176.89$
e. 74.6 ± 12.68

8.18 *b.* 0.386 to 0.514
8.19 *b.* 0.8812 to 0.9128
8.20 *a.* 0.60 ± 0.057
8.21 *a.* $\bar{X} = \$109.82$
      b. $s_x^2 = 179.56$
      c. $\$109.82 \pm 1.72$
      d. $\$109.82 \pm 2.63$
      e. $p = 0.20$
      f. 0.2 ± 0.066
8.22 Assume π is 0.5, $n = 456$
8.23 $\$1 \pm \$0.188$
8.24 0.05 ± 0.0268
8.25 1.50 ± 3.20
8.26 1,067
8.27 0.055 ± 0.057
8.28 10 ± 1.449

CHAPTER 9

9.6 p-value $= 0.0456$ Do not reject
9.8 p-value $= 0.2546$
9.9   Must accept
9.10 p-value $= 0.3085$ Do not reject
9.11 p-value $= 0.146$
9.12 p-value $= 0.03$
9.13 p-value $= 0.038$
9.15 p-value $= 0.2890$
9.16 p-value $= 0.0000$
9.17 p-value $= 0.0307$
9.18 p-value $= 0.78$ Do not reject
9.19 p-value $= 0.1251$
9.21 p-value $= 0.000$
9.22 Accept if $368.5 \le \bar{X} \le 431.5$
9.23 Accept if $384.3 \le \bar{X} \le 415.7$
9.24 0.1978 and 0.7389
9.25 $P(\text{error}|\mu_x = 1.78) = 1 - 0.0375 - 0.0004 = 0.9621$
      $P(\text{error}|\mu_x = 1.76) = 1 - 0.1635 - 0.0000 = 0.8365$
      $P(\text{error}|\mu_x = 1.14) = 0.0000$

CHAPTER 10

10.1 p-value $= 0.0455$
10.2 p-value $= 0.0456$
10.3 $\chi^2 = 5.44$ p-value $= 0.0658$
10.5 *a.* Impossible to accept
      b. p-value $= 0.2440$
10.7 $\bar{X} = 5$ $\chi^2 = 2.28$
      $\nu = 7 - 1 - 1 = 5$
      p-value $= 0.81$
10.8 $\bar{X} = 2.33$ $s_X = 2.06$
      $\chi^2 = 18.3$ $\nu = 7 - 2 - 1 = 4$
      p-value $= 0.0011$
10.9 $\chi^2 = 13.89$ p-value $= 0.0002$
10.10 $\chi^2 = 2.34$ p-value $= 0.67$
10.11 p-value $= 0.96$; Smaller sample size
10.12 $\chi^2 = 2.31$ $\nu = 2$
      p-value $= 0.32$
10.13 $\chi^2 = 0.85$ $\nu = 3$
      p-value $= 0.84$
10.14 $\chi^2 = 6.39$ $\nu = 2$
      p-value $= 0.041$
10.15 *a.* cannot make statistical inference
      b. $\chi^2 = 6.85$ $\nu = 4$
      p-value $= 0.14$

CHAPTER 11

11.2 H_N: $\mu_1 = \mu_2 = \ldots = \mu_J$
11.5 *d.* $F = 3.21$ p-value $= 0.078$
11.6 $F = 7.80$ p-value $= 0.001$
11.10 $F = 3.54$ p-value $= 0.048$
11.11 $F = 5.47$ p-value $= 0.021$
11.12 $F = 15.5$ p-value < 0.003
11.13 No inference is appropriate, as population data are given.

CHAPTER 12

12.6 $\bar{Y}_c = 210.32 + 0.303\,X$
12.7 $s_{YX} = 39.22$; $r^2 = 0.831$
12.8 $t = 1.40$; p-value $= 0.1990$
12.9 171.1 to 249.5
12.10 Nonsense!
12.11 $\$338.19$ to $\$385.45$
12.12 $\$332.94$ to $\$390.70$
12.14 $\bar{Y}_c = 2.943 - 0.01675\,X$
      $r^2 = 0.008$

12.15 $t = -1.067$; p-value $= 0.30$

12.16 $\bar{Y}_e = 2.524 + 8.333X$; for
    $X = 1$, $\bar{Y}_e = 10.857$

12.17 10.367 to 11.347

12.18 9.471 to 12.243

12.19 6.172 to 10.494

12.20 $s_{YX} = 0.8783$
    $r^2 = 0.840$

12.21 p-value $= 0.0024$

CHAPTER 13

13.3 a. $\bar{Y}_c = 50,400$ (Model A)
    $\bar{Y}_c = 50,180$ (Model B)
    e. This would be a forecast
    beyond the range of data.

13.5 b. $\bar{Y}_c = \$3,209.83659 +$
    $\$4.51927\ X_1 + \$1,380.-$
    $53576\ X_2$
    c. $\bar{Y}_c = \$12,573$

13.13 b. p-value $= 0.82$
    c. p-value $= 0.68$

13.14 Note the evidence of multi-
    collinearity.

CHAPTER 14

14.7 10 percent compounded
    yearly

14.8 c. Logarithmic is better.

14.9 $Y = 580.73 + 108.17t$
    (origin, 1973)

14.10 $\log Y = 2.80123 + 0.04931\ t$
    $Y = 1,569.3$ for 1981
    (origin, 1973)

14.11 c. Arithmetic is perhaps
    better.

14.12 $Y = 3.1308 - 0.2132\ t$
    (origin, 1949)
    Y is negative for 1970, which
    is illogical.

14.14 a. 124.6   135.4
    125.0   135.7
    127.2   125.6
    128.6   157.1
    b. Repairing lawnmowers

14.15 125.6

14.16 7,406,900

14.17 Indices: 106.9
    101.1
    89.1
    102.9

CHAPTER 15

15.2

1965	97.78
1966	98.92
1967	100.00
1968	101.00
1969	102.00
1970	103.10

15.3 159.57 for 1965

15.5 USA = 100.00
    Canada = 107.12
    West Germany = 262.37

15.6 a. 100.00
    110.55
    129.76
    88.23

15.7 a.

1970	100.0
1971	72.7
1972	109.1
1973	140.9
1974	159.1

15.9 c.

1974	100.00
1975	98.61
1976	89.48

    d.

1974	100.00
1975	130.08
1976	144.30

15.11

1974	100.0
1975	126.0
1976	129.8

15.12 No

15.15

Sales in 1975 Dollars

1973.............	14,816,106
1974.............	17,377,462
1975.............	16,220,000
1976.............	18,288,443

15.16

1973................	100.0
1974................	117.3
1975................	109.5
1976................	123.4

15.21

	a.	b.	c.
1965.....	95.5	876,440	88.9
1966.....	96.7	957,601	97.1
1967.....	93.9	998,935	101.3
1968.....	90.0	1,030,000	104.5
1969.....	96.3	1,020,768	103.5
1970.....	100.0	986,000	100.0
1971.....	103.3	969,990	98.4
1972.....	104.2	999,040	101.3
1973.....	108.4	970,480	98.4
1974.....	118.9	927,670	94.1
1975.....	127.3	870,385	88.3

CHAPTER 16

16.4 $14, $17, $14, $300
16.5   Don't check by $500 difference
16.6   STOP
16.7   b.   6, 6.7, 6.5, 4.8
        d.   1.6, 0.9, 1.1, 2.8; Do not buy perfect information
16.8   a.   Stock 3 (70¢)
        b.   Stock 2 (52¢)
16.9   Give minor repair to each engine ($60); EOL* = $8
16.11 $531, $528, $531, $245
16.13   New is better by $400
16.15   e. $67,600
16.16   A, then D if good.
16.17   Don't inspect.
16.18   New supplier is $1,300 more attractive.
16.19   Submit $35,000 report

16.20   Buy the ties: EMV = $2,537.50
16.21   B is cheaper by $5,000
16.22   Modify; Seniors next if needed
16.23   Buy at A @ 44¢; B at 44¢ or 48¢; pay what is necessary at C. Expected cost = $0.46952/gal.
16.24   Buy Monday at $2.00; otherwise, buy Tuesday. Expected cost = $2.0128

CHAPTER 17

17.8   0.32
17.9   0.75, 0.25
17.10 $P(F)$, $P(S)$ are priors
        $P(W|F)$, $P(W|S)$ are likelihoods
        $P(F|W)$, $P(S|W)$ are revised probabilities
17.11   a. $P(G) = 0.3862$
        b. $P(E|G') = 0.7603$
            $P(T|G') = 0.0931$
            $P(F|G') = 0.1466$
        c. $P(E|G) = 0.6042$
            $P(T|G) = 0.3699$
            $P(F|G) = 0.0259$
17.12   a.   Expected costs = E, $130.50; T, $130.50; F, $123.00
        c, d, e, f: Regardless of noise, check fuel first.
17.13   a.   0.3833
        b.   0.3913
        c.   0.7568
        d.   Priors: $P(N)$, $P(TV)$
            Likelihoods: $P(P|N)$, $P(P|TV)$, $P(F|TV)$, $P(F|N)$
            Revised: $P(N|P)$, $P(TV|F)$, etc.
17.14   a.   0.021
        b.   ⅓, 0.2857, 0.3810
        c.   0.95889

d. 0.7155, 0.1962, 0.0883

e. 0.04022

f. 0.3446, 0.2894, 0.3660

17.15 $160

17.16 $2.70

17.17 $7

17.19   Use old Form; EOL* = $386.80

Index

This book has been set in 10 and 9 point Times Roman, leaded 2 points. Chapter numbers are 42 point Helvetica Medium and chapter titles are 18 point Helvetica Medium. The size of the type page is 27 by 45½ picas.